INTRODUCTION TO SOCIAL PROBLEMS

EIGHTH EDITION

INTRODUCTION TO SOCIAL PROBLEMS

Thomas J. Sullivan

Northern Michigan University

PEARSON
and

Boston • New York • San Francisco
Mexico City • Montreal • Toronto • London • Madrid • Munich • Paris
Hong Kong • Singapore • Tokyo • Cape Town • Sydney

Executive Editor: *Jeff Lasser*
Series Editorial Assistant: *Courtney Shea*
Senior Marketing Manager: *Kelly May*
Production Supervisor: *Patty Bergin*
Composition and Prepress Buyer: *Linda Cox*
Manufacturing Buyer: *Debbie Rossi*
Cover Administrator: *Linda Knowles*
Photo Researcher: *NK Graphics/Black Dot Group*
Electronic Composition: *NK Graphics/Black Dot Group*

For related titles and support materials, visit our online catalog at www.ablongman.com.

Between the time website information is gathered and then published, it is not unusual for some sites to have closed. Also, the transcription of URLs can result in typographical errors. The publisher would appreciate notification where these errors occur so that they may be corrected in subsequent editions.

Photo credits appear on page 465, which constitutes a continuation of the copyright page.

Library of Congress Cataloging-in-Publication Data

Sullivan, Thomas J.
   Introduction to social problems / Thomas J. Sullivan.—8th ed.
     p. cm.
   Includes bibliographical references and index.
   ISBN-13: 978-0-205-57878-8
   ISBN-10: 0-205-57878-0
  1. Social problems—United States. 2. United States—Social conditions. 3. United States—Social policy. I. Title.
   HN28.S92 2008
   361.10973—dc22
                                      2008002499

Printed in the United States of America
10 9 8 7 6 5 4 3 2 1   RRD/MO 11 10 09 08

For Nancy

CONTENTS

CHAPTER ONE

APPROACHES TO THE STUDY OF SOCIAL PROBLEMS

GROWTH OF CORPORATE AND GOVERNMENT POWER

HEALTH AND ILLNESS

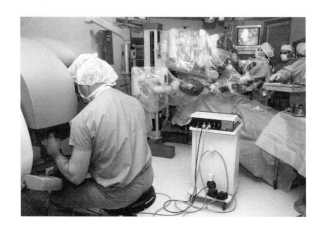

RACE AND ETHNIC RELATIONS

GENDER AND SOCIAL INEQUALITY

AGE, SEXUAL ORIENTATION, AND SOCIAL INEQUALITY

CRIME AND DELINQUENCY

CHAPTER TEN
ALCOHOL AND OTHER DRUGS

PROSTITUTION, PORNOGRAPHY, AND THE SEX TRADE

CHAPTER TWELVE

POPULATION GROWTH AND URBANIZATION

ENVIRONMENTAL PROBLEMS

VIOLENCE, WAR, AND TERRORISM

CHAPTER FIFTEEN

EDUCATION, SCIENCE, AND TECHNOLOGY

PREFACE

At the beginning of the twenty-first century, the study of social problems continues to be one of the most demanding, exciting, and fast-paced fields in sociology and the social sciences. Some remarkable advances have been made: The crime rate has fallen dramatically since 1990; the high school dropout rate among minorities is falling, dramatically in some cases; and women now go into combat as pilots and circle the globe as astronauts aboard space shuttles. And these are just a few examples of the significant advances that have occurred since the first edition of this book was published. At the same time, we should not rejoice for too long, because serious problems persist: The crime rate is still far too high, alarming new evidence suggests that global warming may be a much more severe problem than had previously been thought, the prevalence of poor people of color among the victims of Hurricane Katrina in New Orleans brings home the extent to which class and race still shape opportunities and outcomes in the United States, and the terrorist attacks on New York and Washington, DC, in 2001 remind us of the horrific acts of violence that still occur frequently in the world. So, although some rejoicing is warranted, much important and difficult work still remains.

The work of dealing with such social problems is, of course, a collective effort in which virtually all citizens join at some time and at some level. Many professionals—sociologists, educators, social workers, counselors, and police officers, to name a few—devote their careers to solving social problems. Many other people, with no special training, volunteer their efforts in community centers and other organizations in an effort to alleviate the pain and damage from crime, woman battering, or homophobia. This eighth edition of *Introduction to Social Problems* supports these efforts by providing students who are training for helping professions and any other interested activists with the most current assessment of social problems and their solutions. This book explores the nature and extent of the problems, documents the advances and setbacks, and analyzes what solutions work and don't work.

Sociology and the other social sciences make some special contributions to this battle against social problems. They use scientific research to assess the nature and extent of social problems and the effectiveness of solutions to them. Social science research focuses on questions such as: Why and how do particular social problems emerge? Does a given solution work? Who benefits? What are the negative consequences of a given solution? Is there a way that we can achieve the same gain for less expense? In fact, over the past few decades, the study of social problems has become one of the most exciting and innovative wings of the social sciences because it involves the application of social science research and knowledge to the solutions of some of the most difficult, agonizing, and controversial problems confronting the United States and the world today.

Organization

Many serious social problems confront the United States and the world, too many to cover in a single book. From among these social issues I have chosen to discuss problems that are particularly serious, affect many people, and expose students to a broad array of concerns in varied sectors of life in the United States. By studying these problems, students gain the tools and the insight that enable them to analyze other problems and solutions not explicitly covered in this book.

Chapter 1 introduces students to the sociological analysis of social problems, including a discussion of the theoretical perspectives that are used throughout the book and of the importance of the scientific approach and applied research in the analysis of social problems and their solutions. Chapters 2–4 cover social problems that relate directly to some of the major social institutions in society: government, the economy, the family, and health-care systems. Chapters 5–8 focus on problems that are linked by the common theme of social inequality: poverty; racial and ethnic discrimination; and inequality based on gender, age, or sexual orientation. Chapters 9–11 analyze problems surrounding behavior that some people consider unconventional or deviant: crime and delinquency; alcohol and drug abuse; and prostitution, pornography, and the sex trade. Chapters 12–14 focus on problems involving changes or disruptions in the physical and social world: urban problems and population growth; environmental pollution; violence, war, and terrorism. Finally, Chapter 15 addresses some rapidly changing areas—education, science, and technology—that concern many people in the twenty-first century.

Features in the Eighth Edition

This book goes beyond simply cataloging a set number of social problems. It also provides the student with a framework for analyzing any such problems. This framework is incorporated into a number of special elements of the book.

1. *Theoretical Perspectives.* I have organized the analysis of social problems and their solutions around the three core theoretical perspectives in sociology: functionalism, conflict theory, and interactionism. These perspectives offer tremendous insight into the sources of problems, the effectiveness of solutions, and the ramifications—both obvious and hidden—of adopting particular solutions. These perspectives are used in every chapter of the book to provide the student with a set of tools to analyze any social problem, including problems not directly discussed in this book.

2. *Applied Research inserts.* A theme in this book is that the application of social science research is central to solving problems and evaluating how well solutions work. Therefore, I have included in every chapter an insert titled *Applied Research,* which illustrates how and why this is the case. In this way, I emphasize the point that the choice of solutions to problems, although shaped by personal values and the public policy debate, should be constrained by the assessment of those solutions through systematic and scientific observation. In other words, the choice of solutions to problems should involve an interplay between human values and social research.

3. *Myths and Facts.* To emphasize further the role of research in understanding social problems, I point out some ways in which people's common-sense beliefs about social problems are proved incorrect by research data. This encourages the student to be sensitive to the distinction between myths and facts: beliefs that have no scientific foundation versus knowledge that has been substantiated by observational testing.

4. *Laissez-Faire versus Interventionist Debate.* The debate over social policy and social problems is centered in part on the role of the government in such issues. This long-standing debate is incorporated into the text in the form of two opposing positions. The laissez-faire stance posits that the government is, in most cases, either inefficient at finding or unable to find such solutions and should stand aside and let private enterprise and impersonal economic forces produce solutions. The interventionist position gives the government prime, although not sole, responsibility for finding and initiating solutions to problems. This debate is addressed periodically in the text where it is relevant.

5. *Policy Issues inserts.* Another important theme of this book is that finding solutions to social problems is a political process in which groups differ with one another over which solutions are preferred. One's choice of solutions is influenced in part by one's cultural and subcultural values. Therefore, every chapter includes an insert titled *Policy Issues,* in which contemporary debates on social policy related to that problem are discussed. Both the pros and the cons of policies are debated and in many cases linked to the laissez-faire/interventionist debate.

6. *International Perspectives.* This feature provides students with a global picture of particular social problems and their solutions. One reason this is important is the growing interdependence among the world's peoples and nations. Another reason is that we can gain insight into problems and their solutions when we observe them in societies and cultures that are different from our own. In addition, some social problems are inherently global in nature rather than national or regional.

7. *Social Construction and the Mass Media.* Explicit emphasis is given to the social constructionist perspective on social problems, in many cases by discussing the role of the mass media in constructing problems and their solutions. A section in Chapter 1 discusses the social construction of social problems from the three theoretical perspectives; then, sections on constructionism and the mass media are included in Chapters 2, 3, 6, 7, 9, and 14.

8. *Linkages.* To encourage the student to see the interconnections among social problems, a brief insert at the end of each chapter points out how a problem discussed in that chapter is linked to problems discussed in other chapters. This encourages the student to recognize that the worsening of one problem can mean that other seemingly unconnected conditions may also deteriorate and that alleviating one problem can result in improvements in others.

9. *Study and Review.* At the end of each chapter, a Study and Review section is included to give students an opportunity to test how well they have grasped the material presented in the chapter. Each section contains a chapter summary, list of key terms, multiple-choice questions, true/false questions, fill-in questions, matching questions, and essay questions. Correct answers are also provided (see pp. 458–460). These various testing formats offer an assessment of the different kinds of information found in each chapter and will assist students in organizing their study. Students will thereby have a good measure of how much they have learned and a comprehensive review of the content in the chapter, as well as help in preparing for exams.

10. *Researching Social Problems on the Internet.* Each chapter includes a section, following the Summary, titled *Researching Social Problems on the Internet.* It suggests some ways students can further their knowledge of the topics of that chapter by searching the Internet. It gives some specific Web sites to explore but also suggests some exercises that direct a search for new materials.

Updates and Changes

Although the book's basic organization remains the same in the eighth edition, it has been thoroughly revised and updated to reflect contemporary developments in sociology, as well as new social, political, and economic developments relating to particular social problems. Special attention has been given to ensuring that the data presented on the various social problems are the most current available. The "For Further Reading" sections at the end of each chapter have also been thoroughly updated with challenging books for the student who wishes to pursue a topic in greater depth.

A detailed list of the revisions in each chapter (including the page number where the changes are found in the text) can be found in the *Instructor's Manual* that accompanies this book. The following list highlights the major changes:

- New discussion has been added to Chapter 2 on the role of corporate opposition in the decline of unions (corporate use of litigation and intimidation against unions) and the focus of the global labor movement on the concept of labor rights for all people (to move governments and international trade organizations to recognize as human rights the right to a fair wage, to join a union, and to bargain collectively).

- Although the Applied Research insert in Chapter 2 is mostly the same, new material has been added to expand on the discussion of how media corporations shape public debate over social problems.

- A new discussion is added to the Future Prospects section of Chapter 2 on the trend toward the privatization of government action on social problems (i.e., the tendency to have private contractors do government work); this further expands the attention given in this text to the phenomenon of the privatization of social problems.

- New research is presented in Chapter 3 on the effectiveness (or, rather, lack of effectiveness) of policies promoting abstinence only in sex education programs.

- Where available, data have been added to tables and figures on Asians and Pacific Islanders and, in some cases, Native Americans (Table 6.1 and Figures 5.5, 6.1, 6.3, 7.1, and 8.5).

- In Chapter 6, recent court rulings relating to the school integration and the use of race in assigning students to schools are discussed, including the most recent Supreme Court rulings on this; the social policy implications of these court rulings are discussed in text and in the Social Policy insert.

- Given developments since 9/11, a new section has been included in Chapter 6 on the Arab American experience as an ethnic group and a minority group in the United States, highlighting their experiences with prejudice and discrimination.

- The Applied Research insert in Chapter 8 has been rewritten to include the most recent research and scale development work on scales measuring child well-being in the United States; this current research makes possible a more detailed and complex assessment of the condition of children and youth in the United States.

- The Policy Issues insert in Chapter 11 now includes a discussion of the implications of the most recent Supreme Court rulings relating to censorship on the Internet, especially having to do with restricting the distribution of pornography and using filtering software to control pornography.

- Chapter 13 now gives expanded discussion to research on the problem of global warming and climate change; the section on air pollution has been retitled "Air Pollution, Global Warming, and Climate Change" and now gives expanded discussion to research on and the implications of the broader problem; the section on renewable energy resources is now titled "New Approaches to Energy" and devotes more attention to what can be done to alleviate global warming, including discussion of carbon footprint, carbon tax, carbon trading, and other new ideas related to this issue.

- Figure 13.3 from the seventh edition has been deleted (and other figures renumbered where necessary) in order to make room for a new Figure 13.6, which provides the student with data on the changes over time on the amount and percentage of municipal solid waste that is recycled; this new figure provides students with more important data on the working of environmental programs.

- The discussion of terrorism in Chapter 14 has been updated to take into account developments since the beginning of the Iraq War; Figure 14.2 has been significantly revised to show the growth in terrorist activities in recent years, and the text now mentions terrorist acts in Iraq, Afghanistan, London, and Madrid; in addition, the section titled "Nuclear Annihilation" has been renamed "Nuclear Devastation" and now gives more attention to the danger of terrorists gaining access to nuclear materials and causing devastation rather than annihilation.

- In Chapter 15, new research is presented on the effectiveness of charter schools and vouchers in educating children; sufficient research is now accumulating on these topics that we can begin to draw some solid conclusions.

These and the other additions and revisions called for by world developments in the past few years will make the eighth edition of *Introduction to Social Problems* an even better vehicle for use with students in the study of social problems.

Ancillary Materials

A number of materials have been prepared to assist the instructor and the student in using this textbook. Many of them can be downloaded from the Instructor's Resource Center (www.pearsonhighered.com/educator). More information about these and other materials can be obtained from your Pearson sales representative or from the Pearson Higher Ed Web site.

Instructor's Manual and Test Bank. I have prepared a combined Instructor's Manual and Test Bank to accompany this book. The instructor's manual section contains, for each chapter, a number of materials to assist the instructor in teaching the course: an outline of the chapter, a list of the learning objectives for the chapter, a list of changes in the new edition, a series of suggestions for teaching and discussion, and a list of films that can accompany the chapter. The test bank section contains 10 essay questions, 70 multiple-choice questions, and 15 true/false questions for each chapter.

TestGen EQ: Computerized Test Bank. The test bank is available with the TestGen software for Windows or Macintosh. TestGen can prepare exams that contain questions from the test bank and revisions of those questions or new questions added by the instructor.

PowerPoint Presentation. PowerPoint presentations are available by download or on CD-ROM that provide lecture outlines for the course.

Acknowledgments

Many people have contributed to the completion of this new edition. Jeff Lasser and Karen Hanson served ably as the editors of the last few editions, suggesting timely and sound revisions to make the book even more valuable to students. I would like to thank the following reviewers for their helpful suggestions for this edition: Carole A. Campbell, California State University, Long Beach; William Egelman, Iona College; Anna Hall, Delgado Community College; Liisa Itkonen, Boise State University; and Monique Moleon-Mathews, Indian River Community College. I also received some excellent advice and assistance over the various editions of this book from a number of other colleagues: Gai Berlage, Iona College; Carole A. Campbell, California State University, Long Beach; Susan E. Claxton, Floyd College; Karyn Daniels, Long Beach City College; Mark Evan Edwards, Oregon State University; Chris Girard, Florida International University; George R. Gross, Northern Michigan University; John Hillebrand, Northwestern State Louisiana; Gary Hodge, Collin County Community College; Brad E. Huffaker, Labette Community College; Christine Johnson, Quinsigamond Community College; Kirk A. Johnson, Washburn University; Steven G. Jones, University of Charleston; Daniel C. Morris, Ball State University; G. Alexander Ross, Indian River Community College; Josh Schlenker, University of Maine, Augusta; Bonita Sessing-Matcha, Hudson Valley Community College; Joel Charles Snell, Kirkwood College; Timothy A. Ulrich, Seattle Pacific University; and Anthony W. Zumpetta, West Chester University.

Of all the people who have had an impact on this work, the students in my various classes have probably been the most significant. They have questioned and challenged me; agreed and disagreed with me; and generally forced me to be more careful, analytical, and critical in my teaching and writing than I might otherwise have been. Their collective imprint on this book is greater than they probably imagine.

Thomas J. Sullivan

About the Author

THOMAS J. SULLIVAN is Professor of Sociology at Northern Michigan University, specializing in social psychology, research methods, applied sociology, and medical sociology. He earned his undergraduate degree in sociology from San Francisco State University and his M.A. and Ph.D. in sociology from the University of California at Santa Barbara. He is the author of *Sociology: Concepts and Applications in a Diverse World*, 7th ed. (Allyn and Bacon, 2007), *Methods of Social Research* (Wadsworth, 2001), and *Applied Sociology: Research and Critical Thinking* (Allyn & Bacon, 1992); he is the co-author of *Applied Social Research: Tool for the Human Services*, 7th ed. (Cengage, 2008). He has published articles in *Social Science and Medicine* and *Humboldt Journal of Social Relations*. His applied research has focused on evaluation research of social service delivery in elementary schools and of teen pregnancy prevention and intervention services. He has served in various elected and appointed positions for the American Sociological Association, the Society for Applied Sociology, and the Midwest Sociological Society.

INTRODUCTION TO SOCIAL PROBLEMS

APPROACHES TO THE STUDY OF SOCIAL PROBLEMS

English novelist Charles Dickens characterized life in England and France in the late 1700s with these words: "It was the best of times, it was the worst of times. . . . It was the spring of hope, it was the winter of despair" (1924:1). Dickens was expressing a deep-felt ambivalence held by many people of that era regarding life in their time. England was undergoing industrialization, which promised greater levels of economic productivity, wonderful inventions, and new heights of affluence. For many, however, it also meant agonizing poverty, horrid crowding in filthy cities, and virulent disease. For the entrepreneur, it was a time to dream of riches yet to be made. For the pauper, it was a time to wonder where one's next meal might be found.

At the dawn of the twenty-first century, the United States can be viewed through an equally ambivalent lens. We, too, can find promise of a better life in emerging technologies such as computers, telecommunications, and biotechnology. We, too, have seen remarkable inventions that provide a level of comfort and security thought impossible by our ancestors. Imagine, for example, how you would be limited by the absence of but one amenity of modern living that you probably take for granted: electricity. Yet not much more than one hundred years ago most people lived without it.

But there is a dark side to all this promise—a "winter of despair"—that is the topic of this book. There remain poverty, violence, drug addiction, alcoholism, and a host of other social problems. Perhaps nuclear power provides the best symbol for the contradictions of our time: We use it to produce our electricity, but no one wants its deadly wastes stored near them. And we stand terrified at the specter of death and destruction that would surely accompany the use of nuclear weapons by some nation or terrorist group.

One can understand, then, how life in today's world might be thought of as "the best of times . . . the worst of times." A principal challenge that we face is to conquer these social problems or at least to alleviate their negative impacts on people's lives. In this book, I take a sociological approach to understanding these social problems. **Sociology** is *the scientific study of societies and human social behavior,* and it provides one of the most useful approaches for understanding social problems and a most effective tool for finding solutions to them. In fact, modern sociology might be considered an offspring of industrialization, because it emerged in Europe and the United States in the nineteenth century shortly after the era of which Dickens had written. A major motivation of many early sociologists was to develop a "science of society" to deal with the dislocations, disruptions, poverty, and violence that accompanied industrialization. The same purpose underlies this book: to remove, as best we can, the poverty, crime, violence, and other problems that persist as the United States and the world move into an advanced industrial era. Along with these early sociologists, this book assumes that we *can* do something to improve social conditions and to attack social problems. Furthermore, our actions regarding social problems need to be grounded in *scientific research* on the problems and in *scientific assessments* of the effectiveness of solutions. Uninformed or casual meddling in social problems can create more difficulties than it solves.

This chapter will serve as a framework for the study of specific problems in later chapters. First, what makes a social condition a social problem and why sociology is an essential tool in understanding and solving problems will be discussed. Then consideration will be given to the three major theoretical perspectives in sociology and how they are important in the study of social problems. Finally, it will be shown how scientific research provides the most useful information about problems and their solutions.

What Is a Social Problem?

There are some issues that practically everyone today agrees are social problems, such as crime or racial discrimination. About other issues, however, there is less agreement. There is great debate, for example, over whether water pollution, pornography, or the use of marijuana are social problems. A commonsense approach might define a condition as a social problem if it "harms people" or is "detrimental to society." But this is far too imprecise for our purposes. To develop a more rigorous definition of what is a social problem, it is helpful to distinguish problems that affect individuals from those that involve an entire society.

Personal Troubles, Public Issues, and Social Problems

A distinction made by sociologist C. Wright Mills (1959) between personal troubles and public issues may be the best place to begin. Personal troubles are things that affect individuals and those immediately around them. When parents discover that their daughter has a serious drug problem, theirs is a personal trouble because the values and goals of only that family are threatened. The trouble is seen as being primarily that family's difficulty. Public issues, on the other hand, have an impact on large numbers of people and are matters of public debate; collective solutions, rather than individual or familial ones, are considered. When statistics reveal that our nation loses millions of dollars every year because of accidents, suicide, and worker absenteeism due to drug abuse, we are dealing with a public issue because the values and goals of a large group are threatened. The issue is debated in public forums, and collective solutions are usually proposed. So every condition that adversely affects some individuals is not necessarily an issue of great public concern toward which we should, or could, direct societal resources. Of course, public issues may translate into personal troubles in the lives of some people, but every personal trouble is not a public issue. Mills's distinction between personal troubles and public issues makes us aware that problems need to be viewed in the broad context of their impact on society.

How do we place these issues in a broader societal context? A good start is the following definition: A **social problem** exists when *an influential group defines a social condition as threatening its values; when the condition affects a large number of people; and when the condition can be remedied by collective action* (Loseke, 2003; Spector and Kitsuse, 2000). Let's look briefly at each element in this definition. An *influential group* is one that can have a significant impact on public debate and social policy. For example, groups opposing discrimination against women in employment and other areas have been able to mount a campaign that has forced politicians and the public nationwide to listen to their demands. Groups such as People for the Ethical Treatment of Animals, on the other hand, have not been able to generate significant debate about experimentation with animals or cruelty to animals, and relatively few people consider these to be social problems. Personal troubles do not become public issues, then, unless an influential group so defines them. The mere existence of a social condition does not make it problematic, no matter how harmful it may be. For example, smoking tobacco has been a contributing factor in lung cancer for as long as humans have used the substance, but it was not defined as a social problem until biomedical research made people aware of the link between smoking and lung cancer.

Conditions are viewed as social problems when they threaten a *group's values*. **Values** are *people's ideas about what is good or bad, right or wrong*. We use these values as guidelines for choosing goals and judging behaviors. Because values are necessarily ranked in terms of priority in any group or society, there is disagreement over which conditions will be viewed as social problems. Some groups in the United States, for example, place great value on work and industriousness. Because of this, they may view people who receive welfare with considerable disdain and even consider them threatening to their own way of life. Other groups, emphasizing religious or humanitarian values, might argue that poverty—not poor people—is the real threat and that the poor should be helped, not castigated.

Conditions do not typically become social problems unless they affect *a large number of people*. When they affect relatively few people, they are private issues and there is little public debate over them or search for collective solutions. The more people they affect, the more likely they are to be publicly debated and defined as a problem that society should address. When the unemployment rate is low, for example, relatively few people are adversely affected. It may be a terrible personal hardship for those few who are unemployed, but it does not threaten large or influential groups and there will likely be little societal pressure directed toward alleviating the problem.

Finally, a social condition may satisfy the previous criteria but not be regarded as a social problem because the condition does not have social causes and cannot be *remedied by collective human action*. Earthquakes, tornadoes, and other vagaries of nature, for example, are harmful and frightening natural disasters, but they would not be considered *social* problems because they are not produced by social conditions and cannot be prevented by collective action or changes in social policy.

The Social Context of Social Problems

Social problems differ from personal troubles because the former are public issues rather than personal ones. In addition, social problems are fundamentally social rather than personal in nature because their causes and their solutions have something to do with the workings of society. Social problems may have an impact on individuals, but their roots are found in social life. We will illustrate the social basis of social problems here by briefly describing four distinct social conditions that can play a role in the emergence of social problems: deviation from group values and norms, a decline in the effectiveness of social institutions, extensive social and cultural diversity, and the exercise of power. The importance of these social conditions will be further elaborated in the next section on theoretical perspectives in sociology and throughout this book.

Societies are generally stable and orderly, although change and disruption do occur. This social stability arises in part because societies pass on to their members values and norms that serve to guide people in their behavior. Values have just been defined. **Norms** are much more specific and concrete than values; they are *rules of conduct that guide people's behavior*. They are expectations that people in society share about how they ought to behave. Values are general preferences, whereas norms are specific guidelines for behavior. Norms dictate, for example, that men should wear pants, not dresses, and that motor vehicles are to be driven on the right side of the road rather than the left. Note how norms, like values, can vary from one culture to another and from one group to another. In some societies, men wear dresses and in others people drive on the left side of the road.

Values and norms, then, serve as a script for how to behave, and they enable us, to an extent, to predict how others will behave and to coordinate our behavior with theirs. Thus, values and norms lend stability and orderliness to society. A basic tenet of the sociological view of society is that people live in a socially created reality in which their behavior is shaped by social objects, such as values and norms, as much as by physical objects. However, people do not always behave in conformity with accepted values and norms. *Behaviors or characteristics that violate important group norms and as a consequence are reacted to with social disapproval* are called **deviance**. Laypeople often approach deviant or unconventional behaviors in an absolute way, judging them to be good or bad, right or wrong, by comparing them with some fixed standards, such as some religious teachings. Sociologists view deviance as relative, or based on the social definitions of some group. For sociologists, it is not behaviors or characteristics in themselves that are deviant. Rather, it is the judgments of some group whose norms have been violated that make a behavior unconventional or deviant. This makes deviance relative in the sense that a behavior is deviant only when so defined by some group. So, deviance can be understood only within the context of the norms and values of a particular culture, subculture, or group. As one sociologist put it: "Deviance, like beauty, is in the eyes of the beholder" (Simmons, 1969:4). Deviance does not refer only to the violation of group norms; some stigma, or mark of disgrace, must also be attached to the violation that sets the deviant apart from others. When people violate the values and norms of the influential or powerful, the reaction against the deviant can be very strong. So, some social problems—prostitution, alcoholism, and drug abuse, to name a few—arise in part because they are defined as deviant and stigmatized. Some people are unwilling or unable to conform their behavior to the dictates of influential groups.

Beyond values and norms, another important element of society is **social institutions:** *relatively stable clusters of social relationships that involve people working together to meet some basic needs of society.* The family, for example, is a social institution ensuring that children will be born and raised properly to be contributing members of society. These institutions—the family, religion, politics, education, and others—serve as further guides for people's behavior and also involve social relationships that offer people a sense of community involvement and self-worth. In fact, many behaviors and personal qualities—happiness, mental stability, morality, respect for the law, and others—arise out of such social relationships, out of a sense of community and personal involvement with others. A person who is fired from his job, for example, experiences a social loss that can result in psychological problems as well as physical ailments. Industrialization has threatened such traditional sources of support and authority as the family and religion. Unless their decline is replaced by other sources of support, crime, substance abuse, and other problems may increase. In other words, many social problems arise from the ineffectiveness of social institutions in guiding behavior and offering people a sense of community and self-worth.

As the clothing, hairstyles, and body piercings of these youth in the United States suggest, there is much social and cultural diversity in most societies. Subcultural diversity is an important element in the study of social problems because differing subcultures create the potential for conflicts over values and lifestyles.

Social and cultural diversity is another important element of societies. The United States, for example, is extremely diverse. The norms of the inner-city slum are light-years away from those of the middle-class suburb; the values of the young have little meaning for the elderly; and many beliefs of the affluent are foreign to the poor. One result of all this diversity is that many groups in the United States inhabit their own social worlds, called "subcultures." A **subculture** is *a group within a culture that shares some of the beliefs, values, and norms of the larger culture but also has some that are distinctly its own.* Each of the following could be considered a subculture: teenagers, Cubans in Miami, gays in most large cities, skinheads, the drug set, prison inmates, hip-hop youth of the 1990s, even the few hippies left over from the 1960s. In fact, everyone in the United States belongs to a wide array of subcultures based on age, sex, social standing, religion, leisure pastimes, or other characteristics.

Subcultural diversity is an important element in the study of social problems because it points to the potential for conflict between groups: The values of one group may clash with the values of another. One group, for example, may find the widespread availability of abortion offensive to its religious tenets, whereas another views restrictions on abortion as a threat to women's reproductive choices. Such conflicts are enhanced by **ethnocentrism,** *the tendency to view one's own culture or subculture as the best and to judge other cultures or subcultures in comparison to it.* Because of ethnocentrism, people may view the practices of another subculture as a social problem because they differ from their own practices. For example, are prostitution and the use of marijuana truly problems for society, or are they just offensive to the values of some particular subcultures?

A final element of society to be mentioned here is the exercise of power. **Power** is *the ability of one group to realize its will, even in the face of resistance from other groups* (Boulding, 1989; Weber, 1958, originally published 1919). Power can arise from many sources: the strength of numbers, efficient organization, access to wealth or status, or control of the political and economic institutions that dominate society. Whatever its source, power enables its possessor to compel others to act in a particular fashion. Ultimately, societies can use force or coercion to induce conformity to values and norms or to reduce conflicts or threats to a way of life. **Authority** refers to *legitimate power that is obeyed because people believe it is right and proper that they obey.* For example, most U.S. citizens believe that the Congress and the president, working together, have the legitimate authority to declare war on another country and to compel military service on the part of the citizenry. Many people may prefer not to fight in a war, but they would go because they believe the government has the authority to require that of them. Most social problems are related to the exercise of power and the use of authority, either as forces that intensify problems or as crucial elements in their solution. After all, a group needs some power in order to have a condition defined as a social problem to begin with. Then, which solutions are settled on often depends on which groups can most effectively utilize the power and authority available to them.

This brief description of four elements of society suggests the ways in which social problems are "social" in nature: They are both created and alleviated by social mechanisms. To understand and solve social problems, then, we need to know something about how society works.

The Sociological Imagination

Before going on to a more detailed analysis of the sociological perspective and social problems, it is valuable to step back and consider the implications of this perspective for your own life. The sociological perspective on human beings is a unique and remarkable one, recognizing as it does that human behavior consists of far more than individuals acting independently of one another. It emphasizes the powerful role that group membership and social forces play in shaping behavior. Sociologists focus on social interaction and social relationships rather than on individuals. The sociological perspective offers a special awareness of the world that enables people to approach their own lives with introspection and insight. Peter Berger (1963) referred to the sociological perspective as an "emancipated vista" that can free people from blind submission to social forces that they do not understand. C. Wright Mills (1959) coined the term **sociological imagination** to refer to *the ability to understand the relationship between what is happening in people's personal lives and the social forces that surround them.* For both Berger and Mills, the more people learn about society and social problems, the better equipped they will be to understand their own lives and the impact—both desired and intrusive—of society and social problems on them. To be emancipated, of course, is not always pleasant, because we often learn that social problems hinder us from achieving sought-after goals. Poverty-stricken parents, for example, may not welcome the realization that their children will be penalized by the inequities of the school system in the United States, which has adverse effects on the poor. Nevertheless, it is precisely a better understanding of the role of such inequities that can open the door to making improvements in the educational process. So the sociological imagination offers not only emancipation but also *empowerment:* It assists people in taking control of their lives and circumstances through the struggle against social problems.

Theoretical Perspectives on Social Problems

Every science, including sociology, accumulates knowledge through an interplay between theory and research. First, we need to provide a more detailed account of the theories commonly used in the sociological analysis of social problems. A **theory** is *a set of statements that explains the relationship between phenomena.* The key role of theories is to tell us why something occurred. They help us organize the data from research into a meaningful whole. In this section, we will discuss the most general and important theoretical approaches in sociology. In the next section, we will return to the importance of research.

Some sociological theories focus on specific social problems, such as the causes of juvenile delinquency or the explanations for divorce. We will discuss quite a few of these theories in this book. In addition to these specialized theories, however, there are a number of broader explanations of social reality that are called **theoretical perspectives.** These perspectives are *general views of society that provide some fundamental assumptions about the nature and operation of society and commonly serve as sources of the more specific theories* mentioned previously. Most sociologists today are guided by one or more of the following theoretical perspectives: functionalism, conflict theory, and interactionism. The functionalist and conflict approaches are frequently referred to as *macrosociology* because they focus on large groups and social institutions and on society as a whole. The interactionist perspective falls under the category of *microsociology* because it concentrates on the intimate level of everyday interactions between people. This section first summarizes the perspectives and then suggests how you should use them in analyzing social problems.

The Functionalist Perspective

The functionalist perspective grew out of the similarities early sociologists observed between society and biological organisms. The human body, for example, is composed of many different parts—the heart, the eyes, and the kidneys, to name but three—each of which performs a particular function. The heart pumps blood to the other organs of the body, the eyes transmit information about the external world to the brain, and the kidneys remove waste materials from the blood. These parts of the body do not exist in isolation, however; rather, they are interrelated and interdependent. If one of them ceases to perform its function—if the heart stops, the eyes go blind, or the kidneys fail—the effective operation of the whole body is threatened and survival itself may be in jeopardy.

Society, functionalists argue, operates in a way somewhat analogous to that of a biological organism. According to the **functionalist perspective,** *society is a system made up of a number of interrelated elements, each performing a function that contributes to the operation of the whole* (Parsons, 1951; Turner and Maryanski, 1979). The elements of society include, for example, institutions such as the family, education, and the economy. The family provides for the bearing and rearing of children until they can live on their own. Educational institutions provide training in the various skills needed to fill jobs in society. The economy is responsible for producing food, clothing, and other necessities needed by families to survive, as well as for providing the books and other supplies needed for education. The family and the schools could not survive without the goods provided by the economy, and economic organizations need workers who have been socialized by the family and trained by the schools to work industriously. In addition to institutions, society is also made up of many social roles, social groups, and subcultures, and all these parts fit together into a reasonably well-integrated whole. For functionalists, then, all parts of society are interdependent and function together to provide the things that are essential to maintain society. In addition, there needs to be considerable agreement among the members of society regarding the content of important values and norms.

In a system with all the parts so tightly interdependent, a change in one element of society will probably lead to changes in other parts. For example, the establishment of compulsory education in the United States caused significant alterations in the economic sphere by removing children and eventually adolescents from the labor force, which made more jobs available for adults. Compulsory education also affected the family; with young people no longer working, the financial burden on parents was increased. When children could no longer help support the family financially, a gradual shift to smaller families began. Thus, changes in the educational sphere had important ramifications for family and economic structures. Small changes can usually be absorbed with relative ease, but large or sudden changes can cause major social disruption and lead to problems. Because of this, functionalists argue, social systems are characterized by stability and a tendency toward equilibrium—a state of balance in which the relationships among the various parts of the system remain the same.

A central concern of the functionalist approach is the determination of just what functions each part of society performs. This is not always easy to do because some functions are not as obvious as those in our previous example. In fact, sociologist Robert K. Merton (1968) suggests that there are two different types of functions: manifest and latent. *Manifest functions* are the intended consequences of some action or social process and refer to what most people expect to result. *Latent functions* are consequences that are unexpected or unintended. For example, one of the manifest functions of colleges and universities is to provide people with specialized training. However, institutions of higher education perform a number of latent functions. For instance, they serve as a marriage market, and they reduce unemployment by keeping some adults out of the job market. These latent functions are just as much a part of the system of higher education as its manifest purposes. In addition, some social practices may be *dysfunctional;* that is, they may disrupt social equilibrium rather than contribute to it. For example, encouraging large families, as some religious teachings do, would be dysfunctional in a society that is already overpopulated.

According to the functionalist perspective, a social problem can arise when some element in society becomes dysfunctional and interferes with the efficient operation or stability of the system or the achievement of societal goals. In other words, social problems arise from social disorganization, in which the parts of society work at cross-purposes rather than together. One sign of this disorganization is the decline in the effectiveness of social institutions, discussed in the preceding section. Functionalists search for the sources of this societal breakdown. Consider how divorce might be viewed by functionalists: Marital dissolution involves the breaking up of what is perhaps society's most basic institution, the family. Divorce could be seen as a social problem if those functions that are typically served by the family were to go unperformed, such as children not being raised properly to become contributing members of society (see Chapter 3).

The functionalist perspective is a very useful one, but it tends to overemphasize the extent of stability and order in society and to downplay the fact that social practices that are beneficial to one group in society may be dysfunctional to another. These cautions should be kept in mind when using this perspective.

The Conflict Perspective

Conflict theorists emphasize the inevitability of coercion, domination, conflict, and change in society. The **conflict perspective** is based on *the idea that society consists of different groups who struggle with one another to attain the scarce societal resources that are considered valuable, be they money, power, prestige, or the authority to impose one's values on society.* Karl Marx provided the foundation for the conflict perspective when he viewed society as consisting of different social classes (1967, originally published 1867–1895). The two central classes of his era were the proletariat, or the workers, and the bourgeoisie, or those who owned the businesses, factories, and textile mills in which the proletariat toiled. Marx saw these classes as being in constant struggle with each another to improve their respective positions in society. The workers tried to gain more income and control over their work; the owners tried to make more profits by lowering labor costs and getting workers to work more. For Marx, this conflict was irreconcilable, because what benefits one group necessarily works to the disadvantage of the other. Furthermore, if those in one group can gain an advantage in this struggle, they will use it to dominate and oppress the other group and enhance their own position. They might, for example, gain control of the government and pass legislation that limits the ways the subordinate groups could otherwise compete. A century ago in the United States, for example, it was illegal for workers to organize for the purposes of collective bargaining. This benefited the factory owners because workers were unable to use their strength of numbers to gain higher wages or better working conditions.

Although Marx limited his focus to class conflict, modern versions of conflict theory in sociology hold that domination, coercion, and the exercise of power occur to some degree in all groups and societies because they are the basic social mechanisms for regulating behavior and allocating resources (Collins, 1990; Dahrendorf, 1959; Duke, 1976). In addition to class conflict, groups and subcultures can engage in conflict over contrasting values. For example, some religious groups, such as the Mormons, place great value in family life, whereas other groups view the traditional family as only one of a number of ways people can organize their personal lives. These two perspectives on family are likely to assess social problems such as divorce and childbirth outside marriage in quite different ways. In fact, as we have seen, whether these conditions are even viewed as social problems depends on one's values. Another source of conflict in society is the gap that can arise between values and social practices. The United States, for example, professes to value equality for all. Yet at one time or another, African Americans, Italian Americans, Irish Americans, women, and Jewish Americans, to name but a few, have suffered severe discrimination.

In the conflict view, then, groups exert what power they possess over others when this serves their interests, and society consists of a wide array of such interest groups struggling to acquire a share of societal resources. An **interest group** is *a group whose members share distinct and common concerns and who benefit from similar social policies and practices*. Things that benefit one interest group may work to the disadvantage of others. Some interest groups are formally organized, such as the National Rifle Association, the Sierra Club, the National Manufacturers Association, or the American Civil Liberties Union. Other interest groups are informal, and people may not fully recognize that they are members of them. For example, college students constitute an informal interest group because all college students benefit from such things as lower tuition and increased government funding of student loans. Taxpayers without children of college age, however, might oppose such policies because their taxes would increase.

In the conflict view, social change involves redistributing scarce resources among various interest groups. A *vested interest group* is an interest group that

benefits from existing policies, practices, and social arrangements, and generally resists social changes that might threaten their privileges. However, the inevitable clash of interests ensures that any existing social arrangements eventually will be rearranged. Out of the resulting struggle, new winners will emerge and uneasy truces will be established. These truces, however, will be temporary, because new conflicts will develop that will lead to further struggle and change.

For the conflict theorist, a social problem arises when a group of people, believing that its interests are not being met or that it is not receiving a sufficient share of resources, works to overcome what it perceives as a disadvantage. Unlike functionalists, conflict theorists might view a phenomenon such as divorce as normal under some circumstances because it represents one way of dealing with marital discord. This does not mean that the disruptive effects of divorce are ignored or that divorce is not a social problem. Rather, it means that divorce becomes a social problem when particular groups that have power regard

The conflict perspective makes us aware that people vary substantially in terms of the social and economic resources available to them. The social programs and policies that would benefit the fur-coated woman in this photo are, in all likelihood, quite different from those that would benefit the homeless person huddled under a blanket.

their interests as being threatened by the extent of divorce in society.

Some caution is also called for in using the conflict perspective, especially the tendency to overemphasize the importance of conflict and inequality and to disregard the prevalence of stability and consensus in society. This can lead one to overlook factors important to social problems.

The Interactionist Perspective

Although the functionalist and conflict perspectives offer competing views of social life, the interactionist perspective is more of a supplement to the first two, showing how the social processes described in those perspectives enter into people's daily lives and shape their behavior. The **interactionist perspective** *focuses on everyday social interaction among individuals rather than on large societal structures such as politics, education, and the like* (Blumer, 1962; Hewitt, 2007). For interactionists, society consists of people interacting with one another; to understand society we must understand social interaction. It is through such interactions that groups, organizations, and society as a whole are created, maintained, and changed. The operation of educational institutions can be observed, for example, through students interacting with teachers and through school administrators making decisions. It is these day-to-day interactions that give education its shape and substance.

A central assumption of the interactionist perspective can be summarized in a paraphrase of a statement by sociologists William and Dorothy Thomas (1928): If people define situations as real, they are real in their consequences. In other words, people act on the basis of their beliefs and perceptions about situations. The term **definition of the situation** refers to *people's perceptions and interpretations of what is important in a situation and what actions are appropriate.* A central part of social interaction, then, is people's interpretations or definitions of others' behavior.

This process of definition and interpretation rests on the ability of human beings to use symbols. It is our symbol-using capabilities that enable us to attach complex social meanings to objects, events, or people. A *symbol* is something that stands for, represents, or takes the place of something else. Anything—any object, event, or word—can serve as a symbol. A crucifix, for example, symbolizes the beliefs of Roman Catholicism, whether it is made from wood, metal, or plastic; the Star of David likewise symbolizes Judaism. The meaning attached to a symbol is derived from social consensus; we simply agree that a particular object will represent something.

Because of our ability to use symbols, we live in a world that we create ourselves, through the meanings we attach to phenomena. In other words, we respond to symbolic or social meanings rather than to actual physical objects or actions, and what we do is the result of how we define and interpret those meanings. For example, we attach meanings to people through the use of labels, including deviant labels that carry some stigma with them. We call people "whores," "queers," "crooks," and "crazies." These labels influence how we relate to these people. And when people have been labeled, we come to expect them to behave in certain ways. A central tenet of the interactionist approach is that such social expectations, or norms, tend to influence the behavior of people who have been labeled, especially when the people themselves accept the meaning of the label attached to them. The prostitute, for example, who internalizes the social meaning implied by the label "cheap whore," may not aspire toward any other way of life. Her world and behavior are shaped by the fact that she accepts the stigmatizing label, whether it is true or not. This fact points to another important assertion of the interactionist perspective: What is important is not whether a particular definition of the situation is actually true but rather whether people believe the definition to be true.

Social life rests on the development of consensus about expected behavior. Such shared expectations guide our activities and make cooperative action possible. If this consensus breaks down, some sort of change must occur. Thus, for interactionists, social change involves developing some new consensus with different meanings and expectations.

From the interactionist perspective, a social problem exists when some social condition is defined by an influential group as stigmatizing or threatening to their values and disruptive of normal social expectations. For example, the interactionist would observe that there have been important changes in attitudes toward divorce in industrial societies. In addition to being more common today, divorce has less stigma attached to it than it did one hundred years ago. At the same time, however, divorce is viewed by many groups as a social problem because they see marital dissolution as posing a threat to family stability. If the family is such a basic social institution, divorce may challenge shared meanings and definitions that these groups hold about this institution.

Once again caution is called for in using the perspectives. Because of the emphasis on face-to-face interaction in shaping social reality, the interactionist approach can lead one to de-emphasize the part that social institutions, such as religion and politics, and large-scale social forces, such as industrialization, play in molding human behavior.

Using the Theoretical Perspectives

This discussion of the sociological perspectives is brief and simplified, and more detail will be provided in later chapters. The major elements of each perspective and its view on social problems have been outlined in Table 1.1. The three perspectives should not be viewed as either right or wrong, nor should one select a favorite and ignore the others. Instead, the perspectives should be seen as three different "tools," each of which is useful in analyzing particular social problems. The three perspectives are not equally useful for examining every social problem, nor can any single perspective explain all aspects of human behavior and society. To gain a full understanding of any particular problem, the use of more than one approach may be required.

Constructing Social Problems: The Mass Media and Other Influences

Use of the theoretical perspectives can be illustrated by looking at an important element of the study of social problems: how a social condition becomes a social problem. This chapter has stressed the point that a condition is considered a social problem when an influential group perceives the condition as a threat to its values or way of life and can do something about it. In other words, the existence of a condition alone, even when the condition produces negative conse-

quences, does not make it a social problem; to become a social problem, it must be so defined by some group (Holstein and Miller, 2003; Spector and Kitsuse, 2000). This process of social definition or construction involves a number of elements: how and why groups identify conditions as problems, how the groups develop an understanding of the causes of the problems, and how solutions are developed and implemented. Each of the three perspectives contributes to our understanding of this process.

From the *functionalist perspective,* the social construction of social problems depends, at least in part, on the extent of social disruption or social disorganization produced by a social condition. Conditions that are more disruptive are more likely to be defined as social problems by significant groups or large numbers of people. A highly disruptive condition—a large-scale nuclear war, for example—would be defined as a problem by virtually everyone because the level of social disorganization that results from it is so extensive, universal, and profound. But many social conditions disrupt the lives of only some people, and these conditions may be defined as problems by some groups but not others. In other words, with lower levels of social disruption, the definition of social problems would be characterized by more debate and controversy and less consensus.

The *conflict perspective* helps us recognize that elites and others with access to resources or power play a greater role in this process of social definition: It is the conditions that negatively affect their values and way of life that are most likely to be defined as

TABLE 1.1   An Outline of the Sociological Perspectives

	Functionalism	Conflict Theory	Interactionism
View of Society	A system of interrelated and interdependent parts.	Made up of groups struggling with one another over scarce resources.	Individuals in face-to-face interaction create social consensus.
View of the Individual	People are shaped by society to perform important functions for society.	People are shaped by the position of their groups in society.	People are symbol manipulators who create their social world through social interaction and consensus.
View of Social Change	The social system tends to resist change as disruptive.	Change is inevitable and continuous.	Change occurs when there is no shared consensus about expected behavior and a newly found consensus develops.
View of Social Problems	Caused by dysfunctional activities or disorganization in the social system.	Arise when a group believes its interests are not being served and works to overcome perceived disadvantage.	Arise when a condition is defined as stigmatizing or disruptive of normal social expectations.
Key Concepts	integration, interdependence, stability, equilibrium	interest, power, dominance, conflict, coercion	interpretation, consensus, shared expectations, socially created reality

social problems. Or at least, the views and interests of the powerful will be influential in shaping how all social problems and their solutions are defined, even those problems that affect mostly the less powerful. So, definitions of social problems are constructed out of the clash of competing interest groups.

The *interactionist perspective* recognizes the importance of symbols and social meanings in shaping human life, and it points out that defining a "condition" as a "problem" is a matter of attaching certain negative meanings to the condition. The process of interpretation is central to human social life, and people have to interpret a set of objective conditions as something that is "bad" or "negative" before they will act on it. Beyond defining a condition as a problem, the meaning of the problem can vary from one group to another, and this can affect what kind of solutions are sought. So, divorce may be seen as a problem by two groups, but one group sees the problem as the too easy accessibility of divorce while the other sees the problem as divorce being too difficult to obtain.

This brief illustration of constructing social problems demonstrates how using the three perspectives can provide a more complete understanding of a topic. This social construction of social problems has to do with rhetoric, or persuasive communication: Under what conditions are one group's claims about a social condition accepted by others, and when do those claims serve as the basis for social policy and social action? This social construction process is complex and continuous, and the resulting social definitions are constantly shifting and changing. Although many things play a part in this process of persuasive communication, the mass media are especially influential in the modern, global world. In one fashion or another, media attention has become critical to influencing people's definitions of social problems. Groups with access to the media are much more likely to have their interpretations of social conditions given serious consideration and to have their solutions seriously debated. This text considers the myriad of forces that contribute to the social construction of social problems, and in a number of chapters special attention is devoted to the role of the media in this process.

Research on Social Problems

Until research has been done to test a theory, it is merely speculative. **Research** refers to *the systematic examination of empirical data.* Research can provide the most coherent and objective information about the causes of social problems, their extent, and the effectiveness of solutions. Without a foundation in research, our approach to problems is likely to be surrounded by speculation, misunderstanding, and bias, and we may expend resources in the pursuit of ineffective solutions. If this occurs, we have not only wasted resources but also left the real source of the problem to grow more serious. For these reasons, we must understand what good research is and how we can use its principles in our everyday assessment of social problems.

The Scientific Method

Research conducted by sociologists is based on the scientific method. **Science** is *a method of obtaining objective and systematic knowledge through observation.* The foundation of the scientific approach is the belief that claims about what is correct or incorrect must be demonstrated to be true through some observations in the world (Sullivan, 2001). Intuition, speculation, or common sense can never replace the empirical test of one's claims. Scientific theories are linked to scientific research through **hypotheses,** which are *tentative statements that can be tested regarding relationships between two or more factors.* Hypotheses are statements whose accuracy can be assessed through observation. If hypotheses are verified through observation, this provides support for the theory; if they are not, our confidence in the theory is reduced. The more empirical support there is for a theory, the more useful it is in attacking social problems.

Science is not foolproof, but it is the most effective means available for acquiring systematic, verifiable knowledge about the world and about social problems and their solutions. In the Applied Research insert, science is compared with some other ways of gaining knowledge, showing what makes the scientific approach superior in this realm. Science does have its limitations, however, and it is crucial to understand which issues it cannot resolve. Science is the preferred source of knowledge on issues that can be resolved *through observation.* Some issues are not amenable to such resolution. For example, science cannot verify the existence of a supreme deity or say which religious beliefs are correct because these are not issues that can be settled through observation. They are matters of faith, choice, or revelation but not of science. Likewise, science cannot tell us which personal values are right and preferable because these are again matters of personal choice or judgment.

Conducting Research

In conducting research on social problems, social scientists are very careful and systematic about how they make their observations, which serve as the evidence

Untangling Myths and Facts About Social Problems

Sociologists take the position that scientific research provides the most accurate and useful knowledge for coping with social problems. Science, of course, is not the only way to gain an understanding of the world. For example, people often use tradition as a source of guidance. This might take the form of religious teachings about sex and marriage or proverbs such as "Birds of a feather flock together" and "Two heads are better than one." People also turn to their own personal experience for direction. If we visit a prison and see that most inmates are nonwhite, this can lead us to believe that crime rates are much higher among nonwhites than whites. Knowledge from tradition and experience often accumulates and blends together to form what people call "common sense": practical wisdom that encourages people to make decisions that they believe are sound without having any special training or expertise.

In fact, sociology has been called "the science of common sense" by critics who assume that it merely "proves" what everybody else already knows through common sense. However, research often shows that people's commonsense beliefs about social problems are false, or at least oversimplified. Consider these statements:

1. The crime rate is much higher in the lower class than it is in the middle class.
2. Reading pornography increases the likelihood that men will commit acts of sexual violence against women.
3. Because of the civil rights movement and affirmative action legislation, the gap in income between blacks and whites has narrowed substantially in the past four decades.
4. A person who does not engage in homosexual activities or use drugs intravenously has very little risk of becoming infected with the virus for acquired immune deficiency syndrome (AIDS).

At one time or another, each of us has probably believed that at least some of these statements are true. Yet social science research has shown each one to be false, or at least to be far too simple, as shown by the following:

1. If we use arrest statistics as our data, then this statement is supported, but most people who commit crimes are not arrested. A growing body of evidence based on self-reports of criminal activity suggests that what distinguishes the social classes is not the amount of crime but rather the types of crimes and the likelihood of being arrested. The poor are more likely to commit highly visible crimes, such as homicide or assault, which are likely to be reported to the police and result in arrests. Middle-class people commit crimes such as embezzlement, fraud, or tax evasion that often go unreported (see Chapter 9).
2. There is little convincing evidence that pornography predisposes a person to commit sexual violence, although people who commit such crimes may also read pornography.

for their scientific conclusions. It is important to understand a little about these research methods in order to appreciate and evaluate the scientific conclusions drawn.

Basically, four types of research are conducted (Sullivan, 2001). *Direct observation* is research in which the social scientist sees or hears something himself or herself. This might occur, for example, if the researcher joined in the daily activities of drug sellers, watching how they purchased and sold their drugs, talking to them about how they organized to protect themselves, and observing how they dealt with police interference. These direct observations would then serve as the evidence for verifying hypotheses.

The term *surveys* refers to research in which people are asked questions about their beliefs, attitudes, feelings, or behavior. A study of drug use, for example, might involve showing people a list of illegal drugs and asking them which they had used in the past month. Their answers to the questions are the data or evidence used to test hypotheses. It is important to understand that, with surveys, we have not observed the people's behavior (such as whether they have actually taken drugs) but only what they say about their behavior.

Archival research uses information collected by some organization, agency, or individual for reasons other than research. Studies of drug use, for example,

Much pornography portrays violence against women, and it may well be the violence rather than the sexual content of pornography that encourages violence against women (see Chapter 11).

3. Unfortunately, research shows that the gap has hardly changed over the past three decades. Although many blacks have benefited from such legislation, the gap between the incomes of blacks and whites has been especially impervious to change (see Chapter 6).

4. Although it is true in the United States that most of those who contract AIDS are men who have sex with other men or people who engage in intravenous drug use, heterosexual transmission of AIDS has been growing rapidly, currently accounting for 36 percent of new AIDS cases. And worldwide, 60 percent of HIV infections result from heterosexual intercourse (see Chapter 4).

What is wrong with common sense in these realms? Basically, common sense does not normally involve an empirical and systematic effort to distinguish fact from fiction. Rather, it tends to accept untested and unquestioned assumptions because "everyone knows" they are true. In other words, some commonsense knowledge is a "myth" in that there is little evidence of its truth, although some people still accept it as true. Commonsense knowledge is also very slow to change—even when change seems called for—because the change may threaten cherished values or social patterns.

Even when common sense contains some truth, reality is often vastly more complicated than common sense suggests. Sociological research incorporates procedures that advance our knowledge by establishing facts through observation and by using procedures that reduce bias. Common sense is important and should not be ignored, but an unthinking and unverified acceptance of commonsense beliefs can blind people to social realities. This has important implications for social policy. It is only through the development of an accurate, scientifically verified understanding of social problems that we can hope to overcome them—even if it means relinquishing some of our most cherished commonsense preconceptions.

Each of the remaining chapters includes two features that emphasize these points. At the beginning of each chapter, a Myths and Facts section will contrast some inaccurate or misleading commonsense beliefs about some problem with facts that have been established through research. This comparison encourages students to distinguish between beliefs that have no empirical foundation and may be myths from facts that have been substantiated through observation. Elsewhere in each chapter, an Applied Research section illustrates the use of sociological research in solving problems or evaluating how well solutions work. This emphasizes the theme that the development of social policies about social problems should be influenced by systematic and scientific assessment of their impact as well as by our own personal values.

have been based on criminal justice system records of arrests and convictions for drug possession or selling and of hospital emergency room records of treatment for drug overdoses. If this recorded information is relevant to the research question and available to the researcher, then it can serve as the evidence for testing hypotheses.

The fourth type of research is *experiments,* which are controlled methods of collecting evidence that give us confidence in stating that one factor caused another to happen. If we wanted to assess the effectiveness of a drug education program in reducing drug use among high school students, for example, we could conduct an experiment in which the students' level of drug use is measured both before and after they have been exposed to the program. A decline in drug use after the program would be evidence of its effectiveness, especially if a control group that was not exposed to the program did not show a similar decline. Actually, the term *experiment* refers to a method of organizing observations. The actual observations in an experiment might be done through direct observation, surveys, or archival records.

Whatever kind of research is involved, social scientists tend to follow a series of systematic steps in conducting the research. They first formulate the research problem and develop a detailed research design that describes exactly how the research will be conducted.

This research design is carefully reviewed by other experts to ensure that the problem is one that can be resolved through scientific investigation. These experts also review the design to make sure the researcher used the most modern and effective methods for studying the problem. Then the actual observations are made and the resulting data carefully analyzed to see what conclusions could be drawn from them. The data analysis and conclusions are also carefully reviewed by other experts to make sure that the conclusions are accurate and warranted. Only after this elaborate review process is the research and its results publicly disseminated through publication in a book or professional journal.

This methodical process gives scientists confidence in the accuracy of their conclusions. The process does not guarantee accuracy, but it does make the scientific method more likely than other methods to give us accurate knowledge of the world.

Values, Interest Groups, and Objectivity

An issue that is especially important and quite controversial regarding research on social problems is that of scientific objectivity, or the attempt by scientists to prevent their personal values from affecting the outcome of their research. This does not mean that scientists are without values or passions. Many are intensely concerned about social problems such as crime, divorce, family violence, and nuclear war. At the same time, scientists realize that their personal values can, and probably will, bias their research. Early in the twentieth century, sociologist Max Weber laid out one position on this issue when he argued that sociology should remain as *value free* as possible because human values can distort sound scientific investigation (1958, originally published 1919). Weber argued that sociologists should suspend their personal and political values when engaging in scientific research. Contemporary advocates of Weber's position would concede that such suspension is difficult to accomplish but that abandoning the effort would be disastrous: There would be no means of acquiring an accurate body of knowledge to guide our consideration of ways of alleviating social problems (Gordon, 1988).

Karl Marx (1964, originally published 1848) eloquently stated a position opposite to that of Weber's on this controversy. Marx was a strong champion of the cause of the poor and the downtrodden, and he wanted to use science to improve their plight. He argued that social scientists should bring strong moral commitments to their work and use science to change inequitable or immoral social conditions. Likewise,

there are sociologists today who believe that social research should be guided by personal and political values and directed toward alleviating social ills (Fay, 1987; Shostak, 2001).

Sociologist Alvin Gouldner (1976) has suggested a middle ground between these two positions. He agreed that scientists have values and that the influence of those values on research, which is often very subtle, can never be totally eliminated. But Gouldner proposed that we should deny neither our values nor the negative impact they can have on research. He urged that scientists should be explicit about what their values are. In this way, other scientists are forewarned and are thus better able to spot ways in which research findings may be influenced by personal bias.

The problem of enhancing scientific objectivity can be especially difficult for scientists who are closely associated with some interest group. Close involvement with an interest group can lead, often unknowingly, to distortions and misperceptions that throw into question the scientist's research on topics of interest to that group. For example, sociologists who are actively involved in such environmental groups as Greenpeace or Campaign for the Earth may have difficulty in recognizing ways in which the outcome of their research might be influenced by their personal position on the issues. Any research on environmental issues conducted by these people should be reviewed carefully for such sources of bias.

Assessing Data: Problems and Pitfalls

How can we detect error or bias in what we read? There are, of course, no foolproof guidelines, but we can draw some lessons from scientific research to become better-informed consumers of information.

SAMPLING PROBLEMS A basic question to ask about any set of data is: Upon whom or what were the observations made? In scientific research, collecting data on all the people or events about whom you are interested is normally impossible. In a study of divorce in the United States, for example, interviewing all couples who have divorced would be too expensive and time consuming, because more than a million do so every year. Instead, researchers typically study a **sample,** which consists of *elements that are taken from a group or population and that serve as a source of data.* To be useful, samples should be *representative,* or reflect the group or population that is under study in ways that are considered important.

The sampling problems that can arise when unrepresentative samples are used in the analysis of social problems—and the misleading conclusions that can result—are well illustrated by investigations of homosexuality. In the 1940s and 1950s, studies of gay men by psychologists and psychiatrists typically came to the conclusion that homosexuality is the result of a personality disturbance stemming from disordered relationships with parents during childhood. They also concluded that, as a group, gay men were unhappy and maladjusted individuals. The samples used in these studies consisted of gay men who were the patients of psychologists or psychiatrists. Virtually all the gay men in these samples were unhappy, maladjusted, and had disordered relationships with their parents—a strong association indeed. Yet the problem with the sampling in these studies should be fairly obvious: Gay men who seek psychological counseling are probably not representative of all gay men. People who seek counseling, irrespective of their sexual orientation, do so because they already have personal problems. Gay men who do not have such problems do not seek counseling, and they do not appear in samples of gays collected in this fashion. These early studies, then, contained a built-in bias, caused by poor sampling procedures, toward the conclusion that gay men are psychologically disturbed. Studies using more representative samples have concluded that sexual orientation, by itself, probably does not lead to personality disturbances or unhappiness (Cabaj and Stein, 1996; Ross, Paulsen, and Stalstrom, 1988). When studies do find higher rates of psychological disorders among gays, they are almost always caused by social circumstances, sometimes involving the stigma and hostility that is often directed toward gays. A basic question to ask regarding any data or information, then, is whether it is based on a representative sample.

ASSESSING CAUSALITY One of the major goals in the study of social problems is to find their causes. By **causality,** we mean that *one factor has an effect on or produces a change in some other factor.* Once we have established the causes of a social problem, we are in a better position to determine what programs or policies might alleviate it. However, discovering causal relationships can be a difficult task because causality cannot be directly observed. Rather, we infer causality from the observation of *associations* or *correlations* between things in the world. If changes in one factor are regularly associated with changes in the other factor, then the first factor may be causing those changes.

The early studies of gay men mentioned previously had established an association between sexual orientation and psychological maladjustment, but a little thought will show that this association alone is not sufficient to infer that psychological disturbance causes homosexuality. It is equally logical to infer that being gay, especially in a society in which homosexuality is highly stigmatized, produces psychological disturbance and unhappiness. Thus, in addition to establishing an association, a second criterion to be satisfied before inferring causality is that the *time sequence* be correct: The causal factor must occur before whatever it is presumed to cause.

A third criterion to be satisfied in assessing causality is that the association not be spurious. A *spurious relationship* is one in which the association between two factors occurs because each is independently associated with some third factor. For example, there is a strong association between rates of ice cream consumption and juvenile delinquency, but few people would argue that eating ice cream causes delinquency or vice versa. Obviously, the relationship is a spurious one in which both ice cream consumption and delinquency are related to a third factor, the summer season. School vacations and warm weather offer greater opportunity to eat ice cream and to engage in delinquent acts.

Unfortunately, much research on social problems can satisfy only one or two of the criteria, and this leaves us less confident regarding causality. The central point here is to be cautious and critical about any claims regarding causal relationships.

MEASURING SOCIAL PROBLEMS All scientific research involves *measurement,* which refers to making observations that are presumed to be evidence that something exists or that something has a certain value. The observations that are made are referred to as "indicators." An indicator of juvenile delinquency, for example, might be vandalism at a school gymnasium. Likewise, severe bruises on a child's forearm might be considered indicators of child abuse.

A central concern in the study of social problems is that the indicators of variables have *validity,* or that they accurately measure what they are intended to measure. A thermometer, for example, is a valid measure of temperature but not of volume. The study of child abuse provides illustrations of some of the difficulties of finding valid measures of social problems. If we define child abuse as injuring a child not by accident but in anger or with deliberate intent, then most would agree that a cigarette burn on a child's buttocks is a valid indicator of child abuse; there is no other imaginable reason why such burns should occur (Gelles, 1987). But what about a bruise on the arm? Some groups in our society approve of physically striking a child for disciplinary reasons, even if some bruising results. Other groups define any physical punishment as unacceptable.

Social policy based on conclusions drawn from invalid measures can be very harmful. It may lead us to think we are moving toward alleviating a problem when in fact we are not. Meanwhile, the problem may become more serious as we experiment with untested and ineffective solutions.

ASSESSING CLAIMS If information about sampling, measurement, or causality is not available, what can you do to reduce the chance of deception or distortion? There are a number of additional guidelines that should be kept in mind:

1. Is the claim made by a person or group of people with a strong self-interest in a particular interpretation or conclusion? Their personal interest may be biasing their presentation or interpretation of the data.

2. Can the claim be verified by yourself or others? Even reputable newspapers and magazines sometimes, in good faith, report data that cannot later be verified.

3. Are the claims presented in a propagandistic fashion? There are a number of propaganda techniques that are used to persuade the public. For example, "glittering generalities" involve the use of highly attractive but vague and meaningless words and phrases such as "restoring law and order" or "communism." "Testimonial" is the technique of using famous and respected people to support a program or policy as a means of engendering public support. Any claims using such techniques should be assessed very carefully.

Future Prospects: Solving Social Problems

What Can We Do About Social Problems?

Our goal is not only to understand social problems but also to solve them or at least to alleviate some of their more undesirable consequences. To deal with this aspect of the issue, each chapter in this book concludes with a Future Prospects section where various attempts to deal with the problems discussed in the chapter are explored. Solutions to problems, of course, can take a number of different forms, some rather surprising at first. Solutions to social problems can fall into one of the following categories:

1. *Prevention*. Some efforts focus on preventing a problem from arising in the first place. Drug education programs, for example, attempt to stop young people from taking drugs before they start.

2. *Intervention*. When prevention is not possible or is ineffective, programs often focus on intervening after a problem has emerged with an effort to reduce or eliminate it. Drug treatment programs focus on this—weaning people off drugs after they have become addicted.

3. *Social reform*. Some forms of prevention or intervention focus on social reform, which involves significant change in some social institutions or social practices. Social reform suggests that the problem stems, at least in part, from some serious failings in social organization or social institutions. It suggests that society is not healthy, and the persistence of the social problem is a symptom of this. Widespread drug abuse, for example, may reflect persistent poverty, unemployment, and lack of opportunity among some groups—suggesting that economic institutions are failing to provide a place where all people can work and support themselves and their families. Keep in mind that social reform may be a form of prevention or intervention, but prevention and intervention do not necessarily involve social reform.

4. *Reconstruction*. It may be possible in some cases to alleviate social problems by redefining their nature and extent. Groups that do not consider a particular condition to be a social problem may become more prominent in the arena where social problems are socially constructed. When this happens, they may become influential in changing policies so that fewer societal resources are directed at changing those conditions.

5. *Alleviating consequences*. Whether or not we can solve a particular problem, we may also want to direct attention toward alleviating the negative consequences of the problem. For example, even though the problem of drug abuse persists, we can still do such things as help the victims of crimes that are committed as a part of the problem of drug abuse.

Each Future Prospects section in later chapters explores policies that fall into some or all of these categories.

The Interplay of Social Policy and Research

Solutions to social problems never magically appear. Some action must be taken if solutions are to be effected. These actions develop into what is called **social policy:** *laws, administrative procedures, and other formal and informal social practices that are intended to promote social changes focused on alleviating particular* *social problems* (Jencks, 1992; Koppel, 2002). Social policies are inherently controversial because they are based, in part, on human values. Groups with differing values will often push for very different solutions to the same problem. Or they may, as we have seen, disagree over which social conditions are social problems. This controversy and disagreement is an inevitable feature of the debate over social problems and their solutions.

Within the confines of this debate, however, sociological theory and research can be applied as tools for assessing the validity and effectiveness of particular solutions. Science, as we have seen, cannot tell us what values to hold, but it can help us assess whether the factors we believe underlie a problem are the actual sources of the problem. Scientific observation can also assess whether particular solutions to problems actually work.

To emphasize the role of social policy in identifying and solving social problems, each chapter contains a Policy Issues insert. Each insert explores the different positions on an issue discussed in the chapter and evaluates what support social science research provides for these positions. This serves to stress the theme of the interplay between social policy and social research. The Policy Issues insert in this chapter focuses on solutions to the problem of spouse abuse. Some further linkages between social policy and research are outlined in Table 1.2. In fact, there is a specialty area in the social sciences—variously called applied sociology, applied social research, or evaluation research—that is devoted precisely to this endeavor (Straus, 2002; Sullivan, 1992).

Who Provides Solutions?

Social problems, as we have seen, are conditions that can be remedied through some form of collective action. "Collective action" merely means that people work together toward a solution. In some cases, this takes the form of interest groups working through the normal political process. In the United States, this could occur at the federal, state, or local level. Politicians who are aware of a problem pass legislation to alleviate it, judges make rulings that have an impact on a problem, or private corporations and foundations develop programs to solve a problem. The solution to a problem may even be developed in good part by people who are unaffected, or at best indirectly affected, by it.

Organized protest and social action outside the normal political process represent another way that solutions to social problems can emerge. Groups affected by a problem can strike, riot, or march in the

Organized protest outside the normal political process is one way to shape solutions to social problems. These marchers in Nairobi, Kenya, were participating in the World Social Forum in 2006 and trying to use mass protest to influence the impact of global capitalism on the world.

TABLE 1.2	Linkage Between Social Policy and Social Science Research

Stages in the Policy Process	Possible Research Contribution
Problem Formulation	Assess extent of problem, who is affected, and costs of doing nothing.
Policy Formulation	Assess positive or negative impact of various policy alternatives.
Policy Implementation	Assess whether a program achieves policy goals in an efficient and effective manner.
Evaluation	Assess whether and how a solution has an impact on a problem or on other groups in society; determine whether any new problems are created.
Closure	Assess whether any further policy application would be warranted.

Domestic Violence: How to Intervene?

Domestic violence is a particularly tragic social problem with its jarring intrusion of injury and cruelty into the intimacy of the family. It is also a difficult problem for police officers who are often first on the scene of such violence and whose job it is to make decisions about how to handle the alleged perpetrator of the violence. In the past, such decisions have been left to the discretion and judgment of the officer in the field. Applied social research now offers a basis for developing social policies regarding this issue. Working with the Police Foundation, a research organization in Washington, DC, criminologist Lawrence Sherman and sociologist Richard Berk (1984) designed a study to assess which actions by police officers actually reduce the likelihood that a spouse abuser would be involved in future domestic violence incidents. When police officers respond to a domestic violence call, they have basically three alternatives: arrest the person accused of abuse; separate the couple for a time by ordering the alleged abuser to leave the premises; or attempt to serve as mediators between the parties.

Sherman and Berk asked police officers in Minneapolis to randomly apply one of these three intervention strategies—arrest, separation, or mediation—to each domestic violence call of which they were a part. For ethical and practical reasons, they limited the study to simple, or misdemeanor, assault where there was no severe injury or life-threatening situation. Their measure of the effectiveness of these interventions was whether an alleged abuser was involved in another domestic violence incident in the six months following the original police intervention.

Their basic finding supported the policy of arrest: Those arrested were significantly less likely to be involved in a repeat episode of domestic violence. This was not, however, a result of the fact that being jailed left them with less opportunity than others to commit acts of domestic violence, because those arrested were released very quickly and were thus equally able to engage in such acts as were those who experienced separation or mediation.

After Sherman and Berk reached their conclusions, the Minneapolis and many other police departments established administrative policies encouraging or requiring officers to use the arrest strategy when responding to spouse-abuse calls. Thus, many law enforcement agencies began to take a stronger stand in protecting women from domestic assault, a stand that was shown empirically by Sherman and Berk to have a better chance of reducing the problem.

Because social problems are complicated, sociologists recognize that one research study is not likely to tell us all we need to know. To see if the results would hold up in other places and at other times, variations on the Sherman–Berk study have been done in a number of other cities (Dunford, Huizinga, and Elliott, 1990; Hirschel, Hutchison, and Dean, 1992; Maxwell, Garner, and Fagan, 2001). Generally, the results have been supportive of the efficacy of arrest over other approaches in reducing spouse abuse, but the studies also show that the effect of arrest is not nearly as strong or as consistent as earlier studies had suggested. Why the difference in findings? It may be that Sherman and Berk, given the way they designed their study, inadvertently studied a select group of abusers on whom arrest was particularly effective. This illustrates the concern with sampling problems affecting research, mentioned previously in this chapter. The later studies, looking at a broader sampling of abusers, found that arrest may work well with people whose reputations would be more negatively affected by an arrest, such as the affluent or those with middle-class jobs. On the other hand, for those who are unemployed or irregularly employed, arrest may not be as significant a threat to their reputations or as disruptive to their lifestyles. In addition, research has been extended beyond the issue of arrest to explore such things as severity of sentencing, finding that more severe sentences, such as jail time rather than probation, tend to reduce future episodes of domestic violence (Thistlethwaite, Wooldredge, and Gibbs, 1998). So, sociologists continue to do research in an effort to narrow down their understanding of which batterers of women are deterred by arrest or by severe sentences.

These studies on domestic violence illustrate the continuous interplay between research and policy, showing how social policy emerges, at least in part, from scientifically supported recommendations about how to handle social problems.

streets to force government or private organizations to change their practices. In some cases, a **social movement,** *a collective, organized effort to promote or resist social change through some noninstitutionalized or unconventional means,* may emerge. The civil rights movement, the environmental movement, and the antiglobalization movement are examples of social movements that have used demonstration and protest to force recalcitrant politicians and corporations to change their practices related to social problems. All three of these movements, by the way, have had significant support from college student-led collective action.

In recent years, there has been vigorous debate over the role of the government in identifying and solving social problems. Beginning with the New Deal of the 1930s and continuing through the 1960s, there was considerable support for the government to take responsibility for trying to solve social problems such as crime, poverty, and environmental pollution. In particular, the government used its ability to raise revenue through taxation—its fiscal policy—to attack social problems. For example, it raised money to support such programs as Medicare and Social Security. In addition, in times of economic downturn, the government went into debt, creating a budget deficit, to provide support for the unemployed, stimulate business activity, and create jobs to give people temporary work. The size of the government grew, and many social programs were established. At the risk of oversimplification, we can call this approach to the role of the government in social problems the *interventionist* approach.

With Ronald Reagan's election as president of the United States in 1980, pressure from another direction regarding social problems mounted. This pressure was based on the belief that government can be a hindrance to the solution of many problems and should play only a limited role in attacking them. Rather, the government's primary role should be to create a climate that promotes business expansion, which will in turn produce prosperity that will alleviate many, although certainly not all, social problems. Where possible, solutions to problems should arise from a competitive, market-driven economy. Some even promote the "privatization" of government services and activities, with businesses and corporations doing many things that government once did. Furthermore, many policy analysts support "devolution," or shifting the focus of attention away from higher levels of government, such as the federal level, and toward state and local levels that are closer

to the problems being addressed. Finally, some proponents of this approach argue for reemphasizing the importance of individualism, of people using their own efforts in a competitive environment to improve their lot in life. Social policy, in short, should be less related to government intervention and more dependent on the actions of individuals or private groups and the working of impersonal, economic forces. Again, at the risk of oversimplification, this approach is labeled the *laissez-faire* approach. The French term *laissez-faire,* meaning "to let do" or to leave people alone, refers to the belief that government should intervene as little as possible in people's lives or the workings of society.

Historian Arthur Schlesinger, Jr. (1986) argues that the United States experiences a cyclical shift in national involvement between these extremes—changing from an emphasis on public action to that of private interest and self-fulfillment and back again—every twenty-five years or so. Whether it is cyclical or not, these contrasting views of the government's role in solving social problems certainly have been joined in debate in recent decades as never before. The outcome of this debate shapes which policies will be developed to attack the problems that we will address in later chapters. This book will, therefore, discuss the interventionist and laissez-faire positions at greater length when they are relevant to particular social problems; the discussions in the Policy Issues inserts especially will focus on the extent to which policies are interventionist or laissez-faire in nature.

Should We Solve the Problem?

Once a social condition has been judged to be a social problem, the search for solutions begins. At this point, there may be widespread agreement, at least in the abstract, that the problem should be solved. There are still, however, some final issues that need to be weighed.

1. *Can we accept the costs of a solution?* Because economic resources are limited, money used to clean up the environment is not available to fight crime or build defense weapons. Any effort to solve social ills will mean that fewer resources are available to solve other problems.

2. *Does a solution to one problem create yet other problems?* As we emphasized in discussing the sociological perspectives, a society is a complex intertwining of many parts, and changing one

part may have consequences for other parts. If, for example, we could effectively eliminate prostitution and drug dealing, what would happen to the people who earn a living that way? Would they turn to other crimes to support themselves? There may be times when we decide that the "cure" is worse than the "disease."

3. *Is a particular solution feasible?* Given the political and social climate and the cultural values in the United States, are there some solutions to problems that would be impossible to accomplish because of resistance from some groups? Coping with alcoholism, for example, by banning all use of alcohol is simply not feasible, as the experiment with Prohibition in the 1920s showed.

International Perspectives: Social Problems in Other Societies

People in the United States, of course, tend to be most concerned about social problems in their own country. However, there are three reasons why we should focus some of our attention on social problems in other societies and cultures (Schaeffer, 1997). First of all, we can gain additional insight into problems and their solutions when we observe them in cultures different from our own. Is the nature and extent of some social problem in the United States different from that in other countries? If so, then we can look for the factors unique to the American experience that produce this difference. We can also examine which solutions have worked elsewhere.

This does not mean that they will automatically work here, but it does give us some insight into which solutions to consider.

A second reason for taking an international perspective is that nations today are intertwined in complex relationships in which we all depend on one another to an extent. International trade agreements affect the jobs available to people in Portland, Maine, and Albuquerque, New Mexico; Bolivian farmers survive by growing coca plants, which produce illegal drugs available in the United States; political instability in Southeast Asia sends immigrants to the United States, increasing cultural diversity here and contributing to racial and ethnic conflict. Therefore, to find the causes of and solutions for social problems affecting the United States, it is sometimes necessary to explore social and economic developments in other parts of the world.

A third reason for a more global perspective is that some social problems are inherently global rather than national or regional in nature. This is true of many environmental problems. The sources of acid rain and global warming, for example, are found in many nations, and these problems will affect all the peoples of the world. By their very nature, the spread of such problems will not be stopped by national boundaries.

So, where most appropriate, illustrations of the nature and extent of social problems in other societies and cultures are included in the discussion of problems in the United States. To focus attention on this issue, each chapter contains an International Perspectives insert, which elaborates on some of the global connections and issues relevant to the problem discussed in the particular chapter. Global issues are further explored in the text itself.

LINKAGES

Social problems do not exist in isolation from one another. Rather, problems tend to be linked together such that the worsening of one problem can contribute to the worsening of others. For example, an epidemic disease such as AIDS is a health problem discussed in Chapter 4, whereas the use of crack cocaine is related to drug abuse, discussed in Chapter 10. Yet these two problems are linked because some crack addicts use dirty needles and share equipment, which can contribute to the spread of the AIDS virus. So as intravenous drug use becomes more prevalent, the AIDS virus has a better chance of spreading. Alleviate one problem, and we will have made some progress toward alleviating the other. To encourage this consideration of linkages, each chapter includes a brief insert that suggests one or two of the less obvious ways in which the problems in that chapter are linked to problems in other chapters.

Summary

1. Sociology offers one of the most useful approaches to understanding social problems and finding solutions to them. Social problems involve public issues and are not merely personal troubles. They are fundamentally social in nature because their causes and solutions have to do with the workings of society. Four social conditions that can play a part in the emergence of social problems are deviation from group values and norms, a decline in the effectiveness of social institutions, extensive social and cultural diversity, and the exercise of power.

2. The sociological imagination is the ability to recognize the relationship between what is happening in your own personal life and the social forces that surround you.

3. Sociological insights are formulated into theories. Very general explanations of social reality are called theoretical perspectives. The three major theoretical perspectives in sociology today are functionalism, conflict theory, and interactionism.

4. From the functionalist perspective, society is viewed as a system made up of interrelated and interdependent parts, each performing a function that contributes to the operation of the whole society. Social problems arise when some element of society becomes dysfunctional and interferes with the efficient operation or stability of the system or the achievement of societal goals.

5. From the conflict perspective, society is viewed as consisting of a variety of groups who struggle with one another to attain scarce societal resources that are considered valuable. Social problems arise when a group, believing that its interests are not being met or that it is not receiving sufficient scarce resources, works to overcome what it perceives as a disadvantage.

6. The interactionist perspective focuses on everyday social interaction among people rather than on larger societal structures. It emphasizes the importance of definition and interpretation and the role of shared expectations in shaping behavior. Social problems arise when a condition is defined by an influential group as stigmatizing or threatening to its values and disruptive of normal social expectations.

7. Theories must be tested through research, which for sociologists is based on the scientific method. Science emphasizes objective and systematic observation as a source of knowledge. Theories are linked to research through hypotheses, which are tentative statements that can be tested about the relationship between two or more factors.

8. Although the subject is controversial, most scientists emphasize the importance of objectivity, or the attempt to prevent personal values from affecting the outcome of research. There are a number of factors to watch for in assessing research data, including sampling problems, the assessment of causality, measurement problems, and assessing the claims people make.

9. Solutions to social problems can focus on prevention, intervention, social reform, reconstruction, or alleviating consequences. The best means for finding effective solutions to social problems is through an interplay between the development of social policy and its assessment through scientific research. However, not all problems can or should be solved, because the costs may be too high or there may be disagreement over how to solve them.

Key Terms

authority

causality

conflict perspective

definition of the situation

deviance

ethnocentrism

functionalist perspective

hypotheses

interactionist perspective

interest group

norms

power

research

sample

science

social institutions

social movement

social policy

social problem

sociological imagination

sociology

subculture

theoretical perspectives

theory

values

The Internet has become an invaluable resource in trying to understand social problems and their solutions. Each chapter of this text offers suggestions for useful explorations of the Internet, relevant to the topics in this course. One good way to begin is to look for Web sites relevant to the discipline of sociology and the study of social problems. For example, to learn more about sociology, go to the search vehicle called Yahoo! **(www.yahoo.com)** and select the "more" choice and then "Directory" search category. Then select the "Social Science" category and then "Sociology." At this point, by selecting "Organizations," you will have choices of going to the home pages of many sociological organizations in the United States, Canada, New Zealand, and others. Start by choosing "American Sociological Association" **(www.asanet.org).** The American Sociological Association (ASA) is the main national organization for the discipline of sociology. At its Web site, you can learn more about sociology and about the way in which the national professional organization supports the work of sociologists. Look at some of the other sociology organizations whose links are in the Yahoo! search. What information do you find there relevant to your study of sociology? You can use other search engines, such as Google or AltaVista, to do the same search. Type "sociology" in the search field, and they will locate hundreds of Web pages related to sociology, many of them university departments of sociology.

To learn more about the focus of sociology on the understanding and solution of social problems, go to the Web site of the Society for the Study of Social Problems **(www.sssp1.org).** This is an interdisciplinary organization of researchers engaged in the scientific study of social problems. There, you can read the organization's newsletter, learn about its annual meeting, and find links to other relevant Web sites. Another excellent Web site is Sociosite: Social Science Information System based at the University of Amsterdam **(www.sociosite.net/index.php).** It contains an enormous number of links to other Web sites about particular sociologists, organizations in sociology, newsletters, and journals, as well as information about how sociologists investigate and attempt to find solutions to social problems.

Also, Allyn and Bacon, which publishes this book, maintains a Social Problems Supersite for the use of students in sociology **(http://wps.ablongman.com/ab_socialprob_sprsite_1).** At that site, you will find a variety of materials to assist you in the study of sociology and social problems. One set of materials is a list of Problem Areas in the study of social problems. There is at least one Problem Area for each of the chapters in this book, and you will find additional materials on the chapter topic there.

Multiple-Choice Questions

1. Public issues are different from personal troubles in that public issues
   a. affect large numbers of people.
   b. affect mostly the elite.
   c. lead to the disintegration of family life.
   d. involve the violation of societal values and norms.
   e. involve personal rather than collective solutions.
2. Sociologists refer to rules of conduct that guide people's behavior as
   a. values.
   b. deviance.
   c. authority.
   d. subcultures.
   e. norms.
3. Ethnocentrism can play a role in the emergence of social problems because ethnocentrism
   a. reduces group cohesion.
   b. works at counterpurposes to social institutions.
   c. can enhance conflicts between subcultures.
   d. involves criminal behavior.
4. The term *macrosociology* refers to theoretical perspectives in sociology that
   a. focus on large groups and social institutions and on society as a whole.
   b. derive from the functionalist perspective.
   c. focus on the intimate level of everyday interactions between people.
   d. focus on people's ability to use symbols and to interpret social meanings in social interaction.

5. Which sociological perspective posits that social problems arise from social disorganization in society?
   a. conflict perspective
   b. functionalist perspective
   c. sociological imagination
   d. interactionist perspective
   e. evaluation research
6. Which sociological perspective has at its core the idea that coercion and the exercise of power are basic social mechanisms for regulating behavior and allocating resources?
   a. functionalist perspective
   b. conflict perspective
   c. sociological imagination
   d. interactionist perspective
7. Which of the following statements would be most consistent with the interactionist perspective?
   a. Society is made up of groups struggling with one another over scarce resources.
   b. People are symbol manipulators who create their own world.
   c. Social problems arise when some element in society becomes dysfunctional.
   d. Society is a system made up of interrelated and interdependent parts.
8. In conducting research on social problems, the best kind of sample to use is one that
   a. focuses only on people who are suffering from the problem being studied.
   b. will confirm the hypotheses of the research.
   c. is consistent with the values of the researcher.
   d. represents the population under study.
9. According to the text, commonsense knowledge
   a. is often superior to scientific knowledge.
   b. is based on systematic observation.
   c. usually involves representative samples.
   d. tends to accept untested and unquestioned assumptions.
10. The laissez-faire approach to social problems is based on the idea that
   a. the government should take prime responsibility for solving social problems.
   b. the conflict perspective is most useful in understanding social problems.
   c. the government should play a limited role in seeking solutions to social problems.
   d. most social problems are global in nature rather than national in scope.

True/False Questions

1. According to the text, the definition of a social problem includes both conditions that can be remedied through collective action as well as those that cannot.

2. In comparison to values, norms are much more specific and concrete rules of conduct that guide people's behavior.
3. Authority can also be referred to as "legitimate power."
4. Conflict theory is the sociological perspective that grew out of the similarities sociologists observed between society and biological organisms.
5. One of the core ideas of the interactionist perspective is that society consists of parts that are interrelated and interdependent.
6. The functionalist perspective views social problems as being caused by dysfunctional activities or disorganization in the social system.
7. Max Weber is the sociologist who argued that sociology should remain as value free as possible.
8. Sociologists do not conduct research on commonsense beliefs because they mostly turn out to be true.
9. Social policy is influenced by both scientific research and social and cultural values.
10. The interventionist approach argues that government is generally a hindrance to the solution of many social problems.

Fill-In Questions

1. According to the text, a social problem exists when _____ defines a social condition as threatening its values.
2. Teenagers, skinheads, the elderly, and prison inmates are all examples of _____.
3. The ability to understand the relationship between what is happening in people's personal lives and the social forces that surround them is what C. Wright Mills called _____.
4. According to the functionalist perspective, social practices that disrupt social equilibrium rather than contribute to it are called _____.
5. Two key concepts of the conflict perspective are _____ and _____.
6. The concept of _____ is attributed to sociologists William and Dorothy Thomas and is a key concept of the interactionist perspective.
7. Scientific theories are linked to scientific research through _____, which are tentative statements that can be tested regarding relationships between factors.
8. The three criteria used to assess whether there is a causal relationship between two phenomena are (1) a correlation be found between the two, (2) the correlation not be spurious, and (3) _____.

9. When we consider issues of measurement, a central concern is that the indicators of social problems have _____.
10. The specialty area in the social sciences that is devoted to assessing the effectiveness of solutions to social problems is _____.

Matching Questions

_____ 1. authority
_____ 2. Karl Marx
_____ 3. definition of the situation
_____ 4. value-free sociology
_____ 5. social movement
_____ 6. deviance
_____ 7. functionalist perspective
_____ 8. samples
_____ 9. social institution
_____ 10. norms

A. legitimate power
B. interactionist perspective
C. Max Weber
D. civil rights movement
E. conflict perspective
F. representative
G. macrosociology
H. rules of conduct
I. the family
J. stigma

Essay Questions

1. Give the text's definition of a social problem. Draw out the implications of each element in that definition.
2. How do social institutions and subcultures play a role in the emergence of social problems?
3. What are the basic assumptions of the functionalist perspective regarding the nature and operation of society?
4. Describe how the conflict and interactionist theories would define whether or not a social problem exists.
5. Describe the various positions that sociologists have taken on the issue of scientific objectivity. Include in your answer a discussion of values and interest groups.
6. What is commonsense knowledge? What are its weaknesses? How does scientific knowledge differ from common sense? How does science overcome the weaknesses associated with commonsense knowledge?
7. Describe some of the difficulties that sociologists confront in measuring social problems. Include

in your answer a discussion of the concepts of "measurement" and "validity."
8. Describe the contributions that social science research makes to the social policy process and the search for solutions to social problems.
9. Compare and contrast the interventionist and laissez-faire approaches to understanding and solving social problems.
10. What are some of the considerations that should be taken into account when deciding whether solutions to social problems should be sought at all?

For Further Reading

Robert N. Bellah, Richard Madsen, William M. Sullivan, Ann Swidler, and Steven M. Tipton. *The Good Society.* New York: Alfred A. Knopf, 1991. This is a thought-provoking book about the extent to which the confidence of people in the United States about their society has been shaken. It suggests ways to transform such institutions as the family, politics, and the economy. Such transformations may well be an integral part of the attack on social problems.

Joel Best. *Damned Lies and Statistics: Untangling Numbers from the Media, Politicians, and Activists.* Berkeley: University of California Press, 2001. This is an excellent and readable little book on how statistics about social problems can deceive as well as inform. The author helps the reader to assess when statistical presentations are legitimate.

Randall Collins. *Sociological Insight,* 2d ed. New York: Oxford University Press, 1992. This book, in the vein of Mills's sociological imagination, tries to impart the power and insight of the general perspective of sociology.

Willard Gaylin, Ruth Macklin, and Tabitha Powledge, eds. *Violence and the Politics of Research.* New York: Plenum, 1981. This book raises issues regarding whether researchers should be bound by moral or ethical considerations when they conduct research on social problems and whether they should be responsible for making decisions about these problems.

Robert Heiner. *Social Problems: An Introduction to Critical Constructionism,* 2d ed. New York: Oxford University Press, 2005. This book combines the conflict and the interactionist perspectives into an approach called "critical constructionism," which views social problems as constructed in such a way that they reflect the interests of elites in society to the detriment of those with the least power.

Sam D. Sieber. *Fatal Remedies: The Ironies of Social Intervention.* New York: Plenum, 1981. An excellent book on the many efforts at social intervention that become self-defeating when their outcomes run counter to their intentions. This book preaches a healthy dose of caution when considering social intervention.

Roger A. Straus, ed. *Using Sociology: An Introduction from the Applied and Clinical Perspectives,* 3d ed. Lanham, MD: Rowman & Littlefield, 2002. This book offers an overview of the field of applied and clinical sociology, including many examples of the work of applied sociologists in settings such as health care, the workplace, and the criminal justice field. It describes sociological practitioners actively intervening to improve social conditions.

Thomas J. Sullivan. *Applied Sociology: Research and Critical Thinking.* New York: Macmillan, 1992. This book provides a brief introduction to applied social science research that is easily understandable to the undergraduate. It presents the many ways in which social science research can be used to shape social policy and alleviate social problems.

GROWTH OF CORPORATE AND GOVERNMENT POWER

The culture of the United States places substantial value on the sanctity of the individual and the importance of democratic decision making. In fact, the U.S. political and legal systems go to great lengths—much further than most nations—to protect the rights of people from being intruded upon by the government or other large organizations. In the legal realm, for example, the judicial system is based on the presumption that a person is innocent until proven guilty. It is the government's burden to prove that one is guilty rather than the individual's burden to establish innocence. So people are released on bail before trial on the grounds that the government has no authority to incarcerate people until after guilt has been established. Also, the court system makes it possible for individuals—even those with few economic or other resources—to take on large corporations or the government in the courts. For example, lawyers take some cases on a "contingency fee" basis, which means that they receive payment only if their client wins the case. This means that anyone, even poor people, can hire a lawyer with no financial risk to themselves. With such a system, powerless individuals frequently fight—and sometimes win—battles against corporations with enormous economic clout.

All too often, however, these cultural ideals are threatened by the extreme concentration of power in the hands of a few people in the political and economic realms. The result is often an abuse of power that works to the detriment of many citizens.

To understand this problem, we need to know something about how political and economic institutions work. **Politics** refers to *the agreements in society over who has the right to exercise control over others, who can establish laws to regulate social life, and how conflicting interests in society will be resolved*. By establishing laws and exercising control, political institutions, in effect, determine whose values will predominate and how rewards and resources will be allocated in society. **Economics** refers to *the processes through which goods and services are produced and distributed*. Although politics and economics are distinct institutions, they are closely intertwined. Both focus on a central issue in society: the exercise of power in the allocation of scarce resources. In fact, a classic description of politics could be aptly applied to *both* political and economic institutions: They determine "who gets what, when, and how" (Lasswell, 1936).

The problem associated with these institutions is not the use of power—because this is precisely their purpose in society—but rather the abuse of power: the exercise of power in ways that work against the interests of substantial numbers of less powerful people and result in their exploitation. Abuse of power is often linked with the size and complexity of businesses and government, along with the concentration of power in the hands of a small number of people or organizations.

As we will see, political and economic concentration of power creates many problems. In addition, political and economic institutions are often closely linked with many of the other social problems discussed in this book. So the analysis of political and economic institutions in this chapter serves as a helpful foundation to the remaining chapters in the book.

Types of Economic Systems

To survive, every society must ensure that food, clothing, shelter, and other materials are produced and distributed to the members of society who need them. The rules and social practices governing this production and distribution make up the economic institution of a society. The economies of most nations today are *market economies*, which are based on the exchange of money for goods and services in

---

Myths and Facts

About Business and Government

Myth: The economy of the United States represents a pure form of capitalism.

Fact: There are no pure forms of capitalism in the world today. Even in the United States, the government is involved in controlling and regulating the economy in many different ways.

Myth: Finally, in the 1980s, the growth in the size of government in the United States was halted.

Fact: The federal budget continues to grow larger each year and constitutes close to 20 percent of our gross domestic product. However, the number of full-time government employees has actually dropped slightly since 1970.

Myth: The United States' corporate economy works toward the common good.

Fact: The primary motivation of corporations is to turn a profit and to ensure corporate growth. Corporations have been known to market shoddy, even dangerous, products to the public because a quick profit could be made.

Myth: The economy of the United States has become uncompetitive in world markets because so many workers in the United States are members of powerful unions that force employers to pay unjustifiably high wages.

Fact: At the unions' peak in the 1950s, only one of every four workers in the United States was a member of a union, and that number has dwindled to one out of eight today. The other seven workers have no organized body speaking for them and are on their own when demanding a living wage from their employers.

---

the marketplace. Although modern economies share this market foundation, they differ from one another in significant ways. We will look at three main types of modern economic systems: capitalism, socialism, and mixed economies.

Capitalism

Capitalism contains three features that, taken together, distinguish it from other economic systems: *The means of economic production and distribution are privately held; the profit motive is the primary force guiding people's economic behavior; and there is free competition among both producers and consumers of goods* (Gottlieb, 1988). The proponents of capitalism argue that these features provide for consumer control over the quantity, quality, and price of goods. In its pure form, capitalism works like this. Seeking profits is, in a sense, merely unleashing personal greed. But this is quite appropriate, argue proponents of capitalism, because this gives capitalists the motivation to provide more and better goods and services. If there is a demand for some product, a company will come along and provide it if it can profit from doing so. Furthermore, the profit motive encourages innovation and creativity because there will be entrepreneurs looking for novel goods and services—some that the consumer has not even thought of—that they can sell for a profit. Capitalists must be constantly on the lookout for new products lest someone else beat them to the punch and corner a market. Thus, from this profit-seeking motive, consumers benefit from having more and better goods available. Open competition among capitalists also benefits consumers by enabling them to choose among a number of items, comparing price against quality. If the quality of products is too low or the price too high, people will not buy them and the capitalists will be out of business unless they change. Adam Smith referred to the conjunction of profit seeking with competition as the "invisible hand" of market forces that would ensure that the supply of goods is roughly equivalent to the demand for them and that the public has available the goods that it wants with the highest quality possible.

The role of government in this process, argue those who favor pure capitalism, should be to stand aside and let market forces operate unhindered. The government is necessary to maintain public order and protect against foreign threats, but any effort by the government to regulate the market is regarded as disastrous. Government regulation of prices or wages, for example, would interfere with both the profit motive and the competitive element and thus reduce the incentive to develop new and better products. In short, government policy under capitalism should be

one of laissez-faire: The government should leave the market alone.

There are no pure forms of capitalism in the world today. Even in the United States, the government has always been involved to a degree in controlling and regulating the economy. Despite this, the U.S. economy is still one of the most capitalistic in the world. There is strong resistance to government interference in the economy and little support for government ownership of utilities, railroads, or other industries that are often government owned in other capitalist societies.

Socialism

Socialism refers to *economies in which the means of production and distribution are collectively held so that the goods and services that people need are provided and equitably distributed*. In capitalism, production is based on economic demand: Goods and services are provided if people can afford to purchase them. With socialism, production is based on human need: Goods and services are produced because people need them, irrespective of whether they can afford them (Harrington, 1989; Le Grand and Estrin, 1989). Pure socialist economies reject the profit motive, recognizing that one person's profit is another's loss. In addition, socialists argue, the profit motive provides a built-in incentive for one person to exploit another, for example, by keeping wages low in order to increase profits. In other words, it is inherent in capitalism that one person is set in competition with another—either capitalist against capitalist or capitalist against consumer—and the inevitable outcome is a highly unjust and inequitable distribution of resources.

In socialist economies, the primary motivation for economic activity is to achieve collective goals, such as a higher standard of living for all citizens. To do this, the economy is highly centralized, with decisions about what to produce and how to distribute these products being made for the whole nation by national authorities. Because profit and consumer demands are not key elements in these decisions, the decisions can presumably be made with the collective interests of society as a whole in mind.

As with capitalism, pure socialism is rare. Most socialist economies do allow for the private ownership of some goods, such as personal or household items, and people are allowed to engage in capitalist activity in some economic sectors, such as selling home-grown food in the marketplace. Most means of economic production, however, are collectively rather than privately owned.

At this point, a word needs to be said about *communism*, a term that is routinely misused by many people. **Communism** is the term used by Karl Marx to describe the utopian end stage of the struggle over capitalism. In a communist society, *all goods would be communally owned; people would not work for wages but rather would give according to their abilities; and there would be no scarcity of goods and services, allowing people to receive whatever they needed. In addition, the state would become less important and its role would dwindle.* According to these criteria, nations that were commonly referred to as communist during the Cold War were actually socialist.

Mixed Economies

The economies discussed thus far tend toward pure capitalism or pure socialism, although each includes some elements of the other. Another type of economy, found in England and much of Western Europe, is the **mixed economy,** *in which there are strong elements of both capitalism and socialism* (Brus and Laski, 1989). In mixed economies, most industry is privately owned and oriented toward profit making. In addition, despite considerable government regulation, there is a competitive market economy, and consumer demand determines much of what is produced. However, in mixed economies, many important industries, such as banks, railroads, the communications industry, the media, and hospitals, might be state owned. Mixed economies provide for strong regulation of the private sector by the state. High taxes and an elaborate welfare system are established in hopes of achieving the national goal of a fair and equitable distribution of resources. Through such mechanisms, proponents of mixed economies hope to avoid the extensive social inequality that can accompany capitalism and the economic inefficiency that sometimes afflicts socialist economies.

Understanding these basic economic arrangements is important because the social policy debates relating to social problems often involve the question of which economic arrangements are most likely to achieve specified goals. This debate is introduced in Chapter 1, which discusses the interventionist and laissez-faire approaches. Although we need to be careful about oversimplifying positions, many interventionists argue that we should learn from mixed economies about how government policy can help us achieve goals of fairness and equity. Laissez-faire advocates, on the other hand, argue that an approach closer to that of pure capitalism would lead to greater economic growth and affluence, which would help solve many social problems. As we will see, proposals for solving problems of corporate and government growth tend to follow one of these two approaches.

The Concentration of Economic and Political Power

The Corporate Economy

Capitalism in the United States has undergone considerable change in the past two centuries. The U.S. economy once consisted of small, local businesses and many competitors. Consequently, power in the economic sector was decentralized, diffused, and limited to local or regional levels. It was almost impossible for businesses to accumulate substantial power at the national level. Today, the U.S. economy is very different: It is highly centralized and international in scope, and a small number of people can gain enormous control over wealth and power.

Furthermore, capitalism in the United States is no longer based on the individual ownership of businesses. Rather, the dominant form of business today is the **corporation,** *a business enterprise that is owned by stockholders, most of whom are not involved in running the daily affairs of the business* (Nace, 2003). There are three key things that distinguish corporations from individually owned businesses. First, corporations have access to a much broader source of capital than do individuals, because the former can sell stock to thousands of stockholders. Second, stockholders, who own the corporation, have only a limited liability should the corporation be sued or go bankrupt. Stockholders lose only the funds they have invested. Third, the ownership of corporations is separate from the control of its policies and daily affairs. The corporation is run by professional managers who are ultimately appointed by a board of directors that is elected by the stockholders. These managers may own little or no stock in the company. Legally, the stockholders run the corporation, but for all practical purposes the board and the managers do. Because of these characteristics, the corporate economic structure is extremely attractive to investors. Large amounts of capital can be accumulated with minimum risk to individuals.

Because of the advantages that stem from corporate organization, corporations now dominate the U.S. economy, with a relatively small number of corporations accounting for most business activity (Nace, 2003). There are over three million corporations in the United States, but most are small and have a minor impact on society. Economic resources, and thus influence and power, tend to be concentrated in the larger corporations. As these large corporations have come to dominate the economy, it has become possible for some to control substantial segments of economic life to the point of restricting competition in the market-place. One form of restrictive growth is called a *monopoly*—the control of a product or service by one company. For example, in the early 1990s, Nintendo controlled about 80 percent of the $5 billion video-game market in the United States. Related to the monopoly is the *oligopoly*, in which a few corporations control a market. Some sectors of the U.S. economy are highly oligopolistic, in some cases approaching a monopoly. In a 1980s court case, AT&T was broken up into a number of smaller companies because it had gained almost complete control over local and long-distance telephone service in the United States. In 1998, the government began antitrust proceedings against the Microsoft Corporation because its computer operating system was installed on over 90 percent of computers sold, making it difficult for other software producers to compete in the market.

Another form of corporate growth representing a concentration of economic power is the *conglomerate*, a corporation that owns other companies in fields quite different from that of the parent company. By the late 1990s, for example, a number of conglomerates emerged that centered on the media (television, book publishing, motion pictures, online media, and magazines) but also expanded into ownership of sports teams, farms, factories, and other corporations (Dye, 2002; McChesney, 2004). Some of the holdings of two of these media giants are described in Figure 2.1. Conglomerates are advantageous in that they provide stability through diversity: Losses in one industry can be counterbalanced by the parent company through profits made in an unrelated business.

As corporations have grown over the decades, the larger ones have extended their activities into a number of different countries (Barnet and Cavanagh,

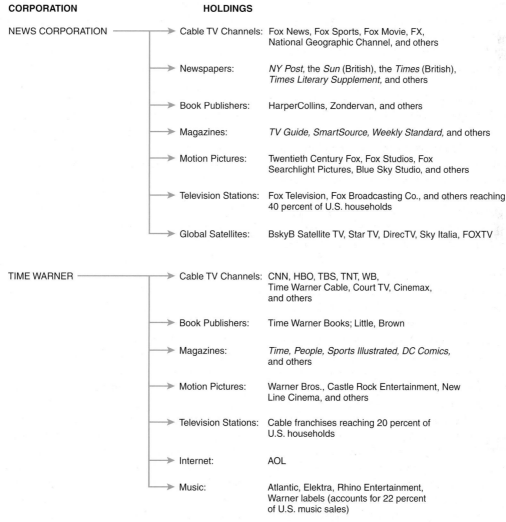

CORPORATION	HOLDINGS	
NEWS CORPORATION	Cable TV Channels:	Fox News, Fox Sports, Fox Movie, FX, National Geographic Channel, and others
	Newspapers:	*NY Post,* the *Sun* (British), the *Times* (British), *Times Literary Supplement,* and others
	Book Publishers:	HarperCollins, Zondervan, and others
	Magazines:	*TV Guide, SmartSource, Weekly Standard,* and others
	Motion Pictures:	Twentieth Century Fox, Fox Studios, Fox Searchlight Pictures, Blue Sky Studio, and others
	Television Stations:	Fox Television, Fox Broadcasting Co., and others reaching 40 percent of U.S. households
	Global Satellites:	BskyB Satellite TV, Star TV, DirecTV, Sky Italia, FOXTV
TIME WARNER	Cable TV Channels:	CNN, HBO, TBS, TNT, WB, Time Warner Cable, Court TV, Cinemax, and others
	Book Publishers:	Time Warner Books; Little, Brown
	Magazines:	*Time, People, Sports Illustrated, DC Comics,* and others
	Motion Pictures:	Warner Bros., Castle Rock Entertainment, New Line Cinema, and others
	Television Stations:	Cable franchises reaching 20 percent of U.S. households
	Internet:	AOL
	Music:	Atlantic, Elektra, Rhino Entertainment, Warner labels (accounts for 22 percent of U.S. music sales)

FIGURE 2.1 **The Holdings of Two Major Media Conglomerates, 2007.**

Sources: www.newscorp.com; www.timewarner.com (accessed May 2007).

1994). By the 1970s, *multinational corporations* had emerged, which made a large commitment of resources in international business and engaged in manufacturing, production, and sales in a number of countries. But these overseas corporate activities tended to involve separate operations in the various countries, often tailored to local social and economic conditions. By the 1990s, *global corporations* had become the prominent actors on the world scene: a few hundred corporations whose economic activities span the globe, using modern financial, industrial, and telecommunications technology to mount a worldwide, integrated system of production and distribution. Corporations have gone multinational, and then global, because enormous profits can be made with such an organization. There are lucrative markets for their goods outside the United States. In addition, the cost of labor, land, and taxes is considerably lower in places such as Mexico, Vietnam, and Indonesia than in the United States. So, U.S. corporations now participate in a "global economy," in which national boundaries have become less important as determinants of or restraints on economic competition. This means that labor and capital in the United States now compete with labor and capital in many countries around the world.

Unionization

It was not until the late nineteenth century, and the emergence of business firms employing thousands of workers, that the labor movement emerged as a significant political force in the U.S. economy. Capitalists, pursuing the profit motive, were inclined to pay workers as little as possible. In response, working people organized to pursue their own interests. Capitalists staunchly opposed the labor movement, believing that higher wages would generate laziness among workers and threaten the "American way of life." The owners' resistance and the workers' determination made U.S. labor history one of the bloodiest and most violent of any industrial nation. However, the workers eventually prevailed, and by the 1930s legislation gave them the right to organize and to bargain collectively with employers.

The number of U.S. workers belonging to labor unions continued to grow, reaching over 22 million people in the 1970s. With the right to strike firmly established for most workers, unions have been in a strong position to gain higher wages and more benefits for their members. Just as businesses formed conglomerates and oligopolies, labor unions from many industries have combined their forces. This enables unions to pool resources and information and to provide mutual support through the refusal of members of one union to cross the picket lines of another.

Although unions have gained considerable power in the United States, their future is uncertain (Craypo and Nissen, 1993). Union membership as a proportion of the workforce has been declining since the mid-1950s and is presently at its lowest point since 1940 (see Figure 2.2). The number of people belonging to unions has declined to less than 16 million. One reason for this decline is that occupations traditionally unionized—blue-collar industrial jobs—have been

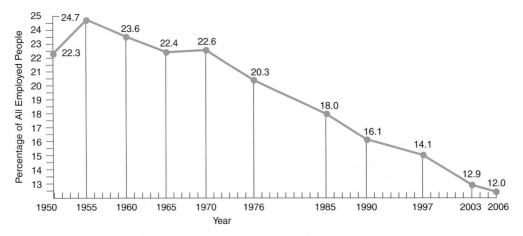

FIGURE 2.2 **Union Membership in the United States as a Percentage of Total People Employed, 1950–2006.**

Sources: U.S. Bureau of the Census, *Statistical Abstract of the United States*, *1948* (Washington, DC: U.S. Government Printing Office, 1983), p. 439; U.S. Department of Labor, Bureau of Labor Statistics, *Employment and Earnings*, January, various years.

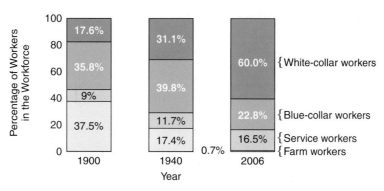

FIGURE 2.3 **Changing Occupational Structure in the United States, 1900–2006.**

Sources: U.S. Bureau of the Census, *Historical Statistics of the United States, Colonial Times to 1970, Bicentennial Edition: Part 2* (Washington, DC: U.S. Government Printing Office, 1970), p. 139; U.S. Department of Labor, Bureau of Labor Statistics, *Employment and Earnings*, 54, No. 1 (January 2007), 219.

declining in numbers, whereas the number of white-collar employees, who have traditionally not unionized, is growing. In fact, the United States is called a "postindustrial" society because a shrinking proportion of its workforce labors in industrial occupations. Because of automation, robotization, and other technological developments, fewer workers are needed to make the products necessary for our lifestyle (see Chapter 15). The largest growth in the workforce has been in white-collar jobs such as sales, management, teaching, or clerical work (see Figure 2.3). A second reason for the decline in unions is that many corporations have relocated in states having weak union organizations or moved overseas where unions are weak or nonexistent and labor costs are low. A third reason for the decline in unions has been the emergence in the past few decades of active opposition to unionization efforts by employers. This opposition is often supported by a phalanx of consulting organizations who specialize in helping employers fight unionization efforts. In their fight to keep unions out of the workplace, employers have sometimes resorted to various forms of intimidation: Union activists are fired, companies threaten to move jobs overseas, and employers engage in lengthy and expensive litigation to keep unions from organizing. Finally, unions have been facing increased hostility from the American public, especially when they demand sizable pay increases in times of high unemployment. This hostility reflects a growing concern that unions have concentrated so much power in their organizations that they can raise wages, and therefore prices, to levels having little relationship to actual worker productivity. Other episodes during the past two decades provided further evidence that the public climate in the United States had become less

favorable for labor unions. Possibly in response to this, labor unions have been noticeably less inclined to use the strike in their struggle with corporations than they were in earlier decades (see Figure 2.4).

Big Government

The founding fathers of the United States intended for the federal government to be small and not extremely powerful. After all, the American Revolution was fueled by hatred for British tyranny over the colonies. After winning independence, the revolutionaries wanted to avoid a domineering federal government. So the role of the central government under the new Constitution was to be limited: to raise an army, to establish a national currency, and to provide an environment in which states and individuals could pursue the common good. And the U.S. government did remain rather small throughout the nineteenth century.

The twentieth century, however, has been witness to a massive growth of government in the United States and other industrial nations. Since 1950, the expenditures for all levels of government—federal, state, and local—in the United States have exploded from $70 billion to over $3 trillion (U.S. Bureau of the Census, 2006:272, 307). This reflects a thirty-fold increase during a period when our population did not even double in size. The federal budget has grown from 10 percent of the gross domestic product just prior to World War II to 20 percent today (see Figure 2.5). However, despite what many people believe, the number of people employed by the federal government has remained about the same since 1970, with the number of full-time employees dropping slightly (U.S. Bureau of the Census, 2006:321).

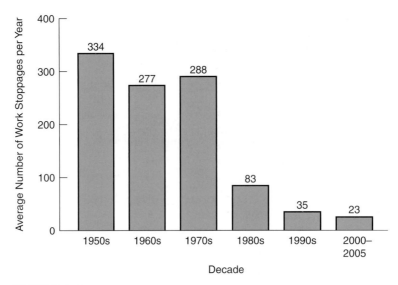

FIGURE 2.4 **Average Number of Work Stoppages per Year Involving 1,000 or More People, 1950–2005.**

Sources: U.S. Bureau of the Census, *Statistical Abstract of the United States, 1989* (Washington, DC: U.S. Government Printing Office, 1989), p. 413; U.S. Bureau of the Census, *Statistical Abstract of the United States, 2007*, (Washington, DC: U.S. Government Printing Office, 2006), p. 422.

Several factors explain this growth in government. A major one is that industrial societies for centuries have been shifting responsibility for regulating social and economic policy to the central government. This shift has occurred because nations have grown so complex and interdependent that some central authority becomes increasingly necessary to regulate economic and social life. In the realm of social policy, for example, the government is now seen as having final responsibility for the sick, the poor, and others who are unable to take care of themselves and do not have families or other support networks to help them.

Responsibility for economic policy has also been shifted to the central government, and this has become

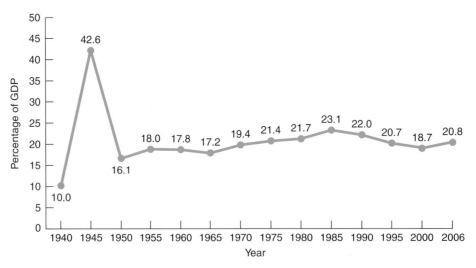

FIGURE 2.5 **Federal Expenditures as a Percentage of the Gross Domestic Product, 1940–2006.**

Sources: U.S. Bureau of the Census, *Statistical Abstract of the United States, 1978* (Washington, DC: U.S. Government Printing Office, 1978), p. 257; U.S. Bureau of the Census, *Statistical Abstract of the United States, 2007* (Washington, DC: U.S. Government Printing Office, 2006), p. 307.

a larger and more complex task as our corporate economy has grown. The freewheeling economic environment of the last century worked reasonably well until business empires became so large that they could monopolize large parts of the economy. Then government had to step in to regulate industry with the interests of the whole society in mind. Also, as technology produced increasingly complex and sometimes dangerous products and services, it grew beyond the ability of the average citizen to evaluate these products, and the government stepped in to offer control and regulation.

A second reason for the growth of government in the United States has been the emergence of the philosophy that social ills can be cured through aggressive spending policies and elaborate government-sponsored programs. This view came to dominate U.S. politics with Franklin D. Roosevelt's New Deal during the Great Depression of the 1930s. In an effort to combat the Depression, Roosevelt used government spending policies extensively to spread money and expand the federal government into many new areas. Massive government spending during World War II continued this infusion of government funds into the economy. This monumental military endeavor called for highly centralized decision making and control over resources, and this further enhanced the size and impact of the federal bureaucracy (see Figure 2.5).

A final reason why government has grown is that people demand many more services from it today than in the past. People rail against the costs of welfare, but they want the government to maintain the national park system, build monuments to Vietnam veterans, and keep our public libraries open and current. Few would want the government to stop providing insurance for individual citizens' deposits in banks and savings and loan institutions, and pleasure boaters whose engines die ten miles from shore are unlikely to rant about excess government expenses when a Coast Guard vessel rescues them.

This discussion of political and economic concentration focuses on the United States, but similar issues of the concentration of resources can be addressed on a global scale. The International Perspectives insert (pp. 36–37) does this.

Perspectives on the Concentration of Power

The recent historical trend, then, has been toward the concentration of power in the hands of large political and economic organizations. Is this inevitable? Is it necessarily bad? This section will analyze these issues using the sociological perspectives.

The Functionalist Perspective

According to the functionalist perspective, societies are made up of interrelated and interdependent parts, including economic and political institutions and practices as well as cultural values. These various parts should be sufficiently integrated so that people can use them to work together toward common goals. As we have seen, cultural values in the United States place emphasis on the sanctity of individuals and their right to control their destiny, the importance of democratic decision making, and the value of free enterprise and private property. Yet mammoth corporations and big government threaten these values. When corporate managers in New York make a decision to close a factory in Pennsylvania and move the work to Malaysia, what should the thousands of displaced workers in Pennsylvania make of the value of individual autonomy and control? What control do they have over their fate? If economic power is concentrated in the hands of a few monopolies or oligopolies, then are free enterprise and competition able to provide the most benefit for the greatest number of people? For functionalists, one of the key elements in the problem of the concentration of power is the inconsistency between cultural values and political and economic reality.

Some inconsistency between values and reality is an expected part of the social disorganization that results from rapid social change. There are good reasons why economic and political organizations have become so large: Large size is functional in providing large numbers of goods and services to many people. For example, producing and distributing the vast array of goods that are a part of our lifestyle would be impossible without organizing ourselves into large nationwide business enterprises. The disorganization results because this bigness can develop in ways that conflict with cherished cultural values and threaten common goals. For functionalists, further change is needed whereby some adaptation and accommodation are made. Cultural values may have to change to recognize the reality and centrality of these mammoth structures in our lives. At the same time, new methods of exercising social control over corporations and government may need to develop to counterbalance their concentration of power.

The Conflict Perspective

From the conflict perspective, there is no necessary harmony among corporations, the government, and the various groups of citizens in society. Rather, society is made up of a variety of different interest groups that come into conflict with one another over the resources available. This conflict of interests is an inherent feature of economic and political life. The accumulation of

Global Economic Concentration

Just as political and economic power is concentrated in the United States, such concentration can be found in the global economy, especially the concentration of power and resources in large corporations. For example, the world's corporate resources are concentrated in the hands of a very few nations—the highly industrialized, capitalist nations of North America, Europe, and Asia, which now dominate the world economy. Most of the largest corporations in the world are headquartered in a small number of nations ("Global 500: World's Largest Corporations," 2004). Looking at the 500 largest corporations in the world, 377 of them—75 percent—are headquartered in the United States, Japan, and three European nations. Even more astonishing, 54 percent of those 500 corporations are found in just two of the world's more than 200 nations: the United States and Japan. So when we talk of global corporations dominating world trade, we really mean that a relatively few nations of the world dominate that trade.

This concentration of corporate wealth has been assisted by some global financial institutions that have emerged during the twentieth century such as the

International Bank for Reconstruction and Development (or World Bank) and the International Monetary Fund (IMF) (Danaher, 2001; Stiglitz, 2006). These global financial institutions lend money, guarantee private investments, help stabilize prices and currencies, and encourage private investment in development. They receive their funding from their member nations (most nations belong), but their decision making and voting power tend to be dominated by the wealthy industrial nations of Europe and North America. In short, they function much as a central bank for the world, lending money and expertise to support economic development in developing nations. However, the support is not free: These global institutions demand that nations organize their economies in ways that support global capitalism and corporate growth. Often this means reducing domestic spending on items such as schools, health care, and social services. It can also require that nations stress export industries rather than production for domestic consumption.

The global concentration of power has also been enhanced by global trade agreements that encourage free trade among

nations and discourage hindrances to trade, such as tariffs, restrictive labor policies, or environmental regulations. The most recent such trade agreements are the North America Free Trade Agreement (NAFTA) of 1994 and the World Trade Organization (WTO) of 1995. There has been much controversy about these trade agreements, especially in terms of who benefits and who loses from them (Stiglitz, 2004; Nace, 2003). In terms of benefits, one of the clear winners has been large, global corporations and their stockholders, who have enjoyed greater profits and more protection from government regulations and other limitations in areas such as environmental, safety, health, and labor policy. These large corporations, after all, have the resources to compete effectively in such a free-for-all trade environment. Also winning are consumers, who often pay lower prices for goods because of the freer trade. Clear losers have been industrial workers in the United States, whose jobs have gone to other countries, and workers in all countries who have fewer environmental, labor, health, and safety protections under these agreements. Also losing have been rural farmers in Mexico and other countries who can't compete against the

power in the hands of a few is the outcome of the struggle for advantage in society. Large corporations and big government become the mechanisms in modern society through which powerful groups maintain their control over resources. From the conflict perspective, a conflict of interests and maldistribution of resources reflect a normal state of affairs.

Concentration of power is not by itself a social problem. It becomes a social problem, from the

conflict perspective, when some influential group of people believes that it is not receiving its fair share of resources and strives to do something about it. These groups sometimes combine their forces and form social movements to improve their lot. Through collective action, they can sometimes redress their grievances. Yet this does not mean that inequalities in power can be, or ever will be, eliminated. From the conflict perspective, collective

Global financial institutions, such as the International Monetary Fund and the World Bank, are controversial elements of the global economic system. Proponents argue that they help spread prosperity around the globe while opponents claim that their policies perpetuate poverty and enhance environmental degradation.

to influence what present and future trade policies will be like.

These global corporations and their supporting organizations subscribe to the ideology that levels of world prosperity are unlimited, that such prosperity can extend to all people, and that economic development and capitalist expansion, largely unfettered by government intervention, is the best means to achieve such global prosperity. In fact, many supporters of these organizations claim that they will eventually eradicate poverty around the world. To support such economic development, world economies have become organized around market-oriented production and continual mass consumption. In such a global economic environment, political boundaries and national allegiances are becoming less important determinants of economic activity. Such global concentration has many ramifications for all nations, including its effects on opportunities for people in the United States. One focus of this chapter and the remainder of this book will be the extent to which people in the United States are affected—sometimes positively but often in a negative way— by this global concentration of power.

large-scale agribusinesses that have taken over. Beyond this shifting of resources from one group to another, these trade agreements may have had little long-term

impact beyond what would have occurred with the previous trade policies. Still, the groups that benefit most from these trade agreements are also in the best position

action leads to a rearrangement of inequalities, not to their elimination. Furthermore, powerful economic interests are most often at a substantial advantage in this struggle. Economic advantage is routinely translated into political advantage, and control of the government can lead to the passage and enforcement of laws that benefit the powerful. The government becomes, in effect, a tool used by the powerful to protect their position.

Is There a Power Elite in the United States?

Researchers of both functionalist and conflict persuasions have conducted research that attempts to assess exactly how concentrated power and decision making actually are in the United States. Out of these efforts, two major models of power in society have been developed: the power elite model and the pluralist model.

THE POWER ELITE MODEL In the 1950s, the sociologist C. Wright Mills (1956) proposed what has come to be called the **power elite model** to explain the exercise of power in the United States. Deriving his approach from the conflict perspective, Mills argued that *there exists a small group of very powerful people who make just about all the important decisions in the United States.* This power elite consists of the people who hold top positions in the government, business, and the military. Included in this group are the president and the cabinet, the executives who run the large corporations, and the generals and admirals who run the Pentagon. According to the power elite model, the government, corporations, and the military dominate our lives today, and it is from controlling these spheres that power is derived.

According to Mills, the power elite is a cohesive group, and the interests of its various members in the government, military, and corporate sectors tend to coincide. There are elaborate social networks that link the members of the elite to one another. For example, they attend a small number of private schools and universities, vacation in the same spots, and go to the same parties. All of this social contact helps them to maintain a consensus about what is in their interests and to develop strategies for ensuring their success. Below the elite, there is a middle level of diverse interest groups including most members of Congress, professional organizations, many lobbyists, and most unions. They participate in making decisions about issues of secondary importance that have little effect on the elite. At the bottom of the political structure in the United States is the great mass of citizens who have virtually no power because they do not belong to those organizations wielding power. These people may vote, but Mills viewed this privilege as meaningless because most elected officials are in middle-level positions, whereas real decision-making power rests with the elite. In addition, the power elite is highly influential in determining which candidates the political parties will place before the electorate. One source of such influence is the mass media. The Applied Research insert analyzes how the media, through concentration and globalization, have become a part of the power elite.

THE PLURALIST MODEL Some sociologists argue that Mills's view of the United States is distorted and overly conspiratorial because there is actually little concentration of power and coincidence of interests among the elite (Kornhauser, 1966; Rose, 1967). Instead, the **pluralist model** views power as *pluralistic, or spread over a large number of groups with divergent values, interests, and goals.* According to to sociologist David Riesman (1961), there are veto groups in society with the ability to block decisions that might adversely affect their positions. For example, labor unions can exert considerable influence on issues affecting their members, such as raising unemployment benefits or minimum-wage laws. Similarly, farmers may fight to stop the lowering of price supports for farm products. To be sure, pluralists recognize that some groups have far more power and other resources than other groups, and there is considerable inequity in society. However, they argue, there is no single, cohesive, dominant elite, and power is not centralized in the hands of a few.

Below the elite, according to the pluralists, is the unorganized, but not entirely powerless, public. With the vote, the public can exercise some constraint over the behavior of those in power. In addition, there are other ways for the public to exert influence on more powerful groups. The environmental movement, for example, has used its ability to organize large numbers of people for public protest as a tool in struggling against corporate power. Especially in the areas of air pollution and the use of pesticides, these groups have organized seemingly powerless people to successfully shape public policy (see Chapter 13). Given these examples, pluralists dispute the power elite view and argue that the mass of the citizenry can effectively exert an influence, even against what seem to be formidable corporate foes.

ASSESSMENT OF THE MODELS Research suggests that the realities of holding power in the United States are more complex than either the power elite or the pluralist models alone suggest. For example, political scientist Thomas R. Dye (2002) reviewed the corporate and governmental sectors in the United States and located approximately seven thousand positions in corporations, the government, and the military that direct most of the nation's economic and social policy. According to Dye, it is this very small group of people who represent Mills's power elite. Sociologist G. William Domhoff (1998) went a step further by studying the social backgrounds of the people who occupy these elite positions. He discovered that members of the upper class participate in an elaborate network of informal social contacts, just as Mills suggested. However, Domhoff did not find the cohesiveness or coincidence of interests among these people that Mills implied. Nevertheless, there are significant linkages and influence peddling among the various sectors of the power elite. Members of the corporate elite, for example, make sizable contributions to both the Republican and Democratic parties in hopes of influencing the decisions of the president, congressional representatives, and other politicians. In fact, some would argue that, because of political contributions, corporate lobbying, and other forms of influence, the corporate elite exercises overwhelming control over politicians, regulatory agencies, and government bureaucrats. In this view, the average citizen has little influence and is largely at the mercy of corporate goals (Greider, 1992).

Research on the power elite has also focused on links between business and the military. In his final speech before leaving office in 1961, former President Dwight D. Eisenhower, himself a five-star general during World War II, spoke of the **military–industrial complex,** referring to *the relationship between the military that wants to purchase weapons and the corporations that produce the weapons. Both the military and the corporations benefit from a large military budget and from policies favoring military solutions to international problems.* The potential danger of a powerful military–industrial complex is that defense decisions and the development of weapons systems may be influenced by what is beneficial to the military and defense industries rather than by what is necessary for national security. One way in which the coincidence of interests among members of the military–industrial complex might occur is if there were a periodic interchange of top-level personnel between the military and defense industries. And, as Mills and other researchers have shown, such interchanges do occur and are extensive (Project on Government Oversight, 2004).

Although there clearly are important links between the military and corporations, suggesting a military–industrial complex, the picture is considerably more complicated than this. Many corporations actually oppose increases in defense spending, fearing that these will adversely affect the economy and result in higher taxes. In addition, the military—industrial complex, although important, does not exist in a vacuum. There are other powerful groups, even among the power elite, with competing interests, and there are less powerful groups that still wield considerable power, especially on domestic issues.

In short, both the power elite and pluralist models offer significant insight into the question of who rules the United States. As the power elite model suggests, a relatively small group of people hold enormous power. It controls much of foreign policy and makes decisions that shape the direction of economic development. This ruling group, although possibly not conspiratorial or completely cohesive, ranks far above most other citizens in political, economic, and social clout. Yet as the pluralist position suggests, many groups that are not a part of this elite can occasionally wield power, especially on domestic social policy and local and regional issues. This is the realm in which many of the battles over solutions to social problems discussed in this book are likely to be fought. And most people in the United States have an opportunity to play a part in these less powerful, but still quite important, groups.

The World Economic System

The power elite and pluralist models can be applied to other nations around the world, and each nation would have its own mosaic of power elitist and pluralist tendencies. Some nations would show more elitist concentration than the United States, whereas others would show less. To understand the emerging world economic system, however, we need to look at some considerations that transcend national boundaries. Although there are a number of reasons for the dramatic concentration of economic resources on a global scale, one important explanation is that it results from the centuries-long historical expansion of capitalist economic systems around the world (Schaeffer, 1997). **World-system theory,** pioneered by the sociologist Immanuel Wallerstein (1979), posits that *the world's nations have become increasingly interdependent, both economically and politically, and are now linked in a worldwide system, with some nations having more power and resources than others.* The major force in this world system is capitalism and its emphasis on market forces, profit making, and surplus accumulation. Capitalism's drive to expand and find new markets creates a pressure to seek out new territories in which to invest. In fact, one of the unique characteristics of capitalism is its commitment to economic growth and expansion. The world expansion of capitalism began in the fifteenth century with the European voyages to the new world to find natural resources and trade that would be profitable for the European colonial nations, and it continues today as corporations seek new markets in a global economy.

Today, corporations' search for new markets has created a global economy with an international stratification system. According to world-system theory, a hierarchy of nations has emerged, divided roughly into *core nations* (capitalist, technologically advanced nations searching for opportunities to expand investment) and *peripheral nations* (less-developed nations that provide cheap labor, produce food, and serve as a source of raw materials). There are also *semiperipheral nations* that are large or have some special resources, and because of this they fall somewhere between the two classifications—less dependent on the core nations, and sometimes acting as core nations themselves (Bornschier and Trezzini, 1997; Chase-Dunn and Grimes, 1995). The peripheral and semiperipheral countries are also sometimes called third-world or less-developed countries.

In this international stratification system, the core nations dominate and exploit peripheral nations. The

Corporate Concentration and Globalization of the Media

That the media are powerful is no secret. The press in the United States, in fact, is intended to be powerful and to serve a free society as an alternative and independent source of power to the government and large corporations. Yet the media are themselves private companies and usually corporate in structure. They pursue greater profits and larger amounts of power in the same fashion as other corporations discussed in this chapter. And, as has occurred in other corporate sectors, there has been a concentration of power among the media. By the early twenty-first century, a race is on, with a few megacorporations trying to control the print, video, and electronic media around the globe. Fewer than ten corporate giants now control most of what appears in the global media: Time Warner, Disney, the News Corporation, General Electric, Viacom, and Bertelsmann (Dye, 2002; McChesney, 2004). Figure 2.1 describes the holdings of two of these corporate superpowers. Together, they own almost all of the fifty most popular cable television channels and most of the daily newspapers in the United States. Despite the existence of more than 25,000 media outlets in the United States, a small number of corporations controls most of the business in daily newspapers, magazines, television, books, and motion pictures.

What is the impact of this global concentration on the role of the media in society and in the

analysis of social problems? We saw in Chapter 1 that the media play an important part in the construction of social problems—shaping people's beliefs about which conditions should be considered social problems, the nature and extent of the problems, and which solutions might be effective and achievable. When capitalist corporations control much of the world communications structure, corporate and capitalist viewpoints on such social problems as the causes of crime and poverty take an increasingly dominant place in public discourse and the media. Competing and dissenting voices emanating from less powerful constituencies are less likely to be heard, especially on a global stage (Bagdikian, 2004; McChesney, 2004).

A related consequence of the corporatization and pervasiveness of the modern media is "hyper-commercialism": the tendency for every aspect of social life and social intercourse to be viewed as a "product" whose production and distribution is determined by its commercial value. In relation to social problems and their solutions, this can especially influence journalism and the production of news. The trend has been a gradual erosion of the wall separating news from the commercial or advertising division of newspapers, television networks, and other media outlets. When this happens, what is presented as "news" depends in part on what is profitable for the corporate owners. So, instead of a free

flow of ideas and information about social problems and their solutions, we have a controlled flow in which problems are defined and solutions assessed on the basis of what benefits a relatively small number of people. Furthermore, the idea that the media should provide some public service has gradually diminished. Instead, what is emerging is a media domain designed to serve mostly private investors rather than the public good.

The media megacorporations shape the public debate over social problems in a number of additional ways. They make large campaign contributions to politicians who support their particular viewpoint on issues. There is also an interchange of personnel between the government and the media as former politicians and government officials take jobs in the media and journalists and media executives gain elected or appointed government offices. The more this phenomenon occurs, the more the line between government and media becomes blurred and the independence of the media is compromised. Also media outlets provide an influential platform from which these corporations can promote their supporters by giving them positive exposure and attacking those with whom they disagree.

Although the trends just described have been identified in much research, additional applied research suggests that reality is more complex and subtle (Demers, 2002). In the newspaper world, for example, as companies become larger, form monopolies, and establish links with the power elite, some develop a viewpoint that has been labeled "corporate liberalism," which tends to look positively on unions, social welfare programs, and government regulation. However, it is not a socialist position, as discussed in this chapter, because corporate liberalism retains the belief that a corporate economy based on private enterprise is the most efficient economic system. In this view, government programs and regulations are intended to protect people from the weaknesses or excesses that can be found in capitalism. In fact, media following this corporate liberal ideology may sometimes be very critical of big government and corporate capitalism, yet this criticism stems not from an opposition to capitalism but from a desire to promote responsible capitalism. One latent function of such criticism is to protect capitalism from challenges and to discourage interest in more radical changes that would significantly threaten corporate control by the power elite.

The great concern, then, of applied social researchers is that concentrated power over public information is potentially antidemocratic. As media specialist Ben Bagdikian put it (2000:x, xv):

With the country's widest disseminators of news, commentary, and ideas firmly entrenched among a small number of the world's wealthiest corporations,

These are some of the media products of Time Inc., the largest magazine publisher in the United States and the United Kingdom. It has brands and franchises in television, satellite radio, cable video on demand, online, mobile devices, and so on. Opponents of such concentration fear that media megacorporations will threaten democratic institutions.

it may not be surprising that their news and commentary is limited to an unrepresentative narrow spectrum of politics. . . . Politicians hesitate to offend the handful of media operators who control how those politicians will be presented—or not presented—to the voters. . . . [T]oday the combination of the media industry and traditional corporate power has reached dimensions former generations could not match.

The additionally disturbing aspect of such a trend is that, as the dissenting voices are silenced, people become less and less aware that they are being presented a distorted view, because they have fewer guideposts with which to measure the accuracy or completeness of what they see, read, and hear.

key to the system is trade, with some nations being goods exporters while others serve primarily as a labor pool and source of natural resources. In fact, some world-system theorists argue that the nature of capitalism is such that it creates social inequalities through its tendency to distribute resources unequally. Such inequalities occur within nations, which have both rich and poor people, and at the international level, where the policies of core nations help keep peripheral nations less developed. The core nations extract natural resources from the peripheral nations and use them as cheap labor pools to produce agricultural and industrial goods that are then exported for profit. Through political, economic, and sometimes military intervention, the core nations encourage the emergence of political and economic elites in the peripheral nations that will support and assist in economic expansion of the core. This elite in the peripheral nations benefits from the world system and supports policies that will maintain its role in the world capitalist system. For example, the political elites in some less developed nations in Latin America have discouraged labor unions that would work to increase the pay and improve the working conditions of citizens of those nations because unions might discourage investment by corporations from core nations that are looking for a cheap and passive labor force. Although elites in the peripheral nations may benefit from this, it tends overall to result in a shift of wealth from the periphery to the core as the corporations of the core nations drain profits from the periphery.

The world economic system, then, divides people into three groups. An international elite of well-to-do people is quite comfortable materially, and some of its members can become very wealthy. An international working class struggles to survive, with its fate determined mostly by decisions made by multinational corporations in core nations; even in this group, people can be thrown out of work and suffer serious economic declines because global corporations shift work to areas with lower labor costs. Finally, an international lower class lives in poverty with little hope of their circumstances improving. It was mentioned earlier that global corporations and their affiliated financial organizations hold the ideology that world capitalism will eliminate poverty. World-system theorists are more skeptical regarding whether this can happen. Looking at the historical record, they see world capitalism benefiting the elites and some others while exploiting many less powerful groups around the world. To this point, research is not terribly supportive of the notion that globalization will benefit all people (World Commission . . . , 2004). Instead, the research shows that the divide between rich and poor nations is growing, that poverty is not declining, that the inequitable distribution of wealth and power around the world persists, and that the increased trade and investment produced by globalization has benefited primarily a relatively small proportion of the world's people.

Problems Created by the Concentration of Power

This section will explore some of the problems created by the concentration of political and economic power, both in the United States and around the world.

Effects on Competition

One of the major problems is that corporate growth can restrict competition, which we have seen is one of the core characteristics of capitalist economies. When economic power becomes concentrated in an oligopolistic or monopolistic fashion, the individual consumer can become a relatively powerless force in the marketplace in comparison to corporations. As has been seen, in an economy based on competition, companies that are inefficient or produce inferior merchandise are likely to be driven out of business because consumers will purchase the less expensive and higher quality products of more efficient competitors. In this kind of economy, consumers have a degree of control over businesses through their discretionary buying power in the marketplace. In a less competitive environment, however, the consumer is at a substantial disadvantage because corporations are able to manipulate prices, quality, and product availability in ways that benefit them and without the controlling force of competition. As these processes continue, power and wealth continue to be concentrated in the hands of a small number of gigantic business enterprises. The larger corporations can offer poorer quality merchandise to enhance their profit structure, and consumers suffer.

Conflict Between Societal and Corporate Goals

The concentration of economic power in corporate structures also raises the issue of whether corporations pursue goals that are broadly beneficial to society or that enhance the narrow interests of particular groups (Schaeffer, 1997). Large corporations control such vast resources that their activities shape in very substantial ways the lives of average people. With the primary goal of corporations being to make and increase profits and to ensure corporate growth, corporations may not necessarily act in the best interests of other groups or of society as a whole. For example, when a corporation leaves the United States for a country that has lower taxes and labor costs, the United States loses jobs and tax revenue, and this loss can bring about increases in unemployment, poverty, and related social problems such as crime and alcoholism. Economic decisions based solely on the criterion of corporate profit, therefore, may create or intensify social problems that have negative effects on other groups in society.

On a global scale, there is considerable controversy over whether the policies of organizations such as the World Bank or the International Monetary Fund (IMF) benefit all, or even most, citizens of the nations in which they operate (Danaher, 2001; Stiglitz, 2006). Although many people do benefit, the policies have also meant drastic reductions in wages for some; lowered expenditures for health, education, and other social services; and devastating degradation of the environment. In some cases, tens of thousands of poor people have been displaced from their homes and resettled, often in less desirable areas, in order to make way for dams, logging activities, or large-scale agricultural and industrial developments. In fact, some dispute whether these organizations have been very successful in their stated goal of promoting development through large loans to governments. Critics of these organizations argue that their practices have dislocated people, exacerbated economic inequality and ethnic tensions, and promoted environmental degradation while benefiting corporations, elites, and a small segment of the workforce.

Threats to Democratic Institutions

The globalization of corporate control in the past century has created new or enhanced threats to democratic practices and institutions around the world (Stiglitz, 2006). These large corporations are sometimes wealthier than the nations in which they operate, giving the corporations enormous power from which to demand that a country adopt policies that are beneficial to the corporation. In fact, governments in smaller nations may deliberately avoid political and economic policies inconsistent with the goals of the corporations. In these ways, social policies in some nations may result not from the democratic wishes of the populace but from implied or explicit demands from powerful corporations. Corporations have intervened in the democratic process of nations by supplying campaign funds to particular political candidates or in a few cases by attempting to overthrow elected officials (Barnet and Cavanagh, 1994).

In the United States, corporations and wealthy individuals have played a very influential part in the political process through the funding of election campaigns. Various laws have been passed over the years to place limits on the amount that businesses and individuals can contribute to political parties and candidates. The most recent such effort is the McCain/Feingold Campaign Finance Reform Act passed in 2002 and upheld by the U.S. Supreme Court in 2003. It strictly limits the amount of money that candidates and political parties can collect from individuals or corporations and restricts the amount of political advertising permissible around election time. However, there are many ways to get around these limits. For example, organizations that are independent of the political parties can still collect unlimited amounts of money from individuals and corporations, and these organizations are replacing the political parties as the vehicles for corporations to exert their influence on elections. In addition, the limits on advertising can be adapted to by shifting funds toward mobilizing voters or direct mail campaigns. So, even with the legal limits, large sums of money will likely still be spent on campaign financing. Because most of this money comes from corporations, they will remain massively influential in U.S. electoral politics. The power of the corporations not only helps elect politicians but also funds public relations campaigns to sway citizens' attitudes on issues from health care, to crime, to welfare reform. In some cases the corporate agenda and viewpoint can overwhelm any competing voices. The danger is, of course, that these few powerful corporate actors will control civic life and public debate to the point that democratic institutions and procedures are undermined. With the globalization of the world economy, this corporate control of political life will operate at an international level.

Global economic institutions, such as the International Monetary Fund and the World Bank, represent very organized threats to the democratic process in some nations. Because these world institutions often operate in secret, ordinary citizens and their governments may have little knowledge of or input into what these international organizations do. Dispensing large amounts of money and making policies at the international level, these organizations have become almost quasi-governments themselves, whose policies affect the lives of people around the world. For example, as a condition of supporting a nation, these organizations often require the establishment of an administrative structure within the government, partly under World Bank or IMF control, that may circumvent or ignore the policies of elected or appointed officials in government.

Corporations and their world financial institutions are private or semiprivate organizations and as such are largely beyond democratic control. The result is that the important economic and political decisions that shape the lives and opportunities of people around the world are in the hands of these powerful private and semiprivate entities. Their decisions often change traditional cultures and ways of life as they push social and political changes that further economic development.

The Dwindling of Unions

Traditionally, unions have enabled employees who have relatively little power unless they organize, to combine their efforts and counter the substantial resources available to their corporate employers. Unions remain powerful in the United States, but, as described earlier in this chapter, the social and economic environment in which they function is shifting. Although predicting an outcome is difficult, many people believe it unlikely that unions will play the same role in a postindustrial society that they did during the industrial period. This may mean that corporations will have a freer hand in establishing wages and working conditions. Especially if unemployment levels rise, as they did in the 1980s, workers will be competing with one another for a limited number of jobs, and union employees willing to strike over labor issues may find themselves replaced by other workers for whom a lower paying job is better than no job at all. This happened in 1992 when 13,000 workers struck the Caterpillar Corporation. Tens of thousands of people applied for jobs to replace the strikers, showing that they would be content to work for wages and benefits the strikers were refusing. The strikers caved in and went back to work out of the fear, probably realistic, that they would be replaced if they pushed their demands. Some companies have been accused of using high unemployment rates as a tool to attack unions and diminish their strength. As this occurs, many workers, especially those with few skills, may find it more difficult to locate jobs that pay what they consider a decent wage, and research shows that, as the extent and power of unions have dwindled in industrial nations, greater levels of social inequality have resulted (Freeman, 1993). This may mean that some people will confront a way of life that is little better than, and possibly worse than, that of previous generations.

Worker Dislocation and Unemployment

Over the past forty years, the percentage of unemployed people in the United States has fluctuated considerably. Today, the unemployment rate is lower than at many points during that period but it is slightly higher than forty years ago (see Figure 2.6). Teenagers, African Americans, and other minority groups are most heavily affected by this problem and exhibit considerably higher unemployment rates than do whites. However, these official unemployment statistics do not include people who are unemployed but have stopped looking for a job—so-called discouraged workers. It also does not include those who are underemployed, working part time, or working at a temporary job that does not pay enough to support a family. When these people are counted, the unemployment problem in the United States is even more grave.

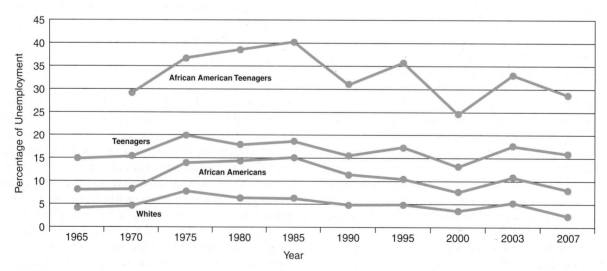

FIGURE 2.6 **Unemployment Rates Among Selected Groups in the United States, 1965–2007.**
Sources: U.S. Department of Labor, Bureau of Labor Statistics, *Employment and Earnings*, January, various years.

One of the reasons for this persistent unemployment in the United States has been increased competition for jobs in the world economic system (Baldwin, 2003). This has resulted in what is variously called "downsizing," "outsourcing," "offshoring," or "offshore outsourcing." Businesses in the United States have closed and moved overseas, or they contract out many tasks to low-wage, usually nonunion manufacturers in the United States or other countries. Countries in Latin America and Asia have been especially receptive to U.S. businesses. The minimum wage in the United States is more than $5 per hour, while well-paid workers on automobile assembly lines can earn $24 per hour. By contrast, global sportswear companies headquartered in the United States pay young girls and women in Indonesia $1.35 per day to assemble sports shoes for export to the United States (Barnet and Cavanagh, 1994). Hundreds of U.S. companies have left the United States and opened up shop in *maquiladoras*, factories in northern Mexico that take advantage of the cheap labor, weak unions, and lax environmental regulations to assemble products and export them to the United States. Many thousands of U.S. jobs have been lost to these *maquiladoras*, which have the best of both worlds—cheap labor and easy access to U.S. markets to sell their products.

This global competition for jobs is no longer limited to manufacturing or blue-collar jobs. The twenty-first century has seen this offshore outsourcing extend into service and technology jobs, including jobs held by well-paid and highly educated professionals (Lohr, 2003). Computer programmers, computer technicians, and even physician-radiologists find themselves competing with less-expensive workers in other countries. After all, writing computer code or interpreting X-rays or MRI scans can be done anywhere and the results communicated around the globe instantaneously. The Internet and modern communications technologies have eliminated the requirement that jobs must be done in particular geographic locales. Projections are that millions of these jobs will be lost to workers in the United States over the next decade (Lohr, 2003). The only jobs that are safe from this trend are those that require face-to-face contact between worker and boss or customer, and in an information-based economy, fewer jobs will have that characteristic.

Although world competition is probably the major factor in the growth in unemployment in the United States, other factors contribute. There has been considerable growth in the teenage labor market, and the number of women joining the workforce has grown over the decades. Still another dimension of the problem is automation, which is discussed in more detail in Chapter 15.

Workers thrown out of work by foreign competition are called "displaced workers," numbering 5 million people between 2001 and 2003, and their ranks continue to grow as more workers are displaced (Moore, 1996; U.S. Bureau of the Census, 2006:387). Some displaced workers never return to the labor force. Those who do often find themselves unemployed for some time—one and a half years, on average—and almost all experience a permanent decline in family income because of their job loss. Many are forced to accept irregular work at low-paying jobs with few fringe benefits. In addition, African Americans and Hispanic Americans are hit much harder by job displacement than whites. These groups are more likely to be displaced, are jobless longer, and are much less likely to be reemployed (Kletzer, 2001; Uchitelle, 2006).

Unemployment, as tragic as it may be, is not the only form in which difficulties confront workers in the United States. A related problem is that the jobs available to them, especially at the low end of the income scale, may not pay as well as they did in the past (Mishel, Bernstein, and Schmitt, 2001; Rank, 2004; Tonelson, 2000). The proportion of jobs that pay poverty-level wages has been increasing for the past three decades, and the new jobs created in recent decades have tended to be at the low end of the pay scale. In addition, corporations have resorted to hiring more temporary and contract workers because they can save on salaries or fringe benefits and have more flexibility in terminating such employees. Unemployment, low pay, and temporary work produce feelings of job insecurity, which can have widespread and negative ramifications for the economy. When work is unstable, workers are less likely to seek training and skills that will enable them to be more productive, and employers are less inclined to invest in such training. So, because advances in employee training promote higher levels of economic productivity and growth, job insecurity thus works against greater economic productivity.

Abuse of Government Authority

There are a number of reasons why massive government bureaucracies can create problems. One reason is the opportunity for the abuse of power by government officials. When government is large and distant from its constituency, isolated bureaucrats are freer to make decisions that benefit themselves and their associates but not necessarily other groups in society. In fact, the growth of big government can become problematic through collusion between government and big business. The Department of Defense, for example, may look the other way when industries with defense contracts have enormous cost overruns. This problem speaks to the very heart of freedom in a democratic

These women are working in *a maquiladora* in Mexico. Such factories often drain jobs out of the United States and exploit workers in Mexico through low wages, long hours, and poor working conditions.

society: Are people able to control the actions of elected or appointed officials? If anything, many people in the United States now assume that their government will keep secrets and hide misdeeds from the citizenry. Beginning with Watergate in the 1970s, the exposure of government misdeeds and cover-ups seems to have become routine. In the 1980s, the Iran-Contra scandal was revealed, in which government officials were said to have diverted funds to support the Nicaraguan contra fighters even though Congress, which represents the people, had voted against this policy. President Clinton was confronted with the Whitewater scandal, with charges that he covered up some of his financial dealings. In 2003, President Bush was charged by some with distorting, if not outright lying about, the evidence of the threat posed by Iraq to the United States in order to gain support for the invasion of Iraq. In a free society, such abusive and sometimes secret exercises of government power are highly detrimental to the democratic process; in a democratic society, the belief that the government is deceiving the people is an insidious cancer that threatens important group values.

A second reason why big government is a problem, according to those who take a laissez-faire stance, is that big government is inherently detrimental to society because it funnels resources away from the private sector where they could be put to better use. Because the government is not constrained by competition and demands to make a profit, it can "afford" to be highly wasteful. Government can lose money and still maintain existing programs if politicians continue to provide tax revenues. If tax money is not available, the government can borrow money and create a deficit. In fact, budget deficits played an important part in the economic and political life of the past few decades. The major concern with budget deficits is that the government must borrow money to operate and thus competes with corporate and other borrowers for the finite amount of loan money available. This competition increases the cost of loan money, which might lead some businesses to forego business expansion or capital improvements. When businesses forego expansion and improvement, there is less economic growth and fewer jobs.

A final reason why large government can create problems involves whether individuals can play significant roles in the decisions shaping their lives. As government grows, most people find themselves further and further removed from those who actually make the decisions. As C. Wright Mills (1956) pointed out, the key decision makers are usually those people who control the large economic and government bureaucracies in modern societies. As the government grows, the values of individualism and autonomy may become increasingly remote and irrelevant. Many groups feel powerless, and there is real danger that their interests will not receive a fair hearing in the halls of political power.

Future Prospects

What—if anything—should be done about big business and big government is highly controversial. The major programs and policies that have been discussed or implemented will be analyzed.

Reducing Government and Deficits

Most politicians are strong supporters of reducing the size of government and also reducing, if not eliminating, the deficit. Yet, the size of the federal budget grows every year, even though the number of government employees has not grown. This persistent growth in the government suggests that the reasons presented earlier in this chapter to explain why government has grown so large during this century remain powerful forces in keeping government large. It is easy to propose reducing government by cutting welfare, but all of the public assistance provided by the federal government amounts to only about 8 percent of the total budget. Defense spending, on the other hand, consumes 16 percent of the budget, and the two major programs for the elderly (Social Security and Medicare) consume one-third of the budget. This does not mean that cuts cannot be made in both the deficit and the size of government, but reducing them is much more difficult and complicated than is often imagined. Because virtually every interest group benefits from some aspect of government spending, serious efforts at it would significantly affect all people in the United States, not just the poor or some other powerless group.

One approach to reducing the size of government is *privatization*: have private corporations provide some of the goods and services previously provided by government agencies. In fact, in the last few decades, this has occurred extensively as the government has paid private contractors to do many things that government employees used to do (Shane, 2007). Today, many more people work under private contract for the government than are actual government employees. However, this solution does not address the overall problem of the size of government and the concentration of power and resources; it merely shifts the growth concentration from government agencies to private corporations. In fact, this may account for why, as discussed earlier, government budgets and deficits continue to grow while the number of government employees remains the same or falls slightly: The government is still doing all these things but using private contractors to achieve them. In addition, privatization may have negative consequences for other problems discussed in this chapter. For example, private contractors tend to pay their workers less than does the government and are much more hostile toward the unionization of employees. So social inequality may be more extensive and workers worse off with privatization. However, privatization has many supporters and is a significant trend in government policy toward social problems today, so its impact will be evaluated in relation to a number of social problems in later chapters.

Government Reorganization

Whether the size of government is reduced or not, measures can be and are being taken to moderate the negative effects of big government.

Politicians and government officials can be made more responsive to the demands of the citizenry. Because of the Watergate scandal and similar political episodes since the 1970s, politicians are now required to disclose a great deal more about their personal finances, and this offers the public greater scrutiny over possible conflicts of interest. There is still, however, much more that can be done. Sociologist Herbert J. Gans (1988), concerned that most people in the United States will not become more politically active, has suggested some creative ways of increasing the responsiveness of elected government officials. One is to increase the staff available to them for providing constituency services. Each official would thus have more workers available to find out what his or her constituents want and to provide the services. A second suggestion is for more, and more diverse, public opinion polling organizations. After all, most such organizations today are very close to the political and economic elites and tend to gather information that those elites find useful. According to Gans, polls should tell elites what the public has on its mind about the issues that are important to it. Polls should tell us what should be on a politician's agenda, not what we think about a politician's already established agenda. All of this would give citizens more input into the workings of government.

Government agencies and officials can be regulated much more closely than at present. This, of course, might mean that we would need more agencies to do the regulating, but not in all cases. Sometimes, bureaucrats in a government agency can do the regulating themselves if they are protected against reprisals should they uncover something detrimental to those heading the agency. In many cases, such whistle-blowers are fired by the agency, but when their cases come to public view, they often find considerable support among the public. Further protections for, and even rewards given to, such internal auditors could make government bureaus more sensitive to decisions that are viewed unfavorably by the public (Project on Government Oversight, 2005).

Government programs can be made more accountable. Policy analysts David Osborne and Ted Gaebler (1992) suggest a shift in focus from government services based on civil service regulations, which try to specify in detail *how* government services should be provided, to an "entrepreneurial government" that focuses on *results*. The idea is to establish measurable performance goals or outcomes as a part of government programs, and then use competition and decentralized authority to achieve the goals. This might call for privatizing some government services if private industry can do the job better than government bureaus can. But Osborne and Gaebler recognize that government is better than private industry at doing some things, especially when issues of fairness and equity come into play. Some programs, such as Head Start (see Chapter 5), currently do focus on results, and privatizing these services has so far not shown any advantages. The problem in the past, they argue, has not been government per se but the inefficient bureaucracy that government had become.

Collective Action by Citizens

In a democracy, one important way of controlling the actions of business and government is through collective, organized actions by citizens' groups to change the law or redirect social policy. In the past few decades, many such groups have emerged as watchdogs over whether government and business are acting in the public interest (Rimmerman, 2005).

Among the most effective citizens' groups over the years have been those originated by consumer advocate Ralph Nader and his associates. Nader first came to public attention in the 1960s when he revealed the extent to which General Motors was willing to make unsafe automobiles in order to increase profits. His campaign resulted in legislation that corrected many of the abuses in the auto industry and also pushed the government into the role of watchdog over automobile safety. Eventually, a whole variety of consumer protection groups—often referred to as "Nader's Raiders"—

grew up around Nader's efforts. Their collective efforts contributed to the passage of consumer protection legislation in many areas: to ensure quality meats, to enhance safety procedures in mining and other occupations, and to restrict the use of chlorinated fluorocarbons, to name just a few.

Concerns about environmental pollution and degradation have also spawned a great deal of collective action by the citizenry. Beginning in the late nineteenth century with the Audubon Society and the Sierra Club and continuing with contemporary groups such as Greenpeace, interest groups have lobbied for social policies to protect and preserve our natural environment. Greenpeace, for example, has focused some of its attention on the more environmentally damaging activities of the World Bank. These collective activities are discussed in Chapter 13.

Some public interest groups, such as Common Cause, have focused on issues of election campaign financing. Its major concern has been that interest groups with substantial economic resources, such as large corporations or wealthy individuals, control the political process by "bribing" public officials with large donations to their campaigns. Recent legislative efforts to control this are mentioned earlier in the chapter, and their limitations are discussed. Reformers have suggested more extreme efforts to limit the influence of the powerful including allowing only public financing of campaigns and limiting the amount each candidate is given, placing spending limits (rather than contribution limits) on political campaigns, or providing free television time to candidates. Some states have implemented some of these reforms, and this is likely to be a continuing area of experimentation in the future. If an effective campaign finance reform plan could be found, it would help to moderate the control of corporations over the political process and return some control to the hands of average citizens.

Globally, collective action is also an important deterrent to government actions, international corporations, and international financial organizations. The term *nongovernmental organizations*, or *NGOs*, is now used to refer to grassroots citizens' organizations that have emerged to fight the intrusive and destructive policies of governments or organizations such as the World Bank and the IMF (Boli and Thomas, 1997). These NGOs use resources they have available, including education, boycotts, and demonstrations, to stop or change activities with detrimental social or environmental consequences. The NGOs are usually small and focus on specific problems that a village or a people confront. International networks of NGOs have emerged to provide mutual help through the exchange of information, resources, and personnel. These NGOs have had some success in alleviating the negative impacts of the actions of corporations or organizations such as the World Bank and the IMF.

In recent years, one of the more active realms for such collective action has had to do with the growing globalization of corporate and economic activity. In places like Seattle in 1999, Genoa, Italy, in 2001, and New York City in 2002, thousands of people gathered to protest these trends toward globalization and to influence the way globalization proceeds around the world. Sometimes called an "antiglobalization movement," this is actually a misrepresentation because most participants involved recognize that globalization in some form will likely be a feature of the modern world. For these participants, the focus is to shape the terms of the debate about globalization rather than to derail the process altogether. The primary strategy at this point is to express divergent positions by massing in large numbers whenever the World Bank, the IMF, the WTO, or other global corporate institutions meet. One of the main demands of the protesters is that the process of globalization be made more democratic, with citizens around the world having input into the process. Currently, globalization is occurring mostly at the direction of global financial institutions, which, as we have seen in this chapter, have no formal mechanisms for citizen input into their decision-making process. The protesters want labor, environmental, human rights, and other groups to sit at the tables where decisions about the global economy are made. Another demand of the protesters is that globalization should promote the reduction of inequalities between the rich and the poor—between the powerful and the powerless—around the world.

Collective action, then, has served as a valuable constraint on the excesses of big business and big government. These efforts have offered ordinary citizens a valuable weapon in pursuing their own interests. The success of these efforts depends on their

1. Ability to appeal to large numbers of people and the financial resources those people provide.
2. Strategic use of legislative and litigation tactics.
3. Effective use of the media for public relations and communication.

Many of the existing public interest groups will undoubtedly continue to function, and more groups will likely emerge in the future as new issues develop and old ones evolve.

The Globalization of Labor Rights

The global economy described earlier in this chapter points to an important world trend: the globalization of labor as labor markets become world rather than simply national or regional phenomena (Moody, 1997; Tonelson, 2000). Although global labor has existed for centuries (consider the Europeans bringing Africans to the Americas as slave laborers), today it is a much more extensive and complete world phenomenon. More so than in the past, corporations roam the globe looking for cheap sources of labor. This means that every worker is potentially competing with the lowest paid workers in the world. The recent trade agreements, the North America Free Trade Agreement (NAFTA) and the World Trade Organization (WTO), work toward reducing barriers to free trade—including tariffs and other barriers that help support high wages for workers in places like the United States.

In response to this trend, some labor unions have recognized that the labor movement must also become transnational: If wages and working conditions are improved for workers around the world, then workers in high-wage nations benefit, because there is less incentive for corporations to relocate. So, some unions in the United States have provided support for unions in less-developed nations to help them organize workers and fight against low wages and poor or dangerous working conditions. In fact, a global network has emerged consisting of workers, union activists, NGOs, and church and community leaders working to promote improved wages and working conditions for working people in all nations. These groups work by negotiating with, or taking labor actions against, global corporations. They also work by pressing for the incorporation of provisions for high labor standards in national constitutions and in international trade agreements, such as NAFTA and the WTO. The goal is to establish, on a global scale, the belief that it is a fundamental right of human beings to be paid a fair wage and have safe working conditions, to join unions, organize at work, and bargain collectively with their employers. To the extent that these efforts are successful, the plight of workers in one nation is linked to the plight of workers in other nations. Through such strategies, international labor organizations may be able to regain some of their strength relative to the concentration of power in corporations.

Economic Reorganization

Some policy analysts suggest that the problems identified in this chapter, such as unemployment and the inequitable distribution of power, can be alleviated only by some fundamental reorganization of economic relations. One approach to such reorganization falls under the general rubric of *worker empowerment*, involving an attempt to provide workers with management authority and responsibility and more control over the operation of corporations (Greider, 2003; Melman, 2001).

In some cases, this has involved employee stock ownerships plans (ESOPs) where workers gain ownership in a company and have a stake in how it is run and in the consequences of their own work performance. Today, 11,000 U.S. firms with 10 million employees have some form of ESOP (The ESOP Association, 2007).

In other cases, worker empowerment has involved changes in the structure of companies so that employees have more of a say in company decision making, more opportunities for advancement, and increased access to powerful people and resources in the organization. Another variation on this takes advantage of the fact that workers have available a substantial amount of capital, mostly in the form of the billions of dollars in their pension funds. Much of this money is invested in purchasing the stocks of corporations, which means that the workers who own these pension funds are part owners of those corporations. Some investment firms now use this worker's capital as a lever to insist that corporations support worker and family-friendly policies. Whatever form it takes, worker empowerment has focused on increasing the power and control that workers exercise over corporations and the workplace. And research shows that worker participation and employee ownership can increase a company's productivity (Blinder, 1990; Rosen and Youngs, 1991).

Another, more radical proposal for dealing with the increasing dominance of corporations over workers and communities is to change the legal structure and responsibilities of corporations in such a way as to produce shifts in the distribution of power (Nace, 2003). Corporations are chartered to operate by federal and state laws that define what they can and cannot do. Currently, these laws define corporations as being owned by the corporate shareholders, and the main legal responsibilities of those running the corporation is to protect the shareholders' interests, which means mostly maintaining and enhancing profits. In this view, only the stockholders, along with the corporate directors and managers, have been seen as stakeholders in the corporation. One approach to shifting the distribution of power, then, is to broaden our conception of who has a stake, and thus should have some say, in the decisions and activities of corporations. Beyond the shareholders, workers and communities also make a long-term commitment to corporations and invest much energy and many resources in the corporation. And both workers and communities often suffer dire consequences from corporate decisions to downsize or relocate a production facility. If such commitment and involvement justify viewing workers and communities as stakeholders in the corporation, then they deserve some input into corporate policies and decisions. This could take, for example, the form of worker and community representation on the boards of directors of corporations. There has in fact been a trend in recent decades toward something called "corporate responsibility," in which corporations voluntarily take the needs of workers and communities into account. However, these voluntary efforts are often justified within the context of profitability: Responsible corporations are more profitable corporations. A more radical approach would involve elevating these other needs to the same level of legal requirement as profitability. Corporate charters could be changed so that corporate managers are legally required to address the needs of workers, the community, and possibly even the environment, in addition to maintaining profitability. This approach is still largely unknown in the United States, although it is found in some European corporations. It requires a radical revision in our view of corporations as purely private entities to a view of corporations as public and community assets. In this new view, corporations would still be private, profit-making corporations, but they would be required by charter to serve public needs, such as providing dignified and secure employment, paying a living wage, respecting the local community, and protecting the environment.

Whether these changes will occur and what their consequences will be remain to be seen, but it is clear that U.S. business institutions are neither perfect nor stagnant. As the United States becomes an advanced industrial economy, the problems it faces are changing, and it is clear that economic arrangements must adapt. In fact, some have suggested that these issues of concentration of power and lack of control will not be ultimately resolved without some fundamental change in the economy. Some argue that it should become more of a mixed economy, with the government taking more control of some economic realms in order to pursue collective goals. Proponents of an extreme power elite position would argue that inequality and exploitation are inherent elements of capitalism, because capitalism is ultimately fueled by personal greed and acquisition. As such, capitalism can work only to benefit the powerful. Some form of a mixed economy would balance the avarice inherent in capitalism by injecting an element of the public good into economic activities and decisions. Others, including some pluralists, would argue that capitalism can benefit most citizens through the checks and balances of competing interest groups. This is not to say that capitalism can achieve equality or that everyone will benefit. But if the government encourages the development of diverse interest groups, large numbers of citizens will be able to pursue their goals. The Policy Issues insert explores different positions on the role of the government in this economic reorganization.

What Role Should Government Play in the Global Economy?

U.S. jobs outsourced overseas. Corporate downsizing. Worker dislocation. All these are pointed to as symptoms of the *deindustrialization* of the U.S. economy in the emerging global economy: aging and deteriorating factories, growth in low-paying service jobs, and an inability to compete with other nations. What role should the governments of the United States and other nations play in dealing with these problems?

The laissez-faire position on this issue is basically that the government should stand aside and let the forces of the market economy work (Finnegan, 2003; Yergin and Stanislaw, 1998). The core idea supporting this position is the belief that privatization, free trade, deregulation, and a competitive marketplace provide the most efficient system for producing and distributing goods and the most promise for improving the economic circumstances of the United States and other nations. Government interference, through tax and spending policies, will only encourage noncompetitive, and thus inefficient, elements to determine the allocation of resources. For example, government intervention to prevent a factory from closing and moving overseas will foster only the continuation of an inefficient business. If this means that some industries in the United States decline and whither, that is acceptable because other industries will replace them. This global economy will be organized and supported by international organizations and treaties, such as the WTO and NAFTA, that will promote and support this economic productivity and efficiency. Such a global economy will produce more jobs and thus reduce poverty and unemployment. For laissez-faire proponents, then, the solution to the problems confronting the U.S. and other economies is an emerging global economy based upon a more unfettered form of capitalism.

Most interventionists accept the reality of a global economy and the global financial institutions that control it (Greider, 2003; Harrison, 1994; Monbiot, 2004). However, they also argue that the global economy is tilted too heavily in favor of corporate control, with corporations having extraordinary protections from government limitations on their actions. The various trade agreements extend extraordinary rights to corporations on a global scale—rights that promote the interests of corporations even though they work to the detriment of many citizens around the globe. The global economy is also very undemocratic, in that most citizens have no input into what decisions are made. Interventionists also assume that national goals may differ from, and even conflict with, the goals pursued by global corporations. Whereas nations may wish to promote notions of social justice or fairness in the distribution of resources, corporations' primary goal is to pursue profits, and deindustrialization has occurred in part because of corporate greed and the pursuit of unreasonably high profit margins. Plants are closed and people thrown out of work not because industries are unprofitable but because profit margins are judged by corporate CEOs to be too low. The role of the government is to promote interests other than the corporate ones and to be a vehicle for bringing more democratic control over economic activity. Some interventionists propose cooperation between government and industry, with the former providing funding and some leadership in promising economic arenas. This could take the form of significant public funding of some industries, as is done in Japan and Europe. Government restrictions on trade might be appropriate to protect some industries in developing nations, and possibly in developed nations, in some cases, so that they can grow and become competitive. Government could also play a central role in setting mandatory international standards for labor, health, and environment that all corporations would have to abide by. Some interventionists even propose a more central government role, such as legislation that restricts the ability of companies to close or relocate, which would prevent the dislocation of workers. Or tax policies could be used to promote national goals, such as giving tax breaks to corporations that strive to keep jobs in the United States. Some interventionists even insist that we need to replace private corporate decision making with more public democratic planning, where workers and the community would participate in corporate decision making. Community ownership of some industries might even be appropriate. For interventionists, then, the emerging global economy should be shaped and controlled by governments that can provide for more democratic input and protect the interests of a broader range of citizens.

The laissez-faire position stresses the superiority of individualism and competition in shaping society and providing benefits to the largest number of people. Interventionists argue that unbridled individualism and dog-eat-dog competition benefit some people but are very disadvantageous for others and can be destructive to families and other parts of society.

Interventionist					Laissez-faire
Community ownership	Factory-closing legislation	Government sets labor, health, and environmental standards	Less government regulation	International financial organizations control	Unfettered market economy

Economic concentration and more low-paying jobs mean that it is harder for families to avoid poverty (Chapter 5). This situation also puts more stress on families, possibly increasing divorce (Chapter 3). It also means that more women are forced to take jobs where they earn less than men, which increases the feminization of poverty (Chapter 7).

STUDY AND REVIEW

Summary

1. Political and economic institutions focus on a central issue in society: the exercise of power in the allocation of scarce resources. The social problem associated with these institutions is the abuse of power.
2. The economies of most nations today are market economies, which are based on the exchange of money for goods and services in the marketplace. The three main types of modern economic systems are capitalism, socialism, and mixed economies.
3. The dominant form of business in modern economies is the corporation, which has many advantages over individually owned businesses. Economic resources have become highly concentrated in a small number of very large corporations. Such concentration can take the form of monopolies, oligopolies, conglomerates, and multinational or global corporations.
4. The number and size of unions in the United States has grown substantially over the past century, but they have declined some in the past few decades.
5. Government has also grown substantially in the past two centuries because it has taken on the responsibility for social and economic policy and because people demand so much more of it. Globally, immense political and economic power is concentrated in a few large corporations and global financial institutions.
6. From the functionalist perspective, big government and big business are problems because they can lead to policies and practices that are inconsistent with cultural values and political and economic reality. From the conflict perspective, concentration of power becomes a social problem when some influential group believes that it is not receiving its fair share of resources and strives to do something about it.
7. There are two major models of power distribution in the United States: the power elite model and the pluralist model. The realities of holding power are more complex than either model suggests. Globally, world-system theory describes how and why political and economic power is concentrated among a small number of nations.
8. The concentration of power creates many problems for society, including a reduction in economic competition, the dominance of corporate profit-making goals over societal goals, threats to democratic institutions, the dwindling of unions, worker dislocation and unemployment, and abuse of government authority.
9. Efforts to alleviate problems stemming from the concentration and abuse of power have focused on a number of policies: shrinking the size of the government and budget deficits, reorganizing government so that abuses are less likely, encouraging collective action by citizens that serves as a counterbalance to government and corporate power, globalizing the labor force, and reorganizing the economy in ways that reduce worker exploitation and unemployment.

Key Terms

capitalism	mixed economy
communism	pluralist model
corporation	politics
economies	power elite model
military–industrial complex	socialism
	world-system theory

Multiple-Choice Questions

1. Which of the following is the central issue in society on which both political and economic institutions focus?
   a. the exercise of power in the allocation of scarce resources
   b. the transition from socialist to capitalist economies
   c. the emergence of market economies in advanced industrial societies
   d. the globalization of labor

The Internet is such a new technology that it is impossible to discern yet what its role in society will ultimately be: a vehicle to be used by large governments and corporations to further extend the concentration of their power, or a vehicle of empowerment enabling dispersed populations to communicate and organize electronically. Certainly, the Internet has made possible more direct, immediate, and interactive contact between citizens and government. Both houses of the U.S. Congress have Web sites: **www.senate.gov** and **www.house.gov.** Logging into the Senate Web site will give you such options as Senators, Legislation & Records, and Committees. The Legislation & Records offers you a number of options for finding what business is currently before the Senate. Browse through this and find topics that relate to issues discussed in this text. Do the same at the House of Representatives' Web site. E-mail your senators or representatives with your thoughts on the topic. Report back to your class any reactions that you get from your senators or representatives. Together with other students in the class, explore both of these Web sites with an eye on how they can be used as tools of citizen influence and empowerment.

The two global organizations discussed in this chapter also have Web sites: the World Bank **(www.worldbank.org)** and the IMF **(www.imf.org).** Explore those sites and report to the class on any information you found that can expand on issues discussed in this chapter.

The Internet can be a very useful tool for discovering the social movement organizations that have arisen to deal with various issues and problems in the world. The reason for this is that these organizations often make themselves prominently visible on the Internet as a way to attract new members and support. Using a search engine, enter key words, such as "globalization" and "organization," or "environment" and "organization." There are many particular problem areas that could be searched. Another approach is to search for "nongovernmental organization" or "NGO." The Economic and Social Council of the United Nations maintains relationships with NGOs around the world. See its long list of NGOs at these Web sites: **www.habitat. igc.org/ngo-rev/status.html** and **www.un.org/esa/ coordination/ngo.** Using these resources, report to the class on what NGOs you have located, the problems they focus on, and their strategies and successes. What conclusions can you draw regarding the effectiveness of these efforts at counterbalancing the concentrated power of corporations and governments?

The Allyn & Bacon Social Problems Supersite **(wps.ablongman.com/ab_socialprob_sprsite_1)** contains material on political and economic institutions and inequality.

2. According to proponents of a pure capitalist economy, the government should do all of the following *except*
   a. maintain public order.
   b. protect against foreign threats.
   c. regulate prices and wages.
   d. Government should do all of these.
   e. Government should do none of these.

3. As used by Karl Marx, the term *communism* refers to
   a. socialist economies in advanced industrial societies.
   b. the utopian end stage of the struggle with capitalism.
   c. the current oligarchical political structures in Russia and China.
   d. the process of bringing corporations under state ownership and control.

4. Global corporations are different from multinational corporations in that
   a. global corporations emerged first.
   b. multinational corporations represent more integrated worldwide systems.
   c. multinational corporations emerged first.
   d. global corporations represent the power elite whereas multinational corporations reflect pluralism.

5. Which of the following is *not* one of the reasons for the decline in the proportion of workers in the United States who are unionized?
   a. Traditionally unionized occupations have declined in number.
   b. Multinational corporations have declined in significance.
   c. Corporations have relocated to states with weak union organizations.
   d. The number of white-collar occupations has been growing.
   e. Unions have faced increasing hostility from the public in the United States.

6. Which of the following is true regarding changes in the occupational structure in the United States in the twentieth century?
   a. The proportion of farm workers has increased.
   b. The proportion of blue-collar workers has increased.
   c. The proportion of service workers has declined.
   d. The proportion of white-collar workers has increased.

7. "Concentration of power becomes a social problem when some influential group believes that it is not receiving its fair share of resources and strives to do something about it." This statement most clearly derives from which sociological perspective?
   a. functionalist
   b. conflict
   c. interactionist
   d. pluralist
   e. capitalist
8. Which of the following statements is consistent with the power elite model?
   a. A small group of powerful people makes most important decisions.
   b. Power is spread over a large number of groups.
   c. There is no significant military–industrial complex in the United States.
   d. Veto groups have the ability to block decisions that adversely affect them.
   e. The unorganized public can exercise constraint over those in power through use of the vote.
9. The problem of unemployment in the United States has grown worse over the decades because
   a. there is increased competition from foreign workers.
   b. the proportion of blue-collar jobs has grown and the proportion of white-collar jobs declined.
   c. the number of women entering the workforce has declined.
   d. U.S. corporations have avoided competing in global markets.
10. The text suggests that some problems of corporate concentration of power can be alleviated if the notion of "stakeholders" in the corporation is expanded to include
   a. corporate managers.
   b. corporate stock owners.
   c. oligopolies.
   d. corporate workers.

True/False Questions

1. Political institutions are the ones through which goods and services are produced and distributed.
2. The primary motivation for economic activities in socialist economies is to earn a profit.
3. Laissez-faire advocates would say that we could learn more about how best to solve social problems from mixed economies than from pure capitalism.
4. In the United States, union membership as a proportion of the workforce has been declining since the 1950s.
5. The number of people employed by the government has doubled in the past thirty years.
6. The pluralist model would argue that the public in the United States has no power or control over what happens at all.

7. In assessing the power elite model, the text concludes that a small group of people in the United States holds enormous power, controls foreign policy, and shapes the direction of our economic development.
8. When economic power is concentrated in a monopolistic fashion, it can result in a less competitive marketplace.
9. Worker dislocation (workers losing their jobs due to competition with foreign workers) has affected white workers more severely than black workers in the 1980s and 1990s.
10. "Corporate responsibility" refers to an arrangement in which corporations are required by law to place public needs ahead of profitability.

Fill-In Questions

1. In capitalist economic systems, _____ is the primary motive guiding people's economic behavior.
2. Economic systems in which there are strong elements of both capitalism and socialism are called _____.
3. If the Ajax Company produces 95 percent of the widgets sold in the world, then this company would be called _____.
4. A _____ is a corporation that owns other companies in economic spheres quite different from that of the parent company.
5. The world's corporate resources are concentrated in _____.
6. Sociologist _____ originally proposed what has come to be called the power elite model of the exercise of power in the United States.
7. The conjunction of the military, which benefits from the purchase of weapons, and the corporations that benefit from producing and selling weapons is referred to as the _____.
8. _____ are workers who have lost their jobs because manufacturing plants in the United States have closed in the face of foreign competition.
9. The _____ approach would argue that the United States economy could be best improved through privatization, free trade, and deregulation.
10. _____ are those who are affected by corporate activities, and thus should have some say in how the corporations are run.

Matching Questions

_____ 1. capitalism
_____ 2. monopoly
_____ 3. power elite model
_____ 4. *maquiladoras*
_____ 5. nongovernmental organizations
_____ 6. mixed economy

_____ 7. World Bank
_____ 8. Dwight D. Eisenhower
_____ 9. deindustrialization
_____ 10. worker empowerment

A. conflict perspective
B. economic production and distribution privately held
C. collective action
D. a company that controls 90 percent of sales in a particular market
E. factories in Mexico producing goods for export to the United States
F. spoke of the "military–industrial complex"
G. aging and deteriorating factories and other productive resources
H. approach to the problem of the inequitable distribution of power
I. global financial institution
J. England

Essay Questions

1. Define capitalism and socialism. Show how each economic system clearly differs from the other in terms of organization and motivation for economic activity.
2. What is a corporation? What are the benefits and disadvantages of corporate organization?
3. What are the major international organizations that work to support the spread of capitalism around the world? How do these organizations achieve their goals?
4. What are the trends in the unionization of workers in the United States? What accounts for these trends?
5. What would the functionalist and conflict perspectives have to say about the concentration of power in societies?
6. Assess how well the power elite and pluralist models describe the exercise of power in the United States. What evidence is presented on this issue in the text?
7. What are "displaced workers"? Who is most likely to be affected by this, and what particular problems do they confront?
8. What does the term *deindustrialization* refer to? Describe the laissez-faire and interventionist stances on how best to tackle this problem.
9. What sort of *government* reorganizations are suggested in the text to alleviate the problems posed by the concentration of power in the United States?
10. What sort of *economic* reorganizations are suggested in the text to alleviate the problems posed by the concentration of power in the United States?

For Further Reading

Amy Chua. *World on Fire: How Exporting Free Market Democracy Breeds Ethnic Hatred and Global Instability.* New York: Doubleday, 2002. This author provides a strong critique of current trends toward globalization, describes its negative consequences, and presents some ideas about a better route.

Charles Derber. *People Before Profit: The New Globalization in an Age of Terror, Big Money, and Economic Crisis.* New York: St. Martin's Press, 2002. This book describes a grassroots resistance to corporate-led globalization and proposes a path based on international democracy and social justice.

Jeff Faux. *The Global Class War: How America's Bipartisan Elite Lost Our Future—And What It Will Take To Win It Back.* Hoboken, NJ: John Wiley & Sons, 2006. This author argues that modern, global capitalism has evolved in such a way that it creates tremendous economic disparities and serves to benefit mainly a small elite. He presents proposals for remedying the situation and reducing the disparities.

Herbert J. Gans. *Democracy and the News.* New York: Oxford University Press, 2003. This author argues that corporatization, among other trends, is causing the vital role of the press and the media in democracy to change in ways that could lead to the disempowerment of people from meaningful participation in civic life.

William Greider. *Fortress America: The American Military and the Consequences of Peace.* New York: Public Affairs, 1998. This book provides an enlightening analysis of how the military–industrial complex has continued to shape defense policy and the distribution of resources in the United States since the end of the Cold War.

Simon Head. *The New Ruthless Economy: Work & Power in the Digital Age.* New York: Oxford University Press, 2003. This eye-opening book argues that the new information technology is producing huge social and economic disparities, as well as other serious problems in the workplace.

Robert Heilbroner. *21st Century Capitalism.* New York: W. W. Norton, 1993. These brief, but thoughtful essays explore what capitalism, which seems likely to be the dominant economic system of the twenty-first century, could be like in the future. The author argues that both capitalism and socialism contain strengths that should be incorporated into a "21st century capitalism."

Russell Mokhiber and Robert Weissman. *Corporate Predators: The Hunt for Megaprofits and the Attack on Democracy.* Monroe, ME: Common Courage Press, 1999. This is a muckraking book that catalogs the negative, exploitative actions of U.S. corporations. Although it is somewhat one-sided, it is also eye opening.

CHAPTER THREE

FAMILY-RELATED PROBLEMS

Problems involving the family interest virtually everyone because we all spend much of our lives in some kind of family unit. And the family, it would seem, is an institution under considerable stress these days. Most of us know someone—a parent, a close friend, possibly ourselves—who has been divorced. Stories of spouses assaulting one another abound in daily newspapers. Some employers today extend health and life insurance benefits to the unmarried domestic partners of their employees, including gay and lesbian couples. So, what had been defined as "family" benefits in the past are now sometimes extended to those in living arrangements that some would not consider "families" at all. In fact, some people view such developments as a virtual assault on the sanctity of the conventional family in society. What is happening to the family in modern societies?

The family is the oldest and most fundamental of all social institutions. In fact, the family has been at the center of political, economic, educational, and religious activities in most human societies throughout history. The position of the family in society today, however, is changing. Before addressing these changes, we need to know what the family is and how it functions in society. The **family** is *a social institution based on kinship that functions to replace members of society and to nurture them.* This seemingly straightforward definition hides considerable complexity and controversy. In fact, there is a great deal of ethnocentrism associated with the family. Most people have strong feelings regarding what "the family" is and how family members should behave. This has a direct impact on social policy when people's conceptions of what the family should be like distort their analysis of family problems and restrict their consideration of ways to solve these problems.

To understand what is happening to the family and assess competing views of family problems, we need to evaluate the role of the family as an institution in society.

The Family in Society

Families can take on many different forms. In some cultures, males wield most power and authority in the family, whereas in other cultures females do. In some cases, a person can have only one marriage partner at a time, whereas other societies permit and even encourage a person to have many spouses simultaneously. In the United States today, cultural norms call for people to practice **monogamy,** *to have only one spouse at a time;* U.S. culture also encourages an **egalitarian family,** in which *power and authority are shared somewhat equally by husband and wife,* although male

dominance may persist in some families. But the family of the past was different. In assessing problems in today's family, we must recognize the changes that have taken place in the family as a consequence of industrialization. At center stage in these changes is the transition from an extended family to a nuclear family.

An **extended family** consists of *three or more generations of people who live together or in close proximity and whose lives and livelihoods are closely intertwined.* Such families are often large and involve strong kinship obligations. Family members are expected to help other family members and to remain loyal to the family. In cultures where extended families are common, prevailing norms stress the importance of the family over that of the individual and his or her goals. Extended families are also often dominated by males, and tasks are divided along age and sex lines. Extended families are more common in preindustrial than in industrial societies.

A **nuclear family** consists of *parents and their children.* In contrast to extended families, nuclear families are small and less likely to be male dominated. Furthermore, cultures in which nuclear families predominate emphasize values of individualism to a greater extent. Nuclear families are the most common family type in industrial societies. Actually, many families found in modern societies are, strictly speaking, neither extended nor nuclear. Rather, they are **modified extended families**, in which *elaborate networks of visitation and support are found even though each nuclear unit lives separately.*

Myths & Facts

About the Family

Myth: Unhappy marriages should be maintained when children are involved—"for the sake of the children."

Fact: Repeated investigations of divorce and its effects on children have failed to demonstrate the psychological benefits to children of maintaining an unhappy marriage. It may, in fact, be more damaging than divorce itself.

Myth: Divorce is a modern phenomenon and was relatively unheard of in premodern societies.

Fact: Not only did divorce exist in primitive societies, but it was sometimes easier to obtain and more common than in the United States today.

Myth: Teenage pregnancies are on the rise in all modern societies because of the decline in traditional values and the rise in sexual promiscuity.

Fact: The United States has many more teenage pregnancies than does any other industrial nation. In societies where effective sex education programs and contraceptives are available to teens, the rate of such pregnancies is two to three times lower than in the United States.

Myth: High rates of childbearing outside marriage along with a decline in family size are unique to the wealthy industrial nations and come from the affluent lifestyle found in those nations.

Fact: The same trends are found in many nations around the world, including less developed countries, and are an outgrowth of industrialization and modernization rather than affluence.

Why does such variation in family types occur from one culture to another or from one time period to another? The answer to this is provided by the three sociological perspectives.

The Functionalist Perspective

Functionalists argue that some form of the family exists in all societies because the family performs certain basic functions that are essential to human survival and the maintenance of society (Eshleman, 2006; Ogburn, 1938). Six major contributions that the family makes to society have been identified.

1. *Regulation of sexual behavior and reproduction.* All societies have rules governing who can engage in sexual activities with whom and under what conditions children should be conceived and born. In most societies, childbearing is limited to marriage and family contexts, which provide a stable setting for having and nurturing children. In this way, the family contributes to the process of replacing people from one generation to the next.

2. *Socialization and education.* All human beings must learn the values, norms, and language of their culture and develop the skills that are necessary to be useful in society. Parents and other family members usually have primary responsibility for ensuring that children are properly socialized. Thus, the family is the major agency of socialization.

3. *Status conferral.* Families confer upon their children a place in society—a position or status relative to other people. By virtue of being born into a particular family, we have certain resources or opportunities available to us. Our racial or ethnic heritage, religion, and social class are determined by the family into which we are born, although some of these characteristics may change later in life. At a minimum, our family confers upon us some initial status in society.

4. *Economic activity.* The family often serves as the basic unit for economic production, with kinship ties defining who is obliged to work together in order to catch game, grow food, or build shelters. Family members work together to accomplish the economic tasks necessary for survival. Kinship ties also determine the distribution and consumption of economic goods by establishing who has a right to a share of the goods produced by a family.

5. *Protection.* Families in all societies provide various forms of care and protection to their members, helping them when they are too young, weak, sick, or old to help themselves.

6. *Affection and companionship.* All human beings need love, affection, and psychological support, and for many people these needs are fulfilled by family members. Such support enables us to develop a positive self-concept and sense of self-worth and to dispel loneliness.

Although these six functions are often performed by the family, they can be accomplished in other ways. In fact, the family and society have been undergoing a major transformation over the past few centuries as a consequence of industrialization, and alternative ways of fulfilling many of these functions are emerging. For example, although most childbearing still occurs in marriages, a growing number of women are having children without marrying. Today, 1.5 million births to unmarried women have been recorded by the U.S. Census Bureau in comparison to about 400,000 in 1970 (U.S. Bureau of the Census, 2006:66). This increase has occurred in part because women in industrial societies are better able to work and support their children without the assistance of a husband or other relatives. With regard to socialization and education, day-care centers, schools, and colleges are becoming increasingly important in transmitting culture and passing on skills and knowledge. Furthermore, people's positions in industrial societies are determined less by family position and more by their achievements than in the past, although family position does give a person a start in life. In terms of economic activity, most people work outside of the home, and the family no longer serves as the center of economic production. Finally, there are hospitals, nursing homes, retirement villages, and many other ways to offer the care and protection that people need.

In other words, the family has become less central in performing these functions as other institutional means of accomplishing them have arisen through industrialization. As a consequence, the traditional roles of family and kinship in society have changed, because they are simply not as important as they once were. As this has occurred, the extended family that performed most of these functions in preindustrial societies has become less common. At the same time, the nuclear family has become more prominent because it is better suited to an urbanized industrial society. Industrialism calls for geographic mobility so that workers can go where the jobs are, and nuclear families with weaker kinship ties make this mobility easier. Industrial societies also emphasize achievement rather than ascription, and these modified kinship relations make it easier for people to be upwardly mobile. Furthermore, large extended families are dysfunctional in urban settings where children are not economic assets. In preindustrial societies, children could work in agricultural settings and therefore contribute economically to the family. Small families are better suited to industrial societies; in fact, the size of the average family in the United States has declined substantially throughout the twentieth century, and people are more likely to be living alone or in nonfamily households (see Figure 3.1).

The part that families play in society, then, has changed with industrialization, and this has contributed to such things as a rising divorce rate and the emergence of a number of alternatives to traditional family lifestyles. These social developments become a social problem when the changes in the family threaten society with disorganization or instability. One of the key debates regarding family problems centers on whether the traditional family functions can be adequately performed by other institutions. Can day care, for example, provide the same kind of socialization to cultural values and development of personality that occurs in the traditional family? This issue is analyzed in the Applied

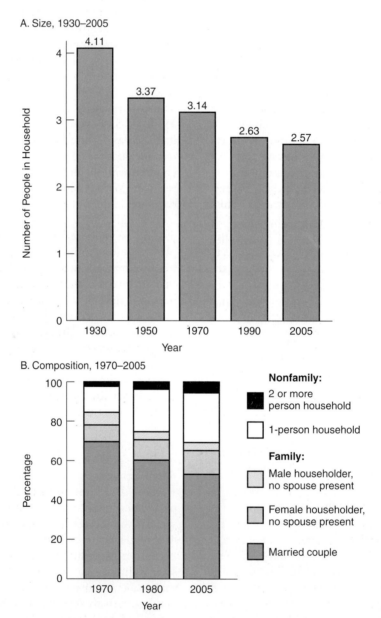

FIGURE 3.1 The Average Size and Composition of Households in the United States, 1930–2005.

Sources: U.S. Bureau of the Census, *Statistical Abstract of the United States, 1982–83* (Washington, DC: U.S. Government Printing Office, 1982), p. 43; U.S. Bureau of the Census, *Statistical Abstract of the United States, 2007* (Washington, DC: U.S. Government Printing Office, 2006), p. 52.

Research insert (pp. 62–63). Do divorced and one-parent families result in less effective socialization and more behavior problems for youth when compared with two-parent families? This question is analyzed later in the chapter. The function of the family that has probably changed least during this process is the provision of affection and companionship, and nuclear families can probably perform this function as well as extended families did. But even this function might be fulfilled in other ways than by the traditional family.

The Conflict Perspective

According to the conflict perspective, the family, along with other social institutions, serves the interests of the dominant groups in society, and there is no reason to assume that a single form of the family would benefit everyone. Rather, the version of the family that is most prominent in society is likely to be the one that is consistent with the values and benefits of the dominant groups. For example, **patriarchy** refers to *a family in which males dominate in the regulation of political and economic decision making, whereas women and children are subordinate*. This is the most common type of authority structure in families, and it serves the interests of men by enabling them to be dominant. In some societies, in fact, women have been so powerless in the family that they were virtual slaves (Chagnon, 1996). In industrial societies, male domination is not this extreme, and fewer women today are willing to accept such a subordinate position; in general, women today demand more egalitarian family roles. However, this change is occurring because women have been accumulating resources that enable them to resist coercion by males. For example, male dominance can be expressed in the form of spouse abuse, which often involves husbands assaulting their wives. However, research indicates that married women with greater economic, social, and educational resources are less likely to be abused and more likely to leave physically abusive husbands (Durfee and Rosenberg, 2004; Gelles, 1997).

The dominant form of the family in society also benefits particular economic interests. For example, the nuclear family serves the interests of capitalist economic institutions because it maximizes the number of consumption-oriented units in society. Each nuclear family buys many consumer items even though some are used only infrequently. Most families, for example, own their own television, stove, food processor, and automobile. A washing machine is used for only a few hours a week, yet most families purchase their own rather than share one with others. In extended or communal families, fewer such consumer goods would be needed because they would be shared, and thus the market for these goods would be smaller, which would hurt the interests of capitalists. Communal families, which are based on the belief in common ownership of at least some material goods, also threaten the basic value of private property on which a capitalist economy rests.

Conflict theorists would also argue that family systems can contribute to the perpetuation of social and economic inequality because inheritance in many societies, especially capitalist ones, is based on kinship. Inheritance makes it possible for a family to accumulate and perpetuate its wealth over generations. Such families as the Carnegies, the Rockefellers, the Bushes, the Kennedys, and the Gettys have amassed enormous fortunes. Anyone who can inherit wealth—of whatever amount—clearly has an advantage over those who come from modest or poor backgrounds. Thus, the family in such societies becomes a vehicle for perpetuating patterns of dominance and subordination.

Conflict theorists argue that the dominant groups protect against threats to their position by teaching people through the schools, the media, and other means that monogamy, nuclear families, family inheritance, and private property are best. Through socialization and education, people internalize these beliefs and they are unlikely, therefore, even to consider other forms of the family, such as communal arrangements. In addition, strong normative pressures motivate people to live in socially acceptable forms of the family. From the conflict perspective, family forms change when new groups acquire the power necessary to gain acceptance for a new form of family. The organization of family life becomes a social problem when groups with the power to make their concerns heard believe that the existing family structure is not serving their interests and they act to change it.

The Interactionist Perspective

Given the many forms of the family, which one is "right"? That, according to the interactionist perspective, is a matter of social definition. Every society has rules and norms that shape family and kin relationships. Once the norms are established, people are socialized to accept their society's form of the family as "natural." In most societies, there is substantial social consensus regarding the proper form of the family and the appropriate way for family members to relate to one another. Most people in the United States, for example, probably consider monogamy to be the most "civilized" type of marriage. Few could accept for themselves the Tibetan practice in which a woman who marries a particular man is considered to be the wife of all of that man's brothers—even brothers yet to

Day Care: Problem or Solution?

Single-parent and dual-earner families have to make arrangements for taking care of their children, and day-care centers have arisen to meet this need. However, the emergence of day care has been controversial. On the one hand, many working parents feel they must work to support their families but do not have friends or relatives available who can assist with child care. On the other hand, some critics of day care argue that only parents can give children the love, attention, and intimate involvement that they need to develop into emotionally healthy and socially competent adults. In fact, critics see the spread of day care as another symptom of the erosion of the family in modern societies. It is in controversies like this, where traditional values and ethnocentric beliefs can lead to biased conclusions, that it is important to turn to social

science research to see what the actual impact of day care on child socialization is.

Decades of such research have now accumulated, comparing children in various types of day-care centers with children raised in the home by parents, relatives, or others. Virtually all this research shows that children sent to day care do at least as well as, and often better than, children raised exclusively in the home by their parents (Belsky, 2006; Burchinal, 1999; Campbell et al., 2001; Loeb et al., 2004; Loeb et al., 2007). Day-care children do as well in verbal and cognitive abilities, creativity, cooperation, psychosocial development, academic achievement, and social competence as do home-raised children; economically disadvantaged children in day care show significant benefits over those not in day care. Day-care children are also as attached to their parents as are children cared for in the home.

Research does suggest a few situations in which day care may not be the best for children (Burchinal, 1999; Loeb et al., 2007; National Institute of Child Health and Human Development Early Child Care Research Network, 2003; Stolberg, 2001). For example, children enrolled in day care for extended periods or at a very young age may become more aggressive and less cooperative, may develop more behavior problems, and may experience more stress; but the effect of day care on these behaviors is small. In addition, economically disadvantaged children are often sent to poor quality day-care centers, which may adversely affect their emotional development. But this mass of research leaves us fairly confident that high-quality day care can do at least as good a job raising children as the parents can. Actually, this should not be surprising because day-care centers have the resources to offer children much

---

be born at the time of the marriage (Goldstein, 1971). Yet strict monogamy is one of the less common forms of the family, being practiced by only about one-quarter of all human societies.

What behavior is acceptable is interpreted in the light of cultural values and societal development. As society and its values change, the interpretations of behavior also change. In an earlier era, for example, when the traditional family was essential to accomplish such things as child rearing, family life was given a sacred or religious meaning, and divorce was highly stigmatized. By expressing shock or disgust at those who divorce, people in their daily lives helped to foster the "reality" that "marriage for life" was the right way to live.

Today, the consensus regarding family and family-related behavior is much less widespread than it once

was. People are faced with issues that in the past were settled by strong social pressures: Should I get married? Should I stay married? Should I have sex, or even children, outside of marriage? Should I take my spouse's name or keep my own? There is a growing inconsistency regarding acceptable behavior in these realms. This creates tension for individuals who must make choices without the clear-cut guidance and support of society. According to the interactionist perspective, when people are not provided with clear expectations for how they should behave, the stability of society is threatened because people may make choices that are defined by others as detrimental to society. Whether such practices are in fact detrimental is, of course, another matter. What *is* essential is that some groups define these practices as threatening to their values and as a social problem.

more—in terms of people to interact with, adults trained in child development and education, and such physical resources as games and educational materials—than does the average home.

Recent research has shifted focus from the issue of whether day care can do a good job to that of the quality of day care in the United States. And that quality is disturbingly low (Morris, 1999; Whitebook, 1999). National surveys of day-care centers found that the care at many of them was barely adequate in terms of developmentally appropriate activities for the children, teacher–child ratios, and the training of teachers. And quality of day care is related to children's development: Children in better quality day care exhibit more cognitive and social development compared with children in lower quality day care. One of the reasons that the quality of day care is often lower than it should be is that we do not pay much for day care. Day-care workers are overwhelmingly female, young, and disproportionately minority. They are a well-educated, dedicated, and committed group of people. They are also paid, on average, poverty-level wages and receive few benefits such as health insurance or retirement (Burchinal and Caskie, 2001; Lewin, 1998b). Higher-quality day care is found where workers have higher wages, more extensive benefits, and better working conditions. Better quality day care is also found when there are low child-to-staff ratios (or more staff for a given number of children), and stability of care, with low turnover among the staff.

What it comes down to is that good day care costs money. This creates a problem, however, because higher costs will price some parents out of the day-care market. So there is a tension between spending more money to improve the quality of day care and keeping day care affordable to parents, especially single parents or those with low incomes. This tension becomes especially noticeable when day-care centers are private, profit-making organizations, which is often the case in the United States. The pressure to increase profit margins can lead to cost-cutting measures that reduce the quality of care. Research shows that for-profit day-care centers, when compared with nonprofit centers, tend to pay lower salaries, have fewer staff per child, provide a lower quality of service, and have more staff turnover (Kagan, 1991; Lewin, 1998b).

Social science research of the sort described in this insert has dispelled the traditional notion that family and maternal care for children is inherently superior to care provided in day-care centers. This research is now serving as a foundation for developing social policy on the future of day care in the United States.

Attitudes Toward Marriage and the Family

Given the changes that have occurred in the role of the family in industrial society, are marriage and family living still popular today? It would seem so: More people in the United States marry than ever before, well over 90 percent. Today, just over 60 percent of all adult men in the United States are married, as are just under 60 percent of all adult women. These figures are about what they were in 1940 but somewhat lower than at any time since 1950 (see Figure 3.2). Surveys reveal that both young people and their parents have quite positive attitudes toward marriage and family (Axinn and Thornton, 2000; Popenoe and Whitehead, 2003). In a national sample of high school seniors, three-quarters reported that marriage and family life were "extremely important" to them, and a survey of young adults aged eighteen to twenty-two found that most of them plan to marry before the age of thirty. The vast majority of them also believed that when people marry, it should be "for life." Despite these positive views of marriage, however, the surveys detected some important changes: Compared with attitudes of the 1960s, young men and women today have fewer negative attitudes toward staying single, see fewer advantages in getting married over remaining single, and are not as certain that having children is the best thing to do. In fact, the people interviewed seemed reluctant to choose either marriage or being single as the preferred alternative. In

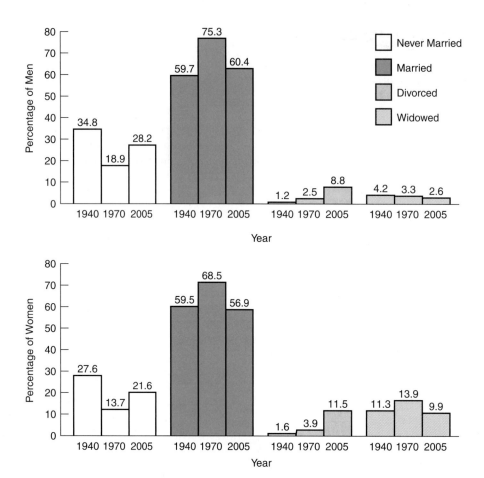

FIGURE 3.2 **Marital Status of Adults in the United States, 1940–2005.**

Sources: U.S. Bureau of the Census, *Statistical Abstract of the United States, 1982–83* (Washington, DC: U.S. Government Printing Office, 1982), p. 38; U.S. Bureau of the Census, *Statistical Abstract of the United States, 2007* (Washington, DC: U.S. Government Printing Office, 2006), p. 50.

short, marriage is viewed quite positively by many people in the United States today, but alternatives to marriage are also becoming more popular.

These attitudes may reflect the culmination of a long transition from "arranged marriages" to "participant-run" romances. In preindustrial societies, in which the extended family and kinship were core social institutions, parents played a key role in deciding when and whom their children would marry. Because the family in these societies was the major institution performing the important functions described in the previous section, it is not surprising that marital decisions were not left to whim or fancy. In many of these societies, *arranged marriages* occurred in which parents would select marriage partners for their children, sometimes shortly after their birth. The selection was based on what was considered best for the family, and the prospective marriage partners had little other choice. Such arranged marriages are still common in India and some other soci-

eties, and their members generally accept this practice as the wisest way to make marital choices.

A modified form of arranged marriage existed in the preindustrial United States, with young people having some choice in selecting a marriage partner but with parents still retaining substantial control over the ultimate decision. Courtship was common, but it occurred under the ever-watchful eyes of parents and other elders in the community. It was a *parent-run* courtship process: Young men and women were allowed to choose from among a pool of partners who were considered acceptable by their parents but were strongly discouraged from going outside that pool (Gordon, 1978).

In modern industrial societies, the selection of a marital partner is based primarily on the individual desires of the prospective mates. Parents can and do play a role in this process, but their influence is typically secondary and often no more important than the suggestions of a close friend. This courtship process, then, is more *participant-run,* with romantic love as a primary factor drawing couples toward marriage. One reason for this declining role of parents over the years is that kinship is less important in modern societies, and one's kin, including one's parents, have considerably less stake in who marries whom. A second reason is that children have a greater degree of economic independence from their parents in industrial societies, and parents therefore have less leverage with which to demand a say in the choice of a marriage partner. In the past, parents could withhold economic support from a couple, which usually made it very difficult for them to establish a household. Today, young people are better able to get jobs independently of their families and to support themselves. As the position of the family in society has changed, then, people have gained more freedom of choice regarding a marriage partner.

Some people see these changing attitudes toward marriage and children as an indication that the family as an institution is in trouble. Other developments suggest trouble for the family, and three of these developments will be reviewed: divorce, lifestyle alternatives to the traditional family, and violence in the family.

Divorce

The Divorce Rate

In calculating the incidence of divorce, most sociologists use a statistic called the **refined divorce rate,** *which is determined by dividing the number of divorces each year by the total number of existing marriages in that year.* This method provides a valid way of comparing the stability of marriages from one year to the next. As Figure 3.3 illustrates, the divorce rate has doubled since 1940, going from 8.8 to about 18 divorces for every 1,000 marriages. As a point of comparison, it has been estimated that there were only 1.2 divorces for every 1,000 marriages in 1869—reflecting a seventeenfold increase during the past century (Saxton, 1980:380). Although the trend in divorce rates over the past sixty years has been up, the divorce rate has actually declined somewhat since its high point around 1980.

The likelihood that a marriage would end in divorce in 1870 was 8 percent. Today, this figure has risen to 50 percent. So, though it may be disturbing to many, the statistical likelihood of a marriage beginning today ending in divorce is about fifty-fifty. However, those people who divorce are apparently not

This four-year-old bride in India is being paraded through a village with her husband. Such arranged marriages were common in some preindustrial societies but have been largely replaced by participant-run marriages in industrial societies.

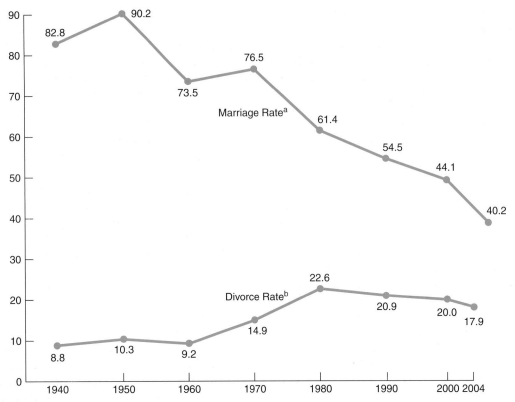

FIGURE 3.3 The Rate of Marriage and Divorce in the United States, 1940–2004.

[a]Marriage per 1,000 unmarried women 15 years old and older.

[b]Divorces and annulments per 1,000 married women 15 years old and older.

Sources: National Center for Health Statistics, *National Vital Statistics Reports* (formerly *Monthly Vital Statistics Report*), various years; U.S. Bureau of the Census, *Statistical Abstract of the United States*, various years, and *Current Population Reports*, various years.

totally disillusioned with marriage because 75 to 80 percent of them will eventually remarry (Coltrane and Collins, 2001).

However, only a portion of marital dissolutions is reflected in the divorce rate. Approximately 3 percent of all marriages end in legal separation, where the partners decide to end their relationship but prefer, perhaps for religious reasons, not to divorce. Desertion is another way in which marriages are dissolved, although it is difficult to know the extent of these. In fact, given these marital practices, we might refer to our marriage system in the United States as one involving serial monogamy rather than monogamy or polygamy. **Serial monogamy** means that *a person is allowed to have more than one spouse, just not at the same time.* **Polygamy** refers to *having more than one spouse at the same time.*

People get divorces for many personal reasons—their spouse has become insensitive, they feel trapped by limited career opportunities, or their sex lives are no longer exciting. However, sociologists prefer to focus on the societal conditions that result in a high divorce rate rather than personal reasons for divorce. At least four such conditions account for the rising divorce rate over the past century.

First, we have seen that the family performs fewer functions today than in the past, which means there are fewer pressures on couples to stay together if they are unhappy. In the past, the same unhappy couple might have remained married because neither spouse felt he or she could raise the children alone or he or she needed the family for support in old age. Today, single parents are better prepared to raise a child, and most people are supported by government or private retirement plans in their old age. In fact, the high levels of affluence afforded by industrialization have made people less dependent on kinship ties for support, with consequent changes in the family as an institution.

Second, the increasing equality between men and women has created both opportunities and tensions that contribute to the divorce rate (Brehm, 1985). In terms of opportunities, many women today are part of the labor force and thus have the economic ability to support themselves and their children without a husband. This reduces the likelihood of women being willing to remain in unsatisfying relationships. In terms of tensions, gender equality has led to a redefining of the roles in the family, which can cause disagreements and stress that may precipitate divorce. A husband, for example, may feel that his wife should do most of the household chores, whereas she feels these tasks should be divided equally. Such conflicts are especially a problem for women who, after marrying, decide to pursue a career. This life change disrupts an established marital pattern and requires a renegotiation of male and female roles in the family, which is sometimes unsuccessful (Houseknecht, Vaughan, and Macke, 1984).

A third reason for the rising divorce rate is that there is considerably less stigma attached to divorce today than in the past (Thornton, 1985). Divorce in the past was often viewed as a serious failing in a person's life, with divorced people frequently labeled as morally inferior. Females in particular bore the stigma of the divorcee as a "fallen" woman. Today, with over 20 million divorced people in the United States, divorce is viewed by many as merely another lifestyle choice rather than a reflection of one's allegedly weak character.

Finally, as negative attitudes toward divorce have eased, pressures have surfaced to simplify the legal process for obtaining a divorce. These developments have encouraged more people to seek dissolution when they encounter marital difficulties.

Who Gets Divorced?

Some couples are at considerably greater risk of getting a divorce than are others (Strong, DeVault, and Cohen, 2008). Couples with an increased likelihood of divorcing have the following characteristics:

1. *Social differences between the couple, such as differences in religion, race, social class background, or values.* These differences can place substantial stress on a marriage.

2. *Low socioeconomic standing, such as low income or education.* Unemployment and other stresses that often accompany low social standing probably make it more difficult to achieve a successful marriage.

3. *Young age at marriage.* Very young couples seem especially ill equipped to have a successful marriage.

4. *Whirlwind romances.* People who have known each other for only a brief period are more likely to choose a partner with whom they will later prove to be incompatible.

The Effects of Divorce

Does divorce make the family unable to perform its functions, such as socializing children and providing emotional support? Does divorce threaten society with severe stress and disorganization? Let us see what some of the effects of divorce are.

Widespread divorce has complicated kinship relationships and brought about what has been called a **blended family:** *a family based on kinship ties that accumulate as a consequence of divorces and remarriages* (Cherlin and Furstenberg, 1994). These families involve relationships that are more complex than the standard nuclear family. For example, a child may live in a family with a full-blood sibling, a half-blood sibling, and a sibling with no blood relation and only marital ties. The same child may have a "real" mother and father as well as a stepfather or stepmother, and three sets of grandparents. Such arrangements, with their attendant complex kinship and legal linkages, can create complications and tensions that are less likely in traditional nuclear or extended family arrangements. In fact, sociologists now speak of "remarried-couple households," defined as married couple households in which one or both spouses have been divorced. Forty-six percent of all marriages in the United States today involve a remarriage by at least one of the partners (U.S. Bureau of the Census, 2000:101).

Divorce can be a disruptive and troubling experience, as those who have experienced it will attest. Marital dissolution often precipitates feelings of failure, loneliness, and rejection, along with intense anger and frustration. For many, it represents an assault on their sense of self-worth. Even when divorce is preferred by a person, an intimate bond is severed nevertheless, and there is often nothing immediately to take its place. Symptoms of psychological distress, sometimes quite severe, are common among the newly divorced. Divorce is also sometimes associated with increased problems of physical health, with divorced people having more serious illnesses, more chronic disabling conditions, and a higher suicide rate than do single or married people (Kiecolt-Glaser et al., 1987; Verbrugge, 1979). Men and women are affected by different elements of the divorce situation: Women's distress is more likely to arise from the fact that divorce leaves them with a lower standard of living and increased parental responsibilities; men's distress tends to arise from their difficulty in maintaining a close and supportive network of personal ties (Gerstel, Riessman, and Rosenfield, 1985).

There has been considerable debate regarding whether the husband or the wife is treated more unfairly in divorce proceedings. Husbands complain about being gouged for alimony or child-support payments, whereas wives protest over allegedly meager or missing payments from husbands. Social scientists have done considerable research on this issue, and the conclusions are remarkably consistent: Women are much more likely than men to suffer economic decline after divorce, and even when men suffer, their economic slide is much less severe and much more short lived than is that of women (Holden and Smock, 1991; McManus and DiPrete, 2001).

One reason women end up worse off is that courts typically divide up only tangible property, such as a home, automobile, or belongings. Less tangible but often far more valuable property, such as a professional license that can translate into considerable income throughout a career, is usually not considered a part of the property settlement. It is the man who is far more likely to possess these less tangible forms of property. There are other reasons for the postdivorce economic decline of women: It is typically the woman who takes custody of children after divorce, and child support awarded by courts is usually meager compared to the father's income; only a minority of fathers comply fully with child-support awards; women earn substantially less than men (see Chapter 7); and women, having child-rearing responsibilities, suffer barriers in looking for jobs and finding child care. Women who are especially likely to suffer from divorce are the homemakers who devoted themselves to the housewife and mother roles and have few marketable skills.

Court rulings could create some change in these realms. For example, some courts have ruled that a spouse divorced after helping support a mate through medical or professional school might be entitled to a share of his or her mate's future earnings. Although these rulings have typically been overturned by a higher court, many experts are predicting that such rulings in the future may result in an expansion of the definition of "property" in divorce cases: Anything that might produce future income, such as a medical or law degree, could be considered property to be shared as a part of a financial settlement.

As far as the children of divorce are concerned, research consistently shows that divorce is without question difficult for children, and living in a loving home is certainly preferable to experiencing an unhappy home or divorce. However, research also shows that children are worse off staying in a conflict-ridden, unhappy home than experiencing the divorce of their parents. The emotional well-being of children is higher when a high-conflict marriage ends in divorce than when the couple stays together (Amato and Booth, 1997; Jekielek, 1998).

When parents do divorce, what are the consequences for the children? There are a number of things that we know about this (Furstenberg and Cherlin, 1991; Wallerstein, Lewis, and Blakeslee, 2000). First, the impact on children depends on their age. Children between five and ten, for example, often feel some responsibility for their parents' divorce, and this may lead to feelings of guilt and failure. Preteens often express tremendous anger toward their parents. Teenagers, on the other hand, are often confronted with the matter of "parental loyalty," feelings that they must take sides in the conflict and form a coalition with one or the other parent. Furthermore, although adolescents are better able to understand the reasons for divorce, they are often very worried about the effects of separation on their future. A second thing we know about the impact of divorce is that children in divorced homes seem more prone to delinquency (Rankin, 1983; Wells and Rankin, 1991). Third, a common consequence of divorce for both boys and girls is a decline in school performance and a higher high school dropout rate. Fourth, it is not the fact of the divorce itself that produces all of the negative consequences; the social and emotional conditions that often surround divorce are also a part of the problem (Amato, 1993; Amato and Rezac, 1994; Furstenberg and Teitler, 1994). The poor parenting, conflict between parents, and economic difficulties that often precede or follow divorce contribute to the negative consequences. In addition, divorce may reduce children's access to and ability to use various resources, such as the emotional support and role modeling of both parents. Finally, research suggests that the impact of divorce on children persists into adulthood and can have negative impacts on the mental health of children of divorce when they are adults (Cherlin, Chase-Lansdale, and McRae, 1998). Children of divorce are also more likely to experience a divorce in their own marriage, especially if their parents' divorce occurred when the offspring were teenagers or young adults.

The impact of divorce on children, however, is not all bad. Research shows that children living in one-parent families sometimes benefit from the experience (Amato, 1987; Dowd, 1997). For example, the single parent sometimes gives his or her teenage offspring more responsibility and a greater role in family decision making. In addition, the experience of divorce is less negative if a child continues to have contact with the parent with whom they no longer live, especially when the divorced parents have a low-conflict relationship.

Emerging Family Lifestyles

The attitudes toward marriage, family, and sexuality discussed earlier in this chapter, along with the increasing incidence of divorce, have led to some significant changes in the kinds of living arrangements that people find themselves in today. The conventional two-spouse nuclear family is not as common as it once was. Those who consider that conventional family form as the preferred one may consider these alternative family lifestyles to be a part of the problems confronting the family today. Yet, despite some problems that do arise, sociologists recognize that increasing numbers of people find themselves in these family arrangements, and they are likely to remain with us for some time. Figure 3.4 illustrates some of the changes in family structure over the past three decades. We now review some of these major alternatives with an eye on what future developments are likely.

Dual-Earner Families

In most nuclear families in the United States in the past, women did not work. Today the norm is for women to work, even in families with young children; so, today, in almost two-thirds of two-parent families, both spouses work. In fact, as Figure 3.5 illustrates, it used to be that women with young children were much less likely to work, but that has changed. Now women are as likely to work in families with children under the age of six as they are in all families. In some families, low wages of a spouse compel women to work in order to provide enough total income to support the family; in other cases, both spouses work because both wish to pursue a career. But when both spouses work, it can put stress on family relations. People who work have less time to spend with their spouses and children. This may stress the spousal relationship as well as contribute to difficulties that children have. Dual-earner families confront another stress: deciding whose career will take precedence. Such disputes can arise, for example, if either husband or wife wants to move in order to advance a career, especially if such a transition would be detrimental to his or her spouse's career. On a routine basis, there may be disagreement over whose career must suffer in order to raise children or to accomplish household chores. Although these tensions suggest that dual-earner marriages are more susceptible to divorce, there is little convincing evidence on this issue so far. Evidence does suggest that women who work out of choice are more satisfied with their marriages than women who work out of a sense of financial obligation, and the men in dual-earner families seem to be

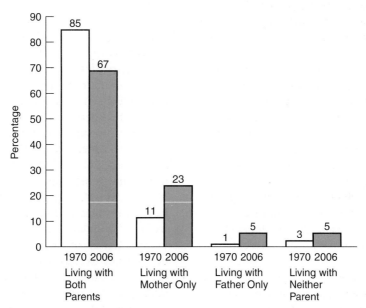

FIGURE 3.4 **Living Arrangements of People in the United States Under Eighteen Years of Age, 1970–2006.**

Sources: From *Statistical Abstract of the United States, 1995*, (p. 66) by U.S. U.S. Bureau of the Census, 1995, Washington, DC: U.S. Government Printing Office; *Current Population Survey*, 2006 Annual Social and Economic Supplement, by U.S. Bureau of the Census, March 2007, Washington, DC: U.S. Government Printing Office.

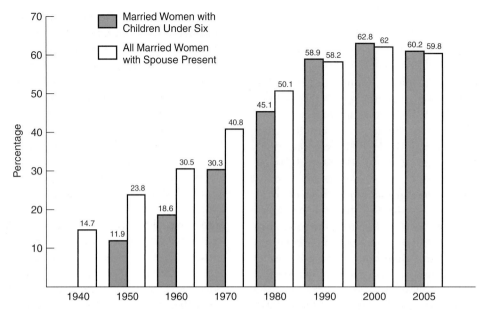

FIGURE 3.5 Percentage of Married Women with Spouse Present Who Are Employed, Among All Such Women and Among Women with Children Under Six Years of Age, 1940–2005.

Sources: U.S. Bureau of the Census, *Statistical Abstract of the United States, 1978* (Washington, DC: U.S. Government Printing Office, 1978), p. 404; U.S. Bureau of the Census, *Statistical Abstract of the United States, 2007* (Washington, DC: U.S. Government Printing Office, 2006), p. 80.

happy with their marriages (Barnett and Rivers, 1996; Vannoy-Hiller and Philliber, 1989). In addition, dual-earner couples are more likely to remain childless, and childless couples tend to have higher levels of marital satisfaction than do couples with children (House-knecht, 1987). An investigation of dual-earner couples working in senior management positions described such marriages as "more equal than others" in that the couples share a more equal partnership, with a more egalitarian decision making structure, than do couples in more traditional marriages (Hertz, 1986).

Higher rates of childlessness among dual-earner families may be an effort to avoid such competing demands. This might create other problems, however. If more people choose careers in the future, it is possible that many will resolve competing demands by choosing not to have children, possibly even choosing not to get married. This may well create a substantial difference in the standard of living between those who devote their energies to careers and those who feel family is important: Careerists will have a substantially more affluent lifestyle, which may make the decision to remain childless appealing to even more people. The outcome, potentially, might be the birth of even fewer children in society. This in turn could lead to a number of problems, such as an increasingly aged and dependent population that would be expensive to support (see Chapter 8).

Singlehood

Today, 54 million adults in the United States have never been married. This figure includes slightly more males than females. Many of these people, of course, will eventually marry, but some will choose single-hood over marriage as a lifelong lifestyle. In addition, although the proportion of our population that is single declined between 1940 and 1970, it has increased considerably since then (see Figure 3.2). Added to these never-married people are the many widowed and divorced who, at least temporarily, are living their lives as single men and women.

Many people who remain single do so because they believe this lifestyle affords them distinct advantages: freedom from unnecessary commitments, economic independence, opportunities to meet new people and develop new relationships, room for personal growth, or the ability to have a more varied sex life that is free of guilt (Macklin, 1987). Remaining single does not mean of course that there is necessarily a lack of emotional involvement with a partner who is at least semiperma-nent. Many singles develop intimate relationships, but they choose not to allow these to become permanent bonds based on marital exclusivity. However, as with childlessness among dual-career couples, singlehood—especially if chosen permanently and in large numbers—may have a long-term effect of lowering the birthrate.

Cohabitation

Cohabitation, or what is commonly called "living together," refers to *relationships in which two people live in the same household and share sexual, emotional, and often economic ties without being legally married*. It is difficult to estimate the number of couples in cohabiting relationships, because it is difficult to clearly define exactly who is cohabiting, and such relationships can change rapidly. The Census Bureau determined that, in 2004, about 5.1 million "unmarried couple" households existed in the United States, with two unrelated adults of the opposite sex sharing the same household (see Figure 3.6). Some of these were not cohabitants, of course, but merely roommates. In addition, 41 percent of women between the ages of fifteen and forty-four in one survey said they had cohabited at some point in their lives, and 7 percent said they were currently in a cohabitation relationship (U.S. Bureau of the Census, 2000: 52–53). These numbers give us some idea of the magnitude of the arrangement. Most of the couples involved are young, but about 5 percent of the Census' "unmarried couple" households involve at least one partner over age sixty-five.

People cohabit for many reasons (Cherlin and Furstenberg, 1994; Loomis and Landale, 1994). For some, it is a "trial marriage," a time for the couple to get to know one another and determine whether they are compatible before establishing the legal bond. For others, cohabitation may be viewed as a replacement for marriage, which some women and men may view as an unnecessary legal tie. In fact, one group among which cohabitation has increased considerably in the past thirty years is the divorced. People increasingly turn to cohabitation rather than remarriage as a vehicle for establishing an intimate relationship after a failed marriage. For these people, cohabitation has come to be seen as acceptable as marriage as a context for family-related activities such as having children. Finally, for some elderly couples, for whom marriage means a reduction in Social Security income, cohabitation may be a matter of economic convenience or necessity.

As the number of cohabiting couples has grown, the stigma associated with this lifestyle has declined. As was mentioned in the beginning of the chapter, some employers, including some city and county governments, have established "domestic partner" provisions that accord cohabitants much the same benefits and rights as married couples. In addition, a number of courts have ruled that the relationship between cohabitants is not unlike that of married couples. For example, cohabitants can make legal arrangements to share their property, and one partner can sue the other for a share of the property and for support payments, or "palimony," should the relationship dissolve. So, although some people continue to see marriage as the preferable route for organizing one's life, a growing number of people are choosing cohabitation, and the courts are establishing a legal framework that sees cohabitation as being very much like marriage.

Single Parenthood

A rapidly growing alternative to the conventional two-parent nuclear family is one with only one parent (Sugarman, 1998). Today, 32 percent of all families

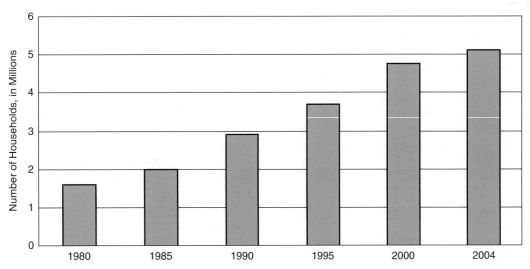

FIGURE 3.6 **Number of Households with Unmarried Couples of the Opposite Sex, 1980–2004.**

Sources: U.S. Bureau of the Census, *Statistical Abstract of the United States, 1998* (Washington, DC: U.S. Government Printing Office, 1998), p. 60; U.S. Bureau of the Census, *Statistical Abstract of the United States, 2007* (Washington, DC: U.S. Government Printing Office, 2006), p. 53.

with children under eighteen years of age are headed by only one parent, mostly by women (U.S. Bureau of the Census, 2006:54). Furthermore, almost one out of every three children lives in a family in which one or both parents are absent (see Figure 3.4), and half of all children may spend at least part of their childhood in a single-parent home. Although some families have only one parent due to the death of a spouse, most are the result of divorce. Increasingly, however, children live with parents, usually mothers, who choose not to marry at all. The number of children living with a mother who had never married increased to 10 percent in 2004 compared to 1 percent in 1970. One-third of all births are to unmarried women today, in comparison with 4 percent in 1950 (U.S. Bureau of the Census, 2006:67). Given these trends in divorce and single motherhood, the proportion of single-parent families is likely to grow considerably in the future. Needless to say, people who view marriage as the only acceptable context for raising children find such developments highly threatening to their values.

The issue of single parenthood has been controversial because suggestions that children raised by a single parent suffer more problems than children raised by both parents have been strongly attacked for implying that mothers are not adequate parents or that parents should not divorce. These suggestions have been interpreted as limiting women's choices in life, a stance that is not popular in this era of gender equality. Yet, the research does suggest, in a qualified way, that children are often worse off when raised by one parent than two, suffering consequences similar to those of children of divorce mentioned earlier (Cancian and Reed, 2001). A summary of this research concluded:

> Growing up with only one biological parent frequently deprives children of important economic, parental, and community resources, and . . . these deprivations ultimately undermine their chances of future success. . . . While living with just one parent increases the risk of . . . negative outcomes, it is not the only, or even the major, cause of them. Growing up with a single parent is just one among many factors that put children at risk of failure. (McLanahan and Sandefur, 1994:2–3)

Not all children in single-parent families will suffer the negative consequences because many factors influence a child's development. The researchers attribute the difficulties of children in single-parent families to three factors: low income, inadequate parental guidance, and less access to community resources. If a single parent can overcome these difficulties, then his or her children can do quite well. For example, when the decision to have a child is well considered by a woman with the social and economic resources to raise the child adequately, the outcome does not raise serious problems for society, although it might clash with the personal or religious values of some groups.

So, the research does not lead necessarily to the conclusion that divorce or single parenthood is bad. However, single parenthood is especially widespread among groups who are more likely to lack the financial resources to support the child, such as minorities and teenagers (Kirby, 2001; Luker, 1996; Zill and Nord, 1994). For example, at least half of all births to African American and Puerto Rican American women are to unmarried women, and both of these groups have some of the highest rates of poverty in the United States. Four out of every ten teenage girls get pregnant at least once before they are twenty years old (Kirby, 2001). Although the teen pregnancy rate in the United States has been falling somewhat recently, the rate is still far higher than in all comparable industrial nations; it is twice as high as in Great Britain and ten times higher than in the Netherlands or Japan. For teenagers in particular, becoming a mother is a difficult burden: They often lack the maturity and economic resources for good child-rearing practices, and the burden often severely limits their educational and employment opportunities.

The Policy Issues insert (pp. 74–75) explores some of the issues and controversies regarding whether gay unions should be considered an emerging family form.

A Global Perspective

Some of the trends in family life found in the United States are also occurring in other nations around the world (United Nations, 2000; United Nations Development Fund for Women, 2002). In the past few decades, for example, the proportion of births to unmarried women has increased in most nations, in some cases dramatically. The proportion has doubled in the United States to 36 percent, but in nations as diverse as Denmark, Norway, and Guam it has increased 300 to 400 percent. In the Seychelles, French Guiana, and Martinique, two out of every three births are to unmarried women. In addition, many households are headed by women: almost 50 percent in nations like Botswana and Barbados and 31 percent in the United States. Household size has also been decreasing in every part of the world, suggesting that the family is becoming a smaller kinship unit. The birthrate in most societies around the world has been declining, and the divorce rate has been increasing. All of these trends suggest the extent to which the form of the family is shaped by the needs of society. Earlier, this chapter pointed out that industrial societies generally tend to weaken kinship and family structures, in part because the family in such societies performs fewer functions and is thus less important. Industrial societies tend to encourage nuclear families and to be more permissive of divorce. Such societies also sometimes split families up as some members must migrate looking for work. In addition, greater gender equality and higher levels of education for women offer them more opportunities in terms of supporting their families. The result, in most nations, is that the family has declined in both size and significance and women have fewer supports with which to take care of themselves and their families. It is a worldwide trend—a by-product of industrialization—although the pace and extent of the developments vary from one society to another.

Violence in the Family

The family is usually viewed as a place where love and affection abound, but one research team concluded that there is a darker side to family life: "Violence between family members is probably as common as love" (Straus, Gelles, and Steinmetz, 1980:13). We will examine the three major types of family violence: intimate partner, child abuse, and abuse of the elderly.

Intimate Partner Violence

Intimate partner violence includes violence between spouses, former spouses, cohabiting partners, boyfriends or girlfriends, and dates. A recent survey by the National Institute of Justice and the Centers for Disease Control and Prevention found that one-quarter of all women and 8 percent of all men reported being the victim of violence by an intimate partner at some point during their life (Tjaden and Thoennes, 2000). Another study found that 20 percent of all nonfatal violence against women is perpetrated by an intimate partner and one-third of all women murder victims are killed by an intimate partner (Rennison, 2003). Possibly as many as one-quarter to one-third of gay men and

These police officers are questioning a victim of intimate partner violence. Such violence is more widespread than many people believe, and it causes serious physical and psychological damage to those who are its victims.

Should Gay and Lesbian Families Be Legitimized?

Attitudes about what is acceptable family life in the United States change as society changes. We have seen this happen with unmarried cohabitation and single-parent families, which were once viewed negatively by many people but have now gained some respectability. Could the same thing happen with gay and lesbian couples, with their partnerships coming to be seen as acceptable families?

Opposition to such a change remains strong. Many religions are vehemently against such a policy, and public opinion in the United States remains firmly against it. Sociologist Alan Wolfe reports on national surveys that show that, although 80 percent of the populace considers a single mother with her children to be a "family," only about a quarter of the public would call a gay couple with children a "family" (Wolfe, 1998). A Gallup Poll in 2006 found that only 42 percent of the public believed that marriages between same-sex people should be recognized as valid with all the same rights as a traditional marriage. In addition, half of Americans supported an amendment to the U.S. Constitution that would define marriage as only involving an opposite-sex couple (Gallup Poll, 2007b). So, traditional beliefs that regard marriage and family as involving members of the opposite sex are still very entrenched, although some change is detectable. Acceptance of cohabitation and single parenthood was also slow in coming, but these family forms do not violate what many people perceive as the fundamentally heterosexual nature of marriage. Although many people have come to accept the idea that gays should have rights and not suffer discrimination, many of those same people still do not see homosexuality as a lifestyle morally equivalent to heterosexuality.

Gay and lesbian couples, of course, do consider their same-sex unions to be "families." From a sociological perspective, the domestic units formed by gay and lesbian couples resemble families because the units perform many of the functions that families perform in society, as described earlier in this chapter (Stacey, 1998). These relationships are often monogamous, the norm for families in the United States, with some degree of permanence and an emphasis on sexual exclusivity. Gay and lesbian couples sometimes have children from previous marriages, or they adopt or conceive through artificial insemination. Estimates are that one-third of lesbians are mothers and between one-quarter and one-half of all gay men are fathers, although many do not have custody of their offspring. In addition, as many as 14 million children are being raised by at least one parent who is gay or lesbian. So, the socialization and educational functions of the family are performed by some gay couples, and research gives no evidence that the children are compromised in any significant way by being raised by a gay parent (Golombok and Tasker, 1996; Johnson and O'Connor, 2002; Stacey and Biblarz, 2001).

Gay couples also often form an economic unit through the common ownership of property, such as a home, and the combining of financial resources. An increasing number of corporate and government employers are extending legitimacy to these relationships by providing benefits and rights to the unmarried domestic partners of their employees, whether a heterosexual couple or a gay couple. As evidence that the relationship is reasonably permanent, some employers look for signs of economic interdependence, such as joint bank accounts or co-owned property. Finally, many gay couples provide the protection and the personal gratification that are among the functions of the units typically called "families."

So, a significant number of gay men and lesbians form relationships that have many of the sociological attributes normally associated with families. To be sure, gay couples face significant stressors, such as discrimination in both occupation and housing (Rodriguez Rust, 2004). They are also likely to be labeled deviant by many and cast into a marginal role. One way in which society marginalizes gays is by denying official legitimation to their bond in the form of marriage ceremonies or licenses that signify societal approval. Some gay couples have ceremonies, sometimes performed by ministers, to mark their commitment to each other; these rituals serve the same functions of public affirmation and legitimation that legally recognized marriage ceremonies do. As of this writing, the Netherlands and Belgium now provide for gay marriages; courts in Canada

lesbians have also been abused by an intimate partner (Durfee and Rosenberg, 2004). All of these figures probably underestimate the amount of intimate partner violence that occurs because people are often reluctant to admit such circumstances in their own relationships. Even so, the numbers demonstrate that a serious problem exists.

How are we to explain this high level of intimate partner violence? One reason for it is that the use of violence to settle disputes is widely accepted in the United States, especially among males. Traditional norms in many subcultures support male domination in marriage. In fact, men with traditional, or nonegalitarian, views toward sex-role relationships are more

A gay family enjoys an outdoor event. The domestic units formed by gay and lesbian couples have many of the sociological attributes normally associated with families; however, significant opposition persists to giving societal legitimation to such unions.

and Massachusetts have ruled that the government must recognize gay marriages; four states (Connecticut, New Hampshire, New Jersey, and Vermont) and the Canadian province of Quebec have civil unions for gay couples, giving them much the same rights and obligations as married couples; in 2003, *Bride's* magazine published an article on same-sex weddings, discussing why gays and lesbians wanted a marriage option available and how guests should behave if invited to such a wedding. All of these develop-ments taken together suggest that a significant shift in attitudes and practices relating to gay families is underway and are certainly testimony to the political clout of the gay community. Yet it is unclear what the future of these devel-opments will be since, as we have seen, strong opposition to them persists. So, there is substantial uncertainty at this point about whether gay and lesbian couples will make additional progress toward being considered married couples living in families.

likely to approve of using violence against a spouse and are more likely to have actually used severe violence against their own spouses. A second reason for intimate partner violence is poverty: Serious violence within families is disproportionately a problem of the poor and economically disadvantaged. Families with low educa-tional and occupational attainment are especially at risk of partner abuse. A third reason for intimate partner violence is sexual inequality (Crossman, Stith, and Bender, 1990; Kalmuss and Straus, 1982). Wife beat-ing is much more likely to occur in families in which power over decision making is concentrated in the hus-band's hands—approximately twenty times the rate found in families in which egalitarian decision making occurs (Straus, Gelles, and Steinmetz, 1980). When women have more social and economic resources, such as a job with which to support themselves, they are less likely to be abused and more likely to leave an abusive husband. A fourth reason for intimate partner violence is an inconsistency between the man's and woman's achievements. So, a high risk of partner violence is found when a man's occupation or educational attainment is significantly lower than his wife's. The husband may feel threatened by this and lash out with physical violence. A final reason for intimate partner violence is social isolation: When a spouse has few contacts with people other than her husband, she is less likely to define the abuse as unjustified and to seek assistance (Stets, 1991).

Child Abuse

Equally if not more disturbing than the conclusions about marital violence are the findings concerning violence by parents against children; more than 60 percent of couples acknowledge performing at least one violent act against a child. One investigation reported that more than twelve of every one thousand children younger than eighteen years are victims of serious abuse or neglect every year, and child abuse and neglect are the leading causes of traumatic death for children aged four and younger (U.S. Department of Health and Human Services, 2002).

Researchers in this field regard these figures as conservative. Some research suggests that the rates of child abuse are increasing in the United States, but this conclusion is controversial and depends on how child abuse is measured. If we look at child abuse reported to police and health-care workers, abuse appears to be up; but if we ask parents if they have shoved, hit, or in other ways hurt their children, rates appear to be down. A definitive conclusion on whether abuse is increasing is just not possible at this time (Egley, 1991; Gelles and Conte, 1990).

As with marital violence, there are economic correlates of child abuse. Investigations have shown that the maltreatment of children is concentrated not only among low-income families but also among the extremely poor. This is especially true for severe violence (Gelles, 1992; Pelton, 1978). For the poor, economic hardships interact with immediate situational stressors—disputes between parents, a burdensome number of children, a child who creates problems for parents—to bring about incidents of child abuse. Especially at risk of using the most abusive forms of violence against their children are poor and young parents, poor parents with young children, and poor single mothers (Gelles, 1992).

Irrespective of social class considerations, it appears that child abuse is a behavior pattern that is passed on from generation to generation in some families. For example, a review of studies on child abuse found that although between 2 percent and 4 percent of parents abuse their children, that rate is as high as 30 percent or more among parents who were themselves abused as children (Gelles and Conte, 1990).

Abuse of the Elderly

The elderly can suffer the same kinds of abuses as do children and spouses: physical violence, psychological abuse such as insults and threats, and neglect of one's important and basic needs of daily living. Estimates are that 32 of every 1,000 older people suffer some type of abuse, with well over half of that being physical violence (Pillemer and Finkelhor, 1988). This means that somewhere between 700,000 and 1.1 million elderly in the United States have suffered abuse. Surprising to some, men are more likely to be victims of elder abuse than are women, and women are more likely to abuse their elder husbands than men are to abuse their elder wives. However, women suffer more injuries and emotional distress when they are abused than do men. Finally, those who live alone or who are not married are less likely to suffer abuse than those who are married or live with others, and those who live with a spouse and an offspring are especially at risk of suffering abuse.

Some abuse of the elderly may arise from the stress of taking care of a dependent older parent or grandparent who is physically or mentally impaired (Flowers, 2000; Steinmetz, 1987). To some extent, abuse of the elderly reflects one of the weaknesses of the modern nuclear family: It lacks the extensive support network and additional helping hands that are available in the extended family or even the modified extended family. As we have seen, we often expect each person in the nuclear family to be a breadwinner, a companion, and so on. When society burdens one person with a wide range of difficult tasks, including taking care of a child or an impaired older parent, the stresses will sometimes accumulate to the point where abuse is likely. Recent research, however, points to a different relationship between dependency and abuse: Abuse is more likely to occur when the caregiver is dependent on the elderly person under his or her care. This is especially true when the caregiver is financially dependent on the elderly person, is personally or emotionally troubled, or abuses alcohol or drugs (Greenberg, McKibben, and Raymond, 1990; Pillemer and Finkelhor, 1989). In these situations, caregivers may be responding to their feelings of powerlessness in the relationship and resorting to one of the few power resources they have available: force and violence.

So, research on abuse of the elderly provides further evidence for the part that inequitable distributions of power and resources play in family violence. Those who are dependent—whether they be children or frail elderly—are at risk of suffering violence at the hands of others. Those with access to economic and social resources, such as wives with careers or the elderly who can live on their own, are better equipped to avoid violence. And those who feel helpless and powerless—such as poor, single mothers or caregivers who are dependent on their elderly charges—may lash out in violence as a reaction to their circumstances.

Constructing Family Problems: Media Images

The mass media have been central to shaping the debate about problems in the modern family through their ability to influence people's beliefs and values about what the family is or should be like in society. Studies of the content of television shows over the decades document the changing portrayals of the family. The portrayals mirror actual family forms in some respects but seriously distort them in other respects (Huston et al., 1992; Robinson and Skill, 2001). Through the 1950s, families on television were always two-parent families, and they had either two or three children or they were a recently married couple who had yet to begin having children. Popular examples of this were *I Love Lucy, Father Knows Best,* and *Ozzie and Harriet.* Although media executives claimed to be merely describing what most families then were like, this is patently untrue because this chapter has shown that family violence was widespread and divorce did occur then. Yet, these social realities were not portrayed on television. Their absence from television helped to foster the belief that the happy, nuclear family with an average of two children was the norm.

In the 1960s and 1970s, more single-parent families began to be portrayed in television; however, most of these families were headed by men, even though in the real world most single-parent families are headed by women. These early portrayals of single-parent families stood out in another regard: The single-parent status resulted from a parental death rather than divorce, even though divorce, then and now, is the far more common cause for a family to have only one parent. Despite the appearance of single-parent families on television during these decades, the predominance of family portrayals were still of tradi-

tional families, often presented in an almost idyllic version, such as *The Waltons* and *Little House on the Prairie.*

Today, the portrayal of families on television has become more realistically diverse, with more single-parent, female-headed families. However, the ratio of male-to-female single-parent families is still much more heavily skewed toward the male end than is the case among actual families. In addition, television still downplays some of the serious problems that confront modern families, such as poverty, access to child care, family conflict and violence, and unemployment.

Another dimension of family life portrayed on television is the kinds of social relationships that exist among parents and children. Although there are exceptions, television portrays mostly affluent, competent, and successful families in which individual family members get along with one another reasonably well (although some superficial conflict does occur). The family members portrayed are far more intelligent, clever, and humorous than is true of the average person. Much less commonly portrayed are very poor families, families immobilized by drug or alcohol addiction on the part of one or both parents, or families with extremely restricted educational or occupational opportunities.

There has also been a substantial growth in the portrayal of gay and lesbian characters in television and movies, to the point where it has become almost routine. However, gay couples or families are still rather scarce in these media, being portrayed in substantially smaller proportions than their real numbers would warrant if the media were attempting to reflect reality. Finally, music must be considered as part of the media technology that shapes images of the family, and some modern music presents a rather negative picture. Musical innovations such as rap and hip hop, for example, sometimes portray positively an aggressive image of masculinity and an almost-misogynistic view of women (Martinez, 1997). This translates at times into a picture of violence between men and women as socially acceptable, or at least tolerable. And, in fact, some research suggests that exposure to rap and hip hop music may reduce some of the inhibitions to committing domestic violence in some people (Barongan and Hall, 1995; Johnson et al., 1995).

These portrayals of family are important because research documents that people's beliefs and values regarding family life are affected by what they see on television (Dorr, Kovaric, and Doubleday, 1990). People tend to see the traditional nuclear family as the norm, despite the enormous diversity that actually exists. To the extent that people use the portrayal on television as a model for understanding family problems in the modern world, their model is likely to be seriously distorted, and people's efforts to understand and find solutions to family problems will be less than realistic. The overall effect of television portrayals of families has probably been to encourage support for policies based on the assumption that most people can and should live in conventional nuclear families and to downplay the extent of the changes occurring in family forms today.

Future Prospects

Most sociologists are confident that the family as a social institution will survive. The family performs important functions in society, and some type of family will undoubtedly continue to perform those functions in the future. But the family is changing, and the real issue is not whether the family will survive but what form it will take. New forms, such as single parenthood, cohabitation, and gay families, are emerging, and these perform some of the sociological functions of families discussed in this chapter. Given these trends, what seems to be emerging in modern industrial societies is a **pluralistic family** in which *a number of different types of family exist side by side, each having an attraction for some people.* So, in the United States today, some people live in traditional extended families, some in nuclear families, some in blended families, and still others in same-sex families. Given the vast diversity in the culture and the changing role of the family, such pluralistic family arrangements are probably more adaptive. They permit people of many occupations, religions, ethnic groups, and lifestyles to find a form of the family that best fits their values and needs. Whereas some people are tolerant of this diversity, others find some of these alternatives to be morally unacceptable, and this conflict will probably persist in the future. Such conflict will be especially salient in the public policy arena in which groups do battle to gain acceptance for their values or way of life. The outcome of this conflict will determine which forms of the family find acceptance at any given moment, and that will likely change from time to time.

Some of these diverse forms of the family, however, can create serious problems for society, and many proposals and programs have been put forth to alleviate these problems.

The Future of Divorce

Despite the rapid rise in divorce in recent decades, the divorce rate will not necessarily continue to rise substantially in the future. In fact, since 1980, the divorce rate in the United States has fallen slightly. In part, this stabilization or decline in the rate is due to a considerable decline in the marriage rate, which has dropped by about half over the past fifty years (see Figure 3.3). However, it may also be that the divorce rate has risen as high as it is likely to in response to changing social conditions resulting from industrialization. On the other hand, there is no reason to believe that the divorce rate will decline significantly in the future. The current divorce rate may well be one that is commensurate with social conditions and the position of the family in a mature industrial society.

In the past, religious teachings, social norms, and practical considerations inhibited people from dissolving their marriages. Today, as we have seen, these factors are less prominent. Yet these traditional controls may be replaced with others. For example, our schools and colleges could offer more and better courses in marriage and family training so that young people would be prepared to make sounder marital choices and work more effectively at maintaining relationships. Such courses could help people identify the factors associated with successful and unsuccessful marriages so that they could use this information in making important life choices. In fact, some states, recognizing that people who marry at a young age are especially likely to divorce, require people younger than eighteen to obtain a court order to marry and to submit to premarital counseling if directed.

Reducing Family Violence

One of the most positive steps toward reducing family violence has been bringing the issue into the open. This has enabled us to concentrate resources on solving this problem. The Child Abuse Prevention and Treatment Act was passed in the mid-1970s and amended in 1988 to help states and communities develop programs for abusive or neglectful parents. The government has also funded research to find the causes of child abuse and the most effective ways of dealing with it. Programs have been established to train parents in "parenting skills" as a way of preventing future episodes of abuse. Prevention can also be enhanced when parents are connected to organizations and services in the community because this increases the chances of getting help before abuse recurs. Substance abuse treatment programs are made available to parents who might be at risk of abusing their children because of the known role of alcohol in child abuse. Self-help groups such as Parents Anonymous, in which a supportive personal relationship is used to help parents stop mistreating their children, have also emerged. Finally, programs such as day care that ease the pressure and burden on parents may reduce the precipitating factors that can initiate episodes of violence.

Spouse abuse has also received much attention recently, and this has resulted in accelerated efforts toward pinning down its sources. As mentioned earlier, the improving economic and social position of women in society will likely make them less vulnerable targets of abuse in the future. Furthermore, spouse abuse centers can now be found in most communities, and these offer sanctuary and support to women who seek to change or leave an abusive relationship. Finally, the Policy Issues section of Chapter 1 pointed out that the criminal justice system today responds much more quickly and aggressively to cases in which spouse abuse is suspected.

Efforts to control abuse of the elderly have not been as extensive as those focusing on other forms of family violence, but some progress has been made (Brownell and Wolden, 2002; Ross, 1991). For example, many states have adopted laws that require reporting of abuse of the elderly to the police. They have also established many protective services for the elderly, increased penalties for abuse or neglect of the elderly, and created provisions for confidentiality in the reporting of cases of elder abuse. Yet there remain substantial restraints on what the authorities can do. Most states have no penalties for many forms of abuse or neglect of a parent. What needs to be done is to establish a range of services that could defuse tensions in the family or help the elderly escape abusive settings.

As family violence has commanded more attention in recent years, various government task forces investigating domestic violence have called for toughening the actions that could be taken to arrest, bring to trial, and imprison offenders (Bohmer, Brandt, and Bronson, 2002; U.S. Advisory Board on Child Abuse and Neglect, 1995). Noting that domestic violence has often been ignored in the past, these task forces make some powerful recommendations, including:

1. Adopting the attitude that family violence in all forms should be regarded as criminal.

2. Establishing arrest as the preferred method of immediately dealing with such crimes.

3. Processing all complaints of family violence as reported criminal offenses.

4. Organizing special units to process family violence cases.

5. Eliminating the requirement that a victim sign a formal complaint before the prosecutor can file charges, unless mandated by state law.

Children and the Family

Social policies designed to deal with the difficulties of single-parent families, especially teenage pregnancies, have been highly controversial because they intrude into some very sensitive areas of family life (Zill and Nord, 1994). One way of reducing teen pregnancies is to make birth control information available to teens, and many family planning agencies have done so without informing the parents of the teens. In fact, countries with low rates of teen pregnancies also have liberal attitudes toward sex, make contraceptives easily available to teenagers, and provide effective sex education programs. Research in this country shows that teen pregnancy can be reduced by providing education in how to prevent conception and access to contraceptives, along with school counseling and job training (Plotnick, 1993). However, such programs are controversial because they rest in part on the assumption that many teenagers will continue to be sexually active. By contrast, federal programs in recent decades have focused on reducing teen pregnancy by promoting sexual abstinence. The 1996 welfare reform law (see Chapter 5), for example, provided money only for abstinence programs and not to teach about contraception. Despite this emphasis on abstinence programs, research to date provides no evidence that these programs reduce levels of sexual activity or age of first sexual activity among teens (Trenholm et al., 2007).

The International Perspectives insert describes the family policies currently being used in some other societies. As that insert points out, social policies in the United States tend to be laissez-faire, with comparatively little government direction regarding families and children. This situation changed somewhat in 1993 when President Clinton signed into law a family leave bill that requires large employers to give their employees unpaid leave to care for newly born children or ill family members. However, the United States is practically alone among industrial nations in not having a national policy that requires *paid* maternity leave (Gornick and Meyers, 2003). So, the U.S. policy on maternity leave to support families provides considerably less protection than that described in the insert for other industrial nations.

Another area in which support for a coherent family policy in the United States has been emerging is day care. In fact, our nation's employers have been developing day-care programs over the past decade (Kate,

Historically, the United States has had a very laissez-faire social policy toward families. This day-care program in the United Kingdom illustrates the much more interventionist family policies in most European industrial nations.

1992). About 3 percent of the nation's employers sponsor day-care centers for their employees' children, and another 9 percent offer at least some employee financial assistance for day care or information and referral services to guide parents in finding day care for their children. Furthermore, 61 percent of employers provide indirect day-care assistance in the form of flexible work schedules, flexible leaves, and part-time work for parents of young children. Not surprisingly, employers with large numbers of women of childbearing age in their workforce are most likely to have some day-care policy, and it is the better-paid and more powerful employees who are most likely to be offered these services by employers. The motivation for employers to sponsor these programs is in good part pragmatic: Research has shown that the problems employees face in arranging care for their children tend to result in absenteeism, tardiness, low morale, and productivity problems. Also, recruiting new employees is easier when an employer can offer child-care services to prospective employees, especially in heavily female segments of the labor market such as nursing. Laissez-faire advocates would argue that this largely private-sector initiative is the most appropriate way to handle day-care policy: Let employers respond to the needs of their employees. Child care should become another fringe benefit—like health-care insurance and vacation time—that is negotiated between employer and employee.

Both the state and the federal governments provide funding for child care, but often as a part of programs with goals separate from child care itself such as the Head Start program (see Chapter 5). Half of the states also provide some support for day care through their tax codes. There are other state and federal supports for child care, but the point is that there is not one coherent policy on the issue as is found commonly in other advanced industrial nations. There is as yet no consensus in the United States that day-care services should be available to all families, irrespective of their economic circumstances (Gornick and Meyers, 2003).

Another controversy in current child-care policy is over *privatization:* Should policies encourage the private sector to develop and provide the services people want, or should the government directly provide the services? Privatization policies provide parents with vouchers to purchase child care or tax credits for money spent on child care, and then parents seek the services where they wish, often from private, profit, or nonprofit centers. Needless to say, laissez-faire advocates support this approach. Interventionists argue that programs such as Head Start, for which the government runs the child-care centers, are preferred because their mission is focused exclusively on provid-

Families and Children in Other Societies

Regarding families and children, social policy in the United States has historically been very laissez-faire, leaving people to get by on their own with little assistance from the government. This contrasts sharply with virtually all other advanced industrial nations, where social policies are based on a consensus that everyone benefits when families and their children are supported (Gornick and Meyers, 2003; Kamerman and Kahn, 1991; Tietze and Cryer, 1999). These nations take responsibility for protecting children, providing good early childhood education, serving children with special needs, supporting mothers' desires to continue working, maintaining family income during and after the birth of a child, and encouraging a birthrate that at least maintains current population size.

To achieve these goals, most industrial nations make publicly funded preschools universally available to children beginning at age three and continuing until the child enters school, irrespective of parents' income or work status. In France and Belgium, for example, the preschools are publicly financed and operated as an integral part of the educational system. All children are eligible, beginning some time after their second birthday, and the schools are free, with parents paying only for things like lunch or certain after-school programs. Similar

programs are found in many other countries, including Israel and Hungary. In Sweden and Finland, preschools are separate from the school system and are heavily subsidized by the government, although parents do pay some fees if they can afford them. The government enforces strict standards regarding such things as staff–child ratios and teacher qualifications in the preschools. Such preschool education is coming to be viewed, by many of these European nations, as a "right" of citizenship, just as one has a right to a basic education.

Almost all advanced industrial nations also provide some level of maternity or parenting leave that enables one or both parents to stay home with their infant for a period after birth. These programs permit the parents to receive some level of their previous income while on leave and protect their job until they return to work. In France, for example, women are given a six-week leave before delivery and ten weeks after delivery, all with pay, and business leaders seem unconcerned about its effects on worker productivity or corporate profits. French parents can also take two years off after having a child without worrying about whether their job will be there when they return.

Given that maternity/parenting leaves enable parents to stay home with their infants, and preschool takes care of children aged three

and older, the only children in need of child care in these industrial nations are those who are one and two years of age. Although child-care programs are much more limited in these countries than are the infant and preschool programs, child care is increasingly being seen as a public responsibility and an entitlement for children. In addition to these programs, most industrial nations also provide publicly funded health care and housing allowances to families, paid leave to parents to care for sick children, and sometimes even direct subsidization of family incomes to reduce the economic disparity between those who choose to have children and those who choose to remain childless.

Despite the fact that United States policy leaves families very much on their own, the need for support seems greater in the United States, with its higher rates of divorce and single parenthood than in these other countries. So, the regulated capitalism of France and Sweden has produced family policies that protect and nurture children because children are seen as key resources for the future. The United States, on the other hand, leaves children to the largely unregulated free market, which has so far meant that many children live in less affluent families and go without while others suffer low quality, inadequate, and possibly damaging preschool experiences.

LINKAGES Changes in the family, especially increases in divorce and single parenthood, have made more women the sole breadwinners for their families, which makes them more vulnerable to discrimination and inequality based on gender (Chapter 7). Family problems are exacerbated by drug and alcohol addiction (Chapter 10) because poor parents are more likely to become addicted, and domestic violence is associated with drug and alcohol addiction.

Summary

1. The family is a social institution, based on kinship, that functions to replace members of society and to nurture them.
2. In the United States today, people practice monogamy, and egalitarianism is encouraged. Families vary in configuration but usually fall into one of three categories: extended, nuclear, or modified extended.
3. The functionalist perspective posits that some form of the family exists in all societies because the family performs certain basic functions that are essential to human survival and the maintenance of society.
4. The conflict perspective views the family as serving the interests of the dominant groups in society, and the version of family most prominent in society is usually the one that is consistent with the values and benefits of the dominant groups. The dominant form of family also benefits particular economic interests.
5. The interactionist perspective points to the fact that what is considered the family is a matter of social definition, becoming a part of the social reality that people create and live by.
6. Marriage and family relationships are popular in the United States today, but these kinds of intimate associations are more likely to be participant controlled rather than parent run.
7. The divorce rate in the United States has risen considerably during this century but has stabilized in the last two decades. Sociologists identify certain changes in society brought about by industrialization as the cause of this rise in the divorce rate. Some couples are at considerably greater risk of experiencing divorce than others. Widespread divorce has some negative consequences, both for the parents and the children.
8. Many different family lifestyles have emerged over the past few decades, some being considered symptomatic of the problems surrounding the family today. Among them are dual-earner families, singlehood, cohabitation, single parenthood, and gay families.
9. Violence among family members is common in the United States, usually occurring between intimate partners or directed at dependent children or the elderly.
10. Most sociologists are confident that the family will survive as a social institution, but that family relationships will be pluralistic in the future.

Key Terms

blended family

cohabitation

egalitarian family

extended family

family

modified extended
  family

monogamy

nuclear family

patriarchy

pluralistic family

polygamy

refined divorce rate

serial monogamy

Multiple-Choice Questions

1. Which of the following perspectives would argue that family institutions exist in society because families make important contributions to human survival and the maintenance of society?
   a. the functionalist perspective
   b. the conflict perspective
   c. the interactionist perspective
   d. the extended family perspective
2. Which of the following is *not* a conclusion of the research regarding the impact of day care cited in the text? In comparison to children raised at home,
   a. day-care children are as attached to their parents.
   b. day-care children do as well in psychosocial development.
   c. day-care children are as socially competent.
   d. children enrolled in day care at a young age may become more aggressive.
   e. all of the above were conclusions cited in the text.
3. By 2005, the most common household had which of the following compositions?
   a. male head of household, no spouse present
   b. female head of household, no spouse present
   c. a one-person household
   d. a married couple household
   e. two or more unrelated people in a household
4. Which of the following statements is true regarding the marital status of people in the United States today as compared to 1940?
   a. A substantially smaller percentage of people are married today.
   b. A substantially larger percentage of people are divorced today.
   c. A substantially larger percentage of people today have never married.
   d. A substantially larger percentage of people are widowed today.

A good starting point for Web resources on family issues is a Web site maintained by the Sociology Department at the University of Colorado (**socsci.colorado.edu/SOC/Research**). You will find many links to other Web sites covering a broad range of family-related issues. Two other useful Web sites that have numerous links to locations related to family problems are the Family Research Council (**www.frc.org**) and the Women's Studies Program at the University of Connecticut (**www.ucc.uconn.edu/~wwwwmst/links.html**).

One of the issues discussed in this chapter is whether gay couples should be considered families. Using the Yahoo! search vehicle, go to the "more" choice and then "Directory" search category; then choose "Cultures and Groups," and then "Lesbians, Gay, Bisexual, and Transgendered." You will then have many options to choose among. Select "Organizations," and you will have choices like "Politics and Civil Rights" and "Marriage and Domestic Partnerships." Explore these various areas and identify all the issues and arguments that relate to gay families.

The chapter also stresses the variety of families that can be found in the United States and in other cultures. Search for Web sites that document and explore that diversity. Can you locate some types of families that were not discussed in this chapter? For an anthropological approach to these issues, try this Web site at the University of Manitoba: **www.umanitoba.ca/faculties/arts/anthropology/knititle.html**. It has an informative tutorial that looks at kinship as an aspect of social organization.

The Allyn & Bacon Social Problems Supersite (**wps.ablongman.com/ab_socialprob_sprsite_1**) contains material on problems related to the family.

5. The likelihood in the United States today that a marriage will end in divorce is closest to which of the following figures?
   a. 15 percent
   b. 30 percent
   c. 50 percent
   d. 65 percent
   e. 85 percent
6. All of the following were identified as placing a couple at a higher risk of divorce *except*
   a. social differences between the couple.
   b. high socioeconomic standing.
   c. young age at marriage.
   d. whirlwind romances.
7. Over the past fifty years, the percentage of married women who work outside the home has
   a. declined steadily.
   b. increased steadily.
   c. increased until 1970 and then declined.
   d. increased until 1970 and then leveled off.
   e. remained level until 1970 and then increased.
8. Which of the following family lifestyles appears to be on the decline?
   a. cohabitation
   b. single parenthood
   c. dual-earner families
   d. none of the above
9. Given the research findings on intimate partner violence, which of the following women would most likely be at risk of being abused by a spouse?
   a. a woman whose spouse has traditional, nonegalitarian views toward sex-role relationships
   b. a woman with high levels of education and other economic resources
   c. a woman with an elaborate social network of friends and relatives
   d. a woman with little education whose husband was well educated
10. Based on the research on family violence, which of the following does the text conclude to be a key element of the abuse of spouses, children, and the elderly?
   a. the high divorce rate
   b. the growth in nuclear families
   c. the inequitable distribution of power and resources in the family
   d. a resurgence in patriarchy

True/False Questions

1. Extended families are more functional in industrial societies than are nuclear families.
2. Of the three sociological perspectives, the functionalist perspective would most clearly take the stance that a particular form of the family exists in society because that family form benefits the powerful groups in society.
3. Young people today, when compared to their parents, have fewer negative attitudes toward staying single.
4. "Parent-run" courtship is more prominent today than it was in preindustrial United States.
5. Even though it is difficult for parents to remain together in a conflict-ridden marriage, research

shows that children are almost always better off when such parents stay together rather than divorce.

6. Children's negative reactions to divorce can be reduced if the amount of conflict between divorcing parents is kept low.

7. More adults are single (never married) today than was the case fifty years ago.

8. Looking at the trends in divorce and single motherhood, the text predicts that the proportion of single-parent families will decline in the future.

9. Levels of child abuse are higher among the poor than they are among the affluent.

10. In comparison to the United States, most other industrial nations take a more extreme laissez-faire position in regard to government support for families and children.

Fill-In Questions

1. The _____ family is one in which elaborate networks of visitation and support are found among extended relatives but each nuclear unit lives separately.

2. Since the 1930s, the average size of households in the United States has _____.

3. When marital partners are chosen primarily on the basis of the individual desires of the prospective mates, this is called a _____ courtship process.

4. A marriage system that allows people to have more than one spouse, but not at the same time, is called _____.

5. In terms of age, it is those who are _____ at the time of marriage who are at the highest risk of experiencing divorce.

6. A _____ family is one that results when people experience a series of divorces and remarriages.

7. The most common living arrangement for children and teenagers in the United States today is to be living with _____.

8. The elderly person who is least likely to experience abuse is the elderly person who lives _____.

9. According to the text, the family organization that seems to be developing in modern industrial societies is the _____ family.

10. In terms of who provides day-care services, laissez-faire advocates would probably support the _____ of day care.

Matching Questions

_____ 1. patriarchy
_____ 2. interactionist perspective
_____ 3. courtship in preindustrial United States
_____ 4. a family system in which people can have more than one spouse at a time
_____ 5. status conferral
_____ 6. palimony
_____ 7. reason for rising divorce rate in United States.
_____ 8. nuclear family
_____ 9. serial monogamy
_____ 10. family inheritance

A. family as socially defined
B. polygamy
C. cohabitant support payments
D. male domination
E. parents and children
F. U.S. marriage system
G. parent-run
H. perpetuation of social inequality
I. increasing gender equality
J. a function of the family

Essay Questions

1. Select one of the sociological perspectives and describe its view of the family as an institution in society. When would that perspective define the family as a social problem?

2. Assess the issue of whether children sent to day care are reared as effectively as children raised in the home. Summarize the research on both sides of the issue.

3. How have attitudes toward marriage and having children changed over the past fifty years in the United States?

4. Describe the four social conditions discussed in the text that account for the rising divorce rate over the past century.

5. What are the social characteristics of couples who are at the greatest risk of experiencing a divorce?

6. Describe the trends in single parenthood in the United States today. Why, and under what conditions, does single parenthood become a social problem?

7. What are the social conditions that increase the likelihood of child abuse in a family?

8. What is likely to happen to divorce rates in the future in the United States? What could be done to bring those rates down?

9. What is being done, and what could be done, to reduce family violence in the United States?

10. What are the differences between the social policies of the United States regarding families and children and the equivalent policies in other industrial nations?

For Further Reading

Stephanie Coontz. *The Way We Really Are: Coming to Terms with America's Changing Families.* New York: Basic Books, 1997. This historian presents research on how well different types of families function and argues in support of the notion that effective families can come in many forms. She encourages people to identify and build on the strengths in their families rather than worrying about what is the "right" kind of family.

Rosanna Hertz. *Single by Chance, Mothers by Choice: How Women Are Choosing Parenthood Without Marriage and Creating the New American Family.* New York: Oxford University Press, 2006. This book challenges conventional conceptions of family by looking at the lives and experiences of women who choose to have children although they are not married. It presents another view on what "the family" is.

Robert B. Hill et al. *Research on the African-American Family: A Holistic Approach.* Westport, CT: Auburn House, 1993. This is a comprehensive review of the current research on the strengths and weaknesses of the black family in the United States today. It gives a thorough review of the social conditions in the black community and society at large that have shaped the black family.

Sana Loue. *Intimate Partner Violence: Societal, Medical, Legal, and Individual Responses.* New York: Kluwer Academic/Plenum Publishers, 2001. This book provides an excellent overview of social science theory and research on the causes of intimate partner violence, how people react to it, and what can be done about it.

Phyllis Moen. *Working Parents: Transformations in Gender Roles and Public Policies in Sweden.* Madison: University of Wisconsin Press, 1989. This book explores some innovative social policies in Sweden that are focused on encouraging women to have children and continue working. Some of the policies might be useful to consider for the United States.

Linda Waite and Maggie Gallagher. *The Case for Marriage: Why Married People are Happier, Healthier, and Better off Financially.* New York: Doubleday, 2000. These authors present data on some of the benefits of marriage over divorce or singlehood. Their data suggest the wide array of ways in which marital status affects people's lives.

Judith Wallerstein, Julia Lewis, and Sandra Blakeslee. *The Unexpected Legacy of Divorce: A 25 Year Landmark Study.* New York: Hyperion, 2000. Although this book has been criticized for using poor research methodology, the authors document some ways in which divorce can negatively affect both children and adults.

HEALTH AND ILLNESS

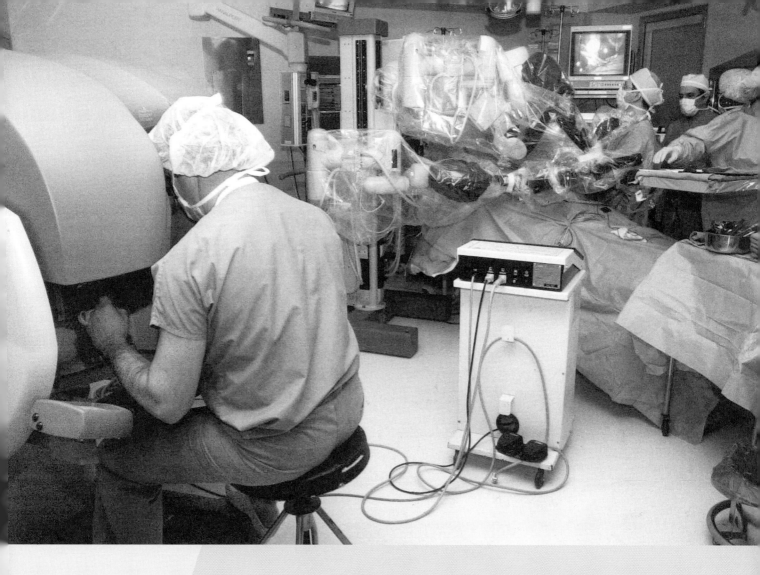

What problems does the United States confront in the area of health and illness? Although the health-care system in the United States can do some marvelous things, Joseph Califano, Jr., who has worked on health-care policy for many decades, summarizes the problems as colossal costs, inefficiency, waste, and abuse (Califano, 1994). The costs of health care have truly skyrocketed. In 1960, health-care expenditures amounted to $142 for each person in the United States; now that amount has exploded to over $6,000! Many billions of dollars are spent each year on coronary bypass surgery, but Califano claims that many of these surgeries could have been avoided by using less invasive—and less expensive—medical procedures to manage patients' conditions.

As all this money is spent on health care, it is not exactly clear what benefit people in the United States receive: They pay twice as much for their per capita health bill as do people in France, yet the French live longer than people in the United States. In addition to costs, another dimension of the problem is whether people have access to the health-care services and resources that they need to remain healthy or overcome illness and injury. Although people in the United States spend billions on coronary bypass surgery, infant mortality rates are distressingly high, especially among minority groups. The infant mortality rate among African Americans in states such as Colorado and Iowa is as high as the infant mortality rate in Sri Lanka and Mexico—countries suffering from severe political dislocation and economic downturn (U.S. Bureau of the Census, 2006:82, 837).

This chapter addresses these and other problems related to health and illness in the United States. Califano (1994) believes that the health-care system in the United States needs radical surgery to overcome the problems. This chapter will assess both the problems and the solutions. It begins by developing an understanding of the role of health-care institutions in society.

Perspectives on Health Care

People tend to view health and illness as biological phenomena. However, health and illness also have a very important social dimension, and this is what we need to focus on as we approach problems surrounding health and health-care delivery. Social factors, for example, influence what diseases people contract, who receives health care, and who benefits from the type of health-care organization that is dominant in society. The sociological perspectives can help us analyze how social factors shape social problems in this area.

The Functionalist Perspective

Disease is a threat to the social order because those who are ill may be unable to make useful contributions to society. People who are sick may not be able to raise food, build houses, drive trucks, or rear children as expected. This makes them burdensome and nonproductive. In extreme cases, ill health can threaten the very survival of society. Many Native American groups, for example, were decimated by infectious diseases, such as venereal disease, during their early contact with European explorers to the Americas. Some people today feel that a nuclear war would cause so much injury and disease that the survival of some societies would be threatened. So disease can be viewed as a social problem when it threatens the ability of a group to survive and prosper.

Given these consequences of disease, sociologist Talcott Parsons (1951) argued that being healthy is the preferred or most functional human condition. When

---

Myths & Facts

About Health and Health Care

Myth: The poor in the United States receive shoddy health care, finding it difficult to see a doctor or gain admission to a hospital.

Fact: Some poor people are quite a bit more likely than the affluent to see a doctor or be hospitalized. Government health insurance for the poor has given some of them far more access to health care than ever before, although it may be of lower quality than the care available to the more affluent.

Myth: Women are healthier than men (or vice versa).

Fact: Reality is complicated on this issue. Men have higher mortality rates, but women are more likely to have acute, non-life-threatening illnesses. Men, on the other hand, tend to have higher rates of serious, chronic illnesses. So the facts on gender and health depend on how one measures "health."

Myth: Controlling physicians' fees would stop the rise in medical costs.

Fact: Although it would help, physicians' services account for less than one of every five dollars spent on health care. And the proportion of the health-care dollar spent on physicians' fees has declined considerably over the past fifty years.

Myth: Thanks to modern science, people today have a healthy diet and can look forward to a long life.

Fact: People in most hunting-and-gathering societies probably had healthier diets than most people in the United States have today. They ate a wide range of fruits, nuts, grains, and other plant foods and relied less on meat. Hunters and gatherers could, if they survived infancy and childhood, look forward to a relatively long life. However, the hunters and gatherers still died at a younger age than most people today, and the quality of their lives in terms of their health status was not nearly as good.

people are ill, they can no longer fulfill their expected role obligations. Society responds to this, Parsons argued, by casting them into a "deviant," or socially disvalued, role. Society must help these deviants to become "normal" again. Ostracizing or imprisoning sick people, which is a common response to many deviant behaviors, is ineffective. Instead, sick people are given a special social role, the sick role, which is intended to facilitate their return to health. The **sick role** refers to *a set of expectations intended to guide the behavior of people who are ill.* People who occupy the sick role are excused from their normal role obligations to the extent that the illness calls for, and they can claim assistance and sympathy from others. However, they are also expected to seek competent care and to cooperate with those who are trying to cure them.

The function of the health-care system, then, is to return people to normal social functioning. The system becomes a social problem when it fails to perform this function effectively. Ideally, people who need health-care services would receive exactly what they need, no more and no less. To the extent that this ideal is not reached, social disorganization exists. This chapter will review the extent to which the health-care system in the United States deviates from this ideal. We will also look for the sources of the disorganization. One source is the lack of integration between different parts of the social system. For example, health care in the United States is operated largely as a profitmaking institution, as is the rest of our economy (see Chapter 2). Because large sums of money can be made from medical services and products, there is considerable abuse in these areas, such as unnecessary surgeries and the overutilization of pharmaceuticals. In addition, people who are unable to pay for services often do not receive adequate medical care. The point is that, in some situations, the profit-making dimension of the health-care system is not well integrated with, and may work against, the goal of achieving the highest possible level of health.

The Conflict Perspective

Health and health care are highly valued in all societies, and they are also scarce resources. Interest groups compete with one another to gain what they feel is their fair share of those resources, as they do with other scarce resources. Staying healthy depends on having access to adequate food, satisfactory employment conditions, clean water, and good health care. Generally, as we shall see, people with higher social and economic standing in society have greater access to these resources, and they are generally healthier than the less affluent. For example, high infant mortality among the poor is not surprising,

from the conflict perspective, because the poor are less able to afford nutritious food, sanitary living conditions, access to prenatal care, and the other things that reduce infant mortality.

In addition to the issue of whether groups receive services is the problem of how much those services will cost—in both monetary and nonmonetary terms—and who benefits most from health-care treatment. In this context, the health-care system is an arena for competition among a variety of groups: health-care consumers, doctors, nurses, hospital administrators, medical technicians, pharmaceutical companies, and a host of others. People must pay, in some fashion, for health-care goods and services, and many people make a living through providing those goods and services. Naturally, what benefits one group, such as low health-care costs for the consumer, may work to the disadvantage of other groups, such as doctors and nurses. Beyond money, prestige and power are also involved in the health-care delivery process.

The inequitable distribution of money, prestige, and power in the health-care system, then, is viewed as a social problem by those groups who feel they are receiving less than their fair share of resources. From the conflict perspective, however, there is no state of the system that is "preferred" or necessarily beneficial to all. If some group gains additional benefits, other groups must lose something. What determines who gains and who loses is the exercise of power. Groups have various power strategies available to them. Nurses and doctors, for example, can go on strike or in other ways withhold their services in order to force concessions from competing groups. Another power strategy is to influence Congress and state legislatures to approve legislation that benefits particular groups. In fact, many interest groups in the health field have formed political action committees to collect contributions and press their interests. The American Medical Association and other physicians' groups have been very effective at lobbying over the years, partly because of the substantial economic resources of their constituents. For example, the AMA has to date successfully fought all efforts to establish a national health insurance program.

The Interactionist Perspective

The interactionist perspective emphasizes that sick people are cast into a social role, part of which has been described as the sick role. This role may include socially devalued and stigmatized elements. A person with venereal disease, for example, may be viewed as immoral, whereas the mentally ill are seen as dangerous. In other words, we attach social meanings—sometimes very negative ones—to various illnesses, and we expect people to behave in conformity to those meanings. For example, some health-care institutions treat people in a dehumanizing and impersonal fashion, which can lead to low self-esteem and a negative self-concept and may drive people away from seeking the health care they really need. Likewise, the staff in a mental hospital expects its patients to be dependent and confused, and the patients often conform to those expectations.

So from the interactionist perspective, the health-care system is considered a social problem when it produces stigmatized and devalued behavior or self-concepts among either the providers or consumers of health care. This perspective is particularly useful in understanding the societal reaction to some diseases, such as acquired immune deficiency syndrome (AIDS), and to mental illness, discussed later in this chapter.

Politics, Stigma, and the AIDS Epidemic

AIDS is now a leading cause of death among young people. Over 300,000 people in the United States have AIDS, and 1 million are infected with the human immunodeficiency virus (HIV); 40,000 new infections occur each year (Centers for Disease Control, 2006). These infections will translate into massive health-care costs as some of these people develop full-blown AIDS. Sadly and outrageously, this devastating epidemic gained a foothold in the United States in part because society failed to show a serious interest in attacking it when it first appeared. The reason for this delay is that the reaction to all diseases, including AIDS, results from a complex intertwining of biology with political, social, and cultural considerations, which the sociological perspectives can help us understand. In particular, the story of AIDS suggests the importance of the conflict view that it is the powerful who influence what happens in society and the interactionist view that people respond to illnesses in terms of the social meanings that the illnesses are given in a particular social and cultural environment.

The impact of social and cultural forces on the treatment of the ill is especially evident in seriously threatening diseases (Sigerist, 1977). Among the Kubu people of Sumatra, for example, serious diseases that produced high fevers were viewed as highly threatening. In fact, they so frightened the Kubu that the sick person was shunned—isolated completely—as if he or she were dead. The ancient Babylonians had a different view of disease: It was punishment for sin and wickedness. The Babylonians believed that people who suffered pain and discomfort were paying for their sins. Because of the spiritually unclean nature of sick people, they were marked by the Babylonians with a stigma. They were not physically shunned, but they were socially isolated until they had made some atonement for their sins. More recently, and continuing into the twentieth century, a disease like leprosy has provoked reactions of both stigmatization and shunning or isolation.

We might be tempted to think that, by the twenty-first century, our reactions to disease have become more "rational" and "scientific" than those of the Kubu or the ancient Babylonians. Yet social life is complex, and people's reactions to disease are no exception. In the case of AIDS, many social and cultural factors came together to produce a significant delay in the attack on the disease (Burkett, 1996; Shilts, 1987). The reasons for this delay were complicated, but some of them are strikingly similar to the reactions to disease among the Kubu and ancient Babylonians. First of all, stigmatization of the supposedly unclean or morally suspect clearly played a role: The disease was linked with homosexuality and illegal drug use. Many people in positions of political and economic power felt either that these were powerless groups whose problems need not be seriously attended to or that they were disreputable groups whose lifestyles ought to be discouraged if not eradicated. In fact, some fundamentalist religious leaders declared that AIDS was punishment for the sins of homosexuals—not a far cry from the ancient Babylonian belief about disease. One conservative columnist wrote: "The poor homosexuals—they have declared war upon nature, and now nature is exacting an awful retribution" (Shilts, 1987:311).

A second reason for the delayed response to AIDS was the Reagan administration's policy of smaller government and greater austerity in social and health programs. The first AIDS victim in the United States appeared in 1980, and the Reagan administration entered office in 1981. The competition for government funds in the early 1980s was fierce, and AIDS researchers typically lost out in the battle. A third reason for the delay had to do with urban politics. New York City had the largest number of AIDS cases in the country, yet New York Mayor Edward Koch refused to do anything about it for a number of years, apparently because of the belief that support for gay causes would link him with the gay rights movement and hurt his chances for reelection. Fourth, the politics of gay communities figured into the delay. There were intense conflicts among gays over how, or whether, to respond to the AIDS epidemic. Some gays proposed closing gay bathhouses on the grounds that these places,

According to the interactionist perspective, people attach social meanings to illnesses and disabilities. When these meanings are negative, people may be stigmatized and discriminated against by others. These attitudes have limited the opportunities of many handicapped people and deprived society of the contributions they have to offer.

where unprotected sex and multiple sexual partners were common, helped spread the disease. The owners of the baths objected strenuously, as did many gays who felt that such a move would be an attack on their sexual freedom and an attempt to restrict the open expression of their sexual orientation. As a consequence, the gay community found itself divided and unable to launch a united campaign for more research and programs on AIDS.

The overall consequence of these political and social factors was that AIDS research and programs were delayed significantly and the disease gained a substantial foothold. Once the cause of the disease and the mode of transmission were established, steps were taken to control it. The gay community, in particular, has emphasized health education, the practice of safe sex, and a change in sexual lifestyles as ways of preventing the spread of the disease. And this effort has resulted in dramatic declines in rates of infection due to male-to-male sexual contact and injection drug use (Centers for Disease Control, 2006). Currently in the United States, only 64 percent of new HIV infections involve male-to-male sexual contact or are due to intravenous drug use. Heterosexual transmission of AIDS is growing, with 36 percent of new infections resulting from heterosex-

ual contact. Worldwide, however, 60 percent of HIV infections result from heterosexual intercourse.

The Applied Research insert (pp. 92–93) points to the role that social science research has played over the decades in understanding the development and spread of the AIDS epidemic.

Health, Illness, and Society

One of the central problems related to health and health care is that there is a variety of social factors—things that we have some control over—that can lead to disease. In this section, we look at how the diseases that are a threat to us have changed over time and how social and lifestyle factors can put us at greater risk of illness.

Health and Societal Development

Most diseases can be classified as acute or chronic. **Acute diseases** are *those with fairly quick, and sometimes dramatic and incapacitating, onset and from*

Combating the Spread of AIDS

Over the past two decades, sociological research has played a critical role in attacking the AIDS epidemic. When AIDS first appeared in the United States in the early 1980s, scientists and doctors were puzzled by it. The first indication of the epidemic was when healthy young men contracted diseases, such as rare forms of skin cancer, not normally found in healthy young people. A first step in understanding a new disease is often to focus on the social characteristics and lifestyles of people who contract it to see if some clues might be found regarding mode of transmission or potential causes. Scientists at the Centers for Disease Control (CDC) in Atlanta did this and noticed something distinctive about the patients: They were either gay males or intravenous drug users. Participating in this

study was William Darrow, a research sociologist at the CDC with expertise in sexually transmitted diseases and the gay community. There was great controversy and confusion about the new disease. Many thought it was relatively unimportant, whereas others thought it might be linked to inhalants that some gays used at the time to enhance sexual pleasure. Darrow, looking at the social characteristics and lifestyle patterns of the early victims, was alarmed and concluded: "It looks more like a sexually transmitted disease than syphilis" (Shilts, 1987:87).

In the first half of the 1980s, Darrow and other CDC scientists attempted to gather evidence that AIDS was sexually transmitted. If they could show that, they could make some recommendations about curing, or at least controlling the

spread of, AIDS. As an important step in establishing that the disease was sexually transmitted, they needed to compare the lifestyles and sexual activities of gay men with the disease to those of gay men without it (Jaffe et al., 1983). They asked health departments, private clinics, and private physicians to provide names of gay men who would be willing to participate in the study. They also asked each AIDS victim to provide the name of a gay male friend who had not been his sexual partner. All these men were interviewed extensively about their lives and sexual behavior. In this pioneering study, Darrow and his colleagues found a link between sexual activities and AIDS: AIDS victims, compared to those free of the disease, were more likely to engage in what is now called unsafe sex, they had many more sexual partners, and they were more likely

---

which a person either dies or recovers. They are often caused by an organism or parasite that infects or invades the body and disrupts its functioning, which is the case with influenza, tuberculosis, and gastroenteritis. **Chronic diseases,** such as heart disease and cancer, *progress over a long period of time and often exist long before they are detected.* Early symptoms of these diseases are often absent or easily ignored. They are usually caused by a mixture of biological, social, and environmental factors.

In preindustrial societies, infectious and parasitic diseases posed some of the more serious health threats (Black, 1978). Diseases such as influenza, diphtheria, and typhoid could strike quickly and were highly contagious and often fatal, especially among infants, the weak, and the elderly. Accidents such as drowning or burns also took their toll, as did cannibalism, infanticide, and human sacrifice. All of these threats added up to a life expectancy in preindustrial societies that was rather short by today's standards, probably around

twenty-five to thirty-five years. However, this short life expectancy was due in good part to high rates of infant and childhood mortality; if one survived the illnesses of infancy and childhood, one had a reasonable chance to live much longer (Antonovsky, 1972).

With the emergence of industrial societies, there has been a dramatic increase in life expectancy, to around seventy-seven in the United States today (U.S. Bureau of the Census, 2006:77). The death rate has also changed appreciably, dropping from 17 deaths per 1,000 people in the United States in 1900 to 8.1 deaths today (see Figure 4.1). The declining death rate and increasing life expectancy can be attributed in good part to two related factors: declines in infant and childhood mortality and changes in lifestyle.

Infant mortality today is far less than it was a century ago. So a newborn infant today has a far better chance of surviving than did infants in earlier times, and this means that someone born today has a better

to find sex partners in bathhouses. In a later study of AIDS among prostitutes, they used a similar sampling procedure: recruiting prostitutes from among women in prison, from venereal disease clinics, and from methadone maintenance clinics. In these studies, they found that the prostitutes at greatest risk of contracting AIDS were those who were also intravenous drug users and who never used condoms (Darrow et al., 1987).

From research such as this, Darrow and other scientists fighting the AIDS battle were able to determine that AIDS was transmitted through contact with bodily fluid, such as blood or semen. Once this fact was established, they could make some critical public health recommendations aimed at controlling the spread of AIDS: Test the blood supply for antibodies to the AIDS virus, educate people about safe sex, and close or closely regulate gay bathhouses and other settings conducive to multiple sex partners.

By the 1990s, the mosaic of AIDS had changed some, but applied research remained important in the battle against it. For example, sociologist Philippe Bourgois and his colleagues have conducted research on homeless heroin addicts in San Francisco (Bourgois, Lettiere, and Quesada, 1997). Intravenous drug use is now one of the major risk factors for the spread of AIDS. Bourgois and colleagues observed the addicts for extended periods over a two-year span to gather direct observational evidence of the risky behaviors they engaged in, especially sharing of needles and other drug paraphernalia. Based on their observations, the researchers concluded that such risky behavior is much more common than other studies had shown and that existing public health efforts to reduce it are ineffective. They showed that the risky behaviors stem in part from the lifestyles of the addicts but also from the demeaning and stigmatized way in which public health workers relate to the addicts. Given this knowledge, policies that focus on merely making clean needles available to addicts are not likely to reduce the risky behaviors a great deal.

So throughout the AIDS crisis, applied sociological research has been central to the development of social policies. In the early years, Darrow's interviews helped to locate causes of the disease and develop interventions, whereas in recent years observational data from Bourgois and others have enabled policy makers to evaluate how effectively interventions are working.

chance of living into old age. For those who survive childhood, however, industrialization has led to considerably smaller increases in longevity over that of their preindustrial counterparts. A study in Massachusetts, for example, revealed that the life expectancy of fifteen-year-olds in 1869 was only five years less than that of fifteen-year-olds a century later (Vinovskis, 1978). Furthermore, there was virtually no increase in the life expectancy of thirty-year-olds between 1869 and 1969. Another study showed that people born in the United States in 2001 could expect to live twenty-eight years longer than those born in 1900. Someone who was twenty years old in 2001, however, could expect to live only about fifteen years longer than a twenty-year-old could in 1900 (Arias, 2004). This illustrates that a major benefit of industrialization in terms of health and longevity is that we have a much greater chance of living through infancy and childhood. Industrialization provides less benefit in terms of longevity once we reach adulthood.

The second key factor in increasing longevity has been changes in people's lifestyles. In fact, this has probably been at least as important as medical treatments offered by modern medicine (McKeown, Brown, and Record, 1972; McKeown, Brown, and Turner, 1975). Industrialization has made available better diets, improved sanitation, better sewage disposal, and cleaner water. Consequently, people are exposed to fewer infectious and parasitic diseases and are better able to resist those to which they are exposed. The death rate for scarlet fever, for example, had dropped to practically zero by the 1940s, when effective medical treatment for this disease first became available (McKinlay and McKinlay, 1977).

Despite declining mortality rates and increasing longevity, we must all die someday, and the diseases we die of today are different from those of the past. In 1900 in the United States, the top three killers were acute infectious diseases, which accounted for well over twice the number of deaths caused by heart

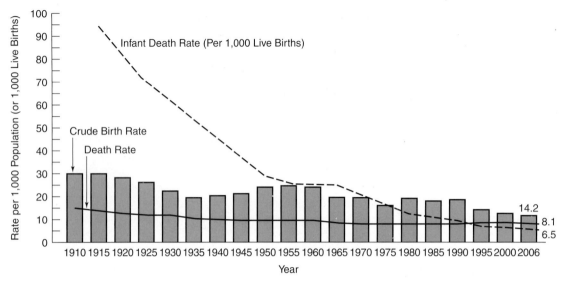

FIGURE 4.1 **Birth and Death Rates in the United States, 1910–2006.**

Sources: U.S. Bureau of the Census, *Statistical Abstract of the United States, 1982–83* (Washington, DC: U.S. Government Printing Office, 1982), p. 60; U.S. Bureau of the Census, *Statistical Abstract of the United States, 1992* (Washington, DC: U.S. Government Printing Office, 1992), p. 64; National Center for Health Statistics, *National Vital Statistics Reports* (Hyattsville, MD: National Center for Health Statistics, various years).

disease and cerebrovascular disease (see Figure 4.2). Today, four of the five leading causes of death are chronic diseases, the fifth being accidents. So acute infectious diseases have become relatively unimportant in terms of mortality, and chronic diseases confront society with a different set of problems than did the acute ones in an earlier era. Chronic diseases develop over a long period of time, may go unnoticed until extensive damage has occurred, and are often associated with people's lifestyles. Effective treatment of such diseases calls for continual rather than intermittent health care and may require that people change their lifestyles. Furthermore, the most effective and least expensive way of dealing with most chronic diseases is probably **preventive medicine,** *changes in lifestyle or other steps that help avoid the occurrence of disease* (McKinlay, 1997). Yet, modern medicine is not organized around prevention but rather toward **curative** or **crisis medicine:** *treating people's illnesses after they become ill.* Modern medicine arose early in the twentieth century when acute infectious diseases were the major health problems, and medical education trained doctors with a "crisis" orientation. This is an effective approach with such infectious diseases as influenza, pneumonia, or diphtheria, in which medical measures introduced after a person becomes ill can often return the person to complete health. With chronic diseases, however, much damage has already been done—and often cannot be reversed—by the time symptoms manifest

themselves and medical intervention occurs. A person who suffers a heart attack, for example, may already have severe blockage of coronary arteries, and the damage typically cannot be completely undone with such modern medical measures as angioplasty or coronary artery bypass surgery. To date in the United States, preventive medicine has had a considerably lower priority—in terms of research and program funding, the construction of medical facilities, and the allocation of health-care personnel—than has crisis-oriented medicine. In fact, Joseph Califano argues that our crisis orientation in the United States has led to a "sick"-care system rather than a "health"-care system, which might be called:

> the obsession of health care reformers with the delivery of medical care for the sick. This love affair has relegated the commonsense alternatives of disease prevention and health promotion to the role of dowdy wallflowers. (1994:130)

He argues that we should move from "sick" care to "health" care by promoting disease prevention and health promotion through changes in people's lifestyles.

So one of the major problem areas in the health-care system in the United States today is that the health-care organization has not adapted to the changing nature of the diseases we face. Another problem is that, although death rates are down and life expectancy is up, people in the United States are

94 **CHAPTER FOUR •** Health and Illness

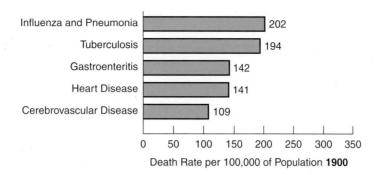

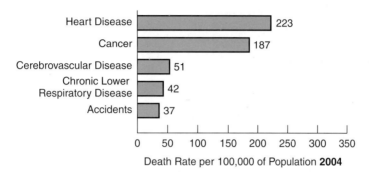

FIGURE 4.2 **Leading Causes of Death in the United States, 1900–2004.**

Sources: U.S. Bureau of the Census, *Vital Statistics Rates in the United States, 1900–1940* (Washington, DC: U.S. Government Printing Office, 1943), p. 210–215; National Center for Health Statistics, *National Vital Statistics Reports*, 54, no. 19 (Hyattsville, MD: National Center for Health Statistics, June 28, 2006).

not so well off when compared with some other countries. For example, the life expectancy of women in twenty-one other nations exceeds that of women in the United States, whereas men in the United States have shorter life spans than their counterparts in twenty-three other nations (see Figure 4.3). Men in Cuba and Costa Rica and women in Puerto Rico and Greece live longer than men and women in the United States. Likewise, the United States has a higher infant mortality rate than at least eleven other nations (see Figure 4.4). In fact, the infant mortality rate in the United States is twice as high as in Japan. Part of the reason the health status of the United States is this low is that certain social and cultural factors have a detrimental impact on the health of many of its people.

Social Factors in Health and Illness

Who suffers from higher rates of illness and death? We will look at the four major sociocultural factors that have the greatest impact on health and illness.

SOCIOECONOMIC STATUS *Socioeconomic status (SES)* refers to people's position in society as measured by their income, educational attainment, and occupational status. The effect of SES on health is very clear: Those who are lower on factors such as income, educational achievement, and occupational status generally have substantially higher disease rates and death rates than do their more affluent counterparts (Aday, 1993; Lynch, Kaplan, and Shema, 1997). With very few exceptions, the incidence of diseases such as cancer, heart disease, diabetes, high blood pressure, arthritis, and many others is higher among those in the lower SES ranges. Infant mortality is also substantially greater among children born into low SES families. One of the major reasons for the substandard health status of the poor is that they live under conditions that substantially increase their general susceptibility to disease. They live under less sanitary conditions, have less nutritious diets, and are less likely to take preventive health actions such as obtaining routine physical examinations. Regarding infant mortality, poor women are less likely to have prenatal checkups and more likely to have poor diets that result in infants with low birth weights. These

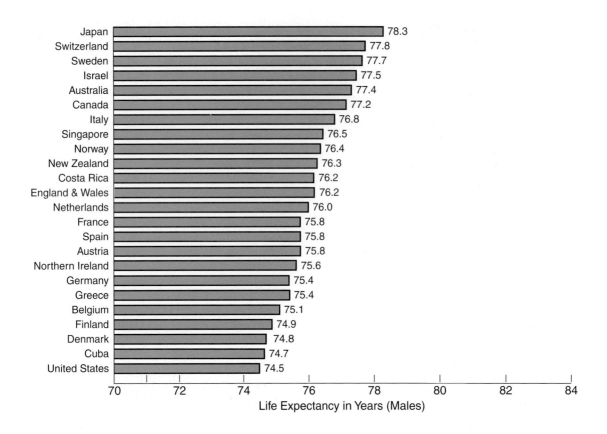

Life Expectancy in Years (Males)

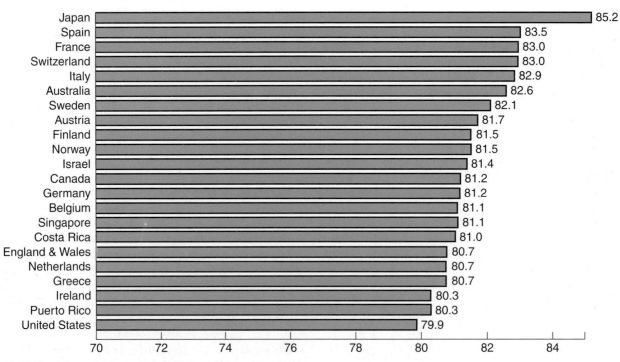

FIGURE 4.3 **Life Expectancy at Birth, By Sex, 2002.**

Source: National Center for Health Statistics, *Health, United States*, 2006 (Hyattsville, MD: National Center for Health Statistics, 2006), p. 174.

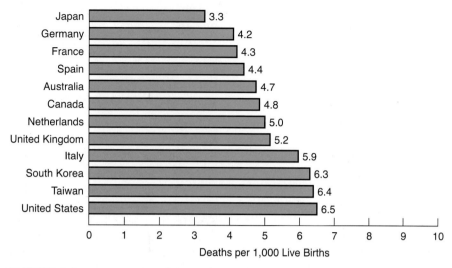

FIGURE 4.4   Infant Mortality Rates: Selected Countries, 2005.

Sources: U.S. Bureau of the Census, *Statistical Abstract of the United States, 2007*. (Washington, DC: U.S. Government Printing Office, 2006), p. 837.

things contribute to infant mortality. Furthermore, despite the considerable advances brought about by Medicare and Medicaid, these programs do not cover many poor people, and some health care still depends on out-of-pocket costs, which the poor usually cannot afford. Finally, the medical care that the poor do receive is likely to be of lower quality. They are more likely to be treated in a hospital outpatient clinic or emergency room where continuity of care, follow-up treatment, and patient education are less common than in a physician's office. And even when the poor have the same health insurance as the more affluent, such as Medicare, the poor do not receive the same level of health care: Poor people receive fewer preventive services, such as influenza immunizations, and less adequate care for chronic diseases (Gornick et al., 1996).

GENDER Women appear to be healthier than men, especially if we consider longevity as the key measure of health. The life expectancy of women today is over five years greater than that of men, compared with less than three years more at the turn of the century (see Figure 4.3). Women also have lower rates of most serious chronic illnesses. What accounts for these differences? First, it may well be that women are biologically more capable of survival than are men (Bird and Rieker, 1999; Waldron, 1997). Males have higher death rates than females at every age, including deaths of fetuses. This suggests that women may have some sort of biological advan-

tage in comparison with men, but the explanation is more complex than this. Higher mortality among males is also due to traditional sex-role definitions that encourage males to be aggressive and to seek more stressful and dangerous occupations where they might, for example, come in contact with industrial carcinogens. In addition, the lifestyles of men have traditionally been less healthy than those of women. For example, men drink more alcohol and smoke more tobacco. Although the gap between men and women in smoking and drinking has narrowed, it is still present. Finally, cultural definitions of women as the "weaker sex" may lead women to respond more quickly to symptoms and to seek medical care earlier in an illness episode. If so, this treatment may enhance the likelihood of effective medical intervention for women.

In the realm of mental illness, women also have higher rates of psychological disorders, especially neuroses, anxiety disturbances, and depression. Part of the reason for this is that sex-role socialization seems to lead men to turn to drugs or alcohol in stressful situations. Women, on the other hand, are more stigmatized for doing this and are more likely to cope with stress through symptoms of depression or other mental disorders. Many of the symptoms of these mental disorders—dependence, withdrawal, self-devaluation, indecisiveness—are characteristics that have traditionally been a part of the stereotype of women. So women have been socialized to behave in ways that, when used as means of coping with situations, are seen as symptomatic of mental illness (Franks and Rothblum, 1983).

RACE Most studies of the relationship between health status and race have involved comparisons between African Americans and Anglo Americans. All these studies reach distressingly similar conclusions: African Americans are at a serious disadvantage when it comes to health, having considerably higher death rates, shorter life expectancies, and more serious life-threatening health conditions such as hypertension and diabetes than do whites (Smedley, Stith, and Nelson, 2002; Williams and Collins, 1995). One major reason for this difference, of course, is that race is associated with socioeconomic status, with blacks being considerably lower in SES on the average than whites. Yet even when researchers control for SES, some racial differences persist. This is probably accounted for by the unique social position of African Americans: The combination of years of racial oppression, poverty, and physically demanding occupations probably works to generate more stress in the lives of blacks than in other racial groups at the same SES level. This stress, in turn, produces greater susceptibility to disease. Minorities other than blacks also suffer substantial health problems. American Indians, especially those on reservations, have disproportionately high mortality rates from such things as accidents, alcoholism, and suicide, and this occurs because of long-standing problems of poverty and unemployment (Young, 1994).

Some of the impact of race on health has to do with discrimination. Research shows that, even when African Americans have the same level of health insurance as whites, they receive fewer and less adequate health-care services, and this undoubtedly contributes to their overall higher levels of illness and health problems (Smedley, Stith, and Nelson, 2002).

LIFESTYLE FACTORS Industrialization has unquestionably improved people's lives, but it has also created health hazards, largely unknown in preindustrial societies, that contribute to death and misery. For example, a substantial proportion of all human cancers are caused in part by environmental conditions, such as air pollution or chemicals in the water and soil. (Solutions to problems of environmental pollution are discussed in Chapter 13.) Occupational stress is linked to heart disease and hypertension (Schnall and Kern, 1986; Thoits, 1995). Unemployment, or even the threat of it, is associated with many physical and mental disorders (Kessler, House, and Turner, 1987). The use of alcohol, tobacco, and

Lifestyle factors, such as the use of tobacco, alcohol, or other drugs, can have serious consequences for people's health status.

other drugs can also cause serious health problems. There even appears to be an association between health and the quality of a person's family life: People who are married and have children are healthier than people who are single or have no children (Verbrugge, 1983). Finally, as Figure 4.2 illustrates, accidents have become one of the leading causes of mortality in modern society.

Mental Illness

In the past forty years, the number of people seeking help for psychological distress, either mild or severe, has increased more than four times. This increase, however, does not necessarily mean that more mental illness exists today. Instead, people are more willing to seek help for psychological distress today because attitudes toward mental illness have changed, and there is less stigma attached to seeking mental health services.

The Nature of Mental Illness

There is substantial agreement about the basic nature of most physical disorders: Some malfunction or pathology has occurred to a person's body. For example, organic malfunction includes such things as a broken leg or an injury to the eye that impairs sight. The cure of such ailments involves, at least in part, some repair work on the person's body, such as setting the leg in a cast or performing surgery on the eye. With mental illness, however, there is more controversy about its basic nature. In fact, there are three positions on this issue (Cockerham, 2006).

THE MEDICAL MODEL One position—very popular among psychiatrists, psychologists, nurses, and other providers of mental health services—is to view mental disorders as having the same basic nature as physical disorders: A person's normal personality and psychological processes have malfunctioned and produced pathological behavior. This behavior is a symptom of the underlying disturbance in the person's psyche, and the mental "disease" can be cured by doing some repair work on the person's psyche, using drugs or possibly surgery. If left untreated, the condition will become progressively worse. Those persons who hold this position may disagree among themselves on the causes of mental disorders. Some would argue they are caused by biochemical imbalances or genetic traits; others would assert that mental illness grows out of disturbed interpersonal relationships. In fact, different disorders might have different causes, some biological in nature and others social. Proponents of the medical model would agree, however, that the disorder is located inside the person and that effective treatment would involve "repairing" the affected individual, possibly through drugs or surgery.

Some mental disorders do appear to have genetic or biochemical causes, at least in part, and the medical model has produced some remarkable advances in treating these disorders. It has also resulted in some effective drugs to treat the symptoms of mental disorders that are caused by environmental factors such as disturbed interpersonal relationships. However, the medical model has its limitations, and if one relies on it too heavily, it can lead to a misunderstanding of some aspects of mental disorders. In particular, its emphasis on the idea that the focus of mental illness is "inside" the person can restrict focus and lead to a disregard for the many factors in the social environment that contribute to mental problems themselves and how we define them. The other two positions on this issue round out the medical model by using the sociological perspectives to place more stress on the processes occurring outside the individual—in social interaction and the social environment.

MENTAL ILLNESS AS DEVIANCE The second position on the nature of mental illness focuses on the fact that the symptoms of mental illness show up in a person's behavior, and human behavior, according to the interactionist perspective, is based on shared social expectations. This insight has led some sociologists to suggest that some of the disordered behavior of the mentally ill reflects not the inner workings of a twisted psyche but a person's efforts to conform to social expectations. Sociologist Thomas Scheff (1999), for example, based his view of mental illness on the interactionist perspective. He argued that the behavior of the mentally disturbed violates normal social conventions, so his view is that of mental illness as "deviance." For example, the person who shouts obscenities on a crowded street violates norms about appropriate behavior in that setting. When we notice these transgressions, we try to understand the behavior, especially if it is threatening, by labeling the person. In this case, we might label the person as drunk. If this individual is not under the influence of alcohol and we cannot come up with another reasonable explanation for his behavior, we might then conclude that the person is mentally disturbed. Why else would he shout obscenities in public? The label of "mental illness" offers us some comfort that we understand the person's behavior and that the world is a predictable and comprehensible place.

Scheff argues that at times everybody engages in behavior that could be labeled as mental illness. In many cases, these behaviors are not noticed by others and are called **primary deviance**: *the violation of social norms in which the violator is not caught or is excused rather than labeled as a deviant.* In other cases, such behavior might be attributed to something other than mental illness, such as overwork, drunkenness, or some physiological ailment. However, in a few cases, people are given the label of "mentally ill," and to be so labeled is to be cast into a social role with certain expectations associated with it. Depending on the circumstances, we may expect those labeled as mentally ill to be dependent, helpless, or even dangerous; we may even make it difficult for them to behave otherwise. For example, we might deprive them of some household or occupational duties. Then, a *self-fulfilling prophecy* may occur as the person begins to live up to our expectations. Scheff calls this **secondary deviance**: *behavior that a person adopts in reaction to being labeled as mentally ill.* This self-fulfilling prophecy is most likely to result when people are experiencing some personal crisis and they are especially sensitive to the reactions of others and vulnerable to any signs of disapproval.

Scheff readily admits that some behavioral disturbances have organic, biological, or psychological causes. His point is that sporadic violations of norms are organized into a stable pattern of behavior when people conform to the expectations of the social role of the mentally ill. Furthermore, he argues that mental disorders with such internal causes can be perpetuated and extended through the emergence of secondary deviance. When mental health professionals label someone as mentally ill, they may be contributing to the emergence of secondary deviance. So Scheff shifts our focus away from the individual in understanding mental disorders and toward social relationships.

MENTAL ILLNESS AS PROBLEMS OF LIVING Psychiatrist Thomas Szasz (1987) provides the third position on the nature of mental illness, and it is very different from those previously discussed. He believes that mental disorders should not be viewed as "illnesses" at all but rather as problems of living: expressions of the fact that human life is a continual struggle to decide how to live and relate to others. Human existence means making choices about what makes life meaningful and valuable. Life is not, says Szasz, without considerable stress, anxiety, and conflict—nor should it be.

Szasz feels that the medical model of mental disorders is not only incorrect but also a potentially dangerous myth that can lead us to seek medical solutions to personal and ethical problems. If a psychiatrist classifies your behavior as a mental disorder, this is a value judgment regarding how you should lead your life. It limits your own exercise of judgment and freedom of choice. Furthermore, defining behaviors as symptoms of a mental disorder can lead to the dangerous step of absolving people of responsibility for their behavior. If one is not responsible for the nausea and fever that accompany influenza, then should a father be held responsible for the rage and child beating that accompany the "illnesses" of personality disorders? Szasz believes that people should be held accountable for the social and ethical choices they make in their lives.

These three positions taken together provide a more complete view of mental disorders than does only one or two of them. Each makes us aware of different things about the problem of mental illness. The medical model suggests that we can clearly define what mental illness is and unambiguously state that certain behaviors are pathological. Scheff and Szasz claim that social reality is more complex than this. What is considered pathological in one context is viewed as normal in another. Furthermore, there is a danger, they argue, that we will abdicate in making moral choices in our own lives by turning the decision over to mental health "professionals" who are more than ready to tell us the "healthiest" way to live our

lives. So it is important to approach the problem of mental illness by using all three perspectives.

The Treatment of Mental Disorders

PROBLEMS WITH DIAGNOSIS Mental health professionals use many concepts to describe the mental disorders that they believe exist: schizophrenia, depression, paranoia, and the like. They assess the existence of these disorders by observing people's behavior. Psychiatric diagnosis basically involves linking the behavioral display of a particular person with one or more diagnostic categories. If this diagnostic process is to be useful, it must be reliable, which means that the same diagnosis is made of the same patient by different professionals.

Unfortunately, psychiatric diagnoses are not nearly as reliable as we would hope. Recent reviews of studies spanning many decades found only a few studies in which reliability of the diagnoses was above the minimum level acceptable for good scientific research (Kirk and Kutchins, 1992; Mirowsky and Ross, 2003). In some cases, psychiatrists reached the same diagnosis in only one of every three cases. In the American Psychiatric Association's most recent version of its *Diagnostic and Statistical Manual of Mental Disorders* (called the DSM-IV), studies of reliability with more positive results are reported, but even here there were few findings with more than 80 percent agreement; a few had as low as 30 percent agreement. In addition, these studies were limited in scope and not well controlled (American Psychiatric Association, 1994; Horwitz, 2002).

The unreliability of psychiatric diagnoses is a serious problem because it throws into question whether mental health professionals can accurately detect mental disorders. If they cannot accurately detect them, can they possibly treat them effectively? Furthermore, with such unreliability, it may well be that some people are being treated for the wrong disorder whereas others are being treated who have no disorder at all. In addition, this unreliability may reflect the fact that the medical model of mental illness, on which these diagnostic categories rest, is not a very useful vehicle for understanding some mental disorders.

COMMUNITY TREATMENT In the past forty years, something called the "community mental health movement" has arisen and has come to play a key role in the delivery of mental health services (Carling, 1995; Cockerham, 2006). Growing in part from the kinds of concerns expressed by people such as Szasz and Scheff, its basic thrust can be summarized in a few statements.

1. Mental health services should be delivered to a total community rather than just to individuals.

2. Services should be delivered in the community where people live rather than in state hospitals or other institutional settings removed from the community.

3. Sources of stress or other problems in the community that have implications for mental health should be detected and attacked.

4. Preventive services should be delivered as well as crisis-oriented ones.

In other words, the community treatment approach assumes that the whole community is its clientele. In addition to traditional therapies such as psychotherapy, community mental health centers should offer vocational placement, compensatory education, or other programs that would alleviate stress and help people lead more fulfilling lives. This should result in improved mental status for individuals. So the community approach tends to promote social change as well as individual adjustment.

Some of the goals of the community mental health movement appear to have been at least partially achieved. There are about as many mental hospitals today as forty years ago, but they are much smaller (U.S. Bureau of the Census, 2006:114–116). Furthermore, although the rate of admission to psychiatric hospitals has not declined, the length of stay has dropped dramatically. Most striking of all, a substantial shift has occurred in where mental health services are delivered. Today, only about 11 percent of psychiatric services are delivered in mental hospitals, compared with 56 percent forty years ago. Today, people are usually treated in the psychiatric wards of general hospitals or as outpatients in hospitals or community mental health centers. In fact, this shift has been so dramatic that it has been called the "deinstitutionalization" of the mentally ill. In addition, the community mental health movement has provided psychiatric services to the aged, the poor, the underprivileged, and other groups that had in the past been underserved in this realm.

Not everyone has been enamored with the community approach (Cockerham, 2006). Some critics have charged that the process of deinstitutionalization did not commence when community mental health centers were first established in the 1960s; rather, it began a decade earlier when drugs that control violence and depression became available. These drugs controlled the most disruptive symptoms of mental disorders, and they made it possible for some of the mentally ill to live in the community. The community mental health approach has also been criticized on the grounds that it does not accomplish many of its innovative goals, such as reducing community stressors or promoting social change, but rather ends up providing the traditional types of therapies to individuals. Yet another criticism of the community mental health approach is that it releases mental patients into the community without regard to the therapeutic value of the setting in which they will live. Living in the community may not always be the most desirable alternative for those who are mentally ill, especially if they do not have supportive homes to live in or coordinated follow-up services available.

Problems in Health Care

Rising Health-Care Costs

For most of the twentieth century, the rise in the cost of health care has been remarkably rapid and consistent. In 1970, it cost about $74 to stay in a major hospital for one day. Today, the average cost of a one-day hospital stay has risen to over $1,400 (U.S. Bureau of the Census, 2006:115). Per capita expenditures for health care have increased over fiftyfold since 1950 (see Table 4.1). We now pay over $6,000 each year for health-care goods and services for each man, woman, and child in the United States—$25,000 a year for a family of four. Inflation accounts for some of this increase, but inflation during the same period increased overall prices only about seven times. A number of factors account for this skyrocketing growth in health-care costs.

First and probably most important is the fact that there has been a growing demand for health-care services, and a basic economic principle is that increasing demand for something tends to push up prices. Our population is larger, more affluent, and older, and these factors tend to increase the demand for a finite

TABLE 4.1 National Health Expenditures in the United States, 1940–2004

	1940	1950	1960	1970	1980	1990	2000	2004
Percentage of GNP	4.0%	4.6%	5.2%	7.2%	9.1%	12.2%	13.0%	16.0%
Per capita expenditures	$29	$78	$148	$357	$1,106	$2,821	$4,729	$6,280

Sources: "National Health Expenditures, Fiscal Year 1977," by Robert M. Gibson and Charles R. Fisher, 1978, *Social Security Bulletin*, 41, p. 15; National Center for Health Statistics, *Health, United States, 2006* (Hyattsville, MD: National Center for Health Statistics, 2006), p. 374.

amount of health-care goods and services. Affluent people can afford more and better health care, and they are more knowledgeable about available services. Older people have more health problems and require more health-care services. These services are also more widely available today because there are more physicians and more hospital services available in suburbs and small towns.

Second, and probably equally important, is the availability of diagnostic and treatment procedures that were unheard of five, ten, or twenty years ago, and these procedures can be very costly. Premature babies who would have died three decades ago are now saved in expensive neonatal intensive care units but at a high cost: from $200,000 to $1 million for an infant who weighs only one pound at birth. Laser surgery, CAT scanners, coronary bypass operations, angioplasty procedures, magnetic resonance imaging—these and many other procedures did not exist a few decades ago. Some feel that heart transplants will be routine in the not too distant future, and they now can cost upwards of $300,000 apiece.

Third, health care is a labor-intensive industry—it requires many people to provide health care—and the cost of health care rises quickly when health-care providers lobby for higher salaries. Nurses, nurses' aides, medical technologists, and many others feel they have been underpaid in the past and are demanding salaries they believe to be commensurate with their training and responsibilities. In addition, physicians' incomes have been rising at a much faster rate than the incomes of most workers. Also, savings through automation are not as easy to achieve in the health field as in other industries. Advances in health technology often involve completely new procedures, which call for new technicians, rather than replacing something that had been done less efficiently by older technology. So, improvements in health technology often result in the need for more, not fewer, workers.

Fourth, economic competition and the check on costs that this can afford are weaker in the health field than in other economic areas. This means that physicians and hospitals can raise costs with less concern about market considerations.

Fifth, there is a tendency to overutilize health-care services and even to perform completely unnecessary diagnostic and treatment procedures. One reason for this overutilization is some of the mechanisms used to pay for health-care services: They can leave both the physician and the patient with little reason to show constraint in the use of services. Until recently, the most common mode of payment was through **third-party medicine,** in which *the patient pays premiums into a fund, and the doctor or hospital is paid from this fund for each treatment provided the patient.* The first two parties in the transaction, of course, are the patient

and the doctor or hospital. The third party might be a private health insurance company or a government program such as Medicare or Medicaid. The basic flaw in such payment schemes is that the party paying the bill—the third-party source of funds—does not participate in the decision about how much or what kinds of services to provide. Patients have already paid their health insurance premiums and do not have to pay more as additional services are rendered, and physicians and hospitals benefit financially when more services are provided. The result was often the performance of too many and sometimes completely unnecessary medical procedures. In 1992, for example, *Consumer Reports* published a study concluding that as much as 20 percent of all surgeries and medical services provided in the United States were unnecessary, costing health-care consumers $130 billion each year (Anstett, 1992).

Finally, there are a number of other factors contributing to increasing costs. The number of malpractice suits and the size of the financial judgments against physicians in these litigations have increased. Consequently, malpractice premiums for physicians rose by a substantial amount each year in the past two decades, with some specialties seeing much greater increases (Jost, 2003). This rise in costs is then passed on to the health-care consumer. In addition, as was mentioned above, crisis medicine tends to be more expensive in the long run than preventive medicine, but our health-care system still tends to emphasize the former. Finally, there are many powerful interest groups benefiting from rising costs: physicians, hospital administrators, the pharmaceutical industry, and so on. Health-care consumers benefit most from controlling costs, but they have yet to organize into a powerful lobby group.

Access to Medical Services

Many people in the United States do not have easy access to medical care when they need it (Quadagno, 2005). Because health care is a commodity sold in the marketplace, those who can afford to pay get medical services, whereas those who cannot afford it are left to fend for themselves. The high cost of health care means that only the wealthiest can afford to pay out of their own pockets for medical services. Most rely on health insurance, either purchased by themselves or provided by an employer. The poor and less well-to-do, who cannot find jobs that provide health insurance, are out in the cold. This situation has been eased somewhat with the introduction of programs of publicly financed health insurance such as Medicaid, but less than one-half of the poor are eligible for Medicaid. As a consequence, fully one-third of the poorest in the United States younger than age sixty-five have no health insurance coverage at all; for them, access to medical care is quite limited. In addition to the poor, there are others

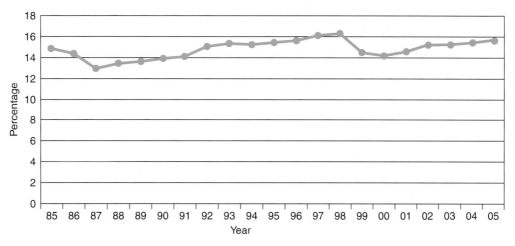

FIGURE 4.5 **People Without Health Insurance for the Entire Year, 1985–2005.**

Source: Robert J. Mills and Shailesh Bhandari, Health Insurance Coverage in the United States: 2002. *Current Population Report*, P60–223; and Current Population Survey, 2005 and 2006. *Annual Social and Economic Supplements* (Washington, DC: U.S. Bureau of the Census, 2007).

who find themselves without health insurance: laid-off employees; people who retire before they are eligible for Medicare; young people who are too old for coverage under their parents' health insurance plan; and widows, widowers, and divorced people who had depended on their spouses' health insurance. Altogether 44 million Americans, or 15 percent of our populace, are without health insurance (see Figure 4.5).

Another dimension of access to health care is the availability of services. In this regard, it has been residents of the inner city and rural areas who are underserved. Physicians prefer to practice in locales where they would like to live and can find a profitable clientele, and neither the inner city nor rural areas can satisfy this preference.

Quality of Medical Services

Rising costs and the intense competition among hospitals may be affecting the quality of health care in the United States. To keep costs down and profits up, hospitals are merging, cutting back on services to patients, and placing heavy workloads on nurses. This has prompted many nurses to leave nursing, making for a significant shortage in nurses (Stolberg, 2002). This has also led to the work of nurses being taken over by lower-paid but less highly trained nursing assistants and technicians. Registered nurses are also given responsibility for supervising these less-trained workers, further taking away from the RNs' direct contact with patients. These and other cutbacks are considered important reasons for a decline in services to the point of increased injury and suffering to patients in some hospitals.

Cutbacks such as these, along with the highly bureaucratic organization of the health-care system, can result in highly impersonal and even dehumanizing health-care services. The standardization and routinization of health care can benefit the health-care system because it is less expensive. Yet, it can lead patients to feel dissatisfied, lonely, and frightened.

Gender Inequality in Health Care

Gender inequality pervades the health-care system in the United States, with widespread ramifications. First, the health-care industry is male dominated, with men holding most of the prestigious, high-paying, and powerful positions (see Figure 4.6). Men make up 68 percent of today's physicians, for example, whereas 91 percent of the registered nurses are women. Most dentists are men, whereas practically all dental assistants and dental hygienists are women. Clearly, the health-care system involves men in positions of authority telling women what to do. This was not always the case. In the nineteenth century, women working as midwives or other types of healers provided much of the medical care for families. As more medical schools opened in the late 1800s, women were excluded from most of them. By the turn of the century, legislation banned the "practice of medicine" by anyone not trained in a state-approved medical school. The result: Women were effectively banned from the practice of medicine. During the first half of the twentieth century, medical schools admitted few, if any, women. Even through the 1960s, medical and dental education were male preserves: Although a few women were admitted, they were often met with hostility or demeaning jokes, making the difficult road through school even tougher. It has not really been until the last thirty years that medical and dental education have opened up to women. Today about two out of every five medical and dental students nationwide are women (see Figure 4.7). There has been much less change, however, in the sparse numbers of men in nursing schools.

One reason for concern about male dominance in the health field is that it has severely restricted women's access to lucrative and prestigious occupations. These issues of economic discrimination are discussed in more detail in Chapter 7. Another reason for concern is that male dominance may have had a detrimental effect on the health and health care of women in the United States (Scully, 1994). Male physicians over the years held the same stereotypes about women that other men did, and this influenced what physicians defined as illness and what treatments they made available. For example, one stereotype viewed menstruation as "unclean" or "abnormal," and physicians contributed to this view by "medicalizing" menstruation or defining it as a medical condition or weakness calling for some intervention. In the nineteenth century and well into the twentieth century, menstruation has been viewed as a pathological condition presumed to have serious consequences and to influence women's ability to think and make decisions. In fact, the reputed ill effects of women's reproductive biology have been an important staple in a sexist ideology justifying the inequitable treatment of women. From the late 1800s until recently, the very process of childbirth itself has been viewed as a medical procedure rather than the profoundly natural and personal event that it really is. Women were routinely given powerful anesthetics that prevented them from experiencing the birth of their children. Then they might not even be permitted to see their infants for a few days after birth, interfering with the bonding that occurs between mother and child soon after birth. More recently, the number of Cesarean births has grown from 5 percent to 27 percent of all births, giving the United States the highest rate of such births (U.S. Bureau of the Census, 2006:69). Some Cesareans, of course, are medically justified, but there is much suspicion that some are performed for the convenience of medical personnel, to protect against malpractice suits, or because doctors and hospitals are reimbursed more for surgical births. In any event, the mother loses control of the birth process when it becomes overly medicalized.

This male doctor discusses cases with the female nurses who work under his direction. While the gender composition of health care providers has changed considerably over the years, the health-care field still tends to be characterized by males holding positions of authority and prestige while females are in more subordinate positions.

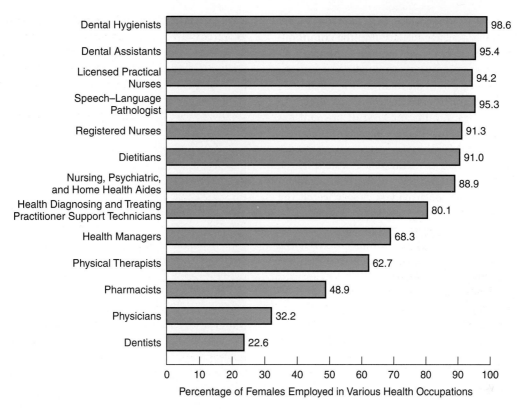

Occupation	Percentage
Dental Hygienists	98.6
Dental Assistants	95.4
Licensed Practical Nurses	94.2
Speech–Language Pathologist	95.3
Registered Nurses	91.3
Dietitians	91.0
Nursing, Psychiatric, and Home Health Aides	88.9
Health Diagnosing and Treating Practitioner Support Technicians	80.1
Health Managers	68.3
Physical Therapists	62.7
Pharmacists	48.9
Physicians	32.2
Dentists	22.6

Percentage of Females Employed in Various Health Occupations

FIGURE 4.6   Men and Women in Health Occupations, 2006.

Sources: U.S. Department of Labor Statistics, *Employment and Earnings*, 54, no. 1. (January 2007), pp. 222–224.

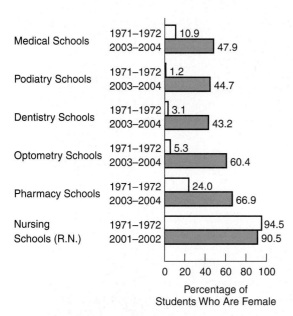

FIGURE 4.7   Enrollment of Women in Schools for Health Occupations, United States, Academic Years 1971–2004.

Sources: National Center for Health Statistics, *Health, United States, 1990*, DHHS Pub. No. (PHS) 91–1232 (Hyattsville, MD: Public Health Service, 1993), p. 172; National Center for Health Statistics, *Health, United States*, 2006 (Hyattsville, MD: National Center for Health Statistics, 2006), p. 363.

The medical procedure that is among those most likely to be performed unnecessarily—the hysterectomy—affects only women. Conservatively, one-third of all hysterectomies over the years were probably medically unjustified, and some studies find as many as 70 percent to be inappropriate (Broder et al., 2000). Some observers have questioned whether a medical profession dominated by women would have so routinely performed such surgeries. In addition, feminists argue that medical research has been dominated by the sexist assumption that it is the woman's responsibility to orchestrate birth control efforts. Consequently, most birth control research has been on female contraceptive devices rather than on finding effective procedures for male contraception.

The Corporatization of Health Care

Some health-care critics argue that the problems just discussed—costs, access, and quality of health care—are due in part to deeper, structural change in the economic organization of health care. Early in the twentieth century in the United States, most hospitals were nonprofit facilities run by religious or charitable organizations or by city or county governments. Their primary motivation was patient care, and they were highly accountable to their patients and the communities they served. The people who ran the hospitals typically lived in the community they served, and the community had a variety of mechanisms for influencing hospital decisions and the allocation of resources. In the last few decades, a different kind of hospital has become more significant: *proprietary hospitals*, which are investor-owned, profit-making corporations. As this transition has occurred, the health-care system in the United States in general has become increasingly profit oriented, and health-care providers closely watch the profit margin when they make medical decisions.

In other words, health-care institutions are increasingly a part of the capitalist economic system of the United States described in Chapter 2. Now this is not new. After all, physicians have been business entrepreneurs in this country since its founding, pharmaceutical companies have always tried to make a profit selling people drugs, and there have always been privately owned hospitals. What is different today is the size and scope of the privatization and corporatization of health care in the United States. Although nonprofit hospitals can still be found, the hospital industry is slowly being taken over by national corporations that own chains of hospitals and manage local hospitals from a centralized business office (one in six acute-care hospitals is now investor owned). In these corporate settings, control and authority over medical decisions and issues are gradually shifting from the hands of patients, physicians, and community leaders to corporate headquarters and medical industry entrepreneurs, and the primary motivation of these corporations is to increase corporate profits. The public sector of community and nonprofit hospitals is being forced to adopt some of the same strategies or be run out of business.

The corporate takeover of hospitals began with the emergence of Medicare and Medicaid, which meant that there were huge profits to be made treating the recipients of these programs. By the 1980s, in the Wall Street world of medicine, patients were known as "revenue bodies," hospitals were "profit centers," and the goal was to "maximize the return on each admission." What has emerged is a rather chilling trend: "Charging every penny that can be charged for patient care and avoiding as much as possible the treatment of patients unable to pay. It also means marketing, or offering paying patients what they *think* they need, while eliminating services a community might *really* need but which aren't profitable" (Lindorff, 1992:18).

There are, of course, benefits to this privatization. Especially for those with good health insurance or the wealthy, who can afford to pay on their own, medicine in the United States provides some excellent services.

Increasingly, health care in the United States is paid for, and sometimes provided by, large corporate health empires that are motivated as much by the need to enhance profits as by a desire to serve patients.

As is described in Chapter 2, capitalism is based on the assumption that competition and profit seeking will work in the interests of the consumer by providing the widest range of goods and services at the lowest price. These incentives should, in theory, encourage private health-care businesses to provide the highest quality, least expensive health care possible to their customers.

However, evidence suggests that it often doesn't work out that way. In areas where many hospitals compete with one another for patients, for example, both for-profit and nonprofit hospitals charge about the same for various procedures; when there is no competition, for-profits actually charge more for services than do the nonprofits (Lindorff, 1992). It seems that, in the absence of competition, the temptation to raise charges, and thus increase profits, is too great for the for-profits to resist. The overall lower costs of non-profit hospitals are especially surprising because they do not dump expensive services such as obstetrics in the way that the for-profits have. Research also shows that investor-owned health insurance plans deliver a demonstrably lower quality of health care than do not-for-profit plans and that investor-owned nursing homes provide lower levels of care to their clients than do not-for-profit nursing homes (Harrington et al., 2001; Himmelstein, Woolhandler, and Hellander, 2001). In addition, there is ample research showing that government health insurance programs such as Medicare are less expensive—or at least, are no more expensive—than health insurance provided by private insurers (Boccuti and Moon, 2003; Gold, 2003). One of the reasons for this is that, surprising to some, the government programs have considerably lower administrative costs.

The privatization and corporatization of health care also mean that those who cannot afford health care—the poor who do not qualify for Medicaid and those who do not have health insurance on the job—do not have access to the health services they need. Even those with Medicaid find that they have limited access to the system because corporate hospitals and doctors prefer to serve those whose insurance will pay higher fees for services than will Medicaid. In addition, expensive medicine, such as obstetrics and emergency medicine, gets dumped onto publicly owned hospitals, which further taxes their ability to provide quality care to their patients.

Dr. Arnold S. Relman (1980), editor of the prestigious *New England Journal of Medicine,* calls this a **medical–industrial complex:** *a coincidence of interests between physicians and other health-care providers and the industries producing health-care goods and services, with both parties profiting from the increased use of these commodities while the health-care consumer pays enormous costs for inadequate care.* This arrangement is analogous to the military–industrial complex discussed in Chapter 2. It can lead to a conflict of interest because many of the businesses are owned by doctors or employ doctors. Like other enterprises, these businesses stand to increase their profits by "selling" as much of their commodity as they can, just as a person who sells cars profits by increasing sales. This situation raises the question of whether health-care decisions are motivated by the health needs of the consumer or by the profit needs of the medical–industrial complex.

Many critics regard the free market and profit-making nature of the U.S. health-care system as a major factor leading people to pay more for lower-quality health care than they should. One problem is that the health-care field is not as subject to the laws of competition and the marketplace, as are other economic realms. Health-care consumers, for example, cannot as readily shop for bargains and are heavily dependent on physicians, who benefit from high health-care expenditures, to tell them what health services they need. Another problem is that health corporations can be tempted to cut back on services, and possibly on necessary health care, in order to increase profits.

Despite these problems, health care is still largely a private-enterprise, profit-making activity in the United States, and we will come back to this issue when we address the future prospects of health care.

Bioethics: Technology and Health

Modern technology has opened up some wonderful opportunities, but it also confronts us with some difficult and potentially frightening issues. The final chapter of this book deals with the impact of science and technology on our lives, but here we need to address a few special concerns that relate to health issues. **Bioethics** refers to *the study of ethical questions that relate to the life and biological well-being of people* (DeVries and Subedi, 1998). It involves an intertwining of ethical, medical, and biological considerations. We will discuss two major issues in this realm: the prolongation of life and the distribution of limited medical resources. Keep in mind that these ethical issues have come to the fore, in part, because of the very success of science and medicine in attacking illness and injury.

The Prolongation of Life

When people die, their respiratory, circulatory, and nervous systems—the major life-sustaining body systems—normally fail at about the same time. With modern technology, however, respiration and circulation can be machine assisted far beyond the point at which the body itself could sustain them. These machines do not provide medical treatment but merely assist the body to stay "alive." Thus, severely injured, critically ill, or very old people can be kept alive for long periods of time.

The expense of such life-support systems can devastate a family's finances. There is also a tremendous psychological burden for the family who has to watch a loved one go through a prolonged period of debilitation before death. Finally, from the individual's perspective, there is the loss of dignity that comes from helplessness. Even if comatose, many would prefer not to end their lives with tubes inserted in their bodies and machines powering their hearts—almost as if the body must fight against modern technology in order to die.

Technology has made the line between life and death more vague. It has become a difficult practical matter to say exactly when death occurs in many cases. The same technology can maintain the lives of terminally ill or comatose people, even when there is little or no hope of recovery. This situation creates a dilemma regarding who should decide whether to discontinue life support. Parents or relatives would seem to be the natural ones to make such decisions, but they could be swayed by such considerations as the psychological or economic costs of maintaining a critically ill relative over time. Medical personnel also play a role in such decisions. But their mission is to save lives, and they may be rightly concerned about civil or even criminal suits resulting from their decisions in such cases. As a consequence, their choices may not be in the patients' best interests.

A number of developments have had an impact on this problem of the artificial prolongation of life. One has been the emergence of social movements whose major theme is "death with dignity." Those involved have lobbied for the acceptance of "living wills," in which people state, while they are still healthy, the conditions under which medical efforts to save their lives should be stopped. A few states have accepted these living wills as legal documents, but their ultimate legality is likely to be debated in the courts. Another development has been the acceptance of a revised definition of death, which used to be defined as the cessation of breathing and heartbeat. The newer approach defines death as the prolonged absence of brain waves, or "brain death." This gives physicians some legal standing in withholding life-sustaining efforts from those who show virtually no possibility of recovery. A final development has been the establishment of panels in hospitals to make recommendations about decisions of whether to withhold treatment or turn off life-support equipment. The panels are made up of doctors, nurses, social workers, psychologists, and even laypeople. These panels relieve physicians of the difficult burden of making such decisions alone, and, by including many different opinions, they reduce the likelihood that personal bias will result in judgments at variance with the patient's interests.

Whom Shall We Treat?

As we have seen, health care is expensive and is becoming more costly all the time. A part of the problem is the growing number of technologically complex and costly procedures that are available. This raises the question of whether we can afford to provide these treatments to everyone with a medical need for them (Merrill and Cohen, 1989; Zussman, 1997). After all,

the money we spend on health care is money we cannot spend on defense, social services, automobiles, and recreation. One option, of course, is to limit the availability of some medical procedures, possibly the more expensive ones. But how do we decide to whom these procedures will be made available? Such decisions rest on some "principle of social justice." There are a number of these principles that can serve as the basis of medical allocation decisions.

1. *Ability to pay.* Offer services to those who can afford to pay part or all of the costs.
2. *Merit.* Offer services on the basis of people's merits, such as their achievements or societal contributions.
3. *Utilitarian.* Offer services to those who would provide the greatest benefit—in economic, personal, or social terms—to the greatest number of people should they live.
4. *Compensatory justice.* Offer services to those who have already suffered some social wrongs or have been deprived of resources.
5. *Egalitarian.* Offer everyone who needs services an equal opportunity to receive them.

Which of these principles, or combinations of principles, would you use to allocate health-care resources? The egalitarian concept is probably the most popular one in the United States. The point, of course, is that, as medical technology becomes more expensive, we may have to decide how to limit its use by adopting some principles of social justice on which to rest the allocation process.

Future Prospects

In terms of social policy on health care, a major focus of attention has been how to finance health care, because this has a big impact on rising costs, access to health care, and the other problems discussed in this chapter.

Publicly Funded Health Insurance

MEDICARE AND MEDICAID Two government programs that have probably had the most profound effects on health-care delivery in the United States are Medicare and Medicaid, both established in 1965. **Medicare** is *government health insurance for those over sixty-five years of age.* This program pays some of the costs for hospitalization, prescription drugs, nursing-home care, and some home-health care. For a monthly fee, the elderly can also purchase medical insurance from

Medicare that will cover other services such as doctors' fees and outpatient services. **Medicaid** is *a joint federal–state program to provide medical care for low-income people of any age.*

These two programs have gone a long way toward reducing the differences in the use of health-care services between the affluent and the poor. Unlike in the past, the poor today visit doctors and enter hospitals more frequently than the well-to-do. To that extent, these two programs have achieved one of their major goals, which was to make health care available to all citizens regardless of financial circumstances. But these plans are not without their problems. First they are very expensive and growing more expensive. Both payment schemes were originally designed as third-party arrangements, and this accounts for some of their high costs. A second problem, especially with Medicaid, has been fraud, committed by both recipients and providers of health care. Some physicians have provided unneeded treatments, and some medical laboratories have routinely charged for tests never performed. Some abuse is inevitable in such large programs, but it has been extensive and expensive (Jesilow, Pontell, and Geis, 1993). A third problem is that some providers have refused to treat Medicaid and Medicare patients because of delays in receiving payments or because the payments were inadequate. Medicare and Medicaid have been criticized over the years for paying physicians too little for services. This problem could create a two-tiered health-care system in which Medicare and Medicaid patients receive lower-quality care by lower-paid physicians in crowded settings, whereas people with private health insurance have good quality services available to them. Finally, as we have seen, the eligibility level for Medicaid in most states is so low that some people who truly need it do not have access to it. Raising the eligibility ceilings would provide health insurance to many who currently have no insurance whatsoever.

A number of efforts have been made to control the skyrocketing costs of Medicaid and Medicare. Some states have developed "preferred provider" programs for Medicaid, in which a hospital or a group of doctors agrees to provide all health-care services to Medicaid recipients in a particular geographic area, receiving, in return, one annual, lump-sum payment. This arrangement encourages the providers to prevent costs from exceeding the annual amount that they are paid because they will not receive any additional payments and are contractually required to provide services. For Medicare, the federal government instituted a new payment mechanism in the early 1980s called diagnostically related groupings, or DRGs. This strategy involves placing each hospitaliza-tion episode into one of about 450 diagnostic group-ings. Then all treatments in a single diagnostic group-ing receive the same reimbursement, whether any particular case actually costs more or less. If a case costs more to treat, the hospital must make up the difference; if it costs less, the hospital keeps the surplus. The purpose is to offer doctors and hospitals a financial incentive for keeping an eye on lowering costs. Opponents of the DRG approach argue that people's illness episodes are too individualized to be treated in this assembly-line fashion: Some people bleed more, others take longer to recuperate, and others are fast healers. Furthermore, doctors would have to consider DRGs when they make diagnoses rather than being guided solely by the condition of their patients. The program seems to have produced a few changes in what doctors and hospitals do: Hospital stays for the elderly are shorter than they used to be, hospitals are trying to draw in more patients to take up the slack, and hospitals have aggressively developed outpatient services (Cockerham, 2007; Freund and McGuire, 1995).

NATIONAL HEALTH INSURANCE Medicare and Medicaid amount to government health insurance for the poor and the elderly. Some have proposed that these benefits be extended as a right to all citizens through **national health insurance:** *government health insurance covering all citizens* (Intriligator, 1993). Great Britain had such a program as early as 1911. In fact, the United States is alone among the industrial nations in not providing some form of national health insurance or health service. National health insurance would alleviate a number of problems. It would ensure health insurance coverage to the many people who do not currently have any, such as low-income people ineligible for Medicaid and people who are between jobs. It would also give the government a more direct means of controlling health-care costs. Finally, it would reduce the likelihood of a two-tiered health-care system. However, national health insurance, if designed as a third-party payment system, could be costly if it did not include some cost containment mechanisms, such as DRGs.

Although some support for a program of national health insurance persists in the United States, such a program has never come close to adoption. The relatively low level of enthusiasm for extending publicly financed health care to all people suggests that some ambivalence remains regarding whether health care is a right or should be a privilege. As the International Perspectives insert points out, this contrasts sharply with the approach taken in many other

Paying for Health Care in Other Societies

Earlier in this chapter, we saw that in comparison to most other industrial nations, people in the United States live shorter lives, lose more infants to death, and pay more for health care. Why do these other nations pay less and get more? Some critics attribute this to the largely unregulated, laissez-faire nature of the U.S. health-care system, which leaves many people with limited or no access to health care.

In Sweden, France, Australia, Germany, Canada, and many other nations, health services are paid for with money collected by the government (Cockerham, 2007). This is similar to Medicare and Medicaid in the United States. Employers and employees pay taxes that are

placed in a fund from which medical bills are paid. Canada, for example, provided hospital insurance for its citizens beginning in 1961 and physician's care insurance in 1971 (Bennett and Adams, 1993). The entire population is covered, and 95 percent of hospital and physician costs are paid by federal or provincial taxes. There are some amenities, such as private hospital rooms and cosmetic surgery, that the system does not pay for. Everything else is covered, and Canadians hardly ever even see a hospital bill. Patients can choose their own physicians, and physicians are private, self-employed practitioners, not government employees. Hospitals operate on a budget that is set

largely by provincial governments. So, Canada has an essentially private health-care system that is paid for almost entirely by public money.

One way in which this universal coverage can be paid for is by keeping costs down. For example, in Canada, the government sets all doctor and hospital fees, and physicians can't charge more for services than the insurance will pay. Canadian physicians do not earn the lucrative incomes that U.S. physicians do, although physicians are still among the highest paid professional groups in Canada. However, Canadian doctors do not have to worry about billing patients, preparing insurance forms, or writing off bad debts.

societies. However, as health-care costs continue to rise in the United States and both employers and employees are squeezed to pay health insurance premiums, people may take another look at national health insurance as a mechanism for spreading the costs out over all people.

Compulsory, Employer-Financed Health Insurance

Some would prefer that the government not get involved in the actual provision of health insurance but rather just ensure that all citizens have access to some health insurance. Because many of the currently uninsured have jobs with no health insurance benefits, one proposal is to have the government require that all employers provide comprehensive health insurance for their employees. The Clinton administration proposed a version of this plan in 1994.

The government could pay the insurance premiums of those who don't work or work for employers who are too small to afford health insurance. Such a program would be expensive, of course, and it would put a burden on small businesses. In addition, the consumer

would pay for it through higher prices for goods and services. Yet, it would provide all people with access to health care. It is also more acceptable than programs such as national health insurance to many laissez-faire advocates because it accomplishes the goal with minimal government involvement. In fact, something like this has been done with Medicare and Medicaid: Instead of the government providing the insurance, the government has encouraged those eligible to join private health maintenance organizations (HMOs) or managed care organizations, with the government paying the premiums for membership. For example, 14 percent of Medicare recipients are enrolled in an HMO (National Center for Health Statistics, 2006).

HMOs and Managed Care

In discussing Medicaid, "preferred provider" programs were mentioned. When these kinds of arrangements emerged many decades ago, they were called health maintenance organizations, or HMOs, and they represented an alternative to traditional health insurance for financing health care. A **health maintenance organization (HMO)** is *an organization that*

Of course, you can't spend less on health care and cover more people, as the Canadians do, without some costs. One cost is that there are sometimes waits for hospital beds and some types of surgical procedures, especially nonemergency surgeries. In addition, some state-of-the-art technology, such as magnetic resonance imaging (MRI) machines, is not as widely available as in the United States. Yet another cost is the higher taxes to pay for the universal government-provided coverage.

Health-care financing programs should be looked at in terms of *who* bears the costs because the costs of any program will have to be borne by someone. Currently, in the United States, those who benefit the most are the affluent, those fortunate enough to have good, employer-provided health insurance, and the elderly with Medicare. A shift to a Canadian-style system would mean redirecting some of the benefits from those groups to the poor, the unemployed, the underemployed, and other marginal groups. So, it comes down to *how* health care will be rationed, not whether it will be rationed. Will some poor and unemployed be denied basic health care, such as prenatal care or frequent doctor visits for sick people? Or will some of the affluent be denied rapid access to elective surgeries or exotic technologies, such as coronary bypass surgery for elderly patients?

Sweden has a truly socialized health-care system, with the government nationalizing most health-care facilities and employing health-care workers. Health services are free to anyone who needs them, and little money changes hands between patient and health-care providers. Taxes support the health-care system, and Sweden does have high taxes. However, the Swedes are also among the healthiest people in the world. They live three years longer than people in the United States and have much lower infant mortality. Sweden is an interesting contrast with both Canada and the United States in that it runs a generally effective, socialized system of health care in a capitalist country.

agrees to provide for all of a person's health-care needs for a fixed, periodic premium. Whereas health insurance is third-party medicine involving a separate payment for each service rendered, HMOs receive a set fee and agree to take care of all of a person's health needs for that fee. In so doing, the HMO assumes a financial risk that the services they give patients might cost more than the premiums the HMO takes in. If this happens, the HMO loses money, so the HMO has an incentive to control costs that the physician or patient in third-party medicine does not have.

In the last two decades, a number of trends discussed in this chapter—the corporatization of health care, increased competition in the health-care field, and rising costs—has led to the emergence of what is now called **managed care:** *a health-care system that focuses on controlling costs by monitoring and controlling the health-care decisions of doctors and patients* (Cockerham, 2007; Draper et al., 2002). HMOs and preferred provider arrangements are variations on managed care, but it also takes numerous other forms. Some managed-care systems own their own hospitals and employ the health-care providers, including physicians. People in managed-care systems typically have a limited choice of doctors from which to select, and the managed-care system exercises tight control over the medical treatments doctors are allowed to employ and the referrals to specialists they are allowed to make. All of this "management" is an effort to control costs. Two-thirds of the people who work at medium and large companies in the United States today are enrolled in some form of managed-care health system rather than traditional health insurance. Whereas most HMOs in the past were not-for-profit organizations, today many HMOs and managed-care systems are for-profit. Insurance companies, traditional HMOs, and hospitals have taken the lead in developing managed-care plans and offering them to employers, usually at a lower price than the employer would pay for traditional health insurance.

One of the motivations for developing HMOs and managed-care systems has been cost containment, and studies of HMOs in earlier decades indicate that they are less expensive than traditional health insurance and provide equivalent levels and quality of services (Brown et al., 1993; Greenfield et al., 1995). HMOs have lower hospitalization rates and do fewer unnecessary surgeries. These benefits may derive from the HMOs' mode of financing, which gives HMOs an incentive to economize, or from their greater utilization of preventive health care. However, it may also be that, in the past when these studies were done, healthier people joined HMOs, which accounted for their lower costs. The managed-care systems of today have not yet been studied as extensively in terms of these outcomes.

However, while managed care arrangements may reduce costs, they have been criticized on a number of other grounds (Himmelstein, Woolhandler, and Hellander, 2001; Ware et al., 1996). For one thing, managed care does nothing to help those without health insurance. Second, its oversight of medical decisions threatens the independence and autonomy of medical practitioners. That independence is also threatened because, in some communities, managed care enrolls so many people that insufficient business is left for physicians who are not part of the managed-care system. To make a living, doctors have little choice other than to sign on with the managed-care system and accept whatever pay and working conditions are dictated. In fact, physicians' incomes have stopped rising and may even have begun to fall, in part because of the cost controls of managed care. Third, managed-care systems aggressively compete for contracts, offering employers low premiums and then pressuring doctors to limit medical procedures and hospitals to cut staff and procedures to come in under cost and make a profit. Patients may suffer from this practice if needed health-care services are not provided. This seems an especially likely outcome when HMOs are investor-owned: Research discussed earlier in this chapter shows that for-profit health insurance plans, such as HMOs, deliver a lower quality of health care to patients than do not-for-profit plans.

A final criticism of managed care is that it represents a dramatic shift in control over medical decisions from the hands of many dispersed doctors and local hospitals to the directors of these huge corporate empires. And these health empires have been merging at a rapid rate, with the result being that the system is moving toward an oligopoly (see Chapter 2). There is little evidence at this point that health-care consumers benefit from these mergers through better care or lower costs (Feldman, Wholey, and Christianson, 1996). Increasingly, the health care people receive today is determined by a contract negotiated between their employer and a national (or global) corporate health-care giant. At this point, it is unclear what all the benefits and disadvantages of such a system are or whether the former outweigh the latter. For the moment, policy action seems focused more on managed care than on other alternatives such as national health insurance. The Policy Issues insert compares managed care and the other modes of financing health care in terms of whether they support the idea of health care as a right or a privilege.

New Health-Care Practitioners

Another approach to lowering costs and increasing accessibility to health care is to expand the types of providers giving primary care and reduce dependence on highly trained and expensive specialists. For example, a new specialty called "family practice" began in the 1960s and was intended to increase the ranks of primary-care physicians. After medical school and a year of internship, family practice physicians go through a residency program in which they receive advanced training in a broad range of medical specialties. This enables them to treat many health problems themselves and to refer more complex cases to the appropriate specialist.

Until recently, there has been a shortage of physicians in the United States, especially in rural and inner-city areas. To alleviate this problem, the government has supported the development of physician extenders, practitioners trained to perform some of the simple and routine health-care tasks traditionally accomplished by physicians. Nurse practitioners (NPs), for example, are registered nurses with advanced training that in some cases includes the master's degree in nursing. Physicians' assistants (PAs) have some medical training and can work only under the supervision of a physician. NPs and PAs do such things as conduct routine physical examinations, provide simple emergency and prenatal care, and the like. They normally work under the guidance of a physician and may serve as the patient's initial contact with the health-care system. In these ways, NPs and PAs provide medical doctors with more time to make complex diagnostic and treatment decisions. Studies show that NPs and PAs can do the things they are trained for as well as physicians can, and at substantially less cost (Horrocks, Anderson, and Salisbury, 2002; Roblin et al., 2004).

Other alternatives exist to highly trained, specialized, and expensive physicians in the delivery of health-care services. Midwives, for example, deliver babies in many rural areas as safely as do physicians in hospitals, especially when life-saving technology is not immediately needed during the delivery (Durand, 1992). In fact, physicians tend to make more life-saving interventions that are not necessary, and this actually increases the risk to the mother and infant. Health policymakers had hoped that alternative healers, such as NPs, PAs, and midwives, would produce less reliance on traditionally trained physicians and thus make health care more accessible and less expensive. This may not be happening, however, to the extent that it could. One reason is that some doctors are reluctant to accept these personnel, believing

Should Health Care Be for Profit?

Underlying this discussion of how to finance health care is an overriding issue: Should health care in the United States be a right or a privilege? A related issue is whether, or to what extent, health care should be a private, for-profit part of the economy.

Proponents of privatization argue that access to health care, like any other economic commodity, should be a privilege of those with the resources to obtain it. This reflects the capitalist and market foundations of the U.S. economy: Health care is another economic service, and it can be most efficiently produced and distributed through open competition in the marketplace. As we saw in Chapter 2, capitalism is based on the assumption that competition and profit seeking will work in the interests of the consumer by providing the widest range of goods and services at the lowest price. These incentives should, in theory, encourage private health-care businesses to provide high-quality, inexpensive health care. Proponents point to aspects of the U.S. health-care system to show the benefits to this privatization. Especially for those with good health insurance or the wealthy who can afford to pay on their own, the health-care system in the United States does provide some excellent services.

The opposing viewpoint is that access to high-quality health care should be a fundamental right of all members of society. Recall the functionalist argument that people's health status is central to the maintenance of society. Aside from any moral demand that we assist people who are sick or injured, society needs to ensure that people are healthy so that they can make contributions to the maintenance of society. So, health care should be a right. Opponents of the privatization and corporatization of health care argue that a private system inevitably deprives some people of care, especially those who cannot afford health care, such as the poor who do not qualify for Medicaid and those who do not have health insurance on the job. Even those with Med-

icaid find that they have limited access to the system because corporate hospitals and doctors prefer to serve those whose insurance will pay higher fees for services than will Medicaid. In addition, expensive medicine, such as obstetrics and emergency medicine, gets dumped onto publicly owned hospitals, which further taxes their ability to provide quality care to their patients. And some question whether profit seeking by doctors and hospitals always works in the best interests of the patient. As one health economist put it: "The real threat to health care is when the doctors' and the hospitals' interests become aligned against the interests of the patient. It's possible that the corporations could usurp the physicians' power" to act as an advocate for the patients (quoted in Lindorff, 1992:86).

There is great controversy about how to resolve this debate. Some critics, such as Ivan Illich (1976) and Robert Sherrill (1995), believe that the capitalist nature of the U.S. health-care system is the fundamental problem and that only a complete restructuring of the system can prevent widespread abuses and exploitation. Some of these critics go so far as to call for a socialized health-care system. Others who see health care as a right argue for a system with both public and private elements, such as a program of national health insurance or an extension of existing Medicare and Medicaid programs, where the government would ensure that all people have access to health care and protect against the difficulties that can arise when profit making is uncontrolled. Current social policy has tended in the direction of support for the profit-oriented nature of the system, as reflected in the growth of largely private managed-care systems in recent years. Yet, strong support persists among the public for the idea of health care as a right. So, although virtually all other industrial nations have policies based on health care as a fundamental right, this issue is not resolved in the United States.

Interventionist			Laissez-Faire
Socialized medicine	National health insurance	Medicare and Medicaid	Privatized managed care and HMOs

that only physicians are competent to provide key medical services. In addition, a surplus of physicians is now emerging, at least in some specialties. As this occurs, physicians may come to see these other providers as competition for a shrinking health-care dollar. So the situation remains unsettled.

Self-Care and Changing Lifestyles

Social commentators such as Ivan Illich (1976) and Joseph Califano (1994) have severely criticized the health-care system in the United States for creating as much illness as it cures. It creates illness, for example, when a hospital patient gets an infection or suffers complications in surgery. This is called *iatrogenic illness:* illness or injury that arises while receiving treatment. However, a more subtle form of iatrogenesis can occur when the health-care system and cultural values convince people that they must rely on medical professionals to remain healthy or to overcome illness. People see themselves as virtually helpless without medical support. When these beliefs predominate, people tend not to do things that might enhance their health status. To overcome this problem, Illich and Califano argue, people should rely more on self-care and lifestyle change as a way to improved health.

We have seen that one of the major causes of many chronic illnesses is the lifestyle of many people today: They eat, drink, and smoke too much; they suffer periodic stresses of divorce or unemployment; and they pollute the environment. People can improve their health status if they attack these problems. In fact, this whole text relates to health problems to the extent that improvements in the physical and social environment have beneficial health consequences.

LINKAGES

Society's health problems are exacerbated by increases in drug abuse (Chapter 10), because intravenous drug users are at a high risk of contracting the AIDS virus and spreading the epidemic by sharing dirty needles. The amount of illness and injury people have to cope with is also increased considerably by environmental pollution (Chapter 13); violent crime (Chapter 9); and violence, war, and terrorism (Chapter 14).

STUDY AND REVIEW

Summary

1. From the functionalist perspective, illness threatens the survival of society because sick people cannot accomplish essential tasks. The health-care system becomes a problem when it fails to return sick people to normal social functioning.

2. From the conflict perspective, health and health care are scarce resources that interest groups compete over. The inequitable distribution of these resources will reflect the overall inequitable distribution of resources in society. This becomes a problem when some group feels that it is not receiving its fair share of these resources.

3. The interactionist perspective recognizes that illnesses involve a network of social meanings and social expectations. Health care can be considered a social problem when it produces stigmatized or devalued self-concepts among consumers of health care.

4. Diseases can be classified as acute or chronic, with the former contributing more to the death rate in preindustrial societies. In industrial societies, the death rate drops substantially and life expectancy increases. This is due largely to declines in infant and childhood mortality and changes in lifestyle.

5. The four major sociocultural factors that affect health and illness are socioeconomic status, gender, race, and lifestyle.

6. There are three positions regarding the nature of mental illness: the medical model, mental illness as deviance, and mental illness as problems of living.

7. Given the unreliability of psychiatric diagnoses, there is some debate over whether mental health professionals can accurately detect mental disorders. There has been a trend over the past thirty years toward a treatment approach known as community mental health.

8. There are a number of problems associated with health and illness in the United States: Health-care costs have been rising rapidly; some people do not have access to the health services that they need; the quality of some health services is low; there is substantial gender inequality in the health-care field; and health services have been privatized and corporatized.

9. Two major bioethical issues are whether to prolong the life of someone who is terminally ill and how to distribute limited medical resources.

10. A central issue in deciding how to attack problems in the health-care field is whether access to health care should be every citizen's right or whether it is a privilege of those who can afford to pay for it. Problems in this field have been attacked through publicly funded health insurance, the emergence of health maintenance organizations and managed-care systems, the development of new health-care practitioner roles, and changes in people's lifestyles.

RESEARCHING SOCIAL PROBLEMS ON THE INTERNET

There are innumerable sources of information about health issues worldwide available on the Internet. Begin by going to the Web page of the World Health Organization, a global organization that conducts research on and runs programs promoting world health: **www.who.ch.** From the WHO home page, select "Publications," then "World Health Report" for the most current year. Explore this document with an eye toward identifying information about the rates of disease and death in various nations and regions, and the impact of social and cultural factors on health and illness. Do the same thing for the United States at the Web sites of the Centers for Disease Control and Prevention **(www.cdc.gov)** and the American Public Health Association **(www.apha.org).**

The Internet also contains many resources regarding AIDS. The WHO, CDC, and APHA sites are very useful for AIDS research. On these sites, identify data on the extent and spread of AIDS currently in the United States and around the world. Are there any new developments since this text was published? In addition, locate organizations that are active in the fight against AIDS. What information can you find at these sites to illustrate issues discussed in this chapter? One of these organizations is the Gay Men's Health Crisis **(www.gmhc.org).**

The Allyn & Bacon Social Problems Supersite **(wps.ablongman.com/ab_socialprob_sprsite_1)** contains material on health and health-care institutions.

Key Terms

acute diseases

bioethics

chronic diseases

crisis medicine

curative medicine

health maintenance organization (HMO)

managed care

Medicaid

medical–industrial complex

Medicare

national health insurance

preventive medicine

primary deviance

secondary deviance

sick role

third-party medicine

Multiple-Choice Questions

1. The concept of the sick role is associated most clearly with which of the following perspectives?
   a. the functionalist perspective
   b. the conflict perspective
   c. the managed-care perspective
   d. the deinstitutionalization perspective

2. Which of the following statements would be most consistent with the interactionist perspective on health-care institutions?
   a. Health and health care are scarce resources, and interest groups compete with one another to gain a share of them.
   b. Disease is a threat to the social order because those who are ill are less able to make useful contributions to society.
   c. People attach social meanings to various illnesses and expect people to behave in conformity with those meanings.
   d. The health-care system involves an inequitable distribution of money, prestige, power, and other resources.

3. The most common cause of death in the United States today is
   a. acute disease.
   b. cancer.
   c. influenza and pneumonia.
   d. heart disease.
   e. cerebrovascular disease.

4. Which of the following statements is true regarding the impact of social factors on health?
   a. Men live longer than women.
   b. The poor have higher death rates than do the affluent.
   c. When looking at African Americans and Anglo Americans in the same social class, no differences in disease or death rates are found.
   d. All of the above are true.
   e. Only b and c are true.

5. Which of the following is *not* a criticism offered in the text for the community mental health approach to treating mental illness?
   a. It relies too heavily on the medical model.
   b. It does not accomplish many of its innovative goals.
   c. It sometimes releases mental patients to community settings that are not therapeutic for the patients.
   d. It does not reduce community stressors or promote social change.

6. Which of the following are factors that have contributed to rising health-care costs?
   a. a growing demand for health-care services

b. the growth of new diagnostic and treatment procedures

c. weak economic competition in the health-care field

d. All of the above are such factors.

e. Only b and c are such factors.

7. Concern over male dominance in the health field has been raised for all of the following reasons *except*

a. it restricts women's access to lucrative occupations.

b. it may have had a detrimental effect on the health care received by women.

c. it contributes to the problem of the medical–industrial complex.

d. it may lead to unnecessary treatments for women's health problems.

8. Which principle of social justice is most commonly used in the United States to decide how to allocate medical treatments?

a. merit

b. egalitarian

c. utilitarian

d. compensatory justice

e. secondary deviance

9. Which type of health-care financing arrangement pays for all of a person's health-care needs for a fixed premium each month or year?

a. medical–industrial complex

b. national health insurance

c. third-party medicine

d. socialized medicine

e. health maintenance organizations

10. Which of the following was *not* cited as a disadvantage in the Canadian health-care system in comparison with the United States?

a. Taxes are higher.

b. Patients sometimes wait for hospital beds.

c. Some advanced technology is not as widely available.

d. Health-care costs are higher.

True/False Questions

1. Worldwide, three-quarters of HIV infections are the result of homosexual intercourse.

2. The transition from preindustrial to industrial societies has been associated with a shift from chronic diseases to acute diseases as the most serious health threat.

3. As far as offering people a longer life, changes in lifestyles associated with industrialization have been at least as important as modern medical treatments.

4. Modern medical practice in the United States is organized more around preventive medicine than around crisis medicine.

5. Thomas Scheff's view of mental illness as "deviance" is based on the interactionist perspective more than the other two sociological perspectives.

6. The medical model of mental illness assumes that the basic nature of mental disorders is directly analogous to physical ailments.

7. National health expenditures today constitute a smaller percentage of the gross national product than was the case fifty years ago.

8. According to the text, the two groups in the United States that have been among the most severely underserved by the health-care system are inner-city residents and those residing in rural areas.

9. One of the problems with the Medicaid program is that eligibility levels are so high that many nonpoor families are eligible for it.

10. According to the text, the health-care system in Canada is an example of a truly socialized health-care system.

Fill-In Questions

1. According to the _____ perspective, the role of the health-care system in society is to return people to their normal social functioning.

2. The kinds of diseases that pose the most serious health threats to preindustrial societies are _____.

3. If a person labeled mentally ill becomes dependent on others for assistance because those others will not let the person do things for him- or herself, this dependence would be an example of _____ deviance.

4. The _____ approach to treating mental disorders assumes that the whole community is the client of the mental health provider.

5. When a patient pays premiums to a fund and the hospital or doctor is paid from this fund for each treatment provided the patient, this is a system of _____ medicine.

6. The _____ is the phenomenon in the health-care field that is analogous to the military–industrial complex.

7. The health occupation that has the largest percentage of females employed in it is _____.

8. The two bioethical issues discussed in the text are _____ and _____.

9. Medicare and Medicaid amount to _____ for the elderly and the poor.

10. _____ is illness or injury that occurs while a person is receiving medical treatment.

Matching Questions

_____ 1. secondary deviance

_____ 2. heart disease

_____ 3. crisis medicine

_____ 4. deinstitutionalization

_____ 5. third party in health financing

_____ **6.** compensatory justice
_____ **7.** Medicare
_____ **8.** Thomas Szasz
_____ **9.** preferred provider programs
_____ **10.** physicians' assistants

A. mental illness as problems of living
B. curative medicine
C. health insurance company
D. government health insurance for the elderly
E. chronic disease
F. HMOs
G. shift in mental health treatment settings
H. self-fulfilling prophecy
I. physician extender
J. principle to allocate health resources

Essay Questions

1. What concepts and assumptions does the interactionist perspective use to analyze and understand social problems in the health-care field? Use the example of AIDS to illustrate your answer.
2. Describe the impact of industrialization on human health and health-care institutions.
3. What is the impact of a person's socioeconomic status on that person's likelihood of getting sick or dying? Why does SES have this impact?
4. How do gender and race influence a person's chances of getting sick or dying? Why do these characteristics have this impact?
5. What is the community mental health approach to the treatment of mental illness? What are its advantages and disadvantages?
6. Explain why health-care costs have been rising in the United States over the past fifty years.
7. How much gender inequality exists in the health-care system in the United States? Why is it considered a problem?
8. Explain what problems are created by the privatization and corporatization of health care in the United States.
9. What are some of the benefits and some of the disadvantages of organizing health care around national health insurance or around health maintenance organizations?
10. What new health-care practitioners have emerged in the past few decades? Why have they emerged and what benefits do they offer?

For Further Reading

Marcia Angell. *The Truth About the Drug Companies: How They Deceive Us and What To Do About It.* New York: Random House, 2004. This is a well-researched and well-written argument about how pharmaceutical companies charge much more than they need to and provide less than people often think. It is a good description of the negative consequences of privatized health care and how one powerful group can influence the government to support them.

Grace Budrys. *Unequal Health: How Inequality Contributes to Health and Illness.* Blue Ridge Summit, PA: Rowman & Littlefield, 2003. This is an excellent overview of the research on how socioeconomic status and other social factors produce health disparities among people in the United States.

Daniel Callahan. *False Hopes: Why America's Quest for Perfect Health Is a Recipe for Failure.* New York: Simon & Schuster, 1998. The author makes a compelling argument for directing more of our resources toward preventive medicine rather than crisis medicine.

Suzanne Gordon. *Nursing Against the Odds: How Health Care Cost Cutting, Media Stereotypes and Medical Hubris Undermine Nurses and Patient Care.* Ithaca, NY: Cornell University Press, 2005. This critical work points to how the position of nurses in the structure of health care impedes the ability of the health care system to deliver top notch care—and how the structure should be changed.

Allan V. Horwitz and Teresa L. Scheid, eds. *A Handbook for the Study of Mental Health: Social Contexts, Theories, and Systems.* New York: Cambridge University Press, 1999. The articles in this book provide a comprehensive and up-to-date overview of the theories and research findings of sociologists on issues of mental health and illness; it covers the causes of mental illness as well as treatments and social policies related to it.

Judith Lorber and Lisa Jean Moore. *Gender and the Social Construction of Illness*, 2d ed. Walnut Creek, CA: Altamira Press, 2002. This book provides a valuable perspective on health and illness by showing how they are created and distributed as social problems based on such factors as gender.

John Mirowsky and Catherine E. Ross. *Social Causes of Psychological Distress*, 2d ed. Hawthorne, NY: Aldine de Gruyter, 2003. These authors present convincing evidence to show that mental illness, especially depression and anxiety, are profoundly influenced by some very important social conditions.

Howard Waitzkin. *At the Front Lines of Medicine: How the Health Care System Alienates Doctors and Mistreats Patients . . . and What We Can Do About It.* Blue Ridge Summit, PA: Rowman & Littlefield, 2004. This is a very thought-provoking critique of our current organization of health care and includes some interesting suggestions for change.

POVERTY

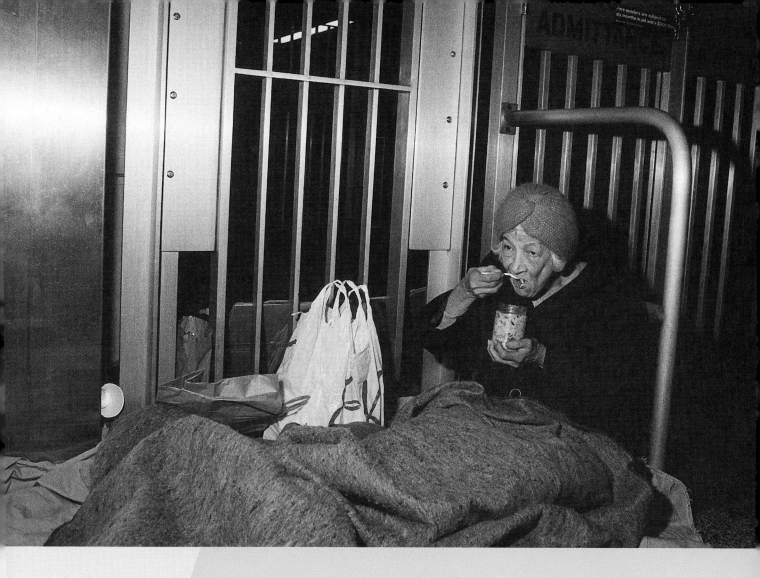

When it comes to economic resources, the United States is truly a nation of contrasts. We are, few would dispute, among the wealthiest nations in the world, and the signs of this opulence are not difficult to find. There are palatial mansions and fine automobiles. Expensive restaurants and clothing stores cater to the whims of those with large sums of money to spend. If not wealthy, most people in the United States are nevertheless quite comfortable materially, with spacious homes, luxurious cars, and more than adequate diets, along with computers, cell phones, and iPods.

Amidst this wealth, however, one in eight people lives below the officially defined poverty level. U.S. Census Bureau data consistently reveal the disturbing fact that one of every four children in Mississippi, Louisiana, New Mexico, Alabama, and Washington, DC, grows up in poverty (U.S. Bureau of the Census, 2006a). Despite the promises of virtually all politicians to ease the problem of poverty, the poverty rate today is at least as high as it was in the late 1960s and 1970s.

Why should we be concerned with the problem of poverty? One reason is that there is a discrepancy between our ideal culture, which calls for equal opportunity for all, and our real culture, in which social forces make it very difficult for some people to improve their lot. Beyond this, there are a number of practical concerns about the widespread existence of poverty: Unemployment, welfare, and other social costs of the poor are a substantial burden on all people; crime, illness, and other costly social conditions are linked with poverty; and poverty is a potential seedbed for social unrest, and even outright rebellion, that could threaten the political and social order.

The Extent of Poverty

Defining Poverty

People often think of poverty in terms of deprivation—being short of food, for example, or not having enough money to buy adequate clothing. This is somewhat misleading, however. There have been many societies in which people, by our standards today, were severely deprived, yet poverty did not really exist. The reason is that virtually everyone was so deprived. In societies in which there was little accumulation of food or material resources, everyone had pretty much the same access to the resources available. When a surplus of resources exists, however, it is possible for some people to accumulate more than others. There then emerges a system of **social stratification,** *the ranking of people into a hierarchy in which the resources considered valuable by society are unequally distributed.* With this development, people could be differentiated from one another based on how much of those valuable resources they possessed. Those with the least could be defined as "poor"—so deficient in resources that they could not maintain a lifestyle considered minimally acceptable in that society. Thus, **poverty** does not refer to a deprivation of resources alone but to *an uneven distribution of the resources available.*

Defining poverty becomes even more complex, however, when we try to specify what a "minimally

Myths & Facts

About the Poor

Myth: The poor are a drain on the public treasury that affluent citizens have to support out of their hard-earned dollars.

Fact: Both the poor and the affluent in the United States are a drain on the treasury, and both pay to support it. Whereas some poor people receive welfare and other government assistance, the affluent receive government handouts such as loans for college students, price-support payments to farmers, and tax deductions for meals and entertainment expenses connected with business. In addition, when all taxes—on income, sales, investments, and so on—are looked at, there is considerable debate over whether the affluent or the working poor pay a larger percentage of their income in taxes. So, the similarity is that both the affluent and the poor receive public assistance in the United States; the difference is that the poor are labeled disreputable and stigmatized for doing so.

Myth: Receiving welfare payments encourages women to have more children, to leave their husbands, and to avoid work.

Fact: Although these beliefs about the negative effects of welfare are strongly entrenched in the public mind, the best social research on the topic suggests that most are wrong (Jencks, 1992; Rank, 1994). Women on welfare actually have a lower birthrate than nonwelfare women of equivalent age and social standing. Welfare also has little effect on whether women marry or divorce. Life on welfare is a difficult struggle, both physically and psychologically, and few people seek it out voluntarily. The one part of the myth that does hold some truth is the work disincentive: Before recent changes in the welfare laws, welfare did encourage people to avoid work but for reasons different from what is often thought. Welfare recipients avoid work because much of what they earn is lost due to reduced welfare benefits and lost government health insurance. So, they simply do not get ahead by working in many cases.

acceptable lifestyle" is. In fact, there is probably no completely satisfactory definition of poverty. Three such definitions are widely used today (Burtless and Smeeding, 2001).

ABSOLUTE DEPRIVATION Some definitions of poverty attempt to establish an economic level below which people are unable to achieve the basic necessities of life. But what are the "necessities" of life? A reliable automobile? A color television with a satellite dish? A summer vacation at the beach? While recognizing that "necessities" is a somewhat relative term, we can nonetheless define it in terms of a diet, clothing, housing, medical care, and the like that will enable people to remain healthy and productive. Nutritionists, for example, can tell us what constitutes a minimally adequate diet. You do not need a steak to maintain health, but the human body does need a certain amount of protein, vitamins, and minerals from some food sources. Likewise, a house without indoor plumbing might be viewed as unacceptable in modern times because of the health hazard it creates. The point of this **absolute definition of poverty** is that *it establishes a fixed economic level below which people are considered poor, and this level does not necessarily change as society on the whole becomes more or less affluent.*

Government programs for the poor in the United States are based on this absolute definition of poverty. For such programs, a fixed annual income cutoff point is established below which people will be unable to purchase what are considered the necessities of life. In the 1960s, Mollie Orshansky, then a social research analyst with the Social Security Administration, developed an ingenious and somewhat objective technique for establishing the poverty level, a technique still in use today (Bernstein, 2003). It is based on how much it costs to buy a nutritionally adequate diet. Once the amount of money necessary for this has been established, it is multiplied by three to arrive at the poverty income, based on the fact that the average family in the United States spends one-third of its income on food. Thus, three times the cost of food is assumed to provide adequate income for food, housing, medical care, and the other necessities of life. Actually, the poverty level is a series of income cutoffs based on factors that can increase a family's cost of living, such as the size of the family.

RELATIVE DEPRIVATION According to the **relative definition of poverty,** *people are poor relative to some standard, and that standard is partially shaped by the lifestyles of other citizens.* A lack of indoor plumbing is considered a sign of poverty today, whereas a century ago that was the norm for many people. But people usually compare themselves with their contemporaries, not their predecessors. People look around and see what most others have and assess their own lives based on that comparison. To take this relative nature of poverty into account, one suggestion might be to define the poor as those families who are on the lowest end of the income scale, say the 15 percent of the people with the lowest income. Or, the poor may be defined as people in those families with incomes less than one-third of the median family income in the United States. In the mid-2000s, this was $20,000 and included about 12 percent of all families. Such a definition means that poverty would always exist, irrespective of how affluent society became. The poor would be those who share least in such affluence. In fact, using the relative definition, poverty could be eliminated only if the inequitable distribution of resources were eliminated.

CULTURAL DEFINITIONS Absolute and relative approaches to poverty define it as the economic resources necessary to achieve a certain lifestyle. However, some have argued that poverty is a cultural as well as an economic condition. The **cultural definition of poverty** *views poverty not only in terms of how many resources people have, but also in terms of why they have failed to achieve a higher economic level.* For example, some people are poor because they have no skills that would enable them to get a job. Others are poor because they have young children at home and cannot afford day care while they work. Still others are poor because they have chosen to go to college and endure temporary low income in order to enhance their earning power in the future.

Using this cultural definition of poverty, the poor are identified as those who are permanently and unwillingly poor. These are people who are likely to remain poor for a long time, possibly generations, and it is toward them that poverty programs should be directed. This would probably include most of the people who are defined as poor when using purely economic criteria, but it would exclude people such as college students who temporarily and willingly choose poverty. The rationale for this is that the real problem of poverty lies with the chronic long-term poor. College students who are poor, although suffering some personal troubles, are not really a societal problem because they will likely improve their circumstances in a relatively brief period. This cultural definition of poverty avoids the rigidities of strict economic definitions and enables us to direct resources toward the entrenched problem of poverty.

Which one of the preceding definitions of poverty is used, of course, depends on people's values. The absolute definition is used in many social policy decisions today, and it reflects widely held values in the United States regarding the role of the government in poverty problems. It especially reflects the belief of many that the government should provide equal opportunities for people to achieve resources rather than ensure an equitable distribution of those resources. In this view, the government's role is to provide people with the minimum necessary resources that will enable them to achieve on their own. Whether people then realize such achievement is regarded by many as a personal matter.

The Extent of Poverty in the United States

The official poverty level in the United States, then, is based on the absolute definition of poverty. In 2005, a family of four people with an annual income of less than $20,144 was considered by the government to be poor (see Table 5.1). This meant that 37 million people in the United States—approximately one out of every eight citizens—were living in poverty. Throughout the 1980s and much of the 1990s, the poverty rate was considerably higher than it had been in the 1970s (see Figure 5.1). In 2005, the poverty rate was 12.6 percent, and more people were poor in 2005 than in 1970. Furthermore, the gap between the nonpoor and the poor has been growing as the median family income has increased at a faster rate than the poverty cutoff. The poverty cutoff income was 54 percent of median family income in 1960, whereas it is 35 percent today. So, using the relative definition of poverty, the poor are worse off today than they were forty years ago.

Another way to assess the status of the poor relative to an earlier time is to look at what percentage of the total income in the United States goes to poor families. Once again, the poor seem worse off today. As Figure 5.2 shows, the percentage of income going to the poorest households has declined since the 1960s. Today, the poorest 20 percent of households receives less than 4 percent of the total income while the wealthiest 20 percent receives over 50 percent. Furthermore, these disparities have increased over the past three decades. In fact, the only group who saw its share of the total income increase is the wealthiest 20 percent of households. The maldistribution of resources is even more striking when one looks at wealth (earned income plus stocks, savings, equity in a home, and other economic resources) rather than just income. The top 20 percent of U.S. households possess 80 percent of the total wealth (Wolff, 1995). This topic has been hotly debated, but most analysts agree with what Figure 5.2 suggests: In the last forty years in the United States, the rich have gotten richer and the poor have gotten poorer (Alperovitz, 2004; Mishel, Bernstein, and Schmitt, 2001). Also, poverty seems to have become more chronic, with people who fall into poverty today remaining poor for longer periods than was true in the 1960s and 1970s. As if all this were not enough, poverty also seems to have become more dysfunctional for the individual and society, with the drug epidemic and the growth in homelessness hindering individual efforts to overcome poverty and confronting society with serious challenges.

The absolute approach to defining poverty provided by the Orshansky poverty cutoffs is used by the government for making social policy decisions, such as who is eligible for various government programs. These cutoffs, however, do have flaws as an accurate measure of people's economic circumstances. One such flaw is that the assumptions for establishing the

TABLE 5.1   People in Poverty in the United States and Poverty Income, 1960–2005

Year	Number of People Below Poverty Level (Millions)	Percentage of Total Population	Poverty Income Cutoff for a Family of Four	Median Family Income of All Families
1960	39.9	22.2	$3,022	$5,620
1970	25.4	12.6	3,968	9,867
1980	29.3	13.0	8,414	21,023
1990	33.6	13.5	13,359	35,353
2000	31.1	11.3	17,463	49,350
2005	36.9	12.6	20,144	57,278

SOURCES: U.S. Bureau of the Census, *Current Population Reports*, Series P60–221, "Money Income in the United States: 2002," (Washington, DC: U.S. Government Printing Office, 2003); U.S. Bureau of the Census, *Current Population Reports*, Series P60–231, "Income, Poverty, and Health Insurance Coverage in the United States: 2005" (Washington, DC: U.S. Government Printing Office, 2006).

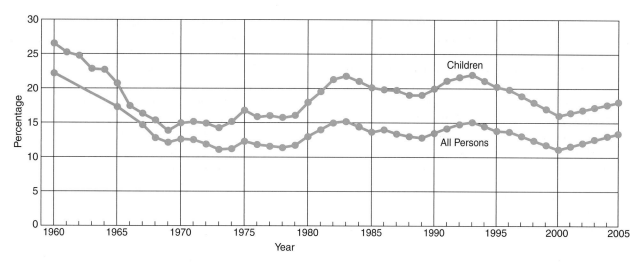

FIGURE 5.1   **Percentage of People Living Below the Poverty Level, Among All People and Among Children Under Eighteen Years of Age, in the United States, 1960–2005.**

Source: U.S. Bureau of the Census, *Current Population Reports*, Series P60–231, "Income, Poverty, and Health Insurance Coverage in the United States: 2005" (Washington, DC: U.S. Government Printing Office, 2006).

poverty thresholds were defined in the 1950s and 1960s based on family consumption patterns and basic needs of that era, and things have changed since then. For example, the poverty index relies on the purchase of food in determining the poverty level. However, for some poor people, especially in urban areas, other expenses such as housing or child care for working parents can consume a larger share of the family income than they do for the average family in the United States. In earlier decades, families spent 34 percent of their income on housing, whereas today it is more like 42 percent. Despite changes such as

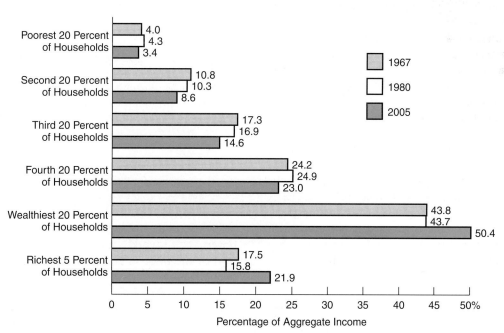

FIGURE 5.2   **Percentage of Aggregate Income to Households from the Poorest 20 Percent to the Richest 5 Percent, 1967–2005.**

Source: U.S. Bureau of the Census, *Current Population Reports*, Series P60–231, "Income, Poverty, and Health Insurance Coverage in the United States: 2005" (Washington, DC: U.S. Government Printing Office, 2006).

these, the poverty cutoffs are still based on the old assumptions. Economists project that today's poverty line would have to be as much as 25 percent higher to be comparable, in terms of the ability to buy food and other basic needs, to the standard established in 1963. If this were the poverty cutoff today, the poverty rate would be 15 percent or more instead of 12 percent (Bernstein, 2003).

A Global View of Poverty

By the standards of many nations around the world, many poor in the United States would be considered reasonably well off. Some people in other nations live in absolute poverty that is so stark and dehumanizing that it is difficult for people in the United States to imagine. For these people, survival itself is a struggle. Few, if any, of the poor in the United States would fall into this category. In nations such as Nicaragua, Zambia, and Madagascar, as many as 50 percent of the people may live in poverty (United Nations, 2006). Compared to these nations, the United States is well off. However, as Figure 5.3 demonstrates, it is not so well off when compared to other industrial nations. In that comparison, U.S. poverty rates tend to be significantly higher, especially among children.

Figure 5.2 shows a very lopsided distribution of wealth in the United States. Are we out of line in this regard in comparison to other nations? It depends on to whom we compare ourselves (Wolff, 1995; World Bank, 2004). In many less-developed countries around the world—such as Paraguay, Pakistan, Brazil, and South Africa—the wealthiest 20 percent of the families earn 60 percent or more of the family income. In Brazil and Paraguay, the poorest 20 percent of the families receive only 2 percent of annual income—a very small share indeed! So, the United States has a more equitable distribution of wealth than do these nations. In comparison to other wealthy nations in the world, however, the U.S. income distribution is somewhat lopsided. In only three of the twenty wealthiest nations do the top 20 percent of the families receive as large a share of income as in the United States; in none of these twenty nations does the bottom fifth receive as small a share as in the United States. For example, the wealthiest 1 percent of households in the United States possesses nearly 40 percent of the nation's wealth. By contrast, the wealthiest 1 percent of households in Britain possesses only 18 percent of that nation's wealth. In addition, trends of the past century have produced higher levels of inequality in the United States while the trend in Britain has been toward reducing levels of inequality (Smeeding, 1997).

FIGURE 5.3 **Poverty Rates in Selected Industrial Nations (data from the mid–1990s).**

Source: Timothy M. Smeeding, Lee Rainwater, and Gary Burtless, "U.S. Poverty in a Cross-National Context." In Sheldon H. Danziger and Robert H. Haverman (eds.), *Understanding Poverty* (New York: Russell Sage Foundation and Harvard University Press, 2001), p. 173. Reprinted with permission of Timothy Smeeding and the Harvard University Press.

Who Are the Poor?

A few years ago, a popular bumper sticker read: "I fight poverty . . . I work!" Implied in this is a characterization of the poor as lazy and somewhat disreputable people who are poor because of their own unwillingness to work for a living. This highly stigmatizing view of the poor is quite popular in the United States, where a majority believes that a willingness to work is the primary ingredient necessary to achieve at least a modest degree of success (Scott and Leonhardt, 2005). Assessing the veracity of these beliefs is central to developing a social policy for the United States regarding poverty. A first step in this direction is understanding who the poor people are in this country.

Social Characteristics

RACIAL AND ETHNIC MINORITIES Contrary to what many people believe, most of the poor in the United States—67 percent—are white (see Figure 5.4). Looking at each racial group separately, however, nonwhites are more likely to be poor than are whites. Although 25 percent of African Americans and 22 percent of Hispanic Americans are below the poverty cutoff, only 8 percent of whites are at that income level (see Figure 5.5). About 25 percent of American Indians have incomes below the official poverty level. Asian Americans as a group have slightly higher levels of poverty than whites—11 percent of Asian and Pacific Islanders. Some Asian groups have quite high poverty levels, however, with 61.5 percent of all first-generation Laotian and Cambodian families living in poverty, as well as 25 percent of all first-generation Vietnamese families. For Asian Americans, poverty is closely linked with the recency of their immigration experience (Lee, 1994). So although nonwhite families constitute a relatively small proportion of our populace, they contribute disproportionately to the ranks of the poor.

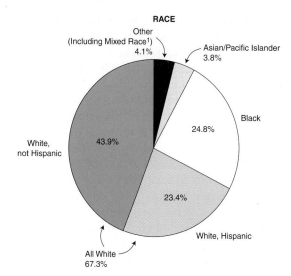

FIGURE 5.4 **People Living Below the Poverty Level by Race as a Percentage of All Poor People, 2005.**

[1]In the Census survey, people were allowed to choose more than one race to identify themselves, if they wished. The relatively few people who did so are included in this category.

Source: U.S. Bureau of the Census, *Current Population Reports*, Series P60–231, "Income, Poverty, and Health Insurance Coverage in the United States: 2005" (Washington, DC: U.S. Government Printing Office, 2006).

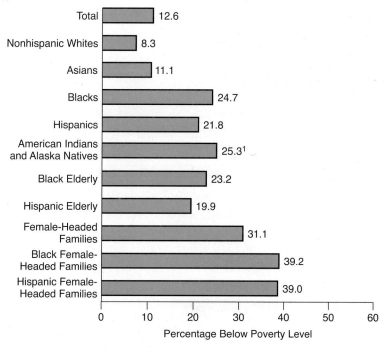

FIGURE 5.5 **Percentage of People in Various Groups Below the Poverty Level, 2005.**

[1]Three-year average, 2003–2005.

Source: U.S. Bureau of the Census, *Current Population Reports*, Series P60–231, "Income, Poverty, and Health Insurance Coverage in the United States: 2005" (Washington, DC: U.S. Government Printing Office, 2006).

The reasons for these racial and ethnic differences are complex and will be dealt with in more detail later in this chapter and in Chapter 6. However, a key factor in all cases has been oppression and discrimination. African Americans have felt the brunt of slavery and, after the abolition of slavery, decades of severe oppression during which it was difficult for black families to advance from poverty. Hispanics, especially those of Mexican and Puerto Rican ancestry, have also experienced a great deal of discrimination in their efforts to establish a niche in the United States. American Indians have confronted some unique problems in the form of the reservation system and the Bureau of Indian Affairs (BIA), which were intended to work for the benefit of Indians but seem instead to have worked to their disadvantage.

CHILDREN Thirty-four percent of the poor are children under the age of eighteen, and more than half of these children live in single-parent families headed by women. Close to one-third of all black and Hispanic children live in poverty, which will make it more difficult for the next generation of racial and ethnic

minorities to lift themselves out of poverty (see Figure 5.6). Children living in large families are especially likely to live in poverty. This is so because economic resources must be spread more thinly in a large family and because the mother is less able to work outside the home when she has many children. The large number of children among the poor serves to deflate the belief that poverty derives from a lack of initiative because we presume that children are not responsible for supporting themselves. This tendency toward poverty shows no sign of ceasing for the youngest of the U.S. citizenry. Poverty rates among children are as high today as they were thirty years ago (see Figure 5.1). A major reason for the persistently high poverty among children is changes in the family structure in the United States—higher divorce rates, more children born to unmarried women, and more female-headed families (Cancian and Reed, 2001). All this means that children today are more likely to live in a single-parent household headed by a woman. Almost half of children living in such families are poor—five times the rate for children in two-parent households (see Figure 5.6). In addition, the parents of poor

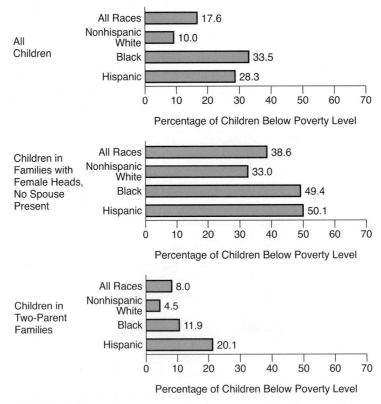

FIGURE 5.6 **Percentage of Children Younger Than Eighteen Living Below the Poverty Level, 2005.**

Source: U.S. Bureau of the Census, *Current Population Survey, 2006: Annual Social and Economic Supplement* (Washington, DC: U.S. Government Printing Office, 2006).

children today are younger—the teenage pregnancy rate is far higher than that in most other industrial nations (see Chapter 3). Finally, young workers today earn relatively less than did young workers in the past. The consequence of all this is that poor children today have fewer resources available to them and live in worse circumstances than did poor children thirty years ago.

THE ELDERLY Although poverty among the elderly is relatively low—slightly lower than among nonelderly adult Americans—the figure is much higher for African American, Hispanic American, and female elderly. The special problems of the elderly are dealt with in more detail in Chapter 8.

WOMEN A development that has been viewed with some alarm in recent years is what has been labeled the "feminization of poverty," referring to the growing number of women among the poor. Despite the increasing emphasis on equality between the sexes in recent years, women, especially those who head their own households, have made little progress. In 2005, for example, 12 percent of all people lived below the poverty level, whereas in single-parent families headed by a woman it was 31 percent (see Figure 5.5). Things may actually be getting worse in some respects: In 1959, 23 percent of all families in poverty were headed by women; today, this figure has grown to just over 50 percent. However, the poverty rate in single-parent female-headed families is now lower than it was in 1959 (see Figure 5.7). As is discussed in Chapter 3, the growth in single-parent female-headed families is due to changes in the structure of the family in the

United States that can be traced back to at least the 1930s. Basically, the family has gotten smaller due to divorce, the decline in extended families, and increasing childbearing by single women. Because of global economic competition and other factors discussed in Chapter 2, young men today are over twice as likely to earn poverty-level wages compared to thirty years ago and thus are less able to support a wife or children. For this and other reasons, husbands, grandmothers, unmarried aunts, and other unattached females have departed from the family, leaving women alone to raise their children. These women alone offer their families substantially less economic support than do women who also have an economically productive husband, grandmother, or aunt living in the family and helping out. In addition, the incomes of women still lag far behind those of men (see Chapter 7). Evidence indicates that growing up in a female-headed family increases the risk that children will still be poor as adults (Cancian and Reed, 2001). However, this is probably caused primarily by the decreased availability of economic and other resources in such families rather than to the absence of a father figure.

CENTRAL-CITY AND RURAL DWELLERS Poverty tends to be concentrated in certain places in the United States, particularly in the centers of cities and in rural areas. Forty percent of the poor live in central-city areas, places with high unemployment and few places to find work (U.S. Bureau of the Census, 2006a). One-quarter of the poor live outside metropolitan areas. Pockets of poverty can be found in rural parts of the South, Southwest, the Ozarks, Appalachia, and the Upper Great Lakes region.

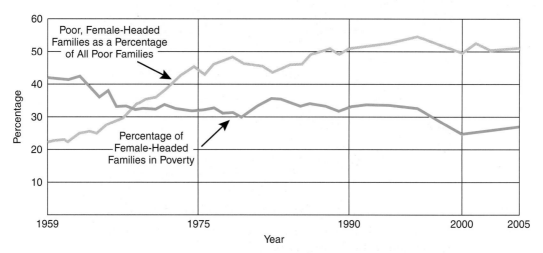

FIGURE 5.7 **Poverty Rate of Single-Parent Families Headed by a Woman, 1959–2005.**
Source: U.S. Bureau of the Census, *Current Population Reports*, Series P60–231, "Income, Poverty, and Health Insurance Coverage in the United States: 2005" (Washington, DC: U.S. Government Printing Office, 2006).

THE DISABLED Poverty is often associated with physical disability (McNeil, 2001). As many as one-third of the poor suffer from severe physical disabilities, while another 7 percent have non-severe disabilities. These disabilities, especially the severe ones, make it impossible for some poor people to work or limit the kinds and amounts of work that other poor people can do.

Social Circumstances

Because most poor are "invisible" or conveniently out of sight to most people in the United States, it is easy to believe that the poor lead a leisurely, if Spartan, lifestyle while feeding at the public trough. Reality is actually quite different from this.

THE WORKING POOR Despite common misconceptions, many adults below the official poverty level actually work for a living (Shipler, 2004). Approximately 60 percent of poor families had at least one family member working, with 24 percent of them having at least one member working full-time year-round (U.S. Bureau of the Census, 2006a). Only one-third of poor families receive cash public assistance income, although others receive such government assistance as unemployment benefits, Social Security payments, disability assistance, government pensions, and the like. Forty percent of all poor families receive no noncash benefits, such as food stamps or Medicaid, from the government. So, income earned from work is essential for many poor families to support themselves.

THE UNEMPLOYED The picture presented of the working poor does not support the popular image that many people have of the poor as able-bodied people who are unwilling to work; to the contrary, many poor people do work at low-paying or part-time jobs (Rank, 1994). In addition, the circumstances of the poor who do not work also do not support this popular image. Many of these unemployed poor are either ill, disabled, retired, or have looked for work but could not find it. Others are prevented from working by child rearing or other family obligations. Still others have given up on trying to find work after years with no success.

The unemployed receive unemployment benefits for a time, but these are exhausted eventually. When they do end, the unemployed person may still have payments to make on a home mortgage or an automobile loan. Some of the unemployed become eligible for welfare assistance when unemployment benefits end, but not all unemployed are

This mother and her children in front of their ramshackle home live in Eastern Kentucky. They illustrate the fact that many of the poor are children living in single-parent families headed by women who can't find work to support their families.

eligible for welfare. To be eligible, people may have to sell their homes and use up most of their savings. Temporary unemployment, then, could devastate a family that had worked and accumulated resources over the years.

THE HOMELESS Some of the poor are homeless, with no permanent residence. The most careful estimates by sociologists are that as many as four hundred thousand people may be homeless in the United States on any given night, with as many as fifty thousand of them being children (Bogard, 2003; Wright, Rubin, and Devine, 1998). Other estimates are higher, but it is a difficult thing to measure with any precision. A more disturbing fact is that 40 percent of the homeless are families—parents and children out on the street—double the percentage of two decades ago. The causes of this disturbing problem can be found in recent social trends, especially the decline in the number of industrial jobs that pay a living wage (see Chapter 2), the flight of jobs from the cities where poor people live, the contraction of social welfare, increases in the numbers of people living in poverty, and the decline in the amount of low-cost housing available. These factors coming together mean that more people are wandering the countryside, searching for a job and living out of their car or truck. Some sleep on park benches, in subway stations, or in steam tunnels. Some eventually land a job and find housing, but others live on the streets for years. Homelessness is also linked with the trends in our health-care institutions: At least one-quarter of the homeless are mentally ill people who in earlier decades had a fair chance of being housed and taken care of in a state or private mental hospital. However, because of the process of "deinstitutionalizing" the mentally ill, which began a number of decades ago (see Chapter 4), very few such mental hospital beds are available today, and so these mentally ill are now treated in community settings. The reality is that many of these mentally ill in the community receive little in the way of psychological or financial assistance and some are homeless, at least for periods of time.

The Causes of Poverty

Programs intended to alleviate poverty must rest on a clear understanding of its causes, and those causes are complex. People often focus on the weaknesses or failures of individuals as the causes of poverty and ignore the role that societal factors play in generating widespread poverty. The three sociological perspectives remedy this.

The Functionalist Perspective

THE STRATIFICATION SYSTEM Functionalists argue that stratification exists because it makes some useful contribution to the ongoing maintenance of society. According to sociologists Kingsley Davis and Wilbert Moore (1945), for instance, all societies must ensure that people will fill essential positions and perform important tasks. Somebody must produce food, build shelter, heal the sick, and raise the young. If these tasks are not accomplished, society cannot survive. However, some positions and tasks are more important or more difficult than others. For example, physicians are more crucial than janitors, and it takes more skill to be a judge than an assembly line worker. Some positions call for scarce natural talents or qualities, whereas others require extensive and difficult training. The stratification system serves to motivate people to occupy and work hard at all of these essential positions. People who fill the more difficult or more essential tasks are given greater rewards—both economic and social—as a consequence.

Thus, the stratification system in society is an essential mechanism for differentially allocating rewards in order to motivate people to perform socially useful tasks. Furthermore, according to the functionalist view, people who do not perform useful tasks should receive fewer rewards. Poverty, then, is society's mechanism to discourage people from neglecting their social duties. If those who do not work were to receive the same rewards as those who do, then many people would choose not to work and society might be threatened.

There has been an ongoing debate over Davis and Moore's functionalist approach to poverty: Are rewards really related to the importance of a position or to the scarcity of qualified personnel to fill it? There does appear to be a relationship between the contributions that people make to society and the rewards they receive (Cullen and Novick, 1979). However, some studies have found that the importance of positions is unrelated to the rewards people receive (Wanner and Lewis, 1978). In addition, a study of public school teachers over a forty-year span showed little support for the functionalist prediction that incomes of teachers would be higher when the supply of teachers was scarce (Betz, Davis, and Miller, 1978). Thus, although these functionalist factors may play a part in causing poverty, there are clearly many exceptions. Even when the functionalist argument is true, it cannot account for the vast disparities between the well-to-do and the poor. Clearly, some people earn far more than would seem warranted by their contribution to society and others make far less. When the link between what a person does and what he or she

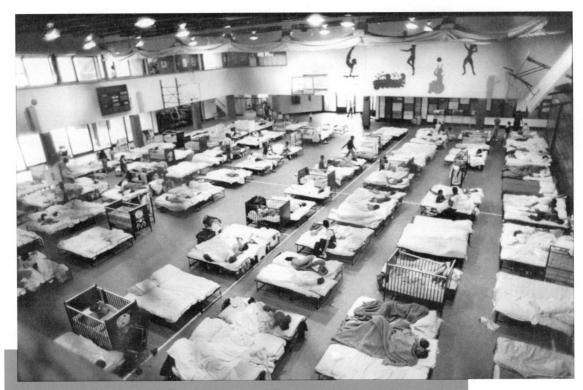

This is a shelter for homeless families in New York City. On any given night in the United States, forty percent of the homeless are families, and as many as fifty thousand are children.

receives becomes vague or broken entirely, then social disorganization can result. People no longer believe that work will be rewarded, and the stratification system no longer serves as the motivation that it is intended to be. In addition, if people are prevented from making a contribution—because of discrimination in the job market, for example—then a similar sense of disorganization can occur.

THE ECONOMY According to the functionalist perspective, society is made up of many interrelated and interdependent parts, and a change in one part can have implications for the other parts. In the realm of poverty, normal and sometimes desirable changes in the economy can affect the level of poverty. One of these changes has to do with inflation. Many economists believe that unemployment is related to inflation. As unemployment drops, more people are working and have money to buy things. This demand for goods causes prices to rise, producing inflation. To reduce inflation, then, it may be necessary at times to let unemployment increase. This was the policy followed by the Reagan Administration in the 1980s. Inflation dropped, but unemployment and poverty increased (see Figure 5.1). In this view, then,

a certain amount of poverty is an unfortunate side effect of maintaining other elements of the economy.

Another important source of economic change has been technological innovation, which has brought such improvements as automation. But automation can throw people out of work and reduce the number of jobs in the economy, contributing to the problem of poverty. In addition to automation, another type of economic change is the rise and decline of various economic sectors. For a good part of this century, heavy industries such as steel and automobile manufacturing were booming. In the past few decades, these industries have been on the decline.

These kinds of changes, some economists argue, are necessary for a healthy economy, but their cumulative impact is to increase rates of unemployment and poverty. This is sometimes called **structural unemployment** because *it is a part of the very structure of the economy.* Some of the growth in economic inequality described previously in this chapter is undoubtedly due to these kinds of structural changes (Rank, 2004).

THE FUNCTIONS OF POVERTY According to some functionalists, one of the reasons that poverty persists is that it performs some positive functions for society or at least for some groups in society. Although it is difficult to think of poverty in this light, this view illustrates a point that has been made elsewhere: Social conditions or practices that some find undesirable or even repugnant, such as poverty or crime, may nonetheless make a positive contribution to society. How can poverty be functional? Herbert J. Gans (1994) suggests that among the benefits to society from poverty are

1. The existence of poverty ensures that society's "dirty work" will be done. There are many boring, underpaid, or undignified occupations that most people would prefer not to do, even though they need to be done. Jobs such as washing dishes, scrubbing floors, or picking farm produce would probably go undone unless people either received high wages to do them or had no other choice. The poor have little choice and are essentially coerced into taking these "dirty" jobs.

2. Poverty subsidizes many of the activities of the more affluent because the poor are willing to work for low wages. For example, the poor do domestic work and housecleaning for the affluent, which frees the affluent to engage in professional, cultural, or leisure activities.

3. Poverty creates jobs for all those people who serve the poor, such as social workers, or who protect society from them, such as police and corrections officers.

4. Poverty creates a market for inferior goods and services that others will not buy. The poor buy day-old bread, run-down automobiles, and secondhand clothes. They also rent deteriorating apartments in run-down neighborhoods that would otherwise go vacant. Needless to say, the people who sell these goods and services benefit from the poor.

5. The poor help to support and symbolize the status of the nonpoor by serving as the official "losers" or "underdogs" in the societal race for success. In a hierarchical society such as ours, some people have to be on the bottom, and this lets everyone else know where they stand. Relative to the poor, the nonpoor can feel that they have "made it."

One function of poverty is that the poor subsidize the lifestyles of the more affluent by working at low-paying jobs, such as this shoe-shine person who makes it possible for the affluent to have such personal services by providing the services for low wages.

Structural Sources of Entrenched Poverty

For some people, poverty is a temporary status out of which they will ultimately move, whereas for others poverty is more permanent, sometimes persisting from one generation to the next. This latter group has presented researchers and policymakers with the greatest challenge in terms of relieving poverty. It is a group whose members are severely disadvantaged, isolated from mainstream society, and living in communities with limited access to the resources that might enable them to improve their lot. For this group, chronic unemployment is the norm, crime is taken for granted, and welfare is a fact of life (Devine and Wright, 1993; Jargowsky, 1997).

Researchers have studied the circumstances of this group in some detail and found out quite a bit about the causes of their plight.

Sociologist William J. Wilson (1987; 1996) traced this group's problems to some fundamental structural changes in the economy over the past several decades, such as the transition from a product-based manufacturing economy to an information-based service economy. The entrenched poor are without the skills or work experience useful in the latter type of economy, which places more emphasis on verbal talent and educational qualifications than on physical brawn and manual labor. Another basic change in the U.S. economy has been the relocation of industries away from the communities where poor people live. This has occurred for a number of reasons, such as government policies providing funds to build new housing in the suburbs and freeways to get there (see Chapter 12). The outcome has been that

factories, businesses, and jobs have fled poor neighborhoods.

The labor market in modern industrial economies has also changed in such a way that people with no work skills or little education are hard pressed to compete successfully for most jobs. At one time, there were ample jobs for people with strong backs and a willingness to work. By contrast, in today's economy, in which a high school degree (and, increasingly, post-high school training) is the entry-level requirement for most jobs, people who lack these credentials are relegated to the lowest-paying jobs or, increasingly, to no jobs at all (Perrucci and Wysong, 2002).

Furthermore, changes in the communities in which poor people live have contributed to the problems of the entrenched poor. In particular, as employers have abandoned the inner city, so too

The Conflict Perspective

Most conflict views of poverty derive at least in part from the view of Karl Marx, and his position contrasts sharply with that of the functionalists. Marx viewed society as involving a constant struggle between social classes over scarce resources, with some groups managing to capture more of these resources than others. This results in the inequitable distribution of resources that makes up the stratification systems of modern societies. Yet this unequal distribution, said Marx, has little to do with rewarding talent or filling important positions. Instead, people gain desirable positions in the stratification system through coercion, exploitation, and possibly inheritance. Once their position is acquired, they work to protect it against inroads by less fortunate groups. This can be done in many ways. For example, employers seek the cheapest labor possible because this increases their profits. The tax system is used to benefit the more affluent who can use tax loopholes, unavailable to the less affluent, to avoid

paying their share of income tax. Even the legal system tends to benefit the affluent. The crimes they commit, such as business fraud, are less likely to be detected and punished than are the crimes of the poor, such as assault and armed robbery.

It should not be surprising that the affluent benefit in these ways, because it is the affluent who write the tax laws, design the legal system, and pay the police to enforce the law. For Marx, the affluent are merely using the resources available to them to protect their own position. There is an even more subtle way in which dominant groups can protect their position: They can convince subordinate groups that the existing distribution of resources is "natural" or preferable to any other. This is done in part by persuading the poor that they, too, can become affluent. Through schools and the media, for example, people can be taught to believe that everyone will be successful if they apply themselves. The implication of this belief, of course, is that poverty is caused by one's not having worked hard enough. Being poor, then, is one's own fault. This

have the working- and middle-class people who held those jobs, leaving behind the poorer residents. When the working people and nonpoor leave, so do many of the small businesses and merchants, who prefer to relocate elsewhere. The consequence is that poor neighborhoods eventually contain mostly the poor and the unemployed. In addition, without working people living in the community, there are fewer respectable role models for the young to look up to. The role models remaining are more commonly those who do not work, who commit crimes, or who abuse drugs. When the youth in poor communities look around, they see little reason to have high aspirations because none of the people they see in their community seems to have achieved much success (Small and Newman, 2001; Wilson, 1991).

Racial discrimination also contributes to the existence of entrenched poverty: Because of stereotyping and racism, some employers are reluctant to hire African Americans. Considerable applied research documents that employers direct hiring efforts toward white neighborhoods and prefer not to recruit inner-city blacks, especially males (Jencks, 1992; Neckerman and Kirschenman, 1991).

Using their research as a foundation, Wilson and other sociologists have made recommendations to Congress and other government agencies about what to do to help the entrenched poor. Their recommendations basically suggest ways in which the negative impact of the economic structural changes on people's lives can be alleviated. In particular, they focus on programs to provide people with the education

and skills necessary to find good jobs in a postindustrial society. They point out that programs that expand job opportunities for those with good job qualifications, such as college graduates, will not have an impact on the entrenched poor. Wilson even criticizes affirmative-action programs on the grounds that they benefit affluent minorities rather than the poor. What is needed are programs to provide people with the basic literacy skills, a high school diploma, or other qualifications needed to gain entry into a modern service-based economy. Research shows that the poor, especially the youth, want to work and are willing to work (Freeman and Holzer, 1986; Newman, 1999). It is not desire or ambition that they lack, but rather the opportunity to find jobs that pay enough to enable them to support their families in a respectable fashion.

belief deflects people's attention from the societal structures and barriers that contribute to maintaining some groups in power. Poverty is viewed as a personal problem rather than a societal one, and the poor are less inclined to demand changes in the system.

Once people have become successful, they tend to pass on their success to their children, and this makes it more difficult for people on the bottom to move up. **Social mobility** refers to *the movement of people from one social position to another in the stratification hierarchy.* Although upward social mobility is fairly widespread in the United States, our stratification system is also characterized by considerable stability with a high degree of occupational inheritance. Most of the mobility that occurs is short range, such as the child of a blue-collar worker who advances to a somewhat better-paying blue-collar job. For the most part, children tend to take jobs that are not too different in socioeconomic status from those of their parents (Featherman and Hauser, 1978; Hout, 1988). Furthermore, children of the affluent have much greater access to a good educa-

tion, which has become a key requirement for success. In addition, growing up poor has devastating consequences for children in terms of academic success, emotional distress, cognitive development, and physical health—all making upward social mobility for poor children a difficult challenge (Duncan and Brooks-Gunn, 1997). In fact, a national tragedy is the fact that our society spends considerably less on the education of poor children, who are more desperately in need of these resources, than it does on the education of affluent children. And relatively little is being done to rectify this (see Chapter 15). All of this means that the poor do not have the same chances for mobility as the more affluent. By virtue of being born poor, they are already at a serious disadvantage. Even the intelligent and capable among the poor suffer such disadvantages, for the stratification system tends to perpetuate itself.

From the conflict perspective, issues of poverty and inequality need to be assessed from a global vantage point, as was done in Chapter 2. The emerging global economy pits large corporations in a competition out of which some people benefit while others suffer from an inability to find a job that will enable them to support themselves and their families in a dignified fashion. The search around the world for higher profits and lower labor costs means persistent, and in some cases grinding, poverty for those who do not have the skills, the social background, or the good fortune that would enable them to benefit from the global economy. For the United States, this loss of good-paying jobs has been one of the reasons for the growth of an entrenched group of poor who do not have the education or skills essential to landing a good job today. For some in this group, poverty has become a permanent, intergenerational problem (see Applied Research insert).

The Interactionist Perspective and Cultural Analysis

The functionalist and conflict perspectives focus on the role of social and economic structures in creating poverty. By contrast, the interactionist perspective focuses on the importance of the subjective element of social reality—how people define themselves and their opportunities through day-to-day social interaction with others around them. This has led to a **cultural analysis of poverty** that focuses on *the values, attitudes, and psychological orientations that may emerge among groups of people who live under conditions of poverty* (Marks, 1991; Small and Newman, 2001). The basic idea is that people who live in poverty develop a cultural orientation that helps them adapt to their life circumstances in a way that enables them to still feel good about themselves. However, elements of this cultural orientation can make it more difficult for poor people to improve their circumstances. Anthropologist Oscar Lewis (1966) was one of the first to speak of a "culture of poverty"—the beliefs, values, and norms that emerge among the long-term poor and help them adapt to their circumstances. The poor tend to be isolated from centers of power and decision making in society and from influential groups and organizations. As a result, their cultural orientation tends to emphasize fatalism and powerlessness, feeling that they have little control over what happens to them. In addition, the experiences of the poor have shown them that, despite their own efforts, the future may not get a lot better for them.

More recently, William J. Wilson (1991) has suggested that prolonged joblessness contributes to this cultural orientation by leaving people with a general sense that they are unable to achieve goals that they might set for themselves, that there is little point in making efforts or taking on challenges. Another element of this cultural context applies to African Americans, whose ancestors were brought to this country against their will, suffered slavery, poverty, and racial oppression over the centuries, and were forcibly kept out of the mainstream in the United States. Among some of these poor people there has developed a conflictual subculture that defines their circumstances as due to the racial oppression and dominance exercised by more powerful groups. As they see it, racism and discrimination control and limit their lives.

With such a cultural orientation, poor people may despair of ever improving their lot. They may see little point in making efforts to change their circumstances because their fate, they believe, is out of their control. They may not sacrifice for the future because they see no link between present effort and future gain. When such a cultural orientation develops, argue proponents of cultural analysis, poverty may become, to a degree, self-perpetuating. The values and norms that make up this orientation may get passed on unwittingly from one generation to the next. When this happens, poverty can become a vicious, difficult-to-break cycle.

Cultural analysis has been criticized because it seems to "blame the victim": Poor people are blamed for their own difficulties by arguing that poverty is due to the character flaws of, or lack of effort by, those affected (Jargowsky, 1997; Small and Newman, 2001). However, that is not the point of cultural analysis. Rather, it argues that certain social conditions— discrimination, lack of opportunity, social isolation—can produce a culture of poverty, and this culture in turn perpetuates the victimization of the poor. It is flaws in the social system, such as those discussed in the Applied Research insert, that are at the root of the problem and that must be changed to combat poverty.

A second criticism of the culture of poverty thesis is that research suggests that it applies only to a limited number of poor people. In fact, the traits that characterize the culture of poverty are probably found among less than half of all poor people and are more common among some poor, such as Hispanics, than among other poor people (Irelan, Moles, and O'Shea, 1969; Kutner and Kutner, 1987; Mead, 1994). Research also shows that some poor people do improve their lives, despite the culture of poverty. So, although the culture of poverty may inhibit some poor people from making things better for themselves, its impact on perpetuating poverty in general is probably limited, although not unimportant.

Future Prospects

Support for the fight against poverty remains high in the United States. A recent survey found that two-thirds of people in the United States felt that the government should make a special effort to help the poor, and the government was identified as the societal

This Head Start program in Oregon is an example of an early childhood educational intervention that has become one of the core efforts to attack the problem of poverty by equipping children with the skills and attitudes that will better enable them to achieve as adults.

institution with the greatest responsibility for assisting the poor (Gallup News Service, 2001). This is the same level of support for government programs for the poor that was found in the 1960s, despite the negative attitudes toward welfare over the past decade (Kull, 1994). However, there has been a dramatic decline over the same period in people's confidence that the government can do the job properly. So, people continue to embrace the values that underlie poverty programs, but they are frustrated with the government's record of achievements in those programs. With these public sentiments in mind, the remainder of the chapter reviews what can be done to alleviate the problem of poverty.

Full Employment

Because poverty is related in part to unemployment, it seems sensible to promote policies that encourage **full employment:** *a situation in which everyone or nearly everyone who wants to work can find a job.* Although most politicians would probably support such a concept, the controversy is over how to do it.

Certainly, any program that proves effective at creating more jobs would probably receive widespread support, but some cautions about such programs are in order. First, many of the poor, as has been seen, are not able-bodied nonworkers. Rather, they are people who would be largely unaffected by the creation of more jobs: children, the elderly, the disabled, and women raising their children alone. Second, many of the jobs created are likely to be low-paying, unskilled, or part-time jobs that will not pull people out of poverty (Rank, 2004). Third, having tried both laissez-faire and interventionist strategies to promote full employment over the decades, it appears that neither is a panacea for the problem of poverty. If anything, unemployment in the United States seems to have increased somewhat over the years despite these policies.

Education, Training, and Jobs

Some social policies aimed at reducing poverty focus on preparing the poor to compete effectively in the job market. The idea is that, for some poor people, the major factor holding them in poverty is that they lack the education, skills, or motivation to find and keep good-paying jobs. A number of programs have been created over the years to focus on these issues.

EARLY CHILDHOOD INTERVENTIONS One approach is to focus on children by providing them with the educational and other experiences at a young age that will increase their ability to find and keep good jobs as adults. Research has shown that such early childhood intervention programs are very beneficial in achieving this goal (Heckman and Lochner, 2000). A program that can serve as an example of this approach is Head Start, which was established by the Economic Opportunity Act of 1964. This program is based on the belief that people fail in life because their access to conventional channels to success—especially education—is blocked. The presumption is that poor children live in an environment, especially at home, that discourages educational achievement, initiative, and a positive self-concept. By intervening on behalf of these poor children, it is argued, the intergenerational cycle of poverty might be broken. Head Start provides preschool children with enrichment and early learning experiences that middle-class children presumably receive at home.

Research over the decades on Head Start and other early childhood educational interventions has shown that such programs do achieve many of their goals (Love et al., 2002; Ramey and Ramey, 2000; Reynolds et al., 2001). Children enrolled in Head Start, for example, when compared with other poor children who do not have such preschool experience, are less likely to be assigned to special education classes or to be kept back a grade in school and are more likely to complete high school. They also do better on mathematics achievement tests and show more improvement in IQ scores, and they are less likely to repeat a grade, get in trouble with the law, or become teenage parents. Head Start children also have a better family life and a more positive self-concept. Finally, as young adults, Head Start children may be more likely to go to college or to hold a steady, skilled job. With benefits such as these, it seems that children who are exposed to such preschool educational experiences will be better equipped to avoid poverty as adults.

JOBS PROGRAMS Whereas Head Start is an indirect, long-term approach to the problem of poverty, other programs have involved more direct and immediate efforts to train people and to find them jobs (Page and Simmons, 2000; Pouncy, 2000). Since the 1960s, programs such as WIN (Work Incentive Program), CETA (Comprehensive Employment and Training Act), and JTPA (Job Training Partnership Act) have provided job training and work experience for people on welfare and assisted them in finding jobs. These programs ended in 2000, and most of their efforts were combined under the Workforce Investment Act (WIA). These programs have provided on-the-job training and temporary public service jobs. They have also provided the young and criminal offenders with special services. Many people, especially women, benefited from these programs, but many people who go through these programs do not find permanent jobs and get off welfare, or the jobs they do get pay less than welfare. The mediocre performance of these programs is due to a number of factors. First, they typically have been seriously underfunded, reaching a relatively small number of the people who are eligible. Second, the programs focus mostly on job skills training and job seeking, and ignore the many other factors (such as health problems, transportation problems, inadequate child care, and lack of a high school education) that make it difficult for people to get and keep jobs. Third, the job training is mostly for low-income jobs that are not likely to move people far out of poverty. Job training programs that overcome these weaknesses would provide more benefits to society in terms of impacting on the problem of poverty.

A job training program that focuses on youth, the Job Corps, run by the U.S. Department of Labor, has proven to be fairly effective. Focused on high school dropouts from poor neighborhoods, the Job Corps gives participants academic education, vocational training, counseling, health education, and job placement assistance. Evaluations of the program have shown that participants, when compared to comparable youth who have not participated in the Job Corps, are much more likely to graduate from high school, be employed, and earn more money; they are less likely to be arrested or receive public assistance benefits (Schochet, Burghardt, and Glazerman, 2000).

In the late 1990s, the then-existing welfare system was replaced with a program called Temporary Assistance for Needy Families (TANF). In this new welfare program, job training has become an integral part of the welfare system in the United States. What has resulted is a major transformation in welfare policy: from an income maintenance system to one with a focus on education and training in order to help people find jobs and get off welfare. This policy change is sufficiently important that the Policy Issues insert is devoted to a description and assessment of it.

Income Maintenance Programs

Modern governments have taken on the responsibility of assisting those in need through a variety of programs that provide them with some minimal level of resources. In the United States, these programs can be divided into two general categories: social insurance and public assistance. **Social insurance** refers to *programs offering benefits to broad categories of people, such as the elderly or injured workers, who presumably were working and paying for the insurance before becoming eligible for it.* There is no "means" test to receive social insurance; that is, there is no income minimum necessary to be eligible. Also, one can receive outside income while insured, and there is little stigma associated with it. In fact, 80 percent of the social welfare dollar is spent on the nonpoor. **Public assistance,** which is what most people mean when they use the term *welfare*, refers to *programs in which a person must pass a "means" test to be eligible.* Those whose assets are above a certain level are not eligible.

There are various social insurance programs in the United States. At both the federal and state levels, over a trillion dollars are spent on such programs each year (U.S. Bureau of the Census, 2006:346–349). Among the best known and most expensive are

1. *Social Security.* Old Age, Survivors, and Disability Insurance (OASDI), commonly referred to as "Social Security," is intended to provide income for retired or disabled workers and their survivors. It also provides unemployment compensation and benefits to workers for on-the-job injuries. Social Security is discussed in more detail in Chapter 8.

2. *Medicare.* Medicare is a health insurance program for the elderly and for some others who are receiving Social Security. It also provides supplementary medical insurance in return for a monthly premium. Medicare is discussed further in Chapters 4 and 8.

There are also a variety of public-assistance programs, costing over $500 billion per year.

1. *Supplemental Security Income (SSI).* SSI is given to certain categories of poor people with little income and few assets. To be eligible, one must be over sixty-five, blind, or disabled.

2. *Temporary Assistance for Needy Families (TANF).* TANF is the federal block grant program that replaced Aid to Families with Dependent Children (AFDC) in 1997. It provides temporary assistance to parents and guardians who do not have the financial resources to support their children, but in return for the assistance the parents must seek work.

3. *General Assistance (GA).* GA is for people ineligible for SSI or TANF. GA is funded by state or local governments, but only about half the states have GA, and the amount of assistance and the eligibility requirements are highly variable from one locale to another.

4. *Medicaid.* Medicaid is a program providing medical and hospital services to people who cannot pay for them themselves. Generally, Medicaid goes to people who meet the means test for other public-assistance programs, but it can also go to people who can provide for their own economic support except for necessary medical care.

5. *Noncash benefits.* A number of public-assistance programs provide poor people with resources that are not direct cash payments, such as food stamps, housing assistance, and a school lunch program.

The history of income-maintenance programs in the United States shows some significant changes in both policies and attitudes toward welfare over the years (Skocpol, 1995). Many modern government support programs, such as Social Security, were established during the New Deal of the 1930s. These programs were clearly designed to assist what some people considered the "deserving" poor, those who had worked to support themselves but who, because of age, disability, or loss of a spouse, were in difficult times. The goal of the programs was to keep these people from falling into poverty or help them out of poverty. Even Aid to Dependent Children, which is what welfare (now TANF) was called then, was originally intended for widowed mothers, not for single or divorced mothers. Single and divorced mothers along with marginally employable men were considered by many to be the "undeserving" poor, who were perceived as being partially responsible for their plight or at least capable of improving their circumstances on their own.

The Great Society programs of the 1960s tended to get away from distinctions between "deserving" and "undeserving" people. Instead they focused on helping all poor people rise out of poverty by providing opportunities to all. Single or divorced mothers and any other poor people could get government assistance. However, since the 1960s, disillusionment has grown among many people in the United States regarding public assistance programs. What has emerged from this disillusionment seems to reflect the earlier distinction between deserving and undeserving people. Although social insurance programs such as Social Security and Medicare have remained popular, public assistance programs have been attacked and their funding slashed. Many people believe that at least some recipients of these programs could make it on their own and don't deserve public support. As a result, many people have been dropped from public-

Welfare Reform: How Well Is It Working?

Traditional welfare in the United States was designed as an entitlement program, which meant that all people who met the income and other eligibility requirements were entitled to receive welfare payments. Some critics of this traditional approach to welfare took a laissez-faire stance and argued that such a welfare program generated a variety of social pathologies: It made people dependent and discouraged initiative (Glazer, 1995; Olasky, 1992). It also made it difficult for people to develop the patterns of hard work, self-sufficiency, and personal demeanor that would assist them in finding and keeping a job. Research has demonstrated that traditional welfare did not produce most of these outcomes, but some critics argued for radical change nonetheless, such as eliminating publicly supported welfare altogether, thereby letting private charities take care of the poor, or requiring that people seek and find work and become independent of government support.

In response to these concerns, in the late 1990s, a new welfare policy was implemented that is no longer an entitlement that guarantees welfare benefits to the poor. Although it doesn't eliminate welfare, the Temporary Assistance for Needy Families (TANF) program is a radical departure from the past. Among its goals are to dramatically reduce the number of people receiving welfare by making the eligibility requirements more stringent, requiring welfare recipients to seek and find work, and placing strict time limits on how long persons and families can receive welfare payments. This "workfare" approach represents the culmination of a shift in public sentiment from viewing welfare as a "right" of those who have fallen on bad times to viewing it as a "privilege" that is limited in duration and can be revoked. Another goal of the TANF program is to shift responsibility for providing welfare from the federal government to the states. So, the previous welfare program was replaced with federal block grants given to the states to provide assistance to the poor. States now have greater control over welfare, and welfare rules and benefits are allowed to vary significantly from state to state. The new

welfare approach requires that most recipients participate in job training programs and find work within two years or lose their benefits. The basic idea behind the new system is that the old system had created a class of people dependent on welfare because there was no incentive for them to work and support themselves. The new system is much more coercive: People will be taken off welfare if they don't participate in job training and find jobs.

Does the new approach to welfare work better than the traditional one? This is a complicated question because the new welfare program is complex and has many impacts on recipients. It is also complicated because it depends on what criteria are used to assess success. Actually, workfare programs of one sort or another have existed for decades, encouraged by the federal government as experiments with various alternative ways of providing welfare. So, this provides us with two major sources of data with which to evaluate TANF: studies of these earlier experiments with workfare and studies of the actual operation of the TANF program in the decade that it has been in existence.

A body of evaluation research on the earlier experiments with workfare now exists that enables us to draw some conclusions about their effectiveness (Friedlander and Burtless, 1995; Greenberg, Linksz, and Mandell, 2003). Generally, workfare programs achieve modest positive outcomes. If the programs are designed well, people in them are more likely to find employment, to earn more, and to get off and stay off welfare than are people on traditional welfare. Workfare forms of welfare seem to especially benefit single-parent families. However, these positive impacts of workfare programs are very modest: Income increases are small, the numbers of people getting off welfare are small, and few of these families are pulled out of poverty by the work programs. In addition, much of the benefit of workfare goes to a small group of participants, whereas many others receive no benefits. Finally, workfare programs show little

assistance rolls in the past two decades. This reaction arose in part from a frustration over the continuing growth in welfare costs and the inability of such programs to reduce levels of poverty significantly. But research is also clear that these programs have lost support since the 1960s because they are perceived as disproportionately supporting members of racial and ethnic minorities (Alesina and Glaeser, 2004).

Yet, the picture of poverty and welfare in the United States is complex because, despite all of this hesitancy, expressed support for poverty programs remains strong in the United States. Recent surveys show that a substantial majority of people in the United States support a host of poverty programs. Furthermore, support for poverty programs is virtually unanimous when these programs are seen as

success with the seriously disadvantaged, who have extreme difficulty finding work.

So, this research on earlier workfare experiments suggests that the effects of switching to a workfare program, such as TANF, are likely to be modestly positive, complicated, and clearly no panacea for poverty. So, what have researchers found with TANF in the years of its operation? Keep in mind that TANF is much more than a workfare program. In fact, its adoption was driven more by political and ideological considerations than by research showing the modest effects of workfare. Its primary goals were to reduce welfare rolls, cut welfare costs, and shift welfare to the states. Many of its elements, such as strict time limits and tightened eligibility requirements, were designed to achieve these goals.

So, what has been the impact of TANF? First, welfare rolls have dropped dramatically (Lewis, Stevens, and Slack, 2002; Lichter and Jayakody, 2002; Weil and Finegold, 2002). Second, many welfare recipients have found work and have improved their lives financially. So, if evaluated by these outcomes, then TANF appears to have been successful because it achieved its goals of reducing welfare rolls and cutting costs. Another positive benefit is on children and adolescents: Youth in TANF families in which the mother finds work report fewer behavioral problems and better academic performance. Again, however, the improvements are modest (Dunifon, Kalil, and Danziger, 2003; Gennetian and Morris, 2003).

However, the picture is more complicated because the drop in welfare rolls began some years before TANF went into effect, and the favorable economy during the past ten years undoubtedly contributed to many people moving off welfare. So, all of the decline in welfare cannot be attributed to TANF. In addition, under TANF, a significant number of poor people find themselves neither working nor on welfare. In some cases, this is because stricter rules make them ineligible for assistance or because they were dropped from the program for failing to follow the job training rules or to find a job in the specified time period. In other cases, people have difficulty finding work because of significant barriers they confront, such as illnesses, psychological problems, or a lack of transportation. These factors result in substantial numbers of people who would have been eligible for assistance under the old welfare system but are neither eligible for assistance under TANF nor can find work. They are worse off than they were before TANF and must scramble to find financial help and housing support from relatives, friends, or anyone else. The most disadvantaged group consists of those removed from welfare who have no job and no spouse or relative to support them. These people report experiencing serious difficulties in life, such as not having money for food or being unable to pay rent and being evicted from their homes.

A major reason why moving people from welfare to work produces only modest improvements is simple: For people with few work skills, there are relatively few jobs that pay enough to support a family. Furthermore, research shows that the effectiveness of workfare depends on resources expended. This means that workfare programs often don't save a lot of money. The programs that actually help people—including TANF—are those that spend a lot on education, training, job search activities, health care, child care, and transportation. So, workfare programs will probably not reduce poverty dramatically as long as the basic structural problems that make it difficult for some people to get decent-paying jobs persist.

Interventionist		**Laissez-Faire**
Traditional welfare as income maintenance	Workfare as privilege	Eliminate welfare

moving people toward productive employment. Thus, almost no one believes that we should cut funds for job training programs, such as the Jobs Corps, or educational programs, such as Head Start.

A major policy product of these conflicting sentiments of support and resistance was the TANF program described in the Policy Issues insert. In addition to the workfare aspects of the TANF program, it also establishes a five-year lifetime limit to how long most recipients can receive assistance (a small percentage can be exempted because of severe hardship), whether they find work or not, and states are allowed to establish shorter time limits. In short, states are required to take people off assistance when they reach the time limit, even if they failed to find a job through no fault of their own. The overall thrust

Poverty and Welfare in Other Societies

Poverty rates tend to be higher in the United States than in many other industrial countries, especially Germany, the Netherlands, and the Scandinavian countries (see Figure 5.3). Practically all of these societies also provide more comprehensive assistance to low-income individuals, the poor, and single parents (Bergmann, 1996; Rodgers, 1990). And they take a very different approach to issues of welfare and public assistance than does the United States. For one thing, these industrial nations focus on preventing social problems, including poverty and crime, by assisting people to avoid poverty. For example, they have housing programs and child or family allowances that go to the nonpoor as well as the poor. In this way, people can avoid tumbling into self-perpetuating poverty if they come on hard times. A second difference is that many of the assistance programs in these nations are universal rather than "means tested" as in the United States. In many countries, for example, all families receive some child or family allowance, although the amount varies by income level. Such universal programs are more effective at preventing social problems, they receive more widespread public support because everyone gains from them, and those who receive "welfare" are less likely to be stigmatized.

A third difference in the approach of these countries is to use public resources and government intervention to keep unemployment as low as possible. Low unemployment can be a significant factor in keeping poverty down. A final difference with the U.S. approach is that all of these other industrial countries make health-care services available to both the poor and the nonpoor. In the United States, many people have stayed on welfare rather than work because they lose Medicaid eligibility if they work. The jobs available to the poor are not likely to have health insurance as a benefit and pay too little to enable them to purchase health insurance, which is quite expensive. So, the choice for the poor in the United States is often either to work but forego health insurance or to get health insurance by not working and remaining eligible for welfare.

Countries that spend more on public assistance don't necessarily have lower rates of poverty (Lawson and George, 1980). This is probably because there are powerful structural and economic determinants of poverty that are unaffected by increasing levels of welfare expenditure. One such structural factor is the number of single-parent families, which is linked with higher poverty levels. In the United States, one-third of all births are to unmarried women as compared to between 10 and 20 percent in most European nations (Federal Interagency Forum on Child and Family Statistics, 2006). Another reason why welfare expenditures don't clearly reduce poverty is that, in many of these industrial countries, a good portion of social welfare dollars is not directed at the poor but at assisting people who work to keep working and achieve a satisfactory lifestyle. For example, we saw in the International Perspectives insert in Chapter 3 that many European societies provide family benefits, such as day care and maternity leave, to everyone, even those who could afford to get them on their own. So, some nations have high public-assistance expenditures and low poverty rates because some of the public assistance is directed at the nonpoor.

So the experiences of these other industrial nations suggest that it is not necessarily the amount of public assistance that reduces poverty but rather the approach taken: universal programs that focus on reducing social problems and unemployment and that make health care available to all.

of current welfare policy, then, is to discourage people from applying for welfare in the first place, to tighten requirements so that fewer people are eligible for welfare, and to push people off welfare as quickly as possible and with little regard to the consequences. The International Perspectives insert explores how welfare issues are dealt with in other societies.

Collective Action

Many of the programs intended to alleviate poverty have been designed by politicians, economists, sociologists, and other experts who are not themselves poor. This raises the question of whether these experts have different interests from the poor or whether they have an accurate and sincere understanding of poverty and its related problems. Leslie Dunbar (1988), who has interviewed many poverty-stricken people at length, believes that policymakers and the general public hold inaccurate stereotypes of the poor as unthinking, unambitious, irresponsible, and possibly even dangerous social misfits. In reality, after listening to poor people speak, Dunbar found that the poor value many of the same things that the nonpoor do, such as ambition, self-reliance, and family life. Most want to work and support themselves, but because of bad luck or circumstances, they find themselves destitute. If policymakers and the public misunderstand the poor and have different interests than they do, then the programs these officials develop may not necessarily further the interests of the poor. So the poor may need to take matters into their own hands through some collective action that would further their interests. In fact,

the poor have done this periodically. The original war on poverty of the 1960s was in part a reaction to the focus of the civil rights movement aimed at the problems of poor African Americans. Since then, groups such as the United Farm Workers Union and the National Welfare Rights Organization have lobbied and protested in support of policies that are in the interests of the poor. Frances Fox Piven and Richard Cloward (1997) suggest that a coalition of poor groups and civil rights organizations could be an effective weapon to bring about change. A strategy such as this has its dangers, of course. It could create a backlash against the poor and result in substantial reductions in public assistance. However, it does illustrate the point that disadvantaged groups in the United States have traditionally used collective action as one avenue to pursue their interests. The poor have not utilized this strategy as much as they might.

LINKAGES   Poor people become more deeply entrenched in poverty when segregation into urban ghettos (Chapter 12) makes it more difficult for them to find jobs and when corporate concentration of power (Chapter 2) makes it easy to close factories and move them away from where the poor live.

STUDY AND REVIEW

Summary

1. Poverty arises not from a deprivation of resources alone but from an uneven distribution of the resources available in a society.

2. There are three widely used definitions of poverty: One is based on absolute deprivation, the second on relative deprivation, and the third on cultural elements. Most social policy on poverty in the United States uses the absolute definition.

3. Poverty is more common among some racial and ethnic minorities, among children, among female-headed households, and among central-city and rural dwellers. Among the poor can also be found the working poor, the unemployed, and the homeless.

4. From the functionalist perspective, poverty exists to discourage people from neglecting their social duties. If people do not contribute to society, they are "punished" by receiving little in terms of wealth, status, or other rewards. In addition, poverty exists because it performs some positive functions for society.

5. From the conflict perspective, poverty exists because some groups are deprived of the opportunity to accumulate the resources that would make possible a minimally acceptable lifestyle.

6. According to the interactionist perspective, living in poverty can lead the poor to define situations or interpret reality in ways that make it more difficult for them to improve their circumstances. A part of this is called the culture of poverty, but this should not be interpreted as a "blame the victim" argument.

7. One approach to reducing poverty is to strive for full employment. How to achieve this, or whether it can be achieved, remains controversial.

8. Another approach is to provide the education and training that will prepare the poor to find and keep jobs. Head Start seems to have been fairly successful at this. Other jobs programs, however, have had mixed success.

9. To assist the poor, a variety of income-maintenance programs has been made available. The two general types are social insurance and public assistance.

The U.S. Census Bureau provides enormous amounts of information about stratification and economic inequality in the United States. Start by going to the Bureau's home page: **www.census.gov.** Click on "People: Poverty," and you will have numerous links to explore. Exploring these sites will provide you with much detailed data on income distribution and inequality in the United States, in some cases going back fifty years. Another useful site is the Office of the Assistant Secretary for Planning and Evaluation of the Department of Health and Human Services **(aspe.hhs.gov/index.shtml).** From these various sites, try to answer these questions: How much income inequality is there? Are the disparities getting wider? How does this information supplement, support, or contradict the data presented in the text? Share what you find with the class.

Explore the issues of stratification and inequality in other cultures. Select one of the search engines and enter some key words that include a particular nation or region that you are interested in, such as "stratification and Russia," "class and Africa," or "inequality and Brazil." Report what you find to the class. The United Nations Development Programme maintains a Web site **(www.undp.org)** where it publishes much data, including its annual publication *Human Development Report.* Also look for Web sites maintained by the World Bank, the International Monetary Fund, and Amnesty International. At all these sites, explore issues of income, wealth, and poverty in nations around the world.

Another source of information is research institutes that conduct and publish research on poverty and welfare issues, such as the Institute for Research on Poverty at the University of Wisconsin **(www.irp.wisc.edu).** Explore what information that site has to offer; then search the Internet for other such sites and share them with your class. Also search for the Web sites of organizations that advocate for the poor, such as the Children's Defense Fund, and bring information about them to your class.

The Allyn & Bacon Social Problems Supersite **(wps. ablongman.com/ab_socialprob_sprsite_1)** contains material on social class, poverty, and inequality.

There is considerable debate over whether welfare is beneficial or detrimental to people and society.

10. Some have argued that the only effective way for the poor to get programs that truly benefit them is through collective action.

Key Terms

absolute definition of poverty

cultural analysis of poverty

cultural definition of poverty

full employment

poverty

public assistance

relative definition of poverty

social insurance

social mobility

social stratification

structural unemployment

Multiple-Choice Questions

1. Cultural definitions of poverty are distinct from the other definitions used because the cultural definitions consider
   a. relative deprivation.
   b. why people have failed to achieve a higher economic level.
   c. an absolute level of deprivation.
   d. a fixed level below which people are considered to be poor.
   e. social stratification to be central.

2. Which of the following statements is true regarding the poverty rate in the United States today?
   a. It is higher than in 1960.
   b. It is at its highest point since 1960.
   c. The poverty rate among children is lower than that among all people in most years.
   d. More people are poor today than in 1970.

3. Which of the following groups has experienced the largest increase in its percentage of the aggregate income in the United States since 1965?
   a. the poorest 20 percent of families
   b. the second 20 percent of families
   c. the third 20 percent of families
   d. the fourth 20 percent of families
   e. the wealthiest 20 percent of families

4. People in which of the following groups have the highest rate of poverty?
   a. African American female-headed families
   b. Hispanic elderly
   c. white elderly
   d. children
   e. Hispanic children in two-parent families

5. Which of these statements is most consistent with the functionalist perspective regarding the reason that poverty exists?
   a. Dominant groups protect their position and resources against inroads by less fortunate groups.
   b. Welfare systems produce dependency in people.
   c. The cultural orientation emerges when people live in conditions of poverty that discourage them from work.
   d. Poverty makes a useful contribution to the ongoing maintenance of society.

6. The cultural analysis of poverty has been controversial for all of the following reasons *except*
   a. it gives support to the functionalist perspective on stratification.
   b. it seems to blame the poor for their own difficulties.
   c. it seems to apply only to a limited number of poor people.
   d. some poor people do improve their lives despite the culture of poverty.

7. For some of the poor, poverty is an entrenched, long-term condition. Sociologists attribute this entrenched poverty in the United States to all of the following *except*
   a. inadequate funding for welfare.
   b. fundamental structural changes in the economy of the United States.
   c. changes in the communities in which poor people live.
   d. the relocation of industries away from the communities where poor people live.

8. Which of the following programs to assist the poor is still in operation?
   a. CETA
   b. WIN
   c. Head Start
   d. All of the above are still operating.
   e. Only a and c are still operating.

9. Which of the following is classified as a "social insurance" program?
   a. Temporary Assistance to Needy Families
   b. Social Security
   c. Medicaid
   d. Supplemental Security Income
   e. General Assistance

10. Which of the following best characterizes the attitudes of people in the United States today regarding poverty programs?
   a. All such programs should be reduced drastically.
   b. Most such programs should be eliminated.
   c. Support is strong for programs that move people toward productive employment.
   d. Programs that help children should be kept but the rest should be eliminated.

True/False Questions

1. Using the absolute definition of poverty, poverty could be eliminated only if the inequitable distribution of resources were to be eliminated.
2. Since 1965, most analysts agree that the distribution of resources among the wealthy and the poor has become more equitable.
3. In making policy decisions, such as who is eligible for various government social programs, the absolute approach to defining poverty is typically used.
4. According to the text, the majority of homeless people are homeless because they suffer from a severe mental disorder that makes it difficult for them to hold a job or maintain a home.
5. Regarding social mobility, sociologists have found that, for the most part, people in the United States tend to take jobs that are not too different in socioeconomic status from those of their parents.
6. Research shows that most people who experience persistent poverty, especially the young, are unwilling to work and this accounts for their poverty status.
7. The text concludes that programs to promote full employment will probably not eliminate the problem of poverty.
8. Evaluations of workfare programs have shown that poor people in such programs are more likely to find employment and get off welfare than people without access to such programs.
9. People in the United States tend to be less supportive of public-assistance programs than they are of social insurance programs.
10. Research shows that nations that spend more on public assistance usually have lower rates of poverty.

Fill-In Questions

1. The _____ definition of poverty compares people to some standard based partially on the lifestyles of other people.
2. The ranking of people into a hierarchy in which the resources considered valuable by society are unequally distributed is called a system of _____.
3. In terms of racial designations, the majority of all poor people in the United States are _____.
4. Davis and Moore's approach to understanding poverty would be classified as deriving from the _____ perspective.
5. Unemployment that occurs because of normal changes in the structure of the United States economy is called _____.

6. The set of beliefs, values, and norms that emerges among the long-term poor and helps them adapt to their circumstances is called the _____.

7. The _____ program was established in 1964 and provides poor preschool children with enrichment and early learning experiences that middle-class children presumably receive at home.

8. Welfare reform legislation of 1996 changed welfare in the United States from _____ to _____.

9. Social Security and Medicare are classified as _____ programs.

10. Two public-assistance programs in the United States are _____ and _____.

Matching Questions

_____ 1. social stratification
_____ 2. cultural analysis of poverty
_____ 3. Head Start
_____ 4. Supplemental Security Income
_____ 5. absolute definition of poverty
_____ 6. homeless mentally ill
_____ 7. functionalist perspective
_____ 8. Medicare
_____ 9. welfare reform of the 1980s and 1990s
_____ 10. functions of poverty

A. interactionist perspective
B. public-assistance program
C. fixed-income cutoffs
D. Kingsley Davis and Wilbert Moore
E. hierarchy of inequality
F. workfare
G. social insurance program
H. Herbert J. Gans
I. deinstitutionalization
J. educational program for poor children

Essay Questions

1. Discuss the different ways of defining poverty, pointing to the drawbacks of each one. Which definition is currently used for social policy decisions in the United States?

2. Summarize the research on the social characteristics of the poor in the United States.

3. What accounts for the increase in homelessness in the United States in recent decades?

4. What answers does the functionalist perspective offer on the issue of why poverty exists in society?

5. What are the positive functions that poverty can perform for society?

6. What criticisms have been made of the cultural analysis of poverty?

7. What recommendations have sociologists made to reduce poverty among the entrenched poor?

8. What are the principles that underlie the workfare approach to public assistance? How well does it work?

9. Make both the laissez-faire and interventionist arguments about which welfare reforms would be appropriate.

10. Describe how policies on poverty and welfare are dealt with differently in industrial societies other than the United States.

For Further Reading

Walter S. DeKeseredy, Shahid Alvi, Martin D. Schwartz, and **E. Andreas Tomaszewski.** *Under Siege: Poverty and Crime in a Public Housing Community.* Lanham, MD: Lexington Books, 2003. These sociologists have written an excellent study of six public housing communities in Canada that illustrates many of the mechanisms discussed in this chapter (disappearance of manufacturing jobs, predatory crime, etc.) that make life difficult for the poor and social advancement very problematic.

Jason DeParle. *American Dream: Three Women, Ten Kids, and a Nation's Drive to End Welfare.* New York: Viking, 2004. This is an intriguing, personal, and detailed look at how welfare and welfare reform impact the lives of three women and their children. It shows how complex the impacts of poverty and social policies are on people's lives.

Barbara Ehrenreich. *Nickel and Dimed: On (Not) Getting by in America.* New York: Metropolitan Books, 2001. This book offers an intriguing, first-hand account of the difficult life of the working poor in the United States. The author, a writer and social commentator, worked the minimum-wage jobs and lived off these earnings in order to gain an understanding of this lifestyle.

Alex Kotlowitz. *There Are No Children Here: The Story of Two Boys Growing Up in the Other America.* New York: Doubleday, 1991. This is a very sensitive and wrenching description of what it is like to grow up poor and African American in Chicago. It helps the reader to see, through the eyes of the poor, what it is like to be poor.

Elliot Liebow. *Tell Them Who I Am: The Lives of Homeless Women.* New York: Free Press, 1993. This is an enlightening and compassionate look at the lives of women who are homeless—how they got that way and how they cope with it. Liebow is an anthropologist who did participant observation research to uncover this aspect of life in the United States.

Katherine Newman. *Declining Fortunes: The Withering of the American Dream.* New York: BasicBooks, 1993. In stratification systems where social mobility occurs, some of that mobility is downward rather than upward. This anthropologist explores the nature, extent, and experience of downward mobility among middle-class, suburban families in the United States.

Kevin Phillips. *Wealth and Democracy: A Political History of the American Rich.* New York: Broadway Books, 2002. This political analyst discusses the growing gap between the rich and the less well-to-do in the United States throughout history and discusses the corrosive negative consequences such a gap can produce.

RACE AND ETHNIC RELATIONS

One of the most fascinating and enriching aspects of life in the United States is the great physical and cultural diversity of the peoples who have settled here. This diversity has provided the United States with a large range of lifestyles. At the same time, however, it has been a major source of divisiveness and conflict for U.S. society. Groups with different traditions, values, and languages have struggled with one another over power, privileges, and prestige. In fact, U.S. history has been a chronicle of unequal treatment of racial and ethnic minorities, stretching from the enslavement of black Africans for the benefit of white Europeans settling the New World to the persisting barriers to advancement that confront some black, Hispanic, and Asian Americans today.

Characteristics such as race and ethnicity are called *ascribed statuses* because they are assigned to people and represent social positions over which people have little or no choice about occupying. Whether the people occupying these statuses like it or not, such positions can and do serve as the basis for unequal treatment of groups, functioning as criteria for allocating resources and determining life chances and lifestyles. Such groups are referred to by sociologists as minority groups, and a discussion of what constitutes a minority group is our first topic in this chapter.

Minority Groups

A **minority group** is *a group whose members share distinct physical or cultural characteristics; are denied access to power and resources available to other groups; and are accorded fewer rights, privileges, and opportunities* (Marden, Meyer, and Engel, 1992). In the United States, black, Hispanic, Vietnamese, and some white ethnic groups such as rural Appalachians are considered minority groups because each has lower levels of educational and occupational attainment than other groups, and each has fewer opportunities. Chapter 7 will show that, despite their numerical majority in our population, women are also considered a minority group because they have been denied equal access to education, jobs, and important positions that men have controlled for some time. Then, Chapter 8 will consider the plight of the young, the old, and gays and lesbians, who can also be considered minorities because they are sometimes exploited and deprived of rights and privileges because of their age or sexual orientation. This chapter, however, focuses only on minorities whose disadvantaged status arises from their racial or ethnic group membership.

The term "minority group," then, refers not to numerical size but to one's position in the stratification system of society. As we saw in Chapter 5, social stratification refers to the ranking of people into a hierarchy in which the resources considered valuable by society are unequally distributed. Ascribed characteristics such as race and ethnicity often determine a person's position in the stratification system in many societies. But the terms "race" and "ethnicity" can be easily misunderstood.

Race and Ethnicity

People use the term *race* quite freely and often with only a vague understanding of its precise meaning. Scientists use it as a biological concept to identify a population that differs from others in terms of certain key genetic, hereditary traits. There is much controversy among anthropologists and biologists, however, over whether there are any traits unique to particular races in the world today. Certainly some traits are more common in some races than others. But with extensive interbreeding among the racial groups throughout human history, genetic traits and characteristics have tended to spread around the world. However, although the biological reality of race may be hazy, its social reality is not. In fact, sociologists' definition of race is based on people's *belief* in racial differences: A **race** is *a group of people who are believed to be a biological group sharing genetically transmitted traits that are defined as important*. Thus, race is a social category because people make important distinctions between people on the basis of such presumed biological differences, even when these differences are actually vague or nonexistent (Montagu, 1998).

An **ethnic group** is *a people who share a common historical and cultural heritage and sense of group identity and belongingness*. Groups that share distinctive cultural traits such as a common language, national origin, religion, or a sense of historical heritage have been a major source of diversity that has enriched all of our lives. Hispanic Americans, Polish Americans, Gypsies, the Amish, and the Jews are but a few of the many ethnic groups in the United States that have made significant contributions to our way of life. On the other hand, some of the tension, conflict, and violence that have been part and parcel of U.S. history and still characterize social life today have focused on ethnic differences.

Racism

The subordination and oppression of minority groups is commonly supported by an ideology that assumes that members of the minority are innately inferior and thus deserving of their subordinate status. **Racism** is *the view that certain racial or ethnic groups are biologically inferior and that practices involving their domination and exploitation are therefore justified*. Racist ideologies in Nazi Germany justified genocidal attacks on the Jews, just as racism in the United States has been at the core of discrimination against African Americans, Asians, and other racial groups. For example, groups such as the skinheads, the Nazis, and the Ku Klux Klan in the United States today are motivated in part by racist beliefs.

Sources of Prejudice and Discrimination

Prejudice and discrimination are closely intertwined, so much so that people are likely to view them as the same thing. In reality, they are quite distinct. A **prejudice** is *an irrational attitude toward certain people based solely*

Some people in the United States still hold racist beliefs, as is illustrated by support for this Ku Klux Klan parade in North Carolina.

on their membership in a particular group (Levin and Levin, 1994). Individuals are "prejudged" on the basis of whatever undesirable characteristics the whole group is presumed to possess. Prejudices can be positive, but they are also often negative. **Discrimination,** on the other hand, refers to *behavior, particularly unequal treatment of people because they are members of a particular group.* The type of discrimination we are most concerned with is the denial of equal access to resources, privileges, or opportunities, practices that are often based on illogical and irrational grounds.

The relationship between prejudice and discrimination is complex. Although they are likely to go together, Robert K. Merton (1949) has demonstrated that sometimes they do not. In fact, people may combine prejudice and discrimination in four different ways. The most desirable combination, from the point of view of political and social values in the United States, is the *unprejudiced nondiscriminator* who accepts other racial or ethnic groups in both belief and practice. The *prejudiced discriminator,* on the other hand, has negative feelings toward a particular group and translates these sentiments into unequal treatment of people in that group. Members of the Ku Klux Klan, for example, have a strong prejudice against blacks and members of other racial groups; they advocate segregated schools and neighborhoods. These first two possibilities involve a consistency between belief and practice, but there are other possibilities. The *prejudiced nondiscriminator* is a kind of "closet bigot" who is prejudiced against members of some groups but does not translate these attitudes into discriminatory practices. A landlord, for example, may be prejudiced against Asian Americans, yet still rent apartments to them because of laws forbidding housing discrimination. Because there are now many laws against discrimination that are strictly enforced, the incidence of this kind of relationship between prejudice and discrimination is probably higher than in the past. The *unprejudiced discriminator* treats the members of some groups unequally because it is convenient or advantageous to do so rather than out of personal antipathy toward them. Salespeople in a real estate agency, for example, may have no personal prejudices but still decline to show houses in certain neighborhoods to African Americans because of the prejudices of people who already live in those neighborhoods.

Social Sources

Problems of poverty and discrimination are closely linked because the result of discrimination is often that minorities are poor, with little access to valued resources. Because of this, prejudice and discrimination can be understood in part through the theoretical explanations of wealth and poverty presented in Chapter 5: the functionalist, conflict, and interactionist perspectives. That discussion is not repeated here. Instead, some additional elements of the perspectives that apply especially well to problems of prejudice and discrimination are presented.

ETHNOCENTRISM **Ethnocentrism** is *the tendency to view one's own group or culture as an in-group that follows the best and the only proper way to live.* An **in-group** is *a group toward which we feel positively and with which we identify, and that produces a "we" feeling.* Feeling positively about one's own group, of course, is good because it gives one a sense of belonging and self-worth. For functionalists, ethnocentrism is functional because it produces loyalty, cohesiveness, and strong group ties. All this helps groups stick together and achieve their goals. It can, however, lead one to believe that other groups—especially those that are very different—have unfavorable characteristics. If one's own way of life is the only proper way to live, it seems that other lifestyles are improper. This can be used to justify unfair, hostile, and even genocidal attacks on other groups. Under Adolf Hitler, for example, the Nazis were so thoroughly convinced of the superiority of the alleged Aryan "race" that the Jews became a despised out-group. Likewise, many Europeans who came to the Americas as colonists believed that their European heritage contained all that was wise and desirable, and these racist beliefs fueled their treatment of the people who already inhabited the New World. So if ethnocentrism gets out of hand, it can become dysfunctional and create social disorganization in the form of hostility, conflict, and discrimination, which can threaten the social order. Although ethnocentrism can have these negative consequences, according to functionalists, such outcomes are not inevitable if people are aware of and guard against them.

COMPETITION According to the conflict perspective, prejudice and discrimination arise when groups find themselves in competition with each other. This competition is often economic, for jobs or land, but it can also be based on non-economic valued resources, such as access to attractive marriage partners or the right to practice a preferred religion. The more intensely groups compete, the more threatening each group becomes to the other and the more likely negative and hostile views are to emerge. When there are obvious differences between the groups, such as in skin color or religious practices, these can become the focus of prejudice. Discriminatory practices may emerge, sanctioned by law or custom, as a way to limit the access of the less powerful group to the scarce resources. Prejudice and discrimination can arise from competitive situations in a number of specific ways (Olzak, 1992).

One type of competitive situation has been called a split labor market by sociologist Edna Bonacich (Bonacich, 1972). A **split labor market** is *one in which there are two groups of workers willing to do the same work, but for different wages.* In a split labor market, lower-priced laborers have a competitive advantage because employers prefer to hire them. Higher-priced workers find their position threatened by those willing to work more cheaply. In such a situation, the higher-priced workers will be inclined to discriminate against the inexpensive laborers in an effort to exclude them from certain occupations. Bonacich argues that this is a key factor in much racial, ethnic, and sexual antagonism because the presumed biological differences between the two groups can serve as the focus of discrimination and can be justified on racist grounds. If people believe that members of a particular racial group are lazy or untrustworthy, then this is a rationale for excluding them from jobs that demand hard work and trustworthiness. Likewise, if people believe that women are best suited for clerical and secretarial positions, then this belief can be used to discriminate against them when they try to get more lucrative jobs in construction or other professions (Bernstein, 1998; Cheng and Bonacich, 1984).

Another type of economic competition is one in which a powerful group exploits a weaker one for its own gain. A clear case of this would be the relationship between the slaveholder and the slave in which the former gains substantially from the relationship, to the detriment of the latter. Slavery in the United States was clearly a form of economic exploitation supported by racist beliefs about the inferiority of blacks. Many of the poor today suffer a similar kind of exploitation because their work at low-paying and demeaning jobs benefits the more affluent in society (see Chapter 5). A variant of this type of exploitation is **internal colonialism,** in which *a subordinate group provides cheap labor that benefits the dominant group and is then further exploited by having to purchase expensive goods and services from the dominant group* (Doob, 1999). For example, the poor in the United States not only provide cheap labor but also purchase health care, televisions, food, and other products that provide substantial profit to dominant groups.

SOCIALIZATION Once patterns of prejudice and discrimination arise, they become incorporated into the values and norms of the group. Prejudice and discrimination toward particular groups then become legitimated, transmitted to new members through the socialization process, and frequently internalized. A study of regional differences in prejudice toward African Americans during the 1960s, for example, found, not surprisingly, that there was greater prejudice in the South, especially within the states of the old Confederacy (Middleton, 1976). It also found, however, that people who lived in the South as children and then moved to other regions were less prejudiced than those who remained in the South. In the same way, people who grew up outside the South and then moved there were more prejudiced than those who remained outside the South. In other words, people tend to adopt the prejudiced beliefs, values, and norms that are considered appropriate in the groups they belong to.

INSTITUTIONALIZED DISCRIMINATION Prejudice and discrimination sometimes become incorporated into social policies and practices, and this can result in the perpetuation of prejudice and discrimination through **institutionalized discrimination:** *the inequitable treatment of a group resulting from practices or policies that are incorporated into social, political, or economic institutions and that operate independently from the prejudices of individuals.* One form of institutionalized discrimination is the use of physical size requirements as qualifications for certain jobs. Many police departments, for example, set minimum height requirements for police officers. Asian Americans have protested against this because Asians are, on the average, shorter than whites and many therefore cannot qualify for police work. Discrimination in this form may not be direct; people may not be excluded from jobs because of their race. Rather, it is the minimum entrance requirements that effectively bar most members of a particular minority group from the jobs while serving as a barrier to only a few people in the dominant group. Through institutionalized discrimination, social inequality can persist long after prejudicial attitudes may have changed. In fact, much of the civil rights effort in the United States over the past fifty years has been concentrated on eliminating this kind of discrimination.

Psychological Sources

STEREOTYPING One psychological factor involves the human tendency to categorize. The physical and social world is sufficiently complex that we need to simplify it by thinking in terms of general categories or by lumping together the elements that have something in common. Categories, however, can become *stereotypes*—rigid and oversimplified images in which each element or person in a category is assumed to possess all the characteristics associated with that category. Because some Jews work in banking, for example, some people might assume that all Jews are proficient in financial matters. Thus, stereotyping can contribute to prejudice and discrimination.

FRUSTRATION AND AGGRESSION Prejudice and discrimination can arise when people become frustrated by their inability to achieve sought-after goals. Psychologists have shown that frustration can lead to aggression in both overt and covert forms (Baron and Richardson, 1994). Aggression can be expressed by direct physical assaults or through prejudice or discrimination. One form this aggression can take is *scapegoating*, or placing the blame for one's troubles on an individual or group incapable of offering effective resistance. This happened, for example, in the southern United States between 1880 and 1930 when thousands of blacks were lynched by angry mobs of whites, many of whom were suffering from unemployment or other economic difficulties. Such racial hatred and discrimination can serve as a form of release for frustrated people, offering the hope, however false, that they are attacking the true source of their difficulties.

THE AUTHORITARIAN PERSONALITY Another psychological approach is to search for personality types that are more prone toward prejudice and discrimination. One such personality type is the **authoritarian personality,** which is characterized by *a rigid adherence to conventional lifestyles and values, admiration of power and toughness in interpersonal relationships, submission to authority, cynicism, an emphasis on obedience, and a fear of things that are different* (Adorno et al., 1950). Authoritarians tend to be suspicious, anti-intellectual, and insecure about their own self-worth. They are also

Among the most severe consequences of prejudice and discrimination are the genocidal attacks that they can sometimes fuel. This mass grave near Sarajevo, in Bosnia and Herzegovina, was unearthed in 2007, revealing the bodies of the many Muslim victims killed by Serb forces over a decade earlier.

likely to be conformists and upset by ambiguities, preferring a world characterized by absolutes with few gray areas. Numerous studies over the years have documented the link between authoritarianism and prejudice. Furthermore, this relationship has been discovered in many cultural contexts, such as white prejudice against blacks, Arab prejudice against Jews, and Israeli prejudice against Arabs (Dekker and Ester, 1991; Hanson, 1975; Kluegel and Bobo, 1991).

The sources of prejudice and discrimination are complex, resulting from the intertwining of numerous sociological and psychological factors. Most sociologists hold that social factors such as ethnocentrism, competition, socialization, and institutionalized discrimination play the most important roles in that these "set the stage" for the operation of psychological mechanisms. Without this social underpinning, prejudice and discrimination resulting from the psychological mechanisms alone would likely be sporadic and unorganized. This is exemplified by the example of lynchings of African Americans by whites mentioned earlier. Research makes clear that the frustration that helped create such horrid aggression was produced in part by the economic competition that existed in some communities in the South between whites and African Americans. In locales where there was less of such competition, lynchings were substantially less common, although they did occur (Soule, 1992). Unfortunately, the social sources of prejudice and discrimination are all too often present, and the consequences can be devastating to both society and individuals.

Consequences of Discrimination

Prejudice by itself can be relatively harmless, but it can become destructive when it fuels discrimination. Discrimination marks the spot where the social problems surrounding race and ethnic relations begin. In modern societies, discrimination against minorities has had a detrimental impact, although some groups benefit in the short run. First and most important, discrimination forces some groups into a disadvantageous position in the stratification system and adversely affects their life chances. Chapter 4 showed that discrimination results in higher rates of illness, injury, and death for minorities. This chapter shows that most minorities in the United States enjoy fewer socioeconomic resources and opportunities than do members of dominant white groups. Being deprived of these opportunities can produce simmering resentments, which periodically erupt in destructive violence.

A second consequence of discrimination is its effect on people's views of themselves. Those who feel the brunt of discrimination may come to accept the devalued and stigmatized view of themselves that is implied by their being powerless and on the bottom of society. Minority youth, for example, often have a more negative self-concept and a poorer sense of self-worth than do nonminority youth. This does not always occur, and the negative consequences can be overcome by supportive families, high-quality schools, and a minority culture that insulates people from the negativism implied by low social standing. Yet, the research is clear that racism can and does result in lower self-esteem among minorities in some contexts (Martinez and Dukes, 1991; Pallas et al., 1990). And people with negative views of themselves and their worth may contribute less to society, and may exacerbate existing social problems through criminal behavior, long-term poverty, domestic violence, child neglect, and the like.

A third consequence of discrimination is that it creates tense, hostile, and sometimes violent encounters between dominant and minority-group members, thus destroying trust, communication, and cooperation. In settings such as school or the workplace where members of different groups interact, discrimination makes it difficult for people to work together (Wilson, 1999).

A final consequence of discrimination is that it can undermine our social and political values and institutions. Because the United States professes to value equality and human dignity, the violation of these values due to racism and discrimination can generate cynicism regarding political and economic institutions. It can also threaten the legitimacy of those institutions if people see them merely as tools to benefit those fortunate enough to have acquired some power in society. From the functionalist perspective, this may represent the most serious of trends to combat: When people begin to lose faith in the system's core values and foundation, that system's survival may be in jeopardy.

Racial and Ethnic Minorities in the United States

The United States is, of course, a land of foreigners. The only difference between groups in this regard is the time of their arrival. Even the group with the deepest roots in American soil, who claim the title "native" Americans, are descendants of immigrants who traversed the Bering Straits land bridge from Asia to the Americas tens of thousands of years ago. Beyond immigrant status, however, there is considerable variation in the positions of racial and ethnic groups in the United States today. (Also, we need to keep in mind that individual people may belong to more than one of these racial and ethnic groups.)

African Americans

African Americans comprise the largest nonwhite minority group in the United States, numbering approximately 38 million, or about 12.8 percent of our total population (U.S. Bureau of the Census, 2006: 15). They are also one of the oldest minority groups, with the first blacks arriving from Africa in 1619, not long after the first permanent European settlers in the New World. They are also the only minority group to have been enslaved in the United States. When the British colonized the New World, they followed the practices of the Spanish and Portuguese before them in bringing black African slaves to the New World (Phillips, 1963; Westermann, 1955).

Technically, all African Americans gained their freedom with the end of the Civil War. However, after a short period during which African Americans exercised a degree of freedom and political control, white Southerners began to reassert their dominance when federal troops left the South in 1877. In 1896, the Supreme Court ruled in *Plessy* v. *Ferguson* that it was constitutional to provide "separate but equal" public facilities for members of different races, and the era of widespread legal segregation began. For six decades, the *Plessy* case served as the foundation for discrimination against African Americans in schools, housing, and other areas. During this time, a split labor market in black–white relations prevailed in the United States (Marks, 1981). Because of deteriorating race relations after the *Plessy* decision and

economic distress in the South, a massive migration of young southern blacks to eastern and midwestern cities began. This was the beginning of large black ghettos in cities such as New York, Detroit, Boston, and Chicago. These concentrations of blacks in cities would later serve as an important mobilizing element in the efforts of African Americans to gain equality.

The 1950s and 1960s were a period of considerable change in the lives of African Americans (Bloom, 1987). In the *Brown* v. *Board of Education of Topeka, Kansas,* decision of 1954, the U.S. Supreme Court ruled that the "separate but equal" doctrine was unconstitutional. The southern states were ordered to integrate their schools "with all deliberate speed," but this process turned out to be rather slow. However, the civil rights movement emerged and, along with more militant black groups, initiated a drive for more economic and social opportunities for African Americans. Out of the demonstrations, protests, and rioting came the Civil Rights Act of 1964 and the Voting Rights Act of 1965. Later, affirmative-action programs and school busing would be used to provide greater opportunities for African Americans.

The position of African Americans has improved substantially over the past three decades (Patterson, 1997). For example, the number of blacks enrolled in college has increased fourteen times since 1960, whereas enrollment of whites has increased only by a factor of five; African Americans now constitute 13 percent of all college students, compared to 6 percent in 1960 (U.S. Bureau of the Census, 2006:176). The number of African Americans in professional occupa-

TABLE 6.1   Income of White, Black, Hispanic, and Asian/Pacific Islander Families, 1960–2004

Year	Median Income			Asian/Pacific Islander	Ratio of Black to White Income	Ratio of Hispanic to White Income
	White	Black	Hispanic			
1960	$5,835	$3,230	NA*	NA*	.55	
1965	7,251	3,993	NA*	NA*	.55	
1970	10,236	6,279	NA*	NA*	.61	
1975	14,268	8,779	$9,551	NA*	.61	.67
1980	21,904	12,674	14,716	NA*	.58	.67
1985	29,152	16,786	19,027	NA*	.58	.65
1990	36,915	21,423	23,431	$42,246	.58	.63
1995	42,646	25,970	24,570	46,356	.61	.58
2000	53,029	33,676	34,442	62,617	.64	.65
2004	56,700	35,158	35,401	65,482	.62	.62

*Data not available

Source: U.S. Bureau of the Census, *Statistical Abstract of the United States, 1985* (Washington, DC: U.S. Government Printing Office, 1984), p. 446; U.S. Bureau of the Census, *Statistical Abstract of the United States, 2007* (Washington, DC: U.S. Government Printing Office, 2006), p. 449.

tions also increased at a much faster rate than among whites. The percentage of blacks registered to vote has doubled, and the number of blacks holding elected political office has increased by five times.

The current picture, however, is by no means one of unblemished progress; African Americans still lag behind many other groups in terms of access to education, power, and economically rewarding jobs (see Table 6.1 and Figure 6.1). For example, although the average income of African Americans has climbed in the past forty years, the income of white people has also increased, and the position of African Americans relative to that of whites has changed very little. The ratio of black-to-white income is virtually the same as it was forty years ago. Although channels of mobility are open to some blacks, others are trapped in poverty or in occupations that offer little prestige or

hope for advancement (see Chapter 5). Today, for example, the number of African Americans in poverty is about the same as in the mid-1960s, with their poverty rate being almost three times as high as for whites.

This lagging achievement is not due to a lack of aspirations, because research shows that African American youth actually have higher educational and occupational aspirations than do white youth (Solorzano, 1991). Somewhere along the way, these high aspirations get sidetracked before becoming reality. However, a clearly overriding factor is that prejudice and discrimination against African Americans have been deeply embedded in U.S. history since the period of slavery and, although improvements have occurred, racism is still a powerful force in the United States (Brown et al., 2003; Feagin, Vera, and Batur-VanderLippe, 2000). Studies have consistently and

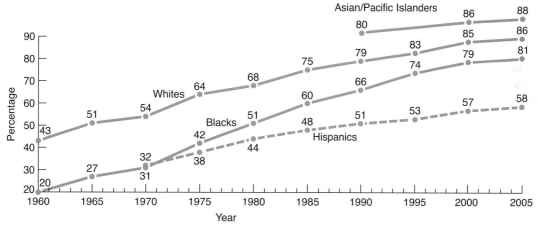

A. People Completing Four Years of High School or More

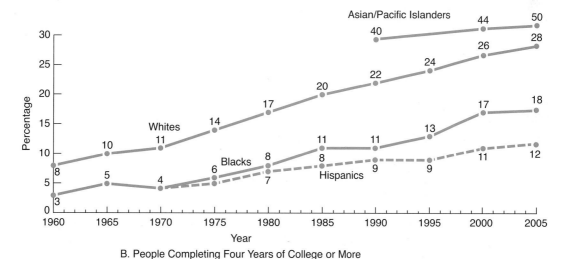

B. People Completing Four Years of College or More

FIGURE 6.1   **Educational Attainment, by Race or Ethnicity, Among People Twenty-Five Years Old and Older, 1960–2005.**

Source: U.S. Bureau of the Census, *Statistical Abstract of the United States, 2007* (Washington, DC: U.S. Government Printing Office, 2006), p. 143.

repeatedly shown that African Americans are discriminated against in jobs, in education, and in the rental and purchase of housing (Neckerman and Kirschenman, 1991; Turner et al., 2002–2003; Yinger, 1995). For example, studies send an African American and a white American with the same income, educational level, and job skills to apply for the same job or inquire about the same housing. As a group, the white Americans are much more likely to get the job or housing than are the African Americans. While most people in the United States today deny being racist or having negative attitudes toward African Americans, the behavior that we observe in these people looks a lot like discrimination and racism. Whatever the reasons for the behavior, the research available clearly suggests that African Americans are still not treated equally, nor are their opportunities the same as those for whites.

HISPANIC AMERICANS Hispanic Americans, or Latinos, are Americans whose ancestral home is Mexico, Central America, South America, or the Caribbean. They include Mexican Americans (Chicanos), Cubans, and Puerto Ricans. (Some members of this ethnic group prefer to be called Hispanic and others Latino; there is no consensus about a proper designation. This text will use Hispanic as the primary designation because it is the term used by the Census Bureau from which much of the data in this chapter were obtained.) There are 42 million Hispanic Americans in the United States, or 14.4 percent of our population. There are also an estimated 3 to 6 million Hispanics in the United States illegally.

The largest Hispanic group in the United States, two-thirds of the total, is the Mexican Americans (see Figure 6.2). This group has a long history of settlement in the United States (Acuna, 1987; Gonzalez, 2000). In fact, there have been Spanish communities located throughout what is now the American Southwest since before Mexican independence from Spain in 1821. However, as the white population in the Southwest grew during the 1800s, the economic prospects for these early settlers declined. Light-skinned, pure Spanish settlers who had adopted the white lifestyle were accepted into the white world, but the darker-skinned settlers who maintained their heritage, especially those with some Indian heritage, were viewed as inferiors and bore the brunt of prejudice and discrimination. Following the Mexican Revolution in 1909, hundreds of thousands of Mexican peasants migrated to the Southwest, where there was much demand for inexpensive labor because of expanding agriculture and railroads. The status of these more recent migrants to the United States, however, was low, although perhaps slightly higher than it had been in Mexico. The depression of

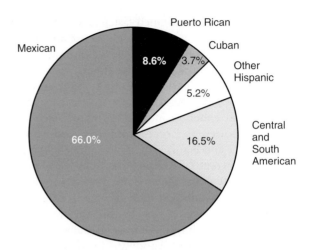

FIGURE 6.2 **Percentage Distribution of Hispanic Americans by Type of Spanish Origin, 2005.**

Source: U.S. Bureau of the Census, *Statistical Abstract of the United States, 2007* (Washington, DC: U.S. Government Printing Office, 2006), p. 44.

the 1930s resulted in a decline in farm work, driving many Mexican Americans into the cities to seek employment or public relief. The first urban *barrios*, or Spanish-speaking neighborhoods, began to spring up in such cities as Denver, Phoenix, and Los Angeles.

Since World War II, the position of Mexican Americans has changed substantially. First, their numbers have grown steadily because of a continuing stream of migrants from Mexico and a high birthrate among Mexican Americans. Today, Hispanics make up one-third of the populations of California and Texas, and almost one-half of New Mexico; they exhibit even larger concentrations in many urban areas: About 75 percent of El Paso, Texas, and Santa Ana, California, residents, for example, are of Spanish heritage as are 65 percent of Miami residents (U.S. Bureau of the Census, 2006:26, 39). Second, in part as an outgrowth of the civil rights movement, the Chicano movement gained support in the 1960s in championing the rights of all Hispanics. Cesar Chavez organized the United Farm Workers to fight for better pay and working conditions for Chicano farm workers, and Reyes Lopez Tijerina started *La Alianza Federal de Mercedes* to demand the return to Chicanos of land in the Southwest deeded to their ancestors in the Treaty of Guadalupe Hidalgo in 1848.

In the past three decades, Mexican American efforts have focused more on conventional politics and consciousness raising than on confrontation. A number of Chicano organizations, such as the Mexican American Political Alliance (MAPA) in California, were founded in the 1960s and continue to be powerful forces on the political scene, pursuing the interests of Mexican

Americans as a group. Consciousness raising and ethnic awareness have been encouraged by Latino student organizations in high schools and colleges and by pressures for bilingual education in communities with large concentrations of Mexican Americans.

Puerto Rican Americans are the second largest Hispanic group in the United States, comprising 8.6 percent of all Hispanics. Puerto Ricans were granted U.S. citizenship, as a group, in 1917. A small number of Puerto Ricans immigrated to the mainland United States before World War II, mostly attracted by farm-labor jobs but a few by factory work in the East. Following World War II, this immigration increased dramatically, in large part because of the chronically depressed economy of Puerto Rico. Puerto Ricans have tended to settle in New York City and Chicago (Fitzpatrick, 1987).

Mexican Americans and Puerto Rican Americans today face much the same problems as African Americans: poverty, low educational levels, and poor health in comparison to Anglos (see Table 6.1 and Figures 6.1 and 6.3). For example, two out of five Puerto Rican families in the United States live in poverty, and just 58 percent of Americans of Hispanic origin have completed four years of high school or more, whereas 86 percent of whites have done so. As with African Americans, the incomes of Hispanic families have persistently lagged behind those of white families, remaining at less than 70 percent of white incomes since the 1970s and actually declining over the years. Hispanics also experience some of the discrimination in housing and jobs that African Americans experience (Turner et al., 2002–2003).

Hispanics in the United States today are a diverse group (Gonzalez, 2000; Suro, 1998). In addition to the variation among groups already mentioned, for example, Cuban Americans have generally been different from other Hispanics in that they come from more middle-class and affluent origins. Despite their diversity, some Hispanic groups may be moving toward a more common Latino ethnic identity and consciousness. Being of a different color, having a common origin in the "South," speaking a common tongue, many sharing the experience of discrimination and outsider status—all this may be forging an ethnic awareness that spans the diversity found in such groups as Mexican Americans and Puerto Ricans. In fact, the term *Latinismo* has been coined to describe a sentimental and ideological identification and loyalty that transcend individual Latin ethnic groups in the United States (Padilla, 1985). This emerging Latin consciousness may be in part political; that is, may reflect a realization that advantage can be gained in the struggle for equality and fair treatment by combining forces behind a common symbol. However, Latinismo also represents an identification with and devotion to the collective concerns of Spanish-speaking peoples in the United States. Groups such as the League of United Latin American Citizens and the National Council of La Raza have emerged to represent all Latin ethnic groups, whereas groups such as MAPA and the Puerto Rican Organization for Political Action devote some attention to the concerns of particular nationalities. All of these groups recognize that Hispanics can become an effective force for political and social change if they can get beyond their differences and combine their forces.

American Indians

During the fifteenth and sixteenth centuries, there were probably between one million and ten million American Indians living in North America (Snipp, 1989). By the late 1800s, there were only about 250,000. After the founding of the United States, the federal government was required by the U.S. Constitution to negotiate treaties with these American Indians, but this did not

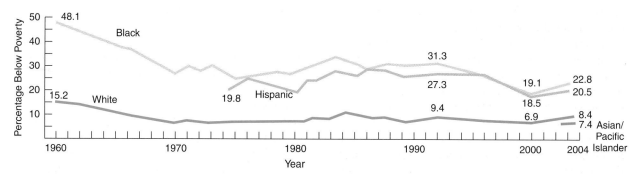

FIGURE 6.3 **Percentage of Families in the United States with Incomes Below the Poverty Level, by Race, 1960–2004.**

Source: U.S. Bureau of the Census, *Current Population Reports Series* P60, "Poverty in the United States." (Washington, DC: U.S. Government Printing Office), various years.

prevent whites from robbing Indians of their land. (Again, there is disagreement about what to call this group. Some members of this minority prefer "Native American" to "American Indian"; others insist that only tribal names, such as Comanche, Cree, and Apache, be used because there is much diversity among the native peoples. This text uses American Indian because it is the term used by the Census Bureau from which much of the data in this chapter were obtained.)

In 1824, the Bureau of Indian Affairs (BIA) was created by Congress as a division of the War Department to seek a military solution to what many congressmen referred to as the "Indian problem." By 1830, Congress succumbed to pressures for opening up more Indian lands to white settlement and ordered the BIA to relocate all Indians west of the Mississippi River. It was not until 1924 that Congress passed the Indian Citizenship Act, granting U.S. citizenship to all American Indians. In 1968, Congress enacted the Indian Civil Rights Act, which extended the basic human rights guaranteed by the Bill of Rights to persons living on tribal lands. Although this undoubtedly had many positive benefits, it may have had the negative effect of undermining tribal control and unity among American Indian groups who possessed their own judicial systems based on tribal customs (Schaefer, 2004).

There are almost 3 million American Indians in the United States (U.S. Bureau of the Census, 2006:15; U.S. Bureau of Indian Affairs, 2005). Two percent of U.S. land (56 million acres) is still managed by the Bureau of Indian Affairs "on behalf of" American Indians. In 2000, there were about 500,000 American Indians, Inuit (Eskimos), and Aleuts living on reservations in the United States (U. S. Bureau of the Census, 2006:43). The BIA, now part of the Department of the Interior, has conservation as its prime directive rather than economic development. This de-emphasis of economic matters has contributed to the problems of American Indians by making it more difficult for them to improve their economic position.

American Indians suffer significant social, economic, and health disadvantages in comparison to other ethnic and racial groups (Snipp, 1989; U.S. Bureau of the Census, 2006:40; Young, 1994). Nonreservation Indians are somewhat better off than their reservation counterparts, but half of all Indians live on reservations in rural areas. They suffer high levels of unemployment, low levels of income, and poverty rates disproportionate to their numbers in the population. They are also less likely to graduate from high school than people in most other groups.

In the 1960s, many minority groups began to resist oppression, and American Indians were among them. In 1969, a group of Indians seized Alcatraz Island to call attention to their exploitation. In 1973, members of the American Indian Movement (AIM) staged an armed takeover of Wounded Knee, South Dakota, where whites had killed hundreds of Indians in the late nineteenth century. These protests may be in part responsible for some recent court decisions ruling that Indian tribes should receive payment for land taken from their ancestors during the nineteenth century. Still, there is a lingering feeling among many American Indians that exploitation continues, albeit in more subtle ways than before (Marks, 1998).

Today, the Indian community in the United States is growing in number and showing renewed pride in its history and culture (Marks, 1998). Although many serious problems persist, a college-educated middle class of American Indians has emerged, and the number of businesses owned by Indians is increasing significantly. Tribes on reservations have been able to exploit gambling and tourism to create jobs, and some have built successful manufacturing businesses. With the economic resources made available by these endeavors, Indians have hired lawyers and lobbyists to go to state capitals and Washington, DC, to fight for the interests of Indians. Some tribes are even struggling to establish tribal sovereignty, which in their view would make tribal lands the equivalent of independent nations. All of these developments together suggest that a cohesive and powerful American Indian community is emerging in the United States that will work to improve the circumstances of Indians both on and off tribal lands.

Asian Americans

Between 1820 and 1969, more than 1 million legal immigrants from China, Japan, the Philippines, Hong Kong, Korea, and India came to the United States—a mere 3.7 percent of all immigration that took place during that period (see Figure 6.4). The heaviest migration of Chinese to the United States occurred between 1849 and 1882 (Daniels, 1988). Although racial prejudices existed toward the Chinese prior to 1849, once their immigration began in large numbers, these sentiments intensified. There was a feeling among many people that the Chinese would deprive whites of jobs in mining and railroading, another illustration of the split labor market discussed earlier. These feelings culminated in the Chinese Exclusion Act of 1882, which prohibited the entrance of Chinese laborers into the United States for ten years.

Between 1882 and World War II, racist attitudes in the United States characterized the Chinese as a "yellow peril." Many Chinese returned to their own country because of this hostility. Those who remained were forced to move to ghettos called Chinatowns. Chinese people were often referred to with the pejorative term "coolies," and the racism toward Chinese often implied biological differences between Chinese and Anglos. An anthropological study in 1877, for

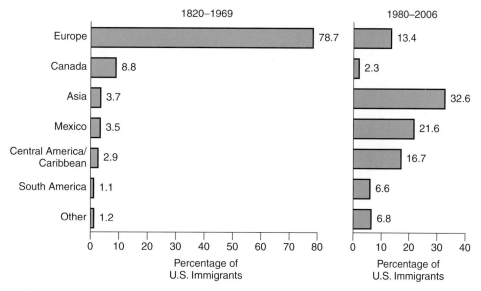

FIGURE 6.4 Immigrants to the United States, by Country of Last Permanent Residence, 1820–2006.

Source: U.S. Department of Homeland Security, *Yearbook of Immigration Statistics, 2006* (Washington, DC: U.S. Government Printing Office, 2007), www.dhs.gov/ximgtn/statistics/publications/yearbook.shtm.

example, concluded, "It is true that ethnologists declare that a brain capacity of less than 85 cubic inches is unfit for free government, which is considerably above that of the coolie as it is below that of the Caucasian" (quoted in Miller, 1969:145).

These anti-Chinese attitudes persisted in the United States until the 1940s. Following Japan's attack on Pearl Harbor, hostilities shifted toward the Japanese, and the Chinese came to be regarded more positively. In 1943, the Chinese remaining in the United States were granted citizenship. Between 1950 and 1970, Chinese Americans became upwardly mobile, with children of the original immigrants attending colleges and universities and moving into professional and technical positions. Today, the socioeconomic status of Chinese Americans, especially those who have been in the United States for some years, is considerably above the average for Americans as a whole (Barringer, Takeuchi, and Xenos, 1990; Hirschman and Wong, 1986).

The peak period of Japanese immigration to the United States began after the Chinese Exclusion Act, between 1880 and 1924. Unlike the Chinese, Japanese immigrants were permitted to bring their wives with them, which aided in the formation of stable Japanese families, and early relations between Americans and the Japanese were positive. After Pearl Harbor, Japanese Americans were the object of considerable discrimination, being forced to sell their property and being interned in concentration camps (Kitano, 1976; O'Brien and Fugita, 1991). Along with the enslavement of blacks and the genocidal attacks on American Indians, the imprisonment of Japanese Americans—none

of whom had been proven disloyal to the United States—stands as one of the darkest examples of racism in U.S. history.

After release from the concentration camps after the war, Japanese Americans led successful lives, exceeding many whites in occupational achievements, and most Americans appear to have a high regard for Japanese Americans today (Barringer, Takeuchi, and Xenos, 1990; Ima, 1982). Still, there are occasional flare-ups of the racism that was so prevalent during World War II.

Significant immigration from Asia to the United States has continued in recent decades (Min, 1994). For example, in the 1970s and 1980s, tens of thousands of refugees entered the United States from Vietnam, Laos, and Cambodia as well as other parts of Asia. These recent immigrants have largely followed the route of their predecessors as far as integrating themselves into the United States, taking undesirable jobs that most workers tend to reject or opening small businesses to make a living. Although there is little widespread discrimination against Asian immigrants, violence does occur. In the 1992 riot in south central Los Angeles, for example, Korean-American businesses were apparently targeted for looting and burning by African American and Hispanic American rioters who were angry over what they perceived as mistreatment of blacks and Hispanics by Korean store owners (Lee, 2002). This reflects the economic sources of racial discrimination and conflict discussed earlier. Blacks and Hispanics find themselves in a position of economic subordination to Korean store owners. This has led to stereotyping on both sides, with Koreans accusing African Americans

Combating Prejudice and Discrimination

The horror of the genocidal attack on Jews and other ethnic groups during World War II dramatically portrayed the extremes to which prejudice and racism might go. One positive spin-off from these atrocities was that they pushed many European and American social scientists to conduct research on the sources of prejudice and discrimination, and many of the results of that research have been summarized in this chapter. The findings of this body of research can also be applied to seeking ways of combating racism.

How do we reduce racist attitudes and encourage people to view members of another racial or ethnic group more positively? A program at a summer camp for children showed one way to achieve this (Clore et al., 1978). The camp included equal numbers of black and white children, and they came from all levels of the socioeconomic hierarchy. In the camp, all children had the same rights and same work duties. There was also an equal mix of blacks and whites among the administrators and counselors in the camp, so the authority structure of the camp was not racially biased. In other words, blacks were as likely to exercise power over the children as were whites. During their one-week stay at the camp, children were required to work on cooperative tasks involving group, rather than individual, goals.

What did the camp accomplish? Basically, children who entered the camp with negative attitudes toward members of the other race showed positive improvements in their views by the end of their stay. Why did this change occur? The results of past research and the outcomes of current programs are very clear in showing that intergroup contact can reduce prejudice if the contact occurs in a particular way (Brewer and Miller, 1996; Pettigrew, 1998).

1. The contact should have high "acquaintance potential," which means that people have the time and opportunity to get to know one another and have some personal and intimate associations.

2. The contact should be between people of equal status, rather than a low-status minority interacting with a higher-status member of the dominant group.

3. The behavior of the minority-group person in the contact should contradict the stereotype held of members of that group.

4. As a part of the contact, the people should work toward cooperative and interdependent goals rather than competitive ones; that is, no one in the

and Hispanics of stealing and African Americans and Hispanics accusing Koreans of selling poor products at high prices and refusing to hire African American or Hispanic employees. Exacerbating this situation is the fact that Koreans have little contact with African Americans and Hispanics outside of this economic (merchant–customer) context. The importance of the nature of the contact that occurs between groups is explored in more detail in the Applied Research insert.

Arab Americans

People are classified as Arab Americans by the U.S. Bureau of the Census if they claim an ancestry from one of the predominantly Arab-speaking countries (such as Lebanon or Iraq) or regions of the world (such as the Middle East) or if they make a general ancestry claim of Arabic. Using this definition, about one-half of 1 percent of the U.S. population would be considered at least part Arabic (U.S. Bureau of the Census, 2005). Although a relatively small ethnic group, Arab Americans give us some additional perspectives on race and

ethnic relations in the United States. One wave of Arab immigration to the United States occurred between 1870 and World War I and involved mostly people seeking better economic opportunities for their families (Read, 2004). This group was predominantly Christian and tended to assimilate into the mainstream after arrival. The second wave of Arab immigration began after World War II and continues today. For this group, immigration has been motivated more by an effort to escape the political turmoil in their native land. This group is predominantly Muslim, better educated, and retains a stronger attachment to their native culture. Despite the diversity in religion and national background of the Arab immigrants, they mostly share a common language and set of cultural values.

Arab Americans as a group are well integrated into life in the United States and have done quite well for themselves (U.S. Bureau of the Census, 2005). As a group, they are considerably better educated than other Americans, have higher incomes, are more likely to be working in management jobs rather than service or blue-collar jobs, and over half of them are

group can achieve his or her individual goals unless everyone works together and achieves their goals.

5. The contact situation should have the support of legitimate authorities, such as a school or church, and should involve social norms dictating friendliness and respect between people.

One can readily see that many of these features were built into the children's summer camp described above. One can also recognize that many everyday interpersonal contacts between members of different races violate these principles. Black and white prison inmates, for example, live together in intimate contact, but it is a very tension-filled contact with little inducement for cooperation or interdependence. Many races intermingle in schools, but school is often highly competitive. And how often is the equal status element violated when a black or Hispanic person deals with a white teacher, a white social worker, or a white prison guard?

We cannot, of course, change all these settings. On a smaller scale, however, we can structure social situations over which we do have control with the above principles of intergroup contact in mind. This was done very well in the children's summer camp. A similar approach has been used successfully many times with adults in the form of small-group interaction and sensitivity training. The goal of these efforts is to bring members of different races together for lectures, discussions, and group activities over a period of days or weeks. Through the use of role playing and other group techniques, participants are encouraged to explore stereotypes, diagnose interracial problems, and cooperatively develop strategies for alleviating those problems. This was done, for example, in Houston in the late 1960s when police–community relations became very tense and hostile following a violent clash between black college students and police in which one police officer was killed. Hundreds of police and community residents participated in the program, and it had a positive effect on people's attitudes and reduced the number of citizen complaints against the police (Bell et al., 1969).

What has been learned about the impact of intergroup contact on prejudice and discrimination can be used to bring about other structural changes in society. School integration, for example, brings students of different races together. The research offers a pretty good idea how to do this so that the positive impact is maximized.

Christians. They are a group of ethnic immigrants who have mostly succeeded in the United States.

However, the Arab American experience has not been all positive. For one thing, they have higher rates of poverty than other Americans, probably reflecting the fact that some in this group are recent immigrants. In addition, Arab Americans have experienced significant prejudice and discrimination since the September 11, 2001 terrorist attacks. Since the war on terrorism has focused substantially on Islamic extremists, many Arabic, Muslim, and Arab-appearing peoples feel that they have been unfairly and unnecessarily targeted with arrest and harassment as a part of the war on terrorism (Henderson et al., 2006). In other words, they feel that one particular ethnic group has become the scapegoat as the United States deals with a very frustrating and amorphous problem. Many Arab Americans feel that their success in the United States is the embodiment of many cultural values and ideals, and yet many also feel that their treatment since 9/11 unveils the prejudices of some Americans against Arabs, Muslims, and people from the Middle East.

Today's Immigrants

In 1965, a totally revamped immigration act removed all racial and ethnic quotas for immigrants to the United States. As a consequence of this act and other trends, today's immigrants are quite unlike those of the past (see Figure 6.4). For most of U.S. history, over three-quarters of the immigrants have been from Europe, with very small proportions coming from Asia or Central and South America. Today, only 13 percent come from Europe, 33 percent come from Asia, and another 45 percent from Mexico and Central and South America.

The Social Construction of Minorities: Media Images

Equally important as the history and circumstances of the major racial and ethnic minorities in the United States, is how others perceive these minorities in society. The media play a key role in this. The images that the

This Cambodian Buddhist Temple in Massachusetts shows the extent to which immigrants to the United States have changed: Today they come mostly from Asia and Central and South America rather than from Europe as in the past.

media present of people of various races and ethnic groups, as the interactionist perspective suggests, help to shape people's perceptions and expectations regarding particular groups. After all, the portrayal of an African American or American Indian on television or in a movie is a cultural image that has some societal legitimacy by virtue of having been given space in the mainstream media. In addition, from the conflict perspective, the media can be considered *contested territory,* which groups attempt to influence and control as a part of the struggle over resources in society. The media are controlled mostly by the dominant racial and ethnic groups in any society, and thus it is their stereotypes of races and ethnic groups that are most likely to find space in the media (Biagi and Kern-Foxworth, 1997; Wilson, Gutiérrez, and Chao, 2004). This means that, in the United States, whites tend to be disproportionately portrayed in the media and to be placed in the more positive roles: the good person, the success, the hero, the winner. In fact, until the 1960s at least, movies and television were pretty much a white landscape: Nonwhites appeared only in minor roles, in menial positions, or as criminals or villains. The images of minorities that the media have presented in the past

three decades have certainly improved. As opportunities for minorities in all areas of society have gotten better, more minorities have begun to work in the media industries that produce culture; there are more minority actors, producers, directors, and newscasters. Media stars such as Spike Lee, Geraldo Rivera, Emilio Estevez, Oprah Winfrey, and Bill Cosby have become influential in shaping the presentation of culture through the media.

Yet, despite these changes, minorities in general are still underrepresented in the media, and Latinos, considering their numbers in the population, may be one of the most underrepresented ethnic groups in the media (Children Now, 2004; National Council of La Raza, 1997). In addition, the image of minorities presented is still often a distorted and negative one. For example, recent studies of local television news stories and reality-based police shows demonstrate the distorted images of race that are presented. African Americans, for example, appear in the local news as violent criminals and in very few other roles (Entman, 1997; Gilliam et al., 1997). Furthermore, African Americans are presented as criminals in these news shows in numbers that are far disproportionate to their actual contribution to the crime problem. African Americans are also portrayed in more dangerous images than are whites, in glowering mug shots or being led around in handcuffs. White criminals are much less frequently shown in such poses. Furthermore, whites are disproportionately portrayed as the victims of black criminals. The overall impression presented in these television shows is that the crime problem is due to blacks and that whites are the victims. Criminologist Katheryn K. Russell concludes that "television's overpowering images of Black deviance—its regularity and frequency—are impossible to ignore. These negative images have been seared into our collective consciousness" (1998:3). As for prejudice and discrimination, these images may well contribute to the negative stereotyping of one racial or ethnic group by another, thus exacerbating the problems discussed in this chapter.

As the twenty-first century begins, the explosion in media, computers, and telecommunications may actually create more opportunities for expression on the part of minorities as more media outlets call for the production of more media products. Because some of these new outlets will be targeted toward minority audiences, this expansion will likely create a demand for minority-produced media materials. This will make it more possible for minorities to find media work, contribute to the portrayal of minorities in the media, and make positive minority role models available. In fact, some of the television networks that have emerged

with the explosion of cable television in the past few decades, such as WB and the Comedy Channel, have targeted programming toward minority audiences as a way to gain a foothold in a very competitive industry.

Future Prospects

Assimilation or Pluralism?

A review of the history of racial and ethnic minorities in the United States shows that relations between minority and dominant groups have taken a number of different forms (Simpson and Yinger, 1985). For blacks, for example, *segregation* from whites in schools, housing, and transportation has been common and still lingers in some realms today. For many minorities, *subjugation*, in the form of subordination and exploitation, has been a major problem. The grisly experiences of American Indians came close to *genocide*, or the annihilation of an entire group. Estimates are that at least two-thirds of the population was annihilated by the direct and indirect actions of white Europeans, with some tribes being completely eliminated. Today, however, the most common relationships between racial and ethnic groups in the United States involve assimilation and pluralism. **Assimilation** is *the process by which a racial or ethnic minority loses its distinctive identity and way of life and*

These merchants in Los Angeles need to post notices in many different languages in order to adequately serve their clientele. This attests to the extent of racial, ethnic, and cultural pluralism that exists in the United States today.

becomes absorbed into the dominant group. Despite the considerable amount of assimilation that has occurred in the United States, there are still many racial and ethnic minorities that preserve their heritage. This pattern of intergroup relations is called **pluralism,** *which exists when a number of racial and ethnic groups live side by side, each retaining a distinct identity and lifestyle while still participating in some aspects of the larger culture.*

Which pattern of minority–majority relations is most desirable in the United States: assimilation, pluralism, or some other? People's response to this question is often colored by a misconception about what has happened historically. The United States is often referred to as a *melting pot* in which the beliefs, values, and lifestyles of many different racial and ethnic groups have been blended together into a unique mix that is called "American." If this had occurred, it would be a form of assimilation in which all groups change to some degree in creating an American identity. Actually, the experience of most immigrants to the United States has come closer to what Milton Gordon has called *Anglo conformity:* To share fully in the American dream, immigrants have been required to renounce their ancestral culture in favor of the beliefs, values, and lifestyle of the dominant WASPs, the white Anglo-Saxon Protestants (Gordon, 1964). These WASPs were among the earliest European immigrants to North America. They came from the British Isles and Germany, and they dominated political, economic, and social life in the United States from the sixteenth through the nineteenth centuries. The WASPs were sufficiently fearful of people who immigrated after them—from places such as Ireland, Italy, and Eastern Europe—that they attempted to "Americanize" them rather than let them build their own social institutions and way of life. Many people today still insist on a version of Anglo conformity by arguing that groups such as Hispanics and Asians should learn English and not be given a bilingual education.

Although Anglo conformity worked for quite a while, it has not persisted. Over time, the original WASP group became such a small minority that it became more difficult for it to force its lifestyle on others. The outcome, at least to this point, is that the United States remains a highly pluralistic society with many distinct racial and ethnic subcultures. Furthermore, some minorities, especially among African Americans and Hispanics, who were never allowed to assimilate by the dominant white groups, prefer it that way. Whether pluralism is desirable, however, is a matter of considerable controversy (Pettigrew, 1988). Many people argue that extensive pluralism will promote tensions that could flare into conflict in the future. They point to the efforts of French Canadians in Quebec to secede from Canada as the kind of problem that pluralism can generate. Proponents of pluralism, on the other hand, contend that racial and ethnic diversity contributes to the richness of U.S. culture and symbolizes the nation's roots as open to the oppressed of all lands. Furthermore, ethnic identity can be a source of pride and positive self-regard for individuals, and speaking in one's native tongue can play an important part in this. Among Latinos, for example, speaking Spanish and having a large and powerful Spanish-language media in the United States are sources of cultural pride and ethnic identity.

The past few decades have generally been a time of considerable improvement in the relationship between minorities and dominant groups in the United States. Many of the more explicit forms of discrimination have been reduced, and these changes have lessened the inequalities that exist in the stratification system. In addition, racial and ethnic minorities in the United States today are more organized, confident, and optimistic than they were in the past.

Race Relations Today: Race or Class?

As discussed earlier, some minority groups, such as African Americans, still lag significantly behind other groups on various indicators of socioeconomic status. There is considerable debate over whether this is because of racial discrimination or because of the class position held by many African Americans, which places them in a weak situation from which to compete for jobs and income.

Sociologist William J. Wilson (1987; 1996) argues that class, rather than race, is the more important factor in determining the social positions of African Americans today. Wilson certainly does not deny that racial antagonism is still with us, or that substantial discrimination against and oppression of African Americans not only has clouded U.S. history but also lingers today. But he points out that the real problem today lies in the continuing existence of a sizable group of poor, marginally skilled African Americans who have little opportunity to obtain the education and skills necessary to succeed in a modern industrial society (see the Applied Research insert in Chapter 5). Such a group of entrenched poor can also be found among Puerto Ricans and some other Hispanic groups (Alex-Assensoh, 1995; Tienda, 1989). Wilson attributes the persistence of this poverty to basic changes in the structure of the U.S. economy, including the relocation of industries away from the communities where many minorities live and a labor market in which people with few job skills or little education are limited to low-paying work with little opportunity for advancement. The primary barrier that this group faces, argues Wilson, is the lack of appropriate job-related skills, not racial discrimination. Blacks or Hispanics with job skills or a college education, he argues, will enjoy opportunities and privileges similar to those of their white counterparts in the class hierarchy and will probably not face significant discrimination even if economic conditions deteriorate.

On the other side of this argument are sociologists Joe Feagin and Melvin Sykes (1994) who argue that racial oppression is still a key factor influencing race relations in the United States. They argue that African Americans are still oppressed and discriminated against because of their race, although the forms and mechanisms of racial oppression may have changed since the 1950s and 1960s. One difference today is that the overt individual racism of the past has declined considerably, but there is still widespread, institutionalized racism in which such things as residential and school segregation place barriers before the advancement of many African Americans but few whites. In addition, many whites find the black urban culture of today alien and threatening (Jencks, 1992). Because of this they are less likely to hire African Americans, particularly young males. In addition, employers have other motivations for discriminating against African Americans in hiring. For example, an employer might believe that an African American employee will drive away white customers. This was done in professional sports for many years when owners and managers believed that white fans would not pay to see black players. This still occurs today when companies refuse to hire African Americans for highly visible positions, such as receptionist or salesperson, when customers are white.

Feagin and Sykes interviewed hundreds of middle-class African Americans, who are presumably the ones least affected by race, according to Wilson. Based on these interviews, Feagin and Sykes concluded that "few middle-class African Americans interviewed . . . see the significance of racism in their lives declining" (1994:12). For all these reasons, Feagin and Sykes argue that race still very much determines the position of African Americans as a group.

So, controversy continues over whether the continuing chasm between the achievements of African Americans and whites is predominately due to class or to race. Although it may be difficult to resolve the proportionate role of each, it is certain that each plays some part. The issues involved are important because the contrasting positions on this controversy point to very different policy recommendations for its solution.

Collective Protest and Civil Rights Legislation

The civil rights movement of the 1950s and 1960s marked the beginning of some significant developments in racial and ethnic discrimination in the United States (Morris, 1984). By the end of the 1960s, as a result of protests and demonstrations, laws had been established that made it illegal to discriminate against people in jobs, housing, schools, or public facilities on the basis of race or ethnicity. Voting rights legislation was also passed to ensure that adults in the United States did not confront barriers to the voting booth. These laws have become the tools for bringing about impressive improvements in the problem of discrimination. Educational, employment, and housing opportunities are now available to minorities who, four decades ago, would have had those doors to opportunity completely closed. Despite advances, however, discrimination persists. Although it is illegal, some employers and landlords still turn away African Americans, Asians, or others because of their race. This discrimination is difficult to eliminate because it is often hard to prove that denial of a job, for example, was motivated by an applicant's minority-group membership rather than by the superior qualifications of another applicant. So civil rights legislation has been a good foundation, but additional efforts have been made to eliminate the lingering effects of discrimination in the form of affirmative action.

Affirmative Action

Affirmative-action programs were first established in the early 1960s, before the Civil Rights acts of the 1960s and at a time when discrimination against African Americans in employment, education, and housing was widespread, overt, and socially sanctioned by many groups. Affirmative action was designed to help remedy this situation. The purpose of affirmative action is to provide opportunities to minorities and to integrate schools and workplaces in the United States (Swain, 2001). As originally designed, it required schools and employers to make active efforts to seek qualified minority applicants for openings and even to establish hiring and admissions practices that gave a preference to minorities. As the program evolved, this resulted in some cases in the establishment of quotas whereby a certain proportion of openings would go to minority applicants, even if that necessitated hiring a less-qualified minority applicant over a more qualified white applicant. The rationale underlying affirmative action was a belief that a school or business with few minority students or employees is itself evidence that discrimination has occurred. The burden is then on the school or the employer to prove that it has not discriminated by actively seeking out minorities.

Over the past three decades, courts and state legislatures have struggled to satisfy the two competing demands in the realms of hiring, promotion, and admission: that all people be treated equally, on the one hand, and that the goal of maintaining racial and ethnic diversity in the civil life of society be encouraged, on the other hand. The overall trend of court rulings and other policies over these years has been toward a weakened affirmative-action policy. In the late 1990s, for example, voters in California passed a referendum that banned the use of race and ethnicity as criteria in state employment and college admissions. In situations where affirmative-action policies have been eliminated, the result has been a decline in the numbers of African Americans, Hispanic Americans, and American Indians admitted to the schools.

In 2003, the U.S. Supreme Court ruled on the constitutionality of affirmative action in a way that gave some support to both sides of the issue. The court supported the position that promoting diversity in student bodies and in work forces was a compelling societal interest because everyone benefited from such diversity. Furthermore, the court ruled that an applicant's race could be used as a factor in admissions decisions in order to achieve this diversity. However, the court also ruled that race must be taken into account in an individualized and holistic way rather than a mechanical way. Strict racial quotas would be mechanical, and therefore unconstitutional, as would be giving every school applicant or job applicant of a particular race a set number of points toward acceptance. On the other hand, considering a person's race along with a variety of other factors—the weight or importance of each factor being assessed individually for each case—would be constitutional. The Policy Issues insert explores some of the positions and policies that have emerged on this issue over the decades.

Affirmative action is a policy that does not ignore race but rather takes it into account when making decisions about hiring, promotion, or entrance into school. The International Perspectives section explores a policy in another society that takes ethnicity into account in an effort to accommodate minorities in a political system.

School Programs and Busing

In 1966, sociologist James Coleman and his colleagues published a report on school segregation that quickly became known as the "Coleman Report." In it, they presented data that showed extensive segre-gation in schools in the United States and that documented that African Americans performed more poorly than other racial or ethnic groups. They also showed that African American students who attend desegregated schools with a better "motivational atmosphere" showed improved academic performance. The motivational atmosphere in the school basically had to do with the proportion of pupils in the school who were lower-class to pupils who were middle-class. African Americans attending schools with a "middle-class" atmosphere did better than African Americans attending schools with a "lower-class" atmosphere. In part because of the Coleman Report, a number of programs were developed to assist minority and white students in improving their academic performance and possibly their career opportunities. Some programs focused on compensatory education to make up for the deficiencies students might experience because of a poor school or home environment. Other programs focused on school integration, sometimes by busing students from one school to another. Such integration, it was believed, would not only improve the performance of minority students, but also reduce prejudice and discrimination in the long run.

Has school integration achieved its goals? In terms of school achievement, some studies have found improvements with integration and others have not (Entwisle and Alexander, 1994; Longshore and Prager, 1985; Rist, 1979). Overall, integration has probably made modest improvements in school achievement by African Americans, especially when students are integrated in the early grades. The reason that the impact has not been more uniformly positive is because so many other factors—socioeconomic status, family background, racial tensions in the schools, and the manner in which integration is accomplished—also influence achievement. However, there are signs that school integration may produce benefits beyond its impact on school achievement. Research suggests that school integration has helped to reduce racial isolation in the United States, and that this will reduce racial tensions and stereotyping in the future (Hawley et al., 1983). Research also suggests that the experience in desegregated schools has an impact on African Americans later in life: They are more likely to attend predominantly white colleges, socialize with whites outside of school, and live in integrated neighborhoods as adults (Braddock, 1985; Braddock, Crain, and McPartland, 1984).

Despite whatever improvements they might have produced, programs of school integration, especially when achieved through mandatory busing, have been controversial. One reason for the controversy is that the programs seem to violate parents' right to send

Should the Government Intervene to Improve Opportunities for Minorities?

Opponents of affirmative action claim that such programs are no longer necessary because the racism that produced unequal opportunities for racial and ethnic minorities is largely a thing of the past. With the dwindling of discrimination based on race or ethnicity, argue some economists such as Thomas Sowell (1981), minorities would be best served by a laissez-faire economic environment in which people compete for jobs on the basis of their own abilities and wits. Immigrant groups of the past, such as Irish and Jewish Americans, struggled against discrimination without government intervention and eventually were able to succeed despite the discrimination. With the decline of racism, the same should be expected of minorities today.

Opponents of government intervention also argue that affirmative action is a form of *reverse discrimination,* where whites are passed over for jobs or positions in school in favor of nonwhites who are sometimes less qualified than the white applicants. In other words, they argue, affirmative action represents not the elimination of racism but rather the use of race to benefit minorities to the detriment of the majority. This has produced considerable resentment among some whites, who feel that they have personally lost opportunities because of such reverse discrimination. It has also resulted in feelings of frustration, resentment, anger, and cynicism among some whites toward social and political institutions and policies. These feelings have been a major factor in the growing opposition to affirmative action.

Supporters of affirmative-action programs argue that such programs have made it possible for many minorities to overcome persisting discrimination and obtain jobs or entrance into schools that they would not have obtained otherwise. Because of this, minorities and women have been integrated into the schools and workforce in the United States to a degree that probably would have been impossible without an effort like affirmative action. Furthermore, a recent study documents that African Americans who enter college through affirmative-action programs succeed very well in their careers and communities as adults and have become a significant part of a growing African American middle class (Bowen and Bok, 1998). In addition, supporters of affirmative action argue, clear-cut cases of reverse discrimination, although they can be found, are relatively rare. Mostly what affirmative action has achieved is to force employers to search out qualified minority applicants and to consider them fairly.

Supporters of affirmative action also argue that, although some minorities have been able to overcome discrimination without affirmative action, African Americans and Hispanic Americans in particular have confronted much more universal and persistent discrimination. And, as documented in this chapter, discrimination against these groups in jobs, education, and housing continues at a significant level today. Under these conditions, equal opportunity and integration of schools and workplaces will be difficult to achieve without some form of affirmative action (Jencks, 1992).

In response to court rulings and other policies prohibiting the use of race as a consideration in hiring, school admission, or school integration, what may be emerging is a search for policies that achieve these goals without the taint of reverse discrimination. One approach might be "soft quotas" that schools and employers make a good effort to meet, but with no precise numerical goals. Related to this is what William Julius Wilson calls "affirmative opportunity": an approach that uses flexible, merit-based criteria for evaluating people for positions in schools or jobs (Wilson, 1999). It doesn't promote equality of outcome and doesn't advocate putting people into positions for which they are not qualified, but it does suggest that one qualified candidate for a position might be given a preference over another qualified candidate if the former had experienced a history of racial discrimination. So, racial background becomes one of a number of criteria used in evaluating people who are qualified for positions.

Another approach, tried by one state, is a plan that allows the automatic admission into the best public colleges in the state for students who are in the top 10 percent of their high school class, irrespective of their SAT scores. Because minorities tend to perform lower on the SATs than do whites, this benefited minority students. Another approach to affirmative action and school integration has been to shift at least some of the attention from race to socioeconomic status on the grounds that it is the poor (of whatever race) who are disadvantaged and need some special assistance. Some programs for school integration, for example, have based student assignment to schools on social class rather than race. Since there is an association between class and race, assignments based on class can help achieve goals of greater racial diversity in the schools.

Interventionist				Laissez-Faire
Affirmative-action quotas	Soft quotas/affirmative opportunity	Use SES or other criteria that support minorities	Improve low-income schools	Open competition for jobs and school entrance

Switzerland: Cooperation in a Multiethnic Society

In 1993, President Clinton proposed Lani Guinier for the post of Assistant Attorney General for Civil Rights and ran into a hailstorm of opposition. Some of the opposition was because Ms. Guinier had explored in her writings some radical proposals for giving minorities some influence on the political system. One alternative she explored, for example, was "cumulative voting," in which voters might cast more than one vote for a single candidate for office. It could work like this: If five city council seats are vacant, each voter could cast five votes. They could cast one vote for each of the five or all five votes for one candidate. By cumulating their votes on one candidate, a racial or ethnic minority that constituted only a small percentage of the population in the city might be able to elect a candidate. Without cumulating, their numbers are so small that they are unlikely to elect any candidate. Cumulative voting and other proposals explored by Guinier were focused on identifying political structures that give minorities a share of political power and that avoid completely disenfranchising groups that happen to be small in size. Such proposals are highly controversial in the United States, but a look at how such issues are handled in other societies can be instructive.

Switzerland is often pointed to as a model of effective pluralism because it is made up of three distinct ethnic groups—German, French, and Italian—that work together peacefully and cooperatively. Prior to the nineteenth century, ethnic conflict in Switzerland was constant and often violent, at times verging on civil war (Schmid, 1981; Steiner, 1990). Intense and bitter religious conflict between Catholics and Protestants also contributed to the strife. The French, who conquered Switzerland in 1798, imposed ethnic and linguistic equality on Switzerland. Finally, a brief civil war in the 1840s ended with the adoption of a Constitution in 1848 that continued the protection of linguistic minorities and created a system of power sharing among ethnic groups that has enabled the Swiss to live in peace and harmony for the last 150 years.

The basic assumption of this power-sharing system is that all three language groups are assured of representation in the government. The Swiss Federal Council, the executive body of Switzerland, and the parliament include members from all three ethnic groups, in rough proportions to their numbers in the population. The chairmanship of the Council, equivalent to the U.S. presidency, is rotated to a different ethnic group each year, assuring each ethnic group a turn in that important position. Civil service positions and military appointments

their children to schools of their choice. Another reason they are controversial is that schools in the United States remain highly segregated, in part because of the high degree of residential segregation that persists between whites and both African Americans and Hispanic Americans (Orfield and Lee, 2004). Residential segregation has persisted, in part, due to "white flight" in reaction to compulsory school busing. White flight refers to white students leaving certain school districts for suburban or private schools to avoid either busing or integration. Research clearly shows that, although busing is not the sole culprit, it has made a significant contribution to the flight of whites from many public school districts (Carr and Zeigler, 1990; Orfield and Lee, 2004; Smock and Wilson, 1991).

The result of all this has been that policies promoting racial integration in schools find less support today. For example, based on the research showing that busing produces white flight and thus helps to resegregate the schools, many courts have terminated court-ordered school desegregation plans, and this termination has probably produced higher levels of school segregation (Orfield and Lee, 2004). Then in 2007, the Supreme Court ruled that it was unconstitutional for schools to explicitly use race as a criterion for assigning students to schools for purposes of achieving racial integration. Such court rulings will make it more difficult to integrate the schools and will probably lead policy makers and educators to search for other ways to achieve some degree of school integration. Some of

are also made with proportional representation in mind. All three languages are considered the national languages of Switzerland. The Swiss political system is one of decentralized federalism, with the governments of each canton, or district, having autonomy in the conduct of many of their affairs. Thus, each canton, dominated by a particular ethnic group, controls its own schools and police.

The pluralist Swiss system amounts to what would be called a quota system in the United States. In contrast to Swiss power sharing, the United States and many other nations tend more toward a system of power competition, according to which each group strives to concentrate as much power in its own hands as it can. Such competition often leaves minorities largely disenfranchised and dissatisfied.

Swiss pluralism works for a number of reasons. First, because the three ethnic groups are of European heritage, they share a lot of common history and culture, despite their differences. Second, the three ethnic groups have been settled in the region for centuries, and compromises and accommodations have been worked out over the years. Third, the Swiss state has been stable for a number of years, without the political instability that can serve as fertile ground for ethnic conflict. Finally, the Swiss ethnic minorities did not have to go through a protracted or bitter struggle for their rights that could have left simmering antagonisms.

Because of these factors, some have argued for Swiss "exceptionalism": The Swiss experience is unique and cannot serve as a model for other societies where conditions make solutions to racial and ethnic conflicts much more difficult to find. But Jurg Steiner (1990), who has studied the Swiss, says they are not a different or "naturally peaceful" people. Rather, from experience over a long period, they have created a system that reduces conflict between groups and produces greater cooperation, stability, and prosperity. As one expert who studied the Swiss experience put it, the lesson to learn from Switzerland is that "successful democratic pluralism depends on minorities being continually accommodated within the political system" (Schmid, 1981:155). The United States is certainly different from Switzerland, and Swiss structures would not necessarily achieve the same outcomes in the United States. However, the Swiss experience does suggest that it could be of value to explore whether new political or social structures could help our pluralist society function with more harmony and less feelings of disenfranchisement among some minorities.

these possibilities are discussed in the Policy Issues insert and in Chapter 15.

Improving the Economy

Those who view contemporary racial problems as a "class" problem and those who take the laissez-faire approach to solving social problems argue that improvements in the U.S. economy will narrow many of the disparities between dominant groups and minorities. Differences in family income, for example, or education or life expectancy can be narrowed if people have access to better jobs and can improve their lifestyles. This does not deny the occurrence of discrimination or exploitation in the past, but it does say that the future calls for different emphases. The government's role in the future, they argue, should be focused on improvements in the economy. Some of the specific proposals have been reviewed in Chapter 5 and need not be repeated here.

There have been many improvements in race relations in the United States in the past two decades. Although there is much in U.S. history to be lamented, people can be proud of the recent advances. Yet there are reasons for uncertainty about the future. Whereas racial violence has been limited of late, periodic outbursts document that such violence is just below the surface. This suggests that the potential for prejudice, discrimination, and racial violence is still very strong and can be rekindled if the proper social conditions arise.

STUDY AND REVIEW

Summary

1. A minority group is a group whose members are viewed by dominant groups as inferior because of certain characteristics. They have less access to power and resources than do other groups, and they are accorded fewer rights, privileges, and opportunities.

2. A race is a group of people who is believed to be a biological group sharing genetically transmitted traits that are defined as important. An ethnic group comprises people who share a common historical and cultural heritage and sense of group identity and belongingness. Racism is the view that certain racial or ethnic groups are biologically inferior and that practices involving their domination and exploitation are therefore justified.

3. Prejudice and discrimination result from different social and psychological sources. Among the social sources are ethnocentrism, competition, socialization, and institutionalized discrimination. Psychological sources include stereotyping, frustration and aggression, and the authoritarian personality.

4. Discrimination has a number of consequences, including an adverse effect on people's life chances and an increase in tension and hostility in society.

5. Among racial and ethnic groups in the United States, African Americans and Hispanics are the largest minorities, and they lag considerably behind other groups in access to education, power, and economically rewarding jobs. One of the most important reasons for this is the long history of discrimination and oppression suffered by both groups, making it difficult for them to improve their position in society.

6. American Indians experience some of the worst conditions of all minority groups in the United States. Some Asian Americans, on the other hand, have been able to attain a degree of affluence despite the substantial prejudice and discrimination they have experienced.

7. Today, the most common types of relationships between dominant and minority groups in the United States are assimilation and pluralism. Although most minority groups have experienced some degree of assimilation, there is considerable emphasis today on the pluralistic nature of society. There is also controversy over whether ongoing socioeconomic differences between the members of dominant and minority groups are a result of racial discrimination or class position.

8. Civil rights legislation, affirmative-action programs, school programs and busing, and efforts to improve the economy are techniques that have been used in trying to improve race and ethnic relations in the United States.

Key Terms

assimilation	internal colonialism
authoritarian personality	minority group
discrimination	pluralism
ethnic group	prejudice
ethnocentrism	race
in-group	racism
institutionalized discrimination	split labor market

Multiple-Choice Questions

1. Polish Americans would most clearly be
   a. a racial group.
   b. an ethnic group.
   c. an authoritarian group.
   d. an example of internal colonialism.
   e. a split labor group.
2. A negative attitude toward certain people based solely on their membership in a particular group is called
   a. prejudice.
   b. discrimination.

The Internet is an excellent place to search for materials on minority groups and on issues of prejudice and discrimination. However, be forewarned that some material you come across may be offensive to some of you. A good way to begin is by dialing in to the Yahoo! search engine. Begin by logging into the Yahoo! search engine. Click "more," then "Directory" search category, then "Society and Culture" and then "Cultures and Groups." Now you have various alternatives, such as "People of Color" and "White Pride and Racialism." As you can begin to see, some of these sites may contain material that is disturbing to certain people, but the reality is that racism and racial hatred are a part of the social reality of race and ethnic relations, and need to be understood.

There is also a box where you can type in various keywords for Yahoo! to search on. You should try to locate materials on minority groups that are not covered in this book or are only briefly covered. You could also search under key words, such as "racism," "hate groups," multiculturalism," "American Indian Move-

ment," or "La Raza." You could also search for particular individuals, such as "Leonard Peltier" or "Russell Means." Don't know who they are? Look them up and report back to the class.

Another approach is to look for organizations that fight against discrimination and for social justice for minorities. One of the largest in the United States is the National Association for the Advancement of Colored People (NAACP) at **www.naacp.org**. At that site, you can find updates on state and national legislation relevant to minorities and social justice, as well as current news events relating to minorities. How many other such organizations can you find on the Internet?

In all of this searching, find information that addresses two additional issues: (1) race and ethnic relations in places other than the United States and (2) viewpoints on issues of race and ethnic relations that are often not found expressed in the mainstream media.

The Allyn & Bacon Social Problems Supersite **(wps.ablongman.com/ab_socialprob_sprsite_1)** contains material on race and ethnic relations.

c. a minority group.

d. pluralism.

e. segregation.

3. Joseph has a negative stereotype toward and dislikes all people from the Middle East, but he does not discriminate against them in hiring for his store because of the laws against it. In Robert Merton's classification, he would be called

a. an unprejudiced nondiscriminator.

b. a prejudiced discriminator.

c. a prejudiced nondiscriminator.

d. an unprejudiced discriminator.

4. Which of the following is a type of economic exploitation between a dominant group and a minority group?

a. ethnocentrism

b. assimilation

c. institutionalized discrimination

d. internal colonialism

e. genocide

5. The split labor market could be best characterized as

a. two groups of workers willing to do the same work but for different wages.

b. exploitation of a subordinate group by a dominant group for the benefit of the dominant group.

c. an unprejudiced person who is a discriminator.

d. institutionalized discrimination by a dominant group against a minority group.

6. All of the following are true about Hispanic Americans *except*

a. some Hispanic groups may be moving toward a common Latino ethnic identity.

b. the largest group among Hispanics is Mexican Americans.

c. they suffer from low educational levels in comparison to whites.

d. the gap between Hispanic and white income has narrowed substantially since the 1970s.

7. Which of the following groups was once placed in concentration camps in the United States?

a. Japanese Americans

b. Chinese Americans

c. African Americans

d. Hispanic Americans

e. Arab Americans

8. Interracial contact would have the *least* likelihood of reducing prejudice if the contact

a. were between people of equal status.

b. were supported by legitimate authorities.

c. supports stereotypes held by majority-group members.

d. has high acquaintance potential.

9. Over the history of the United States, the experience of most immigrants to this country comes closest to

a. a melting pot.

b. ethnocentrism.

    c. Anglo conformity.
    d. genocide.
    e. both a and c.
10. The text concludes which of the following regarding the impact of school integration programs on the performance of minority students?
    a. The amount of white flight from cities is reduced.
    b. Minorities show modest improvement in school performance.
    c. Minorities show dramatic improvement in school performance.
    d. Hostility between minorities and whites increases.

True/False Questions

1. Race and ethnicity are ascribed statuses.
2. Groups such as the Gypsies and Jews would be classified by sociologists as races.
3. From the functionalist perspective, ethnocentrism is always considered to have negative consequences for members of an in-group.
4. The text concludes that racism does lower the self-esteem of minorities in some contexts.
5. African Americans were the only minority group to be enslaved in the United States.
6. Because of casino gambling and other economic enterprises on Indian reservations, income and educational levels on reservations now approach those for society as a whole.
7. According to the text, the most common relationship between racial and ethnic groups in the United States today is segregation and subjugation.
8. Contact between different racial and ethnic groups can reduce prejudice if the contact has high "acquaintance potential."
9. The text concludes that race is more important than class in determining the social position of African Americans in the United States today.
10. The civil rights legislation established in the 1960s has virtually eliminated discrimination on the basis of race and ethnicity.

Fill-In Questions

1. Sociologists' definition of race is based on people's _____ that there are biological differences between the races.
2. _____ is the view that certain racial or ethnic groups are biologically inferior and can be discriminated against because of this.
3. Fred and Mary believe that their high school is superior to all the other high schools in their district. This is an example of the tendency toward _____.

4. In a split labor market, the people who receive the brunt of the discrimination is the _____.
5. The ruling in which the U.S. Supreme Court declared the "separate but equal" doctrine to be unconstitutional was _____.
6. U.S. citizenship was granted to all American Indians in the decade of the _____.
7. In recent decades, the largest percentage of immigrants to the United States has come from the geographical region of _____.
8. Proponents of _____ contend that racial and ethnic diversity make positive contributions to U.S. culture.
9. _____ discrimination occurs when affirmative-action quotas result in qualified majority-group members being excluded from a job because of their race.
10. _____ occurs when white students leave a school district for suburban or private schools in order to avoid school busing or school integration.

Matching Questions

_____ 1. MAPA
_____ 2. mass media
_____ 3. competition causes discrimination
_____ 4. psychological source of prejudice and discrimination
_____ 5. soft quotas
_____ 6. Cesar Chavez
_____ 7. assimilation
_____ 8. WASPs
_____ 9. ethnocentrism
_____ 10. James Coleman

A. contested territory
B. affirmative action
C. a blending of racial and ethnic identities
D. the authoritarian personality
E. Hispanic political group
F. study of segregation in schools
G. Hispanic labor organizer
H. in-group feeling
I. earliest European immigrants to North America
J. conflict perspective

Essay Questions

1. What is ethnocentrism? What role does it play in prejudice and discrimination?
2. How does socialization influence prejudice and discrimination?
3. According to the text, what detrimental consequences does discrimination have for society?

4. Describe the prejudice and discrimination experienced by Japanese Americans and Chinese Americans since first immigrating to this country.

5. What are the social circumstances of African Americans and Hispanic Americans in comparison to one another and to whites?

6. Characterize the patterns of minority–majority relations in the United States today and in the past.

7. What characteristics of the contact between racial groups are most likely to reduce prejudice between the groups?

8. What are the arguments for and against affirmative-action programs?

9. Is the situation of African Americans in the United States today mostly a function of "race" or "class"? Make arguments for both sides of this issue.

10. What does the text conclude regarding whether racial integration of the schools has achieved its goals?

For Further Reading

Dalton Conley. *Being Black, Living in the Red: Race, Wealth, and Social Policy in America.* Berkeley: University of California Press, 1999. This sociologist provides an in-depth analysis of the role of both race and class in determining the social and economic position of whites and blacks in the United States today.

Joe R. Feagin and Karyn D. McKinney. *The Many Costs of Racism.* Lanham, MD: Rowman & Littlefield, 2003. This book provides an excellent overview of how racism has substantial negative impacts on people and community.

Stephen S. Fugita and David J. O'Brien. *Japanese American Ethnicity: The Persistence of Community.* Seattle and London: University of Washington Press, 1991. Focusing on the experiences of Japanese Americans, these sociologists investigate the factors that influence whether an immigrant group maintains a viable community or becomes completely assimilated by the dominant group.

Paula Mitchell Marks. *In a Barren Land: American Indian Dispossession and Survival.* New York: William Morrow, 1998. This is an excellent and readable history of Indians in the New World. It comes all the way to the present and suggests the complexity of factors that have shaped the status of Indians in the United States.

Randall Robinson. *Defending the Spirit: A Black Life in America.* New York: Dutton, 1998. This is an eye-opening memoir by a Harvard-educated African American lawyer about what it is like to grow up black in the United States. Robinson describes the insult and humiliation that he has suffered and the rage that can result.

Earl Shorris. *Latinos: A Biography of the People.* New York: W. W. Norton, 1992. This excellent book explores the lives and history of the fastest growing minority group in the United States, the descendants of the Spanish conquest of the Native American peoples. Through wonderfully insightful biographical sketches, the author communicates the complex diversity today in the group that is given the single designation of "Latino."

Debra Van Ausdale and Joe R. Feagin. *The First R: How Children Learn Race and Racism.* Lanham, MD: Rowman & Littlefield, 2002. Based on direct observations of children interacting with one another, these sociologists explain how children learn and use racial identities in their lives.

William Julius Wilson and Richard P. Taub. *There Goes the Neighborhood: Racial, Ethnic, and Class Tensions in Four Chicago Neighborhoods and Their Meaning for America.* New York: Knopf, 2006. Using Chicago as a case study, these sociologists explore the complexity of race and ethnic relations in the United States today, looking at sources of tension and conflict between various groups and proposing ways of bringing these diverse communities together.

GENDER AND SOCIAL INEQUALITY

omen have made some remarkable advances in the past few decades in the struggle for gender equality. More women hold elective office than ever before, female astronauts now routinely orbit the earth, and as many women graduate from law school and medical school each year as men. Yet, despite these advances, evidence can also be found attesting to the fact that the United States still falls short of according full equality to women. In 1998, for example, the Southern Baptist Convention voted overwhelmingly in support of adding to its essential statement of beliefs the amendment that a woman's proper role in the family is to "submit graciously" to her husband's leadership and that the husband should provide for, protect, and lead the family. As another example, even today, female soldiers in the United States routinely experience sexual harassment, sexual assault, and even rape at the hands of their fellow soldiers. Whether it be in the military academies, in the barracks, or in the war zones of Iraq and Afghanistan, such soldier-victims have often found it difficult, if not impossible, to bring their assailants to justice.

Sexual harassment and job discrimination are two elements of the problem of social inequality based on sexual status. This chapter will review the reasons why such inequality occurs, its dimensions in the United States, and what can be done to alleviate it.

Men and Women in Society

Sex is an *ascribed status:* It is a position in society that is assigned to a person; people have virtually no control over their ascribed statuses. Unlike achieved statuses, such as one's educational level or occupation, there is little, if anything, that people can do to alter their sexual status. Sex is also a *master status* because it has considerable social significance in all societies. It is a central determinant of how people view themselves and how others respond to them, and it frequently serves as a basis for social differentiation. In fact, gender inequality is an important element of the stratification system in society. In some societies discrimination based on sexual status is so irrevocable that women have virtually no chance to improve their status. Gender inequalities are typically justified by **sexism,** *an ideology based on the belief that one sex is superior to and should dominate the other sex.* To understand how sexual status shapes the structure of society, it is helpful to understand why sex is an element of social differentiation in societies at all. This chapter will examine four different views on this issue.

The Biological Perspective

One perspective on the role of sexual status in determining one's position in society is that innate biological differences between men and women shape the contributions each can make to society. One question this raises, of course, is: What precisely are the biological differences between the sexes? Modern research has documented some differences and shown that other differences are not supported by the available evidence. For example, evidence exists that men are more aggressive and violent and have greater upper body strength than women. Men also seem to excel in visual–spatial abilities, whereas women do particularly well in verbal skills and creativity. As far as personality characteristics such as sociability, emotionality, dependence, or self-esteem, no consistent evidence exists that the genders differ. Are the differences found in research caused by biology? In only a few realms is there any evidence that they are (Fausto-Sterling, 1992; McCoy, 1985). Higher levels of aggressiveness in males, for example, are very common in other species, such as rhesus monkeys, and

Myths & Facts

About Gender Inequality

Myth: Women have taken their place in the workforce with men, holding more varied jobs and earning higher pay relative to men than ever before.

Fact: More women work, but their pay still lags significantly behind that of men doing the same work. This is true in virtually all industrial nations, with women in Japan earning only half of what men do. Also, many low-paying, low-prestige jobs are still female ghettos, with 97 percent of secretaries, 93 percent of receptionists, and 98 percent of dental hygienists in the United States being women.

Myth: More women are seeking political office than ever before.

Fact: Women, who make up 51 percent of the U.S. population, held 16 percent of the seats in the U.S. Senate and 17 in the House of Representatives in 2007. Women do well in Cuba and Finland, where they hold one-third of the parliamentary seats, but in some African and Arab nations, there are no women in parliament.

Myth: By the 1990s, the United States had become solidly supportive of equal rights for women.

Fact: The Equal Rights Amendment to the Constitution, which would prohibit discrimination on the basis of gender, has yet to be approved.

Myth: The courts have ruled that barring women from service and community organizations such as Rotary and the Kiwanis violates antidiscrimination laws. Thus, women now have the same access as men to community and business arenas.

Fact: This is true in communities that have antidiscrimination laws. In the thousands of communities where there are no such laws, however, women can be and are excluded from such organizations.

it is almost universal in human cultures. Levels of aggressiveness can also be affected by changes in sex hormones. Thus, there is the suggestion, but by no means conclusive proof, that higher levels of aggressiveness in males are in part biological. In terms of the differences in verbal and spatial–visual ability, some evidence suggests that the brains of males and females are organized differently in this regard. In men, verbal skills are focused on one side of the brain and spatial–visual skills on the other. In women, each skill can be found on both sides of the brain. This difference in the organization of the brain may account for why women tend to have more verbal skills and men are more adept at spatial–visual tasks. With regard to greater upper-body strength, this is probably attributable to the higher levels of the hormone testosterone among males.

So there undoubtedly are some biological differences between men and women that have implications for social behavior. However, the differences are far fewer and much smaller than were once thought to be the case. Furthermore, the differences appear to relate to general tendencies, such as aggressiveness, rather than to specific social behaviors, such as fighting or playing football. In addition, despite any biological differences, men and women are highly flexible and extremely malleable in terms of what they are capable of doing. Most of our behavior is learned rather than biologically programmed, which means that men can learn to behave in a stereotypically female fashion, and women can learn to behave in ways that we would expect men to behave (Tavris, 1992). A final point is that the differences between men and women refer to average levels of performance, which ignores the significant overlap between the sexes. Many women, for example, are more aggressive than some men, and some men are less aggressive than many women. Because of this, sexual status alone is a rather poor basis for establishing social policy or allocating social tasks and rewards.

The Functionalist Perspective

Functionalists argue that some tasks were allocated to men and others to women in preindustrial societies because such arrangements were more convenient and practical (Ford, 1970; Giele, 1978). On the whole, males are physically stronger than women and free of the responsibility of bearing and nursing children. Women, on the other hand, were expected to have many children during their lives and to spend much of their adult lives either pregnant or rearing their children. In addition, women were a more valuable reproductive resource in that the loss of a woman, as in war, would reduce the reproductive potential of society. The loss of a man, on the other hand, could easily be made up for through increased sexual activity on the part of other men. There would be no loss in the overall reproductive potential of society. Given these considerations, functionalists argue, it was more practical in preindustrial societies to assign to men tasks, such as hunting or felling trees, that are physically demanding and might draw one away from home for long periods. Men were also assigned the dangerous tasks, such as protecting the group against attack from enemies. Women, on the other hand, who were limited by pregnancy and the need to nurse their young, were considered better suited to such tasks as gathering roots or berries, cooking food, and making pottery. Once these sex-role distinctions had become firmly established as a part of a group's tradition, they were then supported by strong group norms that made these differences independent of their origins. They came to be seen as the "natural" ways for men and women to behave rather than as practical means of accomplishing societal tasks (Brown, 1970; O'Kelly and Carney, 1986).

Industrialization ushered in a number of significant social changes: the separation of work from family life, smaller families, and a longer life expectancy. As a consequence, women tended to be isolated in the family and given prime responsibility for homemaking and child-rearing duties, whereas men went out and worked. Sex roles became divided along the lines of instrumental and expressive tasks (Parsons, 1951). **Instrumental tasks** refer to *the goal-oriented activities of the group, such as hunting, building something, or managing a work team.* Males were seen as having responsibility for most of these tasks. **Expressive tasks** refer to *activities focused on the relationships between people—maintaining happiness, harmony, and emotional stability.* These tasks were seen as primarily a woman's responsibility. In fact, for men, it became a status symbol to have a wife who did not work—an indication of how capable the man was at producing economically and supporting his family. To justify this division of tasks, sexist beliefs emerged that a woman's place was in the home and that women were not biologically equipped for most forms of male work. However, in most preindustrial societies, women were not removed from economically productive roles. Much of what they did, such as gathering roots, tending crops, or herding flocks, contributed significantly to the economic support of the group. They were by no means limited to child rearing or expressive tasks. Likewise, men were by no means limited to instrumental tasks in preindustrial societies.

From the functionalist perspective, then, a social problem exists when the sex-role division of labor is no longer consistent with the needs of a particular society. To confine women to child rearing or expressive activities would waste a valuable resource. In industrial societies, families have few children today, and they have many supports, such as day care, to help in raising them. So it is no longer necessary for adults—either male or female—to devote their lives to such tasks. It would be better if they used their intellectual, creative, and productive abilities to make additional contributions to society. Because the birthrate is low and most jobs in industrial societies are not dangerous, there is no need to protect women as a reproductive resource, as was the case in the past. In addition, great physical strength is no longer necessary for most jobs in a highly automated, technological society. For all of these reasons, functionalists argue, it is not particularly useful to use sex as a criterion for allocating jobs today. It would be more functional to assign tasks based on individual abilities.

The Conflict Perspective

Many sociologists have questioned whether the fact of a woman having children is the central element in shaping sex roles in society and especially whether it explains the continued existence of sex stratification. For example, sociologist Randall Collins (1971) has argued that there is an inherent conflict of interest between men and women and that sex roles can serve as a mechanism by which one group dominates the other. In part, this domination results because males in general are physically stronger than women, which better equips them to use power to their own advantage and gain dominance. But the situation is more complex than this. Through the socialization process, a subtler form of power is exerted and control achieved: People learn to want those things that are in the interests of the dominant group in society. In most societies, women have learned to accept the dominance of males and their own subordinate positions because they believe such dominance is appropriate and even desirable or because they feel they have no other choice.

The economic competition discussed in Chapter 6 also contributes to sexual inequality. In simple hunting and gathering societies, there is a division of labor based on sex, as we have seen, but there is also considerable equality between men and women. The reason for this is that women produce as much as and sometimes more than men. Gathering nuts, roots, and berries produces a steady and dependable food supply, whereas the results of hunting can be very sporadic. It might be days or weeks before men can fell some game. In the interim, women provide food for the group. In agricultural societies, men tend to dominate economic productivity, in good part because their physical strength and freedom from child-bearing duties enable them to engage in extensive, heavy labor

that might take them away from home for hours or days at a time. This leaves women economically subordinate and unequal. As functionalists point out, this inequality continues into early industrial societies as men work and women stay home. This arrangement benefits men, of course, because they have a corner on the prestigious and powerful positions in society, and most men wish to continue those social practices.

From the conflict perspective, then, sexual differentiation becomes the "battleground" for a struggle over scarce resources—in this case, for jobs and prestige. However, this economic competition for jobs—a form of the split labor market discussed in Chapter 6 because women are typically paid less than men—was translated into the sexist ideology that women were incapable of performing the jobs as well as the men.

From the conflict view, sexual inequality becomes a social problem when some group—in this case, women—realizes it is being exploited and that something can be done about it. In the past half century,

Women were allowed to hold many traditionally male jobs in the United States during World War II when the men were unavailable, but the women were forced out of the jobs when the men returned—a clear reflection of gender dominance and inequality, according to the conflict perspective.

women have come to realize that their inferior status has been caused by male domination, not biological inheritance. Once this realization emerged, sexual inequality came to be viewed as a social problem and entered the arena of public debate.

The Interactionist Perspective

According to the interactionist perspective, human beings relate to one another on the basis of symbols that have social meaning within a given culture or society. Those social meanings are created, communicated, and reinforced as people interact with one another on a daily basis. So we can understand a lot about the creation and maintenance of gender inequality if we watch how men and women interact in various settings. Probably the most important symbol system for human beings is language. Interactionists point out that many values, beliefs, and social meanings find expression in different language forms. For example, the sex-specific pronouns *he* and *his* can be used when referring to both men and women, and this convention in English may be a veiled way of maintaining male dominance. Research suggests that such sexist language is still very much with us and shows conclusively that use of the generic *he* does create predominantly male images in people's minds, especially for men (Gastil, 1990; Switzer, 1990). When people read or hear "he," instead of "she" or "they," they think of men, and this can be a symbolic reinforcement of the exclusion of women from many aspects of society. This linguistic usage, then, may reinforce and help perpetuate sexist thought and action, especially among men, by encouraging a predominantly male imagery when thinking about activities or realms of which both men and women might be a part.

The conversational styles of men and women can also reflect and reinforce gender patterns of dominance and subordination (Spencer and Drass, 1989; Tannen, 1994). Such styles, for example, can have direct implications for gaining and keeping positions of leadership in groups. One investigation focused on the order in which people speak in mixed-sex groups (Aries, 1996). In general, men initiate more conversation and receive more interaction than women. People who initiate the most interaction in groups take up the most time and are considered by others in the group to be leaders. So if women are taught to be submissive or timid around men, they may be less likely or less able to assume leadership in groups. As another example of the effect of conversational styles, it is widely believed in the United States that women talk more than men (the stereotype has it that women "chatter on" about frivolous subjects), yet many investigations of conversational behavior in mixed groups show that men talk more than women and interrupt while others are talking more than women do. Men also answer questions not addressed to them and continue talking when there is an overlap in conversation.

So it is through interaction patterns such as these that beliefs and practices regarding gender inequality are maintained and reinforced. In preindustrial societies, the roles of men and women were relatively clear cut and accepted by most people, even though those roles reflected substantial inequality. In modern industrial society, however, the social structure is changing at a rapid pace, and forms of sexual differentiation formerly accepted are now challenged by many people. So gender inequality becomes a social problem when there is a lack of consensus and a lack of shared expectations about the roles of men and women in society.

The Socialization of Men and Women

Scientific research has demonstrated that much of our behavior as males and females is not a function of biology but rather of learning. This leads to the distinction that sociologists make between *sex* and *gender*. *Male* and *female* are used as sex-related terms—the innate, biological feature of sexual identity. **Sex** refers to *the biological role that each of us plays, such as in reproduction. Masculine* and *feminine,* on the other hand, are used as gender-specific terms. **Gender** refers to *learned behavior involving how we are expected to act as males and females in society.* One of the key issues in analyzing gender inequality is how we learn to be masculine and feminine and how this learning contributes to sexual differentiation and inequality. This learning occurs in good part through three major agencies of socialization: the family, the schools, and the media.

The Family

Infancy represents a crucial period for human development and for the establishment of beliefs about appropriate masculine and feminine behavior. A growing body of literature clearly demonstrates how parents are likely to treat male and female infants and young children in ways consistent with how they view masculinity and femininity. For example, fathers are typically "rougher" with boys and gentler with girls, and both mothers and fathers tend to speak more softly to girls than to boys (MacDonald and Parke, 1986; Rossi, 1984).

By the age of three, children have acquired a gender identity, which means that they can correctly label themselves as male or female. But at this point, their identity is oversimplified and highly stereotyped. It is also based more on such things as hairstyle or dress than on an accurate awareness of genital differences between the sexes. Once the child's gender identity has been established, he or she then attempts to master the behaviors that are associated with that gender. Behaving "like a boy" or "like a girl" becomes rewarding because it brings approval from adults and peers. Parents today still tend to encourage boys to engage in instrumental play, such as building something, whereas girls are encouraged toward expressive play, such as making themselves look attractive.

Even in childhood, it appears that male activities are valued more than female ones. For example, girls often display a fondness for the higher prestige of the masculine role by becoming "tomboys" (Burn, O'Neil, and Nederend, 1996; Martin, 1990). "Tomboyism" is acceptable to a much greater extent than a little boy's being a "sissy." In fact, girls are more prominent in boys' games than boys are in girls' games—testimony to the less negative reactions to tomboys than to sissies. Other investigators have discovered that boys play more competitive games than girls and that girls typically do not learn how to deal with direct competition (Berliner, 1988; Best, 1983).

Research shows that parents today do interact with their children differently from parents of a few decades ago. Parents today are more aware of the negative consequences of gender stereotyping, and they make greater efforts to treat all their offspring alike, regardless of gender. Yet, gender and traditional cultural ways of relating to males and females are powerful forces, and parents still relate to their male and female offspring differently. This is true even of parents who consider themselves egalitarian in terms of gender relations (Weisner, Garnier, and Loucky, 1994).

The Schools

A very significant part of the socialization process occurs in the schools. School systems are characteristically staffed in such a way that children's perceptions of masculinity and femininity are reinforced. Although most elementary schoolteachers are female, most elementary school principals are male. Thus, from the beginning of school, children see men in positions of authority and dominance over women (Richmond-Abbott, 1992). In addition, schools and teachers treat children very differently based on their gender, with significant consequences for what children learn about gender (Benokraitis and Feagin, 1995; Thorne, 1993). Investigations have shown that female teachers are more likely to encourage independence and assertion in boys than

in girls. Teachers also tend to provide less attention to girls, and to reward female students for conforming and male students for being aggressive. The way teachers do this is quite subtle. Dependence in girls, for example, is encouraged by not sending them off to work on their own, although boys often work alone. So teachers, often without realizing it, reward their students for behaving in a fashion consistent with their own sex-role stereotypes.

Two or more decades ago, the images of males and females presented in school textbooks typically reinforced traditional stereotypes: Males were pictured far more often than females, males were pictured in many occupations and women in few of them, and female pronouns such as *her* were uncommon. But have there not been changes in all this in the past twenty years? Not as many as one might think. Things have improved, especially when efforts are made to produce materials that are nonsexist in their presentation. However, some stereotyping still persists. Studies of children's picture books, for example, find that more women are portrayed than in the past but still less often than men, women are less likely to be portrayed as working outside the home, women are still shown in fewer occupations than men, and women are portrayed as less brave and adventurous and more helpless (Clark, Lennon, and Morris, 1993; Crabb and Bielawski, 1994; Peterson and Lach, 1990; Purcell and Stewart, 1990). Furthermore, although men are sometimes portrayed as expressing their emotions, denying one's feelings is still characterized in these books as a normal aspect of maleness.

Even college textbooks are not immune to these influences. Studies of the pictorial content of texts for college-level psychology and sociology courses found that women are shown less often than men and are portrayed more passively and negatively than men (Ferree and Hall, 1990; Peterson and Kroner, 1992). For example, the psychology texts portray women as the victims of mental disorders and the clients in therapy, whereas men are pictured as the therapists. All these portrayals help to perpetuate the cultural stereotype that men tend to be stronger, more active, and working in the world to solve problems, whereas women are more likely to be weaker, more passive, and focusing their interests around home and family.

Evidence shows that sexist treatment in the schools does result in lower self-esteem for female grade school and high school students (Martinez and Dukes, 1991; Sadker and Sadker, 1994). Even at the college level, as the Applied Research insert in this chapter suggests, the interaction between faculty and female students can involve strong doses of sexism, with potentially detrimental influences on female students' performance.

Fighting Sexism in Higher Education

The manner in which men and women are treated in college classrooms can amount to gender discrimination if women are treated in such a way that the classroom contains a powerful negative educational atmosphere for them. Some behaviors that are offensive to women are fairly obvious, such as professors using sexual humor to "spice up" dull lectures. Although most college professors probably avoid such blatantly offensive behaviors, there may still be subtle ways in which male students are favored in the classroom over female students, even though many professors and students may not be consciously aware of them. In fact, a report by the Association of American Colleges' Program on the Status and Education of Women (1982) suggested twenty years ago that there was a "chilly climate" in the college classroom for women. It cited the following behaviors by professors as instances of sexism that help create that chilling effect:

- Calling directly on male students but not on female students.

- "Coaching" male but not female students to work toward a fuller answer by probing for additional elaboration or explanation.

- Waiting longer for men than for women to answer a question before going on to another student.

- Interrupting women students or allowing them to be disproportionately interrupted by peers.

- Using classroom examples that reflect stereotyped ideas about men's and women's social and professional roles, as when the scientist, doctor, or accountant is always "he" and the lab assistant, patient, or secretary is always "she."

- Using the generic *he* or *man* to represent both men and women, as in "When a writer is truly innovative, what criteria can we use to measure his achievement?"

The report provoked considerable debate and numerous research efforts to assess the extent and exact forms that such chilly behaviors might take (Canada and Pringle, 1995; Crawford and MacLeod, 1990; Fritschner, 2000; Howard and Henney, 1998). The research shows that, at least in some colleges and in some contexts, male students do dominate college classroom discussions. However, there is less evidence that it is the chilly behavior of male college professors that discourages participation by female students. Some colleges may have a classroom atmosphere that is generally friendlier to male students, but in most colleges the sex of the professor does not seem to be a big factor in producing the dominance of males—it occurs in the classrooms of both male and female professors. It may be that males come to college more prepared to project themselves actively and aggressively into classroom discussions, and the professors in turn may respond more positively to those students, irrespective of sex, who show such initiative and speak up in the classroom. Male college students may behave differently from their female counterparts in this regard because of the general socialization experiences discussed elsewhere in this chapter, or because they were encouraged to do so in grade school and high school classrooms.

Whatever the reasons for gender differences in the classroom, colleges and professors need to look at things they can do to encourage more classroom participation from female students. A helpful finding in some of this research is that female professors create an atmosphere in the classroom in which students feel more comfortable interacting, and they elicit more student participation than do male professors. Female professors seem to be more aware of the interpersonal dynamics in the classroom that might discourage participation. Their male counterparts might be able to learn something from them.

So, this sexist atmosphere in the classroom, subtle though it is, can impact women students in a negative way. By exploring the sources and nature of the sexism through research, we will be better able to design interventions to fight it.

The Media

The media are an extremely important influence on gender-role socialization through their portrayals of men and women, with perhaps the most significant for young people being television. It has been estimated that between kindergarten and sixth grade, children watch from ten to twenty-five hours of television every week. In fact, "children spend more time watching television than they do reading books, listening to the radio, or going to the movies" (Richmond-Abbott, 1992:98). Despite the fact that television has "cleaned up its act" to some extent, this powerful medium still overwhelmingly portrays stereotyped gender roles. Investigations of television programs reveal that many of them present a grossly distorted view of family life. Over the past three decades, only 20 percent of the characters on prime time television shows were female, and most of the women shown were young, unemployed, family bound, and in comic roles (Richmond-Abbott, 1992).

There have, of course, been improvements in the portrayal of women in the movies and on television over the past decades. Some popular network shows in recent years—*L.A. Law*, *West Wing*, and *First Monday* come to mind—have featured strong and positive female characters in their starring roles. Yet studies repeatedly document that only one out of three roles in prime time is played by women and that anchors, newsmakers, and authorities on television news shows are overwhelmingly white men (Howard, 2002; Smith, 1997). Women are more likely to be shown as preoccupied with romance, dating, and personal appearance rather than with work or education. The portrayal of women in children's shows was even more lopsided, according to the reports.

So, some of the old stereotypes linger, and evidence shows that they affect youngsters' attitudes about these matters. Research demonstrates that children do model what they see on television, and they identify with same-sex characters (Lindsey, 1997). Boys are attending to the strong and virile male characters, whereas

Although things have changed over the decades, the roles on prime time television still often perpetuate stereotyped images of women and men, as this advertisement for *Desperate Housewives* seems to do with its heavy emphasis on physical beauty and sexuality as central aspects of female identity.

girls respond to the beautiful female portrayals. In addition, the teenagers most strongly affected by gender-role portrayals on television are those with the least sexist attitudes to begin with: Fairly intelligent girls show the most change toward sexist attitudes. This again illustrates the subtle ways in which people can develop views of the world that help maintain patterns of dominance and subordination.

Music is also a powerful medium for communicating to young people about gender, and much of what has been said about portrayals of gender in other media formats is true for music (Lindsey, 1997). Although one can find practically any message—including strongly egalitarian and feminist ones—in some musical formats, the predominant portrayals tend to be of men who are dominant, strong, and aggressive, and of women who are young, physically attractive, and sexually alluring. The images that predominate are those of the sexual temptress, the virginal girl next door, and the subordinate woman whose fulfillment is dependent on the actions of a man. Portrayals of the assertive, independent woman are far less common. Whatever the musical form—rock, country and western, rap, hip hop, and so on—male performers predominate in numbers over female performers, and the female performers who become successful typically must perform and dress in a sexually provocative way. Heavy metal, rap, hip hop, and rock videos also often combine sexual images with images of male aggression and violence, sometimes perpetrated against women (Barongan and Hall, 1995; Smitherman, 1997; Sommers-Flanagan, Sommers-Flanagan, and Davis, 1993). Similar images predominate in video games: They are suffused with images of male conquest, males protecting fragile and dependent women, and men saving women from unsavory ends (Gilmore and Crissman, 1997). What little research there is on the impact of exposure to such images suggests that they do reinforce traditional sex-role stereotypes, promote attitudes of indifference toward violence against women, and might actually promote such violence. These are issues that will need to be explored through further research in the future.

The Extent of Gender Inequality in the United States

Although women are a numerical majority in the United States, they comprise a minority group, and there are a number of important similarities between women and other minorities (see Chapter 6). Like African Americans, women still have unequal access to valued resources and suffer discrimination on many fronts. Although this chapter focuses primarily on the way in which women suffer from gender inequality, it also looks at some ways in which men have been discriminated against by unreasonable differentiation based on sex.

Economic Discrimination

Women occupy a subordinate position in comparison to men on virtually every dimension of socioeconomic status (SES). The three main dimensions of SES are education, occupation, and income.

EDUCATION Until about 1850, women were almost completely excluded from colleges. It was assumed that women needed less education because their careers would be as homemakers and mothers. In fact, in 1873, the U.S. Supreme Court ruled that an Illinois woman could be denied a license to practice law on the grounds that she was female. One Supreme Court justice of the era defended this stance by saying, "the paramount mission and destiny of women are to fill the noble and benign offices of wife and mother. This is the law of the Creator" (The Brethren's First Sister, 1981:17).

Since 1950, the number of people twenty-five years of age and older with some college training has quadrupled, and there have been dramatic increases in the proportion of women who pursue some form of advanced education in the United States. The percentage of doctoral degrees going to women has grown from 10 percent in 1960 to 48 percent today, and 49 percent of law degrees go to women today, compared with only 5 percent in 1970 (U.S. Bureau of the Census, 2006:183–186). Still, more men attain these degrees than do women, and as Figure 7.1 illustrates, the percentage of men who complete college still exceeds that of women, at least among whites and Asians and Pacific Islanders. Although women have gained on men in college graduation rates in the past half century, a significant gap still exists. Furthermore, a very substantial gender gap persists in particular educational fields, such as science, mathematics, computers, and engineering (U.S. Department of Education, 2004b). For example, only 18 percent of bachelor's degrees in engineering are awarded to women. An interesting related issue is that among African Americans, men are slightly worse off in terms of educational achievement than women, suggesting that decades of oppression and racial discrimination have made it especially difficult for black males to be upwardly mobile (see Chapter 6).

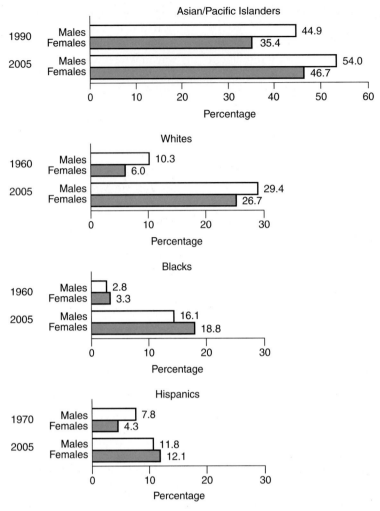

FIGURE 7.1 Percentage of People, Age Twenty-Five Years or Older, Completing Four Years or More of College, by Sex and Race, 1960 and 2005.

Source: U.S. Bureau of the Census, *Statistical Abstract of the United States, 2007* (Washington, DC: U.S. Government Printing Office, 2006), p. 143.

WORK AND THE WORKPLACE Although women constitute about 46 percent of the labor force in the United States, they are concentrated at the lower end of the status hierarchy. Table 7.1 illustrates that women tend to hold jobs such as secretary or receptionist, which provide relatively low income and prestige. The better occupations, such as physician or engineer, are held primarily by men. Evidence suggests that some of this difference, even today, is the result of discrimination in hiring practices. Some employers still prefer to hire men for jobs requiring technical or managerial skills based on the gender-role stereotype that men are more competent at such tasks. This is especially true when there is no evidence to suggest superior job performance on the part of either the male or female applicant for a job (DeLaat, 1999; Zebrowitz, Tenenbaum,

and Goldstein, 1991). Table 7.1 illustrates that the job opportunities for women have improved since the 1970s, with considerably more women moving into such lucrative jobs as lawyer, physician, and engineer. But the dark side of the issue is that many of the low-paying and low-prestige jobs are still almost exclusively filled by women. In addition, research shows women who take traditionally male, blue-collar jobs encounter a very hostile climate in terms of how they are treated by their male coworkers and supervisors. These women, as a result, are less satisfied with their jobs and experience more stress at work than do women in traditionally female jobs (Mansfield et al., 1991).

Despite an upsurge in the number of women lawyers in recent years—from 2.8 percent of the profession in 1970 to about 30 percent today—women still

TABLE 7.1

TABLE 7.1   Employment Positions Held by Women, 1976 and 2006

Some Jobs Show Changes			Some Jobs Show Little Change		
	Percentage of Jobs Held by Women			Percentage of Jobs Held by Women	
Employment Positions	1976	2006	Employment Positions	1976	2006
Cashiers	87.7%	74.8%	Secretaries	99.0%	96.9%
Food counter clerks	85.5	66.2	Receptionists	96.2	92.7
Food service workers	68.7	56.6	Child-care workers	98.2	94.2
Real estate sales	41.2	59.9	Word processors and typists	96.7	91.2
Accountants and auditors	26.9	60.2	Bank tellers	91.9	84.8
Financial managers	24.7	55.0	Bookkeepers	90.0	90.3
College and university teachers	31.3	46.3	Health-service workers	86.2	89.4
Lawyers	9.2	32.6	Hairdressers, cosmetologists	88.0	93.4
Physicians	12.8	32.2	Librarians	82.4	84.2
Police	3.7	12.8	File clerks	85.5	79.2
Civil Engineers	1.2	11.9	Elementary and middle school teachers	84.2	82.2
Firefighters	0.0	3.5	Construction trades	1.6	3.1
			Brick mason, block mason, and stone mason	0.0	1.6

Source: U.S. Department of Labor, Bureau of Labor Statistics, *Employment and Earnings*, 24, no. 1 (January, 1977), 8–9; U.S. Department of Labor, Bureau of Labor Statistics, *Employment and Earnings*, 54, no. 1 (January, 2007), 222–227.

make up only about 5 percent of the managing partners in large law firms, and research documents that women lawyers still are paid less than male lawyers at every level of legal practice and are discriminated against in promotions in major U.S. law firms (Kay & Hagan, 1998; Rhode, 2001). A number of government studies have found evidence that women are less likely to be promoted to senior management positions in industry (Glass Ceiling Commission, 1995; U.S. General Accounting Office, 2001). Although women make up 46 percent of the workforce, they constitute less than 5 percent of senior managers. In addition, the reports find evidence that the disparity is due to discrimination: Male senior managers refuse to promote women and other minorities because they view such promotions as a direct threat to their own advancement.

Another obstacle that women face in the occupational realm is that they tend to be saddled, more so than men, with familial obligations (Ferree, 1991; Lewin, 1998a). Even when both spouses work, and even though men have taken on more responsibilities for these tasks in recent decades, women are still expected to take on more responsibility for raising the children, keeping up the home, and taking care of sick relatives. In fact, research shows that the cost of child care is an important reason why women sometimes quit the jobs they do get (Maume, 1991). Even among

college-educated people, it is the rare couple who has a truly symmetrical relationship in which both partners share equally in household and work responsibilities.

INCOME Classical economic theory claims that wages are determined by the competitive forces of supply and demand. Employers are rational and pay workers what they are worth in terms of the employer's ability to produce goods and services for a price that consumers are willing to pay. In this view, discrimination in pay based on gender or other characteristics is irrational and thus will not persist in the long run. Many economists and much sociological research suggest that this is a very simplistic view of the factors that influence the setting of wages (Blau, Ferber, and Winkler, 1998; Peterson, 1990). In addition to market forces, income levels are also influenced by how much power different groups of workers possess and by cultural stereotypes of what different workers are worth as well as by the traditional levels of pay for different jobs. The effect of these "irrational" factors on women has been that they are paid considerably less than men.

In 2005, the median income for males working year round and full time in the United States was $41,386; for females, it was only $31,858. Women's income is now about 77 percent of men's income

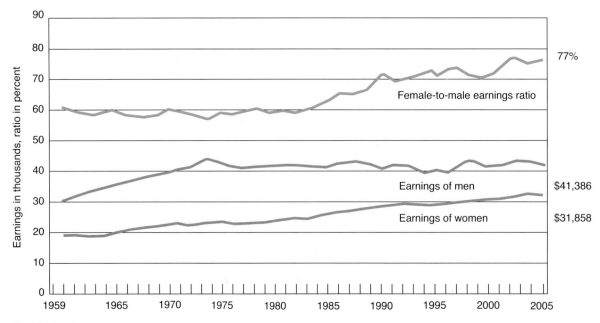

FIGURE 7.2 Median Earnings of Year-Round, Full-Time Workers, by Sex, and Ratio of Female-to-Male Earnings, 1960–2005 (Earnings in 2005 dollars).

Source: U.S. Bureau of the Census, Current Population Reports, P60–231, *Income, Poverty, and Health Insurance Coverage in the United States: 2005* (Washington, DC: U.S. Government Printing Office, 2006), p. 11.

among people who worked full time for the whole year. This shows some improvement—up from about 60 percent forty years ago (see Figure 7.2). However, much of the improvement in this earnings ratio is due to declines in men's earnings rather than increases in women's earnings: Since the early 1970s, the median income of men has either stagnated or fallen. This gender inequality in income is found in virtually all industrial nations, with women in Sweden earning 81 percent of what men make and in Japan, 44 percent of men's incomes (United Nations, 2006). This is a substantial difference. Even if we look at income levels of male and female workers in the same occupa-

tional categories who work year round and full time, women earn substantially less than men in every job category (see Table 7.2). Some of these differences in income result from the fact that most men have been working longer than women and thus have gained seniority and salary increases that have boosted their income. However, studies that have taken this into account still conclude that women have tended to earn less than men for doing the same job. A study by the U.S. Department of Education, for example, looked at the experiences of men and women who graduated from high school in 1972 and thus would be in the middle of their careers at the time of the

TABLE 7.2 Median Weekly Income for Year-Round Full-Time Workers, by Sex and Occupational Category, 2006

Occupational Group	Female Income	Male Income	Ratio Women/Men
Professional and related occupations	$816	$1,109	0.74
Sales	487	761	0.64
Service occupations	390	494	0.79
Office and Administrative support occupations	557	619	0.90
Transportation and material moving	414	581	0.71
Farming, forestry, and fishing	342	401	0.85
Management, and Professional and related occupations	840	1,154	0.73
Construction and Extraction occupations	533	621	0.86
Protective service occupations	557	737	0.76

Source: U.S. Department of Labor, Bureau of Labor Statistics, *Employment and Earnings*, 54, no. 1 (January, 2007), 260–266.

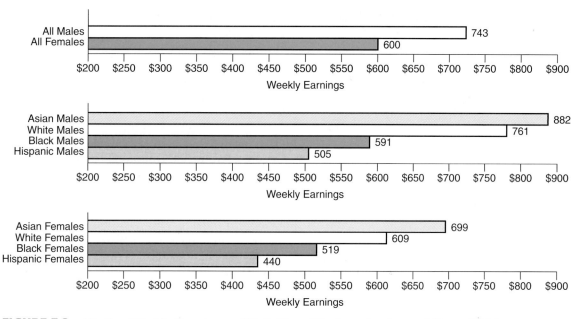

FIGURE 7.3 **Median Weekly Earnings of Full-Time Workers, by Sex and Race, 2006.**

Source: U.S. Department of Labor, Bureau of Labor Statistics, *Employment and Earnings*, 54, no. 1 (January, 2007), 260.

study (Adelman, 1991). What they found was that women on the whole did better in high school and college than men did, they finished college faster, and they had more positive attitudes toward their educational experience. However, by the midpoint in their careers, the women earned less than the men and were more likely to be unemployed. The study looked at comparable men and women, such as those who had no children and had been working equal lengths of time, but still found pay inequities: In only seven of the thirty-three occupations studied did pay equity between men and women occur. The other twenty-six occupations showed men making significantly more than women. No occupation showed women making more than men. It is safe to say, then, that while some improvement has occurred, the prospects for complete income equality in the near future are not great.

Chapter 6 discussed social inequality based on race and ethnicity. People in whom a subordinate racial or ethnic status is combined with a subordinate sexual status are even worse off than women in general. Forty-four percent of elderly black women who live alone are living in poverty, and minority women who work earn less than do their male counterparts or white women (see Figures 7.3 and 8.6).

Discrimination in the Military

Even women who choose the military as a career do not have the same opportunities as men. Although they constitute 15 percent of the armed services, they are currently barred from serving in many combat positions. In 1993, the Clinton Administration opened some, but not all, combat positions to women. This is important because serving in combat positions is one of the best ways to advance one's career in the military. The partial ban on women in combat units continues despite the fact that, during the Gulf War of 1991 and the Iraq War of 2003, female soldiers found themselves in combat, performed well by all standards, and were killed in action and taken prisoner by enemy troops. In fact, in a poll taken in 2005, 72 percent of the U.S. public favors women serving with support troops in combat zones and 44 percent favor women serving with ground troops doing most of the fighting (Carlson, 2005). The major arguments against women in combat positions, especially ground infantry units, is that they do not have the physical strength or aggressive nature needed for the job, that they would disrupt the cohesiveness and "bonding" that occurs among men in combat and is important to combat success, and that it violates deep-seated cultural values regarding manhood and womanhood in Western civilization. Supporters of equal opportunities for women argue that women can be trained for the strength and aggressiveness and that they proved themselves in recent wars. Furthermore, there is no reason to believe that women could not "bond" in a military unit as well as men. The major stumbling block, according to this view, is that fighting and military combat are one of the last bastions where men can maintain a separate "male" world into which women are not allowed. Of course, a major factor fueling the movement of women into the military over the past thirty years has been the needs of the military itself, which is ultimately concerned with finding a sufficient number of educated and motivated recruits. Along these lines, three factors are propelling the greater utilization of women: the all-volunteer military; the increasingly high-tech workplace, which calls for brains and dexterity more than brawn; and the increasing feminization of the workforce. Given these trends, the military may see that it is in its own interests to expand opportunities for women, maybe by opening up more combat positions to them in the future.

Other Types of Discrimination

Discrimination on the basis of gender is not confined to education, occupation, and income. There are various other ways in which women are placed at a disadvantage in the United States. For example, the U.S. legal system has built into it a great deal of discrimination against women. Until recently, many states did not consider it a crime for husbands to rape their wives. Although all states today prohibit marital rape, thirty-three states still provide husbands with some loopholes to avoid prosecution for raping their wives (Bergen, 1999). Depending on the state, for example, a man cannot be charged with raping his wife if the wife is unable to consent to having sex because she is physically impaired, asleep, or unconscious. Only seventeen states accord wives the same protection as other women by treating marital rape like any other rape.

Women have also experienced discrimination in the realm of retirement income. Retirement plans have traditionally paid women a smaller monthly income than they pay to men with the same accumulated retirement assets. This inequity has been based on the fact that women live longer, on the average, than men. The rationale has been that women will draw the same total assets from their retirement plan as men, but they will draw it out in smaller amounts over a longer period. Women, of course, have complained that this penalizes them for being healthy. They have also argued that there are many other criteria than gender that could be used to determine retirement income, such as genetic susceptibility to disease such as heart disease or behavioral factors such as smoking.

Gender Inequality Involving Males

Most discussions of gender inequality focus on women, but men also suffer from unreasonable gender differentiation. Some have even spoken of a "masculine mystique" and the "myth of masculinity": a set of stereotypes about men, such as their being strong, dominant, tough, unemotional, and so forth (Kimmel, 1996). Socially imposed expectations concerning male behavior can be as limiting for men as the stereotypes involving females have been for women. In terms of professional careers, for example, male secretaries were often regarded as social oddities not that long ago. Men who entered such unconventional male roles had to be prepared for incredulous and sometimes even abusive reactions from others. At that time, most men probably did not even consider a profession such as nurse or secretary, even at times when jobs for college graduates in nursing were plentiful and other jobs were scarce. Still, today, very few men go into nursing (see Chapter 4).

Other forms of discrimination against men can be found. For example, some states have laws that make it a punishable offense for men (and presumably other women) to use obscene language in the presence of females. Many insurance companies charge higher automobile insurance premiums to young males because of the higher rate of automobile accidents among that group. Thus, a young man who is a careful driver is penalized by virtue of his gender. Finally, men but not women are required to register for the military draft, and only men could be inducted into the military should the draft itself be reinstated.

A Global Perspective on Gender Inequality

The general patterns of gender inequality found in the United States are reproduced in other societies around the globe: Overall, the majority of women still lag far behind men in power, wealth, and opportunity. Over the past few decades, a growing number of women have entered the workforce, but in some areas their share of the labor force is still quite small: 14 percent in Saudi Arabia, 13 percent in Oman, and 19 percent in Iran (United Nations, 2006; World Bank, 2003). In the United States, it is 41 percent. However, women are also the most affected by economic recession: They are hired later when jobs are expanding and are let go quicker when jobs contract. For the women who do work, they generally have the less prestigious and lowest-paying jobs, a situation found in nations at all levels of development. In industrialized nations, such as Japan and South Korea, women earn about one-half of what men do, but this is also true in less developed nations, for example, Malaysia. In Iceland, women earn 71 percent of what men do, compared to 62 percent in the

United States (this figure is different from the one reported in Figure 7.2 because this figure includes all workers, not just year-round, full-time workers).

In all parts of the world, the rate of illiteracy is higher among women than men, with the rate almost twice as high for women in Asia. Also, in most places women lag behind men in enrollment in high school and college, although in 33 countries more women enroll in higher education than men (including the United States and many nations in Asia, Latin America, and the Caribbean). In addition, around the world, women in educational occupations tend to be employed at the lower levels, teaching in primary schools rather than in the more prestigious and higher-paying postsecondary school positions.

Worldwide, women are poorly represented in political positions where important decisions are made (United Nations, 2006). Women make up fewer than 10 percent of all members of parliaments or congresses in the world. Women do fairly well in some countries: Finland, Norway, Costa Rica, and Cuba have one-third of their parliamentary seats filled by women; the parliaments of Sweden and Rwanda are 45 percent female. Some African and Arab nations have no women in parliament, and Japan's Diet is 10 percent female. The United States does a little better than this, with 15 percent representation, but it still lags significantly behind the more advanced nations.

Finally, poor women in many developing nations have been among the major victims of the capitalist world economy. As described in Chapter 2, the spread of capitalism to many nations has uprooted people from their traditional lands, with many migrating to towns or cities, looking for work. The women among these migrants have been a significant source of cheap and docile labor for agribusiness and export industries. Traditional cultures do not encourage women to seek high levels of education or pursue careers. Yet their families permit, and sometimes encourage, them to seek the low-paying factory or agricultural jobs they can get because the families desperately need the income. Traditional gender roles encourage the women to be subservient to their fathers and husbands and to provide whatever economic support they can. Women who cannot find such jobs sometimes resort to joining the burgeoning sex industry in nations such as Thailand. Thus, patriarchy and traditional gender relations conspire to push these women into exploitative jobs in the global economy, and global corporations take advantage of this in order to maximize profits and exercise control over labor.

The International Perspectives section (pp. 190–191) explores the issue of gender equality in various societies and suggests some reasons for variations in the levels of such inequality.

Future Prospects
Collective Action and the Feminist Movement: A Global Struggle

The **feminist movement,** or **women's movement,** refers to *the collective activities of individuals, groups, and organizations whose goal is the fair and equal treatment of women and men around the world.* This movement has not been limited to the United States, or even Western democracies. Certainly, the democratic, egalitarian, and individualist ideologies that emerged in Europe and the United States in the seventeenth and eighteenth centuries have been influential in many parts of the world. However, many nations have used their own religious beliefs and traditions, combined with ideas from elsewhere, to justify gender equality. The Arab world, for example, was certainly influenced by European belief and example in the 1800s and early 1900s (Barakat, 1993; Hourani, 1991). Yet, many in the Arab world argue that Islamic traditions themselves support the emancipation of women and that the substantial subordination of women in the Arab world is the result of a misinterpretation of the Koran, the Islamic holy book. For instance, one of the pioneers of Arab feminism, Qassem Amin, published a book in 1899 titled *The Liberation of Women,* which called for extending to women most of the same rights that men enjoyed. Anticolonialist movements in places such as Palestine, Egypt, and Iraq mobilized women in support of nationalist causes, and this effort produced a variety of women's organizations that have continued the struggle for gender equality (Najjar, 1992). In 1923, Arab feminists convened at a women's conference in Rome, and in 1944 an Arab women's conference held in Cairo called for women to have the same marital rights as men, including the right to initiate divorce. Even such tradition-bound societies as China and Cuba have an active feminist movement, which has at times gained significant support from the Communist government (O'Kelly and Carney, 1986).

Stirrings of feminist activity could also be found in the United States in the 1800s when women such as Susan B. Anthony and Elizabeth Cady Stanton campaigned for women's right to vote. Finally, in 1920, the Nineteenth Amendment to the Constitution—the Women's Suffrage Amendment—was passed. In the late 1940s, fueled by women's work experience during World War II, women renewed the campaign for equal rights, but were beaten back by the conservative champions of another movement: the "return to normalcy." Women were pressured to relinquish jobs to men returning from war.

The Treatment of Women in Other Societies

When we look at cultures other than our own, it is not hard to find women being treated, even today, in ways that people in the United States would find abhorrent. In Bangladesh, for example, mothers with limited resources give their sons the first pick of the food available whereas daughters have to be satisfied with what is left over. Because Bangladeshi culture discourages women from doing paid work outside the home, males are seen as the more important breadwinners in the family and are thus fed and cared for with more zeal. Hence, Bangladeshi girls are often underfed and suffer stunted growth. In Saudi Arabia, religious police, or Mutawin, patrol in jeeps looking for women who are not properly attired according to the Islamic code. Unacceptable attire, which might mean having an ankle visible beneath the mandatory long black robes, is met with harassment and in some cases arrest (Hijab, 1988; Sadik, 1989). In some African societies, young girls are subject to female circumcision or female genital mutilation, in which parts of the female genitalia are surgically removed, often without benefit of anesthesia or sterile equipment and procedures. Such cultural beliefs and practices are reflected in women's and men's opportunities in the workplace. In Bangladesh, less than 10 percent of adult women work, compared to half of women in the United States. In Saudi Arabia, women and men are segregated in many workplaces and schools.

A close look at these and other examples of gender inequalities makes one thing clear: Although gender inequality is pervasive, and often more extensive than in the United States, it is also complicated and influenced by many factors. One such factor is religion. Bangladesh, Saudi Arabia, and some of the countries where female circumcision are common are Islamic countries, and Islamic societies have tended to keep women subordinate and out of the labor force. At the same time, there are many modern and well-educated women in such Islamic countries and many Muslim men who support greater education of and opportunities for women (Hourani, 1991). In fact, many Muslims interpret parts of the Koran (the Islamic holy book) as giving religious affirmation to gender equality. So, the picture in many societies is one of a tension between an admittedly very strong and pervasive social custom of male dominance on the one hand, and the desire of some women and men to open up a broader range of opportunities for

In 1963, a well-known advocate of women's rights, Betty Friedan, wrote a book titled *The Feminine Mystique*. She took issue with the assumption that women "belong in the home," and her argument became the classic indictment of the presumption that women function best as mothers and homemakers. In 1966, Friedan and other feminists organized the National Organization for Women (NOW). At the time, this body of activist women was regarded as radical in mission, but many observers feel that "its style was actually somewhat conservative, and it stressed working through established legislative channels to achieve rights for women" (Richmond-Abbott, 1992:354).

NOW concentrated much of its efforts toward passage of the Equal Rights Amendment (ERA), a constitutional amendment that would have banned discrimination based on sex. The ERA stated very simply: "Equality of rights under the law shall not be denied or abridged by the United States or any state on account of sex." In 1982, the deadline for ratification passed on the ERA because an insufficient number of states were willing to endorse it. The ERA was viewed by many as the Emancipation Proclamation for women. Proponents of the ERA viewed its defeat as a significant setback for the women's rights movement, and it certainly suggests that sentiment still lingers in the United States against complete equality for women. But again, reality is probably more complex than this. Some people opposed the ERA because they believed that existing legislation protected women adequately and that the amendment was redundant, whereas others thought it would produce unisex bathrooms and sanction same-sex marriages. Some women opposed it because they did not want to give up special privileges that they do receive, such as preference in child custody and divorce award cases. So, people opposed the ERA for many reasons, some of them having little to do with resistance to equality for women (Richmond-Abbott, 1992).

both genders on the other hand. Which of these tendencies predominates shifts over time. But this fluctuation in attitude is also true in the United States. We have documented in this chapter a move toward greater gender equality in the United States. Yet some people have detected a backlash against equality that seems to have brought considerable resistance to further advances for women (Faludi, 1991). Also, as alluded to in the beginning of the chapter, religion can be an obstacle to gender equality in the United States. In 1998, the Southern Baptist Convention stated that the proper role of women in the family is to submit to her husband whereas the husband's proper role is one of leadership in the family. Women are still prohibited in Roman Catholicism from becoming priests—the most devout position in the church and a critical stepping-stone to positions of power. So, the United States also experiences a tension regarding gender equality like that in Islamic countries, although at a different level.

Another factor that influences gender equality is wealth and modernization, with the wealthier and more industrialized nations according more equal opportunities to women. Yet, Saudi Arabia, one of the wealthiest nations in the world, is also one of the more patriarchal. In addition, many anthropological studies have shown us that high levels of gender equality are sometimes found in hunting-and-gathering and horticultural societies (O'Kelly and Carney, 1986). Even among the industrialized nations, levels of gender equality vary. In countries like the United States, Canada, and Sweden, for example, over two-thirds of all women work. However, in Italy and Spain—modern, industrial nations—less than one-half of adult women are in the workforce (United Nations, 2006). In these two countries, religion plays a part in that they are heavily Roman Catholic countries.

So, patterns of gender inequality are complex and influenced by many elements of a culture, such as religious beliefs, wealth, level of industrialization, and other factors. How much gender inequality exists in a particular society depends on its unique blend of all those elements at a given time. This cross-cultural and international viewpoint serves as a warning not to oversimplify the reasons for gender inequality or the patterns that it can take. It also suggests caution against the easy assumption that the United States is on an unchanging trajectory toward greater gender equality, because there are social forces that might push in the other direction.

Seen from another perspective, the ERA issue is one of *status politics:* Opposition to or support for the amendment is in part a controversy over who has the power to enforce its definition of appropriate sex-role behavior on society. Beyond any practical effect it might have, passage of the ERA would symbolically demonstrate the power of NOW and other feminist groups. Likewise, the defeat of the ERA shows that people supporting more traditional definitions of the sexes have the power to draw the line somewhere. According to the status politics point of view, the passage of legislation is as important as a symbolic demonstration of the exercise of power as it is for its practical outcome (Scott, 1985).

Despite these developments, feminists in the United States and around the world have created a global network to work toward gender equality, often working through international organizations like the United Nations or independent nongovernmental organizations (NGOs) discussed in Chapter 2.

The United Nations formed its Commission on the Status of Women in 1946 to monitor the treatment of women and promote women's rights in all nations (United Nations, 2000). There followed a series of steps to expand the arenas in which nations were to be encouraged to accord equal treatment to women. In 1952, for example, the Convention on the Political Rights of Women established the mandate that all women should have the right to vote, hold office, and exercise public functions. In later years, United Nations conventions or conferences were held in Nairobi in 1985, Beijing in 1995, and New York in 2000. Each time, additional plans were established to encourage governments to extend more rights to women. Specifically targeted were efforts to encourage governments to ensure that women have equal rights in education, training, and employment; to attack negative stereotypes and perceptions of women; to encourage men and women to share domestic responsibilities; and to collect statistics to

Some Islamic societies have tended to keep women in a subordinate status, symbolized by the required wearing of long black gowns that fully cover the body, veils that cover the face, and separate lines for male and female customers at this fast-food restaurant in Riyadh, Saudi Arabia.

monitor the situation of women. Of course, all member nations of the United Nations are not strongly enthusiastic about the advancement of gender equality, but a host of women's NGOs has maintained pressure on the United Nations to encourage nations on these issues. The outcome of these pressures has been the achievement of important victories in the quest for gender equality in many nations, although much gender inequality still persists on a global scale.

Changes in the Law

Over the past thirty years in the United States, a significant amount of legislation has been approved that contributes to the reduction of gender inequality. Legislation prohibits discrimination in loan eligibility based on sex or marital status. Title VII of the 1964 Civil Rights Act makes illegal any sex discrimination in employment practices. Title IX of the Educational Amendments Act specifies that any educational institution discriminating on the basis of sex will be denied

federal aid. Other examples of legislation that helps women are the Displaced Homemaker Act (which assists women who have divorced but have few skills with which to support themselves) and legal provisions for wives who have been abused by their husbands.

A new idea for reducing the economic inequities suffered by women has emerged, called "comparable worth." The basic idea is that people whose jobs make equivalent demands on them and that call for similar skills, education, or responsibility should receive roughly similar pay; in other words, "equal pay for comparable worth" (England, 1992; Levine, 2001). For example, a judge in Seattle ruled in 1983 that the state government was in violation of Title VII of the 1964 Civil Rights Act because it routinely paid jobs performed mostly by women less than those performed mostly by men. His ruling was based in part on a comparison of state jobs in terms of "worth points," with points given for such things as knowledge and skills required, mental demands, accountability, and working conditions. Since then, twenty-two states have begun to reassess their pay schedules with these ideas in mind.

Comparable worth has been a highly controversial development with opponents arguing that it is impossible really to compare the "worth" of different jobs and that the free market should determine what people are paid. These opponents argue that, if women are dissatisfied with the low pay in some jobs, they should compete for the higher-paying jobs. Some even suggest that such interference with market mechanisms would disrupt the whole economic system. Supporters argue that women face more barriers in the competition for jobs than do men and that comparable worth would help overcome generations of discrimination in the way salaries are set. So far, comparable worth has not substantially altered the position of women in society.

Changes in the Workplace

Research has clearly documented that two factors have been, and will continue to be, vital to improving opportunities for women in the workplace. One factor is government regulations and programs of affirmative action that encourage employers to hire and promote women. The second factor is the increasing numbers of women in the workplace (Cohen, Broschak, and Haveman, 1998). As more women enter low-level jobs, they gain the skills and get the opportunities to be promoted to higher-level positions; as more women enter higher-level positions where they participate in decisions about hiring and promotions, women's chances of being hired or promoted are substantially greater than when such decisions are made mostly by men.

However, the picture of women in the workplace is not one of unimpeded progress. In fact, as the number of women in the work force has increased and as they have moved into more traditionally male occupations, some new issues have risen to prominence. For example, some research disputes the belief that sexism in the workplace has declined as more women are employed. Resistance to women declines at first, but as the proportion of women in the work setting passes 15 percent, renewed resistance emerges because men feel their opportunities are being reduced due to competition with women. Research has also found that, when many women are employed in the same job, that job comes to be defined as a "woman's job." Once this happens, the job tends to be devalued, with less pay and a smaller budget than when more men held that position (Baron and Newman, 1990; Maume, 1998).

Another emerging reality concerning women in executive management positions is that some who occupy these positions are "bailing out" of the managerial workforce because trying to combine full-time, demanding careers with being wives and mothers has proved too difficult. The rate of turnover in management positions is considerably higher among women than among men, and many women who take maternity leave do not return to work (Conlin, 2002). In addition, young women appear to be less drawn to high-powered business careers today than they were in the 1970s and 1980s. For example, female enrollment in business programs at universities is stuck at about 30 percent, despite substantial efforts to increase it (Alsop, 2001). It seems that today's women are less willing to make as many compromises in the family area as some young women did twenty years ago.

To alleviate this tension between work and child rearing, many employers have established "family-friendly" policies, such as flextime or a "mommy" career track, which would enable men or women to pursue their careers as well as spend time with their families. One career track, for example, called career-primary, would involve the traditional expectations placed on male employees: Career comes first, no time out for personal reasons, and work on nights and weekends if corporate needs demand it. The second track, called career-and-family or the "mommy track," would allow employees to pursue careers while also devoting themselves to their families. For example, maternity leave would not be frowned on and excessive demands would not be placed on women's free time. Critics of such policies argue that those in the mommy track are discriminated against in any event through smaller pay increases or reduced opportunity for promotion. In fact, research shows that women who interrupt their careers for family reasons never catch up, in terms of income or promotions, to their female counterparts who stay on the job (Dobrzynski, 1996; Jacobsen and Levin, 1992). Apparently, their employers think they are not as serious about or as committed to their jobs. Also, corporations with family-friendly policies have few women in their top positions, whereas corporations without such policies have more women at the top—suggesting that if women are to get to the top of the corporate ladder, they have the best chance of doing so by following the traditional male career path.

Despite this, we can predict that women will continue to join the workforce in even larger numbers. Substantial improvement is already observable. One-quarter of all businesses in the United States today are owned by women, and some labor experts project that this may hit 40 percent before too long (U.S. Department of Commerce, 2001). This growth has been impressive, and credit and capital are now more available to women who wish to start or expand a business. In addition, research shows that college-educated

Fighting Sexual Harassment in the Workplace

In 2003, it came out that a number of women cadets attending the United States Air Force Academy were sexually harassed, molested, and even raped by fellow cadets. Such behavior is now more likely to come under the harsh glare of publicity than it was a few decades ago, and lawsuits have made sexual harassment expensive for employers to ignore. In 1980, the Equal Employment Opportunity Commission placed sexual harassment under the Civil Rights Act of 1964 as a form of civil rights violation (Lindsey, 1997). The Civil Rights Act of 1991 provided beefed-up protection and additional legal weapons in the fight against sexual harassment in the workplace. Some states also have strong antidiscrimination statutes that include sexual harassment. However, because of stringent standards set by the courts, winning a sexual harassment case is not easy. In particular, many courts require that harassment be so severe that a "reasonable employee" would find her or his psychological well-being and work performance seriously affected because of it, but some of the behaviors that women find demeaning and disturbing are not perceived by judges and juries to be that serious.

Part of the problem with sexual harassment is that men and women tend to perceive behaviors quite differently. Most men and women agree that demanding sexual favors as a condition of employment or promotion is wrong. However, the Equal Employment Opportunity Commission also defines as harassment behaviors that create a "hostile" environment that makes it more difficult for people to do their job. So, repeated sexual advances by a coworker, even if not linked to employment or promotion, could constitute harassment because they are disturbing to the woman (as they might be to some men) and create an environment in which it is difficult for her to work (Gregory, 2003). And this is where men's and women's perceptions tend to differ. Many men see such behaviors as relatively harmless and claim they would even be flattered if they were the recipients of such actions by coworkers. Most women, on the other hand, find such behaviors disturbing, insulting, and offensive, and such

women are becoming much more like their male counterparts in terms of the emphasis they place on work as being essential to a person's life and happiness (Fiorentine, 1988). As these changes occur, mechanisms are developing to overcome some of the barriers that women have faced in the past. For example, women are excluded from fewer of the social and business networks that can assist one in a career or business. Because of court challenges based on antidiscrimination legislation, women have gained access to some chapters of such organizations as Rotary, the Lions Club, and the Kiwanis where businesspeople often gather. In addition, new networks have emerged to help women. For example, WomenVenture is a nationwide organization that offers seminars and workshops to women on how to start or expand a business, as well as financial backing to twenty-five hundred businesswomen each year. Numerous Web sites on the Internet offer business advice and assistance to women. Such organizations and contacts can make the difference between advancement and stagnation in one's business or career. The opportunities for advancement for women in the twenty-first century will undoubtedly improve with the further availability of such supports for women. However, thousands of clubs and organizations still do not admit women because there are no state or local antidiscrimination laws to force them to do so.

Sexual harassment and assault are serious problems that women face in the workplace, and as the Policy Issues insert shows, some important strides have been made in overcoming these problems.

The Changing Face of Politics

The stark reality is that, although women make up 51 percent of our populace, very few of them are among our elected representatives at the national level. Of the one hundred senators, the number of women among them fluctuated from a low of none to a high of two between 1970 and 1992, rising to 16 in the 2006 election (see Figure 7.4). However, this rather modest change hides some dramatic gains that women have made in politics over the past few decades. In 1970, only 25 women ran for seats in the U.S. House of Representatives; by 2002, this had increased six times, to 150 women. Although only 17 percent of the House of Representatives in 2007 were women, that is four times greater than the 3 to 4 percent female representation of the 1970s. Gains

behaviors do create a "hostile" atmosphere in many women's minds. This is why we repeatedly hear women exclaim about men, "They just don't get it!" In other words, men simply fail to understand why women find such behaviors offensive, demeaning, and maybe even frightening.

To give both men and women a better perspective on women's views of these issues, attorneys William Petrocelli and Barbara Kate Repa (1992), experts on the legal issues of sexual harassment, suggest the following simple test to help decide whether a remark or a behavior is appropriate:

1. Would you say or do the same thing in front of your spouse?

2. How would you feel if the same remarks or behavior were directed at your mother, sister, wife, or daughter?

3. How would you feel if a man made the same remarks or took the same actions toward you?

If your reaction to any one of these questions is negative, then the remark or behavior might well be seen as inappropriate harassment by a female coworker.

Many employers have been taking steps that experts recognize will reduce the likelihood of sexual harassment or assault occurring in the workplace: 1) Have a written and publicized policy against such actions; 2) Vigorously enforce the policy; 3) Educate employees about what constitutes harassment and how to file a complaint about it; and 4) Provide sincere and significant top-management support for the policy (Gregory, 2003). Such steps should make the workplace of the twenty-first century a much more hospitable one for women. However, as we saw in Chapter 6, discrimination, as well as harassment, tends to rear its ugly head when competition between groups grows fierce. As more women take jobs traditionally held by men, harassment may emerge as a response to threatened losses. So additional vigilance may be necessary to alleviate this problem.

have been especially impressive at the state and local levels. In 1971, women made up less than 5 percent of all state legislators, compared with 23 percent today (Center for American Women and Politics, 2007). (The best state for women running for the legislature in 2007 was Vermont with 37 percent of its legislature being women; South Carolina was on the bottom with a meager 9 percent.) Thirty years ago, a paltry 1 percent of mayors of large cities in the United States were women; today it is 17 percent. Although women are still far underrepresented in politics, they are beginning to move into more powerful and nationwide political positions. It takes time to get significant numbers of women entrenched in

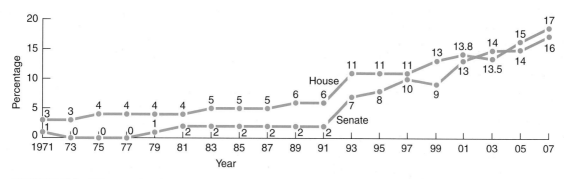

FIGURE 7.4 **Women in the U.S. Senate and House of Representatives, as a Percentage of Each Body, 1971–2007.**

Source: U.S. Bureau of the Census, *Statistical Abstract of the United States, 1982–1983* (Washington, DC: U.S. Government Printing Office, 1982), p. 485; U.S. Bureau of the Census, *Statistical Abstract of the United States, 2007* (Washington, DC: U.S. Government Printing Office, 2006), p. 251.

the political system to the point where they can make a run for a Senate seat. We will likely see more women in politics in the future.

Masculine, Feminine, or Human?

Some of the problems surrounding gender inequality may arise in part because of the oversimplified view that people tend to have of gender, seeing things as either male or female, but not both. In reality, each individual can be seen as a combination of both feminine and masculine characteristics. In fact, masculinity and femininity may not be polar opposites but rather two independent sets of characteristics. So, for example, some very feminine women may have few masculine characteristics, whereas other very feminine women might have many masculine traits. In fact, the word **androgyny** (from the Greek *andro*, "male," and *gyn*, "female") has been coined to describe *a condition where male and female characteristics are not rigidly assigned and there is a blending of the traits, attitudes, and roles of both sexes.* From this perspective, people explore a broad range of gender-role possibilities and choose emotions and behaviors without regard to gender stereotypes. This does not mean that gender distinctions disappear but that one's biological sex becomes a less rigid determinant of which masculine and feminine traits a particular individual will exhibit. This means that people can be more flexible in their role playing and express themselves in a variety of ways other than the traditionally masculine or feminine ways. The trends toward gender equality discussed in this chapter may make more of this flexibility possible in the future.

LINKAGES Gender inequality and fewer opportunities for women can lead some poor women (Chapter 5) toward prostitution and pornography (Chapter 11) as ways to support themselves and their families. This is especially tempting for poor single mothers whose opportunities are severely limited.

STUDY AND REVIEW

Summary

1. Sex is an ascribed and a master status. The text examines four different views of sex as an element of social differentiation: the biological perspective, which assumes that innate biological differences between men and women shape the contributions that each can make to society; the functionalist perspective, which argues that a problem exists when the sex-role division of labor is no longer consistent with the needs of a particular society; the conflict perspective, which views sexual inequality as a problem when some group (women) realizes it is being exploited and strives to do something to change the situation; and the interactionist perspective, which emphasizes social definitions and symbolic representations of appropriate behavior for males and females in trying to understand sexual inequality.

2. *Male* and *female* are sex-related terms; gender refers to learned behavior involving how we are expected to act as males and females in society. One of the key issues in analyzing gender inequality is how we learn to be masculine and feminine and how this contributes to sexual differentiation and inequality. This learning occurs primarily through the three major agencies of socialization: the family, the schools, and the media.

3. Sexual inequality is widespread in the United States and around the world. Women occupy a subordinate position in comparison to men on virtually every dimension of socioeconomic status (SES). Discrimination on the basis of sex is not confined to education, occupation, and income. Women also experience unequal treatment in the military and before the courts. Sexual inequality also affects men when they are discouraged from pursuing certain kinds of jobs and can be drafted into the military when no equivalent service is asked of women.

4. The future of gender inequality will depend on the progression of the feminist movement and how much collective action is mobilized around the world to deal with the various forms of discrimination. Changes in the law and new legislation affecting women, such as comparable worth, will also be important. The workplace is changing, with increasing numbers of women joining the labor force. Any meaningful changes in the situation surrounding sexual inequality will involve a redefinition of both masculinity and femininity.

The Census Bureau (**www.census.gov**) has much data available on women and their role in society. Use its alphabetical listing of subject categories to find the listings for women. From there, you can go to parts of the Census Web page that have information on women's education, women's income, businesses owned by women, and so on.

For a Web site that focuses primarily on women's issues in the United States, go to the site maintained by the National Organization for Women (**www.now.org**). This site is up to date on current social issues and legislation that affect women. For a more global perspective, take a look at the Web site of the Feminist Majority Foundation Online (**www.feminist.org**). This site has links to feminist issues and organizations around the world, including the Feminist Internet Gateway (lots of Web links), Feminist Research Centers, and Women and Girls in Sports. A different global perspective can be gained by going to the Web page of the United Nations' Department of Economic and Social Development (**www.un.org/esa**) and then clicking on "Advancement of Women." This will enable you to find out what the United Nations is doing in relation to gender issues around the globe. Also look for non-governmental organizations that address women's issues at this Web site.

A good way to learn about policies and practices related to sexual harassment is to do a Web search for "sexual harassment." Among the most relevant sites I found when doing this were Sociologists Against Sexual Harassment (SASH), a professional organization of sociologists whose research and social policy development focus on issues of sexual harassment, and the sexual harassment policies of a variety of universities and private companies. See if your university policy is displayed. What issues are commonly addressed in these policies? From all the sites you visit in this search, describe the social network of groups and organizations that have emerged to deal with the issue of sexual harassment.

The Allyn & Bacon Social Problems Supersite (**http://wps.ablongman.com/ab_socialprob_sprsite_1**) contains material on gender and gender inequality.

Key Terms

androgyny	instrumental tasks
expressive tasks	sex
feminist movement	sexism
gender	women's movement

Multiple-Choice Questions

1. Regarding biological differences between men and women, the text draws which of the following conclusions?
   a. The differences are actually larger than was once thought.
   b. The differences refer to averages which ignore the significant overlap between the sexes.
   c. Relatively little human behavior is learned through socialization.
   d. There has not been much research on the differences between the sexes.

2. Which of these statements would be most consistent with the conflict perspective?
   a. The sex-role division of labor is a social problem when it is no longer consistent with the needs of society.
   b. Sexual differentiation is a "battleground" for the struggle over scarce resources.
   c. Beliefs about sexual inequality are maintained and reinforced through patterns of social interaction.
   d. Innate biological differences between men and women shape the contributions each can make to society.

3. Research on conversational styles supports the conclusion that
   a. men talk more than women in mixed-sex conversations.
   b. women talk more than men in mixed-sex conversations.
   c. women interrupt more than men do in mixed-sex conversations.
   d. both a and c are supported.
   e. both b and c are supported.

4. Which of the following is *not* an agency of socialization that the text considers primarily responsible for learning during the socialization process?
   a. the family
   b. the media
   c. the schools
   d. the churches

5. Regarding the socialization of children, the text concludes that
   a. boys are more prominent in girls' games than girls are in boys' games.

b. most elementary school teachers treat boy students and girl students the same.

c. in childhood, male activities tend to be more valued than female activities.

d. children's books have eliminated most stereotyped images of the sexes.

6. Among which of the following groups does a higher percentage of women graduate from college in the United States than the percentage among men?
   a. the elderly
   b. whites
   c. Hispanic Americans
   d. the poor

7. Classical economic theory claims that wages are determined by which of the following?
   a. the competitive forces of supply and demand
   b. how much power different groups of workers possess
   c. cultural stereotypes of what different groups of workers are worth
   d. Both a and b are consistent with classical economic theory.
   e. a, b, and c are consistent with classical economic theory.

8. Which of the following is *not* true regarding the gender inequalities suffered by males in the United States today?
   a. Men but not women must register for the military draft.
   b. More women attend law school than do men.
   c. Men are sometimes charged more for automobile insurance than are women.
   d. Socially imposed expectations limit the freedom of men to choose stereotypically female occupations.

9. Which of the following is currently *not* being implemented as a social policy in the United States?
   a. comparable worth
   b. the 1964 Civil Rights Act
   c. the Equal Rights Amendment
   d. Title IX of the Educational Amendment Act

10. A situation in which male and female characteristics are not rigidly assigned but instead there is a blending of the traits of both sexes is called
   a. a master status
   b. comparable worth
   c. sexism
   d. androgyny
   e. instrumental tasks

True/False Questions

1. Gender is an ascribed status, but it is not a master status.

2. The text concludes that there are no biological differences between men and women that have any social significance.

3. The functionalist perspective argues that it is more functional in industrial societies to assign tasks to people on the basis of individual abilities rather than ascribed characteristics.

4. Stereotyped views of gender roles have been largely eliminated in children's text books but can still be found in college-level textbooks.

5. Male predominance in social interaction in college classrooms does not seem to occur in the classrooms of male professors only but is also found in classrooms with female professors.

6. There is a higher proportion of college graduates among women today than among men.

7. The percentage of secretaries who are men has remained virtually unchanged over the past twenty-five years.

8. One argument that is made for not allowing women into combat units in the military is that their presence would interfere with the male bonding that is important to combat success.

9. The quest for gender equality is a global movement rather than one limited to western or industrial nations.

10. According to the text, androgyny is a thing of the past.

Fill-In Questions

1. A person's educational level is an/a _____ status.

2. _____ is an ideology that justifies the domination of one sex over the other because of the presumed biological inferiority of the subordinate.

3. Building a house or managing the activities of a work team are tasks that sociologists call _____ tasks.

4. The study of the conversational styles of men and women provides evidence for the _____ perspective.

5. The learned behavior involving how we are expected to act as males and females is referred to by sociologists as_____.

6. The three main dimensions of socioeconomic status are education, _____, and _____.

7. The employment position that has the highest percentage of jobs held by women is _____.

8. Currently, among people who work year-round and full time, women earn approximately _____ percent of the income of men in the United States.

9. The idea that people whose jobs make equivalent demands on them should receive roughly similar pay is called _____.

10. Women currently constitute _____ percent of the United States Senate.

Matching Questions

_____ 1. Equal Rights Amendment
_____ 2. NGOs
_____ 3. a person's occupation
_____ 4. maintaining harmony in a family
_____ 5. agency of socialization
_____ 6. Beijing
_____ 7. blending of traits of both sexes
_____ 8. WomenVenture
_____ 9. prohibits gender discrimination in education
_____ 10. myth of masculinity

A. international pressure groups
B. expressive task
C. UN Conference on Women
D. androgyny
E. achieved status
F. Title IX of the Educational Amendments Act
G. stereotypes about men
H. status politics
I. the media
J. helps women in business

Essay Questions

1. What conclusions does the text draw regarding the impact of biological differences between men and women on social behavior?
2. According to the conflict perspective, what are the reasons for sex stratification in society?
3. What does research show about the impact of gender on conversational styles? What is the importance of these gender differences?
4. Describe the ways in which schools contribute to the problem of gender inequality.
5. What is the "chilly climate" in the classroom described in the text? Why does it happen and what are its consequences?
6. Describe the impact of gender and race on people's educational opportunities and accomplishments in the United States.
7. What are the arguments for and against women serving in combat positions in the military?
8. Describe the kinds of gender inequality that confront women in third-world nations around the globe.
9. What are ways to reduce levels of sexual harassment in the workplace?
10. What changes have occurred in the workplace in the United States as far as gender inequality is concerned?

For Further Reading

Deborah Blum. *Sex on the Brain: The Biological Differences Between Men and Women.* New York: Viking, 1997. This is a thorough and readable summary of the research on whether behavioral differences between men and women are due to biology or to cultural experiences.

Nancy Bonvillain. *Women and Men: Cultural Constructs of Gender,* 4th ed. Upper Saddle River, NJ: Prentice Hall, 2007. This book explores issues of gender and gender inequality in many cultures around the globe and in societies at many different levels of development, providing a complete and sophisticated view of the role of gender in society.

Michael S. Kimmel and Michael A. Messner. *Men's Lives,* 6th ed. Boston: Allyn & Bacon, 2004. This book approaches issues of gender from the male perspective, focusing on inequality, discrimination, socialization, and masculinity in general.

Ethel Klein. *Gender Politics: From Consciousness to Mass Politics.* Cambridge, MA: Harvard University Press, 1984. An excellent overview of the use of the political process to achieve more equality for women. This is a good historical overview of the women's rights movement.

Peggy Orenstein. *Schoolgirls: Young Women, Self-Esteem, and the Confidence Gap.* New York: Doubleday, 1994. This book documents the decline in self-esteem and self-confidence that many girls experience as they go through adolescence by looking in-depth at the lives of girls at two schools.

Irene Padavic and Barbara F. Reskin. *Women and Men at Work,* 2d ed. Thousand Oaks, CA: Sage, 2007. This book provides a detailed analysis of how men and women fare in the workplace. It is enlightening and includes some material from other cultures and from the minority experience.

Deborah Tannen. *Talking from 9 to 5: How Women's and Men's Conversational Styles Affect Who Gets Heard, Who Gets Credit, and What Gets Done at Work.* New York: William Morrow, 1994. Building on the interactionist perspective's focus on conversational styles shaping and reinforcing gender patterns in society, this excellent book describes some of the complexity of these processes in the workplace and the consequences they can have.

Julia T. Wood. *Gendered Lives: Communication, Gender, and Culture,* 6th ed. Belmont, CA: Wadsworth, 2005. This book provides a comprehensive overview of the multitude of ways that gender pervades our lives and profoundly shapes our thoughts, feelings, and behaviors—often in ways of which we are totally unaware.

AGE, SEXUAL ORIENTATION, AND SOCIAL INEQUALITY

The preceding two chapters focused on the extent to which people experience social inequality because of their race, ethnicity, or gender. This chapter focuses on two additional characteristics that are often associated with social inequality today: age and sexual orientation. Other characteristics, of course, are linked with social inequality, but the ones that are the focus of these three chapters are the ones where inequality is prominent and where significant groups have seen the inequality as a serious problem and have taken steps to place the problem on the public agenda. To begin, we will focus on age and explore the way in which age—an ascribed status like race and sex—influences a person's position in society.

Age, Life Course, and Social Structure

Gerontology is the *scientific study of aging* (Atchley and Barusch, 2004). It studies people of all ages because the process of aging begins the day we are born. As people age, societies tend to carve out their lives into a series of stages, each with its own set of expectations. The content of these stages depends on a person's biological age and the social needs of a particular society. All these stages taken together constitute the **life course** or **life stages,** which is *a succession of statuses and roles that people in a particular society experience in a fairly predictable pattern as they grow older.* Biology plays an important role in the life course, especially at the beginning and the end. As infants and young children, each of us is highly dependent on others for our survival, and thus the statuses that are open to us are limited. In very old age, physical deterioration may limit our capabilities and again make us dependent on others. Society cannot rely on us during these periods to the extent that it can during other stages of the life span. Between infancy and very old age, however, the social structure is more important than biology in shaping the life span. Thus, although biology does play a role, we should be cautious about viewing life-span stages as biologically created. Rather, they make up a socially approved sequence of stages, adjusted for certain biological limitations, that guides people's behavior as they live their lives. The sociological perspectives provide insight into how society shapes the life course.

The Functionalist Perspective

Functionalists argue that the stages of the life course are intimately related to the social needs of particular societies. For this reason, the stages that occur may differ substantially from society to society (Aries, 1962). In preindustrial societies, for example, people usually learn how to fill adult positions fairly early in life. The technology is relatively simple, so little training or education is required. People do not need to know how to read or write in order to make contributions to society. So the transition from childhood to adulthood generally occurs early, somewhere between age eight and the mid-teens. People continue to work as they grow old, being limited only by physical infirmity. Only among small groups within society, such as a ruling group or a

Myths and Facts

About Age and Sexual Orientation

Myth: Teenagers are too young to have achieved maturity, and this is why they are required to stay in school rather than work for a living or begin raising a family.

Fact: In preindustrial societies, most people have joined the adult world of work by their teenage years and may have even begun raising a family. Industrial societies have created a new social category called adolescence, consisting of people who are biologically mature but still considered dependent and emotionally immature. The purpose of this category is to allow for an extended period of education and to reduce competition with adults for existing jobs.

Myth: The exploitation of child labor in the United States is largely a thing of the past.

Fact: Although child-labor problems have been reduced, there are currently few restrictions on youngsters working in some jobs, such as farm laborers. It is estimated that one-quarter of the farm laborers in the United States may be under age sixteen.

Myth: Because most people in the United States today have retirement plans where they work, retirement income for the elderly in the future will not be a problem.

Fact: Less than half of working people today have retirement plans. In addition, some people do not work for a company long enough to have retirement funds vested (or become their own personal property), so they end up with meager pension resources.

Myth: In the last few decades, gay men and lesbians have found much wider acceptance in the United States than in previous decades.

Fact: Although there have been improvements, much negative sentiment toward gays still exists. Almost one-half of adults in the United States still believe that sexual contact between people of the same sex should be illegal, and some communities have been rescinding statutes that ban discrimination in jobs and housing because of sexual orientation.

priesthood, is inactivity or nonproductivity common among older adults.

Industrial societies, on the other hand, with a complex technology and an elaborate division of labor, need a highly educated and well-trained workforce. Thus, training and education must be more extensive than in preindustrial societies. Furthermore, the sophisticated technology of industrial societies makes it possible for a small number of people to provide all of the goods and services that are needed. As a consequence, it is not necessary for all adults to participate in the workforce. These factors contribute to two major differences in the life course of industrial societies in contrast to preindustrial ones. First, the age at which people are allowed to enter the adult world is postponed in industrial societies (Kett, 1977). Childhood continues into the early teens and is followed by a new stage in life, adolescence, which runs roughly from thirteen to eighteen years of age. Adolescence is viewed as a time of preparation for adulthood, in terms of both education and psychological maturation. Adolescents are not considered adults and are not expected to assume adult responsibilities, such as supporting a family. They are also not accorded many adult privileges, such as being able to vote or join the adult workforce on a full-time basis. The second difference between the life stages of industrial and preindustrial societies involves old age (Plakans, 1994). In industrial societies, most men and women are encouraged to leave the workforce, or forced from it, long before they die, often when they are still healthy and capable of working. Presumably, younger workers are healthier and more vigorous and make a better contribution to the work world. But irrespective of the capabilities of older workers, retirement serves as a way of reducing the number of workers who are competing for a limited number of jobs.

From the functionalist perspective, the treatment of the young and the old becomes a social problem when it is inconsistent with their capabilities and development, both biological and social. When age is used as an arbitrary criterion for inequitable treatment, it is dysfunctional and can lead to social disorganization. If young people, for example, are prevented from gaining prestige by joining the work world, they may turn to drugs or crime as a way of gaining a sense of self-importance. Likewise, forced retirement among the elderly can lead to depression and alcoholism. So societies need to provide socially acceptable statuses for their members at every stage of life and make available opportunities to achieve socially desired goals (Riley, Kahn, and Foner, 1994). People need to feel that they are making an important contribution to society. With the transition from a preindustrial to an industrial social order, however, something has been lost. A degree of social disorganization has arisen as there are more and more young and old people with fewer and fewer contributions that they are allowed to make to society. They do not work, head families, or rear children.

The Conflict Perspective

The position of the young and the old in modern societies is not unlike that of other minority groups (see Chapters 6 and 7). They have less access to social, political, and economic power, and they are dominated by groups with more resources. This has not always been the case. In most preindustrial societies, the elderly held considerably more power because they owned and controlled many economic resources, especially property. In addition, kinship ties were much more important then than today, and people often needed the support of their parents to get a start in life. It was from their parents that young adults learned a trade or acquired some land to farm. This meant that sons and daughters were economically dependent on their parents. In such a situation, social customs and laws tended to support and reinforce the dominant position of the elderly in society. In other words, respect for the elderly in preindustrial societies flowed from their control over political, social, and economic resources.

In industrial societies, people are not as heavily dependent on their parents to make a living. Trades can be learned in school, and most people will be salaried employees of a corporation or government agency. So, entry-level positions in the economy can be gained with little if any parental support. In addition, family ties in general have become less important. As a consequence, kinship ties are not a source of power and prestige for many elderly. The outcome of all this is that the status of the elderly has declined because they no longer hold positions of economic power, and their children are no longer dependent on them for their economic livelihood.

From the conflict perspective, then, the position of any age group in society is determined by the social, political, and economic resources that group has access to. The access of the young and old to jobs and other sources of social and economic reward has been restricted because this exclusion benefits the large group of people in early to middle adulthood. In an economic system with a scarcity of jobs, this helps to reduce competition. Fewer young workers enter the labor market, and older workers are forced out by retirement in order to open positions for younger adults.

Society, of course, does not couch these social practices in such contentious terms. Rather, cultural norms hold that the restrictions placed on the young and old are for their own benefit. An ideology emerges to legitimize these social practices, just as sexism justifies discrimination against women and racism justifies the domination of particular racial groups. **Ageism** refers to *an ideology or set of beliefs holding that people in a particular age group are inferior, have negative attributes, and can be dominated and exploited because of their age* (Laws, 1995). The term was originally coined to describe reactions to the elderly, but it applies to any age group that experiences such prejudice and discrimination. In addition, like sexism and racism, ageism is often defended on biological grounds, pointing to the immaturity of the young and the senility of the old. With such beliefs, age becomes an important factor in differentiating among people in society.

The Age Structure of Society

Demography is *the study of the size, composition, and distribution of human populations and how these factors change over time*. Demographers have found that societies vary in the proportions of their populations that are at different stages in the life cycle. They refer to this as the **age structure** of society, *the distribution of people into various age categories*. In preindustrial societies, such as the United States of more than a century ago, the age structure is "bottom heavy," with young people representing a large proportion of the population (see Figure 8.1). In such societies, as much as 40 to 50 percent of the populace might be fifteen years of age or under with less than 6 percent being older than age 65. The reason for this, which will be discussed in more detail in Chapter 12, is that preindustrial societies have high birthrates and high death rates. Many people are born, but a smaller proportion of them live into old age than in industrial societies. Industrial societies, with lower birthrates and a longer life expectancy, tend to "age," making their populations "top heavy." Older people make up a growing proportion of the populace. Today, 24 percent of the United States population is under age eighteen, compared with 13 percent sixty-five and older (see Figure 8.2). This is quite a dramatic shift from a preindustrial United States, and this trend will intensify. By the year 2050, when the younger students reading this book will be approaching senior citizenship, the young and the old will come very close to constituting equal proportions of our populace: 23 percent and 20 percent, respectively. In that year, there will be eighty-six million people over age sixty-five in the

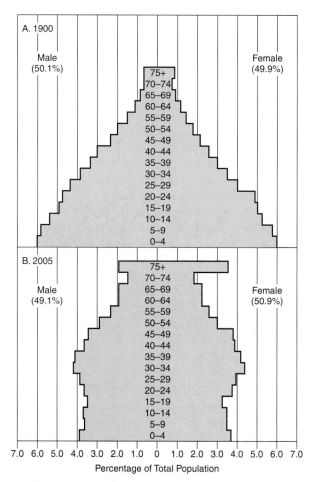

FIGURE 8.1 **Age–Sex Population Pyramids for the United States, 1900 and 2005.**

Source: U.S. Bureau of the Census, *Census of Population: Characteristics of the Population* (Washington, DC: U.S. Government Printing Office, 1940, 1970); U.S. Bureau of the Census, *Statistical Abstract of the United States, 2007* (Washington, DC: U.S. Government Printing Office, 2006), p. 12.

United States, compared with only three million in 1900 and forty million today.

From their analysis of the age structure of society, demographers develop a very important statistic called the **dependency ratio,** which *shows the relative size of the group in our society that is economically dependent for support on others who are working*. The dependency ratio is often calculated by comparing the number of people over sixty-five with the number between eighteen and sixty-four (see Figure 8.3). In 1900, the dependency ratio in the United States was 7, meaning that there were seven older people for each one hundred people between eighteen and sixty-four. Today the ratio is about 19. By the year 2050, projections suggest that it will be about 33 and rise to 40 by 2100, when there will be four older persons for every ten adults of working age. So, as society ages,

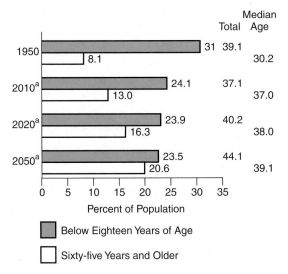

FIGURE 8.2 **The Distribution of Young and Old in the United States, 1950–2050.**

aEstimates based on middle-level projections

Source: U.S. Bureau of the Census, *Statistical Abstract of the United States, 1978* (Washington, DC: U.S. Government Printing Office, 1978), pp. 8–9; U.S. Bureau of the Census, *Statistical Abstract of the United States, 2007* (Washington, DC: U.S. Government Printing Office, 2006), p. 13.

those who are dependent become a significantly larger proportion of the populace.

The major concern about this issue, of course, is whether or at what level society can or will support such a large dependent population. Later in this chap-

ter, we will address some possible solutions to the problems created by shifts in the age structure of the United States.

Problems of the Young

Human beings remain dependent on others after birth for much longer than is the case with most species. This dependence places the young at considerable risk of being discriminated against or exploited.

Economic Exploitation

Children in most societies participate in some form of economic productivity, but it is usually by joining with family members in hunting or farming. In some cases, however, children work in nonfamily settings as wage laborers (U.S. Department of Labor, 2000). They work in mines, in factories, and as self-employed workers engaging in street trades. Many of these children confront terrible economic exploitation: working long hours in potentially harmful environments for relatively little pay. In nineteenth-century England and the United States, for example, children worked in factories for eleven or more hours per day. Toddlers barely three years old worked in cotton mills.

Such severe economic exploitation of children is not often found in the United States today, but it is, unfortunately, all too common in many nations around the globe, especially in developing countries

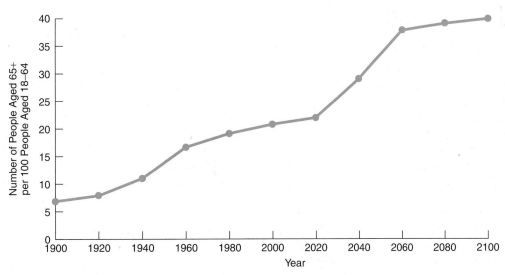

FIGURE 8.3 **Dependency Ratio in the United States, 1900–2100.**

Source: U.S. Department of Health and Human Services, *Aging America: Trends and Projections*, DHHS Pub. No. (FCoA) 91-28001 (Washington, DC: Department of Health and Human Services, 1991), pp. 18–19; U.S. Bureau of the Census, Population Division Working Paper No. 38, *Methodology and Assumptions for the Population Projections of the United States: 1999–2100* (Washington, DC: U.S. Government Printing Office, 2000).

(U.S. Department of Labor, 2000). In Africa, one-third of all children work; in Latin America 15 to 20 percent of children work. Although it is impossible to say exactly what proportion of these children are exploited, the great majority work long hours for substandard wages in conditions that are often unhealthy. Child workers are often beaten or otherwise abused, and they typically do not receive an adequate education that would better prepare them to support themselves as adults. In some cases, children are in debt bondage, which occurs when, to secure a loan, a person offers his or her own labor or the labor of others in payment of a loan. If interest on the loan is sufficiently high, the labor will never be able to pay it off, and the person is, in effect, a slave. Parents in places such as India and Pakistan sometimes offer their children's labor to secure such loans, placing their child in virtual slavery.

There are a number of reasons why such child exploitation exists. For one thing, poverty forces families to exploit their children to survive. For another, factory owners find children an easy and profitable group to exploit. Children are much more vulnerable than adults and far less likely to protest their conditions successfully. With the intense competition in the world economy described in Chapter 2, some employers find it impossible to resist the temptation to exploit children. A third reason why child workers are exploited is that the public is often indifferent to the issue or, in some nations, believes that child labor among the poor is just "the way things are."

Legislation has been adopted in most countries in the past fifty years to control the labor exploitation of the young (U.S. Department of Labor, 2000). The International Labour Organization runs a program called International Program on the Elimination of Child Labor that finances efforts in many countries to collect data on the extent and problems with child labor, to remove children from exploitative child labor, and to protect children from exploitation in the sex industry. The United States contributes funds and other resources to these efforts.

In the United States, the Fair Labor Standards Act of 1938 outlaws the employment of people younger than sixteen years in many settings, especially occupations with hazardous conditions (U.S. Department of Labor, 2001). However, child labor is by no means a thing of the past. In fact, families sometimes have to put everyone to work—including the children—to keep out of poverty. Recent government investigations of child labor found a case where a thirteen-year-old worker was run over and killed by a piece of farm equipment being towed by a tractor. Another seventeen-year-old worker was killed when hit by the bucket of a front-end loader. A ten-year-old boy was killed when a tractor he was working on overturned. The number of violations of federal child-labor laws more than doubled during the 1980s, mostly for working youngsters too many hours per day, too late at night, or in hazardous jobs with dangerous equipment. By the year 2000, the number of such violations declined significantly because of increased government oversight. However, current legislation places few restrictions on youngsters working in some jobs, including that of farm laborer. It is estimated that one-quarter of the farm laborers in the United States may be under age sixteen. These children work in hot, unpleasant conditions for low wages and receive few, if any, benefits such as retirement or health insurance. Many agricultural states have no minimum age for farm laborers, and state laws often do not apply to the children of migratory farm laborers.

In many less developed nations, young children are sometimes forced to work for long hours for low wages, as are these children who are paid to haul bricks in Colombia. Such exploitation occurs because, among other reasons, poverty forces families to use their children in this way to earn enough money to support the family.

Family Instability

Many young people in the United States and other nations grow up in family settings that are less stable and supportive than would be desirable for effective child rearing. Chapter 3 reviews the extent of divorce and single parenthood and the problems associated with them. Children often suffer when a divorce occurs, even if the divorce is necessary. Many children of divorce have strong emotional problems, do less well in school, and are more prone to delinquency and other kinds of behavior problems. This is not to say that a single parent cannot provide the necessary environment for good child rearing; they can and some do. However, the research does suggest that children are often worse off when raised by one parent rather than two (Bruce, Lloyd, and Leonard, 1995; McLanahan and Sandefur, 1994). The difficulties of children in single-parent families are due to three factors: low income, inadequate parental guidance, and less access to community resources. If single parents can overcome these difficulties, then their children can do quite well.

Poverty

Partly because of the higher rates of divorce and single parenthood, many young people today are at risk of growing up in poverty. The statistics on poverty among children are reviewed in Chapter 5. The poverty rate among children is higher today than it was forty years ago: 17 percent today as compared to 14 percent in 1969. And it is almost twice as high as the poverty rate among the elderly. One-third of all African American children live in poverty, and half of all African American and Hispanic American children in single-parent families live below the poverty level.

One-third of the nation's poor people are under the age of sixteen, and the children of the United States are worse off than children in most other industrial nations (see Figure 5.3). What accounts for these appalling circumstances among our nation's young? Although some teens earn income, the economic circumstances of children are determined almost entirely by that of their parents—another manifestation of their dependency. And some critical trends of the past few decades, already reviewed in Chapters 3 and 5, have contributed to the growing poverty among children. Unemployment has increased and family incomes have not grown and in many cases have declined. More children today live in single-parent families, which have much higher poverty rates than two-parent families. These economic circumstances that children confront are especially troubling because children, for the most part, cannot walk away from them or work to improve their lives as some adults can. They are heavily dependent on adults. Poverty is simply something they must live with until they become adults, and often they face further poverty in adulthood because their poverty-stricken childhood failed to provide them with the resources and the motivation to achieve as adults.

Sexual Exploitation

One common form of sexual exploitation of the young is sexual assault by a parent, adult relative, or guardian (Estes and Weiner, 2001). Sexual assault can involve sexual intercourse, fondling, or indecent exposure. Once again, the young are at a disadvantage, especially when assaulted by a family member or relative, because the attack is often couched as an expression of love or affection. This often inhibits the child from reporting the assault. Such attacks can continue for years because children are often afraid of hurting the adult by reporting the incidents.

Adolescents are susceptible to yet another version of sexual exploitation: prostitution and pornography (Estes and Weiner, 2001; Flowers, 2001a). Teenage runaways, for example, find it difficult to support themselves through legitimate jobs, which are likely to be either unavailable or low paying. Such teenagers are sought after by pimps and pornographers because they are defenseless and exploitable. The teenagers are afraid to go to the police and have no other adults to protect them. In large cities, prostitutes as young as twelve years old—both male and female—can be found. There are even organized rings nationwide to provide the services of young prostitutes to those who desire them. Such youngsters typically lack the economic and social resources necessary to extricate themselves from these situations and are likely to continue being exploited until arrested.

Child Abuse

Because of their dependent status, it is often children who experience the brunt of their parents' frustrations or failures. Too often, this reaction takes the form of child abuse. As with sexual exploitation, children are usually too weak and defenseless to protect themselves against such abuse. In addition, their fear of their parents is often mixed with love, making it especially difficult for them to seek assistance. The problem of child abuse is discussed in more detail in Chapter 3.

The Applied Research insert in this chapter discusses some of the evidence that social scientists use to document the condition of children and youth and assess whether things are getting better or worse.

How Well Off Are Children and Youth in the United States?

Are children and youth in the United States better off in the early twenty-first century compared to earlier decades? Many have computers, cell phones, and Palm Pilots, along with many other luxuries and technological wonders of the age. But, overall, has life for the young gotten better or worse? A few years ago, economists Victor R. Fuchs and Diane M. Reklis gave a gloomy answer to this question: "American children are in trouble. . . . Many observers consider today's children to be worse off than their parents' generation in several important dimensions of physical, mental, and emotional well-being" (1992:41). They reached this conclusion by looking at statistics that could give a glimpse of prevailing social trends:

- The performance of children and youth on standardized aptitude tests in the United States was lower in the 1990s than in the 1960s.

- Since 1960, obesity was up sharply, especially among children.

- Since 1960, the proportion of children who lived in a household without an adult male present had tripled.

Is this still true today? Since Fuchs and Reklis' time, social scientists have made significant advances in the development of sophisticated measures of social phenomena. They can now combine data on drug abuse, high school dropout rates, and a variety of other social problems to create a composite score measuring what might be called the "social health" of children and youth. It is a summary measure of how well children in the United States are doing on a variety of social and economic dimensions (Land, 2007; Miringoff and Miringoff, 1999). It is analogous to using the consumer price index and the Dow Jones average as measures of the state of the economy.

One such measure, the Child Well-Being Index (CWI), shows a dramatic decline in the overall index from the mid-1970s to the mid-1990s, indicating that social conditions for children and youth were worsening. Since 1995, the composite index has risen, but it has barely climbed back to where it was in 1975, suggesting that, overall, children are no better off today than they were decades ago.

When we look at the various parts that make up the overall index,

however, a more complicated picture appears, showing children and youth being better off on some dimensions but distressingly worse off on other dimensions. For example, many risky behaviors have shown a fairly steady decline (fewer teen pregnancies, less use of drugs and alcohol). In other realms, things have gotten worse, sometimes dramatically. The worst realm is health, with disturbing increases in child and youth obesity and declines in the improvement of child mortality. There has also been an increase in the proportions of children living in single-parent families and in numbers of children experiencing residential mobility. These factors affect children's ability to establish fulfilling relationships with others

So, on the whole, and despite the substantial affluence in the United States, life for its children and teenagers has not gotten unequivocally better over the years. Some positive trends have occurred, of course, but the number of negative trends is disturbing, especially in what is one of the most affluent nations in the world. Also, some of these indicators, such as teen suicide and rises in obesity, clearly point to the significant failure of our society to provide for its young.

Problems of the Elderly

Work and Retirement

In all societies, what people do to make a living is important to them. Work provides an economic livelihood, and it is a major source of self-esteem and sense of personal self-worth. Yet, many people have been, and some still are, forced out of work because of their age. Actually, mandatory retirement was largely eliminated in the United States when the Age Discrimination in Employment Act of 1967 was amended in 1986. In only a few occupations, such as airline pilot, does mandatory retirement still exist. Yet, some people still find themselves forced out of a job because of their age. Companies may do this as a way of reducing costs or saving on retirement benefits. After all, younger workers are cheaper than older workers because younger workers have smaller incomes and place less strain on company resources such as health costs. Companies may deliberately "restructure" as an excuse for the wholesale dismissal of older workers. Over 14,000 complaints of such age discrimination are made to the Equal Employment Opportunity Commission each year (U.S. Equal Employment Opportunity Commission, 2004).

Although there is no mandatory retirement today, few people continue working after age sixty-five: only about 19 percent of all men and 11 percent of all women (U.S. Bureau of the Census, 2006:373). In contrast, 60 percent of the men older than sixty-five in 1900 continued working. Since most older people are retired, a major concern is whether retirement has a beneficial or detrimental impact on people's lives. One view is that occupational roles and identities are so important and pervasive that their loss has very negative consequences. In their place, the retiree is left with an ambiguous status that gives life little direction and whose social prestige is difficult to determine. In fact, gerontologist Ethel Shanas (1972) has called retirement a "roleless" role to emphasize the point that what society expects of a retiree is much less well defined than are most social roles. Despite this, however, retirement for many is a positive experience (Atchley and Barusch, 2004; Rowe and Kahn, 1998). According to a summary of research on the topic, people are likely to enjoy retirement if

1. retirement is voluntary rather than forced;
2. one's income and health are good enough to live comfortably in retirement;
3. work is not the most important thing in one's life; and
4. some preparation and planning for retirement have occurred. (McConnell, 1983:340)

Poverty and Financial Problems

The poverty rate among people over sixty-five years of age in the United States was 10.1 percent in 2005, slightly below that of people between the ages of eighteen and sixty-four (see Figure 8.4). This represents astonishing progress over forty years ago when over 25 percent of the elderly were poor—almost three times higher than nonelderly adults. So the elderly have come a long way. However, as Figure 8.5 illustrates, the annual income of a family headed by a person sixty-five years of age or older is considerably less than that of other families. In addition, Figure 8.6 demonstrates that some groups among the elderly are not doing so well. Poverty rates are still unacceptably high among older women living alone, older African Americans, and older Hispanics. Three-quarters of the poor among the elderly are women.

There is reason to be cautious, however, in comparing the economic circumstances of older and younger people. When we look at total wealth or total net worth, the elderly are in some ways better off than younger adults (Peterson, 1991). During the 1980s, for example, the net worth of families headed by someone over sixty-five increased, whereas the net worth of families headed by someone fifty-five or younger decreased. In addition, the share of the total wealth going to the elderly went from 26 percent in the 1960s to 33 percent today, whereas adults aged thirty-five or younger got only 6 percent of that wealth then and today.

When the elderly do experience economic difficulties, it is usually for one of two reasons. First, the

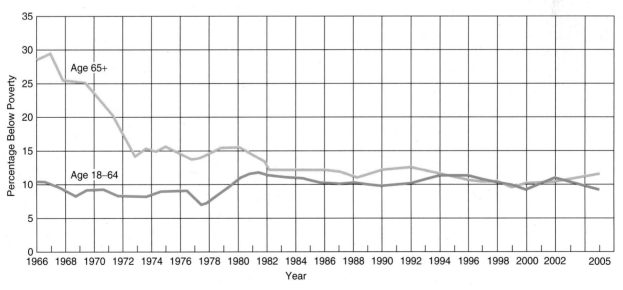

FIGURE 8.4 **Poverty Rates of Elderly and Nonelderly Adults, 1966–2005.**

Source: U.S. Bureau of the Census, *Current Population Reports*, Series P60-231 *Income, Poverty, and Health Insurance Coverage in the U.S.: 2005* (Washington, DC: U.S. Government Printing Office, 2006), p. 16.

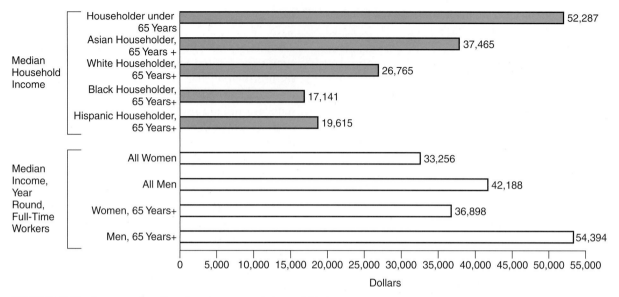

FIGURE 8.5 **Income by Gender, Race, and Age, 2005.**

Source: U.S. Bureau of the Census, *Current Population Survey, 2006 Annual Social and Economic Supplement* (Washington, DC: U.S. Government Printing Office, 2006).

elderly are more likely than other adults to be outside the workforce and thus prevented from earning a high income. Only 26 percent of the income of people aged sixty-five years or older comes from earnings (see Figure 8.7). The rest of their income is from Social Security, retirement benefits, assets, or public assistance. The elderly who do work full-time earn as much as, if not more than, younger workers (see Figure 8.5).

A second reason for the economic difficulties of some elderly is that they have worked for years at jobs with no retirement pension plan or with few benefits. In 1960, for example, only 37 percent of all nongovernmental employees had retirement programs where they worked; by the end of the 1990s, this had increased to only 50 percent (U.S. Bureau of the Census, 1978:344; U.S. Bureau of the Census, 2006:354). This could continue as a problem in the future because, in the 1980s and 1990s, companies have cut costs by reducing the amounts that they put into employee retirement plans and

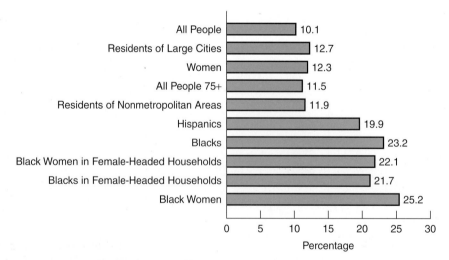

FIGURE 8.6 **Percentage of Elderly Below the Poverty Level, by Selected Characteristics, 2005.***

*Unless otherwise noted, data are for age 65+.

Source: U.S. Bureau of the Census, *Current Population Survey, 2006 Annual Social and Economic Supplement* (Washington, DC: U.S. Government Printing Office, 2006).

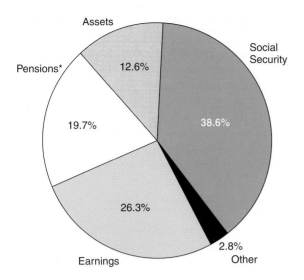

FIGURE 8.7 **Share of Income from Various Sources for People Aged Sixty-five and Older, 2004.**

*Includes private and government pensions, annuities, and IRA, Keough, and 401(k) payments.

Source: Social Security Administration, *Income of the Population 55 or Older, 2004* (Washington, DC: U.S. Government Printing Office, 2006). www.ssa.gov/policy/docs/statcomps/income_pop55/

requiring employees to match contributions. Also, many companies have dropped pension plans that make the company responsible for paying a set annual income to a retiree (called "defined benefit plans") and replaced them with plans that provide less security and fewer guarantees regarding what a retiree's income will be (called "defined contribution plans"). Basically, this change entails shifting the costs, responsibilities, and risks of providing employees with retirement from the employer to the shoulders of the employees. Only one-fifth of all income available to the elderly comes from pensions (see Figure 8.7). As a consequence, some elderly find themselves heavily dependent on Social Security or other transfer income from the government. What is ironic about this situation is that, from its inception in 1935, Social Security has not been intended to serve as a person's sole retirement income, but rather as a supplement to other sources of financial support. Social Security payments are low, therefore, and those solely dependent on them are in difficult financial straits.

Social Isolation

In preindustrial societies, older people normally remained with their families because few other alternatives existed. Today, however, an aging person is much more likely to live apart from family: Thirty percent of the elderly lived alone in 2005 compared with 18 percent in 1960 (see Figure 8.8). Living alone is especially common among women and the very old. Yet, living alone does not automatically mean loneliness or social isolation. In fact, research indicates that loneliness and isolation are not a problem for most elderly, at least not most of the time (Atchley and Barusch, 2004). Older people maintain relatively extensive contacts and involvements with friends and acquaintances, albeit fewer than do younger people. People in advanced old age (older than seventy-five years) and those with serious physical ailments are most likely to suffer from severe social isolation. It is these elderly who are least likely to visit friends, go to the library, or attend social events. In addition, socioeconomic status plays an important part in this. Middle-class elderly have more friends, are more likely to develop new friendships, and visit their friends more often than do their working- and lower-class counterparts (Atchley and Barusch, 2004). The differences are not a result of financial status but rather are attributable to the social skills acquired by middle-class people that enable them to develop and maintain friendships more easily.

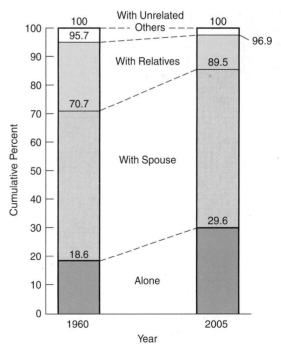

FIGURE 8.8 **Distribution of the Elderly by Living Arrangements, 1960 and 2005.**

Sources: Congressional Budget Office, *Changes in the Living Arrangements of the Elderly: 1960–2030* (Washington, DC: U.S. Government Printing Office, March 1988), p. 3; U.S. Bureau of the Census, *Statistical Abstract of the United States, 2007* (Washington, DC: U.S. Government Printing Office, 2006), p. 39.

Domestic Violence

Chapter 3 discusses the problem of the physical and psychological abuse of older people by their caretakers. Just as the dependence of the young makes them vulnerable to abuse, the elderly who are dependent on others for care face the same problem. Some abuse of the elderly results from the stress or frustration of taking care of an older parent or grandparent who is physically or mentally impaired. The burden at times becomes too much, and the nuclear family does not provide the extensive support network that would help spread these stresses over many people. Abuse of the elderly also occurs when it is the caretakers who are dependent on those they care for, possibly for financial support. The dependence of a younger adult on an older adult can lead to pent-up frustration that may find release in violence, especially when the caretaker has personal or financial problems or abuses drugs or alcohol.

Health Problems

Health is one of the major problems faced by the elderly. Paying for the health care of the elderly poses considerable difficulty for society as a whole, as the discussion of Medicare in Chapter 4 demonstrates. Medicare currently costs over $300 billion each year, which translates into $1,000 for every man, woman, and child in the United States. Forty percent of all hospital beds occupied each day are filled by people older than sixty-five years. Almost half of people older than sixty-five years in the United States experience some limitation in their activities because of chronic illnesses, with many of these limitations being major ones. Overall, the health-care expenditures of the elderly are three and one-half times greater than those of people under sixty-five. Medicare and other government health insurance pays for many of these costs, but 20 percent of the health expenditures of the elderly are paid out of their own pockets (National Center for Health Statistics, 2006). These costs are likely to increase in the future as the number of very old people, those over eighty years of age, increases.

Fear of Crime

Older people commit relatively few crimes. Instead, the elderly tend to be the victims of crime, or at least many elderly fear that they will be. Although the rate of crime perpetration against the elderly has dropped over the past two decades, the elderly do tend to be disproportionately the victims of property crimes, so their fears have some basis in reality (U.S. Department of Justice, 2006). Surveys find that crime is considered by many older people to be one of the more serious problems they face, especially for minority elderly and those who live in low-income communities. The fear seems to stem, in good part, from feelings of vulnerability—the belief that they would be unable to protect themselves from younger and more physically able predators (Joseph, 1997; Killias and Clerici, 2000). These feelings are exacerbated by the fact that some older people find themselves living in neighborhoods that, although once middle class and respectable, have deteriorated over the years.

Institutions and Nursing Homes

There are more than 16,000 nursing homes in the United States with 1.5 million residents (U.S. Bureau of the Census, 2006:113). Yet, most older people do not live in nursing homes or other extended-care facilities. In fact, only about 5 percent do. However, between 40 percent and 60 percent of the elderly will live in a nursing home for at least some time before they die. So the reality for most elderly in the United States is that they will likely spend their final days, if not their last years, in such institutions. This is especially true for women, those with fewer financial resources, and people with fewer social ties in the community.

The overriding concern with nursing homes is whether they offer the elderly a pleasant and healthy environment (Bates, 1999). Many residents are sick and vulnerable, making them easy targets for exploitation by the unscrupulous. In some homes, the elderly suffer from unappetizing and poorly prepared food, dark corridors and stairwells, and severe boredom and apathy. Sometimes basic physical care, such as prompt assistance to the bathroom, is slow or lacking. Elderly nursing-home residents also sometimes suffer from physical and psychological abuse at the hands of nursing-home personnel. Medical care can be poor and dental care scarce.

Such conditions exist for a number of reasons. First, in profit-making, or proprietary, institutions, there is a tension between the necessity of making a profit and the desire to provide services to the residents, and two-thirds of the nursing homes in the United States are proprietary, or investor-owned, institutions. Medicaid and private insurance carriers pay for people's nursing-home care on a flat-fee basis, meaning a set per diem charge for each resident. If the facility actually spends less to care for a resident, it keeps the difference. This means that the less care provided, the greater the institution's profits. Recent research documents that investor-owned nursing homes provide a lower quality of care, are more likely to have situations where patients are harmed, and have fewer nursing staff than not-for-profit nursing homes (Harrington et al., 2001).

A second reason for poor conditions in nursing

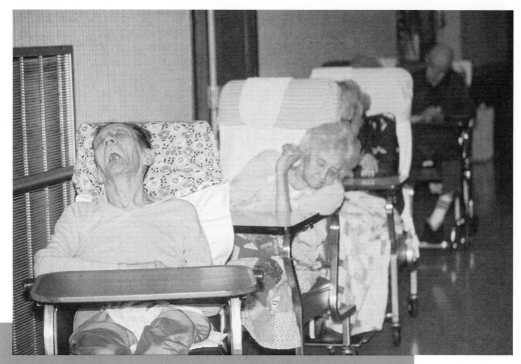

Approximately one-half of the elderly will live in a nursing home for some time before they die, and nursing homes are often unpleasant, and sometimes unhealthy, places for the elderly to be.

homes is that they have difficulty hiring and keeping qualified staff. People with little or no training in health care or gerontology are often hired because they will accept low salaries and cannot find other work. Such people are not likely to have the empathy that can lead to good care or the professionalism that will result in innovative programs in the home. Because of low pay and poor working conditions in nursing homes, there is often a high turnover rate among the skilled nursing staff. This makes it extremely difficult to maintain the continuity of care and the leadership that would help sustain adequate and innovative services.

Homosexuality and Homophobia

Homosexuality refers to *sexual feelings, attractions, and actions directed toward members of the same sex.* Estimates of the extent of homosexuality have to be viewed with some caution because people do not always report truthfully about their sexual behavior when asked by an interviewer. Especially with homosexuality, which is still stigmatized by some groups in society, some people will not honestly report their experiences. Despite these problems, best estimates are that between 1 and 5 percent of adult males in the United States are predominantly or exclusively gay (Billy et al., 1993; Laumann et al., 1994; Strong et al., 2008). **Lesbians,** or *female homosexuals,* are probably about half as common. In addition, somewhere between 5 percent and possibly as much as 25 percent of all males have had at least one homosexual encounter.

Theories of Sexual Orientation

Why do some people become attracted to members of the opposite sex whereas others are attracted to members of the same sex? Numerous attempts have been made to explain sexual orientation, although there is much that we still do not know. A major issue in the debate is whether people are born with tendencies in one direction or the other or whether sexual orientation is a product of learning through experiences while growing up.

The last few decades have produced a number of research studies that suggest, but do not definitively prove, that sexual orientation may be determined, at least in part, by a person's genetic inheritance (Hamer and Copeland, 1994; Rahman and Wilson, 2003). A study of twins, for example, found that twins who share the same genetic material (monozygotic twins) are much more likely to both be gay than twins who do not share the exact same genetic material (dizygotic twins) or two adopted brothers who share no genetic material. However, to date, these research efforts have not been able to discover exactly what is inherited. It may be that what is inherited is not sexual orientation directly but rather behaviors that can be shaped into homosexuality in the proper environment. For example, people may inherit a tendency toward gender nonconformity, that is, the tendency for young boys to behave in a girlish fashion, or be "sissies." Then the reactions of others to that gender nonconformity may encourage ways of thinking and behaving that come to be defined as "homosexual." So a genetic predisposition may get shaped by the social interaction during childhood and teenage years. There is still a lot that we do not know about this, and we have no idea whether all, or only some, homosexuality is biologically linked.

Another explanation for homosexuality suggests that it arises from some psychological maladjustment, possibly stemming from a poor parent–child relationship (Lewes, 1988). In fact, the American Psychiatric Association listed homosexuality as a mental disorder until 1973. Despite their popularity, however, psychological explanations have been subject to many criticisms. One criticism is that some studies have observed no personality differences between homosexuals and nonhomosexuals. In addition, many children with poor relationships with their parents do not become homosexual (Bell and Weinberg, 1978; Hooker, 1969). Another investigation involving more than three hundred gay men and women determined that two-thirds of these people perceived their relationships with their fathers as satisfactory, and three-quarters of those in the sample felt that they maintained a satisfactory relationship with their mothers (Robinson et al., 1982). In part because of these criticisms, in 1973, the American Psychiatric Association removed homosexuality from its list of mental disorders. At present, there is no scientific proof that homosexuality is either a psychiatric malady or an indication of poor psychological adjustment (Ross, Paulsen, and Stalstrom, 1988).

Sociologists have argued that some social or situational factors may influence people to engage in homosexual acts and that certain social contingencies influence whether a person adopts a homosexual lifestyle (Goode, 2001). Sociological theories of homosexuality suggest that, like heterosexuality, homosexuality can be the result of learning through interaction with others. In some cases, homosexual acts are a consequence of experimentation. Human sexuality is flexible and exploratory. Some people engage in homosexual acts because they are new and different, and most of these people do not consider themselves homosexuals. In other cases, homosexual acts occur because there are no heterosexual outlets available. In prison, for example, homosexuality is common, but most prisoners who engage in homosexual acts do not consider themselves to be homosexuals and they return to heterosexuality when released from prison.

Some people not only engage in homosexuality but also come to view themselves as homosexuals. To understand this, we need to look at the process of self-definition in developing a homosexual identity (Troiden, 1989). Labeling theory points out that our self-concepts derive in part from how others treat us. If a person is labeled as a homosexual by others, especially if his or her sexual identity is not yet clearly formed, it increases the likelihood that the person will eventually accept that label (see Chapter 9). If a person is labeled a homosexual by others, the person may think that the assessment of those others is accurate. In addition, the labeling may create a stigma that makes it more difficult to associate with heterosexuals and precipitates a drift into contacts with homosexuals. Let us say that a teenage male has sex with another male and finds the experience pleasurable. This does not mean he is "gay" because, as we have seen, many mostly heterosexual men gain release at times from homosexual contacts. Further suppose that his friends find out about it and react in a negative and hostile way. They may even pull away from associating with him for fear that others will think they are gay. His friends' reaction may lead the boy to question in his own mind whether he is heterosexual or homosexual. "If my friends think I am gay," he wonders, "that must mean I am, and I did enjoy it." In addition, the boy is likely to find acceptance and support among other gays. He will also find additional opportunities to explore homosexuality among them. So the labeling may precipitate a gradual changing of the boy's self-concept along with a growing association with people in the gay community. These changes in turn may help solidify his self-definition of himself as gay. In a sense, what has occurred is a self-fulfilling prophecy: The boy has become what his friends thought they were merely discovering when they first labeled him "gay." The point here is not that all people develop their sexual orientation through this route but that this is one route to becoming straight or gay. Even if sexual orientation involves some biological predisposition, as discussed earlier, it may be partly through a social vehicle such as the labeling process that the predisposition actually becomes a reality.

Societal Reaction to Homosexuality

ATTITUDES TOWARD HOMOSEXUALITY Is homosexuality deviant behavior and can it be considered a social problem itself? Recall from Chapter 1 that deviance is in the eye of the beholder: It is a group's judgment about the worth or acceptability of a behavior or a lifestyle. So, we would likely get a different answer to our question in San Francisco than we would in rural Mississippi. Nationally, the attitudes of people in the United States toward homosexuality have tended toward the negative. Although the media seem to devote more attention to and present more positive images of gays and lesbians today than in the past, the public still harbors some fairly negative views (Gallup Poll, 2007b; Wolfe, 1998). As Figure 8.9 shows, 40 percent of people in the United States believe that homosexual relations should be illegal, and this figure is about what it was twenty-five years ago. Furthermore, 39 percent of the public believes that homosexuality should not be considered an acceptable lifestyle. In 1977, only 56 percent approved of equal job rights for gays, but by 2006 that had risen to 89 percent (see Figure 8.9). In addition, people have become more tolerant of having gays and lesbians work in various occupations (see Figure 8.10). But although 9 out of 10 people today believe that gays should be allowed to hold sales positions, only about 6 out of 10 think they should be in the clergy or work as elementary school teachers. Generally, men, older people, religious people, and those with lower educations and incomes are more likely to be intolerant of homosexuality. Negative sentiment toward gays is also greater among those with traditional social values (Loftus, 2001; Saad, 1997).

DISCRIMINATION AGAINST GAY MEN AND LESBIANS Many of the problems surrounding sexual orientation have to do with the negative reactions of many heterosexuals to gay men and lesbians. In fact, the circumstances of gays, in many respects, are similar to those of racial, ethnic, and gender minorities discussed in Chapters 6 and 7. One difference, of course, is that their minority status is based on behaviors that are considered unconventional by the majority rather than on ascribed and unchangeable characteristics such as sex and race. This makes it easier for gays to avoid some of those negative reactions. But if they wish to live openly and honestly as gays, they may face strong negative reactions from some people in the United States.

Two areas in which gays face problems are in employment and housing, where discrimination is still strong, although things have improved. Many states, counties, and municipalities in the United States have given explicit protection against discrimination in housing and employment to gays. However, several locales, and at least one state, rescinded those protections, suggesting that many people still want the option of discriminating against gays in these realms. The attitudes

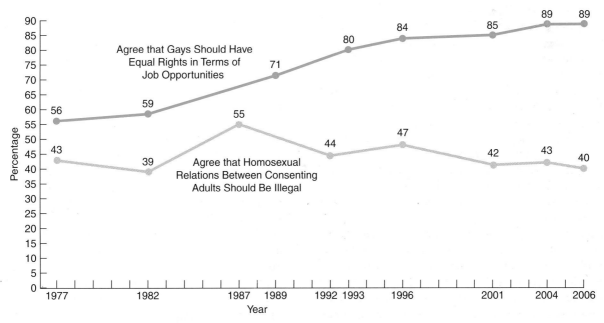

FIGURE 8.9 **Attitudes on Gay Issues in the United States, 1977–2006.**

Source: The Gallup Poll, *Poll Topics A to Z: Homosexual Relations.* Princeton, NJ: Gallup News Service, April 10, 2007, www.gallup.com/content/default.aspx?ci=11755.

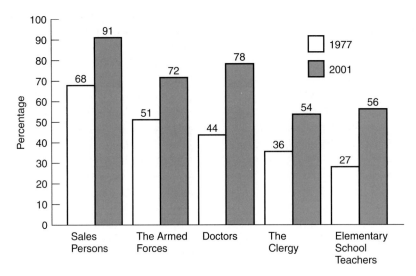

FIGURE 8.10 **Percentages of People in the United States Agreeing that Homosexuals Should Be Hired in Various Occupations, 1977–2001.**

Source: Gallup News Service, *Gallup Poll Topics A–Z: Homosexual Relations.* Princeton, NJ: The Gallup Organization, www.gallup.com/poll/indicators/indhomosexual.asp, 2001.

expressed in Figure 8.10 support this: Although things have improved in the past twenty years, there is still considerable support for keeping gays out of many jobs.

A particularly disturbing reaction by some against gay men and lesbians is the use of violence (Berrill, 1992; Jenness and Broad, 1997). Thousands of episodes of harassment, intimidation, assault, vandalism, and murder occur every year in which the victim's sexual orientation is the reason for the violence. Surveys document that between 9 percent and 24 percent of gays have been physically assaulted because of their sexual orientation. Most gays expect to be the target of antigay harassment or violence, and one-half to three-quarters fear for their safety. So, the reality is that gay men and lesbians are the subject of much hostility from their fellow citizens. Antigay murders are especially brutal and bloody, often involving "overkill" or multiple shooting or stabbing of the victim. The director of the New York City Gay and Lesbian Anti-Violence Project commented, "The level of violence in these homicides is really gruesome" (Dunlap, 1994:A10). Such excessive violence is seemingly a product of a deep rage against gays. As with so many other things, gender plays a part here: Gay males are more likely to be attacked or threatened by strangers or people they are not related to or harassed in school or by the police. Lesbians, on the other hand, are more likely to experience verbal harassment from their families. Gay adolescents also suffer a high rate of victimization, and this seems to contribute to a disturbingly high number of attempted suicides among them. Most "gay-bashers" are young males,

attacking in a group with other young males, and they are strangers to the victim. An increase in the reported cases of violence against gays has been seen in the 1980s and 1990s, but whether this represents an increase in actual violence or just more extensive reporting of it is not known.

Another area of discrimination against gays is in the military, which has traditionally maintained a strict policy of viewing homosexuality as incompatible with the mission of the armed services (Scott and Stanley, 1994). This position is based on the notion that gays constitute a security risk and that they would be a disruptive element in military units that must work and fight together in close quarters. Actually, there is no reason to believe that gay soldiers are a security risk, especially when gays can admit their sexual orientation without fear of punishment or assault. As for the second assertion, there is no evidence of any disruptive influence. The reality is that thousands of gays have served in the armed forces over the years without causing such disruption, although they were forced to keep their sexual orientation secret. President Clinton attempted to open the military to gays but met hostile resistance to such a policy. The compromise policy that resulted (dubbed the "don't ask, don't tell" policy) is one that allows gay men and women to serve in the military as long as they hide their sexual orientation. If their sexual orientation becomes known, they are discharged. In recent decades, 600 to 1,200 soldiers per year have been forced from the military under this policy over the past decade (Servicemembers Legal Defense Network, 2007). Given this policy, the extent to which the military today and in the future will present a legitimate career path for the openly gay person is questionable.

SOURCES OF HOMOPHOBIA The term **homophobia** has been adopted to refer to *an intense dislike of or prejudice against homosexuals.* What accounts for the homophobia that seems to underlie the attitudes and discriminatory behaviors described previously? A part of the answer is Western Christian theology, which defines homosexuality as sin (Britton, 1990; Greenberg, 1988). Strong condemnation of homosexuality has been an integral part of much of the Christian history and heritage, and this attitude has been pervasive in the United States. This negative reaction is often justified on the grounds that homosexuality is a threat to the family or to the reproductive potential of society. Once these norms regarding family life and sexual reproduction are established, they become powerful controls over people's behavior. Other ways of organizing one's personal or sexual life come to be seen as a threat. As one argument goes, if all or most people practiced homosexuality, how could society maintain its numbers? People make this argument despite the fact that maintaining population size has never been a problem in the many societies that have permitted homosexuality to be practiced in one form or another. But the homophobic reaction comes not from rational consideration of the evidence but from a perceived threat to a lifestyle based on deeply held cultural norms and values.

This negative attitude sometimes gets expressed in nonreligious realms. Freudian psychology, for example, sees homosexuality as an immature and underdeveloped form of adult sexuality. Only heterosexuality is seen as mature and "healthy." These psychological theories provide a scientific legitimation for viewing homosexuality in a negative light. With these pervasive and deeply held values, open displays of homosexuality are highly threatening to the dominant group and could, if left unchallenged, spread. Reactions against homosexuality then become boundary-maintaining mechanisms that highlight the prevailing norms and show people what behaviors are acceptable. As with attacks on racial or ethnic minorities, attacks on gays show symbolically who is the dominant group and show others the costs to crossing over into the realm of unacceptable behavior.

Most perpetrators of antigay violence are adolescent or very young adult males, which suggests another source of this violence: the marginalized status of some adolescents and young adults (Comstock, 1991). Recall from the earlier discussion in this chapter that modern industrial societies tend not to incorporate young people into the adult world of work and status until they are in their late teens and sometimes into the early to mid-twenties if they go to college.

Homophobic responses to gay men and lesbians are all too common in the United States, as is illustrated by these antigay protestors in Washington, DC, and sometimes lead to acts of intimidation and violence.

Because they cannot achieve status and a sense of self-worth through adult avenues, they may search for other ways of doing so, such as drinking alcohol, joy riding in cars, or other thrill-seeking ventures where they can demonstrate strength, bravery, daring, or other positive qualities. Add to this the strong emphasis on male dominance and aggression in our culture along with the negative attitude toward gays expressed by many churches and other legitimate societal institutions, and the ground is set for some of those adolescents to seek adventure, recreation, or relief from boredom through attacks on gays.

Some evidence also suggests that homophobia is associated with rigid and deep-seated negative feelings about human sexuality where sex is seen as dirty and a threat to the social order (Ficarrotto, 1990). The AIDS crisis of the 1980s has also intensified the homophobic reaction among some people (Young et al., 1991). Finally, homophobic attitudes and behavior are associated with many of the same things that lead to prejudice and discrimination against racial and ethnic minorities: authoritarianism, intolerance of differences, and dogmatism (Stark, 1991).

So, the societal reaction to homosexuality in the United States still has a strongly negative element to it. For gays this is where the social problem lies: in the stigmatization and discrimination that they face in many spheres of their lives. In this regard, the conflict perspective offers some insight. Although movements such as gay liberation have increased gay input into political decision making, especially in some cities with a large gay population, straight society's interest groups are still much more powerful and have a distinct heterosexual bias.

The Gay Community

Some neighborhoods of some cities in the United States have become distinctly gay and lesbian territories. In some cases, these were depressed, run-down neighborhoods that were taken over because few other groups wanted to live there. In fact, gays produced a certain amount of the gentrification of U.S. cities that is discussed in Chapter 12. One reason for the emergence of these gay communities is protection: They feel safer from the assaults and gain some degree of distance from homophobia when living among others like themselves (Jenness and Broad, 1997). The second reason for their emergence is that they enable gays to live among others who share their lifestyle and values. A third reason is that they afford them a degree of political power. By numerically dominating a community, they can elect city and state politicians who support their interests. An additional reason is that gays are sometimes discouraged from living in neighborhoods dominated by the majority, especially those who wish to live an openly gay life. All these reasons, by the way, are the same reasons racial and ethnic minorities often gravitate to one community.

The gay community, then, is a subculture that reproduces the cultural and institutional frameworks of the larger culture but casts them in a light of acceptance and support for gays and their way of life. Bookstores, restaurants, retail establishments, bowling and baseball teams, political organizations, support groups, hiking clubs, and Alcoholics Anonymous (AA) groups—all these organizations are found in the gay community, but they adapt to the needs, aspirations, and lifestyles of gays. Bookstores, for example, would stock books and magazines of interest to gays, and people in gay AA groups could talk openly about how their addictions have an impact on their same-sex partner. In all these settings, there is less worry about hostile contacts with "straights," and the overall climate enhances a positive sense of self-regard for gays. As with other groups that bear the burden of hostility from dominant groups, the gay subculture can provide a safe haven in a hostile world.

Future Prospects

Reducing Risks for Children and Youth

Many social policies over the past few decades have focused on reducing the risk that children and youth will be exposed to poverty, family violence, sexual exploitation, and other forms of discrimination and exploitation (see Chapters 3, 4, and 5). One of the major emphases in the United States has been to provide the supports to children and their families that will make child development and socialization a more positive and fruitful experience (Danziger and Waldfogel, 2000). In addition, in 1997, President Clinton established the Federal Interagency Forum on Child and Family Statistics (2006), which is to publish an annual report that documents the state of children in the United States and suggests policy directions for improvements. However, one important fact has made all of these efforts less effective than they might be: In the struggle for a share of society's resources, children and youth in the United States have not done nearly as well as some other interest groups. Although the United States spends more on government programs for children now than thirty years ago, government programs that benefit adults have grown at a much faster pace. In addition, people over age sixty-five have gained the largest increase in government support. The government spends more on the health-care needs of the

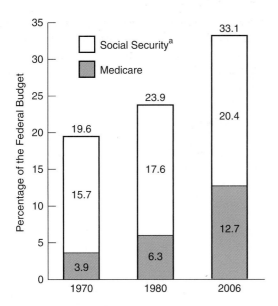

FIGURE 8.11 **Medicare and Social Security as a Percentage of the Total Federal Budget, 1970–2006.**

Source: U.S. Bureau of the Census, *Statistical Abstract of the United States, 2007* (Washington, DC: U.S. Government Printing Office, 2006), p. 309.

elderly during the last year of life than it spends on *all* the health care of *all* children. Overall, the government spends eleven times as much on each person over sixty-five as on each under eighteen (Hewlett, 1991). As Figure 8.11 demonstrates, Social Security and Medicare programs, which direct funds mostly to the elderly, have grown considerably over the past three decades—to the point now where they consume one-third of the federal budget. The Policy Issues insert (p. 220) explores the issue of whether the current allocation of resources to different age groups is the most effective.

Economic Resources of the Elderly

Social policy regarding retirement in the United States rests on the assumption that the elderly's economic support will consist of three elements: personal pensions, Social Security, and accumulated savings and assets.

RETIREMENT PENSIONS As has been seen, some elderly have little or no income from personal retirement pensions. In the 1970s, the government tried to alleviate this problem by passing legislation that requires employers with more than ten employees to offer their workers a pension plan. This legislation also regulated the "vesting" of pensions. A "vested" pension is one that is the property of the employee rather than the

company, so that the employee keeps the accumulated funds in the plan even if he or she no longer works for that company. In the past, some pension plans were never vested so that people had to keep working for a particular company until they retired in order to receive retirement benefits. All too often, people would work for a company for many years, only to be laid off in their fifties and lose all their retirement income. In fact, some companies have been accused of purposely laying off older workers to save the pension money. Federal legislation now requires that pensions be vested in the employee after five years of employment.

Legislation has also been enacted to protect some older women, especially those who were homemakers throughout their lives and never established a pension plan of their own (Rankin, 1985). Such women are dependent on their husbands' retirement, but some husbands chose—without consulting their wives—to have retirement benefits end at their death. These women, who often outlive their husbands, find themselves with no pension after their husbands die. The Retirement Equity Act of 1984 requires employees to take their retirement in a form that provides the spouse with a pension after the worker's death, unless the spouse agrees in writing to another arrangement.

Current legislation involving retirement plans is a vast improvement over the far less regulated environment of the past. Still, however, many people find themselves with few accumulated pension funds when they retire. Some people jump from one job to another every few years and never achieve a vested pension plan. This problem could be considerably alleviated by shortening the vesting period to two to four years of employment. This would provide many more workers with retirement income, but it would also cost employers more and possibly increase prices.

SOCIAL SECURITY The Old-Age, Survivors, Disability, and Health Insurance Program (OASDI) is discussed briefly in Chapter 5. OASDI, popularly known as Social Security, was first established by Congress in 1935. It is a compulsory retirement insurance program, meaning that all qualified employees and their employers must contribute. Currently, income up to $90,000 is taxed for Social Security at a rate of 15 percent. (If you pay Social Security taxes, the amount is shown in the box labeled "FICA" on your pay stub.) The employer and the employee each pay half of the tax, with self-employed persons paying the full tax. When people retire, they receive monthly benefits based mainly on total contributions they made to Social Security over the years.

Social Security income constitutes 38 percent of all the income available to the elderly. Although Social Security was never intended to be a person's sole

Should Medicare or Social Security Be Based on Age Rather than Need?

Many social programs are based on age in that a person must be in at least a general age category in order to be eligible. Thus, with Medicare and Social Security, a person must be at least sixty-five years of age to receive full benefits from Social Security. Supporters of this age-based approach argue that this is appropriate for Medicare and Social Security because older people have more needs and different circumstances from the young. There was a time, not too many decades ago, when the elderly were much worse off financially than today and undoubtedly deserved a large share of societal largess. Although the financial circumstances of the elderly have improved, they still face significant limitation in comparison to others: They have a much more limited ability to increase their income through earnings from work, and they face much more serious health problems than do the young.

Opponents of age-based policies, on the other hand, argue that the circumstances of the elderly have changed over the past forty years (Crystal, 1986; Longman, 1987). Many elderly today are financially comfortable, with retirement plans that offer them a lifestyle that they enjoy. In fact, as we have seen, most elderly people do not view financial problems as being among their more serious concerns. This has led gerontologist Bernice Neugarten to comment that "age itself is becoming a poor indicator of an older person's circumstances and needs" (1982:25). Some elderly, as we have seen, are still very much in need; but age-based services, because they provide support to all people in an age category, may actually draw resources away from those elderly who are in most desperate need of help. It also draws resources away from other groups whose needs may be greater than the needs of some elderly. Earlier, this chapter demonstrated that the social health of youth in the United States has deteriorated over the past few decades. If Neugarten's policy of focusing on need rather than age were to be adopted, then resources now flowing to the elderly might be redirected toward needy youth. Resources must be spread more thinly if they have to cover a whole age category, such as all elderly, rather than being directed toward those with identifiable needs irrespective of age.

Opponents of age-based policies also argue that such policies may perpetuate ageism and age discrimination at the same time that they claim to be advocates for the elderly. This can occur because age-based policies can contribute to the misperception of "the old" as a homogeneous group with numerous problems not experienced by other age groups in society. This can reinforce the notion that "being old" is a problem in itself rather than focusing on those conditions, such as poverty or physical infirmity, that can be found among all age groups, although possibly more often among the old. Thus, Neugarten argues, we should focus on poverty, not old age, as the key social problem in devising social policy.

Neugarten's position could translate into social policy in a number of possible ways:

1. Medicare could be made available to all people over sixty-five, but the financially independent elderly might pay a higher deductible, a larger percentage of their charges, or possibly monthly premiums for the coverage.

2. Social Security could be based on need, with the poor elderly receiving larger payments and the well-to-do elderly receiving little or no Social Security.

Changing policies to be need-based rather than age-based is a controversial one because there are many groups whose interests would be threatened by such policies. This position is also a complex one because it causes us to assess the many other ways in which age is used as a legal and administrative criterion. Is it equitable, for example, to allow sixteen-year-olds to drive a car but prohibit fifteen-year-olds from doing so? Or to require teens to attend school until a certain age? Of course, good reasons for such age-based policies can be located, but the point here is that these practices raise critical questions of equity: Is it fair to treat members of a group in this fashion merely because of their age? Once one begins to view age as an ascribed status that may be an inappropriate criterion for allocating most resources and privileges, many social practices may need scrutiny.

retirement income, it is for some people, and Social Security payments are barely sufficient to live on. For example, the average benefit for a retired worker and spouse is about $19,920—poverty-level income (U.S. Bureau of the Census, 2006:351). Many elderly receive much less than this average. So retirees who must rely exclusively on Social Security are in desperate straits.

Social Security is organized such that the benefits paid to the elderly today are taken from money collected from current workers; it is not an investment program where workers invest money today to fund their retirement years from now. Because of this, Social Security periodically runs into trouble as the number of elderly receiving benefits from the program grows (Baker and Weisbrot, 2001; Diamond and Orszag, 2004). In some years, the system has paid out more than it collected. Over the years, changes have been made to alleviate this problem: trimming benefits, raising Social Security taxes, lowering benefits to early retirees, and raising the age at which full benefits could be received. These changes have kept Social Security solvent, and it now collects more than it pays out. The basic problem remains, however: The population is aging, with the elderly growing in proportion to those still working. If nothing is done, expenditures will eventually exceed collections. Although this is not projected to occur for at least forty years, there are a variety of proposals for preventing this from occurring. Some propose modest changes, such as raising the retirement age or raising the minimum income that is subject to Social Security taxes; at the other extreme, radical plans have been proposed to turn it into a private investment program where workers' contributions are placed in private accounts for them to invest for their future retirement. Although changes in Social Security will undoubtedly be made, it is unclear at this point what the nature of those changes will be.

SAVINGS AND ASSETS Savings and accumulated assets, such as stocks and bonds, are a third source of economic support in retirement, but many elderly do not have any significant amount of such assets (Springstead and Wilson, 2000). This is especially true for minority elderly, among whom probably less than 20 percent have such assets. If people who are able could be encouraged to save and accumulate assets while working—beyond money put into a pension or Social Security—this would help alleviate the financial problems of some older people. In the past two decades, the government has encouraged this by allowing various types of tax-deferred savings and investment plans, such as Individual Retirement Accounts (IRAs), 401(k) plans, and self-employment pensions (SEPs). There are limits on how much money can be placed into these plans and penalties if any of the money is withdrawn before a person is fifty-nine and one-half years old.

These tax-deferred savings and investment plans have become very popular and will be an important element in the economic picture of many retired people in the future. In fact, the government could further encourage such personal saving for retirement by allowing people to put a larger proportion of their income into such plans than they currently can.

However, such encouragements to save only help those with money to save; that is, the more affluent. In fact, the investors in such programs are predominantly white, affluent, and well educated (Investment Company Institute, 2001). For example, only two out of five households have established an IRA (U.S. Bureau of the Census, 2006:356). The less affluent and minority groups such as African Americans have low participation rates in such retirement plans.

Health Care of the Elderly

The availability of health care to the elderly has been vastly improved through the Medicare and Medicaid programs (see Chapter 4). These programs have gone a long way toward relieving the financial burden of health care for the elderly, and they have made the decision of whether to seek health services an easier one for older people to make.

These programs, however, are not without their problems. First, they do not cover all services. The elderly still pay substantial out-of-pocket health-care costs. A second problem is that Medicare is very costly for society. However, despite the budget cutting that hit social programs in recent decades, Medicare emerged relatively unscathed. This suggests that the benefits provided are not likely to be significantly reduced in the future, although expenditures for additional benefits will probably be scrutinized very closely.

Living Arrangements of the Elderly

Because old people are increasingly unlikely to live with and be cared for by their children, where do they live? A number of alternative living arrangements have arisen.

AGE-INTEGRATED HOUSING Maggie Kuhn, founder of the Gray Panthers, an advocacy group for the elderly, promoted what she called "shared housing" arrangements for herself and other old people (Danigelis and Fengler, 1990). Shared housing involves a number of people, both young and old, sharing a home and the various chores and responsibilities of home ownership. Proponents of such arrangements believe they offer many advantages to the elderly, including social ties to replace the family. In a shared housing setting, there are young people to make difficult repairs and do hard labor; there are people present to alleviate feelings of isolation; and there is help for the elderly if they develop some activity limitations. These arrangements also reduce the segregation and stereotyping that may result from age-segregated housing.

Public and Familial Assistance for the Elderly in Other Societies

Throughout history, families have provided much of the support people need in their old age, and we often hear calls in the United States for a return to family values. However, today's families may not be able to play such a central role because family structures have weakened in virtually all societies in the modern world (Kosberg, 1992). Families have become smaller, the elderly are less revered and more likely to live alone, and marital disruption is more common. In addition, in all societies, some elderly do not have families, while some families are too poor to offer much assistance. Finally, in societies as different as Argentina, Sweden, and the United States, surveys show that many elderly do not *want* to be dependent on their adult children or other family members. For all these reasons, a shift of responsibility for caring for the elderly has been occurring in all societies, with the government becoming increasingly active in providing this assistance.

One form of government assistance to the elderly is public pensions. The United States has one of the lowest mandatory contribution rates to a public pension plan (Social Security) of all the industrialized countries. Furthermore, our public pension policy leaves some elderly with little or no pension income because the amount of income a person receives from Social Security depends on his or her lifetime work and earnings. Such a policy discriminates against those, often women, who never worked or who worked part-time or intermittently. Societies such as Israel, the United Kingdom, and the Scandinavian countries try to alleviate this problem by also providing a universal pension that is payable to all citizens who reach a certain age, irrespective of whether or how much they have worked (Cnaan, Olsson, and Wetle, 1990; Nusberg, Gibson, and Peace, 1984). Swedish policy provides for three sources of income: a flat-rate pension for all citizens, an earnings-related pension for those who have worked, and mandatory worker pensions provided by employers and trade union organizations. With this system, destitution among Swedish elderly is practically nonexistent.

Because public pensions are rarely large enough to provide for all the needs of the elderly, many industrial nations, like France, Switzerland, and Sweden, require almost universal private pension

Age-integrated housing arrangements can take forms other than shared housing. They might involve a community with separate houses or apartments that are available to people of all ages. Proponents of such living arrangements argue that they offer the elderly stimulation, novelty, and the delight of relating to people of all age groups. However, the evidence is not clear on whether age-integrated settings or age-segregated settings are more beneficial to the elderly (Burby and Rohe, 1990). The elderly in age-segregated housing seem more satisfied with how their living arrangements are managed and are more active and involved with people around them. But the impact is not great, and there are some negatives, such as a greater fear of crime in age-segregated settings.

GOVERNMENT-SUBSIDIZED HOUSING The housing priority of the many elderly with low or moderate incomes is very basic: to find a place to live that is safe, clean, and affordable. The government has offered assistance in this area for many years, including such things as building low-income housing, offering rent supplements for private apartments, and providing mortgage insurance for elderly with low or moderate incomes (Kerschner and Hirschfield, 1983). However, crime is still a sizable problem in the deteriorating neighborhoods and public housing projects in which many elderly people live. In addition, much of the public housing already constructed is beginning to deteriorate and is badly in need of repairs.

SUPPORTED-LIVING ENVIRONMENTS The physical infirmities that can accompany aging have a particular impact on the ability of people to live independently. Family members, especially adult daughters, provide most of the care for aging parents in the United States (Abel, 1991). This places a considerable burden on those family members, and some supports for them have developed, such as in-home physical therapy or other assistance.

In addition, a variety of institutional settings has emerged to help the infirm elderly cope (Struyk et al., 1989). Taken together, they are called *supported-living environments* because all provide some level of support for people who cannot or do not want to live independently. Some of these homes are nonprofit

coverage for employees through nationally negotiated agreements. Whereas less than one-half of U.S. workers have private pension coverage, 90 percent of workers in Sweden and 80 percent in the Netherlands have that coverage.

To provide protection for women and men with meager work histories, Germany, New Zealand, and Canada split pension credits accumulated during a marriage at the time of a divorce. So, a nonworking spouse shares in the pension accumulation of the working spouse. For earnings-related public pensions, Switzerland and the United Kingdom permit people to use a deceased or former spouse's earnings record at the time the marriage ended to calculate retirement benefits. In some cases, if a wife's earnings record does not qualify her for a pension, she can combine it with her husband's earnings record.

In addition, to ensure that all work contributes to a worker's retirement pay, many societies have much more liberal vesting policies. In Sweden and Switzerland, for example, for workers who have reached their late twenties, full vesting occurs as soon as one begins to work or within a few years of employment. This means that people who switch jobs after a few years still accumulate some retirement funds that are permanently their own. This especially benefits women, who are more likely to work for short periods and to switch jobs.

All industrialized countries recognize the value of maintaining the elderly in their own homes because it is more humane and less expensive than caring for them in a nursing home or other institutional setting. Denmark, Norway, and Sweden, for example, provide such things as chore and escort services, meals-on-wheels, laundry services, counseling, transportation, friendly visiting services, and other supports that allow older people to continue living in their homes. In some cases, these services are universal rather than age-based or income-based— anyone with functional impairments is eligible for them. This increases political support for them and encourages people to view them as a right of citizenship rather than a welfare handout. Some of these services are available to the elderly in the United States, but these other societies have a much more elaborate infrastructure of such services.

institutions run by religious groups, business organizations, or labor unions for the benefit of their members. Others are commercial or proprietary institutions that are run to make a profit for their owners. The range of support they provide is quite varied. At one extreme are homes for the aged that care for reasonably healthy people who no longer want responsibility for running a home and caring for themselves. At the other extreme are nursing homes that take people who have severe physical limitations and require extensive support. In some homes, people purchase or rent an apartment with cooking facilities and can either cook for themselves or eat in a dining area with the other residents. Some homes provide the whole range of support. People can enter when they are reasonably healthy and be assured of support by the community if their physical status deteriorates.

The care and programs available in these living environments are quite variable. Generally, the non-profit homes run by religious groups or labor unions have the financial resources and the motivation to provide excellent care and a wide range of services. Other homes charge high fees and still find it difficult to provide high-quality care. This is especially true of proprietary institutions that cater to low- and moderate-income groups. To alleviate these problems, the government has developed an elaborate set of regulations to be followed in order for a home to be licensed. It has also developed programs to train nursing-home personnel and nursing-home inspectors.

The International Perspectives insert provides a comparison of financial and other services available to elderly in the United States with those in some other societies.

Collective Action by the Elderly

There is little doubt that it has been older people themselves who have been the most vocal about the treatment of the elderly in the United States. The elderly have shown, and continue to show, signs of increasing political activism, and even radical militancy, focused on changing traditional conceptions of old age and advocating social policies that might alleviate the problems of the elderly. Two popular organizations promoting the interests of the elderly are the AARP (formerly called the American Association of Retired Persons) and the National Retired Teachers Association (NRTA). These groups offer many programs and services for the elderly, such as courses in income tax preparation and public speaking. They have also been very active at the local, state, and national levels in lobbying for programs that are beneficial to the elderly.

The Gray Panthers, a group that is considerably more extreme than AARP or NRTA, believes that the problems of the aged stem from some basic defects in the social structure (Brown, 1998a). The most fundamental defect, it argues, is our emphasis on materialism and the consumption of goods and services, rather than on the quality of life and personal relationships. In a materialist society, the elderly are viewed as useless because they are less economically productive. Because of this, they are abandoned, like worn-out automobiles. The Gray Panthers hope to liberate people from what they perceive as outmoded ways of thinking about the elderly and to encourage independence and self-determination among the elderly.

These various groups and social movements have been quite successful in protecting and advancing the interests of the elderly. For example, when many social programs were being severely trimmed by the government, Medicare and Social Security suffered the least. A primary reason for this was that politicians were concerned about the strong reaction they could expect from the very well-organized groups backing the elderly. Such successes are likely to enhance support for groups such as AARP, NRTA, and the Gray Panthers. In addition, the elderly have more financial and economic resources available today than they did decades ago, and this will be even truer in the future. They also have more time to pursue their interests than do younger people who must work. Finally, older people take their duty to vote much more seriously than do younger people. In presidential elections, only 40 percent of people in their early twenties bothered to vote, whereas 68 percent of people over sixty-five did so (U.S. Bureau of the Census, 2006:256). This affords the elderly considerably more political clout. People between fifty and sixty-five also vote in large numbers, and these people are also concerned about issues related to the elderly because they will soon be in that group. This group of people aged fifty and older comprises a substantial voting bloc.

So collective action on the part of the elderly is likely to continue as one of the most powerful forces working against ageist attitudes and social policies in the United States.

Collective Action by Gays and Lesbians

We have seen that, although homosexuality is still regarded by many as unacceptable, it has also gained more public notice and probably more respectability in the past twenty years. At the very least, more people are now aware of how widespread homosexuality is (Loftus, 2001). And research shows that familiarity with gays and the gay lifestyle leads to more positive attitudes toward homosexuality. Also, more educated people are more accepting of gays. So, as educational levels in the United States rise and as more gay men and lesbians lead their lives openly, we can expect attitudes toward homosexuality to become even more positive.

The extensive and effective use of collective action in the political arena has had an impact on the discrimination and violence meted out against gays and lesbians (Button, Rienzo, and Wald, 1997; Jenness and Broad, 1997). Local, state, and national organizations that promote gay rights have been working to change laws, make sure that the criminal justice system deals with violence against gays, and promote positive images of gays and lesbians in the media and elsewhere. Over the past twenty years, there have been significant changes in the direction of more equitable treatment of gay men and lesbians. As we have seen, a number of places around the country now ban discrimination against gays in employment and housing. In addition, a number of employers have extended benefits to gay couples that had previously been available only to married couples (see Chapter 3). These "domestic partner" benefits can include health insurance, retirement plans, and so forth.

However, strong opposition to such policies persists. In 1992, a statewide ballot in Oregon would have permitted discrimination against gays, would have prohibited gay state employees from holding any position where they worked with children, and would have made it official state policy that homosexuality is "unnatural" and a "perversion." Although the ballot measure lost, 43 percent of Oregon voters voted in favor of this extreme measure. In 1998, the voters in Maine voted to repeal that state's law protecting gays from discrimination, leaving only ten states with statewide gay-rights laws still on the books. On top of all these things, we have seen that gays still suffer physical attacks in unacceptable numbers because of their sexual orientation. The tolerance for gays that has emerged for many people seems to be an acceptance of individual gays in jobs or social settings but a rejection, sometimes strongly, of homosexuality as an identity or acceptable way of life (Wolfe, 1998). So there is still real tension in the United States over this issue, and, although many predict the future will bring greater acceptance of gays, there is still much uncertainty about this. Gays have become a much more powerful political force than they were twenty years ago, so they will be better able to protect themselves against threats.

As gays have gone more public with their lifestyle and become more politically active, they have become more effective at getting societal institutions, such as schools, government, and corporations, to establish policies and practices that better serve the interests of gays. This has created new arenas for conflict with those who feel that society should not support, or even condone, homosexuality. One of the most contentious issues in this regard is whether society should provide for gay marriages or some sort of civil unions for gays which legitimize their relationships and extend to gay couples most or all of the privileges that marriage affords to heterosexual couples. (Issues regarding gay marriages and families are discussed in the Policy Issues section of Chapter 3.) A few countries now provide for gay marriages, and some countries and states in the United States now provide civil unions to gay couples that do much the same thing. The fact that even one state has passed legislation to provide for civil unions is impressive testimony to the political resources that the gay community has accumulated. Yet, it is unclear whether these policies will be maintained, let alone advanced. There is strong support to abolish the civil unions in states where they have been provided, and other groups are promoting an amendment to the U.S. Constitution that would define marriage as only involving an opposite-sex couple. So, although gays have made significant gains in this regard, what the future holds is still very unclear.

LINKAGES Providing support and assistance to the elderly has contributed to skyrocketing health-care costs because Medicare has become so expensive and increased demand considerably for health-care services (Chapter 4). At the same time, the elderly are more likely to be battered and injured by a caretaker who abuses drugs or alcohol (Chapter 10).

STUDY AND REVIEW

Summary

1. Gerontology is the scientific study of aging. All societies carve out people's lives into a series of social stages, and this is called the life course. The life course is determined in part by biology and in part by the needs of a particular society.

2. Functionalists argue that the stages of the life cycle are intimately related to the social needs of a particular society. The life cycle in preindustrial societies differs significantly from that in industrial societies. From the conflict perspective, the position of the young and old in society is related to their access to social, political, and economic power.

3. Ageism refers to the ideology holding that people in a particular age group are inferior, have negative attributes, and can be dominated and exploited because of their age. The age structure of industrial societies is becoming more "top heavy" as these societies age and their dependency ratios grow larger.

4. The major problems facing the young are economic exploitation, family instability, poverty, sexual exploitation, and child abuse.

5. The elderly in the United States face a number of serious problems: They are less likely to work and have to adapt to retirement; they confront some financial problems; they suffer from social isolation, especially when they are very old; they are sometimes victims of domestic violence; they have more health problems than others; they fear being the victims of crime; and they are in danger of being exploited in poorly run nursing homes.

6. There are biological, psychological, and sociological explanations of sexual orientation. Homosexuals in the United States experience inequitable treatment in the form of discrimination, hostility, and violence. Homophobia has many sources, including condemnation of homosexuality by Christianity, the marginalized status of young males, and characteristics such as authoritarianism, intolerance of differences, and dogmatism.

Two particular types of information can be found on the Internet in relation to age and sexual orientation. One type is data that will assist you in assessing the extent of problems society confronts in relation to age or sexual orientation. One valuable site in this regard is the U.S. Census Bureau **(www.census.gov)**. Much valuable information can be found there about both the young and the old (rates of poverty and so on). For information specifically about the elderly, the Web site of AARP is especially valuable **(www.aarp.org)**. From that site you can also link to the page maintained by the NRTA. Are there sites that provide factual information about gay men and lesbians and the problems they confront? Does the Federal Bureau of Investigation provide any information about crimes against gays **(www.fbi.gov)?**

Many organizations advocate for particular constituencies, such as the young, the old, gays, or bisexuals. These advocacy organizations play an important role in the social construction of social problems and in implementing solutions to them. These advocacy organizations have taken to the Internet like ducks to water because the Internet is such an effective tool for communicating with a large but geographically dispersed constituency. Find the Web sites of as many such organizations as you can. Evaluate them in terms of which groups they advocate for, what problems in particular

they focus on, what policies they propose as solutions to the problems, and whether they present any scientific evidence to support their contention that these policies would work. Assess the material presented in these Web sites in terms of how they contribute to the construction of problems surrounding age or sexual orientation. Child Trends is an organization that supports research on and services to children and youth. Part of its focus is on the positive and negative consequences of a variety of socialization practices. At its Web page **(www.childtrendsdatabank.org)**, you can find some very useful data and visual presentations on a wide range of topics relevant to children and youth. It includes information on indicators of child and youth well being, foster care, youth sexual activity, contraceptive use, and much more. Review some of these data and explore ways in which the problems suggested by the data might be alleviated through changes in socialization practices.

As a final exercise, search the Web for sites that focus on these issues in other nations. What can you learn at those Web sites that might be useful in dealing with these problems in the United States?

The Allyn & Bacon Social Problems Supersite **(wps.ablongman.com/ab_socialprob_sprsite_1)** contains material on issues of age and sexual orientation.

7. Efforts to improve the status of the young focus on finding a more equitable distribution of resources between the young and the old. Efforts to improve the status of the elderly have focused on ensuring that more people have adequate access to financial resources (pensions, Social Security, and savings and assets) for retirement, better health care, and adequate living arrangements. The elderly have used collective action very effectively to advance their interests.

8. In good part because of the effective use of collective action by gays and lesbians, homosexuality is more public and accepted today and is more protected from discrimination and other negative reactions. However, significant sources of homophobia persist.

Key Terms

ageism

age structure

demography

dependency ratio

gerontology

homophobia

homosexuality

lesbians

life course

life stages

Multiple-Choice Questions

1. According to the functionalist perspective, the treatment of the young and the old is considered a social problem when
   a. it leads to social disorganization.
   b. the young and the old have little power.
   c. there is an absence of ageism.
   d. the young and the old believe they do not have a fair share of society's resources.

2. Ageism is like racism in that both
   a. use race as a criterion for discrimination.
   b. use both race and age as criteria for discrimination.
   c. derive from the functionalist perspective.
   d. use biological grounds to defend inequitable treatment of groups.

3. The dependency ratio in the United States today is approximately _____ people older than age sixty-five for each one hundred people between ages eighteen and sixty-four.
   a. three
   b. twenty
   c. sixty
   d. eighty
   e. Cannot be determined.
4. In the United States today, which of the following is true regarding retirement policies?
   a. Retirement is mandatory at age sixty-five.
   b. Retirement is mandatory at age seventy.
   c. Retirement is not mandatory at any age for people in most occupations.
   d. All companies are required to provide pensions for their employees.
5. Which of the following is true of poverty rates among those older than sixty-five years of age in the United States today?
   a. The rates are slightly higher than those for adults aged eighteen to sixty-four.
   b. The rates are much higher than those for adults aged eighteen to sixty-four.
   c. The rates are higher than they were thirty years ago.
   d. The rates are slightly lower than those for adults aged eighteen to sixty-four.
6. The largest source of income for people older than age sixty-five in the United States is
   a. pensions.
   b. Social Security.
   c. assets.
   d. earnings from work.
   e. Medicare.
7. Research on the biological basis of sexual orientation has reached the conclusion that
   a. sexual orientation is definitely caused by genetic inheritance.
   b. sexual orientation is definitely not caused by genetic inheritance.
   c. sexual orientation may be determined, in part, by genetic inheritance.
   d. sexual orientation is caused by problems children have in their families while growing up.
8. Physical assaults on gay males are most likely to be perpetrated by
   a. young males.
   b. solitary criminals.
   c. young females.
   d. middle-aged males.
   e. minority-group males.
9. What proportion of the total federal government budget is consumed by Medicare and Social Security together?
   a. 5 percent
   b. 15 percent
   c. 33 percent
   d. 55 percent
10. Age-segregated housing for the elderly produces which of the following outcomes in comparison with age-integrated housing?
    a. less fear of crime among the residents
    b. less activity and involvement for the residents
    c. more satisfaction with living arrangements
    d. higher rates of crime among the residents

True/False Questions

1. According to sociologists, biology plays a relatively small role in shaping the life course in human societies.
2. The transition from childhood to adulthood occurs earlier in life in industrial societies than it does in preindustrial societies.
3. As societies industrialize, their age structures tend to become more "top heavy" rather than "bottom heavy."
4. One of the reasons that children in single-parent families face difficulties is that such families are more likely to have low incomes.
5. Research shows that retirement for most elderly is a negative experience.
6. When one looks at total wealth and not just annual income, the elderly are better off than younger adults.
7. The largest share of the income of people older than sixty-five years comes from earned income from work.
8. Approximately one-half of all older people will live in a nursing home at some point before they die.
9. One criticism of age-integrated housing for the elderly is that it promotes stereotyping of the elderly.
10. The elderly are much more likely to vote in elections than are people in their early twenties.

Fill-In Questions

1. The _____ is a succession of statuses and roles that people in a particular society experience in a fairly predictable pattern as they grow older.
2. The new stage in the life course that is found in industrial societies but not preindustrial ones is called _____.
3. The dependency ratio in preindustrial societies tends to be _____ than the same ratio in industrial societies.

4. Because what society expects of people who retire is much less well defined than are most social roles, retirement has been called a _____ role.

5. A _____ is a pension that is the property of an employee rather than the company for which the employee works.

6. _____ is an intense dislike of or prejudice against homosexuals.

7. _____ are tax-deferred savings or investment plans.

8. _____ is a government health-insurance program for people older than age sixty-five.

9. _____ is a popular organization promoting the interests of the elderly.

10. Political activism and radical militancy on the part of the elderly themselves are examples of _____ among the elderly.

Matching Questions

_____ 1. Age Discrimination in Employment Act
_____ 2. adolescence
_____ 3. subculture
_____ 4. an aging population
_____ 5. shared housing
_____ 6. ageism
_____ 7. demography
_____ 8. child exploitation
_____ 9. IRAs
_____ 10. Gray Panthers

A. stage in the life course
B. a higher dependency ratio
C. gay community
D. prejudice
E. debt bondage
F. retirement savings
G. study of human populations
H. radical activism for the elderly
I. age-integrated housing
J. eliminates mandatory retirement

Essay Questions

1. How do the life stages in industrial societies differ from the life stages in preindustrial societies? Why do these differences occur?

2. Describe the age structure and the dependency ratio in preindustrial and industrial societies. How do they differ from one another?

3. Explain why the economic exploitation of child laborers occurs in the United States and other nations.

4. Explain why children in the United States are at such risk of living in poverty.

5. Is retirement a good or a bad thing? Make the argument for both sides of this issue.

6. What is the poverty status of the elderly? What other kinds of financial difficulties do they confront?

7. Describe what problems are found in nursing homes, and explain why these problems exist.

8. What are the sources of homophobia in the United States?

9. What is the policy debate over whether programs for the elderly should be based on age or need? What arguments are there in favor of need-based policies?

10. In what kinds of collective action have the elderly and gays and lesbians engaged? How effective have they been and why?

For Further Reading

Phillippe Aries. *Centuries of Childhood: A Social History of Childhood.* New York: Random House, 1962. An excellent history of how childhood has been viewed in many different cultures.

Carroll L. Estes. *The Long Term Care Crisis: Elders Trapped in the No-Care Zone.* Newbury Park, CA: Sage Publications, 1993. This sociologist explores the problems with institutional care of the elderly in hospitals or nursing homes and suggests improvements in current policies.

Jacob S. Hacker. *The Great Risk Shift: The Assault on American Jobs, Families, Health Care, and Retirement and How You Can Fight Back.* New York: Oxford University Press, 2006. This author documents how economic forces have promoted changes in social policy that shift the risk of supporting people and their families (in terms of paying for health care or providing retirement pensions) from the government and employers to the backs of individuals, leaving people more vulnerable and less secure than in the past.

Daniel Harris. *The Rise and Fall of Gay Culture.* New York: Hyperion, 1997. This work describes how the gay community in the United States arose as a reaction to the discrimination, hostility, and assaults that straights thrust upon gays. It also talks about the changes in gay community and culture that may be occurring.

Jonathan Kozol. *Amazing Grace: The Lives of Children and the Conscience of a Nation.* New York: Crown, 1995. This is a passionate and eye-opening account of the lives of poor children in the United States. The author persuasively argues that we need to redistribute some of our vast resources to the problems of poor children.

Carl Husemoller Nightingale. *On the Edge: A History of Poor Black Children and Their American Dreams.* New York: Basic Books, 1993. This is a thought-provoking book about the circumstances of

African American children today—showing how they are very much products of their culture, but the culture conspires against their advancement.

Valerie Polakow (ed.). *The Public Assault on America's Children: Poverty, Violence, and Juvenile Injustice.* New York: Teachers College Press, 2000. The readings in this book provide an in-depth examination of child abuse, poverty, health, and other problems that affect children and youth and how some social policies actually help to perpetuate these conditions.

Alissa Quart. *Branded: The Buying and Selling of Teenagers.* New York: Perseus, 2002. This disturbing book, written by a journalist, documents the extent to which teenagers today are the targets of a comprehensive and sophisticated marketing campaign to get them to buy products. Quart explores the idea that this constitutes an unparalleled exploitation of the young.

CHAPTER NINE

CRIME AND DELINQUENCY

One doesn't have to look very hard to find statistics that seem to document the importance of crime and delinquency as social problems in the United States:

- The rate of violent crime is twice as high today as it was in the 1960s.

- The rate of incarceration in prison is four times higher today, one of the highest rates of any nation in the world.

- If current rates of incarceration continue, an African American male has an almost one-in-three chance of being put in a state or federal prison at some time during his life.

- There may be as many as 16,000 gangs in the United States, committing over half a million gang-related crimes each year.

Yet, these statistics, as disturbing as they are, are part of a much more complicated picture that makes up the reality of crime in the United States today. This chapter will flesh out that picture, exploring the causes of crime and delinquency as well as solutions to the problem. We will see that these statistics are a part of the problem, but that not all crime is violent—crimes are also committed by people in business suits and in corporate boardrooms and by corporations themselves. And this white-collar crime can be as harmful to people and society as violent street crime. We will also see that people are often misinformed about the nature and extent of the crime problem, with the media playing a part in their distorted view.

Explanations of Crime

Like all behavior, crime and delinquency are complex, and many people find them hard to understand. In fact, because crime and delinquency are often so frightening, it is tempting to settle for overly simple explanations of them. Over the years, many people have sought *biological explanations* of crime, which view criminal behavior as arising, at least in part, from a person's physical or biological makeup. Some people, it is argued, are simply biologically less capable of conforming their behavior to conventional norms. Decades of research results, however, have shown that biology makes, if anything, only a small contribution to the crime problem. Criminologists today agree that criminal behavior is for the most part due to psychological and social forces (Chambliss, 1991).

Unlike their biological counterparts, *psychological approaches* to crime still receive considerable support (Adler, Mueller, and Laufer, 2007). From this perspective, criminality is linked to personality disorder or maladjustment, often developing during childhood. Evidence in support of such connections comes from research on personality defects and disorders among delinquents, mental disease in prisoners, and studies of psychopathic and sociopathic personalities (Eysenck and Gudjonsson, 1989). Although sociologists recognize the importance of personality and psychological processes in people's lives, such explanations offer only a partial understanding of crime and delinquency. In many cases, people who commit crimes are free from the psychological disorders that are presumed to cause crime, and people with those disorders often do not commit crimes. In other cases, it can be the criminal lifestyle, along with the stigma and fear of imprisonment, that leads people to develop unique personality characteristics rather than the other way around. In addition, many of the psychological maladjustments that lead to crime are the products of social circumstances, and social conditions also contribute to the cause of crime in many cases where psychological factors do not come into play. So, social conditions contribute substantially to the level of crime in society. Therefore, policy designed to reduce crime needs to

Myths & Facts

About Crime

Myth: There is a clear line between the "criminal element" in society and the law-abiding and respectable people. If we could put that criminal element behind bars, the crime problem would be solved.

Fact: Once again, social reality is far more complex than many commonsense beliefs would have it. It turns out that many crimes are committed by people who are otherwise considered quite respectable by themselves and many others. For example, who commits vandalism? Teenage punks? Hostile and alienated losers? Social psychologist Philip Zimbardo conducted an intriguing study of people who vandalized automobiles in New York City (Zimbardo, 1973). After seeing many stripped and battered automobiles on his way to work, he decided to observe who the vandals were. He bought an old car, left it on a street near New York University, and watched from a hidden location. Within ten minutes, the first vandals appeared: a father, mother, and their eight-year-old son! The mother

served as lookout while the father and son removed the battery and radiator. Later, another vandal was pushing an infant in a baby carriage. There followed a virtual parade of people who removed everything of value from the car and then began battering what was left. These vandals were often well dressed and chatted amiably with passersby as they toiled.

Myth: Crimes are committed by the less educated members of society, whereas those fortunate enough to attend college understand the importance of obeying the law.

Fact: College students in the state of Michigan were asked to indicate which criminal activities they had engaged in. Their responses showed that every student who responded could have been jailed for offenses he or she had committed. Michigan is probably no different in this regard than any other state. Some groups may commit more crimes than others, or more of certain types of crime, but the crime problem is by no means limited to one or a few groups.

focus on the social conditions that produce it, and the sociological approaches to crime provide the basis for doing this. These perspectives emphasize the role of culture, social structure, and social interaction in bringing about criminal and delinquent behavior.

The Functionalist Perspective

An early functionalist, Emile Durkheim, provided one of the explanations for high levels of crime in industrial societies. One of the key features of industrial societies, he argued, is the weakening of many of the social bonds important in preindustrial societies. Ties to family, community, and church become less important in industrial societies as families become smaller and workers more mobile and independent of their families (see Chapter 3). People are freer to pursue their own needs and fulfill their own desires; they are less constrained by the need to please relatives or account to a priest or minister. But this freedom has its costs. The reduction in social constraints also results in a degree of social disorganization as people pursue needs and goals that may be detrimental to the overall good of society. After all, bonds to family and church were one of the key mechanisms constraining people from committing crimes or engaging in other socially disapproved activities. When those bonds are weakened or removed, a certain amount of crime and social disorder will result. For Durkheim, then, crime is one of the costs that we pay to live in the type of society that we do, and recent research comparing many different societies supports his theory (Leavitt, 1992). More recently, Durkheim's views have been applied to juvenile delinquency in the form of a "social control" theory of delinquency. The basic idea is that the chances of delinquency occurring can be reduced if youngsters maintain attachments and commitments to the conventional world of their parents, schools, and peers (Agnew, 1991; Hirschi, 1969).

Another influential functionalist approach to crime and delinquency is sociologist Robert K. Merton's **anomie theory** (1968), which posits that *inconsistencies and contradictions in the social system contribute to many forms of crime.* Merton observed that *people in the United States are taught to strive for certain goals but are not always provided with the culturally approved means necessary to attain these goals.* Merton referred to *such inconsistencies and the confusion they can cause in people* as **anomie.** In the United States, for example, an important cultural goal is success, which is defined largely in material terms. One culturally approved way to become successful is to get an education and work in some legitimate occupation. Some people, however, are prevented from succeeding in this fashion because of poverty, discrimination, or some other social condition. When

people are thus hindered from achieving desired goals, deviance in one of its many forms may result. Deviance is the person's "mode of adaptation" to the anomie, although the person may not think of it this way.

Merton called the most common mode of adaptation to anomie *innovation,* according to which people pursue the cultural goals through illegal or other socially disapproved means. This is likely to occur when people feel that legitimate routes to success are closed and that their only option is to turn to illegitimate ones. People who are unemployed or underemployed, for example, can provide for their families and themselves through robbery or burglary. Likewise, a person running a marginal business concern can survive by cheating on taxes or using deceptive advertising practices. Recent research on crime supports anomie theory. For example, crime rates, especially for property crimes, are higher in communities with greater economic inequality or with a larger disparity between incomes among groups. In such cities, the less fortunate can readily see the affluence around them, and some turn to crime to improve their own circumstances (Simons and Gray, 1989). Crime also goes up when there is an economic recession (Devine, Sheley, and Smith, 1988). Crime rates are high among the unemployed and low among the employed (Allan and Steffensmeier, 1989).

The importance of anomie theory for understanding crime should be clear: Much criminal activity derives from the social and economic conditions of U.S. society. With high unemployment and reduced government spending on social services, economic disparities are exacerbated. In fact, criminologist Elliott Currie has argued that the low crime rate in industrial societies such as Japan results in part from their programs promoting high employment and the fact that income disparities are much smaller than in the United States (Currie, 1985).

The functionalist perspective also emphasizes the interrelatedness of the various parts of the social system. Changes in one part bring about changes in other seemingly unrelated parts. Certain social trends and changes that are found in affluent industrial societies have increased the opportunities for committing certain kinds of crime, particularly burglary, larceny, and theft (Cohen and Felson, 1979; Miller and Ohlin, 1985). For example, the number of women working has increased dramatically in the past four decades; there has been an increase in the number of households with only one adult member; and people take more vacations now than in the past. The result of these three trends is that homes are much more likely to be left unattended for a part of the day and therefore become tempting targets for burglars. There has also been tremendous growth in consumer spending for items such as televisions and automobiles, which are likely objects for theft. In short, the rise in crime results in part from the increasing opportunities to commit crimes made available by trends that many people view as desirable. Unless alternative means of controlling such crimes are found, people may have to settle for the realization that some crimes represent an unfortunate by-product of an affluent and leisured lifestyle.

The Conflict Perspective

In reviewing the functionalist argument, conflict theorists observe that the analysis of the "crime and delinquency problem" tends to focus heavily on criminal behavior that is more likely to occur among the less powerful groups in society: the young, the poor, and the nonwhite. In fact, the Federal Bureau of Investigation's Crime Index, the most widely publicized statistic on the amount of crime, emphasizes crimes such as assault, which the less well-to-do are more likely to commit, rather than embezzlement, gambling, or tax evasion, which are committed more by middle-class and "respectable" people. The so-called crime and delinquency problem, then, as it is defined by the police, the courts, and the public, results from the activities of the less fortunate in society.

From the conflict perspective, the legal and criminal justice systems are geared to benefit the dominant groups in society (Kennedy, 1990; Quinney and Shelden, 2001). Laws, after all, are mechanisms whereby some groups exercise control over the activities of other groups. Generally, it is the powerful who establish legislation defining what activities will be considered criminal and who decide what the penalties will be for those crimes. Thus, removing a television from a store is regarded as criminal, whereas polluting a stream may not be. Armed robbery can bring a fifteen-year prison sentence, whereas price fixing that costs the public millions of dollars in excess expenditures may be punished with a light prison sentence or a fine.

It is also the powerful who can get the police to enforce the laws against some crimes while ignoring other infractions of the law. The powerful also determine the extent of resources that will be devoted to controlling particular types of crime. There are, for example, periodic and highly publicized drives against robbery, prostitution, and drug offenses. For twenty years, the government has declared "war" on illegal drugs, proclaiming that this problem was the United States' number-one crime issue. One is less likely to see, however, a politician launch such a campaign against corporate crime. From the conflict perspective, then, the social problem of crime is not simply a matter of social disorganization; it is also influenced by the preferences, predilections, and interests of various groups in society.

Conflict theorists who have been influenced by the writings of Karl Marx view the causes of crime very differently from the functionalists. These conflict theorists blame certain characteristics of capitalism as an economic system (Headley, 1991). Capitalism is characterized by a constant search for greater profits, or at least a struggle against falling profits. This process can be especially fierce in a global economy such as we have today, where countries at many different levels of development compete with one another. In the process, capitalists search for ways to enhance profits by reducing costs through mechanization or automation of work or through relocation to areas where resources and labor are cheaper. Both mechanization and relocation put people out of work or force people into competition for lower-wage jobs. Because this process is a continual one, capitalism inevitably contains recurring cycles in which people are thrown out of work and communities are decimated by the loss of jobs. These inherent features of capitalism, then, mean that certain levels of poverty and the crime associated with it will always be with us, although which groups or communities are affected may shift over time.

In addition, capitalists need to sell their goods to make a profit, so capitalists must instill in people a desire for the many products that capitalism can produce. At the same time, capitalists attempt to keep wages low to reduce the costs of production. A mass of unemployed people also benefits a capitalist economy by serving as a cheap labor force when new workers are needed. The unemployed also serve as a lesson to employed workers: Do not demand too high a salary or you, too, may be among the unemployed. The result, according to sociologist William Chambliss, is a contradiction: "Capitalism creates both the desire to consume and—for a large mass of people—an inability to earn the money necessary to purchase the items they have been taught to want" (1975:151). For these people, crime is one way of resolving this dilemma. Unlike anomie theory, however, Marxian conflict theory does not assume that the problem can be alleviated through full employment; rather, it sees these contradictions as inherent in a capitalist economy.

The Interactionist Perspective

Interactionist approaches do not dispute the sources of crime pointed to by the functionalist and conflict views. But interactionists see these views as incomplete because they do not explain how a person becomes criminal or why one poor person responds to anomie through crime and another does not. To understand this, we need to look at the socialization and interaction processes that influence people's daily lives.

Cultural transmission theories posit that *crime and delinquency are learned and culturally transmitted through socialization.* The most influential of these theories is the **differential association theory,** developed by criminologist Edwin Sutherland in the 1920s and 1930s. According to Sutherland, *crime and delinquency are learned in interaction with other people, for the most part within intimate primary groups such as families and peer groups* (Sutherland and Cressey, 1978). There are two elements of this learning process. First, people learn the specific techniques for engaging in criminal behavior. For example, by becoming a member of a delinquent gang, a person might learn how to buy drugs or where to obtain weapons. Learning these things makes it more possible and likely that a person will engage in some criminal or delinquent acts. Second, people learn to value criminality more highly than conventional behavior. By associating with other people who engage in criminal behavior, people are more likely to learn to view these activities as desirable and learn a rationale for why they are preferable to a more conventional way of life. Delinquent gangs or prison inmates, for example, may value a lifestyle in which a person makes money the "easy way"—through crime—and to denigrate the "chumps" who work every day for a small wage. Someone who falls in with groups such as these may well be influenced by their values. Whether people become criminals or delinquents depends on the extent and intensity of contacts with groups that value a particular form of criminality and on the age at which the contacts occur. It also depends on whether a person identifies with these criminals. Association with such people without identification is not likely to result in valuing criminal behavior.

According to cultural transmission theories, then, learning to be criminal or delinquent involves mechanisms of socialization similar to those associated with learning any social status. If people have close group ties with others who conform to established group values, they are likely to learn to conform to that lifestyle. Those who associate with criminal or delinquent groups are more likely to adopt criminal or delinquent values.

Another interactionist approach to understanding crime and delinquency is labeling theory, which shifts attention away from the individual transgressor and toward the ways that others react to the deviant (Cavender, 1991). **Labeling theory** suggests that *whether other people define or label a person as deviant is a critical determinant in the development of a pattern of deviant behavior.* According to this theory, many people engage in activities that are defined as criminal, at least occasionally. In all likelihood, you have engaged in a few actions that could be so defined, as probably have most other college students. Few of us, however, are caught and labeled—either by our friends or by official agencies—as criminals or delinquents. Labeling theorists refer to this *violation of social norms in which a person is not caught or is excused rather than labeled as a deviant* as **primary deviance** (Lemert, 1951). But the theory does not attempt to explain this type of behavior. Labeling theory concentrates on **secondary** or **career deviance**—*the deviant behavior that a person adopts in response to the reaction of others to his or her primary deviance.* Consider how this could happen.

We know that shoplifting among teenagers, at least of small items, is not uncommon. Imagine that a teenager, possibly out of curiosity or on a dare from peers, engages in a single act of shoplifting. This would constitute primary deviance, because there has been no labeling and no change in the teenager's or the community's image of him or her. If, however, the young person's shoplifting is brought to the attention of the police, they may begin the labeling process by notifying the young person's parents. If this label becomes "public," it is quite likely that some stigma will attach to this teenager's reputation—perhaps a criminal record.

One key consequence of this labeling process is its effect on a person's self-concept: Because the teenage years are formative ones in terms of personal identity, the person may respond to others' reactions, at least in part, by accepting their judgment. After all, the stigma associated with deviant labels such as "criminal" and "delinquent" implies something very negative about people who behave in that fashion. The terms "murderer," "thug," "robber," and "thief" suggest the strong emotions that underlie these deviant labels, and such labels can affect the way people view themselves. A second key consequence of labeling involves the effect that labeling has on people's social relationships. If the criminal activity becomes publicly known, some of the person's conventional friends may shun him or her out of fear for their own reputations. The person may also find it difficult to develop new friends, at least among conventional peers, finding acceptance, instead, among youngsters who are already engaging in delinquent or criminal actions on a widespread scale.

As a result of these changes in self-concept and social contacts, labeling theorists argue, the likelihood of a deviant career developing is increased. Thus, labeling can perpetuate crime and delinquency because, once people have been labeled, they have fewer alternatives, and the deviance becomes a part of their social identity. This represents secondary deviance because it results from a person's efforts to cope with the responses of others to their primary deviation. It also represents, in a sense, a *self-fulfilling prophecy* in that the deviant label helps to bring about the pattern of career deviance that people thought they were merely identifying when they first attached the label (Heimer and Matsueda, 1994).

These sociological theories of crime and delinquency help us to better understand why sociologists take the position that criminal behavior is *relative*, a notion first introduced in the discussion of deviance in Chapter 1. It is not the act itself that is deviant; rather it is people's interpretation of it or judgment about it that makes it deviant. Deviance or crime exists in the social context of an event rather than in the act itself. So, according to anomie theory, what is defined as criminal or delinquent depends on what are considered socially approved means and goals in a particular society. Conflict theorists see crime and delinquency within a framework of definitions and judgments that are formulated and enforced by those people in powerful positions in society. For cultural transmission theory, criminality is a result of socialization, and people are capable of learning a wide variety of things. Finally, labeling theory makes us aware that being identified as deviant depends, among other things, on the resources a person possesses and his or her ability to avoid the negative aspects of being labeled. As we review the different types of crime, keep in mind that the line between criminal and acceptable behavior, between delinquency and nondelinquency, is shifting and vague rather than clear and obvious.

Types of Crime

A **crime** is *an act that violates a criminal code enacted by an officially constituted political authority*. The Federal Bureau of Investigation (FBI) publishes an annual document called the Uniform Crime Reports (UCR) that summarizes crime statistics collected by the FBI each month from law enforcement authorities in more than 16,000 cities and towns. In the UCR, the FBI distinguishes between what are called Part I, or more serious criminal offenses, and Part II, or less serious offenses (see Table 9.1). Part I offenses are considered more serious because many believe they pose the greatest and most direct threat to personal safety and property. The FBI also publishes the Crime Index, the official crime rate typically reported in the media. The Crime Index comprises the number of Part I offenses known to the police for every 100,000 people in the United States.

TABLE 9.1 Classification of Criminal Offenses by the Federal Bureau of Investigation

Part I Offenses		Part II Offenses
Murder and nonnegligent manslaughter	Violent crimes	Other assaults
Forcible rape		Forgery and counterfeiting
Robbery		Fraud
Aggravated assault		Embezzlement
		Stolen property; buying, receiving, possessing
		Vandalism
Burglary	Property crimes	Weapons; carrying, possessing, and so on
Larceny-theft		Prostitution and commercialized vice
Motor vehicle theft		Sex offenses (except forcible rape and prostitution)
Arson		Drug abuse violations
		Gambling
		Offenses against family and children
		Driving under the influence
		Liquor laws
		Drunkenness
		Disorderly conduct
		Vagrancy
		All other offenses (except traffic)
		Suspicion
		Curfew and loitering law violations
		Runaways

Violent and Property Crime

Violent crimes such as murder, assault, robbery, and rape are clear violations of group norms and the law. There were 16,000 murders committed in 2005, along with almost 1 million aggravated assaults (Federal Bureau of Investigation, 2006). Many murders are situational, in that they occur as a result of some dispute, frequently trivial, over money or some element of personal demeanor; they are only rarely planned in advance. The victim is often a relative, friend, or acquaintance of the assailant. In 2005, one-quarter of all homicides arose from an argument, whereas only 17 percent occurred during the commission of a felony. However, the reasons for and circumstances surrounding homicide have changed some over the past few decades; today, homicide is more often related to the drug trade, juvenile gang killings, and robbery or debt settlement among strangers rather than growing out of a dispute among people known to one another (Lattimore et al., 1997). Assaults are much more likely to involve strangers than are murders. In addition to these offenses, there are a half million robberies every year, some of which involve personal injury to the victims.

Forcible rape, another violent criminal offense, occurs when an assailant sexually assaults another person. In 2005, there were almost one hundred thousand rapes known to the police in the United States, but many estimates place the actual number much higher because victims may be reluctant to report the crime. According to survey results, rape is the crime that women, particularly those under 35 years of age, fear the most. Especially in urban areas, this fear affects their daily lives as they avoid going out alone, refuse to enter certain neighborhoods, and install deadbolt locks in their homes (Stanko, 1995). In addition to physical danger and degradation experienced by rape victims, the act also has a political element in that it symbolizes and reinforces the power and domination of the assailant over the victim. As one social scientist put it regarding female rape victims: "Rape is to women as lynching was to blacks: the ultimate physical threat" (Brownmiller, 1975:254). As discussed in Chapter 7, only in recent decades, because of pressure from women's groups, have states made raping one's wife a crime (Bergen, 1999).

Although people are most alarmed about violent crime, they are much more likely to be victims of property crimes in which the costs are usually economic rather than physical. Two million burglaries, 7 million thefts, and 1 million auto thefts are reported to the police each year. The hidden costs of property crime are frequently underestimated, such as the enormous amount of money that citizens pay in insurance premiums to protect property from burglary, theft, and arson.

Organized Crime

Much of the crime so far described is sporadic and individualized in nature, such as the lone mugger or the small group of juveniles who rob homes. There are, however, forms of criminal activity that benefit from large-scale organization. For example, gambling and prostitution can be highly profitable to those who organize them. Other crimes, such as drug smuggling, involve large overhead costs (front money to purchase the drugs, for instance) that are difficult to fund without some organization. This leads to organized crime or *syndicates*: criminal operations in which several criminal groups coordinate their illegal activities.

Although a great deal of criminal activity in the United States is organized to some degree, there is considerable debate about the structure and extent of this kind of crime (Abadinsky, 2007; Kleinknecht, 1996). One view is illustrated by the image of the Mafia, consisting of a nationwide alliance of families, based on kinship and ethnic solidarity, that coordinates its criminal actions and controls large areas of criminal activity. Whether the Mafia or La Cosa Nostra was ever as powerful and consolidated as its portrayal in the media suggests is subject to debate, but it is probably not nearly that large, cohesive, or controlling today. Organized crime today also includes many other racially or ethnically based criminal gangs, including Asian organized crime, Colombian drug trafficking organizations, and Hispanic street gangs. Many of these gangs operate in local or regional criminal markets, although some do gain a national reach. In addition to illegal activities, organized crime also develops interests in legitimate business, such as real estate, trucking, and food processing, at least in part as mechanisms to launder the vast sums earned through their illegal activities.

White-Collar Crime

White-collar crimes are offenses committed by people in positions of respect and responsibility during the ordinary course of their business (Coleman, 2005). One such offense is antitrust violations, or attempts by businesses to monopolize a segment of the economy. White-collar crime can also take the form of price fixing, in which competitors agree to sell their products for a price higher than they would be able to in a truly competitive market. In the mid-1970s, for example, a price-fixing scheme involving the four major breakfast cereal makers in the United States is estimated to have cost the public some $128 million. Another type of white-collar crime is the fraudulent use of funds. A number of offenses of this sort came to light in the early 2000s when the top executives of a number of large corporations were accused of using their corporations to make illegal, off-the-balance-sheet loans to themselves of millions of dollars. For example, a number of Enron Corporation executives were accused of using Enron to engage in sham business with companies in which the executives had invested. This sham business made the companies look like they were growing and thus increased the companies' stock price and the value of the companies' stock, in which the executives had invested. Because of these and other illegal or shady practices, Enron collapsed into bankruptcy, which meant that thousands of people lost their jobs and saw their retirement savings dwindle significantly.

As these illustrations should make clear, white-collar crime can be very costly to society and damaging to many people. In fact, white-collar crime may actually hurt more people than does street crime (Reiman, 2007). Despite this cost, the Federal Bureau of Investigation classifies most white-collar crimes as less serious offenses. The public in both the United States and Canada also seems to view most white-collar crimes as less serious than other crimes (Cullen, Link, and Polanzi, 1982; Goff and Nason-Clark, 1989). Occasionally, corporate criminals go to jail, as has happened in the past few years to some of the corporate executives involved in the corporate scandals mentioned in the previous paragraph. But critics argue that these tend to be the exception rather than the rule and that the law is very lenient on white-collar criminals, especially the influential ones.

Victimless Crime

Victimless crimes are offenses such as gambling, drug violations, and prostitution, in which the "victims" are willing participants in the crime (Stitt, 1988). In 2005, close to 2 million arrests were made for these crimes (Federal Bureau of Investigation, 2006). There are obviously far more victimless crimes than these statistics suggest because many offenses are never reported to the police. Although no accurate estimates of the total number of victimless crimes are available, it is safe to say that most people in the United States have participated in such offenses, if only by betting in a football pool or purchasing small quantities of marijuana. When highly desired goods and services are made illegal, a black market is likely to develop to provide them. One of the controversies about having victimless crimes on the books is whether the government ought to be controlling what some people feel are personal or moral issues, such as gambling, drug use, or prostitution. A second controversy is that, because victimless crimes are illegal, people sometimes

commit additional crimes, called "secondary crimes," while doing the victimless crime. Thus, an addict may rob to buy drugs, which are very expensive in part because they are illegal. If the victimless crimes were legal, less secondary crime might occur. Finally, victimless crimes are related to public corruption in that bribes are sometimes given to police or other public officials to ignore the illegal flow of drugs, sex, or gambling.

Juvenile Delinquency

A juvenile delinquent is a young person who has committed a crime or has violated a juvenile code. *Youthful offenders* are young people, in most states between the ages of seven and seventeen, who commit offenses for which, if they were adults, they could be tried in a criminal court. *Status offenders* are young people who commit specific acts that are prohibited by the juvenile code, such as running away from home, incorrigibility, truancy, or sexual promiscuity. Status offenses are not considered criminal when committed by an adult.

According to official statistics, juveniles under the age of eighteen are responsible for committing 23 percent of all Part 1, or serious, crimes, although youth between 10 and 17 years of age make up only about 11 percent of our population (Federal Bureau of Investigation, 2006). They are arrested for over 37 percent of the vandalism, 25 percent of auto thefts, and 25 percent of the robberies in our society. People in this age category are responsible for 9 percent of all murders, 26 percent of all burglaries, and around 14 percent of rapes and aggravated assaults. And the rate of delinquency may be on the rise. In 1960, there were twenty cases of delinquency before the courts for every thousand young people. By 2002, that number had increased to fifty-two cases for each one thousand juveniles each year (U.S. Bureau of the Census, 1984:182; U.S. Bureau of the Census, 2006:207). Most delinquent acts, however, are status offenses.

The Crime Rate in the United States

Between 1970 and 1980, according to the FBI, the rate of Crime Index offenses rose by a startling 49 percent. However, the 1980s were another story: Crime Index offenses actually dropped by 2 percent between 1980 and 1990. Most of this drop was accounted for by the drop in property crimes. During the 1980s, violent crimes rose by 22 percent, but this was less of an increase than the 64 percent rise in the 1970s (see Figure 9.1). Since 1990, the crime rate

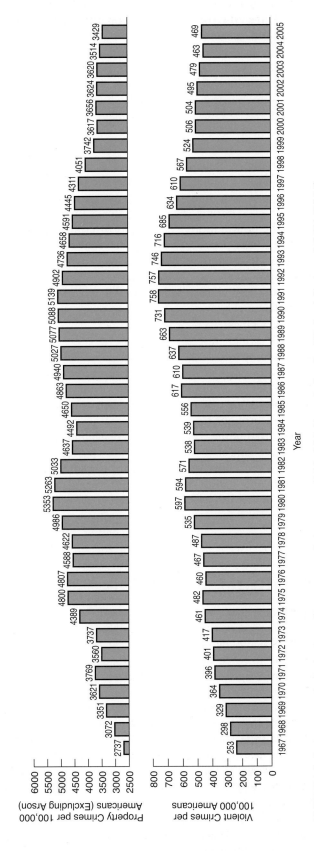

FIGURE 9.1 Rates of Violent and Property Crimes per 100,000 People in the United States, 1967–2005.

Source: Federal Bureau of Investigation, *Uniform Crime Reports: Crime in the United States* (Washington, DC: U.S. Government Printing Office, various years).

has shown a steady and significant decline: a decline of 38 percent in violent crimes and 33 percent in property crimes between 1991 and 2005. Yet the crime rate is still far higher than in earlier decades. If crimes were evenly spaced throughout the day, in 2005, there would have been one property crime about every three seconds of each day and one violent crime approximately every twenty-two seconds (Federal Bureau of Investigation, 2006).

Some of these increases, however, need to be placed in perspective. They may in part reflect changes in the likelihood of reporting crimes rather than actual increases in crime. Rape, for example, has traditionally been a vastly underreported crime. With more public discussion of rape in recent decades and strong pressure from feminist groups, both the police and the public have become more sensitive to the problems of rape victims. Many hospitals provide counseling for rape victims, and many states have rules that limit the use of information about a victim's previous sexual activities as evidence in court. These changes have encouraged more women to report rapes, and this undoubtedly accounts for some, although not all, of the increase in reported rapes compared to earlier decades.

Another reason for caution about UCR crime statistics is that they are based on crimes known to the police, and considerable crime is not brought to the attention of the police. Such unreported crime is not reflected in these statistics, which are conservative indicators of the crime problem in the United States. It is estimated, for example, that only half of the violent crimes are reported to the police and as few as 30 percent of the thefts (Maguire and Pastore, 2004:210).

Who Are the Criminals?

At the outset, it is important to recognize that patterns of criminality are not to be confused with the causes of crime. The reason for this is that the members of some social groups may be more likely to be arrested and processed by criminal justice agencies, thus injecting an element of bias into crime statistics. For example, some crimes such as embezzlement are "hidden crimes" in that they are less likely than homicide or assault to come to the attention of the police. When an embezzler is discovered, the victim, the employer, may not call the police for fear that it will hurt the business's reputation. Homicide, on the other hand, is virtually always brought to the attention of the police by someone. So people committing hidden crimes are less likely to be arrested than people committing more noticeable crimes. If members of

one group are more likely to commit hidden crimes and members of another group commit more open crimes, then the latter group will get arrested more often. So especially when using arrest records, one group will appear to be more criminal than another because of its differential treatment by the police and the courts. With these thoughts in mind, we will look at four social characteristics that are closely associated with crime.

Gender

Gender is the single social factor that is most predictive of patterns of criminal behavior. Males have higher rates of involvement than females in practically all forms of criminality. In 2005, 82 percent of all people arrested for violent crimes were males—five times as many males as females—and 68 percent of all those arrested for property crimes were male (see Figure 9.2). There are approximately four boys referred to the juvenile court for every girl so referred. Even crimes that do not involve aggressiveness or violence—larceny, fraud, embezzlement—are still more likely to be committed by males. The only offenses that females are more likely to be involved in are prostitution and being runaways. Although it is possible that women receive preferential treatment in the criminal justice system or that women are more likely to engage in "hidden" crimes, there is evidence against this (Bishop and Frazier, 1984; Steffensmeier and Allan, 1988). Males are disproportionately represented in most forms of criminal activity even if such sex preferentials occur. The male propensity toward crime is probably in part a function of the male's role in which daring, action, and aggressiveness are viewed positively and sometimes take a criminal form. However, with some crimes, such as fraud, forgery, and auto theft, crime rates are growing much faster among women than men.

Age

Figure 9.2 shows the percentage of all people arrested in 2005 who were younger than various ages. To put the numbers in this figure in perspective, people between the ages of 10 and 24 constitute only 21 percent of the U.S. population but account for 45 percent of all arrests for violent offenses and 54 percent of all arrests for property offenses. Figure 9.3 illustrates the considerably higher involvement in crime by teens, as measured by arrest rates for violent crimes, over the past three decades. The arrest rate for teens is three to four times that of adults. Figure 9.3 also shows the significant decline in the crime rate since the mid-1990s. Clearly, crime is a "young person's

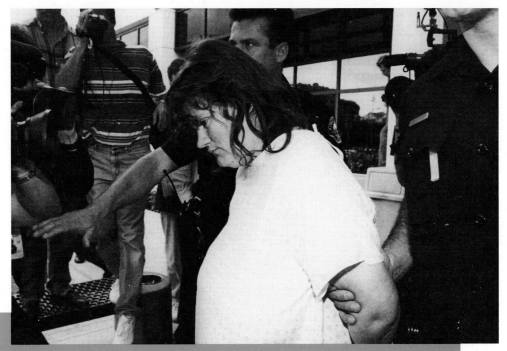

This woman is being arrested for suspected homicide, but she is unusual: The vast majority of crimes, including homicide, are committed by young males.

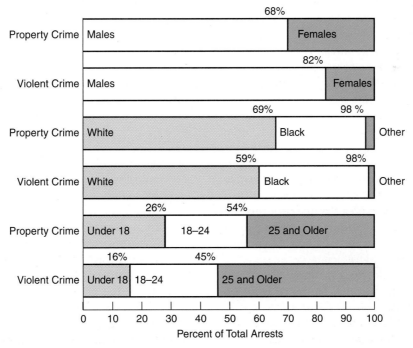

FIGURE 9.2 **Total Arrests for Violent Crimes and Property Crimes by Gender, Race, and Age, 2005.**

Source: Federal Bureau of Investigation, *Uniform Crime Reports: Crime in the United States, 2005* (Washington, DC: U.S. Government Printing Office, 2006) <www.fbi.gov/ucr/05cius>.

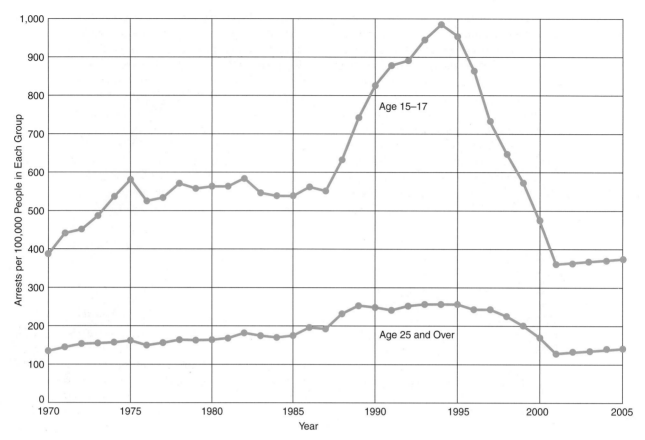

FIGURE 9.3 Arrest Rates for Violent Crimes by Age, 1970–2005.

Source: Federal Bureau of Investigation, *Uniform Crime Reports: Crime in the United States* (Washington, DC: U.S. Government Printing Office, annual).

game." There are a number of possible explanations for this. It may be that young people are more likely to be arrested for committing a crime than are older people. Or it may be that older people are actually less likely to engage in criminal activity (Rowe and Tittle, 1977). Young people's higher rates of criminal conduct may be due to opportunity and physical capability: Young people are more likely to commit visible offenses, such as property crimes and robbery, than "hidden" crimes, such as embezzlement, price fixing, or corporate malfeasance. In addition, young people have the strength, agility, and stamina to commit crimes such as burglary and robbery.

Important social policy considerations flow from the link between age and crime. Crime rates go up when teens and young adults, who commit lots of crimes, grow as a proportion of the population. This is what happened in the 1960s and 1970s: People 14 to 24 years of age grew from 15 percent of the U.S. populace to 20 percent in 1980, and the crime rate doubled during that period (see Figure 9.1). Since 1980, the proportion of people in that same age group has dropped to 15 percent. So, as young people constitute

a smaller proportion of the populace, the crime rate has tended to go down, or at least go up less rapidly, since the 1980s.

Socioeconomic Status

The relationship between socioeconomic status (SES) and criminality has been one of the more controversial issues in modern-day criminology. Some research has shown that lower-class people have higher rates of crime commission than do middle-class and more affluent people; other research concludes that little evidence exists for a consistent or strong association between SES and rates of crime commission (Elliott and Huizinga, 1983; Tittle and Meier, 1990). So, the relationship between social class and crime is probably more complicated than a straightforward association. Official crime statistics show that lower-class people are more likely to commit crimes, but research shows clearly that lower-class people are also more likely to be arrested. Therefore, it may be that arrest is more common among the lower class rather than that actual rates of crime commission are higher. In addition, lower-class people are more likely to commit highly visible and violent crimes, such as homicide or assault, that are more frequently reported to the police (Huff-Corzine, Corzine, and Moore, 1991), whereas some hidden crimes, such as embezzlement and fraud, may be more common among the middle class. Other hidden crimes, such as vice offenses, may be as common in the lower class as in the middle class. Therefore, there may be some social class variation in the types of crimes committed but not in the overall numbers of criminal acts committed. At this point, a reasonable conclusion is that the relationship between SES and crime is weak and complicated.

Race

As we indicated at the outset of this discussion, official statistics show that African Americans are disproportionately involved in crime (Tonry, 1995). They make up about 13 percent of our population but account for 30 percent of all arrests for property crimes and 39 percent of all arrests for violent crimes (see Figure 9.2). African Americans are particularly likely to be arrested for robbery, murder, and gambling. Only in the cases of liquor law violations and driving under the influence of alcohol are their arrest rates proportionate to or lower than what would be expected given their numbers in the populace.

Detailed analysis through victimization surveys indicates that black–white differences in criminal behavior are real, rather than merely reflecting criminal justice system biases such as the likelihood of arrest (Hindelang, 1981). Still, as was pointed out earlier, this does not imply that race is a causal variable. The social environment of African Americans is primarily responsible for crime rate differences (Duster, 1987). In addition, African Americans are lower in socioeconomic standing, so they are less likely to be involved with "hidden" and "respectable" crimes, which we have seen result in greater economic losses than all other types of criminality combined. Because we are aware of black–white differences in criminal behavior, African Americans may be more closely watched than whites by law enforcement agencies, which would lead to higher arrest rates.

Who Are the Victims?

We sometimes focus so closely on people who commit crimes that we forget the victims of their actions. Twenty-three out of every thousand Americans are crime victims each year (U.S. Bureau of the Census, 2006:195–201). But race and sex play a part in this, with males and blacks considerably more likely to be victims. Homicide rates, especially, show the gruesome consequences of race. Black males are eight times more likely to be the victims of homicide than are white males, and black females are four times more likely to be victims than white females. For some crimes, such as robbery and larceny, poorer households were more likely to be victimized, whereas the affluent were more likely to experience auto theft.

One very important correlate of victimization is its relationship to participation in criminal and delinquent activities: Offenders are often the victims of other criminals (Fagan, Piper, and Cheng, 1987).

The Criminal Justice System

The criminal justice system includes the police, the courts, the prisons, and other institutions whose task is to control crime in society. The goals of this system are to deter people from committing crimes, to provide society with some retribution against people who have violated important societal rules and norms, and to rehabilitate those who have committed such violations. There is much debate over how effectively the criminal justice system in the United States achieves its goals.

The Police

When a crime is committed, the first and perhaps most crucial link that most citizens have with the criminal justice system is the police. In the United States, police have a great deal of discretion in dealing with offenses that come to their attention. Sometimes, the police may even help to negotiate some type of informal agreement between the complainant and the accused, a procedure that is well short of actually arresting and booking a suspect. This may appear surprising to some, because it is often assumed that police take pride in "busting" all crimes. In fact, there are so many minor violations of the law occurring on a daily basis that the criminal justice system would be helplessly swamped if the police tried to pursue every one of them. One investigation found only one arrest for every five felonies known to the police in the United States (Maguire and Pastore, 2004:373). In some of these cases, the police undoubtedly chose not to pursue the case, possibly realizing that they had little chance of solving it. However, the exercise of discretion by the police is not influenced solely by judgments of the seriousness or solvability of the crime, as one might expect, but also by subtle social factors. For example, a study of police response to domestic disputes found that police were far more likely to arrest someone when the dispute occurred in a poor neighborhood (Smith and Klein, 1984). In middle-class neighborhoods, police put in more effort to find solutions to the dispute short of arrest. Thus, social factors influence the discretionary behavior of police in ways that affect the crime statistics discussed earlier.

The Courts

As illustrated in Figure 9.4, there is substantial case attrition following arrest. Of 100 typical felony arrests brought by the police to the prosecutor, fewer than 75 result in conviction. After arrests are made by the police, the court system utilizes an adversary model in evaluating guilt or innocence. The prosecution is pitted against the defense, and a judge or jury is utilized to settle the "dispute" (Sykes and Cullen, 1992). The office of prosecuting attorney is perhaps the most powerful position in the criminal justice system. Prosecuting attorneys have the power to determine which cases will be pursued and with how much vigor. Most importantly, prosecuting attorneys are political figures—they are either elected or appointed to office—and have a keen awareness of how they achieved their positions in the first place. To keep influential groups or their elective constituencies happy, prosecutors exert enormous pressure on the police. One criterion used to evaluate police departments is the number of arrests that eventually result in convictions. Should a prosecuting attorney see fit not to seek convictions for a particular type of

offense, then the police will spend little time dealing with cases of this type. By like token, if a prosecutor shows favoritism for a given offense, then police will regard these as "good busts" and alter their law enforcement patterns accordingly. Once again, discretionary elements enter into the battle against crime. As we have seen, it is usually more politically profitable to attack "street" crime committed by the less fortunate because this is the crime that frightens the middle class and affluent groups who put prosecuting attorneys in office.

Defense attorneys represent the other part of the court system. Ideally, counsel for the defense is responsible for representing their client's interests before the criminal justice system. In reality, there are considerable pressures on defense attorneys to place as much emphasis on "negotiating justice" as on ensuring due process for their clients. Defense attorneys often have close ties with judges, prosecuting attorneys, police, and others working in the criminal justice system. They work daily with these people on many cases and need their cooperation and good will to do their work. Because of this, they come under considerable pressure to help the system run smoothly, which may mean encouraging their clients to accept a guilty plea or a plea bargain. If they do not appear cooperative, the prosecutor's office has many resources that can be used or assistance that can be withheld that could make the defense attorney's job more difficult. So, negotiation between the prosecutor and the defense counsel becomes the most sensible alternative open to many of those charged with a crime, but the defendant's best interests may not be served

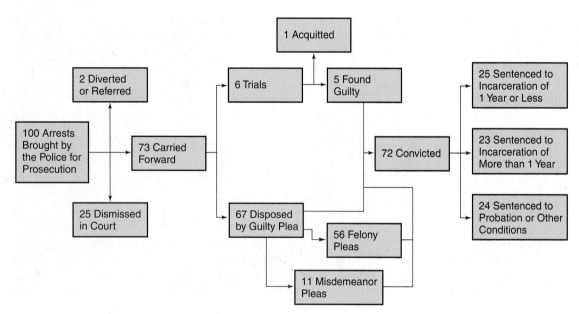

FIGURE 9.4 **Typical Disposition of One Hundred Urban Felony Arrests.**

Source: Adapted from Brian A. Reeves, *Felony Defendants in Large Urban Counties, 1994*, NCJ-164616 (Washington, DC: Department of Justice, Bureau of Justice Statistics, 1998).

when the overriding pressure on both prosecution and defense is to dispose of cases on a crowded court docket quickly and smoothly.

Another element of the court system is plea bargaining: an informal agreement among the defense, the prosecution, and the court that is not legally binding. Plea bargaining is involved in over 90 percent of all convictions for criminal offenses. In exchange for a plea of guilty, suspects may receive special considerations from the court, such as the dropping of some charges, a more lenient sentence, or the reduction of a charge to a lesser offense. This accounts for further attrition in the criminal justice system (see Figure 9.4). Approximately 6 percent of all felony arrests result in a trial verdict of guilty or innocent. Plea bargaining has been criticized because it involves an "informal dispensing of justice," as issues such as local politics, community norms, and the perceived needs of criminal justice bureaucracies take precedence over established judicial principles such as due process of law.

Sentencing and Punishment

In the past few decades, the criminal justice system has become considerably more punitive in its response to crime, as legislators have passed laws that send more people to prison and for longer sentences. One example of this is an approach popularly dubbed "three strikes and you're out." The basic idea is that, when people commit a third felony (a third "strike"), they are sentenced to life in prison (Clark, Austin, and Henry, 1997; King and Mauer, 2001). It is difficult to assess how well these policies work in terms of reducing crime because they are relatively new and affect a relatively small number of people in most states. In addition, most states, prior to having three-strikes legislation, had other laws dealing with habitual offenders, usually by giving them more severe punishments. So the new laws are often just extensions of existing policies. Current research suggests that "three-strike" policies have not reduced the crime rate. However, the laws have produced more crowded court dockets and local jails because suspects who come under three-strikes legislation, facing life in prison without parole, are more likely to go to trial rather than plea bargain. In addition, in some states, it has produced more prison crowding as more people are sent to prison for longer periods. The Applied Research insert (pp. 246–247) takes a look at the research on the effectiveness of one punitive response to crime—capital punishment.

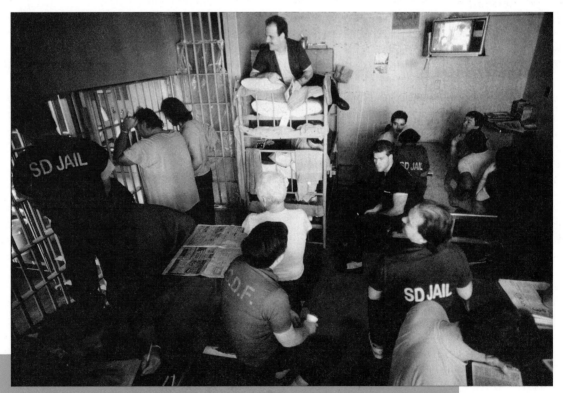

Trends in both crime and sentencing practices have produced a skyrocketing prison population in the United States. The resulting crowding in prisons is dangerous and, at times, inhumane.

Does the Death Penalty Deter Crime?

One of the more controversial elements of the criminal justice system in the United States is the use of the death penalty for certain crimes. The number of executions is relatively small—there were 60 in 2005—but the number is growing, and there were 3300 prisoners on death row that year (U.S. Bureau of the Census, 2006: 211). Forty-one percent of them were nonwhite, and this points to one of the arguments against the death penalty: The poor and nonwhite are more likely to be executed than are affluent whites. It seems that the well-to-do can afford the legal battle to avoid the death sentence, and prosecutors, judges, and juries—which are mostly white—may be more inclined to sentence nonwhites to death. Another argument made against the death penalty is that it does not achieve one of the goals of punishment: to deter others from committing crimes. Over the past 50 years, quite a lot of social research has focused on the latter issue.

If capital punishment deters crime, then states with capital punishment should have lower homicide rates than do states without capital punishment. Another approach would be to look at states that once had the death penalty but abolished it and states that were once without it and instituted it. Once again, this before–after comparison should show lower homicide rates when a state has capital punishment, if such punishment deters crime. The overall conclusion from many studies of these types is that the death penalty seems to have no deterrent effect, or at least we cannot find much evidence of it (Bailey, 1974; Bonner and Fessenden, 2000; Cochran, Chamlin, and Seth, 1994; Costanzo, 1997; Galliher, 2004).

Although many states have the death penalty on the books, some states are much more likely actually to execute people for certain crimes. Maybe it is the death penalty in action that deters crime rather than its mere existence in law. To evaluate this possibility, we can compare the number of murderers who have actually been executed in each state. Studies that have done this find no relationship between the use of capital punishment and homicide rates or at best a very weak and confusing relationship (Lempert, 1983; Peterson and Bailey, 1991). Where a relationship is found, it is small and sometimes in the opposite direction: States with many executions actually have higher homicide rates than states with fewer executions. Finally, perhaps the use of the death penalty has to be widely publicized for it to deter crime. Once again, research findings have been inconsistent on this (Bailey, 1990; Stack, 1990).

So, we cannot clearly say at this point whether or under what conditions the death penalty does deter homicide. However, the research clearly does show that

---

Another reflection of the more punitive direction of policy has been a response to the rise in juvenile crime. In the past, juveniles were adjudicated in juvenile courts where punishments were different from those given to adult criminals. An increasing number of states have gone to "blended sentencing," in which a juvenile offender is given a combination of adult and juvenile sanctions and is sometimes under the jurisdiction of the adult criminal court rather than the juvenile court (Torbet et al., 1996). The focus in blended sentencing is more on punishment and retribution rather than rehabilitation, and the severity of punishment is determined more by the seriousness of the offense than by the needs or developmental level of the offender.

In addition to long prison sentences, federal and state legislators have devised many additional punishments that can be given to people convicted of crimes (Mauer and Chesney-Lind, 2002). Some states take away the voting rights of convicted felons, even after they have finished serving their prison sentences; other states bar ex-offenders from obtaining state licenses to work in a variety of occupations and professions; other states strip them of their driver's license, at least for a period of time; and still other states deny them eligibility for welfare or public housing. All of this serves the goals of punishment and retribution, but it probably works against the goal of rehabilitation. It makes it much more difficult for newly released inmates to find and keep a job, support their families, and follow a law-abiding life. Long sentences make it difficult for inmates to maintain contact with their children and partners—in effect, punishing the whole family. In

homicide rates are linked to a variety of social factors. For example, states with low income and educational levels, high unemployment, and a highly urbanized population tend to have higher homicide rates. Directing our resources toward these problems is likely to make a more significant impact on homicide rates than would executing more murderers. As Elliott Currie suggests, overreliance on a punishment-based criminal justice policy may not be the most efficient utilization of resources for all crimes (Currie, 1985).

Through applied research efforts such as these, we can assemble a body of observations about the outcome of various strategies and policies related to social problems. This is not the whole story, however, because there may well be reasons other than deterrence for having capital punishment. The death penalty can satisfy people's needs for retribution against someone who has committed the most heinous of crimes, and it may serve to affirm symbolically society's moral outrage over such offenses and support for those who are victims of such crimes. At this point, however, observational evidence suggests that capital punishment does not serve as a deterrent to homicide.

Protestors oppose the execution of terrorist bomber Timothy McVeigh in 2001. There is much controversy over whether capital punishment is an effective deterrent against crime.

addition, many states send their inmates to prisons in other states—often thousands of miles from where the inmate's family lives—where the inmates can be kept less expensively. But this geographic separation can make it almost impossible for inmates and their families to maintain ties and further reduces the likelihood of rehabilitation. These problems have been especially burdensome to the African American community because of the high incarceration rates among black males (Lanier, 2003).

In addition to lengthy sentences and excessive punishments, there also appears to be considerable inequity in punishments (Blume, Eisenberg, and Wells, 2004; Petersilia, 1985; Walker, Spohn, and DeLone, 2003). With homicides, for example, one would expect the same crime to receive the same punishment. But there is much disparity. A person is far more likely to receive the death penalty for homicide—in some states, more than eight times as likely—when the victim is white rather than black. Studies of sentencing in a number of states document that African Americans and Hispanics are given heavier sentences by judges than are whites and serve more time in prison than do whites, especially when a black criminal is convicted of a crime against a white person. This is true even when comparing those who have committed comparable felonies and have similar criminal records. All this discriminatory treatment may reflect unconscious racism on the part of prosecutors, judges, and juries, or it may be that mostly white jurors tend to identify with white victims and deal more harshly with those who victimize whites. In either case, it leads many people to question whether justice is fairly and impartially dealt by the courts.

The Prisons

The United States currently imprisons a far larger proportion of its population than ever before, with the rate of incarceration having quadrupled since 1975 (see Figure 9.5). For much of this century, the rate of incarceration was fairly steady, and less than one-fourth of what it is now, even in the difficult economic times of the Great Depression of the 1930s. Since 1975, the rate has increased steadily and disturbingly. Even more distressing is that the United States now incarcerates more of its citizens than almost any other nation in the world and far more than any of the other modern industrial nations (Austin and Irwin, 2001). These shocking statistics are partly due to a rising crime rate, of course. However, another contributing factor was the emergence of crack cocaine in the 1980s and the explosion in drug arrests. More people were taking drugs, and the drug use led to more secondary crimes to support people's drug habits. In addition, the federal government put millions of dollars into the war on drugs, which encouraged the police and other officials to aggressively pursue drug users. Yet another factor contributing to the explosion in incarceration is a growing frustration with and anger against crime felt by many people, which in turn has made "getting tough on crime" very popular. People in the United States have become very receptive to sending more people to prison for longer periods of time as a way of controlling crime. This has produced a crisis of overcrowding in many of our prisons unheard of in our history.

This overcrowding is dangerous because it increases unrest among inmates and produces a climate in which violence is more likely. Riots, escapes, and hostage taking become more of a problem. Prison overcrowding also makes it more difficult for correctional officers and prison administrators to manage the prisons. All this makes prisons more costly to run. In addition, many question whether it is moral to imprison people in circumstances that are cruel and unusual; that may promote mental disorders; where degrading sexual assaults are common; and where stabbings, beatings, extortion, and murder are routine and rampant.

Prison crowding also makes it far more difficult for prisons to achieve one of their major goals: the rehabilitation of the inmates. So far, prisons have failed miserably at rehabilitation. **Recidivism** refers to *the repeat of an offense after having been convicted of a crime*, and the rate of recidivism is very high. Two-thirds to three-quarters of all inmates in state and federal prisons are recidivists—they have been con-

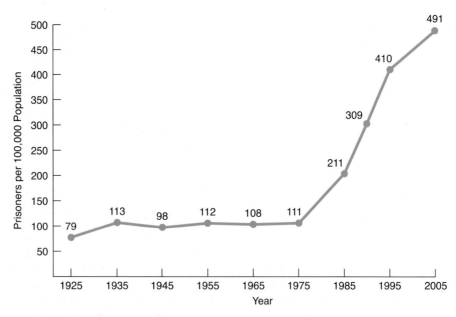

FIGURE 9.5 **Sentenced Prisoners in State and Federal Institutions, 1925–2005.**

Sources: *Prisons, 1925–1981*, (Washington, DC: Department of Justice, Bureau of Justice Statistics, 1982); "Prisons in 2005," *Bureau of Justice Statistics Bulletin* (Washington, DC: U.S. Government Printing Office, November 2006).

victed and sentenced for a crime before the one currently sending them to prison (Maguire and Pastore, 2004). Two-thirds of people released from prison are rearrested for a felony within three years. Critics of the criminal justice system point to these figures as evidence that prisons have failed in their efforts to rehabilitate. One controversial development that might affect these problems is discussed in the Policy Issues insert in this chapter.

Constructing the Crime Problem: The Role of the Mass Media

Earlier in this chapter, the interactionist perspective was used to explain why some people might engage in deviant behavior or commit crimes. This perspective also provides insight into the process whereby things like deviance and crime come to be defined as important public issues toward which people and policymakers should direct their attention. In modern societies, the mass media play an important role in this process of reality construction because many people gain much of their information about crime from newspapers, magazines, or television (Cuklanz, 1996; Kooistra, Mahoney, and Westervelt, 1998; Sacco, 1995). Overall, crime coverage consumes a significant amount of space in the media, anywhere from 5 percent to 25 percent of all news coverage, depending on the particular type of media. The media devote more attention to covering crime than to reporting on the U.S. Congress or the president.

In terms of shaping the public's definition of crime, the picture of crime portrayed in the media is in some ways a significant distortion of reality. Comparing the media portrayals with the statistics and research on crime that social scientists have accumulated, the media give the distinct impression that the volume of crime is much higher than it actually is. Furthermore, media reports suggest that violent crime is more common than nonviolent crime, whereas crime statistics clearly indicate the reverse is true. The vast majority of crimes reported in the media are crimes committed by individuals, such as homicide or robbery, rather than crimes committed by organizations or corporations, such as price fixing, securities violations, or the violation of environmental regulations.

In regard to the criminal justice system, the media present the police as more effective in solving crimes and apprehending criminals than the statistics suggest they actually are. The media also tend to feature the police quite prominently in news reports, but other facets of the criminal justice system (the courts, prisons, probation officers, and so on) are given less attention than their role in controlling crime would seem to warrant. Finally, the media often present a distorted image of crime victims, portraying all citizens as equally likely to become victims when, in reality, poor minorities in inner-city communities are the most likely victims. The chance that an affluent suburbanite will become a victim of, say, drug violence is actually quite small. Yet portraying victimization as randomly spread through the community is more likely to generate general concern about crime and lead people to see it as an important social problem.

The reasons the media present this image of crime and criminal justice have a lot to do with the organizational processes of news production and the position of the media in the political and economic institutions of society. First of all, the media are mostly private companies motivated by profit, and they devote attention to crimes they see as profitable—crimes that increase the sales of newspapers and magazines and the audience of television news and shows. To attract large numbers of readers or viewers, they prefer stories that are short, simple, and personal. Crimes committed by individuals tend to be much simpler and can be focused on individuals such as the victim and the offender. Organizational and corporate crimes tend to be more complex and harder to explain to an audience unfamiliar with the complicated legalities of antitrust laws or securities violations. Uncomplicated crime stories are also easier for news organizations to write and produce, and this is important when shows or stories must be produced under rigid, daily deadlines. It also helps, especially for television, if the crime can be captured in a short, dramatic video segment that will appeal to audiences. This is why television is so fond of portraying drug raids: It is dramatic to see police officers with shotguns and combat dress bash in doors of apartments and apprehend startled suspects. Nonviolent crime or corporate crime often cannot be captured in such visually appealing images, nor do they have the same drama as some individual crimes.

Another aspect of news organizations that influences the reporting of crime is that journalists and newsmakers sometimes try to organize individual stories around a broader news "theme" in order to legitimize the presentation of particular stories. After all, one reason for reporting about a particular crime, which may seem of little significance by itself, is that it is a part of a "crime wave"—that is, this crime is symptomatic of a broader news issue that the public needs to be aware of. One study in New York, for example, found journalists reporting increasing numbers of

Should States Let Private Companies Run Correctional Facilities?

Prisons and jails in the United States have historically been under the jurisdiction of federal, state, or local governments. Recently, however, there has been a trend toward contracting with privately owned, profit-oriented companies to provide these services. This move began during the 1980s, when government-run facilities were fast becoming overcrowded and some jurisdictions turned to the private sector to help them out. Hundreds of private corrections facilities are now either operating or being developed, now holding over one hundred thousand inmates—7 percent of all federal and state prisoners in the United States (Harrison and Beck, 2006; Perrone and Pratt, 2003).

Supporters of privatization in the prison industry claim that they can do the job more cheaply than the government does. Proponents also claim that they are free of political interference and patronage that make public prisons costly and inefficient. They also point to the high recidivism rate to show that public prisons have not done such a hot job at corrections work.

Many experts in the field, however, are skeptical of whether privately owned detention facilities should be used at all (Austin and Irwin, 2001). One general concern is whether it is ethical to allow a private company to oversee the removal of the rights and freedoms of a human being. Because it is only the legally constituted government that can take away a person's freedom, some question the

constitutionality of giving private individuals the state's authority to deprive people of their freedom. Supporters of the privatization of prisons recognize that these issues are important but also argue that the state does not abdicate any authority when it contracts with private corporations to run prisons. It is still the state that *imposes* punishment by determining who will go to prison and for how long. The state then delegates to a private corporation the power to *administer* the punishment. Yet, opponents of privatization argue that the correctional staff, even a private one, performs a quasi-judicial function when it disciplines inmates, metes out punishment, and advises parole boards. Some of this disciplining and punishing is a part of the day-to-day operation of the prison and is neither mandated nor reviewed by the courts or other state authorities.

Opponents of privatization also argue that a profit-oriented institution would inevitably be tempted to enhance its profit margin by reducing services to inmates. The fear is that the residents and their rehabilitation will suffer in order to achieve lower costs and greater profits. Recall the discussion of capitalism, competition, and free enterprise in Chapter 2. Unlike other realms in which private enterprise operates, however, the recipients of services in this realm—the inmates—do not have the freedom to "shop around" for the best proprietors of correctional services. In fact, some opponents fear that a **prison–industrial complex** is emerging in which

crimes against the elderly as part of a growing "crime wave" in the city (Fishman, 1978). Yet, reviews of actual crime statistics and criminal victimization of the elderly could detect no actual increases in these types of crimes. The process of competitive journalism also contributes to this tendency. Once one news source reports such a crime wave, other newspapers or television news organizations feel some pressure to follow suit in the competition for audiences (Orcutt and Turner, 1993).

Technological developments have expanded the opportunities to show crime and police activities on television. Video recording equipment is now small, inexpensive, and mobile, and it is in the hands of many police and civilians. Some police cars are now permanently equipped with video cameras. As a result, many crimes and police activities get recorded, and a spate of reality-based crime shows has emerged on television,

such as *Cops, America's Most Wanted,* and *NYPD 24/7.* Some of these shows use actors to reenact actual crimes, but all use as much live video footage as they can locate. The result is that television viewers can be repeatedly exposed to live criminal activities, sometimes in a very dramatic and frightening portrayal. And these shows affect people's attitudes: People who watch reality-based police programs make higher estimates of how prevalent crime is (Oliver and Armstrong, 1998). Many of these shows also contain a preponderance of images of African Americans as the criminals, and this affects attitudes: People who watch these shows make higher estimates of the prevalence of crime among African Americans. So, these programs are shaping people's definitions of reality, even when those definitions are not consistent with the facts.

Given all of these considerations, it is not surprising that the media present a distorted image of crime.

correctional corporations and authorities, along with correctional officers and the communities in which prisons are built, see it to their advantage when more people are sent to prison and given longer sentences (Hooks et al., 2004). Communities compete with one another to have prisons built in their locales in hopes that it will create jobs and economic development. All of this creates more demand for the services of the prison industry and greater profits and has led the prison industry to lobby politicians to pass laws that are tougher on criminals. So, irrespective of whether longer sentences reduce crime, they do bring economic advantages to the prison–industrial complex.

What does the research show about private prisons? Most research concludes that the private outfits pay their correctional officers less than public ones, provide more meager training and fringe benefits, and have fewer services, such as psychological counseling, for residents (Camp et al., 2002; Harding, 1997; Perrone and Pratt, 2003). Some private prisons also tend to reduce the quality and number of staff and programs as a way to maintain profits. However, it is unclear whether the overall quality and effectiveness of the job done is higher in public or private prisons. Private prisons come off better in

some studies and worse in others, depending in part on how each study measures quality and effectiveness. On the other hand, most studies show that both types of prisons have about the same level of recidivism and that, overall, private correctional facilities exhibit somewhat lower costs than do public facilities (Bales et al., 2003; Perrone and Pratt, 2003). However, these conclusions must be highly qualified at this point because relatively few research evaluations have been done and because the research often suffers from serious methodological weaknesses. In addition, the lower costs of private prisons might arise, in part, because they have the option of sending sick or troublesome inmates—who are the more expensive inmates—back to public institutions.

So, research does not provide any clear answers to this policy issue yet, and some aspects of the issue—such as the ethical ones—cannot be resolved through research. One way to view this privatization trend is as a process of "market testing" where public prisons and private prisons compete with one another to see what niche of the correctional field each can best fill. The ultimate outcome will likely not be the privatization of all prisons but rather some mix of public and private prisons.

Interventionist		Laissez-Faire
Public prisons	A public–private mix of prison services	Private prisons

This image, once presented, is a powerful force in shaping the public's definition of the "crime problem." The police and other criminal justice authorities also play an important part in creating this definition because the media are heavily dependent on the police for access to news about crime. The police are typically the people who have most information about crimes and access to offenders, victims, and crime scenes; the police are also credible sources of information, which is important for the media. In giving information to the media, the police tend to portray themselves in the most positive light, by dwelling on cases they have successfully solved. One social scientist concluded, "The police role as the dominant gatekeeper means that crime news is often police news and that the advancement of a police perspective on crime and its solution is facilitated" (Sacco, 1995:146).

Future Prospects

Social Reform

Given the role of poverty and economic inequities in fostering crime, it is plausible that reducing poverty and the economic disparity between the affluent and the poor would help reduce some forms of crime and delinquency. Especially important along these lines would be to provide equal educational and occupational opportunities for all Americans. Given Elliott Currie's analysis of crime in Japan (International Perspectives insert), it may be possible to reduce poverty and economic disparity through programs that encourage fuller employment—government and private-sector programs to create new jobs and to provide job training to those without adequate job skills (Currie, 1998).

Crime in Other Societies

It is sad to admit, but the United States is a disturbingly crime-ridden society when compared to most societies around the world. If we compare the United States with Japan, another affluent, industrial nation, the United States comes off poorly (Currie, 1985; Hendry, 1995; Thornton and Endo, 1992). Overall, there are twelve hundred crimes committed for each one hundred thousand persons in Japan; this compares to almost five thousand crimes per one hundred thousand people in the United States! The United States has eighteen times more rapes, ten times more homicides, six times more burglaries, and nine times more drug-related offenses.

What accounts for this dramatic contrast? To answer this question, we need to look at how Japanese culture and society differ from our own. One widely recognized difference is that Japanese society places much more emphasis on the importance of group and family whereas the United States emphasizes individualism and personal autonomy. Individual Japanese feel a strong obligation to their family and society, and families feel a strong sense of responsibility for the behavior of their members. Each family member bears a share of the responsibility for preserving the reputation of the family and avoiding bringing disgrace to it by doing something that might be socially disapproved, like committing a crime. This means that informal mechanisms of social control, such as threatened exclusion from the group, can more effectively control crime in Japan than in the United States.

Another difference is that Japanese culture instills a strong sense of respect for laws, rules, and customs. Respect for and obedience to the law is seen as part of a citizen's social obligation, probably deriving from Confucian teachings about uprightness, duty, and obligation. In Japan, people obey the law because of this obligation, not just out of fear of authority or punishment; in the United States, people are more inclined toward cynical violation of the law if they feel they can get away with it.

A third difference between Japan and the United States is that Japan is a much more racially and

---

In addition, the jobs people get must pay a living wage so that people can support their families. Furthermore, sociologist Mark Colvin (1991) recommends that we fight crime by investing in the institutions that prepare people for productive roles in society: families and schools. Many of these proposals, such as job training programs, Head Start, and so on, have been discussed in other chapters in this book. It is failures in educational institutions and families that have contributed to the inability of many young people to find and make use of legitimate avenues to opportunity. These calls for social reform are an attempt to attack the social and structural conditions that have created much, although not all, of our crime problem. The International Perspectives insert explores in more depth the differences between Japan and the United States in this regard.

Legalization of Some Crimes

Some have proposed that we should legalize many of the victimless crimes, such as gambling, prostitution, and some drug violations. This would reduce the secondary crime associated with these offenses and free the police and courts to attack more serious and dangerous crimes. This measure would also remove these activities from the black market and the hands of organized crime and place them in the public realm, where they can be regulated and taxed. Legalizing these "crimes without victims" does not imply societal support of such activities; they might still be considered by many as serious social problems. Rather, legalization involves the recognition that the criminal justice system should deal with controlling behavior that threatens public order, not with regulating people's morality. Legalization is also an admission that the criminal justice system has been unable to control these crimes effectively.

Better Law Enforcement

Arresting people who commit crimes reduces the likelihood that those individuals will commit crimes in the future. Society should provide the resources that enable the police to do their job. In fact, we have

culturally homogeneous society where there is considerable consensus regarding desirable values and appropriate behaviors. This removes one important source of misunderstanding, tension, and conflict that exists in the United States. Without these social fault lines, Japan offers its citizens a much more cohesive and supportive neighborhood and community environment.

A final difference is that Japanese society is much more *supportive* of individuals and their families than is the United States. Through economic and social policies, Japan strives toward full employment of its workers and tries to create a stable connection of workers to the workplace. Consequently, the income distribution in Japan is much more equitable than in the United States, and no severely deprived and permanently disadvantaged class exists. These supportive policies create the foundation for the emergence of strong and stable family and neighborhood ties, which in turn exert strong social controls over misbehavior. In addition, Japan, along with many Western European industrial nations, has social policies that cushion the disruptions and hardships that can accompany the loss of work. These nations, for example, give more generous unemployment benefits and distribute them to more unemployed workers than does the United States. Because of this, less disruption of family and communal roles accompanies unemployment. This is important because it is not just economic circumstances that motivate crime; the weakening of family and communal supports that can accompany unemployment also reduces controls over misbehavior and aggravates the impact of economic insecurity on crime.

When considered separately, each of these elements of Japanese culture may make only a small contribution to the low Japanese crime rate; however, in combination they provide considerable understanding of the yawning gulf between crime in the United States and crime in Japan. They also emphasize the sociological perspective on crime—namely, that crime emerges from particular social and cultural conditions and that crime can be reduced by changing those conditions.

made considerable strides in the past few decades toward a better-equipped, better-trained, and more highly educated police force in the United States. An increasing number of police departments, for example, require their officers to have a college education. Whether this makes them more effective at controlling crime we will only know through future research (U.S. Department of Justice, 1992a).

Policymakers now have available a wide array of research studies evaluating the effectiveness of various law enforcement activities in controlling crime (Sherman, 1997). These studies have shown that some things don't seem to work very well: neighborhood watch programs, arresting juveniles for minor offenses, and community policing where the focus is putting more police into a community rather than providing police with tasks that focus on specific factors that increase crime. The research also shows what does reduce crime: more intensive police patrols of crime "hot spots," devoting resources to arresting serious repeat offenders, and police efforts to seize guns carried in public. The results of research such as this offer criminal justice authorities and politicians a basis for deciding what would be effective in the fight against crime. Many police jurisdictions, for example, have responded to the finding that arresting repeat offenders is effective by using computers and other modern technologies to locate and arrest the relatively small number of people who commit large numbers of robberies and burglaries. Putting these people in jail has a much bigger impact on the crime problem than does imprisoning someone who commits a crime only occasionally.

Judicial Reform

There are a number of reforms that might be considered for our judicial system to enhance its effectiveness in controlling crime (U.S. Department of Justice, 1992a).

1. Provide swift, certain, and fair punishment. Swift and certain punishment is more effective in controlling crime than are overly long and

counterproductive prison sentences. There is little evidence that severity of punishment reduces crime or the rate of recidivism.

2. Provide equitable punishment, whether the crime occurs on a slum street or in a corporate boardroom. Disparities in punishment resulting from the racial, sexual, or socioeconomic characteristics of the offender should be carefully monitored and controlled. This means that society needs to make a serious effort to control white-collar crime, which we have been rather lax about until now. Disparities in punishment lead those who are punished to view the criminal justice system with a jaundiced eye. As more than one inmate has been heard to say: "I'm not in prison because I committed a crime; I'm here because I'm poor (or black)."

3. Narrow the discretionary options of police officers, prosecutors, and judges and develop procedures to hold them accountable to the public for the fairness and reasonableness of their decisions and actions.

4. Provide all criminal defendants with truly equal legal counsel to reduce the inequities in convictions and sentences.

Alternatives to Prison

Professor of law and criminology Norval Morris argues that people in the United States "have an exaggerated belief in the efficacy of imprisonment" to control crime (quoted in Butterfield, 1992:4). The simple notion is that throwing more people in prison for a longer period of time will significantly reduce the crime problem. Many criminologists feel that such a prison-based criminal justice policy is a costly delusion (Austin and Irwin, 2001; Currie, 1998). Although the prison population has quadrupled since 1975, the crime rate has gone down only slightly (see Figures 9.1 and 9.5). This and other evidence suggest that excessive punishments, especially for nonviolent crimes, do not provide adequate payback in the form of reduced crime. Furthermore, such a policy is enormously expensive. And prison expansions bleed funds away from social programs that might decrease crime by attacking its roots, such as programs to provide job training for the unemployed. Some states today, for example, pay more to run their prison systems than their colleges and universities. Finally, imprisoning people causes untold human suffering and dislocation to both the prisoners and their families.

Given these problems with a prison-based policy, prison sentences should be used only when necessary for public safety or when it has proven deterrent value.

In addition, this policy should be balanced by efforts to change the conditions that produce crime and to find alternatives to prison for punishing or rehabilitating people who have committed crimes. Alternatives that have proven effective are such things as putting people on probation under intensive supervision, using house arrest with monitoring by electronic bracelets, and placing criminals in drug treatment programs (Anderson, 1998). These alternatives are especially effective with nonviolent and drug offenders.

Prison Reform

When people are sent to prison, prisons and their programs should be designed so that they have the greatest chance of rehabilitating prisoners and reducing recidivism. Research has shown that some things seem to work (Gendreau and Ross, 1987; MacKenzie, 1997). For example, effective rehabilitation programs focus on changing behaviors and beliefs conducive to crime, such as drug use and high levels of anger. Effective programs also provide carefully planned and structured activities that do not reinforce criminal responses, and they concentrate resources on offenders who are most likely to return to crime. Correctional programs should promote rather than undermine personal responsibility and provide offenders with real opportunities to succeed in legitimate occupations. These might include increased occupational training and counseling while imprisoned or work-release programs. Research documents that prisoners who receive vocational or academic education while in prison are more likely to stay out of prison and to find a job and support themselves once released (Steurer and Smith, 2003).

The crowding in prisons should be reduced to eliminate the degrading conditions under which many prison inmates live. Some prisons and juvenile detention facilities have tried to deter crime or rehabilitate criminals through the imposition of military discipline and structure into people's lives or by shocking them into an awareness of the dire consequences of getting caught at crime. However, research has shown that these "boot camps," shock probation, or Scared Straight approaches do not reduce crime or recidivism (Anderson, 1998; MacKenzie, 1997).

Environmental Opportunities

Efforts should be made to reduce the environmental opportunities for committing crime (Crowe, 1991). This can take the form of better physical security, such as burglarproof locks; better detection of crime through such mechanisms as burglar alarms and antishoplifting tags in stores; and improved surveillance, such as better street lighting. (The Applied Research insert in Chapter 12 suggests some other ways in which environmental planning and urban design can be tools in the fight against crime.)

Victim Restitution

States should be encouraged to establish victim restitution programs in which the victims of crime are provided with some compensation for their loss. Often the victims of crime feel more assaulted by the criminal justice system than by the perpetrator. Once the many social sources of crime are recognized, it should be clear that society has some responsibility to the victims who unwittingly suffer as a consequence of society's failings.

Which of the reforms discussed in this chapter will have the most beneficial effect on the crime problem and on inadequacies in the criminal justice system can be determined only after programs have been initiated and evaluated. What should be clear is that only a broad-based and coordinated attack is likely to have a significant impact. If all these suggestions were incorporated into our attack on the crime problem, we would undoubtedly make a significant dent in it.

LINKAGES The level of crime in the United States is significantly increased by the persistence of entrenched poverty (Chapter 5) and the spread of illegal drugs (Chapter 10). At the same time, high rates of crime make parts of our cities into dangerous places to live (Chapter 12), and throwing criminals in prison can disrupt family lives (Chapter 3).

STUDY AND REVIEW

Summary

1. Biological explanations of crime, which view crime as arising from people's physical constitution or genetic makeup, have been largely discounted by criminologists today. Psychological approaches receive more support, but they are seen as offering only a partial understanding of crime and delinquency. Social policy designed to reduce crime needs to focus on the social conditions that produce it.

2. The functionalist perspective views crime as arising in part from the weakened impact of bonds to family, church, and community. Another functionalist approach is anomie theory, which views crime as a consequence of the inconsistency or confusion between the goals people are taught to strive for and the culturally approved means they have available to achieve these goals.

3. Conflict theorists point out that the powerful groups in society decide which crimes will be considered serious problems and who will be arrested and sent to jail for committing crimes. Conflict theorists also blame certain contradictions in capitalism as a source of crime.

4. The interactionist perspective emphasizes the differential association theory, which points to how people learn whether to value criminal or conventional behavior. Labeling theory shows how a pattern of criminal behavior (career deviance) can result from a person being labeled as a deviant or criminal by the police or others.

5. The crime and delinquency rates in the United States have been rising for a number of decades, but the rise appears to have leveled off some in the 1980s and declined a little in the 1990s. Four social characteristics are associated with crime: gender, age, socioeconomic status, and race.

6. There are a number of problems associated with the criminal justice system in the United States. The police have a great deal of discretion—maybe too much—in how they do their job, and police feel they do not receive the support of the public or the courts. The courts exercise discretion regarding which cases will be pursued and with how much vigor, and there is much "negotiated justice." Prisons are overcrowded and do not seem to be very successful at rehabilitation.

7. To control crime, we need most of all to carry out social reforms that will have an impact on the social conditions that cause crime in the first place. Some crimes could be legalized, thus freeing the police to deal with more serious crimes. The police could institute new

Government agencies now make a lot of data about crime, crime victims, and criminal justice issues available at their Web sites. Take a look at the Web sites of the FBI (www.fbi.gov), the Bureau of Justice Statistics at the Department of Justice (www.ojp.usdoj.gov/bjs), and the Bureau of Prisons (www.bop.gov). Many of the documents and data sets at these sites can be downloaded to your computer, and some require special software such as Acrobat Reader. For example, the FBI's *Uniform Crime Report* is available at its Web site, and the Bureau of Justice Statistics' *Sourcebook of Criminal Justice Statistics* can be found at its Web site or at www.albany.edu/sourcebook. Gather data at those sites to update and supplement the information in this chapter. Share the data with your class.

There is also a Web site that contains the results of a nationwide survey that is conducted in the United States each year. Called the General Social Survey, it is conducted by the National Opinion Research Center at the University of Chicago. The survey is based on a large sample of adults and is considered to be one of the most scientifically sound sources of data about social issues available. You can access the survey results at

www.norc.org/GSS+Website/. Once there, click on "Search." Now you can look for questions asked in the survey that are relevant to a topic of interest to you. For example, type in "capital punishment." This displays a list of abbreviated names, each identifying a question that was asked relating to the subject of capital punishment. Click on the name CAPPUN. This will provide you with people's responses to the question of whether they favor or oppose capital punishment. How much support is there for capital punishment in the United States? How has that support changed over the past two decades? Go back to the Search screen and look for other topics related to crime, deviance, or the criminal justice system.

You can also explore the Internet for information about white-collar and corporate crime. Use the search engines to locate Web sites on these topics. One of Ralph Nader's public interest groups maintains a Web site on recent episodes of corporate crime: www.citizenworks.org/enron/corp-scandal.php.

The Allyn & Bacon Social Problems Supersite (http://wps.ablongman.com/ab_socialprob_sprsite_1) contains material on crime and the criminal justice system.

law enforcement procedures that would enable them to catch serious criminals. Many judicial reforms could be carried out that would make the courts more effective. We could also reform our prisons, reduce the opportunities to commit crimes, and provide for victim restitution.

Key Terms

anomie

anomie theory

career deviance

crime

cultural transmission theories

differential association theory

labeling theory

primary deviance

prison–industrial complex

recidivism

secondary deviance

Multiple-Choice Questions

1. With regard to biological explanations of crime, sociologists have concluded that
   a. biology explains a substantial amount of crime.
   b. biology plays no role in causing crime.
   c. biology makes, at best, only a small contribution to the crime problem.
   d. biological explanations are more important than psychological ones in understanding crime.
2. The concept of "anomie" is linked with which theoretical perspective in sociology?
   a. the functionalist perspective
   b. the conflict perspective
   c. the interactionist perspective
   d. the biological perspective
   e. the psychological perspective
3. Conflict theorists argue that the causes of crime can be found in
   a. the labeling process.
   b. certain characteristics of capitalism.
   c. biological inadequacies of individuals.
   d. weakened social bonds in industrial societies.

4. A violation of social norms for which a person is not caught, or is excused rather than labeled, is referred to as
   a. relative deviance.
   b. secondary deviance.
   c. tertiary deviance.
   d. career deviance.
   e. primary deviance.
5. Which of the following is true of homicides?
   a. They are rarely planned in advance.
   b. The majority occur during the commission of a felony.
   c. The majority of homicide victims are strangers to their assailants.
   d. The majority are committed as a part of organized crime activities.
6. Which of the following are considered victimless crimes?
   a. gambling
   b. prostitution
   c. white-collar crimes
   d. all of the above
   e. only a and b
7. Regarding the relationship between socioeconomic status and crime, the text concludes that
   a. lower-class people commit more of almost all types of hidden crimes.
   b. the relationship between SES and crime is a strong one.
   c. there is social class variation in the numbers of criminal acts committed but not the types of criminal acts committed.
   d. lower-class people are more likely to commit highly visible and violent crimes.
8. A person is sent to prison for committing a felony, is released, and then commits another felony after release. This would make this person
   a. a primary deviant.
   b. an anomie deviant.
   c. a recidivist.
   d. a secondary deviant.
9. The text recommends all of the following to help in the fight against crime and delinquency *except*
   a. reduce poverty.
   b. give longer prison sentences for most crimes.
   c. legalize some crimes.
   d. promote personal responsibility among prison inmates.
10. According to the text, prisons and prison programs should be designed so that they
   a. rehabilitate prisoners.
   b. increase recidivism.
   c. reinforce criminal responses.
   d. increase secondary deviance.

True/False Questions

1. For sociologists, a behavior can be inherently deviant, without regard to people's interpretation or judgment of the behavior.
2. Anomie theory can lead to the conclusion that large disparities between income groups can cause crime.
3. Cultural transmission theories posit that crime can be blamed on certain characteristics of capitalism as an economic system.
4. People in the United States view most white-collar crimes as less serious than other crimes.
5. Crime rates are rising faster among men than among women for all types of crime.
6. When responding to a domestic dispute, police are more likely to arrest a suspected abuser in a poor neighborhood than in a middle-class neighborhood.
7. People are more likely to receive the death penalty for homicide when the victim is white rather than when the victim is black.
8. Prison populations in the United States have grown in part because people are receptive to giving criminals longer prison sentences.
9. Effective rehabilitation programs in prisons are those that concentrate resources on offenders who are most likely to return to crime.
10. Research has shown that states that institute the death penalty experience a significant drop in their homicide rates.

Fill-In Questions

1. According to _____ approaches to crime, criminality is linked to personality disorders or maladjustments.
2. _____ refers to the inconsistencies and contradictions in the social system and the resulting confusion experienced by people.
3. The most important mode of adaptation, according to Robert Merton, and the one that might take the form of crime, is called _____.
4. The differential association theory of crime is one example of a/an _____ theory.
5. If a drug user is discovered and responds to the discovery by becoming more closely involved with other drug users, this would be an example of _____ deviance.
6. Antitrust violations are one type of _____ crime.
7. Young people who commit acts that are prohibited by the juvenile code but are not considered criminal when committed by an adult are called _____ offenders.

8. The single social factor that is most predictive of patterns of criminal behavior is _____.
9. The U.S. court system utilizes a/an _____ model in evaluating guilt or innocence.
10. According to the text, the criminal justice system should provide punishment that is _____ and _____.

Matching Questions

_____ 1. organized crime
_____ 2. recidivist
_____ 3. sociopathic personalities
_____ 4. Emile Durkheim
_____ 5. plea bargaining
_____ 6. forcible rape
_____ 7. fraudulent use of funds
_____ 8. prison–industrial complex
_____ 9. social reform
_____ 10. labeling theory

A. syndicates
B. psychological approaches to crime
C. Part I offense
D. white-collar crime
E. repeat offender
F. functionalist perspective
G. private prisons
H. reducing poverty
I. informal dispensing of justice
J. interactionist perspective

Essay Questions

1. Describe the psychological approaches to crime. How do sociologists assess them as explanations of crime?
2. Explain crime from the conflict perspective.
3. According to the differential association theory, what is the explanation for why some people commit crimes and others do not?
4. Describe the effect of gender and age on people's likelihood of committing crimes.
5. Describe the relationship between socioeconomic status and crime.
6. What are the causes of the burgeoning prison population in the United States since 1980?
7. Make arguments both for and against the use of private prisons in the United States. What does research show about how well these prisons work?
8. Why is the crime rate in Japan so much lower than it is in the United States?
9. What social reforms are suggested in the text to help reduce the crime rate in the United States?
10. Make arguments both for and against the use of the death penalty for some crimes in the United States. What does research show about the impact of the death penalty?

For Further Reading

K. C. Carceral. *Prison, Inc.: A Convict Exposes Life Inside a Private Prison.* Edited by Thomas J. Bernard. New York: New York University Press, 2005. This is an excellent and personal account of life inside a privately owned prison, as recounted by the inmates.

David Cole. *No Equal Justice: Race and Class in the American Criminal Justice System.* New York: The New Press, 1999. This author, a law professor, reviews the abysmal treatment of racial minorities and people of low economic standing by the U.S. criminal justice system. He proposes various remedies, especially suggesting that the system move away from the punitive and toward the rehabilitative.

Joel Dyer. *The Perpetual Prisoner Machine: How America Profits from Crime.* Boulder, CO: Westview Press, 2000. This book identifies the groups that profit from high incarceration rates in the United States and suggests how fears of crime can be used to maintain and enhance those profits.

Stephen P. Garvey, ed. *Beyond Repair? America's Death Penalty.* Durham, NC: Duke University Press, 2003. The readings in this book provide a balanced and thorough overview of the research and policy issues relating to capital punishment in the United States today.

Michael Jacobson. *Downsizing Prisons: How To Reduce Crime and End Mass Incarceration.* New York: New York University Press, 2005. This book calls for some significant changes in social policy regarding sentencing and parole that, the author argues, will reduce crime, reduce correctional budgets, and reduce recidivism

Russell Mokhiber. *Corporate Crime and Violence: Big Business Power and the Abuse of the Public Trust.* San Francisco: Sierra Club Books, 1988. A muckraker's view of white-collar and corporate crime. Thirty-six cases are described in which corporate misconduct killed people or significantly harmed the environment.

Mary Pattillo, David Weiman, and Bruce Western, eds. *Imprisoning America: The Social Effects of Mass Incarceration.* New York: Russell Sage Foundation, 2004. The readings in this book explore the many negative consequences of incarcerating people—to families, communities, and others—and argue for policies that promote less incarceration of criminals and incarcerate only when the benefits clearly outweigh the costs.

David R. Simon. *Elite Deviance,* 8th ed. Boston: Allyn & Bacon, 2006. An excellent antidote to the myth that deviance occurs mostly among poor and disreputable people, this book chronicles the deviant activities of the rich and powerful.

ALCOHOL AND OTHER DRUGS

In 1982, well-known actor and former *Saturday Night Live* star John Belushi died from an injection of heroin and cocaine, a combination known as a "speedball" in drug circles. In 1984, David Kennedy, the 28-year-old son of Senator Robert F. Kennedy and nephew of President John F. Kennedy, died in a hotel room from a combined dose of cocaine, a narcotic painkiller called Demerol, and an antipsychotic tranquilizer known as Mellaril, which had been prescribed for Mr. Kennedy by a physician. In 1993, the movie star River Phoenix died of an overdose of cocaine and heroin or morphine. In 1995, Jerry Garcia, leader of the rock group The Grateful Dead, died while a resident in a drug treatment program, and baseball great Mickey Mantle died of cancer, partly the result of years of alcohol abuse. These deaths stand out from the others that are attributable to drug abuse because these men were wealthy and famous; however, deaths related to drug abuse or overdose occur routinely in the United States, although rarely with the attention surrounding these cases. The notoriety of the people mentioned publicized the horrible consequences that can result—to people of both high and low social standing—when drug use gets out of control.

Use of drugs in one form or another is widespread in human societies (Davenport-Hines, 2002). Most societies condone the use of certain drugs, at least by some groups. Such drug use is generally regulated, either through law or social convention, because the unregulated use of mind-altering substances can have damaging effects on society. This common societal ambivalence toward drug use—condoning it on the one hand, but controlling it on the other—points to one of the controversial elements of the problem of alcohol and drug use: drawing the line between what is acceptable use and what is not. Chapters 1 and 9 describe the relative nature of deviant behavior. This chapter focuses on this issue specifically in the context of drug use. In the United States, opinions about drug use vary widely. At one extreme, some groups call for a complete ban on all drugs, including alcohol. Other groups believe that some drugs—alcohol and marijuana are most commonly mentioned—can be used safely by mature people. At the other extreme, a few groups argue that adults should be free to use any drug they please as long as they do not become a danger to others.

These issues of social definition are central to understanding the problem of drug abuse in the United States and to developing sensible social policies to deal with it. These issues will be addressed first, before considering the extent and nature of the drug problem in the United States.

Drugs and Their Consequences

What is a drug? Strictly speaking, a **drug** is *any substance that, when consumed, alters one or more of the functions of the human body* (Kuhn, Swartzwelder, and Wilson, 1998). This definition covers a wide range of substances, from cocaine to medicines for the control of cancer or high blood pressure. It also includes many everyday foods along with beverages such as tea, coffee, and cola that contain the mild stimulant caffeine. Does this make your aunt, who drinks two six-packs of caffeine-laced cola each day, a drug addict? Not by most definitions. The effects of most of these everyday substances are rather mild, and their use or withdrawal does not normally create major disruptions in people's lives. The drugs that constitute a social problem are typically limited to the **psychoactive drugs**: *those that can produce major alterations in the mood, emotions, perceptions, or brain functioning of the person who takes them* (Schuckit, 2006).

Drug Use and Abuse

The use of psychoactive drugs is not, by itself, a social problem. After all, as we have noted, most societies approve the use of some such drugs. Where, then, is the line between acceptable drug use and drug abuse? This is a very controversial question. The World Health Organization (WHO) defines drug abuse as

Myths & Facts

About Drug Abuse

Myth: The drug abuse problem in the United States today is of epidemic proportions, with more people using and abusing drugs than ever.

Fact: Although today's drug abuse problem is serious, it is probably not a lot more serious than it was a century ago. Then, marijuana, cocaine, and various narcotics were legal and widely available, and many people were addicted to drugs.

Myth: Heavy use of heroin clouds judgment and reduces inhibitions, and this is the prime reason heroin addicts commit crimes.

Fact: Heroin addicts are as likely to be high on alcohol as heroin when they commit crimes, and in fact many

heroin addicts drink alcohol before committing crimes in order to bolster their courage.

Myth: The most serious drug problem that the United States faces is the flow of heroin, cocaine, and marijuana into the United States from overseas.

Fact: In terms of the number of people affected and the economic costs to society, most specialists on drug problems consider alcohol abuse to be the most severe drug problem we have. In addition, a drug such as heroin is probably less harmful to its user's health than is alcohol, and many have argued that heroin should be treated by society like alcohol: as a legal but highly controlled substance.

the excessive use of a drug in a way that is inconsistent with medical practice. However, this definition, with its emphasis on the medical consequences of behavior, seems overly broad. Heavy smoking, for example, would by this definition be drug abuse because physicians warn against it, but few are likely to call heavy smokers "drug addicts." Rather, we need to consider drug use in the context of particular cultural or subcultural norms and values. From this viewpoint, **drug abuse** is *the continued use of a psychoactive substance at a level that violates approved social practices.* Typically, use of a substance meets social disapproval when it has negative consequences for people's health, endangers their relationships with other people, or is threatening to others in society. Even people's belief that the substance has these consequences can produce social disapproval. As we will see, cultural norms regarding drug abuse are by no means completely rational. These norms are influenced as much by history, religion, and cultural values as they are by the actual damage drugs do to a person's health or social relationships.

Much of the concern about drugs of abuse relates to their effects on people. Some drugs produce **dependence,** or *a mental or physical craving for a drug and withdrawal symptoms when use of the drug is stopped.* Dependence and its withdrawal symptoms can be physical, psychological, or both. Alcohol withdrawal, for example, can lead to convulsions, hallucinations, and insomnia on the physical level and nervousness and a reduced sense of self-worth on the psychological level. The withdrawal symptoms of a drug are often the opposite of the effects of taking the drug. For example, alcohol, which helps a person relax, can lead to insomnia and anxiety when use is discontinued. Drug dependence and drug abuse are not the same thing, although they are often related. A severely depressed person, for example, may become highly dependent on antidepressant medications prescribed by a physician, but this would not be considered drug abuse because the physician's diagnosis and treatment prescription make this a socially approved use of a drug. Neither are drug abuse and drug addiction synonymous. **Drug addiction,** as used by professionals in the field, refers to *physical dependence on a drug.* Although most drugs of abuse are physically addicting, some, such as the hallucinogens, are not.

Often associated with dependence on a drug is **tolerance:** *physical changes that result in the need for higher and higher doses of the drug to achieve the same effect.* This occurs because, with continual use of some drugs, the liver destroys the drug more quickly and the nervous system's response to

the drug is diminished. So more of the drug is needed for the same "boost." It is also possible to develop cross-dependence and cross-tolerance. **Cross-dependence** occurs when *the withdrawal symptoms of one drug are alleviated by another drug in the same pharmacological class.* **Cross-tolerance** is found when *a tolerance built up to one drug leads to a reduced response to another drug in the same pharmacological class.*

The Societal Costs of Drug Abuse

The consumption of alcohol and other drugs takes a costly toll from society.

1. *Accidents.* Each year, one-third to one-half of the drivers in fatal traffic accidents have been drinking, and between sixteen thousand and thirty thousand people die in traffic accidents involving alcohol (U.S. Bureau of the Census, 2006: 693–695). Alcohol consumption is also associated with airplane and occupational accidents. Marijuana impairs motor skills, reduces judgment, and affects time and distance estimation, and thus increases the danger of accidents (Kuhn, Swartzwelder, and Wilson, 1998).

2. *Crime.* In well over half of the homicides in the United States, either the victim, the perpetrator, or both were drinking at the time of the crime. People who commit rape are also disproportionately likely to have been drinking before the crime or to be alcoholics. Studies of heroin addicts in treatment programs have found that most addicts commit crimes to support their habit (Inciardi, Horowitz, and Pottieger, 1993). Thirty-four percent of all convictions for federal offenses in the United States today are for drug offenses, up from 18 percent in 1980 (U.S. Bureau of the Census, 2003:214). In most large cities, over half of the people arrested for all crimes test positive for some illegal drugs.

3. *Family problems.* Alcoholics are seven times more likely to become separated or divorced from their spouses than are other people, and 40 percent of the family court problems involve alcohol in some fashion. Studies find that between 29 and 71 percent of spouse abusers were drinking at the time of the attack (Martin, 1993).

4. *Work problems.* People who abuse alcohol or illicit drugs have twice the rate of work absenteeism as other workers and are much more likely to jump from one job to another, to be fired by their boss,

and to be involved in a workplace accident (Hoffmann, Larison, and Sanderson, 1997).

5. *Health problems.* Most psychoactive drugs, especially if taken continually or in large quantities, produce severe health problems and even death. Alcoholics and heroin addicts, for example, have far higher death rates from many illnesses than do people who abuse neither drug.

Placing a dollar figure on these and other costs of drug abuse is necessarily approximate and tentative, but it helps to highlight the dimensions of the problem. One congressional estimate of the core costs for drug and alcohol abuse in the United States was $246 billion! This is what it cost society to diagnose, treat, and care for alcohol or drug-related illnesses and deaths and to cover the costs of lowered work productivity (Ramstad, 2000).

The Extent of Drug Abuse in the United States

People in the United States consume many different kinds of drugs. These drugs differ from one another in their chemical composition and their social, psychological, and medical consequences. The major classes of drugs that are problems in the United States will be discussed.

Alcohol

Alcohol is a psychoactive drug that any adult in the United States can purchase legally without a prescription. There is little debate that it constitutes our most severe drug problem. According to a survey conducted by the National Institute on Drug Abuse, 7 percent of all adult Americans are heavy drinkers, consuming five or more drinks at one sitting at five or more times each month (U.S. Department of Health and Human Services, 2006). Overall, people 14 years of age and older in the United States consume an average of 2.7 gallons of pure alcohol per person per year. This is a particularly impressive amount considering that about one-third of the adult population drinks no alcoholic beverages whatsoever. Furthermore, the young also drink a lot. Four percent of all high school seniors drink every day, and almost one-third of all high school seniors reported episodes of heavy drinking in the preceding two weeks (see Figure 10.1).

The consumption of alcohol by itself is not a social problem. Many people use it throughout their lives without running into any difficulties, or at least the particular effects are not defined as problems. However, the continuous or excessive consumption of alcohol, commonly termed "alcoholism," is likely to create problems. Actually, attempts to define alcoholism have created much controversy. One approach is to define it by the amount of alcohol consumed or the alcohol blood levels of a person. However, many alcoholism treatment specialists feel that these definitions have weaknesses because they ignore the social definitions of what is considered too much alcohol or the social consequences of consuming a certain amount of alcohol. The most popular definition of **alcoholism** is *the consumption of alcohol at a level that produces serious personal, social, or health consequences, such as marital problems, occupational difficulties, accidents, or arrests* (Ray and Ksir, 2004; Schuckit, 2006). In this definition, there is no set level of alcohol consumption that distinguishes the alcoholic from the nonalcoholic. Alcoholics are people who cannot stop drinking before the detrimental consequences, such as losing their jobs or being arrested, occur.

An estimated 15 percent of male drinkers and 6 percent of female drinkers in the United States become alcohol abusers. This means that about 18 million people in the United States are either addicted to alcohol or drink enough to cause problems for themselves and other people. Who are these alcoholics? Alcoholism counselors are quick to point out that alcoholism knows no age, sex, race, or social class bounds, and this is certainly true to the extent that alcoholics can be found in virtually all social groups. Yet, this statement also hides the reality that people with certain social characteristics are more likely to become alcoholics (Flewelling, Rachal, and Marsden, 1992; Haglund and Schuckit, 1981):

1. *Sex.* Men are far more likely to become alcoholics than are women. This is due in part to the fact that alcohol consumption and drunkenness have been more socially acceptable for men than for women.

2. *Socioeconomic status.* Rates of alcoholism are higher among people with lower levels of income and education. This may be due in part to the abilities of people with higher socioeconomic standing to avoid being publicly labeled as alcoholics.

3. *Religion.* There are strong associations between religion and alcohol consumption. Most Jews, for example, consume alcohol, but heavy drinking among this group is relatively infrequent. Catholics, on the other hand, have many drinkers and much higher rates of heavy

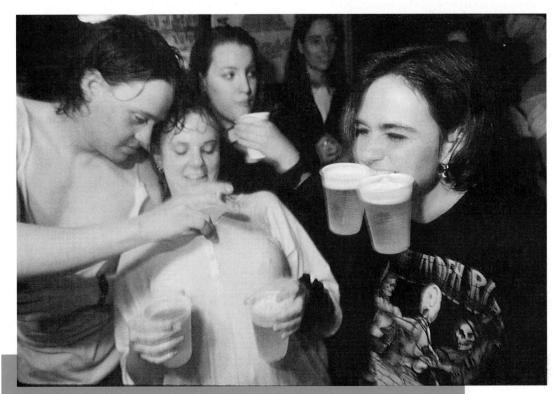

While alcohol abuse can be found among people of all ages, it is a much more serious problem among the young, such as these college students at a party.

drinking, especially among French and Irish Catholics.

4. *Age.* Alcohol abuse is a more serious problem among younger than older people. Among people between the ages of 18 and 34, one-quarter to one-half admit to having some alcohol-related problems, such as automobile accidents while drunk or missing work because of drinking (Schuckit, 2006). After age 34, heavy drinking declines, and by age 65 the proportion of heavy drinkers is about one-third what it is in the younger groups. Half of high school seniors have used alcohol in the last month, and over 40 percent of college students have consumed five or more drinks in one sitting during the previous two weeks. However, surveys over the past three decades suggest that alcohol consumption among adolescents as well as adults has declined, but with a modest increase in the past few years (see Figures 10.1 and 10.2).

Marijuana and Hashish

Marijuana is a preparation made from a plant of the genus *Cannabis*, usually consumed by smoking it like tobacco (Kuhn, Swartzwelder, and Wilson, 1998). The primary psychoactive ingredient of *Cannabis* is tetrahydrocannabinol, or THC, which is concentrated in the resin of the plant. The potency of marijuana depends on how much of the resin is present. Hashish is a concentrated form of the resin taken from the flowers of the plant. It is either eaten or smoked and is very potent. It is difficult to classify marijuana in relationship to other psychoactive drugs. It has sedative properties at the doses usually consumed in cigarette form, but it also has definite hallucinogenic properties when taken in stronger doses.

The level of marijuana use in the United States is far lower than that of alcohol. Approximately 5 percent of college students use marijuana on a daily basis, and somewhere between one-third and one-half of all adults have ever used marijuana (see Figures 10.1 and 10.3 and Table 10.1). Rates of marijuana use are far higher among younger than older people. Among those between eighteen and twenty-five years of age, 17 percent are current users, compared with only 3 percent of those over thirty-five. Although these levels of use are much higher than those prior to the 1970s, usage peaked in the late 1970s and declined steadily and substantially since then (see Table 10.1 and

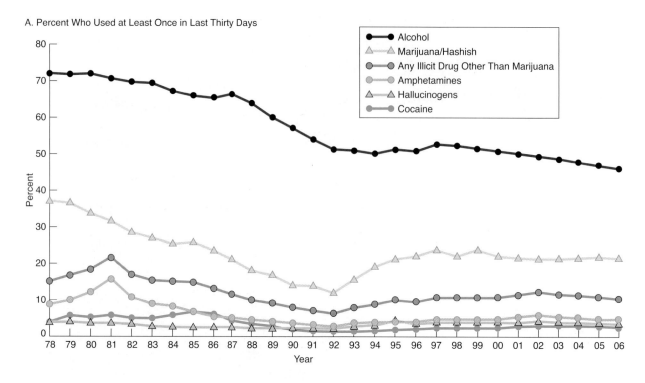

A. Percent Who Used at Least Once in Last Thirty Days

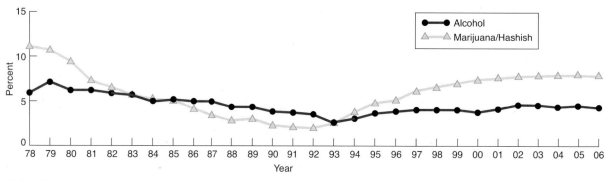

B. Percent Who Used Twenty or More Times in Last Thirty Days

FIGURE 10.1 **Drug Use Among High School Seniors, 1978–2006.**

Source: Lloyd D. Johnston, Patrick M. O'Malley, Jerald G. Bachman, and John E. Schulenberg, *Monitoring the Future: National Survey Results on Drug Use, Volume 1: Secondary School Students*. Bethesda, MD: National Institute on Drug Abuse, various years), www.monitoringthefuture.org.

Figure 10.1). Usage rates had increased somewhat by the late 1990s among teenagers. These patterns reflect the overall trends in the use of any illicit drugs since the 1970s (see Figure 10.4). Males are also more likely to use marijuana than are females, and it is less common among college students than noncollege adults.

In the low potencies found in some marijuana, the drug produces feelings of pleasant euphoria and well-being, along with sleepiness, heightened sexual arousal, increased sense awareness, difficulty in keeping track of time, and a decrease in short-term memory. Marijuana intoxication can also impair a person's ability to carry out complex tasks. However,

some marijuana today is far more potent than the marijuana of earlier decades, and large amounts of this highly potent marijuana can lead to intense emotional reactions, substantial distortions in perception, a "panic" that one has lost control of oneself, and vivid hallucinations. It can even lead to a psychotic reaction, usually in people with a history of mental instability. Long-term marijuana use may also damage the lungs and immune system and affect long-term memory. However, marijuana is a fairly mild drug when used in moderation and in low potency. Its use leads to only mild levels of tolerance. Some argue that there is no physical dependence at all with marijuana.

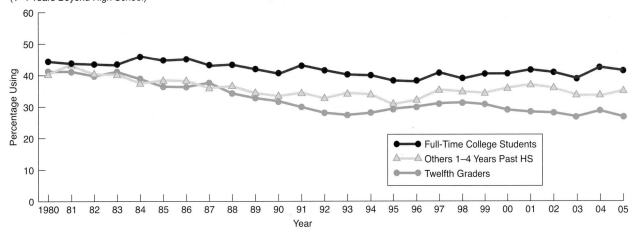

A. Trends in Two-Week Prevalence of Five or More Drinks in a Row Among College Students vs. Others
(1–4 Years Beyond High School)

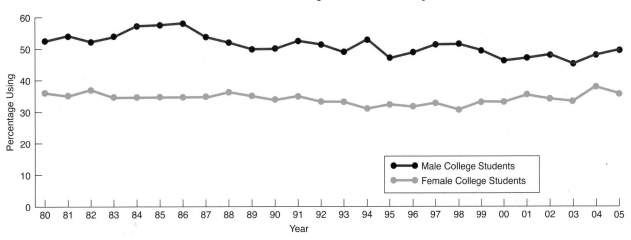

B. Trends in Two-Week Prevalence of Five or More Drinks in a Row Among Male and Female College Students

FIGURE 10.2   **Use of Alcohol Among College Students, 1980–2005.**

Source: Lloyd D. Johnston, Patrick M. O'Malley, Jerald G. Bachman, and John E. Schulenberg, *Monitoring the Future: National Survey Results on Drug Use, 1975–2005: Vol. II: College Students and Adults, 19–45* (NIH Publication No. 06–5884). Bethesda, MD: National Institute on Drug Abuse, 2006), www.monitoringthefuture.org.

Withdrawal symptoms, if they occur at all, appear to be quite mild.

Some studies have concluded that chronic marijuana users, especially among adolescents, may develop what has been called an amotivational syndrome, characterized by a lack of goals, apathy, sluggish mental responses, and mental confusion (Zimmer and Morgan, 1997). Such investigations have been criticized, however, on the grounds that many of the behaviors associated with this syndrome are socially acceptable and even valued in the subculture of some chronic drug users. So these behaviors may

not be responses to the drug but to the social expectations present in a subcultural milieu. In addition, this syndrome probably affects a small number of chronic users—one study estimates 3 percent—and it disappears without any treatment being given for it, even when marijuana use is continued.

There has been some debate over the years about whether marijuana use can lead to the use of other drugs such as cocaine or heroin (Zimmer and Morgan, 1997). Clearly, people who use these other drugs often use marijuana first. However, there is no convincing evidence that marijuana itself causes a

A. Trends in Thirty-Day Prevalence of Daily Use Among College Students vs. Others (1–4 Years Beyond High School)

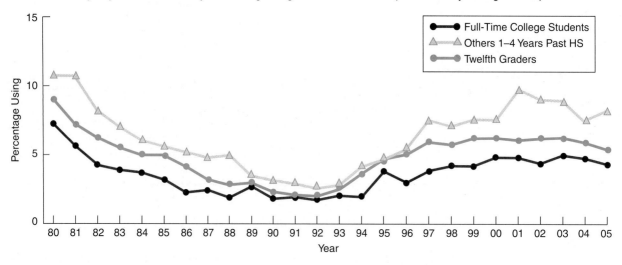

B. Trends in Thirty-Day Prevalence of Daily Use Among Male and Female College Students

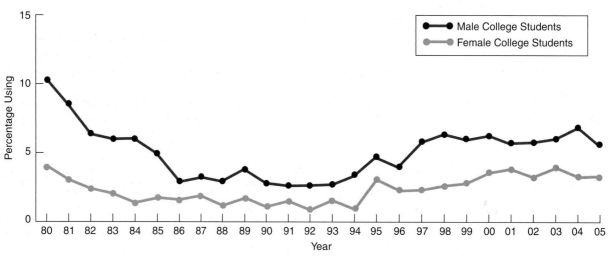

FIGURE 10.3 **Marijuana Use Among College Students, 1980–2005.**

Source: Lloyd D. Johnston, Patrick M. O'Malley, Jerald G. Bachman, and John E. Schulenberg, *Monitoring the Future: National Survey Results on Drug Use, 1975–2005: Vol. II: College Students and Adults, 19–45* (NIH Publication No. 06–5884). Bethesda, MD: National Institute on Drug Abuse, 2006), www.monitoringthefuture.org.

person to turn to these other drugs. Rather, the social circumstances or personal problems that incline certain people toward drug abuse probably lead to marijuana first, possibly because of its accessibility. Even if marijuana were not available, such people would probably abuse other drugs eventually, such as alcohol, heroin, or cocaine. In addition, obtaining marijuana often brings the user into contact with people who also know how to obtain and use other drugs. It is probably these associations, not the marijuana itself, that produce the link between use of one drug and use of another.

Stimulants

There are enough stimulants produced legally in the United States each year to provide fifty doses to every person. About one-half of these legal stimulants find their way into the illegal drug trade (Schuckit, 2006). The term **stimulants** refers to the many *drugs whose major effect is to stimulate the central nervous system.* They can increase one's alertness, reduce fatigue, enhance a person's mood, and create a sense of excitement. They can also produce euphoria, confidence, a heightened sense of sexuality, increased energy, and

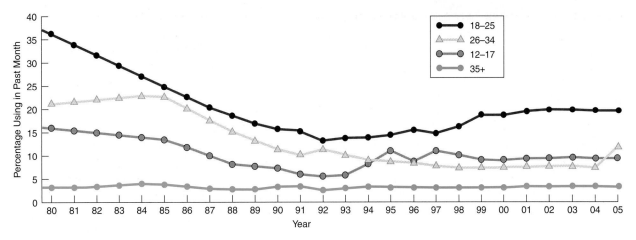

FIGURE 10.4 Percentage of People Who Have Used Any Illicit Drugs in the Past Month, by Age, 1980–2005.

Source: Substance and Mental Health Services Administration, Office of Applied Studies, *National Survey on Drug Use and Health* (formerly *National Household Survey on Drug Abuse*), (Washington, DC: U.S. Department of Health and Human Services, various years), <www.oas.SAMHSA.gov/NHSDA.htm>.

restlessness. Low doses of some stimulants, such as cocaine, can lead to enhanced motor performance, but higher doses result in a deterioration in performance and, at an extreme, convulsions. The stimulants produce tolerance, cross-tolerance, and physical and psychological dependence. Stimulants have many legitimate medical uses in the treatment of narcolepsy (falling asleep without warning), hyperactivity in children, and obesity. However, they are also widely abused.

Cocaine is a stimulant derived from coca leaves and has become the third most popular psychoactive drug

TABLE 10.1 Percentage Reporting Illicit Drug and Alcohol Use in the Past Month, by Type of Drug and Age Group, 1979–2005

Drug	1979	1985	1990	1995	2005
Marijuana/Hashish					
12–17	14.2	10.2	4.4	8.2	6.8
18–25	35.6	21.7	12.7	12.0	16.6
26–34	19.7	19.0	9.5	6.7	8.6
35+	2.9	2.6	2.4	1.8	3.0
Cocaine					
12–17	1.5	1.5	0.6	0.8	0.6
18–25	9.9	8.1	2.3	1.3	2.6
26–34	3.0	6.3	1.9	1.2	1.3
35+	0.2	0.5	0.2	0.4	0.6
Alcohol					
12–17	49.6	41.2	32.5	21.1	16.5
18–25	75.1	70.1	62.8	61.3	60.9
26–34	71.6	70.6	64.4	63.0	62.5
35+	59.7	57.5	49.5	52.6	53.3

SOURCE: Substance and Mental Health Services Administration, Office of Applied Studies, *National Survey on Drug Use and Health* (formerly *National Household Survey on Drug Abuse*), (Washington, DC: U.S. Department of Health and Human Services, various years), www.oas.SAMHSA.gov/NHSDA.htm.

in the United States after alcohol and marijuana. Today, one in six adults aged 26 to 34 have tried cocaine, compared with one in eight in the late 1970s. Among young people aged 18 to 25 years old, 13 percent had used it compared with 27 percent in 1979. However, there seem to be fewer current users now: Only 2 percent of the 18- to 25-year-olds used cocaine in the last month in 2005 compared with 9.9 percent in 1979. In fact, cocaine use seemed to have peaked between 1980 and 1985 and has shown a substantial decline since then (see Table 10.1 and Figures 10.1 and 10.5). However, there is evidence that the decline in cocaine use is among casual users rather than heavy users or addicts. For example, the rate of daily use of cocaine has not dropped much, whereas the rate among those who used cocaine in the last 30 days—presumably the casual users—has dropped significantly. In addition, although equal proportions of whites, African Americans, and Hispanic Americans have tried cocaine, whites are less likely to be current users than are the other two groups. So, cocaine use among whites tends to be more short-lived and probably more experimental (U.S. Department of Health and Human Services, 2006).

Cocaine used to be an expensive drug, and this limited its use. However, drug entrepreneurs discovered ways to produce cheap and potent drugs from cocaine, such as crack cocaine (Kuhn, Swartzwelder,

A. Trends in Annual Prevalence Among College Students vs. Others (1–4 Years Beyond High School)

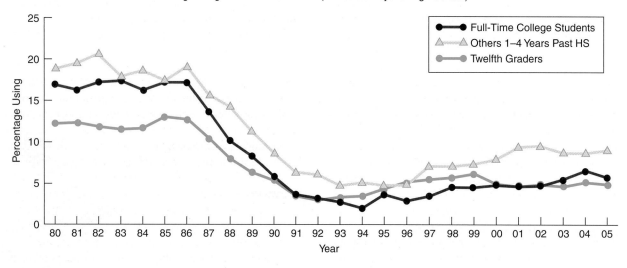

B. Trends in Annual Prevalence Among Male and Female College Students

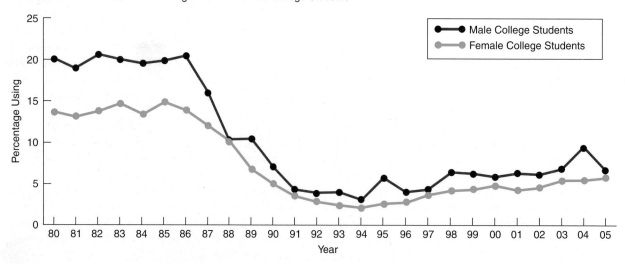

FIGURE 10.5 **Cocaine Use Among College Students, 1980–2005.**

Source: Lloyd D. Johnston, Patrick M. O'Malley, Jerald G. Bachman, and John E. Schulenberg, *Monitoring the Future: National Survey Results on Drug Use, 1975–2005: Vol. II: College Students and Adults, 19–45* (NIH Publication No. 06–5884). Bethesda, MD: National Institute on Drug Abuse, 2006), www.monitoringthefuture.org.

and Wilson, 1998). Crack gives an intense high—almost instantaneously because it is smoked—and is extremely addictive. Crack addicts sometimes engage in "binging," taking high doses in rapid succession, as often as every 10 minutes. Crack is sometimes used with other drugs, such as when combined with heroin to make a "speedball" that gives a quick and potent high. It is also cheap enough to be available even to poor people with a few extra dollars in their pocket. Because of this, crack has been an especially cruel plague for many poor communities. Even mothers receiving welfare can afford crack if they neglect their personal needs and those of their families. Consequently, some poor women have become addicted to crack, given birth to children who are addicted, and then neglected and even abandoned their children as their crack habits spun out of control. Under these circumstances, the problems of poverty and drug abuse become intertwined and mutually reinforcing.

High doses or chronic use of cocaine can produce a schizophrenia-like or paranoid psychotic reaction, manic-like states, severe depression, and panic states. Crack especially can be extremely dangerous. For example, the heart rates of users can increase abnormally, which in some cases can lead to cardiac arrest and death. Cocaine can produce as much dependence, tolerance, and withdrawal in those who use it as does heroin. Finally, for those who take cocaine intravenously, there is the danger of AIDS infection when dirty needles are shared with other users.

Other addictive drugs, called amphetamines, are synthetic central nervous system stimulants. One type of amphetamine, methamphetamine, is the most prevalent synthetic controlled substance clandestinely manufactured in the United States (Office of National Drug Control Policy, 2007). The effects of amphetamines are longer lasting than cocaine, but the two types of stimulants are quite similar in other respects. Some amphetamine abuse arises when people use these stimulants to help them accomplish socially acceptable tasks, such as studying long hours for an examination or putting in extra hours at work. For these people, the drug may have been obtained through medical prescriptions, or it might have been bought on the black market. These socially acceptable uses of amphetamines, however, can readily become abuses. Because tolerance develops, legitimate users may increase the dosage to the point at which withdrawal symptoms occur if use is discontinued. In addition, amphetamines are highly addicting, which can make quitting very difficult. A far more destructive type of amphetamine abuse is by "speed freaks" who take massive doses, often through intravenous injections, several times a day. This "run" might result in the person staying awake for many days (Milhorn, 1994). Sleeping and eating very little, people's judgment becomes impaired, and they feel overconfident, paranoid, and nervous. The feelings of overconfidence can lead to accidents. At the end of a "run," users will "crash," sleeping for long periods.

The use of stimulants such as cocaine and amphetamines has been linked with high levels of crime and violence, and the Applied Research insert explores this issue.

Depressants

The main effect of **depressants** is the opposite of stimulants: *They depress the central nervous system (CNS), along with having some analgesic, or painkilling, properties* (Schuckit, 2006). Alcohol is a depressant that we have discussed in a separate section. In addition, depressants include almost all sleeping medications (hypnotics or barbiturates) and antianxiety drugs (or the minor tranquilizers).

Barbiturates are a class of CNS depressants that are used as sedatives or painkillers. They can have effects similar to alcohol, particularly in reducing people's inhibitions. This can lead some to relax and others to become highly active, even aggressive. Their effects range from slight lethargy or sleepiness, to various levels of anesthesia, and finally to death from respiratory and heart depression. They can produce physical addiction, tolerance, cross-tolerance, and psychological dependence. Addiction to barbiturates is so severe that withdrawal is more dangerous than withdrawing from narcotics. Withdrawal can be accompanied by anxiety, nausea, cramps, hallucinations, and even fatal convulsions. Another serious problem with barbiturates is overdose. Especially with someone who uses a lot of depressants, including alcohol, it is easy to forget how much one has taken and inadvertently take too much. With their depressant effect, an overdose of barbiturates can slow a person's breathing and heart rate to the point where coma or death occurs. An overdose of barbiturates is also a common means of committing suicide.

An especially serious problem with barbiturates and other depressants is what drug abuse specialists call *potentiation*. This refers to what occurs when two depressants are taken at the same time: The effect of the combination is greater than would be expected from the action of either drug separately. The outcome can be an unexpected lethal dose. For example, people who consume a lot of alcohol—a depressant drug—and then decide to take a few sedative pills to sleep may inadvertently kill themselves due to respiratory failure or go into an irreversible coma. This lethal combination of barbiturates and alcohol is not uncommon.

Discovering the Role of Drugs in Crime and Violence

One of the enduring concerns with regard to drug use is the extent to which drugs are associated with crime and violence. Sociologists have studied this relationship in a number of different ways, both by interviewing drug users and by observing them as they buy and use drugs. What they have found about the link between drugs, crime, and violence is complicated and in some respects surprising.

Heavy users of stimulants, especially cocaine and amphetamines, are much more likely to commit crimes and be involved in violence than are users of most other psychoactive drugs (Lattimore et al., 1997). Part of the reason for this has to do with the effect of the drug: They are stimulants that can make people aggressive and lead them to feel overly confident,

paranoid, and impulsive. However, the biological effect of the drug is only part of the picture. Equally if not more important are the social circumstances that surround drug taking and drug dealing. For example, the link with violent crimes has to do in part with the criminal subculture in which "speed freaks" and crack cocaine users often participate—the hustles, fraud, and coercion that are a part of the illegal drug business (Brownstein, 2000; U.S. Department of Justice, 1992b). The street trade in cocaine illustrates this. Much more so than other illegal drugs and alcohol, cocaine, and especially crack, is bought in street-corner transactions where the buyer and seller do not know one another; it is a highly competitive market, users purchase drugs frequently in order to support their habit, and they often do not have a primary supplier with whom they

have a long-term relationship. This market situation provides many opportunities for violence and contains fewer inhibitions, such as a personal relationship between a buyer and a seller, which might prevent violence from occurring. In addition, prostitution, robbery, and violent crimes are ways of getting money to buy drugs and support oneself.

Among some drug users, gender has an interesting impact on the link between drugs and violence. Heavy drug users among males are most likely to be the perpetrators of violence, whereas among women drug users are the victims of violence. To oversimplify somewhat, the male users robbed stores or assaulted people, and the female users got beat up by their spouses or boyfriends.

Heavy users of heroin and cocaine tend to be polydrug users,

In earlier decades, barbiturates were often obtained legally through a physician's prescription and then used in ways for which they were not medically prescribed. Today, however, barbiturates are not prescribed as commonly as in the past, having been replaced by other drugs, including tranquilizers (Milhorn, 1994). As a consequence, use of barbiturates has declined, especially among the young.

The minor tranquilizers have many of the same effects as barbiturates, but in addition they can reduce anxiety and tension and produce a sense of wellbeing. The minor tranquilizers are also characterized by addiction, tolerance, and severe withdrawal symptoms. Medical use of tranquilizers is more common than sedatives. For many, this means taking tranquilizers to relieve the stresses and anxieties and to get over the "rough spots" of modern life. The danger, of course, is that a pattern of abuse can set in, often before the person realizes what has happened. Also, the combination of tranquilizers with other depressants can be deadly: A combination of alcohol and tranquilizers can produce coma and death.

The nonmedical use of sedatives and tranquilizers is more common among young adults and among whites than among nonwhites (U.S. Department of Health and Human Services, 2006).

Some barbiturate-like drugs were developed as nonaddicting and safe substitutes for barbiturates. Most have turned out to be very different indeed, sharing many dangers with barbiturates. This is especially true for methaqualone (Quaalude, Sopors), which has been widely abused.

Narcotics

Narcotics or **opiates** are *drugs whose main use is as analgesics or painkillers.* These include natural substances (opium, morphine, and codeine), minor chemical alterations of those natural substances (heroin, Dilaudid, and Percodan), and synthetic drugs (Darvon and Demerol). In addition to reducing pain, they produce drowsiness, mood changes, euphoria, and reduced mental functioning with high doses. They also depress the central nervous system

including heavy alcohol use. Social researchers at the Interdisciplinary Research Center for the Study of the Relations of Drugs and Alcohol to Crime interviewed heroin users recruited from the streets of Manhattan regarding the nondrug-related crimes that they had committed (Strug et al., 1984). These users reported committing many nondrug crimes during the thirty-six hours before the interviews. The investigators also asked about the users' drug and alcohol consumption patterns before and after committing crimes. It turned out that alcohol, not heroin, was the drug that these addicts had used most frequently during the thirty days before being interviewed, and they were more likely to report being under the influence of alcohol than any other drug. Regarding crime, the respondents reported being high on some drug during 37 percent of the crimes they committed. Of the crimes committed while on drugs, the perpetrator was high on alcohol alone or alcohol in combination with other drugs 63 percent of the time. The men reported that consuming alcohol near the time of their crimes "provided them with calmness and courage, and allowed them to take bigger risks, which, in their opinion, also allowed them to perform better" (Strug et al., 1984:561). Other studies of cocaine users reach the same conclusion: Alcohol has a stronger effect in causing crime and violence than does cocaine or heroin (Martin, Maxwell, and White, 2004). With respect to the use of money gained through criminal activities, the studies show that polydrug users are as likely to spend their criminal income on alcohol as on heroin. Researchers have also discovered that the need for money to buy alcohol was one of the motives for these men to commit their crimes. Although the general public tends to think that the high cost of heroin makes heroin addicts particularly prone to committing income-producing crimes, the economic resources of these addicts are so meager that the regular use of alcohol alone can generate the need to commit crimes.

This research, then, suggests ways in which popular stereotypes may be misleading. It shows how the complicated social fabric that surrounds drug selling, buying, and using can affect the commission of crimes and violence. It also demonstrates how the illegal drugs affect crime and behavior not simply because of the drug's detrimental affect on the body, but also because illegality changes the social context within which drugs are purchased and used.

and heart activity. The opiates produce tolerance and cross-tolerance. They are also highly addictive, with physical dependence developing very quickly.

Some opiate abusers misuse painkillers that they began taking for medical reasons. Health-care providers, especially physicians and nurses, have a high rate of such analgesic abuse, possibly because of its easy availability to them. Other opiate abusers purchase their narcotics in the street market. Many street abusers begin with the occasional use of opiates and then progress to daily use, with tolerance and dependence growing rapidly (Office of National Drug Control Policy, 1997). Daily heroin users who are physically addicted may spend $50 to $100 per day to support their habits. However, the image of the addicted narcotic addict should not be overdrawn. Some heroin users never progress beyond occasional use, called "chipping," and they continue this for many years, without physical addiction, and while maintaining a family, a circle of friends, and a job. They may spend as little as $15 to $20 for heroin on the days that they use it. This suggests that opiates, like alcohol, can be used semiregularly by some people while maintaining respectability and social stability and without contributing to a social problem (Kuhn, Swartzwelder, and Wilson, 1998). As for the link between crime and heroin abuse, it is clear that heroin addicts commit many crimes. However, as the Applied Research insert indicates, alcohol—a legal psychoactive drug—plays an important role in this criminal behavior.

There are probably eight hundred thousand heroin addicts in the United States (Office of National Drug Control Policy, 2007). Yet relatively few people have ever tried heroin. Among young adults—the heaviest users—only 1 percent claim to have ever used it, and that figure may be declining. There are other indications that heroin use has declined. For example, the number of arrests involving opiates has dropped, as has the number of cases of hepatitis and opiate-related mortalities. Still, the morbidity and mortality rate for street abusers of opiates is high, usually due to dirty needles and impure drugs. In addition, addicts who are accustomed to heavily diluted heroin may suffer an overdose if they happen to purchase some high-quality heroin. Finally, because of sharing dirty needles with HIV-infected drug users, heroin addicts run a considerable risk of HIV infection and thus contracting AIDS.

Heroin and many other opiates are far less damaging to the human body than are alcohol and tobacco (Trebach, 1982). Withdrawal from the opiates is also less dangerous than withdrawal from barbiturates or alcohol. In fact, opiate addicts can lead reasonably normal lives if they have a steady supply of the drug, use clean equipment, and know how to administer it properly. Many of the street abusers' problems arise from the illegality of the drugs: the high prices of black market drugs, the violence associated with the street drug trade, the varying quality and purity of drugs bought on the street, and the difficulty of keeping injection equipment sterile.

Hallucinogens

Hallucinogens, also called **psychedelics,** are *drugs that produce hallucinations, often of a visual nature.* Unlike marijuana, whose effect at normal doses is to change a person's mood or feelings, the hallucinogens produce illusions and hallucinations even at low doses. Awareness of sensory input and mental activity is intensified, thoughts are turned inward, and users are less able to differentiate between themselves and their surroundings. Hallucinogens have no accepted medical use in which their benefits outweigh their disadvantages. Examples of hallucinogens are lysergic acid diethylamide (LSD), psilocybin, peyote, mescaline, and a phenylisopropylamine known as DOM or STP. Some, such as LSD and STP, are synthetic, whereas others are plant products (peyote and mescaline come from cacti, and psilocybin comes from mushrooms—although not the ones sold by your friendly grocer). All are taken orally. Tolerance to hallucinogens builds up rapidly, and there is cross-tolerance between most hallucinogens (although not, as some believe, between hallucinogens and marijuana). There is no physical dependence or withdrawal.

The popularity of hallucinogens peaked in the 1960s, and their use has since been somewhat supplanted by stimulants and depressants. One problem with hallucinogens bought on the street is that you may not know what drug has actually been purchased. What a seller hawks as mescaline may actually be PCP or LSD. In addition, hallucinogens are sometimes adulterated with other drugs, such as amphetamines. This makes it difficult for users to know exactly what drug they are taking, and thus their reaction to it may be unpredictable, unpleasant, or dangerous. Another problem with hallucinogens is that usage can precipitate psychoses, with wild hallucinations, paranoid delusions, and mania. These psychoses are not common and usually clear within hours or days. If the psychoses persist, it is usually because of a preexisting psychiatric condition.

One of the most widely abused drugs, after alcohol, cocaine, and marijuana, is phencyclidine (PCP). It is inexpensive and relatively easy to synthesize by amateurs (Kuhn, Swartzwelder, and Wilson, 1998). The usual way of taking PCP is orally or through smoking, but it can also be injected or sprayed on other drugs. The evidence is still unclear as to whether PCP causes physical or psychological dependence, and there do not seem to be any withdrawal symptoms.

PCP in low doses creates a sense of euphoria, a lack of coordination, and an agitated emotional state. Moderate doses create a drunken-like condition with perceptual illusions. At still higher doses, PCP can produce psychosis. Especially with people who go on "runs" of two or three days of continual PCP ingestion, highly agitated and even violent behavior can occur. These people are often seen in hospital emergency rooms. Law enforcement officials experience serious problems in subduing suspects who are using PCP, because the suspects are often very difficult and dangerous to stop.

Another hallucinogen, which also has properties of an amphetamine, is methylenedioxymethamphetamine (MDMA), or "ecstasy." It reduces inhibitions and provides a euphoric rush like some amphetamines, but it also has some of the mind-expanding qualities of hallucinogens. However, many experts believe it is psychologically addictive and can cause cardiac problems as well as produce panic attacks, paranoia, and psychosis. As Figure 10.6 shows, use of ecstasy has increased substantially in recent years, especially among teenagers and young adults. It has become popular on the nightclub circuit and at all-night dance parties known as "raves." Also, organized drug traffickers have begun to market it aggressively because it is cheap to manufacture and produces large profits.

Explanations of Drug Abuse

Drug abuse is a very complicated process. Many factors—biological, psychological, social, and cultural—contribute to the problem. There is no one source of the problem and no one quick fix that will solve it.

Biological Explanations

There is now impressive evidence to suggest that heredity influences the likelihood of some people becoming

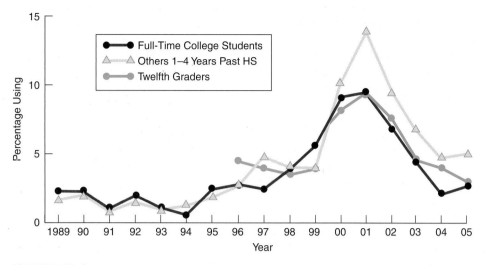

FIGURE 10.6 MDMA (Ecstasy) Use Among Teenagers and Young Adults, 1989–2005.

Source: Lloyd D. Johnston, Patrick M. O'Malley, Jerald G. Bachman, and John E. Schulenberg, *Monitoring the Future: National Survey Results on Drug Use, 1975–2005: Vol. II: College Students and Adults, 19–45* (NIH Publication No. 06–5884). Bethesda, MD: National Institute on Drug Abuse, 2006), www.monitoringthefuture.org.

alcoholic (Blum and Payne, 1991; Milhorn, 1994). People with an alcoholic parent are as much as six times more likely to become alcoholic themselves, even when raised apart from their biological parents in a nonalcoholic family. Although this heritability is found among men, it is not yet clear whether it applies to women.

The reasons for this susceptibility are still under debate (Schuckit, 2006). Alcoholics may develop a tolerance to alcohol more quickly, they may metabolize alcohol more quickly, or they may possess an inherited nutritional deficiency that is made up by alcohol. However, one very important point—especially when considering social policy relating to alcoholism—is that 60 to 65 percent of alcoholics do not exhibit this genetic link, and some alcoholics with the genetic link only became heavy drinkers under certain environmental conditions. As for biological mechanisms involved in addiction to drugs other than alcohol, there are a number of theories relating to tolerance, drug metabolism, and the like, but there is little evidence that such factors make some people more biologically susceptible to drug addiction.

Psychological Explanations

Psychological approaches to drug abuse posit that abuse arises from some psychological process or is the result of some emotional or personality disorder.

Social learning or reinforcement theories, for example, argue that people will repeat those actions that provide them with some reward or pleasure (Ray, 1988). Drugs provide experiences that some people find pleasurable: euphoria, relaxation, ease of tension, even hallucinations might be enjoyable to some. So people who feel uncomfortable at parties, for example, may find that alcohol, marijuana, or a depressant relaxes them so that they can talk, dance, and enjoy themselves. Drug use may then become a habitual way they relax or enjoy themselves. Given the number of stressful and tense situations that some people face in their daily lives, it is not surprising that the reinforcing properties of alcohol and other drugs can have these effects.

Psychodynamic theories claim that drug abuse is a consequence of flaws or weaknesses in people's personalities (Light, 1986). It may be, for example, that alcoholics are exceedingly dependent personalities who experienced rejection by their parents during childhood and have a compulsive need for love. The excessive use of alcohol can serve as a means of relieving anxiety when those unrealistic needs are not met. Another psychodynamic approach claims that it is a need for power, not dependency, that underlies excessive alcohol use. While drinking, men can fantasize about how strong and powerful they are and thus ignore feelings of weakness and inadequacy. Many studies have found that opiate addicts have very high rates of mental disorders, especially depression (Rounsaville et al., 1984).

Although personality and psychological processes are undoubtedly important in the lives of individuals, they are probably not sufficient, by themselves, to explain a deviant behavior such as drug abuse. For one thing, psychological factors by themselves would produce an abuse problem that is sporadic and intermittent. Yet, the societal drug problem is continuous and persistent because there are many social and cultural factors contributing to it. In addition, psychological problems have social sources, often in family experiences, and these social factors should be the focus of social policy. Finally, research results on the psychology of addiction have been contradictory. Some addicts exhibit psychological maladjustment, whereas others do not.

Sociological Explanations

Sociological explanations of drug abuse focus on the role of culture, social structure, and social interaction in precipitating drug abuse. We will review the insights that the three sociological perspectives shed on this problem.

THE FUNCTIONALIST PERSPECTIVE The functionalist approach focuses on the strains, inconsistencies, and contradictions in the social system that can contribute to the drug problem. In Chapter 9, Robert Merton's anomie theory of deviance and crime was discussed. It posits, in brief, that an inconsistency occurs when people are taught through the socialization process to pursue certain socially approved goals, such as success, but then are denied access to socially approved means of achieving those goals. Examples of people in anomic situations would be those who want to go to college but cannot afford it, a person whose business has failed, or a parent whose child has died. People can adapt to this anomie in many ways, such as crime, resignation, or outrage. Merton labeled one mode of adaptation *retreatism*: the rejection of the culturally approved goals and the importance of achieving them through the culturally approved means. Retreatists "drop out" or try to escape, and for some, this means using drugs or alcohol in the search for solace and forgetfulness.

Another mode of adaptation to anomie, discussed in Chapter 9, is *innovation:* an acceptance of the cultural goal of success but the use of socially disapproved, possibly illegal, means to achieve it. People in poor communities might be drawn into the illegal drug trade as a way to attain material success that would be more difficult or impossible to attain in conventional ways. Their benefiting from the drug trade helps to perpetuate the illegal drug business.

THE CONFLICT PERSPECTIVE The drug abuse problem is shaped in part by the exercise of social, political, and economic power. As we saw in Chapter 9, it is powerful groups in society that are in a position to define which crimes or which drugs will be sanctioned and made illegal. Over the years, powerful and respectable people have used alcohol, and it was not, until recently, even considered a "drug" to be linked with substances such as heroin and cocaine. In the 1980s and 1990s, the War on Drugs did not attack alcohol but rather cocaine and heroin. In fact, drug enforcement authorities have been criticized for what appears to be a war against mostly young male African Americans and Hispanics. The vast majority of those arrested in the War on Drugs are African American and Hispanic even though there are as many white drug users as African American and Hispanic. This could be interpreted to mean that the authorities may be more interested in creating the appearance of fighting drugs by attacking drug use among poor and minorities while largely ignoring the much more considerable drug use, both legal and illegal, among more affluent and influential groups. In the past thirty years, marijuana has gained a more respectable status—and legal penalties for its use have been reduced in many jurisdictions—primarily because middle-class, college-educated people have taken up its use. So what is considered a dangerous drug whose use is to be sanctioned by society depends on which groups have most control over the political and legal apparatus.

The conflict perspective points to another element of the drug abuse problem: Some groups benefit in economic and other ways from the consumption of drugs by others, and it is in their interests to make drugs available and to encourage their use. This issue is discussed in the International Perspectives insert in this chapter.

THE INTERACTIONIST PERSPECTIVE The interactionist approach is based on the premise that drug use and abuse arises from the social influences and pressures that can be found in particular contexts. Recall from Chapter 9 that cultural transmission theories view crime and drug abuse as learned behaviors that are transmitted through the socialization process of a particular culture or subculture. This learning occurs mainly in intimate groups, such as with family or friends, where people learn what drugs to use, where to buy them, how to use them, and even what the "high" from a particular drug is supposed to feel like. They also learn to value the use of particular drugs.

A person being introduced to cocaine, for instance, might be told by experienced users that cocaine is good because it makes one more perceptive, creative, and energetic, whereas alcohol is a downer. In other words, drug subcultures are important in promoting and maintaining patterns of abuse. People must have the opportunity and encouragement to use drugs and the willingness to take the consequences. Sociologists Richard Cloward and Lloyd Ohlin (1960), for example, have argued that youngsters with close ties to conventional groups and little access to drugs will not respond to teenage adjustment problems by turning to drugs. Instead, they will find other outlets for their energies or anxieties. It is the youths without access to legitimate opportunities and with some entrance into a drug subculture who are in danger of developing a pattern of drug abuse. Even an "alcoholic personality" may be somewhat immune from becoming an alcoholic if he or she is involved in a subculture in which drinking is severely sanctioned.

This cultural transmission of values regarding drug use can be illustrated by comparing patterns of alcohol use among some ethnic groups in the United States. Some groups, such as Jews and Italians, incorporate alcohol into family activities in a closely regulated fashion. Alcohol is consumed in moderation as a part of family rituals such as meals or picnics. This teaches youngsters to value the moderate use of alcohol and to view alcohol consumption as appropriate only in particular social contexts. Among such groups, many people use alcohol, but rates of alcoholism are fairly low. Among the Irish, on the other hand, it is acceptable for males to drink outside of the family context, and drinking is viewed as an approved way of reducing frustrations or tensions.

Future Prospects

Drug abuse is a serious and complex problem for which there is no quick and easy solution. Yet, some things can be done to keep it under reasonable control and to mitigate some of its more serious consequences. These programs focus on prevention, redefining the nature of the problem, or treatment.

Prohibition: The War on Drugs and Alcohol

One of the major preventive efforts of current social policy toward drugs of abuse is the legal prohibition of their use. Most such drugs, with the exception of alcohol, are illegal (when not used for medical reasons) and carry criminal penalties for their use. Does prohi-

bition work? Not by most assessments (Davenport-Hines, 2002; Miron, 2004). The effort to prohibit the use of alcohol through the Eighteenth Amendment to the U.S. Constitution (ratified in 1920) was an abysmal failure. People continued to drink, and organized crime flourished by supplying the "bootleg" liquor. The amendment also produced a certain cynicism toward law and government, as violations of the law were open and flagrant. The hypocrisy of the law was finally recognized by 1933 when the Eighteenth Amendment was repealed.

A similar experience has occurred over the past few decades as marijuana has become more popular. Although still illegal just about everywhere in the United States and carrying stiff prison terms in some jurisdictions, the use of marijuana flourishes. It is cheap, easy to obtain, and few people are punished for using it. There are lessons to be learned from our experience with alcohol and marijuana. When a practice is widespread, viewed as socially acceptable and even desirable by powerful groups, and brings economic gain to some interests, it is extremely difficult to eradicate through legislation. Laws will probably stop some people from using and abusing these drugs, and proponents of prohibition support it for this reason: They believe that it reduces the drug problem to below what it would be without such prohibition.

In fact, the War on Drugs was carved into law in the Anti-Drug Abuse Act of 1988. More police and narcotics agents have been sent out to track down drug users, stiffer and mandatory prison sentences have been given to those convicted, and boats and planes have swarmed over the Caribbean and Central America to catch drug importers. Despite spending billions of dollars each year, not much has changed. Casual use is down compared to the early 1980s, but up slightly in the past decade, and the crack cocaine and heroin epidemics are still blighting parts of our cities, and our prisons are bursting at the seams with people doing time for drug offenses. There are probably as many hard-core addicts as before, and there are as many drugs being produced in, or shipped into, this country as before. Illegal drugs are as easy to get today as before the War on Drugs. In addition, experts who have studied the changing trends in drug use do not attribute the decline in drug use since the early 1980s to vigorous law enforcement (Jacobsen and Hanneman, 1992). Instead, the drop in use has probably been due to the decline in the social acceptance of drugs, which had an impact on the casual users but not the serious drug addicts. Yet, despite the doubts of experts regarding the effectiveness of prohibition to control drug use, this policy still attracts considerable public support.

The Political Economy of the Global Drug Trade

Two young lawyers in San Francisco lay out some lines of cocaine for their friends at a party while thousands of miles away a Colombian peasant family, children and all, trudges along a dusty path into an isolated field. The two scenes seem worlds apart, but they are intimately linked through the political economy of the worldwide drug trade. The term *political economy* refers to the way in which politics and the exercise of power influence the production and distribution of economic resources. Colombia exports billions of dollars of cocaine each year—its biggest single export (Forero, 2006; U.S. Department of State, 2007). For a poor country like Colombia, that is big business. For thousands of Colombian peasants, their very survival depends on cultivating the drugs that feed the acquired illicit tastes of those lawyers along with the many other people in the United States who use cocaine or smoke marijuana. Marijuana and cocaine produce more foreign exchange for Colombia than do coffee and cut flowers, the country's two chief legal exports. Thousands of Colombians depend on the coca trade for their livelihood. Illicit drugs worldwide may generate annual revenues of $500 billion. As one South American peasant farmer put it, "I don't care how much pressure [the United

States] puts on us to stop growing coca, we will never give this up because we have no other means to survive" (Sims, 1995). Farmers in many other countries that export illegal drugs to the United States would echo those sentiments.

All coca leaf and much marijuana are grown in Central and South American countries, primarily Bolivia, Colombia, Ecuador, Jamaica, Mexico, and Peru (Forero, 2006; U.S. Department of State, 2007). In Asia, the major drug producers are Myanmar (formerly Burma), Cambodia, Laos, Thailand, Pakistan, and Afghanistan. This is where most opium poppies are grown. One goal of American drug enforcement policy is to reduce the overseas production of drugs and their importation into the United States. In fact, by law, the president of the United States is required to cut off foreign aid to countries that do not make progress in reducing their drug crops. This leaves the United States with the dilemma of whether to cut economic assistance and other types of foreign aid to countries that do not cooperate. Such cuts may exacerbate a major factor underlying the international drug trade: Poverty and economic underdevelopment make the growing and selling of

drugs a way for some people to survive.

Why do these countries refuse to cooperate? Part of the reason is the difficulty of controlling the illicit growing of marijuana, coca, and opium poppies. Much of the cultivation takes place in isolated, hard-to-reach parts of these countries, and the law enforcement authorities are often not equal to the task. In addition, the criminals running the illegal drug traffic are powerful, sometimes more powerful than the government. In Bolivia and Myanmar, for example, wealthy and well-organized drug traffickers have actually taken control of the areas where drugs are produced, killing government officials or soldiers who enter without permission. In Colombia, many judges, politicians, police officers, and other government officials have died in drug-related assassinations. Often, the governments have been corrupted by bribes from drug traffickers or by direct participation of government officials in the traffic. Finally, the drug crops, although illegal, are often a significant source of economic support and foreign dollars. To successfully control the drug trade would be a severe economic blow to these countries.

When we understand the extent to which the drug problem in the United States is linked with

Legalization

Opponents of prohibition point not only to its ineffectiveness but also to the fact that it infringes on the rights of people who use drugs without abusing them (Miron, 2004). As we have seen, many people use

alcohol, marijuana, cocaine, LSD, and even narcotics in a limited and periodic fashion for recreational purposes, without creating a health or addiction hazard. In addition, efforts at prohibition have contributed to a swelling prison population that is expensive to maintain and that ruins many lives and families. Over half a

Afghan farm workers walk through a field of opium poppy plants. Poppies are also used to produce heroin, and Afghanistan is one of the largest suppliers of opium and heroin to the world drug trade.

worldwide political and economic issues, the complexity of the problem becomes clearer. Lest we think that the political economy of drugs is primarily a foreign problem, estimates place marijuana as one of the largest, if not the largest, cash crop in California, Kentucky, West Virginia, and Tennessee, and 25 percent of the demand for marijuana in the United States is satisfied by marijuana grown in the United States (Clines, 2001). For some remote counties of northern California and rural Appalachia, growing marijuana is very lucrative for those willing to take the risk, and their profits help support other local businesses, such as small-town banks.

So, a key element of the drug problem in the United States is the many sources—domestic and international—that give people a host of opportunities to purchase and use drugs. Controlling the drug problem depends on our ability to reduce these sources of supply. Yet, so many powerful interest groups benefit from policies that make it difficult to reduce the supply that there is some pessimism about how successful these efforts can be.

million people are arrested for possession (not sale) of marijuana each year, getting a lifelong criminal record as well as possibly spending time in prison. Finally, whether inadvertently or by design, African Americans and Hispanic Americans have borne the brunt of the War on Drugs, being much more likely to be caught and sent to prison for illegal drug use than are white drug users.

Responding to these and other problems with the prohibition strategy, some policy analysts suggest that the "single-minded pursuit of a 'drug-free society' is quixotic" (Nadelmann, 1998:112). Instead, we need to recognize that drugs, although certainly not desirable, are probably here to stay. Some of these policymakers call for a "harm reduction" approach: learning to live with drugs in such a way that they cause the least harm. To this end, some proponents argue for giving marijuana and a few other drugs the same status as alcohol: legal but highly controlled substances. A more popular stance is to *decriminalize* the use of these drugs by making simple possession of them for one's own use either a misdemeanor or a noncriminal offense punishable by a fine. In fact, at one time or another in the past thirty years, eleven states decriminalized marijuana, although some have rescinded those changes.

Proponents of legalization also point to the problems created because of the illegality of some drugs—their high cost and the crime and violence associated with obtaining them. Legalization, they argue, is one way of alleviating these problems. Both with the prohibition of alcohol in the 1920s and with the illegal drugs today, powerful and violent crime syndicates emerged to supply these substances. Because of the enormous amount of money involved, such organized crime can also have a corrupting influence on law enforcement agencies and elected officials. This has happened in South America and in the United States, where some drug enforcement agents have been found guilty of drug trafficking. If drugs were legal, they could be supplied by legitimate corporations; crime syndicates would not move in and other problems created by the illegality of drugs would be reduced. It has also been suggested that legalizing marijuana, the mildest of the illicit drugs, would have another advantage: It would help sever the connection of marijuana use with drug dealers. If marijuana could be purchased legally, one less incentive for involvement with drug pushers would exist. The Policy Issues insert explores the experiences of some other societies that have legalized or decriminalized some drugs.

The closest the United States comes to legalizing drugs (other than alcohol) are drug maintenance programs, which provide addicts with drugs to substitute for the illegal drugs they were taking. The most common such drug is methadone, a synthetic opiate that

POLICY ISSUES

Should Drug Use Be Decriminalized in the United States?

The issue of whether to prohibit, decriminalize, or legalize some drugs in the United States has been a long-standing one. Insight into the pros and cons of doing so can be gained by looking at the experiences of other nations that have pursued one version or another of these policies (Bertram et al., 1996; Nadelmann, 1998; Zimmer and Morgan, 1997). The Netherlands decriminalized drugs in 1976. Drug users and small-time dealers are not prosecuted, whereas large drug dealers and those who sell to minors are. Drug use in the Netherlands since then has not increased and may have declined somewhat. The consumption of marijuana and hashish, for example, declined after decriminalization. With marijuana and hashish widely available in Dutch cities, consumption of more serious drugs such as heroin has also declined. The Netherlands has fewer hard-drug addicts than other Western European countries, far less of a drug problem, and a significantly lower death rate due to drug overdose than does the United States. There is also a very low incidence of AIDS among intravenous drug users. The Netherlands treats drug addiction as a health problem rather than a criminal one, and this creates a climate in which addicts can be open about their drug use and seek treatment for both their health and addiction problems.

Great Britain has experimented with policies to make drugs legally available, but in a somewhat different way from the Netherlands. Throughout the 1960s, physicians in Britain could prescribe opiates and cocaine for their patients if they needed them, even if the need was to prevent the physical or mental symptoms that the person would suffer if the drug were withdrawn. In other words, physicians could prescribe drugs to maintain an addiction, although they had to be convinced that maintaining the addiction was in the patient's best interest, possibly because there was little chance of successfully kicking the habit. There was still a black market in drugs in Great Britain because some addicts could not get a physician's prescription whereas others sought higher dosages than the government would permit.

By the end of the 1960s, Britain had begun its own "war on drugs" in response to an increase in the illegal use of stimulants, sedatives, and hallucinogens. Greater limitations were placed on physicians' ability to prescribe heroin and cocaine. Physicians could still prescribe these drugs to nonaddicts and to addicts in limited circumstances, but special licenses were needed to prescribe addiction maintenance doses to addicts, and the licenses were given only to practitioners in drug abuse clinics. Official government policy was that addicts are to be weaned off drugs as quickly as possible. However, by the late 1980s, in part in

is prescribed for addicts who enroll in government-sponsored treatment programs. Methadone is itself highly addicting and leads to withdrawal, but its benefits over heroin are that the effects of methadone last longer (twenty-four hours as opposed to six hours for heroin) and people do not develop tolerance to methadone. What is called a "blocking dose" of methadone will block the euphoric effects of heroin, thus negating the motivation for continuing heroin use. The goal of the methadone maintenance program is to lower the dosage of methadone to a "maintenance" level at which withdrawal symptoms are prevented and there are few undesirable side effects. Methadone also does not induce much of a "high," so the person is sufficiently clear-headed and coherent to hold a job and lead a normal life.

Methadone maintenance programs are highly controversial. Critics argue that they merely replace one addiction with another, which is true, and that many addicts return to heroin and other drugs (Belluk, 2003). There is also a black market in methadone supplied in part by addicts in treatment who sell rather than take their methadone, and some methadone addicts get high by taking nonopiates, such as cocaine, whose effects are not blocked by methadone. Supporters argue that many addicts in methadone programs are free of any addiction, including methadone, after two years and are much less likely to be arrested and more likely to hold a job. Other studies show that addicts in maintenance programs use less heroin and other drugs, are less likely to become HIV positive, and have lower death rates than those not enrolled in such programs (Nadelmann, 1998; Yancovitz et al., 1991). New maintenance drugs are being developed that alleviate the craving for or blunt the euphoria of alcohol or drugs but that also have fewer negative effects than does methadone.

Primary Prevention

As used by drug abuse specialists, the term **primary prevention** refers to *preventing drug problems before they begin*. The government has established a three-front drug war focusing on primary prevention. One effort is to use educational programs to alert

response to the spread of AIDS among addicts sharing needles, drug policy in Great Britain has swung partially back to a less restrictive approach. Doctors have been given more authority to dispense drugs to addicts.

Since tightening up the drug laws, addiction rates have risen substantially in Great Britain. However, this may be due to worsening social conditions for lower-income groups during the 1970s and 1980s, with declining economic productivity and fewer resources going into education, job-training, child-care, housing, and health-care programs. Drugs seem to be a common refuge when other problems—poverty, racism, family dissolution—become more severe.

Portugal recently launched a drug policy based on the idea that drug abusers are victims who need help rather than criminals who need jail (Holley, 2001). Portugal decriminalized all drug possession and use when there is no drug selling involved. Anyone caught with drugs is brought before a commission that can impose punishments such as a fine, loss of a driver's license, or community service. The commission also directs users toward services that will help with their medical and addiction problems. Those who sell drugs still go to prison.

These less punitive approaches seem to work reasonably well for countries like the Netherlands and Great Britain. (Portugal's is too new to be assessed.) They have far fewer narcotics addicts than the United States does, and crime, death, and health problems associated with the use of narcotics are lower there than in the United States. Would such policies work in the United States? They might have some benefits, especially in terms of lowering the very high crime rate linked with heroin and cocaine use. Experience in these and other countries does suggest that decriminalization or legalization of illegal drugs could produce a modest increase in drug use, but not a lot, and most of the increase would be among people who tend to use drugs whether they are illegal or not (Miller, 1991). However, such policies would be no panacea: They would by no means eliminate, and possibly not even reduce, drug abuse. But the harsh, punitive approach currently applied in the United States hasn't been notably successful either.

Interventionist		Laissez-Faire
Prohibition on drugs	Decriminalize drugs	Legalize drugs

people to the dangers of drugs and instill responsible attitudes toward drug use. The second front is to interdict the drug traffic now flowing across our borders from overseas, and the third is to reduce production of drug crops by other nations.

Most experts agree that the best way to attack the drug problem is to reduce the demand for drugs. Educational programs try to do this by teaching youth that drugs are risky and dangerous, by using peers and adults to serve as role models to influence youth against the use of drugs, and by providing tips for how to resist the temptation of drugs (Botvin, 1998; Ellickson, 1998). Research on these programs shows that they can and do work and that more resources devoted to them would be useful in keeping young people off drugs. However, each program needs to be carefully evaluated and monitored because some of them don't work, some don't work with all young people, and some are not effective with all drugs. For example, one of the more popular such programs in recent years has been Drug Abuse Resistance Education or D.A.R.E. (Dukes, Stein, and Ullman, 1997; Wysong and Wright, 1995). The overall assessment of this program is that is has little effect. It has been impossible to this point, for example, to show that D.A.R.E. produces lower rates of drug use, at least for most drugs. Supporters of programs like D.A.R.E., who have a significant stake in seeing their programs as effective, have criticized the research as poorly done. Yet, the bottom line is that no good research currently exists that shows these programs to be effective. However, other drug prevention educational programs have been shown to work.

Border interdiction of drugs focuses on reducing the supply of drugs, and the results here have been meager. Experts estimate that only 10 percent of the drugs smuggled into the United States are seized (Miron, 2004). The illegal drug trade is so lucrative that people are willing to risk substantial punishments, and profits can be made even when 50 to 90 percent of a smuggler's drugs are confiscated. Controlling drug production overseas has been discussed earlier in the International Perspectives insert.

Rehabilitation and Therapeutic Communities

Many drug abusers can be rehabilitated if they are given proper treatment, such as counseling, methadone maintenance, or job training. Among adolescents at high risk of abusing drugs, school-based social support programs have proven that they can reduce the likelihood of future involvement in drugs (Eggert and Herting, 1991). By enhancing communication, empathy, and helping between students and teachers, these programs offer students an alternative to drugs. Most experts agree that making drug treatment programs available to all who desire them is more effective and less expensive in controlling drug use than either drug interdiction or law enforcement efforts to arrest and convict drug users. Expanding drug treatment programs would be an important step toward significantly reducing the drug problem (Goldstein and Kalant, 1990). However, all these rehabilitation programs cost money, and much of the funds for the War on Drugs have been channeled into law enforcement and drug interdiction, leaving relatively little for rehabilitation. A real weak spot is in the provision of drug treatment programs for prison inmates. Even though drug and alcohol abuse are strong contributing factors in the commission of many crimes, fewer than one in five prisoners who need drug treatment receive any care at all before being released (Wren, 1998).

One of the more widespread types of treatment programs for drug addicts is the therapeutic community in which group involvement, social support, and group pressure are used to help addicts quit taking drugs (De Leon, 1995). These programs are often run by addicts who are drug free. One of the best known therapeutic communities is Alcoholics Anonymous (AA), which was established by two alcoholics in 1935 to help them quit drinking. AA has more than a half million members. The first step in the AA program is for people to admit publicly that they are alcoholics, helpless before alcohol, and need help from others. AA is organized and run by volunteers and costs nothing. Meetings are open to anyone, drunk or sober, and even in small towns there are meetings held practically every day. At these meetings, people talk about their problems, what alcohol has done to them, and their fears of returning to drink. Others provide emotional support and encouragement and help members deal with their problems. There are also groups for the spouses of alcoholics (Al-Anon) and the children of alcoholics (Alateen).

There are also therapeutic communities for abusers of drugs other than alcohol. Narcotics Anonymous is very similar to AA but focuses on narcotics addicts. The Odyssey House, Phoenix House, and Daytop Village are therapeutic communities that provide housing, counseling, and work for people trying to shake the drug habit. Many of these programs depart from the AA approach in that people must sever ties with former associates and live for a time in the community itself. This regulation is based on the assumption that these former associations may have contributed to the person's drug problem, and it also

These U.S. Coast Guard personnel are seizing drugs that were about to enter the United States. Such drug interdiction efforts are an expensive and not very effective means of primary prevention of drug problems.

gives the community considerable control over its members. Acceptance by peers is a prime force in these communities. They offer strong emotional support, but some have been accused of being highly authoritarian, demanding complete conformity to the rules of the group.

Research on the effectiveness of therapeutic communities is difficult to conduct because of problems in finding representative samples of members and of non-member addicts to compare them with. The available evidence, however, clearly suggests that these programs work for many. Although relapse (a return to the use of drugs) is common, many members successfully refrain from using alcohol and other drugs for long periods. Those people with the best likelihood of success are older addicts who are married, have a job, and have a history of relatively few delinquent or criminal acts. However, therapeutic communities are completely ineffective with the millions of addicts who do not believe they have a problem with drugs.

Behavior Modification

The social learning theory of drug abuse says that people become addicted because drugs provide them with personal pleasure or rewards. One therapeutic approach suggests that addicts might be weaned from drugs by making drug taking unpleasant. This is known to drug abuse professionals as behavior modification. One form of this technique, used to treat alcoholism, is aversion therapy, in which the act of drinking alcohol is associated with some unpleasant experience. In some cases, a drug called Antabuse is used because it induces nausea and vomiting if the person taking it drinks any alcohol. A more controversial form of aversion therapy uses electrical shocks administered to a person each time he or she takes a drink of alcohol. The theory behind these treatments is that associating alcohol consumption with a painful or unpleasant experience will eventually lead the person to perceive alcohol consumption itself as undesirable. Aversion therapy is of limited utility because it depends on the cooperation of the alcoholic, but it has been helpful for some addicts who have not had success with other approaches.

Social Policy and Public Pressure

A few decades ago, the problem of alcoholism was shrouded by guilt and shame. Many alcoholics were unwilling to admit that they had a problem, and their families and friends were so embarrassed that they covered for the alcoholic when he or she got into trouble. Public sentiment has changed considerably. Alcoholism is now viewed as a medical problem that

This meeting of Alcoholics Anonymous represents one type of therapeutic community. While it is difficult to conduct research on the overall effectiveness of such communities, they are clearly useful in helping some people stay clean of alcohol and other drugs.

can be treated with tested methods. Government support, along with funding from private sources, has helped in the development of an extensive network of support services dealing with problems of drug abuse. Today, considerably less stigma is attached to the problem, and there are many places to seek help. Employers have pitched in with employee assistance programs (EAPs) that offer confidential help for employees with drug or alcohol problems. Employers have found that they benefit by rehabilitating, rather than terminating, a trained and experienced employee.

There has also been considerable public pressure to do something about the public dangers created by some forms of drug usage, such as those who drink alcohol and drive. Groups such as Mothers Against Drunk Driving (MADD) and Students Against Drunk Driving (SADD) have lobbied effectively at both the state and the national level for laws that have an impact on the problem. In response, states have raised the drinking age to twenty-one, and some have even outlawed such things as "two-for-one" happy-hour specials. Bartenders can now be held legally responsible if they serve liquor to someone who is drunk and the person gets into a traffic accident. State courts have even ruled that

the host of a party is responsible for the behavior of a guest if the host serves the guest enough alcohol to get drunk (Mincer, 1985). In short, the courts, the legislatures, and the public are taking an increasingly tough posture toward some drug problems, such as drunk driving.

Still another hotly contested social policy issue that has involved much public pressure is drug testing. The Drug-Free Workplace Act of 1988 requires companies with federal contracts to make an effort to maintain a drug-free workplace. Some companies do random testing of their employees whereas other companies limit testing to hiring or when there is an accident or some other indication of a drug problem. Half of all full-time workers are employed in settings where some form of testing occurs (Zhang, Huang, and Brittingham, 1999). Drug testing in the workplace, it is claimed, would help locate those with substance abuse problems and offer them assistance. The American Civil Liberties Union (ACLU) and other opponents of routine drug testing, on the other hand, maintain that drug testing violates rights of privacy and the Constitution's prohibition against unreasonable search and seizure. Furthermore, the ACLU questions the accuracy, validity, and reliability of such tests. In addition, the testing detects relatively few drug users, and most of those are occasional marijuana users who are probably not bad workers and no threat on the job. Drug testing is likely to remain a hotly debated issue over the next few years.

Social Reform

Although all the things discussed thus far are important in the effort to control drug abuse, probably the most difficult step is to recognize that a serious and widespread drug problem says something about the United States. As one expert on drug issues put it:

> Endemic drug abuse tells us that something is fundamentally amiss in our *social* organization.

Healthy societies are not overwhelmed by hard drugs. Those that *are* overwhelmed, around the world, are invariably riddled with other preventable social problems. (Currie, 1993:280)

Many of those problems, of course, are the topic of this book: fractured families, inequities based on race or ethnicity or gender, high levels of violence, a lack of economic opportunity for many people, and so on. Not all drug abuse is caused by these conditions, but the pervasiveness of the problem in the United States is in part due to people's reactions to the negative social conditions they confront. As the United States makes progress in alleviating these problems, the drug problem will also likely ease.

LINKAGES The drug epidemic has ravaged parts of our cities with unacceptably high rates of crime (Chapter 12) and helped spread diseases such as AIDS through the sharing of dirty needles (Chapter 4). Drug addiction has also destabilized many families (Chapter 3), when poor parents become addicted to crack cocaine, heroin, or alcohol.

STUDY AND REVIEW

Summary

1. The use of drugs in one form or another is widespread in human societies. Opinions about drug use vary widely, with some groups arguing for a complete ban on all drugs and others opting for the freedom to use drugs as people see fit. Drug use by itself is not a social problem; drug abuse refers to the continued use of psychoactive substances at a level violating approved social practices. Drug abuse is costly to society in terms of accidents; crime; and family, work, and health problems.

2. People in the United States consume many different kinds of drugs; some are legal, whereas others are illegal. A legal drug, alcohol, is regarded as the United States' most severe drug problem when it is used to excess. The level of marijuana use in society is far lower than that of alcohol. Debate continues regarding how damaging marijuana really is to society. Stimulants refer to the many drugs that stimulate the central nervous system, including cocaine and amphetamines. Depressants, most notably the barbiturates and tranquilizers, have the opposite effect, depressing the central nervous system, and have some painkilling properties. Narcotics are drugs whose main use is as analgesics or painkillers. Hallu-

cinogens or psychedelics are drugs that produce hallucinations, often of a visual nature.

3. There are different explanations of drug abuse. Biological explanations suggest that hereditary factors may help make some people prone to addiction to various drugs. Psychological approaches to drug abuse posit that abuse arises from some psychological process or is the result of some emotional or personality disorder. Sociological explanations focus on the role of culture, social structure, and social interaction in precipitating drug abuse.

4. Drug abuse is a serious and complex problem for which there is no quick and easy solution. Most programs involving such solutions focus on either prevention, redefining the nature of the problem, or treatment. One major preventive effort of current social policy is legal prohibition. Opponents of this approach favor legalization, including such alternative drug treatment programs as methadone maintenance. Another strategy is primary prevention, which refers to preventing drug problems before they begin. One of the more widespread types of treatment programs for drug addicts is the therapeutic community. Another approach involves behavior modification in the form of aversion therapy. Social policy and public pressure are also

Many groups are actively promoting social policies relating to drug and alcohol abuse, and today these groups typically use the Internet to spread their proposals and recruit new members. Search for Web sites maintained by such organizations. Alcoholics Anonymous maintains a Web site **(www.alcoholics-anonymous.org)** where, among other things, you can test your knowledge of alcoholism. The group Common Sense for Drug Policy **(www.csdp.org)** raises many questions about our existing drug policies and tries to educate the public about alternative policies. Two other organizations to look for would be Drug Abuse Resistance Education (D.A.R.E.), which educates schoolchildren to avoid drug use entirely, and National Organization for the Reform of Marijuana Laws (NORML), which promotes easing the restrictions against the use of marijuana. There are, of course, many other organizations. For each of the organizations you find, describe its basic policy regarding drug use and abuse and whether it is basically an interventionist or laissez-faire stance. Also determine the extent to which its position on drug issues is supported by valid research.

It is also valuable to explore the various Web sites mentioned in Chapter 9 that relate to crime and the criminal justice system. You can explore the complex issue of to what extent crime is related to or caused by the use of illegal drugs.

This chapter contrasted U.S. drug policy with the policies of some European nations that approach the issue as more of a health problem than a crime problem. You can learn more about these harm-reduction policies at the Web site of the Netherlands Institute of Mental Health and Addiction **(www.trimbos.nl).** This site has links to online academic journals as well as research and other organizations focusing on drug and alcohol problems. The World Health Organization also has a Web site **(www.who.int)** where you can learn about European policies on drugs and alcohol. As an exercise, it would be useful to look for other Web sites that explore the drug policies of nations other than the United States.

The Allyn & Bacon Social Problems Supersite **(http://wps.ablongman.com/ab_socialprob_sprsite_1)** contains material on drug problems.

important in the future prospects on drug abuse. Groups such as Mothers Against Drunk Driving (MADD) and Students Against Drunk Driving (SADD) are current examples.

Key Terms

alcoholism	hallucinogens
cross-dependence	narcotics
cross-tolerance	opiates
dependence	primary prevention
depressants	psychedelics
drug	psychoactive drugs
drug abuse	stimulants
drug addiction	tolerance

Multiple-Choice Questions

1. The drugs that constitute a social problem are typically limited to
   a. medically prescribed drugs.
   b. illegal drugs.
   c. psychoactive drugs.
   d. stimulants, depressants, and opiates.
2. As used by professionals in the field, the term *drug addiction* refers to
   a. physical dependence on a drug.
   b. both tolerance and dependence on a drug.
   c. either tolerance or dependence on a drug.
   d. the excessive use of a drug that violates socially approved practices.
3. Which of the following represents the most severe drug problem in the United States?
   a. heroin
   b. alcohol
   c. cocaine
   d. amphetamines
   e. stimulants

4. Which of the following statements is true regarding the social characteristics of those at risk of becoming an alcoholic?
   a. Women are at greater risk than men.
   b. Lower SES people are at greater risk than higher SES people.
   c. The old are at greater risk than the young.
   d. Jews are at greater risk than Catholics.
5. Since 1980, the percentage of college students who use marijuana has
   a. skyrocketed.
   b. increased gradually.
   c. stayed fairly steady.
   d. declined somewhat.
6. Cocaine would be classified as a
   a. stimulant.
   b. depressant.
   c. hallucinogen.
   d. narcotic.
7. Which category of drugs has the least likelihood of producing physical dependence?
   a. alcohol
   b. cocaine
   c. heroin
   d. hallucinogens
8. According to the functionalist perspective, drug abuse occurs because
   a. people carry inherited tendencies toward addiction.
   b. some people benefit in economic ways when others become addicted to drugs.
   c. strains, inconsistencies, and contradictions in the social system affect people.
   d. childhood experiences lead people to develop an "addictive personality."
9. Methadone maintenance is a program for treating
   a. alcohol addiction.
   b. addiction to hallucinogens.
   c. heroin addiction.
   d. cocaine addiction.
   e. amphetamine addiction.
10. Therapeutic communities would probably be least effective in treating which category of drug addict?
   a. alcoholics
   b. heroin addicts
   c. young addicts
   d. addicts who do not believe they have a problem with drugs
   e. addicts who have been taking drugs for a long time

True/False Questions

1. According to the text, caffeine is one of the drugs that is considered to contribute to the social problem of drug abuse.
2. According to the text, drug dependence and drug abuse are the same thing.
3. The percentage of people in the United States who use marijuana is about the same as the percentage who use alcohol.
4. Heroin is classified as an opiate.
5. Crack addicts are more likely to be highly active and paranoid while high than are heroin addicts.
6. The nonmedical use of sedatives and tranquilizers is more common among the elderly than the young.
7. MDMA, or ecstasy, is a hallucinogen.
8. Social scientists have concluded that there is very little evidence to support the idea that genetics or biology plays a part in who becomes addicted to alcohol or other drugs.
9. Only about 10 percent of the drugs smuggled into the United States are seized by border interdiction programs.
10. Research has shown that school-based social support programs for adolescents at risk of abusing drugs can reduce involvement in drugs.

Fill-In Questions

1. _____ refers to a situation in which higher and higher doses of a drug are needed to achieve the same effect.
2. If the withdrawal symptoms of one drug are alleviated by taking another drug in the same pharmacological class, then the first drug possesses _____.
3. Drugs whose major effect is to stimulate the central nervous system are called _____.
4. Amphetamines are classified as a _____.
5. Methaqualone, or Quaalude, is classified as a _____.
6. The term "chipping" refers to _____.
7. _____ theories argue that people become addicted to drugs because they gain some reward or pleasure from using drugs repeatedly.
8. The _____ perspective posits that patterns of drug use and abuse are due to the cultural transmission of values.
9. _____ is a synthetic opiate that is sometimes prescribed for heroin addicts.

10. The three-front focus of primary prevention of drug use in the United States is (a) border interdiction, (b) reduction of overseas production, and (c) _____.

Matching Questions

_____ 1. aversion therapy
_____ 2. potentiation
_____ 3. dependence
_____ 4. stimulant
_____ 5. speed freak
_____ 6. marijuana
_____ 7. LSD
_____ 8. psychodynamic theory
_____ 9. narcotics anonymous
_____ 10. primary prevention

A. craving for a drug
B. amphetamine abuser
C. alcoholism treatment
D. a psychedelic
E. therapeutic community
F. combined effect of two depressants
G. has both sedative and hallucinogenic properties
H. border interdiction
I. psychological explanation of drug abuse
J. produce tolerance and dependence

Essay Questions

1. Define the terms *drug, drug abuse,* and *drug addiction.* What do the terms *tolerance* and *dependence* mean in this context?
2. Summarize the costs that society must pay because of alcohol and drug abuse.
3. What are the social characteristics of people who are at a greater risk of becoming alcoholics?
4. What are the problems that the use of marijuana can produce for people?
5. Why are stimulants such as cocaine and amphetamines often associated with violence?
6. Describe the political economy of drug use in the world. Link it up with the conflict perspective.
7. What are the pros and cons of attempting to prohibit the use of drugs such as alcohol and marijuana?
8. What are the pros and cons of legalizing the drugs that are currently illegal?
9. What efforts have been made in the realm of the primary prevention of drug abuse? How effective have they been?
10. Summarize the research on the effectiveness of therapeutic communities in treating addictions to alcohol and other drugs.

For Further Reading

Howard Abadinsky. *Drugs: An Introduction,* 5th ed. Belmont, CA: Wadsworth/Thomson Learning, 2004. This book provides an excellent overview of the drug problem in modern societies, covering history, causes, treatment, and social policy.

William Adler. *Land of Opportunity: One Family's Quest for the American Dream in the Age of Crack.* New York: Atlantic Monthly Press, 1995. This is a fascinating tale of one family's involvement in the drug trade in Detroit, detailing both fortunes made and prison time earned. It illuminates how the illegal drug trade operates.

David J. Hanson. *Preventing Alcohol Abuse: Alcohol, Culture, and Control.* Westport, CT: Praeger, 1995. This book reviews data about drinking and drinking problems from around the world and uses them to develop a social policy for the United States that will avoid the pitfalls of current policies.

Philip Jenkins. *Synthetic Panics: The Symbolic Politics of Designer Drugs.* New York: New York University Press, 1999. This book takes a social constructionist approach, looking at the social process involved in how certain kinds of drugs and drug use become defined as social problems.

Craig Reinarman and Harry G. Levine, eds. *Crack in America: Demon Drugs and Social Justice.* Berkeley: University of California Press, 1997. This book of readings offers an excellent overview of the social, political, and legal issues involved in the policy decision of whether to prohibit, decriminalize, or legalize crack cocaine.

Peter Dale Scott and Jonathan Marshall. *Cocaine Politics: Drugs, Armies, and the CIA in Central America.* Berkeley: University of California Press, 1991. The very controversial thesis of this book is that the War on Drugs is a sham and that the United States encourages the world drug trade as long as it advances our political goals abroad—a new wrinkle on the political economy of the drug trade.

William Weir. *In the Shadow of the Dope Fiend: America's War on Drugs.* New Haven, CT: Archon Books, 1995. In addition to providing a good account of current drug problems and policies in the United States, this book also provides an interesting social history of the various crusades against drugs in U.S. history.

Terry Williams. *The Cocaine Kids: The Inside Story of a Teenage Drug Ring.* Reading, MA: Addison-Wesley, 1989. Sociologist Williams spent a great deal of time over a five-year period with a group of teenage drug dealers in New York's Spanish Harlem. He provides a fascinating picture of the drug trade and offers some startling revelations, such as the extent to which these drug dealers maintain a deep belief in the American dream of hard work and success.

PROSTITUTION, PORNOGRAPHY, AND THE SEX TRADE

The varieties of human sexual expression are almost endless, and practically all of them have been condemned, by some group at some time or other, as deviant. However, this chapter, despite its title, is only partly about sex; it is also about people's reactions to various forms of sexual expression. Recall from Chapters 1 and 9 that behaviors are classified as deviant by sociologists when some group in society defines the behaviors as wrong and stigmatizes people who engage in those behaviors. So deviance is not a characteristic of a behavior but rather involves the judgments about a behavior by some individual or group. The types of sexual behavior that are condemned will change from time to time, but what persists is the tendency to condemn groups that are different—whether the difference arises from race, ethnicity, gender, or sexual expression. In Chapter 6, the text discusses what the sociological perspectives have to say about prejudice and discrimination, and that discussion is not repeated here. Instead, this chapter focuses on the special issues that arise when discrimination and condemnation are founded on differences of sexual expression.

The two preceding chapters explored forms of deviance, such as crime and drug abuse, that have more clearly demonstrable negative consequences for society, at least in some realms. With the behaviors discussed in this chapter, however, it is not as easy to find clearly negative consequences. Some consequences of things like prostitution and pornography will be explored, but it is much more controversial whether these are detrimental to society. Of course, some groups have moral objections to prostitution, pornography, and other elements of the sex trade; they may like to see them banned for that reason. But our focus is on the social problem: the extent to which such sexual deviance causes problems for some groups or the extent to which the societal reaction to this deviance negatively impacts on some groups. The chapter will first discuss sexual behavior in general and then focus on issues having to do with prostitution, pornography, and the global sex trade.

Variety in Human Sexuality

A Cross-Cultural View

Many people believe that there is a "natural" or "instinctive" expression of sexuality that people are aware of largely or completely without learning. Reflecting this belief, some people refer to variant sexual acts as "violations of nature." So for many people in the United States, "natural" sex is sex between a man and a woman who are married. Some would even extend this "naturalness" to the sexual position assumed: genital contact in the "missionary" position (face to face with the male on top). Yet studies of other cultures indicate that socially acceptable sex takes far more forms than this. Consider one such culture:

> Sex—sex for pleasure and sex for procreation— is a principal concern of the Polynesian people on tiny Mangaia. . . . They demonstrate that concern in the startling numbers of children born to unmarried parents, and in the statistics on frequency of orgasm and numbers of sexual partners. But that concern is simple fact-of-life—*not* morbid preoccupation. . . . There is great directness about sex, but the approach to sex is correspondingly indirect. Among the young, there is no dating, no tentative necking in the American sense. A flick of the eye, a raised eyebrow in a crowd, can lead to copulation—without a word. There is no social contact between the sexes, no rendezvous that does not lead directly to coitus—copulation is the only imaginable outcome of heterosexual contact. The sexual intimacy of copulation precedes personal affection. . . . (Marshall, 1974:26–27)

Myths & Facts

About Prostitution and Pornography

Myth: Prostitution is one of the categories of crime in which women far outnumber men as perpetrators.

Fact: This is true, but it is also the case that the gender disparity in arrests for prostitution is not nearly as large as many imagine. One-third of all people arrested for prostitution and commercialized vice in the United States are male.

Myth: Pornographic materials that portray people in highly erotic and sexually explicit settings are dangerous to society because they lead to other social problems such as rape and other forms of sexual violence against women.

Fact: The latest research suggests that exposure to sexually explicit or arousing materials that have no aggressive content does not seem to produce negative effects. It is the aggressive content of some pornography that may lead some people to view violence against women as acceptable or desirable.

Myth: Pornography tends to be popular in communities where there is much hostility toward women and where women are discriminated against in occupational and other arenas.

Fact: Actually, research shows the reverse: Communities with high levels of gender equality have higher circulation rates for pornography than do communities with lower amounts of gender equality (Baron, 1990). This is probably because both pornography and gender equality flourish in politically tolerant communities.

So Mangaians have what many people in the United States would call an extremely permissive attitude toward sexual behavior. Although sexual intercourse among unmarried persons is accepted by many people today, multiple partners and casual sex tend to be frowned upon, especially for women. If there is a natural or instinctive form of sexual expression, what are we to make of the Mangaians? Consider some other examples (Bullough, 1976; Davenport, 1977). In Tahiti, young people were encouraged to masturbate. In the Truk Islands of the Pacific, sexual gratification is associated with pain and frustration, and sexual foreplay involves lovers inflicting pain on each other. Among most human groups, the female breasts are considered erotic, but this is not universal. Among the Mangaians mentioned previously, the breasts are not involved in foreplay and sexual arousal. Kissing is also a part of sexual expression in most human societies, but there are people among whom sexual intercourse occurs completely without kissing. The Siriono of Bolivia even find kissing to be a disgusting act. Prostitution and pornography—the forms of sexual behavior we will discuss in this chapter—are also highly variable. In some societies, prostitution is considered an accepted sexual outlet, whereas in others it is banned. What many people in the United States would consider pornographic—such as explicit portrayals of sexual intercourse—are considered public art and even religious symbols in some societies.

From this review of sexuality in other cultures, we can see that sexual norms are similar to all other societal rules: They are learned from others through social interaction. Through the socialization process, people learn what is acceptable sexuality in their group or culture. There is nothing "instinctive" about it beyond a general, undirected biological drive. Who to have sex with, when, and in what fashion—these are all behaviors that people learn. If these responses were instinctive, we would not see the variation that occurs from one culture to another. Consequently, what constitutes sexual deviance in different societies depends less on the act itself and more on how that action fits with societal values and norms. This is not to suggest that one should adopt an "anything goes" attitude toward sex. Sex is part of culture, and it must be integrated with other cultural practices such as the form of the family and child-rearing needs. At the same time, we can recognize the flexible nature of human sexual expression. In a diverse society, this can create a tension between the sexual practices of one group and those of another group. This situation creates the possibility that some forms of sexuality might be viewed by some people as social problems and may produce conflict that exacerbates other social problems.

Sexual Standards and Variety in the United States

There is variety in human sexuality, not only between cultures or societies, but also from group to group and from time to time within the same culture or society. Many Western religions, such as Roman Catholicism, prohibit all sexual activity outside the marital bond. Such a complete prohibition on premarital sex is found in only about one-third of human societies. Anthropologists who have looked at many societies, both today and in the past, estimate that about one-third of human societies allow almost completely unrestricted premarital sex, and almost another third allow premarital sex with some restrictions, such as avoiding pregnancy (Murdock, 1967).

Today, people in the United States are more divided than in the past over premarital sexuality (Coltrane and Collins, 2001; Davis and Smith, 2004; Gallup, 2003). In the 1960s, only 20 percent believed that premarital sex was acceptable; today, just over half of the people in the United States view it as permissible. Young people are much more likely to approve of premarital sex, as are those who are less religious and have more egalitarian sex-role attitudes. However, as in so many other realms, attitudes and behavior are sometimes at variance; because people *approve* of a behavior does not mean that they *engage* in it themselves. Sexual behavior is very sensitive, so information about it is not always easy to get. However, putting together the best information from surveys that we have, we can conclude that sex before marriage, which was once considered taboo in the United States, especially for women, has become routine. Today, 80 to 85 percent of women and 95 percent of men have had sex before marriage. This compares with about half of women and two-thirds of men in the 1920s. So, there has been a gradual increase since the 1920s, but the change is less dramatic than many believe because at least half of all men and women in the 1920s had premarital sexual experience. If there has been a sexual "revolution," it is among women. Whereas the numbers of women having premarital experience gradually increased throughout the century, they did show a leap in the 1960s and 1970s.

These changes in premarital sexual behavior are often misunderstood and exaggerated. There has been a dramatic change in how publicly we discuss sex and in how openly we recognize the reality of premarital sex. We are also less likely to insist that sex be limited to the marital context. However, changes in actual sexual behavior, although real, have not been as dramatic as many believe, especially if we treat cohabitation as similar to marriage. Among some in the United States today, cohabitation has come to be viewed as a socially acceptable bonding between two people (see Chapter 3). If we treat cohabitors like married couples and remove their sexual activity from the premarital category, the sexual "revolution" looks even less dramatic. In addition, some experts conclude that the most significant change has been the elimination of the "double standard" that permitted men to engage in premarital sex ("sow a few wild oats") without sanction but strongly discouraged the same behavior in women (Milhausen and Herold, 1999). Although there are still differences, women's sexual behavior has become much more similar to that of men's in the past few decades.

What accounts for these changes in sexual behavior? One important factor, certainly, is the emergence of easy to use, unobtrusive, and very reliable contraceptives. This has eased women's fears of pregnancy and widened their options as far as sexual behavior is concerned. A second major factor has been the feminist movement, which emphasizes that women should gain control of their lives and be able to make decisions for themselves. It also demands that women's choices not be limited by sexist or stereotypical views of gender. Without question, many traditional views of women's sexuality were sexist, stereotyped, and very wrong. A third factor producing changing sexual practices has been technological developments, such as the automobile, that provide young people with more freedom and the means to escape surveillance by adults. A final factor producing changes in sexual behavior is the trend toward **secularization**: *the process through which the influence of religion is removed from many institutions in society and dispersed into private and personal realms.* When religion as an institution was stronger and more pervasive, it controlled more of people's sexual behavior. As religion has come to exercise less control, people have become more willing to engage in previously condemned forms of sexuality.

Despite these changes, people in the United States are still not at the level of permissiveness of the Mangaians. Prostitution is still illegal in most states, and the Supreme Court has ruled that such prohibitions are constitutional. Strong pressures persist to ban most or all pornography. In addition, changes in sexual standards are not uniform throughout society, and depending on the group or subculture involved, attitudes about what is normal or deviant can vary substantially.

Prostitution

Prostitution has been called the "world's oldest profession," because it seems to have been with us throughout recorded history. **Prostitution** refers to *sexual activity in exchange for money or goods, in which the primary motivation for the prostitute is neither sexual nor affectional.* Prostitution can take many different forms. Some prostitutes are known in the trade as "streetwalkers": They solicit clients by walking the streets. These prostitutes—both men and women—generally engage in sexual behavior with their customers in clients' automobiles or in cheap hotel rooms. Most of these practitioners of the trade work for a pimp, who may "manage" from one to twenty women (Diana, 1985). Pimps offer protection and bail money in exchange for the allegiance of the prostitutes in their "stable." Pimps frequently resort to violence as a means of enforcing obedience, and they can garner nearly 100 percent of their employees' earnings. Other prostitutes work in what at one time was the most common environment for the trade: the house of prostitution, brothel, or "whorehouse." In these cases, a "madam" acts as supervisor of a number of prostitutes and negotiates with clients who enter the facility. Unlike pimps, madams usually garner about 50 percent of their "ladies" proceeds. Prostitution is legal in some counties in Nevada, and brothels flourish. They are run like any other business, to the point of accepting credit cards and traveler's checks.

Still other members of the trade operate out of bars, taverns, and massage parlors. The type of prostitute commanding the highest status within the trade is the escort or "call girl" who might operate independently or be part of a larger operation. Escort services have expanded considerably in the past decade, using modern technologies such as cellular phones and pagers to keep track of prostitutes and customers and arrange liaisons (Roane, 1998). The New York City Yellow Pages now has over fifty pages of ads for escort services, many of which are fronts for prostitution. Prostitutes have also begun to utilize the Internet to advertise themselves and arrange meetings with customers. For the cost of a computer, a modem, and an online account, a prostitute or a pimp can be in business. This technology makes it easier for prostitutes to operate on their own, often not even considering themselves to be prostitutes but rather business entrepreneurs innovating with new technology. Escort services and online prostitution also make it much easier for sex workers to avoid contact with the police, especially in comparison to the visibility of the streetwalker. Among male prostitutes, a similar stratification system exists, ranging from the street hustler to the bar hustler to the escort prostitute (Luckenbill, 1989).

Extent of Prostitution

Precise figures on the incidence of prostitution are impossible to obtain. Much prostitution goes on unreported, and there are women and men who engage in the trade on a part-time basis, with some of these individuals occupying otherwise respectable positions in their communities. Furthermore, arrests for prostitution are highly susceptible to political manipulation. In some jurisdictions, for example, the trade may be more or less tolerated, whereas in others police agencies may be motivated to "crack down," thus creating the impression that prostitution is on the rise, when in fact it is merely law enforcement activity that has increased (Clinard and Meier, 2004). And prostitution tends to flourish "indoors" and in other settings where the police have a difficult time observing it and making arrests. A New York City police captain described it this way:

> You have some people who have no alternative but the street. But there are a whole lot of people that we never deal with, working out of offices, apartments and the Internet. And if they are acting behind closed doors and are discreet, we will never hear about them. (quoted in Roane, 1998:1.)

Considering these problems, the best estimates place the number of prostitutes in the United States at between one hundred thousand and five hundred thousand and the money generated each year at between $1 billion and $10 billion (Thio, 2004). There are about one hundred thousand arrests for prostitution and commercialized vice offenses each year. Sixty-one percent of the people involved were female. Considering the degree of nonreporting alluded to earlier, these figures are conservative. The trade is clearly thriving, and the explanation is primarily economic: There are people willing to pay for the services and others who are willing to supply them for a price.

A particularly disturbing form of prostitution appeared with the emergence of the crack cocaine epidemic in the past two decades (see Chapter 10). In crack houses, crack-addicted women, and in a few cases men, would engage in quick sex with many men to get crack or the money to buy crack (Inciardi, Horowitz, and Pottieger, 1993). This is typically unprotected sex and involves multiple partners, with

many IV-drug users among the partners. The women go from one sexual contact to another for a hit of crack and in some cases have literally thousands of sexual contacts a year. In fact, some of the women who engage repeatedly in quick oral sex with many men to get crack did not even consider this to be prostitution. This behavior entails a very high risk of spreading the AIDS virus.

Considerable controversy exists regarding whether prostitution should be regarded as a social problem or even a crime, for that matter (Carpenter, 2000). Generally, only about one in four adults believes that prostitution should be legal in his or her state (see Figure 11.1). Women, those with lower income and educational levels, and the elderly tend to be most opposed to legalizing prostitution. Those who favor legalizing prostitution argue that this activity is a "victimless crime" and that what goes on between consenting adults in private should not be a matter of legal enforcement (Albert, 2001). (This is the same argument discussed in Chapter 10 to support the legalization of some psychoactive drugs.) In fact, prostitution is legal in 11 counties in Nevada, where houses of prostitution are privately owned and regulated by the state. Another argument in favor of legalizing prostitution is that illegal prostitution causes problems such as the spread of venereal disease and AIDS and may come under the control of organized crime. It also leads to other related crimes, such as assaults on customers and the use of drugs.

Where prostitution is legal, such as Nevada and some countries in Europe, these problems can be monitored and fairly effectively controlled among the legal prostitutes (Campbell, 1991). Nevada, for example, requires licensed brothel prostitutes to be tested for gonorrhea, syphilis, and AIDS at least once a month. If they test positive for AIDS, they cannot work as a legal prostitute in Nevada. Nevada also requires that condoms be used at all licensed brothels, and brothel owners will not employ women who are IV-drug users. As a consequence, no brothel prostitute in Nevada has ever tested positive for the AIDS virus, whereas in some cities where prostitution is illegal, 20 to 40 percent of prostitutes are infected. However, it is not clear how much of this infection is due to prostitution itself and how much is due to prostitutes taking drugs intravenously or having sex with IV-drug users. Nonetheless, legalized and monitored prostitution does provide significant protection against sexually transmitted diseases for both the prostitute and the customer. In addition, there is no evidence of serious crime problems accompanying legalized prostitution in Nevada. This leads proponents of legalization to argue that everyone—the prostitute, the customer, and society—would be

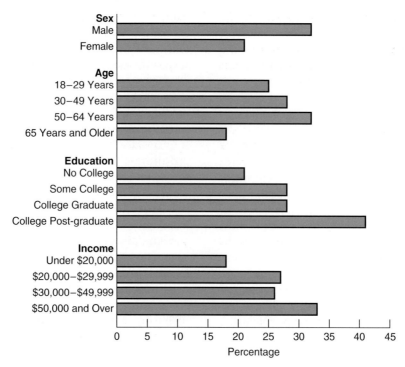

FIGURE 11.1 **Percentage of Adults Agreeing that Prostitution Should Be Legal in Their State, 1996.**

Source: Kathleen Maguire and Ann L. Pastore, eds. *Sourcebook of Criminal Justice Statistics, 1996.* U.S. Department of Justice, Bureau of Justice Statistics (Washington, DC: U.S. Government Printing Office, 1997), p. 204.

better off if prostitution were legal and subject to government regulation. A variant on this position has been taken by a variety of organizations formed to pursue the interests of prostitutes, such as COYOTE (Call Off Your Old Tired Ethics), PONY (Prostitutes of New York), and SWAC (Sex Workers Action Coalition). These advocates argue that basic issues of work rights and women's self-determination are involved: Prostitution is legitimate work and women have the right to control their own bodies, including the selling of sexual favors. COYOTE, for example, agrees that women should not be forced into prostitution, but it also believes that the right to choose prostitution freely is a basic civil right for women. Although COYOTE has not achieved some of its major goals, such as decriminalizing prostitution, it has worked to protect prostitutes from harassment by police and courts and to bring educational programs about AIDS to prostitutes.

Critics of legalization argue that legalizing prostitution does not stop the health and crime problems associated with prostitution but simply pushes it into the illegal trade. Prostitutes who get involved in crime, use drugs, or have a sexually transmitted disease continue to work, but on the street rather than in the legal brothels. In fact, this seems to be true

because illegal prostitution continues in Nevada. However, having legal prostitution available does reduce the amount of illegal prostitution. Other critics of legalized prostitution, including some feminists, argue that prostitution does create victims: the prostitutes themselves. Prostitution, they claim, involves an exploitation of women so that men can have unrestricted access to sexual pleasure. As one critic of legalized prostitution put it, "Prostitution is a culturally sanctioned system of oppression that uses women, children, and young men as sexual objects. . . . The sex industry uses power and control tactics to supply its customers with human beings who are used as sexual toys. Prostitution is dehumanizing to everyone involved in the industry" (Greenman, 1990:111). Although prostitutes appear to be willing partners, they are really coerced into prostitution because of poverty, few job opportunities, or a sexist ideology that defines women primarily in terms of their sexuality rather than other skills and qualities.

Who Becomes a Prostitute?

There is a widespread myth that most prostitutes get their start through a kind of "white slave" trade—that young women are coerced by profit-oriented adults and forced into selling their sexual services for money. Although this does occur, as in the case of teenage runaways who gravitate toward major cities in an attempt to make a living, forced prostitution is rare in the United States—no more than 4 percent could be said to have been railroaded into the trade (Thio, 2004).

How, then, do most prostitutes get into the trade? An important step in becoming a prostitute is knowing others who are involved in the trade or who are on its fringe. As differential association theory discussed in Chapter 9 suggests, people learn prostitution from others who are involved. Many prostitutes first learn about prostitution from close friends or relatives, whereas others have contact with a pimp or prostitute who convinces them to "turn out," as the first move into the ranks of prostitutes is called (Flowers, 2001a; Weisberg, 1985). Contacts with other prostitutes or with a pimp are also important in developing a clientele. Associating with prostitutes or pimps who idealize the life of the prostitute as exciting and glamorous and extol its virtues in terms of making "easy money" also encourages potential recruits to "turn out." These recruits learn attitudes that espouse prostitution as a desirable way of life. They also learn that prostitution might bring lucrative economic rewards and an independence rarely found in other occupations. So "contacts" appear to be the most important ingredient in becoming a prostitute, once again underscoring the importance of learning a deviant lifestyle through intimate group associations. The learning process is similar to how "respectable" people learn to adopt socially acceptable ways of life.

Quite obviously, being young and physically attractive are also valuable assets for joining the ranks of prostitution, whether legal or illegal (Diana, 1985). Consequently, the vast majority of female practitioners are between 17 and 24 years of age, with the peak earning age being around 22 (Clinard and Meier, 2004). Prostitutes also often have early and frequent promiscuous sexual experiences. They often have their first sexual intercourse by 10 to 13 years of age and develop a pattern of having sex with several men, often after very brief acquaintanceships. More than any other single factor, entrance into prostitution for women is linked to poverty: Poor women are far more likely to become prostitutes than are affluent women. Two other important precursors to prostitution are a history of juvenile delinquency and being sexually abused as a child (Widom and Kuhns, 1996).

Male prostitutes tend to come from two distinct subcultures (Luckenbill, 1989; Weisberg, 1985). One is the peer-delinquent subculture, which consists of boys from lower-class backgrounds who never define themselves as homosexuals. For them, prostitution is exclusively a way of making money, not achieving sexual gratification, and they also engage in other criminal activity. The other subculture is the gay subculture, involving boys who consider themselves homosexual or bisexual. These prostitutes are more likely to work the gay neighborhoods of cities. They are also more likely than the peer-delinquents to come from the middle class. Gay prostitutes engage in prostitution as a way of interacting with gay people and achieving sexual gratification as well as making money. Adolescent male prostitutes come from unstable families and are likely to have experienced physical abuse and sometimes sexual abuse by their caretakers. For gay prostitutes, conflicts with parents over their sexual orientation often lead them to run away and turn to prostitution to support themselves.

Leaving prostitution can be difficult, especially for women who have been in the trade for some time (Greenman, 1990). For one thing, prostitution isolates women from the "straight" community and from their families and friends. This means they have few supports to turn to when they need help, except the pimp and others in the trade in whose interest it is to see them continue as prostitutes. Often, pimps encourage prostitutes to participate in other illegal actions such as drug trafficking or forgery, and this creates additional barriers to going back to the straight world. In addition, the women are often battered by their pimps or assaulted by customers. They often have alcohol and drug problems, no high school degree, no safe and affordable housing, no marketable skills, and no recent work experience to be cited when applying for legitimate jobs. All this can make prostitutes feel as though they are on a dead-end, one-way street with few alternatives: all in all, not a very glamorous life. This section has looked at the life of prostitutes in the United States; the International Perspectives insert (pp. 298–299) explores the world of the prostitute in the global sex trade.

Pornography

A few years ago, an issue of a magazine, which routinely contained very sexually explicit photos, advertised that it contained "the most obscene photographs ever published." Not surprisingly, this issue enjoyed particularly vigorous sales on the magazine stands. Rather than sexually explicit photos, however, the photographs were extremely vivid portrayals of combat in Vietnam. This episode highlights an important question in the social controversy pertaining to pornography: What is obscenity? Another dimension of this issue involves the debate over whether adults should have the right to choose what they see and read about.

The Global Sex Industry

During the Vietnam War, burgeoning sex industries erupted outside U.S. military bases in Korea, Vietnam, Thailand, the Philippines and Okinawa. Rest and Recreation ("R & R") actually created new cities and added much-needed capital to the overall economy of each nation. It is estimated that by the mid-'80s, the sex industries around U.S. bases in the Philippines had generated more than $500 million. At the end of the war in Vietnam, Saigon had 500,000 prostituted women—equal to the total population of Saigon before the war. (Mirkinson, 1997:30)

So, huge U.S. military bases around the world helped build and support what would become a global sex industry, where today tens of thousands of women and children are virtually enslaved as sex workers fulfilling the desires of the affluent from many nations. Of course, many other factors have contributed to the growth of this burgeoning sex industry. One major factor is the poverty that has pushed desperate individuals and families in poor countries toward the sex trade as a way of surviving (Bales, K., 2003). Families might run their own small-scale prostitution business, supplying their daughters to customers. Sometimes, young boys or girls leave their families, or are driven out, because the family has too many mouths to feed. In a surprisingly large number of cases, families actually sell their children to sex rings as a way of getting money for the family to survive. This happens in the Philippines, India, Cambodia, Thailand, and other places. When sold to a sex boss, the child becomes the property of the boss, in a form of debt bondage discussed in Chapter 8 when assessing the economic exploitation of children. In debt bondage, the child belongs to the boss until a family's debt is paid off, and if interest on the loan is high enough, it may be many years, or never, before the debt is paid off.

Another factor contributing to the global sex industry is the emergence of tourism as a huge industry since World War II (Brennan, 2003). With growing levels of affluence in many parts of the world and a rapid and affordable means of global transportation, millions of people now move around the world taking vacations, and whole infrastructures have emerged to service and make a profit off them. A part of that tourism industry is the sex industry, which consists of brothels, sex clubs, pornography peddlers, and striptease bars that cater to tourists who are looking, at least in part, for sexual services. Organized sex tours take people from Europe, Japan, and the United States to places like Thailand for vacation and sex. In addition, poor young women from Thailand and Malaysia are brought illegally to Canada and other Western nations and forced into prostitution. The hotels, airlines, and credit-card industries also benefit from this worldwide sex trade. Enormous resources are put into marketing this industry to expand the number of clients who are seeking these services and willing to travel to find them.

Yet another reason for the global sex trade is economic demand: When large numbers of men gather together away from their homes—whether they are soldiers, businessmen, or tourists—the demand for prostitutes grows. With profits to be made, someone will offer services to fill that demand. All too often, it is highly organized, international sex cartels that fill the demand by exploiting mostly poor and defenseless children and women.

The global sex industry is constantly recruiting children as young as fifteen, and in extreme cases as young as eight, into the ranks of prostitutes (Estes and Weiner, 2001; Flowers, 2001b). How many such child prostitutes there are is impossible to say with accuracy, but estimates worldwide run from a low of a few hundred thousand to a high of a million. These younger recruits have appeal for a number of reasons. One reason is that such young children, especially when abandoned by their families, are extremely defenseless and thus easily manipulated, controlled, or coerced into doing whatever their bosses need. It is not unheard of for children in the sex industry to be beaten, starved, and imprisoned as means of coercion. Another reason why young recruits have appeal is that many customers demand young prostitutes. In some cultures, sex with a virgin is highly prized, and thus the appeal of youth in the industry. However, youth also has

These women in Rome in 2007 are part of the global sex industry, in which traffickers force young women from poor countries to engage in prostitution in more affluent nations. The industry thrives because of the great demand for the services and the poverty that forces women into these occupations.

appeal because of the fear of AIDS. Many customers believe that a younger prostitute is less likely to be infected with the HIV virus. Some European countries have become sufficiently appalled by this exploitation of children that they have passed laws enabling them to arrest their citizens for using children and adolescents sexually, even if the sexual activity occurs on another continent and previously out of the reach of their laws.

The Internet has also become a part of the global sex trade. It is very effective at helping people learn of sex tours or other opportunities in the sex trade around the world. The Internet has also become a vehicle for the worldwide distribution of pornography. Dutch police discovered a ring of pornographers who used the Internet to send pictures of the sexual abuse of children and even infants to clients in Europe, Russia, and the United States. Apparently, the pornographers took advantage of the collapse of the Soviet Union and the resulting turmoil in some eastern European countries by using vulnerable children from those countries in their pictures and movies.

Defining Pornography

The term **pornography** was first applied to characterizations of prostitution, but as currently utilized, it describes *"sexually 'explicit' writings, still or motion pictures and similar products designed to be sexually arousing"* (Sobel, 1979:2). *Obscene* is a term that originally implied "filth." Today, obscene material is generally thought of as "lustful material that offends prevailing senses of decency and morality" (Sheley, 1985:119). Feminist Gloria Steinem has commented that it is the *dehumanizing* aspect of pornography that distinguishes it from *erotic* materials. For Steinem, the message in pornography "is violence, dominance, and conquest," whereas erotica portrays "mutually pleasurable, sexual expression between people who have enough power to be there by positive choice" (Steinem, 1980:37). Clearly, what is obscene to one person may be considered by another person to be a work of art.

Particularly vivid examples of the controversy involving different definitions of obscenity or pornography are found in attempts by various moral interest groups to ban such literary classics as James Joyce's *Ulysses* and J. D. Salinger's *Catcher in the Rye.* In 1948, novelist Norman Mailer published *The Naked and the Dead.* In that book, although with an obviously deliberate misspelling ("fug"), a four-letter, Anglo-Saxon word, previously regarded as taboo in printed material, was used frequently. Three years later, James Jones released his classic *From Here to Eternity,* and in that book, this same word was used with equal frequency in its correct spelling. Today this very same expression is used frequently in various publications, quite regularly in motion pictures, and increasingly on television.

Over the years, the U.S. Supreme Court has ruled that obscenity lies outside of the free speech protection of the First Amendment to the Constitution, but the courts have had considerable difficulty in trying to determine what is and is not "obscene." The current legal status of pornography was established in the 1973 Supreme Court case *Miller* v. *California.* According to the *Miller* test, material must meet three conditions in order to be considered legally obscene (Hawkins and Zimring, 1988).

1. The average person applying community standards considers the material as a whole to appeal to prurient interests.
2. The material depicts sexual conduct, specifically defined by state or federal law, in a patently offensive way.
3. The work lacks serious artistic, literary, political, or scientific value.

Since the *Miller* ruling, a large body of court rulings has emerged in an effort to specify more clearly such things as who the "average person" is, which "community" standards are to be applied, and what is "patently offensive." The issue has become vastly more complex with the advent of online pornography, which raises the possibility that a "community" is not a limited geographic region but rather a national or international audience that is connected electronically. So, much dispute remains about what is obscene, and, except in the most extreme cases, judgments about obscenity will inevitably be subjective and influenced by personal or religious values. Because of this, antiobscenity legislation is essentially in the hands of the more powerful political elements and interest groups of particular states and communities. Very often, what is and is not considered "obscene" is reduced to a single decision by a judge or jury. What is clear, however, is that pornography—sexually explicit materials designed to be sexually arousing—is not obscene according to the *Miller* test and thus is protected free speech under the First Amendment to the Constitution.

Pornography and Censorship

One of the key issues in the debate over pornography as a social problem is whether and to what extent it should be censored. Proponents of antipornography statutes argue that society must be protected from these "immoral vices." They contend that, unless there is censorship, such materials will fall into the hands of impressionable youth. In addition, they point out, pornographic materials frequently involve the exploitation of women and children, sometimes treating them as "property" or mere sex objects. Because of this, some feminists have joined with more conservative groups in making a case for a ban on pornography. For example, law professor Catharine MacKinnon and author Andrea Dworkin have pioneered a new approach to pornography that views it as a violation of the civil rights of women (MacKinnon, 1993). In their view, when women are portrayed as sex objects and in degrading and subjugated roles, it helps to perpetuate sexist cultural beliefs that it is appropriate to treat women as property or as mere sexual objects. Because pornography portrays women as subordinate, submissive, and often the recipients of violence, it encourages sexual assault and the abuse of women. So, because pornography helps to create a hostile environment for women with negative outcomes, in their view, it violates their civil rights. These ideas have been incorporated into the laws of some municipalities, but the courts have struck down such laws as unconstitutional.

During the 1980s, the controversy over pornography experienced renewed energy and momentum, fueled by the Reagan administration's call for a national commission on pornography legislation. In 1986, the Attorney General's Commission on Pornography, the Meese Commission, ended its one-year investigation of pornography in this country and issued a report that condemned violence and degradation in sexually explicit films, magazines, and books. The report also called for more aggressive prosecution of those who sell what it called obscene materials in order to keep them out of circulation. In addition, the Attorney General threatened to publish a list of pornography distributors in the United States. This threat led an estimated ten thousand stores nationwide to stop selling adult magazines such as *Playboy, Penthouse,* and *Hustler.* In some cases, major retail chains such as B. Dalton Bookseller were picketed. Although the Meese Commission Report attacked primarily violent pornography, opponents of pornography have used the report as a club with which to attack all pornography.

Those opposed to censoring pornography argue that people should be free to decide for themselves what they wish to read or watch (Strossen, 1995). There is virtual unanimity in the United States, among both men and women, that pornography should be kept out of the hands of children, and those who oppose censoring pornography agree with this. However, they argue that adults' fundamental right to choose whether they want to consume these materials should not be interfered with. If censorship were to become common, it would be difficult to draw the line between works without "redeeming value" and those having literary or other worth, as the examples discussed earlier illustrate. Antipornography legislation, they argue, would open the doors to banning much literature and art because it is offensive to some group. When children are involved, however, the matter of exploitation is very clear. Those who are opposed to antipornography legislation strongly agree that pornography involving children should be banned.

There is an ironic contradiction in people's stance toward pornography in the United States. On the one hand, powerful interest groups have maintained steady and strong pressure to limit the distribution of pornography, even to adults. At the same time, the pornography industry flourishes, and many people avail themselves of pornographic materials. Only 37 percent of people in the United States believe that laws should forbid the distribution of pornography to adults as well as children, with about one-half of women and one-quarter of men taking this stance (see Figure 11.2). These percentages have remained fairly steady since 1980. Approximately one-third of all men and 16 percent of all women admit to having seen a pornographic movie in the past year (see Figure 11.3). This likelihood of seeing a pornographic movie is considerably higher among men than women, and it has increased, especially among men, over the past three decades. One reason for this increase is that modern technology has expanded considerably the ways in which people can access pornographic materials (Egan, 2000). In earlier decades, access was limited to magazines and movie theaters. Today, people can rent or buy videos to watch in their homes, they can access

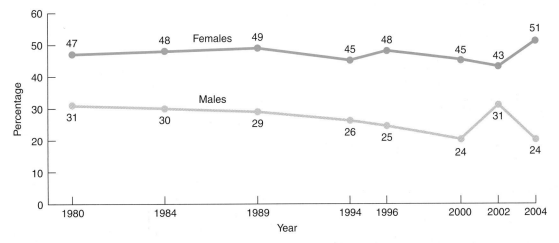

FIGURE 11.2 **Percentage of People Agreeing that Laws Should Forbid Distribution of Pornography to People of Any Age, by Gender, 1980–2004.**

Source: James A. Davis and Tom W. Smith. *General Social Surveys, 1972–2004.* Chicago, National Opinion Research Center (producer); Storrs, CT: The Roper Center for Public Opinion Research, University of Connecticut (distributor); www.icpsr.umich.edu/GSS.

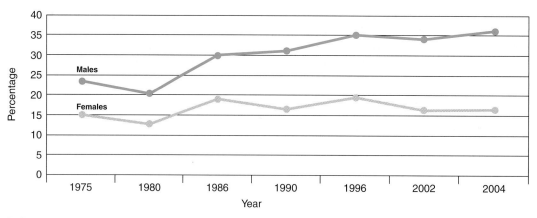

FIGURE 11.3 **Percentage of People Who Say They Have Seen a Pornographic Movie in the Past Year, by Gender, 1975–2004.**

Source: James A. Davis and Tom W. Smith. *General Social Surveys, 1972–2004.* Chicago, National Opinion Research Center (producer); Storrs, CT: The Roper Center for Public Opinion Research, University of Connecticut (distributor); www.icpsr.umich.edu/GSS.

sexual videos from their cable or satellite television providers, and they can watch pornographic movies on the pay-per-view channels in many hotels (major hotel chains are the largest purveyors of pornographic materials in the United States today). In addition, people today can download pornographic pictures and videos in digital format from the Internet.

Pornography and Sexual Violence

There is stronger opposition to the distribution of pornography that features violence or the degradation of women. In fact, as has been seen, the pornography issue has become a battleground on which some feminists and the religious right have joined forces to push for a ban on pornographic materials on the grounds that they lead to sexual aggression, sexual assault, and other forms of violence against women by men (Segal, 1990). About one-half of people in the United States agree that pornography leads men to commit rape, with women considerably more likely to agree with this than men (Davis and Smith, 2004). The slogan "Pornography Is the Theory, Rape Is the Practice" embodies the belief that pornography is the ideology that fuels not only violence against women but all forms of female exploitation and oppression. For some feminists, these are core issues, and they rest on an assertion that can be subjected to empirical testing: Viewing pornography increases men's levels of violence against women. The role of applied research in social policy is sufficiently important in this realm that the Applied Research insert (pp. 304–305) is devoted to evaluating that assertion and the turmoil that swirls around it.

Perspectives on Sexual Deviance

The Functionalist Perspective

As is pointed out in Chapters 1 and 5, the functionalist perspective suggests that social practices such as prostitution and pornography can contribute to the maintenance of society even though they are viewed very negatively by many people. In other words, even though many claim to want to rid society of such practices, the practices may perform positive functions for society nonetheless (Davis, 1971; Thio, 2004). One of the functions that the sex trade serves is to help establish the boundaries of acceptable morality for society. By calling prostitution, pornography, or other deviant sexual practices immoral and by stigmatizing those who engage in such practices, society is making a statement about what it is moral for respectable people to do—it is drawing the boundaries beyond which people who consider themselves respectable should not wander. Another function of the sex trade is to provide for a wide array of sexual outlets and services in a society that places restrictions on what is acceptable sexual conduct. In the sex trade, people can find the sexual activities they desire without putting undue pressure on spouses or other partners to engage in sex that they may find distasteful or immoral. Forcing these partners to engage in oral or anal intercourse or sado-masochism when they are resistant to doing so may threaten family or other important relationships. Or, a person who is unattached or away from home can find sexual outlets in the sex trade without engaging in force or using other socially disruptive strategies to find sexual release. So, a sex worker who provides these services is, in a sense, helping maintain the social order by reducing tensions and conflicts that might occur in the absence of a sex trade. At the same time, the sex workers are defined as disreputable because they engage in morally condemned behavior.

The Conflict Perspective

From the conflict perspective, the sex trade is closely related to issues of social inequality and the exercise of power. At one level, the sex trade represents gender inequality in a patriarchal society, because it mostly involves men gaining rewards through the domination and exploitation of women. Whether the men be the owners and organizers of the sex trade or the recipients of the sexual services, they are the main benefactors of the sex industry; the mainly young and female sex workers, as we have seen, are heavily exploited. At another level, the sex trade has to do with poverty, because this industry could exist on a widespread scale only on the backs of poor women

around the world. Poverty provides a sizable and docile labor force for the sex industry. In short, the sex trade reflects and reproduces the patterns of dominance and subordination that the conflict perspective says are at the core of social life.

Another way to view the sex trade is in terms of who controls whether various kinds of sexual activities are legal or illegal. It is the dominant groups in society who have the power to criminalize various behaviors, and in so doing they can assert their own cultural dominance. In the United States, this struggle is closely tied to religion because various religious groups have fought hard to keep such things as prostitution and pornography illegal. In so doing, they symbolically establish their continuing power in society—at least on the surface, because the sex trade, even when prohibited, often thrives just below the surface.

The Interactionist Perspective

The interactionist perspective stresses the point that social life revolves around varying definitions of reality and this influences the nature of a social

These protestors are expressing strong opposition to pornography, which many people feel is morally offensive, degrading to women, and may promote violence against women.

Does Pornography Lead to Violence Against Women?

The issue of whether pornography leads to increased levels of violence against women is a very volatile topic because some groups feel very passionately about anything that might seem to increase violence against women. In general, however, the research has not been very supportive of the notion that pornography causes sexual violence. Research in the 1960s and 1970s generally failed to document any link between pornography and sexually violent behavior, and the 1970 report of the president's National Commission on Obscenity and Pornography rejected the conclusion that exposure to erotic materials is a factor in causing sex crimes and sexual delinquency (Segal, 1990). Nine years later, the Committee on Obscenity and Film Censorship in the United Kingdom came to the same conclusion.

Some research, however, does suggest a link between pornography and sexual violence. For example, a few laboratory experiments on how people respond to pornographic images found such a link. As one example, psychologist Edward Donnerstein and his colleagues showed pornographic films to college-age males and then asked them to judge simulated rape trials (Donnerstein, Linz, and Penrod, 1987). They found that men who watch sexually violent films are less likely to vote for conviction of a rapist than men who see nonviolent pornographic films

or nonpornographic films. The researchers concluded that the men who watch sexually violent films develop more calloused attitudes toward women and attitudes that trivialize rape. The men also show more acceptance of rape myths, such as that female hitchhikers or provocatively dressed women deserve to be raped. Donnerstein and his colleagues also found that portrayals of sexual violence produce higher levels of sexual arousal than erotic but nonviolent sexual imagery, greater acceptance of violence against women, and a greater likelihood that men will state that they would rape someone themselves if they could get away with it.

Donnerstein concludes from his research that it is the aggressiveness and violence in some pornography, rather than its sexual explicitness, that makes men more likely to express negative attitudes toward women and positive attitudes about rape. In fact, when he removes the sexual content from the films and leaves the aggressiveness, the negative consequences of watching the films seem the same. Other research generally supports this conclusion: Nonviolent pornography does not increase sexual violence for most men; it is the violence rather than the eroticism that creates the problem (Boeringer, 1994; Malamuth, Addison, and Koss, 2000). However, pornography of any sort may increase tendencies

toward violence in men who are very aggressive to begin with. Or it may be that these men have a greater attraction to pornography.

Even though some analysts have interpreted this research as providing some support for policies to control pornography, the research has been criticized on a number of grounds. First, none of this experimental or survey research actually observes sexual violence against women. All they observe is changes in responses to hypothetical situations such as rape trials or changes in some attitudes. Whether any of the men in these experiments would actually go out and commit sexual violence against women is unknown. A second criticism is that the experiments are done in highly artificial situations that may have little to do with the real causes of sexual violence. There is a huge difference between saying in a purely hypothetical and anonymous context that you might assault a woman if you could get away with it and actually assaulting a real human being. A third criticism is that these studies typically observe only short-term effects—what the men say or feel immediately after viewing the films. That effect may not last more than a few minutes, a few hours, or a few days and thus may have little influence on their behavior in the real world. So, the weaknesses of the research, along with the fact that other research does not find a link, lead social

problem. In a culture that defines women in a subordinate and somewhat negative role, the self-worth of many women may be such that they are more receptive to entering the sex trade. They may see this as a proper thing for women to do or as

one of the few things that women are capable of doing. This is especially true considering that many women in the sex trade have been sexually abused as children or adolescents. This treatment may have left them vulnerable to defining themselves as pow-

scientists to be very cautious about drawing conclusions, especially when changes in social policy are at stake.

Another approach to research on this issue is to see what pornography does to actual rapists. Again the results are less than supportive of a ban on pornography (Kutchinsky, 1991). Rapists have less experience with pornography in their teenage years than do nonrapists, and rapists do not use pornography more than others as adults. They also are not more aroused by pornography or more likely to engage in sexual behavior after exposure to pornography. In addition, as with ordinary men, rapists are less aroused by viewing forced sex than by viewing consenting sex.

Another line of research has been to see whether rates of rape and other sex offenses increase when more pornographic materials are available. Some studies have found positive correlations: In the United States, states that have higher rates of circulation of adult magazines have higher rates of rape. However, a recent study at the city, rather than state, level failed to support this: There was no correlation between level of circulation of pornographic magazines in a city and the rape rate in that city (Gentry, 1991). In addition, even if rapes are higher in locales with more pornographic materials around, the pornography may not be the cause of the rapes. It could be that the interest in pornography and the incidence of rape are both affected by the same thing: sexist and demeaning attitudes toward women. Remove the pornography and those attitudes would still be there. Actually, other research shows that communities with high circulation rates for pornography have higher levels of gender equality than communities with low pornography levels (Baron, 1990). This is probably because both pornography and gender equality flourish in politically tolerant communities. Furthermore, a longitudinal study of changing rates of rape in Denmark, Sweden, and West Germany—all three of which legalized pornography in the early 1970s—could find no increase in rape associated with the growing availability of pornographic materials (Kutchinsky, 1991). Likewise, in the United States, where both violent and nonviolent pornography have become much more widely available since the 1970s, there has been no increase in rape associated with it.

So, where does all this leave us? There is little scientific proof at this point that pornography causes sexual violence. Nevertheless, some of the research shows that men's attitudes and actions toward women may be changed by viewing violence against women, and this helps focus the debate on the realm that may be problematic—the violence rather than the sexual explicitness. Research should continue into all these areas.

Which brings us to the final issue: the politics of scientific research. Advocates of both sides of this issue would like to use scientific research to show that their position on the issue is correct. This can lead to distortions or misrepresentations of the research. For example, the U.S. Attorney General's Commission on Pornography of 1986 used Donnerstein's research as a basis for its conclusion that pornography plays a role in causing sexual violence and aggression, even though Donnerstein and his colleagues strongly disagree with that conclusion (Linz and Donnerstein, 1992). For reasons discussed in this insert, Donnerstein and his colleagues are much more cautious about what their research shows: only that violent pornography may temporarily change some of men's attitudes toward women or change some of their behavior in artificial, laboratory settings. They do not believe this can justify social policies that curtail the distribution of all sexually explicit materials. It appears that the Commission had an agenda when it started—to curtail the circulation of pornography in the United States—and it was simply searching for any evidence that might seem to support its position. This is why scientists need to be very careful in doing their research, so that distorted or misinformed representations of the results can be minimized.

erless or morally degraded. Once in the sex trade, prostitutes and other sex workers may accept the stigmatized stereotype that society at large holds of them, and this may lead them to be less able to leave the business. They may lack the sense of self-worth that could enable them to attain the education or job skills that could move them into more respectable positions in society.

The interactionist perspective also argues that a social condition becomes a social problem when it is defined by an influential group as threatening their values or disruptive of normal social expectations. Yet, while some respectable members of society may see the sex trade as threatening to family life or other parts of society, a degree of ambivalence can also be detected because many respectable people purchase services provided by the sex trade. In addition, prostitutes often define what they do as providing an essential service to society. So, in a sense, we might consider this to involve a competition among a variety of "moral entrepreneurs," with each trying to impose its definition of what is moral on society as a whole.

Future Prospects

Social policy regarding various forms of sexual behavior remains highly controversial. There is strong, universal disapproval, of course, of sexual behavior that involves the use of force or violence against an unwilling victim. Equally strong disapproval is found for child molestation, whether force is involved or not, because of the dependence and vulnerability of the child. However, these instances of forced sex are addressed in Chapter 9 as crimes. The sexual behaviors addressed in this chapter generally involve consenting adults (except in the cases of child pornography and teenage prostitution). Social disapproval of sexual behavior involving consenting adults is generally less severe, although prostitution, pornography, and other elements of the sex industry are viewed negatively by many people in the United States.

One approach to these forms of sexual behavior, then, would be to attempt to rid society of them by criminalizing them. This has been tried with prostitution and, to a lesser extent, pornography. It has not worked—both behaviors flourish. In addition, many people are hurt unfairly by punishment for their choice of a sexual outlet with another consenting adult. Furthermore, such criminalization seems unjustified because these sexual behaviors involve few negative consequences for society. Of course, future research could show a causal link between pornography and violence, and such a development would warrant rethinking social policies. In addition, prostitutes are often exploited because of their poverty and the sexist attitudes in society, but that is really a matter of poverty and gender inequality (Chapters 5 and 7), not of sexuality. So, although the criminalization policy is still pursued, at least to some degree, controversy and conflict persist over what to do about prostitution and pornography.

As for prostitution, it is legal in many counties in Nevada with no apparent damaging effects. It is illegal elsewhere but flourishes nonetheless. It is legal in some European nations and subject to government controls that seem to minimize the problems that arise, such as the spread of disease or control by organized crime. These facts suggest that we might want to reexamine our policy of criminalizing prostitution. The various policies proposed on this issue reflect, in one way or another, the laissez-faire or interventionist position on social problems. Helen Reynolds (1986) proposes these four different models of how government could approach prostitution:

1. *Laissez-faire model.* Prostitution is illegal but no active enforcement or prosecution is pursued; the risk of arrest is low for prostitutes, and competition flourishes among many different types of prostitutes.
2. *Regulation model.* Prostitution is legal, but only in settings that are licensed by authorities, such as brothels; prostitution in unlicensed settings is attacked by police.
3. *Zoning model.* Prostitution is permitted in particular areas of a community; prostitution may be legal or illegal in these areas, but the police would arrest prostitutes only outside these neighborhoods.
4. *Control model.* Prostitution is illegal and enforcement and prosecution are actively pursued everywhere; the risk of arrest is high everywhere and much prostitution is forced underground.

The first model represents the laissez-faire approach in which society does little to control prostitution, even though it is illegal; a kind of "hands-off" policy is encouraged. The last model represents a strong interventionist position in which authorities make significant efforts to control prostitution in all settings. The other two models represent more moderate interventionist models in which the authorities attempt to control some types of prostitutes, or prostitution in some settings, but let other types of prostitution flourish. These four models make clear that social policy on prostitution need not focus only on whether it is legal or illegal. More complex alternatives exist.

Most authorities would agree that prostitution is very hard to stop even when it is illegal. With a demand for the services and lots of money to be made, people are very creative in figuring out how to get around whatever barriers the police and other authorities are likely to put up. One approach that does show some promise focuses on the street trade: use coordinated and multileveled efforts to discourage prostitution in particular neighborhoods (Lowman, 1992). This could involve intensive efforts by police to arrest prostitutes and their customers, community groups that take control of the streets and discourage customers from coming around, and road closures and traffic diversions to make it difficult for customers to drive near where the prostitutes congregate. In some places, legislation makes it illegal to communicate about the purchase or sale of sexual services in public, which gives the police an extra tool with which to convict prostitutes and their customers. For some prostitutes and many customers, participating in the trade is a matter of how easy it is to do so, and coordinated efforts such as this seem to push them out of the trade. More committed prostitutes, however, such as those who need money to support a drug habit, tend to move elsewhere in response to such police interventions. So, whether these programs reduce prostitution in a particular area depends on how committed the prostitutes are to the trade. In some cases, these efforts just send prostitutes into other neighborhoods to ply their trade.

Legalization of prostitution does not eliminate the fact that some women are forced into prostitution because of poverty and sexism in society. For these reasons, society may still wish to reduce the amount of prostitution, even though it is legal. To do this, we need to recognize that society implicitly condones and encourages prostitution by perpetuating certain fallacies about it. One fallacy is that people "choose" to be prostitutes. Once we recognize that many people are forced by their poverty, vulnerability, and lack of opportunities into the trade and prevented from leaving by equally powerful forces, then all who participate in the trade become partners in that oppression. Another myth is that prostitution protects respectable women and children from sexual assault or unwanted sexual demands. This gives a noble sound to what is really a mechanism to ensure men the widest possible sexual access to women. The effort to control prostitution needs to begin by challenging these fallacies by ending the implicit support of a practice that it explicitly condemns. Another thing that could be done is to provide prostitutes with a way out of the trade: drug and alcohol rehabilitation, job referrals and job training, safe and affordable housing, assistance in completing high school or going to college, admission to programs for battered women, and whatever other assistance would help them get respectable and well-paying jobs.

During the 1970s, our laws took on new levels of tolerance for various forms of pornography, and this tolerance manifested itself in greater acceptance of nudity and overt displays of sexual conduct in public settings. The feminist movement of the 1980s and 1990s expressed renewed concern about pornography—especially sexually explicit materials that involve sexual violence. The most recent research available suggests that there may be a link between certain pornographic materials, especially those portraying violence against women, and attitudes about violence toward women. We can detect a definite trend of vacillation here between liberal attitudes and conservative responses. Through it all, actual research data are less than conclusive about the effects of pornography. One thing is certain: Lawmakers are responding to public concern about pornography and other elements of the sex industry with restrictive rulings. For example, a number of cities have used zoning ordinances to severely restrict sex-oriented video and book stores and X-rated movie theatres (Myers, 1994). The regulations limit, for example, how many such businesses may open and where, with the result that fewer are opened than would be the case with no regulations. The U.S. Supreme Court has ruled that, although sexually explicit materials are a form of speech protected under the Constitution, local authorities can restrict their activities if they can demonstrate that such businesses have some harmful impacts. The distribution of pornography on the Internet has produced a whole new set of issues and concerns (see the Policy Issues insert pp. 308–309).

Sex is a core and very emotional aspect of people's lives, and it rouses the passions. In addition, it is deeply linked to long-standing religious and cultural traditions. This is fertile ground for biased misperception and zealous overreaction, and social policies aimed at controlling one form or another of sexual behavior often result. Social policy should be based on the demonstrated negative impact of such behaviors on society or groups in society, not on the efforts of some powerful group to impose its personal or moral beliefs on others. As has been seen in this chapter, research to date fails to show that prostitution or pornography is, in and of itself, detrimental to society at large, although some groups are exploited by the sex trade. However, the societal reactions to these types of sexual behavior can create problems.

Should We Censor Pornography on the Internet?

In the years before computers and the Internet, the distribution of pornography was limited by the technology then used, namely magazines or videos that a person had to purchase in person or through the mail. Pornography was found in "adult" stores from which children and teenagers were excluded, or it was on a top shelf, out of sight except if one were looking for it. Because of this level of technology, pornography was largely out of reach of children or those who preferred not to be exposed to it. The Internet changed this because information is so freely accessible in cyberland. Through Web sites, e-mail, chat rooms, and news groups, all kinds of information, including pornography, are now easily available. Even children and those who prefer not to see pornography can find themselves exposed to it when they do an innocent Web search or go into a new chat room. Although some adults are likely to be stunned and offended by the hard-core pornography they can be exposed to inadvertently, parents are especially concerned that their children will be harmed by what they see. These developments have prompted a rousing debate over whether and how materials on the Internet should be censored (Godwin, 1998; Hick and Halpin, 2001).

Opponents of such censorship argue that it violates the protection of free speech that is provided for in the Constitution. Censorship, especially by central political authorities, will enable them to control the content of the Internet, editing or even eliminating information about unpopular or minority groups or the opinions and tastes of such groups. Although the immediate focus may be to control pornography, opponents argue, that merely opens the door for powerful interests to extend the control into other realms. In fact, the U.S. Supreme Court has seemed to support some of these arguments in its rulings over the last decade. Congress has passed a number of laws to limit the distribution of pornographic or obscene materials over the Internet, but the Supreme Court has consistently ruled that broad restrictions outlawing making pornography available on Web sites, even when children can gain access to it, is unconstitutional (Urbina, 2007).

Proponents of some degree of censorship argue that the new technology is so much more intrusive and pervasive than earlier print and film media that some efforts to enable people to control what they are exposed to must be made. While recognizing the importance of protecting free speech, they also believe that some compromises must be made to control what employers, families, and children are exposed to. In fact, the Internet is not currently the open, anarchic realm that some claim that it is. Most Internet service providers (ISPs) today do control what their users can gain access to, stopping access to illegal materials such as child pornography. In addition, software is widely available that will block access to adult-oriented sites, and many ISPs, such as America Online, enable their users to program their access to filter out certain kinds of Web sites or chat rooms. So, when a child logs on, the software or the ISP might prevent him or her from going to an adult chat room. This gives individuals and families some control over unwanted materials, and the Supreme Court has so far ruled that the use of such filtering software does not violate the Constitution. However, the filtering is very crude, and some useful material is undoubtedly also filtered out. Some proponents of censorship have suggested the development of a ratings system similar to what is currently used for films and videos. Each Web site or chat room could be rated for its sexual content, violence, or other criteria. Then each user could program his or her access to filter out Web sites with characteristics that he or she prefers not to be exposed to. One of the controversies with ratings systems, of course, is who will do the rating. The government could do it, but this brings up images of "big brother" controlling where people go on the Internet and has not been a popular way to rate films and videos. Web sites could voluntarily rate themselves, but that is ripe for abuse because Web sites that want to gain the widest access possible may downplay the extent of their sexual content or violence. The ISPs could cooperate in the development and application of a ratings system, as is currently done with films and videos.

Some opponents of censorship argue against filters and ratings systems. Filters are imprecise and block access to much useful and valuable information as well as to the unwanted information. Also, they argue, ratings systems inevitably expand in ways that will limit people's access unreasonably. In fact, the efforts at censorship could significantly change the Internet from a single

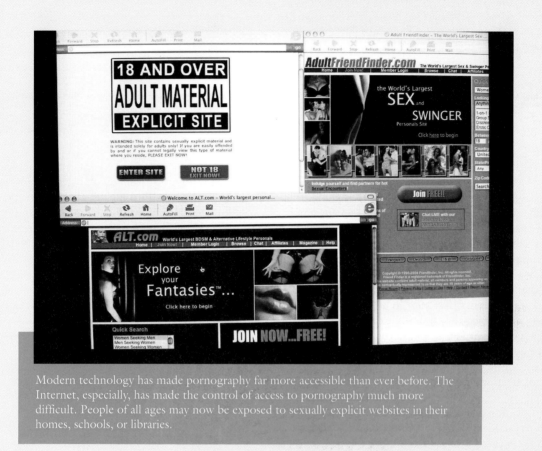

Modern technology has made pornography far more accessible than ever before. The Internet, especially, has made the control of access to pornography much more difficult. People of all ages may now be exposed to sexually explicit websites in their homes, schools, or libraries.

superhighway with everyone having access to everything into a series of "white-listing services"—Internet services that give a subscriber access only to a limited part of the Internet that has been approved by some organization or that has met some criteria. So, you might subscribe to a service that gave you access only to sites that had been approved by the Catholic Church or the Democratic Party or the Microsoft Corporation.

Some proponents of censorship argue that the ISPs should not serve as the "cops" of the Internet and that

rating systems may help but will not completely solve the problem. Thus, they call for federal legislation that would make it illegal to distribute certain materials on the Internet, especially materials that would be harmful to minors. These supporters of censorship believe that effective control will be achieved only when the government can fine or imprison those who distribute inappropriate material on the Internet. To date, however, the courts have thrown out legislative efforts to do this as unconstitutional.

Interventionist			Laissez-Faire
Government censors content of Internet	ISPs developing rating systems	Individuals and families purchase filtering software	No censorship at all

Prostitution increased when the crack cocaine epidemic in the 1980s (Chapter 10) led some desperate, crack-addicted women to engage in multiple sex acts in order to purchase the drug. This increased health problems (Chapter 4) because their unprotected sex with multiple partners, many of whom were IV-drug users, helped spread the AIDS virus. In addition, both prostitution and pornography are seen by some as reflecting sexual inequality: They are remnants of the patriarchal control that men still exercise over women (Chapter 7).

STUDY AND REVIEW

Summary

1. The varieties of human sexual expression are almost endless, and most of them have been condemned at one time or another as deviant. Prostitution and pornography are forms of sexual expression over which there is intense debate.

2. Sexual attitudes and behavior vary from culture to culture. There is also variety in human sexuality from group to group within the same culture or society. Sexual attitudes and behaviors have changed over time in the direction of greater permissiveness, and this trend is explained by secularization, increased technological sophistication, and the growing demand for equal rights.

3. Prostitution takes different forms: from streetwalkers to call girls to male prostitutes. Precise figures on the incidence of prostitution are impossible to obtain. There are arguments for and against the legalization of prostitution, although in eleven counties in the state of Nevada prostitution is already legal.

4. There is tremendous controversy about what is and is not pornographic and about what kinds of materials, if any, should be censored. The U.S. Attorney General's Commission on Pornography reported in 1986 that sexually explicit materials are directly linked with violence. This conclusion is disputed by current research on pornography.

5. From the functionalist perspective, deviant behaviors such as prostitution and pornography continue to exist because they perform important functions for society. From the conflict perspective, the sex trade is closely related to issues of social inequality and the exercise of power. From the interactionist perspective, sexual deviance has to do with varying definitions of reality and with the impact of labeling and stigmatization on self-concept and self-worth.

6. Disapproval of various forms of sexual behavior is greater when force is involved, or when one partner is not an adult. There has been a lot of change and conflict in this realm in the last few decades. Some argue that prostitution should be legal and that no problems are created when it is legal and regulated. When illegal, prostitution is very difficult to control. Although more pornographic materials are available today, there is also growing pressure to restrict their distribution.

7. Research fails to show that prostitution and pornography, in and of themselves, are detrimental to society. Problems arise from the hostile reactions that some groups have toward these forms of sexual expression.

Key Terms

pornography   secularization
prostitution

Multiple-Choice Questions

1. A complete prohibition on premarital sex is
   a. found in almost all preindustrial societies.
   b. found in about one-third of all human societies.
   c. not supported by most Western religions today.
   d. found in very few preindustrial societies.

2. According to the text, the most significant change in sexual behavior in the United States in the twentieth century has been
   a. a decline in premarital sex.
   b. an increase in homosexuality.
   c. the elimination of the "double standard."
   d. the decline in the use of prostitutes.
   e. the increase in the use of prostitutes by women.

3. Which of the following factors was *not* mentioned as something that accounts for the changes in sexual behavior in the United States in the late twentieth century?

You should be forewarned before doing a search of the Internet for topics relating to this chapter that almost any such search that includes terms such as "prostitution" and "sex" will probably generate sexually explicit or pornographic materials. This problem is discussed in the Policy Issues insert in this chapter. With this warning, if you wish to push ahead, there are two Web sites that approach the issues from quite different directions. The Prostitutes' Education Network **(www.bayswan.org/index.html)** argues for the legalization of prostitution but also for the protection of prostitutes from assault and disease. It offers advice, information, and contacts for prostitutes. The organization Femisa maintains a Web site that supports feminist positions in general and argues against the exploitation of women in its many forms, including prostitution and pornography. At the Femisa Web site, use its search engine to find materials specifically on prostitution and pornography.

Data on subjects like prostitution in the United States can be found at the Federal Bureau of Investigation Web site **(www.fbi.gov)**. Gather as much information as you can about prostitution from that site. Also, the Bureau of Justice Statistics at the Department of Justice **(www.ojp.usdoj.gov/bjs)** publishes a volume called the *Sourcebook of Criminal Justice Statistics*, which is available at this Web site: **www.albany.edu/sourcebook**. Some of the data on prostitution and pornography in this chapter were taken from the *Sourcebook*. Update that data, if you can, and also look for other data on prostitution, pornography, or other forms of sexual deviance.

The Allyn & Bacon Social Problems Supersite **(http://wps.ablongman.com/ab_socialprob_sprsite_1)** contains material on various forms of sexual behavior.

---

    a. secularization
    b. reliable contraceptives
    c. the feminist movement
    d. the growth in single-parent families

4. _____ are less likely to agree that prostitution should be legal than are _____.
    a. Men . . . women
    b. The elderly . . . the young
    c. People with higher incomes . . . people with lower incomes
    d. People with more education . . . people with less education

5. Those who support the legalization of prostitution argue that prostitution is
    a. a self-fulfilling prophecy.
    b. homophobia.
    c. secondary deviance.
    d. primary deviance.
    e. a victimless crime.

6. Where prostitution is legal in the United States
    a. illegal prostitution still persists.
    b. AIDS is rampant.
    c. it mostly takes the form of streetwalkers.
    d. it is hard to regulate.

7. All of the following have contributed to the growth of the global sex industry *except*
    a. the downsizing of the U.S. military.
    b. poverty in Third-World countries.
    c. the growth of the tourism industry since World War II.

    d. the economic demand for sexual services.
    e. All of the above contributed to the growth.

8. "Sexually explicit materials that are designed to be sexually arousing" is a definition of
    a. pornography.
    b. obscenity.
    c. homophobia.
    d. self-fulfilling prophecy.

9. Which of the following was found in research investigating the link between pornography and violence against women?
    a. Rapists read more pornography than do nonrapists.
    b. Violent pornography changes some men's attitudes in artificial, laboratory settings.
    c. Nonviolent pornography is as harmful as violent pornography.
    d. Sex offenses decline in locales where pornography is in heavy circulation.

10. Which of these models of prostitution represents the strongest interventionist approach?
    a. laissez-faire model
    b. regulation model
    c. control model
    d. zoning model

True/False Questions

1. The social problem with the sexual behaviors discussed in this chapter is that the behaviors themselves have very harmful consequences for society.
2. The Mangaians described in the text have what many people in the United States would call a very permissive attitude toward sexual behavior.
3. Young people today are more likely to view premarital sex as socially acceptable than are older people.
4. Over the past few decades, the amount of sexual behavior engaged in by men and women has been growing apart.
5. The prostitute with the highest status in the prostitute world is the streetwalker.
6. Compared to streetwalkers, escort services and online prostitutes find it harder to avoid contact with the police.
7. Escort prostitutes are not found in male prostitution.
8. According to the text, the prostitution trade in the United States is thriving.
9. The courts in the United States have ruled that obscenity lies outside of the free speech protection of the First Amendment to the Constitution.
10. The Supreme Court has ruled that local authorities can restrict where sex shops can open for business if they can demonstrate that such businesses have harmful impacts.

Fill-In Questions

1. Changes in premarital sexual behavior during the twentieth century have often been referred to as the "sexual _____."
2. The _____ refers to a situation where men are allowed more sexual freedom than women are.
3. The process of _____ involves the dispersal of religion into private and personal realms.
4. Most "streetwalkers" work for a _____.
5. Best estimates place the number of prostitutes working in the United States at between _____ and _____.
6. In the United States, prostitution is legal in parts of the state of _____.
7. Male prostitutes tend to come from two distinct subcultures: the _____ subculture and the _____ subculture.
8. More than any other single factor, entrance into prostitution for women is linked to _____.
9. _____ is lustful material that offends prevailing senses of decency and morality.
10. Approximately _____ percent of people in the United States believe that laws should forbid the distribution of pornography to adults as well as children.

Matching Questions

_____ 1. secularization
_____ 2. zoning model
_____ 3. peer-delinquent subculture
_____ 4. Internet
_____ 5. madam
_____ 6. call girl
_____ 7. COYOTE
_____ 8. *Miller* test
_____ 9. Catharine MacKinnon
_____ 10. U.S. Attorney General's Commission or Meese Commission

A. supervisor of prostitutes
B. decline in religion
C. prostitute interest group
D. male prostitutes
E. worldwide distribution of pornography
F. pornography report
G. feminist opponent of pornography
H. escort prostitute
I. government approach to prostitution
J. conditions of legal obscenity

Essay Questions

1. Describe some of the variety in sexual behavior among human beings. What accounts for this variety?
2. What accounts for the increase in premarital sexual behavior in the United States in the twentieth century?
3. Describe the different kinds of prostitutes that can be found in the United States. Which ones are easier for the police to control and why?
4. What are the arguments for and against legalizing prostitution in the United States?
5. How and why do women become prostitutes? What sociological theories were used to explain the process?
6. Describe the global sex industry. What factors have contributed to its emergence?
7. What are the arguments for and against the censorship of pornography for adults in the United States?
8. Summarize the research evidence regarding the issue of whether pornography leads to violence against women.
9. What are the arguments for and against a social policy that controls prostitution and pornography by criminalizing them?
10. Describe the four different models of how the government could approach prostitution. How does each model relate to the interventionist and laissez-faire positions?

For Further Reading

John Gagnon and William Simon. *Sexual Conduct,* 2d ed. New York: Aldine de Gruyter, 2004. This new edition of a classic book describes how sociologists approach issues of human sexuality and especially develops a social constructionist approach to sexuality.

Cecil Greek and William Thompson. *Porn Wars: The Battle Over Pornography in England and America.* New York: Aldine de Gruyter, 1995. This is an excellent history and analysis of the battle against pornography by religious fundamentalists, conservative politicians, and some feminists. The authors view these groups as "moral entrepreneurs" in a battle over whose values will prevail.

Valerie Jenness. *Making It Work: The Prostitutes' Rights Movement in Perspective.* Hawthorne, NY: Aldine de Gruyter, 1993. This book analyzes why prostitution is considered deviant by many and describes a social movement that has attempted to reduce the stigma associated with the activity and "normalize" it.

Daniel Linz and Neil Malamuth. *Pornography.* Newbury Park, CA: Sage Publications, 1993. This book offers a good summary of the different stances that have been taken on the issue of pornography and an excellent summary of the research on the effects of pornography on people and society.

Robert T. Michael, John H. Gagnon, Edward O. Laumann, and Gina Kolata. *Sex in America: A Definitive Survey.* Boston: Little, Brown, 1994. This book is a shortened version of the National Health and Social Life Survey reported on in this chapter. It presents interesting information about human sexuality in the United States and deflates a number of myths along the way.

D. Kelly Weisberg. *Children of the Night: A Study of Adolescent Prostitution.* Lexington, MA: Lexington Books/D.C. Heath, 1985. Provides excellent coverage of adolescent prostitution, with excerpts from interviews with teenage participants in the "trade."

POPULATION GROWTH AND URBANIZATION

In the early 1800s, world population reached one billion people. It took one million years to reach this number. In the next 160 years—by 1960—the world's population had tripled in size to approximately three billion people. Then, with incredible speed, another billion people were added during the fifteen years between 1960 and 1975 and yet another billion by the late 1980s. It is projected that another two billion people will be added to the world population by the year 2025 (see Figure 12.1). Demographers caution that long-range projections concerning future world population size are speculative but that it could well exceed nine billion people sometime in the twenty-first century. This population explosion has many consequences, as will be seen, such as crowding, starvation, and the depletion of natural resources. Population growth also has consequences for the earth's environment, which is the topic of Chapter 13. In fact, if humankind fails to control population growth, the world could be heading for a catastrophe of stunning proportions.

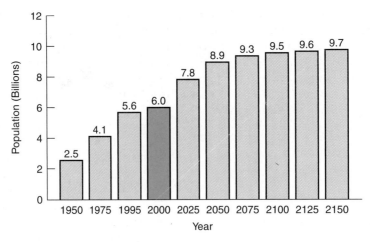

FIGURE 12.1 **World Population, 1950–2150 (based on a medium-fertility scenario).**

Source: Population Division of the Department of Economic and Social Affairs, United Nations Secretariat, *Long-Range World Population Projections: Based on the 1998 Revision* (New York: United Nations, 2002), www.un.org/esa/population/publications/longrange/longrange.htm.

Myths & Facts

About Population Growth and Urbanization

Myth: The most important factor in controlling world population growth is technology: Modern contraceptive technology is essential if people are to control their fertility.

Fact: The most crucial ingredient in world population growth is human values and desires. Effective contraception procedures have been available for some time, but as long as people place a high value on having many children, world population will continue to grow. At times in U.S. history, before modern contraceptives were available, the birthrate has been quite low because people chose to have fewer children.

Myth: The United States achieved zero population growth (ZPG) when the birthrate dropped below replacement level in the 1970s.

Fact: Although the U.S. birthrate has been dropping steadily and has remained below replacement level for some time, this rate will have to continue for another generation before the country reaches ZPG.

Myth: Suburban growth in the United States began early in the twentieth century because people wanted larger homes and more land, and entrepreneurial real estate developers satisfied that desire.

Fact: Although these played a part, the suburbs are equally an invention of government policies. The U.S.

government built the interstate highway system, which made it possible for people to live in the suburbs and still get to work in the city; the government also provided low-interest, guaranteed mortgage loans for new homes, which were most often built in the suburbs because most cities had little space for new homes. The government did not provide such loans to build apartments in cities, which would have encouraged people to stay in the cities. The result was a strong government incentive for people to move to the suburbs.

Myth: Our cities are segregated today because whites and nonwhites just do not want to live together in the same neighborhood.

Fact: Through the 1950s, the government discouraged blacks and whites from living in the same communities by actively discouraging real estate developers from selling homes in white suburbs to African Americans. At the same time, the government discouraged lenders from making home mortgage loans to people living in African American communities on the grounds that people in such communities are bad credit risks. So the seeds of today's segregated urban landscape were planted many years ago by government policies.

Accompanying the growth in world population over the centuries has been a change in the size of the human communities in which most people live, from small villages and rural areas to large and crowded cities. Most people in the United States live in cities or the suburbs that surround them. The chapter will begin with an analysis of population growth and the problems associated with it; following that, urban problems will be the focus of attention.

Population Growth

Elements of Demographic Change

Demography is *the study of the size, composition, and distribution of human populations and how these factors change over time.* Each one of us participates in at least two "demographic acts" that affect human population—we are born and we will eventually die. Many of us also engage in other demographic acts, such as having children of our own. All these individual decisions and activities combine into an enormous wave of actions that make the world population what it is today. The term **population** refers to *the total number of people inhabiting a particular geographic area at a specified time.* Three basic elements shape the size, composition, and distribution of human populations: fertility, mortality, and migration.

FERTILITY **Fertility** refers to *the actual number of children born.* This is distinguished from **fecundity,** or *the biological maximum number of children that could be born.* Because women rarely have the maximum number of children they are capable of bearing, the fertility of a society is normally quite a bit lower than its fecundity. The simplest measure of fertility is the *crude birthrate,* the number of live births occurring in a particular population during a given year for each one thousand people in that population. Figure 4.1 on page 94 shows the changes in the crude birthrate in the United States since 1910.

MORTALITY **Mortality** refers to *the number of deaths that occur in a particular population.* As with fertility, mortality in a society can be described in a number of ways. The *crude death rate* refers to the total number of deaths for every one thousand people (see Figure 4.1). The crude death rate in the United States has declined substantially over the past century from seventeen deaths per one thousand people in 1900 to about eight today. However, as can be seen in Figure 4.1, there has been relatively little change in the past three decades. The crude death rate does not take into account the fact that people of some ages, such as the

very young, are much more likely to die. It is therefore useful to look at the *infant mortality rate,* which is the rate of death among infants under one year of age. Infants have experienced the greatest decline in death rates of all age groups in the United States: dropping from one hundred deaths per one thousand infants in 1915 to fewer than seven today. Another way to describe the mortality of a populace is with the *life expectancy,* which refers to the number of years, on the average, that people can expect to live. People in the United States have experienced a substantial increase in life expectancy during the past century, as Table 12.1 illustrates. As can be seen, the life expectancy of women has increased more than that of men. The difference in life expectancy between the sexes was only one year in 1920, whereas it is almost six years today.

When we combine the results of the crude birthrate and the crude death rate, we derive an indication of the growth of a population, and the difference between these two figures is referred to as the *rate of natural increase.* For example, in 2005, the crude birthrate of the United States was 14.2 and the crude death rate was 8.1, yielding a rate of natural increase of 0.61 percent.

MIGRATION On the most general level, **migration** refers to *a permanent change of residence.* The term *immigration* refers to movement into a particular country, whereas *emigration* involves moving out. In analyzing migration, demographers look for "push" and "pull" factors. Sometimes people are pushed out of one country because of poor economic

TABLE 12.1 Expectation of Life at Birth in the United States, 1920–2010

Year	Total	Male	Female
1920	54.1	53.6	54.6
1930	59.7	58.1	61.6
1940	62.9	60.8	65.2
1950	68.2	65.6	71.1
1960	69.7	66.6	73.1
1970	70.8	67.1	74.7
1980	73.7	70.0	77.5
1990	75.4	71.8	78.8
2000	77.0	74.3	79.7
2010[a]	78.5	75.6	81.4

[a]Projection

SOURCES: U.S. Bureau of the Census, *Statistical Abstract of the United States, 1978* (Washington, DC: U.S. Government Printing Office, 1978), p. 69; U.S. Bureau of the Census, *Statistical Abstract of the United States,* 2007 (Washington, DC: U.S. Government Printing Office, 2006), p. 75.

times, unstable political conditions, and the like. Many Southeast Asians migrated to the United States in the 1970s and 1980s, for example, because of the unpredictable political situation in that part of the world. In other cases, there is a "pull" or attraction that leads people to migrate to a particular place. Many Europeans migrated to the United States in the belief that they would have better economic and social opportunities.

Migration is also an important variable in the population within a particular nation. For example, the population density of the southern and western states in the United States has risen dramatically in recent decades because of in-migration from other states. Likewise, the number of people living in some other states has declined because of out-migration. Between 1980 and 2005, North Dakota, West Virginia, and Washington, D.C., experienced a net decline in population, and some states, such as Iowa, showed almost no increase (U.S. Bureau of the Census, 2006:20). All other states showed some increase. These shifts contribute to high rates of unemployment and fewer job opportunities in the states showing little growth (see Chapter 2).

World Population Growth

In analyzing world population problems, migration, for obvious reasons, is not a critical element of overall population growth and change, although it can have an impact on the fortunes of particular regions. Fertility and mortality, however, are key elements, and this discussion will focus on them.

Most of human history has passed on an earth that was only sparsely populated by people. It has been estimated, for example, that there were fewer people on the whole earth seven thousand years ago than there are in larger cities such as New York or Tokyo today. At the time of Christ, approximately two thousand years ago, there were probably not many more people alive than currently live in the United States. In Figure 12.2, you can readily see that, prior to the 1700s, world population was small and growth was slow. After 1750, world population began to increase at a more rapid rate, and it continues to grow even more rapidly today. Only in the last two centuries has world population exceeded one billion, with a current population of about six billion (see Figure 12.1). The largest nation in the world today is China, with a little over 1.3 billion people.

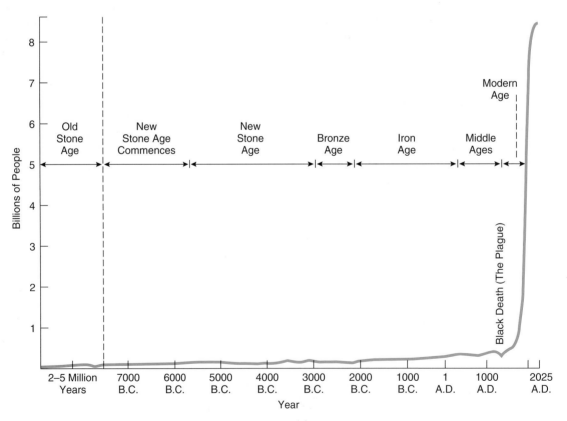

FIGURE 12.2 **World Population Growth Through History.**

Source: Population Reference Bureau, *World Population: Fundamentals of Growth*, 3d ed., 1995.

The United States is the third largest nation, with a population of 300 million, behind China and India.

The primary reason for the low rate of population growth in the world prior to 1750 was the relatively high death rate that existed in practically every society. For example, until 1600, the average life expectancy in European countries was little more than 35 years, in comparison to more than 70 years in industrial societies today. One important factor in the high death rate at that time was the extremely high infant mortality rate. In some societies, as many as 50 percent of the infants born would die within their first year of life (Antonovsky, 1972). The two most important factors producing these high death rates were disease and famine. In fact, disease has accounted for more deaths in the Western world than any other factor, and this has been the case throughout history. Famine at times has led to astonishingly high death rates. For example, a severe famine in China in 1877 and 1878 was responsible for the death of between 9 million and 13 million people (Petersen, 1975). Before the modern era, knowledge and technology related to medicine, sanitation, and agriculture were not sufficiently advanced to lower the death rate and thus increase life expectancy.

The Demographic Transition

What explains the rapid world population growth of the past few centuries? In an effort to answer this question, demographers point to a process known as the **demographic transition**, *the changing patterns of birth and death rates brought about by industrialization* (Ginn Daugherty and Kammeyer, 1995). The reasons for this transition are complex. It is most useful to divide the demographic transition into four stages (see Figure 12.3). The *preindustrial stage* is characterized by high birthrates and high death rates, resulting in a population that grows slowly, if at all.

Throughout much of human history, societies have been in this preindustrial stage.

For most Western nations, including the United States, the preindustrial stage existed until the onset of industrialization between 1750 and 1850, when the *transitional,* or *early industrial, stage* begins. This stage is characterized by continuing high birthrates but declining death rates. The falling death rates occur because of improvements in lifestyle resulting from industrial development (see Chapter 4). More and better food was available, for example, that helped people resist infectious diseases and reduced infant mortality. In addition, improvements in transportation, communication, and sanitation contributed to a lowering of the death rate. However, cultural values still encouraged people to have large families, so the birthrate stayed high. *The gap between the high birthrates and low death rates*—commonly called a **demographic gap**—resulted in explosive population growth during the early industrial period (Brown, 1987). The death rate was too low to keep population size stable when the birthrate remained high.

The third stage is called the *industrial stage* and is characterized by a continued decline in the death rate and a declining birthrate. During this stage medicine became more effective in controlling acute and chronic diseases and thus contributed to additional declines in the death rate. In addition, industrial technology made it possible for people to lead cleaner and healthier lives. The decline in the birthrate was a response to the impact of industrialization on cultural values regarding childbearing. Urbanization and increasing education, for example, led couples to desire smaller families than in the past.

The *postindustrial stage* of the demographic transition, which some demographers prefer to consider a continuation of the industrial stage, is characterized by low birthrates and low death rates, once again

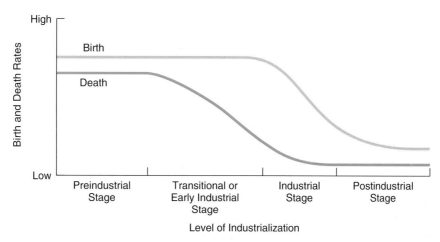

FIGURE 12.3 **The Demographic Transition.**

a roughly stable population with little growth. The industrialized nations, such as the United States, Japan, and some European countries, may be currently entering this stage, although how low their birthrates and death rates will remain and for how long is a matter of some speculation.

The Extent of Overpopulation

The fully industrialized nations in the world today, including the United States, have experienced the demographic transition and now exhibit relatively low birthrates and death rates. If these low rates continue, then the populations of these countries will eventually stabilize, with little if any subsequent growth (assuming no immigration). However, many nations in the world are considerably less industrialized and have not yet gone through this transition in birthrates and death rates, and this is where the largest increases in the world's population can be found today. In these nations, the death rate has dropped considerably, due in large part to the introduction of modern medicine, sanitation, and public health efforts. Insecticides, better transportation, and improved agricultural practices, for example, have made more and better food available. The impact of these changes on mortality has frequently

been dramatic. In Sri Lanka between 1945 and 1949, the crude death rate declined from 22 deaths per one thousand people to 12 per one thousand; in 1947 alone, the life expectancy rose from 43 to 52.

Although declines in the death rate in these countries have been substantial, the birthrate has remained high, resulting in a continuing and large demographic gap. Afghanistan and Jordan, for example, are projected to have rates of natural increase of over 2 percent in 2010 compared to half a percent in the United States (U.S. Bureau of the Census, 2006:837). In today's industrialized nations, the death rate has declined slowly over many decades, so population growth has been gradual, allowing cultural values regarding childbearing and family size to change, yielding smaller families. The developing nations of today, however, have seen their death rates drop rapidly, and cultural values do not change that quickly. Thus, the developing regions of the world are expected to grow at an annual rate of 1.5 to 2.0 percent, as compared with 0.5 percent in the fully industrialized nations (United Nations, 2006). Figure 12.4 shows the impact of these differing rates of natural increase: Europe and North America, where most of the industrial nations are, will contain a dwindling proportion of the world's population, whereas Africa, Asia, and Latin America, containing mostly

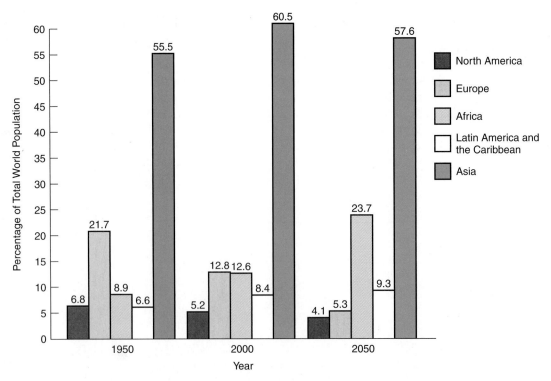

FIGURE 12.4 **Percentage Distribution of the World's Population in Various Geographic Areas, 1950–2050 (based on a medium-fertility scenario).**

Source: Population Division of the Department of Economic and Social Affairs, United Nations Secretariat, *Long-Range World Population Projections: Based on the 1998 Revision* (New York: United Nations, 2002), www.un.org/esa/population/publications/longrange/longrange.htm.

developing nations, will see their proportion of the world's population grow significantly.

The impact of all this can be better understood if we examine the number of years required for the world's population to double in size. Demographers refer to this figure as the *doubling time*. From the beginning of the Christian era, it took 1,650 years for the population to double. By comparison, if current rates of world population growth continue, only 200 years will pass until world population again doubles its size! Will the developing nations of the world today lower their birthrates before world population grows disastrously out of control? Keep in mind that the demographic transition is a description of a long historical trend found in some nations, all of which have experienced occasional changes in birthrates or death rates that go against this trend. We do not know if the developing nations of today will follow the same path. However, one thing is clear. In a preindustrial era, population growth, or the lack of it, was determined primarily by a high death rate, over which people had little control at that time. Today, growth is determined to a large extent by factors, especially fertility, over which people do have some control. Thus, the attention of those concerned about overpopulation today has been focused on issues of fertility control.

The Growth of Cities

All humans organize their lives into **communities,** which are *groups of people who share a common territory and a sense of identity or belonging and who interact with one another* (Lyon, 1999). The earliest human communities were small hunting and gathering bands, usually consisting of between forty and one hundred people, roaming the land in search of food and game. Approximately ten thousand years ago, people discovered how to cultivate plants and domesticate animals. This afforded them with greater control over their food supply and permitted a growing surplus of food. The result was the emergence of agricultural villages, and later cities, in fertile river valleys around the world. A **city** is *a relatively large, permanent community of people who rely on surrounding agricultural communities for their food supply.* As a consequence of developing agriculture, then, human communities grew enormously in size. At the height of the Roman Empire, Rome is estimated to have had as many as one million residents (Hawley, 1971).

Urbanization

Industrialization ushered in ever-increasing urbanization, with cities growing far larger than their preindustrial predecessors. By the mid-twentieth century, cities such as New York, Chicago, and Los Angeles had many millions of inhabitants. Two hundred years ago, only 5 percent of all people in the United States lived in urban areas, in contrast to 79 percent today (see Figure 12.5). The New York metropolitan area has 18 million people, and Los Angeles 13 million. Why has this extensive urbanization occurred? One of the main reasons is that most economic activity in

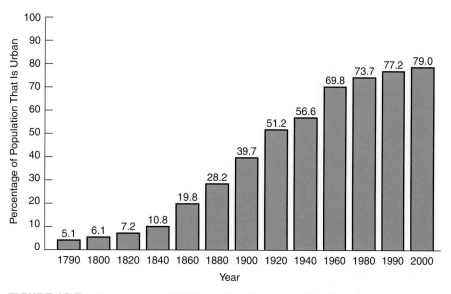

FIGURE 12.5 **Percentage of Urban Population in the United States, 1790–2000.**

Sources: U.S. Bureau of the Census, *Statistical Abstract of the United States, 1991* (Washington, DC: U.S. Government Printing Office, 1991), pp. 17, 27; and *Statistical Abstract of the United States, 2007* (Washington, DC: U.S. Government Printing Office, 2006), p. 36.

industrial societies is nonagricultural, and such activity benefits from being concentrated geographically. With industry and jobs located in cities, people are drawn to the cities to find work.

Suburbanization

Equally as important as the growth in size of cities has been the growth of **suburbs,** *less densely populated areas, primarily residential in nature, on the outskirts of a city.* Mass suburbanization is a relatively recent development. In the United States, it arose out of a complex set of social factors (Banfield, 1990). One factor was the economic and technological developments that made it possible for people to live far from where they worked. Early in the twentieth century, most people were limited in where they could live by the need to find transportation to work. This meant that most had to live in the cities, near where the jobs were. By the 1940s and 1950s, the increasing affluence in the United States, along with the automobile, made it feasible for people to live farther from work and opened up suburban life to the middle class.

In addition to these economic developments, government policy also contributed to suburbanization.

For example, the federal government paid 80 percent of the cost of developing the interstate highway system. Another encouragement to the development of suburbs were policies of the Federal Housing Administration (FHA), established in 1934, and the Veterans Administration (VA) (Bullock, Anderson, and Brady, 1983). Beginning in the 1930s, the FHA and the VA made available federally guaranteed mortgage loans for the purchase of new homes. Because land outside the cities was both inexpensive and available, this was where much of the construction took place. The FHA and VA did not provide loans to purchase existing homes or build apartments, policies that would have encouraged people to continue living in the cities. Keep in mind that this suburbanization occurred not simply because people wanted to move to the suburbs. It also depended on the development of new transportation technologies and on federal social policy on housing and transportation. The manifest function of the social policies was to stimulate economic development. Their latent function was to encourage decentralization of urban areas and to bring about the eventual decline of many cities. Clearly, all the ramifications of these policies were not considered when they were established.

Government policies that assisted people in purchasing new homes in the suburbs rather than existing housing in the city encouraged the suburbanization of cities such as Los Angeles. Urban sprawl and severe air pollution were among the eventual results.

These same developments eventually made it possible for businesses and factories also to move outside of cities. A labor force and highways were available in the suburbs. In addition, suburban land was typically less expensive, taxes were lower, and affluent suburbs could afford to offer tax breaks to industries to relocate. Increasing crowding and congestion in cities, along with the growth of numerous problems, also made the suburbs popular as a "rural refuge" from the hustle and bustle of the city. In their early development, suburbs were not economically self-supporting, because many residents made their livelihood in the cities. By the 1970s, however, this had changed, with 75 percent of all suburban residents both living and working in the suburbs and only about 25 percent commuting to the central city to work. Today, the United States is a nation of suburbanites, with 60 percent of its metropolitan population living in the suburbs.

The Postindustrial City

Although people and some jobs have left the city, other jobs have remained. Many cities have retained or increased jobs in the financial service industries, those related to the functioning of corporate headquarters, telecommunications and publishing, and those involving nonprofit and governmental activities (Abrahamson, 2004). In other words, the changes in cities reflect the changes in the economy discussed in Chapter 2: the stagnation in the manufacturing sector and the growth of the service sector.

However, recent technological developments may reduce the need for corporations or service industries to concentrate their workers in one locale. Computers, microwave transmission, fax machines, and communications satellites make it possible for people to communicate over long distances instantly and inexpensively. There will still be some need for centralization, however.

Perspectives on Population and Urban Problems

The Functionalist Perspective

A major assumption of the functionalist perspective is that both societies and cities are systems made up of interdependent parts and that changes in one part of the system may have consequences for the other parts. In the case of society as a whole, the parts include the size and characteristics of its population along with the food supply and other elements of the environment that support that population. One of the earliest attempts to understand population dynamics was basically functionalist in nature. An English clergyman named Thomas Robert Malthus (1960, originally published 1798) became concerned with population problems around the beginning of the industrial revolution in Europe. Malthus viewed population size and food supplies as two parts of a system that should be in balance if society is to function properly. He argued that there exists an immutable passion between the sexes that leads to reproduction, and this leads to a constant pressure toward population growth. He also said that societies have a limited ability to produce food. If the tendency toward population growth continues unchecked, then populations will eventually grow larger than the food supply can support. Malthus believed that human beings could intercede in this process and control population growth by postponing marriage or remaining celibate, but he was pessimistic about whether human intervention would completely save the day. He thought populations would continue to grow, ultimately being checked by deaths due to starvation, disease, and war.

Like Malthus, modern-day functionalists view population growth as a social problem in terms of the relationship between uncontrolled population growth and the exhaustion of available resources. Population growth becomes a social problem when it becomes dysfunctional and leads to social disorganization. This occurs when population growth interferes with the ability to achieve societal goals, such as providing adequate food and housing or keeping illness rates at an acceptable level. Cities have also confronted social disorganization resulting from changes in some parts of the urban system. Some of these significant changes have just been discussed: the flight of people and jobs to the suburbs, changes in the occupational structure of an advanced industrial society, and developments in technology, such as the automobile, highways, and computers. The problems of cities in the United States arise, at least in part, because these changes have produced some degree of social disorganization, with people dislocated because of the changes and problems such as crime and violence arising. All these changes have been beneficial in many respects, of course, but they have also had highly dysfunctional effects for many cities.

It may be, of course, that the central cities are no longer functional for modern economies and should be abandoned, especially considering that businesses find it cheaper to locate elsewhere and people prefer to live elsewhere. Yet the cities are still an important part of the social system: People live, work, and shop there and are adversely affected by the crime and other urban problems. Many societal resources in the form of buildings, transportation networks, and people are tied up there. So ignoring the problems of the cities does not alleviate their impact on people's lives.

The Conflict Perspective

From the conflict perspective, population and urban problems are due more to an inequitable distribution of resources than to a lack of resources. In regard to population problems, for example, Karl Marx argued that powerful groups in society, namely, the capitalists, benefit from restrictions in the food supply and other scarce resources. Recall from Chapter 2 that capitalism is based on profit making. Because of this, food and other goods are not produced unless someone can make a profit from producing and selling them. Less food may be produced than people actually need so that the low supply of food will increase the price. With an economy based on producing food for human need rather than profit, Marx argued, technology could be harnessed to produce a sufficient amount of food for a growing population.

From the conflict perspective, then, population becomes a social problem when those who control the economic system take steps to limit artificially the resources available in order to benefit a particular group of people. The solution to these problems does not focus on limiting the number of people born but rather on enacting changes in the systems of production and distribution that would lead to a broader and more equitable distribution of resources among groups. Elements of this conflict perspective can be found in the stance of some developing nations today. They argue that world population growth is not the real problem but rather that resources are unevenly distributed among the various nations. For example, the United States could grow far more food than it currently does, and in fact the United States withholds much good cropland from production to lower food surpluses and raise prices.

From the conflict perspective, cities have deteriorated because the groups most directly affected—people living in the cities—have not had the political and economic resources to thwart the changes under way (Feagin, 1998). As we have seen, federal legislation encouraged the shift of people and jobs to the suburbs. The people who left the cities were the middle class and the affluent—the very people with the power to do something about the decline of the cities if they wished. But, of course, once they left, they were no longer interested in urban problems. In fact, these people tended not to understand the part their own actions played in bringing about the problems. The poor and minorities who were left in the cities had few political and economic resources with which to attack the problems.

The Interactionist Perspective

The interactionist perspective stresses the importance of social definition and social meaning, and thus population and urban problems are as much about *subjective* definitions of reality as they are about *objective* conditions. People in the United States have become used to rather spacious surroundings—the ranch-style suburban house on a large lot. In an equally industrialized but much more crowded nation such as Japan, on the other hand, most people have become accustomed to substantially less living space. People in the United States might well regard the amount of space available to the average Japanese family as "crowded." Likewise, the United States today could be regarded as overpopulated if the amount of land available to farmers during the preindustrial period is compared with the amount available to most people today. On the other hand, even the most spartan living conditions available to many poor people in the United States would appear luxurious to the poor (and some nonpoor) in a crowded, less developed nation such as India.

So, the interactionist perspective stresses that population conditions become social problems, in part, because of people's social definition of what is desirable or essential in their lives. The same is true regarding assessments of urban problems. In many respects, cities in the United States are far better off than they have ever been (Banfield, 1990). They are less crowded and have better sanitation, and the schools have improved in comparison to pre-World War II cities. Even their finances are in pretty good shape when compared with cities in earlier eras. Yet the interactionist perspective points to the importance of subjective definitions of social reality. People have come to expect much more than they once did. In addition, people tend to assess cities today in comparison with the immediate past that many of them can recall. The period between World War II and 1970 was one of considerable economic expansion and social prosperity for cities. By contrast, the urban experience of the 1980s and 1990s seems to have been a highly disruptive downturn in the fortunes of cities (Clark and Walter, 1991). It is this contrast that often leads people to perceive the problems of cities as much more severe than objective conditions would warrant. Yet, the important issue from the interactionist perspective is that people define these conditions as a social problem.

Consequences of World Population Growth

Has population growth had adverse consequences for people? In looking at this issue, a useful concept is that of **carrying capacity:** *an upper-size limit that is imposed on a population by its environmental resources and that cannot be permanently exceeded* (Cohen, 1995). The idea of carrying capacity parallels some Malthusian ideas about population dynamics: A point is reached at which environmental resources in a geographic region are insufficient to allow further population growth, at least not without a change or decline in lifestyle. A geographic area such as the United States has a large carrying capacity, in part because of its abundant natural resources. In contrast, an area such as Ethiopia has a much lower carrying capacity because of its comparatively scarce resources and lack of technology. Advances in technology can increase the carrying capacity of an area. Improvements in agriculture, for example, might enable Ethiopia to support more people than it once did. But there is always a limit to how much growth can occur. After an extensive review of the data available on the subject, one expert concluded that:

> The human population of the Earth now travels in the zone where a substantial fraction of scholars have estimated upper limits on human population size. . . . The possibility must be considered seriously that the number of people on the Earth has reached, or will reach within half a century, the maximum number the Earth can support in modes of life that we and our children and their children will choose to want. (Cohen, 1995:367)

Whether we have reached the carrying capacity or not is still controversial, but we can begin to see some of the consequences of coming closer to that carrying capacity.

Crowding

One important consequence of population growth is crowding. Studies of animals have shown that extreme crowding can have adverse consequences, including increases in aggression and erratic behavior. Animal studies, however, are only suggestive of how crowding may affect human beings, because it would depend on people's past experiences and their expectations. In addition, living quarters and work areas can be designed so that density is high but people do not have the *impression* of being crowded, and potentially negative effects could be avoided (Baum and Davis, 1976). In fact, psychologist Jonathan Freedman (1975) has argued that crowding by itself does not have negative consequences. Instead, crowding is usually associated with other social conditions, such as poverty, that produce increases in crime or aggression (Ehrlich and Ehrlich, 1990). Thus, there is considerable controversy over the impact of crowding. Yet if world population doubles in the next 200 years and doubles again after that, we will experience serious overcrowding by most people's standards.

Food Shortages

Another consequence of population growth is the potential for food shortages. Especially in developing nations that are experiencing rapid population growth, increasing agricultural production sufficiently to keep up with population expansion is difficult. As a consequence, millions of people die each year from starvation and malnutrition. Concern over this has provoked substantial efforts over the years to expand the world food supply. These efforts have focused on three key areas: the sea, farmland expansion, and yield increases (Brown, 1998b; McGinn, 1998).

According to most observers, the sea will not be a very important source of expanding food supplies in the years to come. It is possible through intensive efforts to increase fish production of the oceans to some degree, but the costs of such a move could outweigh the benefits to be gained. As for farmland expansion, it may be possible to increase the amount of land under cultivation so that we can produce more food overall. So far, however, population growth has proved to be so relentless that the world is undergoing a steady reduction in the amount of farmland available. Therefore, yield increases appear to hold the best prospect for increased food production. Efforts to increase yields have pursued a number of strategies: introduction of new crops, reduction of turnaround time between harvesting and replanting, improved management of the crop environment, and development of higher-yielding plant varieties.

In fact, the last mentioned strategy was labeled the Green Revolution, and many hoped it would head off the threat of massive famine by making it possible to produce far larger crops from the same amount of land. Time revealed, however, that the Green Revolution and the other strategies to increase food production were not the panacea to the world food problem. Although it is true that world grain production has increased every year since 1950, this production level barely stayed even with population

Population growth along with other problems, such as global warming, will produce a serious depletion of some resources in the near future. Water will likely be one of these depleted resources, as illustrated by this boy in India waiting to be allocated a share of water from a public tap.

growth in the years to follow. Per capita consumption levels dropped off in the most disadvantaged nations, food prices increased by leaps and bounds, and well over one hundred countries of the world confronted critical food deficits. By the 1980s and 1990s, these problems coalesced into an increasingly serious crisis, with some developing nations experiencing starvation. In addition, the Green Revolution and other intensive agricultural programs have had some negative effects: By emphasizing a narrow range of crops, they have pushed biological uniformity to dangerous levels, they have relied on heavy utilization of chemical pesticides, and the expanding farmlands have eaten into forests and wetlands and depleted water supplies (Repetto, 1994).

The biotechnology revolution of recent decades offers some new possibilities for expanding the food supply (Rifkin, 1998). Through gene splicing and other techniques, discussed in Chapter 15, it is now possible to produce modified species that grow faster, reproduce quicker, or provide larger quantities of proteins or other nutrients than do naturally occurring species. Although these new developments hold considerable promise, it is too early to assess how much they will expand the food supply and whether their negative consequences may not outweigh the benefits.

Depletion of Resources

Beyond food, population growth can threaten the depletion of other world resources. There is considerable debate, however, about how serious this problem is. A few decades back, a group of concerned business leaders, political leaders, and scientists, calling themselves the Club of Rome, initiated the controversy by publishing two very pessimistic assessments about the future supply of the world's resources (Mesarovic and Pestel, 1974). Based on estimates of world supplies of various resources and the rates of their use, the reports forecast a grim future. For example, petroleum, natural gas, and aluminum were all estimated to be exhausted in fifty years or less.

More recent assessments are generally more optimistic because they take into account new discoveries of supplies of the resources and changing estimates of rates of use of the resources (Bartsch and Müller, 2000; Cohen, 1995; Goodstein, 2004). For example, some assessments conclude that many minerals can be maintained at desirable levels through judicious use and discoveries of new sources. However, many assessments still warn of serious shortages at some point during the twenty-first century. Oil supplies may begin to decline within the next decade or two, which could result in dramatic shortages in supply and a substantial increase in price. We may begin to run out of fossil fuels completely by the end of this century. This could dramatically change many people's lifestyle. On the other hand, coal is plentiful and could replace some of the depleted fuels. But coal has its own problems, in terms of environmental destruction when it is mined and serious pollution when it is burned. Beyond fossil fuels, new technologies based on nuclear fusion, solar power, or wind power may be able to replace fossil fuels as they are depleted.

So, even today, not all experts agree about what the future holds in terms of depletion of resources. The point is that no one knows for sure. However, most agree that the most prudent course is to begin to plan for the possibility that some of our most important resources will be in short supply in the not-too-distant future.

Intergroup Conflict

The struggle for scarce resources intensifies when population increases. One way to cope with scarcity is to increase production of resources to satisfy demand. However, given that there are finite limits to expansion and growth, regulated competition could escalate to unregulated conflict. This might lead to one of Malthus's positive checks on population growth: war. People confronted with famine or disease may not sit idly by and accept starvation and death. If competition intensifies to conflict, the result may be all-out struggle for dwindling resources, such as living space and food. This is an especially ominous prospect in a nuclear world in which increasing numbers of nations have access to nuclear weapons.

Problems in Cities of the United States

The focus of attention on urban problems tends to be on those conditions found in the central cities of large metropolitan areas. To be sure, the central cities do suffer most severely from problems such as crime, poverty, and deteriorating housing. Yet many of these problems can be found in smaller towns, and some suburban communities find themselves beset with similar difficulties.

Economic Decline

One of the premier problems that some cities in the United States confront is that they are in a state of economic stagnation or decline. In fact, in the past two decades, a number of cities, especially in the Northeast and Midwest, have been on the brink of financial collapse (Caraley, 1992; Feagin, 1998). During the recession of the early 1980s, Boston and Detroit were so short of funds that their governments had to consider not paying for essential city services such as fire and police protection. In more recent years, many cities have had to cut fire and police services as well as social services and raise local taxes in order to make up for cuts in federal support for cities and to pay for the increased cost of homeland security.

One major cause of these financial problems has been the flight of people and jobs from many cities since World War II. Of the twenty largest cities in 2005, five have lost population since 1950. Of the 20 largest in 1950, 16 have lost people (U.S. Bureau of the Census, 1978; U.S. Bureau of the Census, 2006). And population growth has been much slower in the central cities than elsewhere. As is pointed out in Chapter 2, the centralization of economic organization in the United States has meant that a relatively small number of corporations account for an increasingly large share of economic activity. When one of these large business enterprises leaves a city, the departure has a ripple effect as smaller companies that support it also move. As businesses and affluent residents leave the cities, the tax roles decline. The poor and elderly who remain pay fewer taxes and use more city services than do the well-to-do who left. As a result, many cities have faced severe financial crises over the past few decades, and these economic difficulties contribute to all the other problems of the cities.

The economic difficulties of cities, then, arise in part from the capitalist nature of the economy of which the cities are a part (Costells, 1977; Feagin, 1998). Corporations pursue profits, and if that corporate activity benefits a particular city, then that city does well. If corporate profit-making activities do not benefit a city—if it results in jobs leaving the city—then the city suffers.

The plight of cities in the United States and around the world also needs to be placed in the context of the global economic competition discussed in Chapter 2. That chapter discusses the dramatic transition of the United States economy from a goods, production-based system to an information-based service economy. This has meant that, for the urban poor, unskilled manual labor jobs that are more common in a goods-production industrial economy have become less common in a service-oriented economy. This has dramatically reduced the ability of cities to provide jobs that pay sufficiently to support a family at a decent level. The problems created by the shift in the U.S. economy are exacerbated by the global competition among capitalist corporations. Cities in the United States have to compete with cities and nations around the globe for jobs, and the result for many cities has been fewer jobs, especially well-paying jobs.

Housing

Two visible symbols of the economic problems of cities are the deterioration and in some cases abandonment of housing in many neighborhoods, and the inability of the poor to find affordable housing (National Low Income Housing Coalition, 2006). The result is that many people—often the minorities, the elderly, and the poor—live in buildings with dangerous structural defects, inadequate plumbing and heating, poor sanitation, overcrowding, exposed wiring, rotting floors, and inadequate toilet facilities. Other people cannot find any housing that they can afford. The problem of homelessness, discussed in Chapter 5, is due in part to the unavailability of sufficient rental units at a price that low-income families can afford.

The government provides housing vouchers to low-income families to help them pay for acceptable housing. The government has also built low-income housing projects across the country, and most of these efforts have provided adequate and safe shelter for poor families. However, low-cost housing is in distressingly short supply.

Segregation

The population shifts in cities in the United States have led to considerable residential segregation of racial and ethnic minorities. The term **ghetto** refers to *a neighborhood inhabited largely by members of a single ethnic or racial group*. In the early part of this century, Jews and Italians lived in urban ghettos; today, African Americans, Hispanics, and Asians are the primary ghetto residents. Although African Americans make up about 13 percent of our populace and Hispanics another 14 percent, they constitute far larger proportions of the residents of our largest cities (see Table 12.2). They are concentrated in the central-city areas with the most severe urban problems. Although 25 percent of all whites live in central cities, 56 percent of African Americans and 53 percent of Hispanics live there (U.S. Bureau of the Census, 2003a).

This segregation of people of color, especially African Americans, did not occur by chance (Feagin, 1998; Judd, 1991). In fact, it was encouraged by the FHA and VA policies discussed earlier in the chapter. During the 1930s and 1940s, administrators of these programs actively promoted the idea that neighborhoods should be racially segregated because, in their

TABLE 12.2 The Racial Composition of the Twenty Largest Cities in the United States, 1960–2000

City	Percent Black		Percent Hispanic	
	1960	2000	1980	2000
Austin, TX	13.1	10.0	18.7	30.5
Baltimore	34.7	64.4	1.0	1.7
Boston	9.1	25.3	6.4	14.4
Chicago	22.9	36.8	14.0	26.0
Columbus, Ohio	16.4	24.5	0.8	2.5
Dallas	19.0	25.9	12.3	35.6
Detroit	28.9	81.5	2.4	5.0
Houston	22.9	25.3	17.6	37.4
Indianapolis	20.6	25.5	0.9	3.9
Jacksonville, FL	23.2	29.0	1.8	4.2
Los Angeles	13.5	11.2	27.5	46.5
Memphis	37.0	61.4	0.8	3.0
Milwaukee	8.4	37.2	4.1	12.0
New York	14.0	26.6	19.9	27.0
Philadelphia	26.4	43.2	3.8	8.5
Phoenix	4.8	5.1	14.8	34.1
San Antonio	7.1	6.8	53.7	58.7
San Diego	6.0	7.8	14.9	25.4
San Francisco	10.0	7.7	12.3	14.1
San Jose	1.0	3.5	22.3	30.2

Sources: U.S. Bureau of the Census, *Statistical Abstract of the United States, 1978* (Washington, DC: U.S. Government Printing Office, 1978), p. 24–26; U.S. Bureau of the Census, *Statistical Abstract of the United States, 1985* (Washington, DC: U.S. Government Printing Office, 1985), pp. 23–25; U.S. Bureau of the Census, *Statistical Abstract of the United States, 2002* (Washington, DC: U.S. Government Printing Office, 2001), pp. 39–40.

eyes, this promoted more neighborhood stability and higher property values. As the FHA *Underwriting Manual* of 1938 put it: "If a neighborhood is to retain stability, it is necessary that properties shall continue to be occupied by the same social and racial classes" (quoted in Judd, 1991:740). The result: African Americans were almost completely excluded from the federally insured mortgage market and from the suburbs that it was helping to create. In part as a consequence of these policies, African Americans today tend to be residentially isolated from whites. In assessing whether the United States has moved any closer to the goal of residential integration by the 2000s, most assessments conclude that little real progress toward that goal has been made (Massey, 2001).

There has been some movement of African Americans and Hispanic Americans to the suburbs in the past two decades; however, they tend to move only to a small number of suburban areas that typically have existing black or Hispanic populations (Phelan and Schneider, 1996). Most suburbanites still fear that an influx of African American or Hispanic American residents will produce white flight and declining property values.

This concentration of minorities in ghettos can create some serious difficulties for urban areas. For example, residential segregation exacerbates both poverty and economic deprivation for both African Americans and Hispanics. Minorities who live in segregated urban neighborhoods have more difficulties finding jobs or taking advantage of educational opportunities that are available. Segregation also concentrates the problem of poverty into a few neighborhoods rather than spreading it more evenly around a metropolitan area. Such dispersal could spread the burden of assisting the poor throughout the metropolitan area. Residential segregation can also enhance tensions between racial groups. For example, ghettos isolate racial groups from one another so that they have little contact and believe they have little in common. Much research has shown that such segregation can lead to negative stereotyping, hostility, and prejudice. Sympathy and understanding decline without social contact between groups. The outcome is mutual mistrust and suspicion that make working toward solutions for urban problems even more difficult.

Crime

Crime is probably one of the urban problems that the average citizen thinks about most. Although crime can be found everywhere, it is far more common in cities. As Table 12.3 illustrates, the rate of violent crime is five times greater in the largest cities of the United States than it is in rural areas; the rate of property crime is three times greater. The greatest disparity is for robbery, which occurs at a rate at least 43 times greater in large cities than in rural areas! Also, the larger the city, the higher the crime rate. And suburban areas have lower crime rates than all but the smallest cities. Even within cities, crime is not evenly distributed. Crime is more likely in central-city areas where the poor and minorities live. Low-income and minority people are also more likely to be the victims of crimes.

The massive crime rate that exists in some urban neighborhoods exacerbates many of the other problems that these communities confront: the lack of economic development, the growing group of entrenched poor, and physical deterioration. Simply stated, the growing crime rate in a neighborhood ripples through the community with devastating effect. New busi-

TABLE 12.3	Crime Rates in Urban and Rural Areas, 2005

Area	Crimes Known to the Police per 100,000 People
Violent Crimes	
Cities with population of:	
250,000 or more	941
100,000–249,999	616
50,000–99,999	474
25,000–49,999	374
10,000–24,999	303
10,000 or less	330
Suburbs	316
Rural Areas	218
Property Crimes	
Cities with population of:	
250,000 or more	4,797
100,00–249,999	4,648
50,000–99,999	3,895
25,000–49,999	3,632
10,000–24,999	3,327
10,000 or less	3,635
Suburbs	2,800
Rural Areas	1,743

SOURCE: Federal Bureau of Investigation, *Uniform Crime Reports: Crime in the United States, 2005* (Washington, DC: U.S. Government Printing Office, 2006), www.fbi.gov.

nesses refuse to move in and old ones relocate, making it even more difficult for community residents to support themselves. The chaos and violence produced by crime and drug use can pervade the schools, with disorder making it more difficult for students to achieve scholastically. With a high crime rate, many of a community's males may be in jail, which means fewer partners for women to marry and help to provide for their children. In short, the economic, educational, and familial structures of the community are compromised in a highly crime-ridden environment. The Applied Research insert (pp. 330–331) discusses some elements of this problem and what the research suggests could be done about it.

The sources of crime and programs to control it are analyzed extensively in Chapter 9, and that discussion will not be repeated here. Without question, the high crime rates in cities are in part a function of unemployment and the general lack of legitimate opportunities for success. Any programs that successfully reduce crime will have a beneficial effect on urban life.

As Chapter 9 and this chapter have documented, there is little question but that the quality of life in cities is lowered by crime, fear of crime, and the restrictions that city residents impose on their daily routines as a consequence. Chapter 9, for example, showed that the crime most feared by women who live in cities is rape. The fear of crime directly affects women's daily lives as they avoid going out alone, avoid going to certain neighborhoods, and install security devices in their houses or apartments. The other crimes women fear most are robbery and burglary. Another study found that one-half of the women in large cities felt that it was unsafe to be out in their neighborhood after dark (Davis and Smith, 2004; Stanko, 1995). Social science research has proved very useful to urban planners by pointing to ways to design cities that make urban life safer, more enjoyable, and more fulfilling.

One focus of attention for applied researchers has been urban residents' relationship to their community, especially people's involvement in their community and the crime-fighting effort in their neighborhood (Adams and Serpe, 2000; Bennett, 1995). Research shows that the existence of formally organized local community associations can diminish fear and self-imposed limitations on activities. Neighborhood watch programs, for example, or programs in which residents can meet the police officers assigned to their neighborhood help to get people involved in their community. In the absence of such formal efforts, some urban dwellers develop informal techniques for dealing with fear and victimization. For example, such techniques might include casual gatherings to air mutual concerns about crime and to discuss possible strategies for protection. Research investigations have shown that urban residents who are more integrated into the social fabric of a neighborhood—the ones active in formal and informal community organizations—are less fearful of crime and place fewer restrictions on their behavior. So programs to encourage such formal and informal activities will improve the quality of urban life.

Based on years of study of crime in cities, sociologists and urban planners have come to recognize that architecture and urban design play a part in the crime problem. These policy analysts have developed a new approach to designing cities that has come to be called the *defensible space* strategy because it focuses on changes in the physical environment that make it easier for neighborhoods and communities to defend themselves against crime (Cisneros, 1995; Donnelly and Kimble, 1997; Newman, 1972). This approach is based on the recognition that many criminals are, to a degree, rational; they calculate how they can obtain the greatest gain

Educational Problems

The United States often turns to education as a way of mastering social problems. Education, for example, has been the route for most immigrants to achieve upward mobility. In many cities today, however, the schools are not up to this task (Kozol, 2005). One major hurdle is financial. Poor communities and financially pressed cities simply cannot afford the educational expenses of the more affluent suburbs. Central-city schools must contend with old buildings, less equipment, archaic educational technology, high rates of teacher turnover, and low staff morale.

Teachers are often ill equipped to deal with the problems of inner-city schools. Low pay and other problems of the teaching profession have been much discussed in the past few years. Beyond this, teachers often confront a degree of culture shock in inner-city schools as the teacher's middle-class training and upbringing come face-to-face with the world of lower-class minorities. The subcultural values, personal demeanor, and even the language of many of the teachers' students are likely to be strange and possibly seen as threatening. There may even be a tendency, based on racial or ethnic stereotypes, to label many of these students as incapable of great achievements. When this occurs, a self-fulfilling prophecy can set in, especially when the students accept the teachers' judgment of them. Problems in education in the United States are discussed at greater length in Chapter 15.

for the least risk. As the likelihood of getting caught increases, criminals either commit crimes somewhere else or avoid committing crimes. In addition, many neighborhoods and buildings in cities are designed in such a way that they discourage social interaction and social participation on the part of residents. They isolate people from one another, which tends to increase the opportunities for criminals to operate unobserved. So, the defensible space strategy designs locations so that intruders believe that they will be observed, be identified, and have difficulty escaping if they commit a crime. With such ideas in mind, sociologists and urban planners suggest a few design considerations that would make crime less likely:

1. Buildings should have only a small number of units sharing the same entryway off the street. In this way, residents know who lives there, who has a right to be there, and who is a stranger.

2. Windows, lighting, entryways, and paths should be designed so that there is continuous surveillance by the residents. This reduces the number of isolated spots where crime can occur unobserved.

3. Lobbies should be designed not merely as entryways to buildings but as social centers where people congregate. This might be done by having newsstands or recreation items in or near the lobby.

4. Buildings should be low-rise with fewer residents to reduce feelings of anonymity, isolation, and lack of identity with the building. Research shows that the crime rate is higher in taller and more populous buildings.

5. Neighborhoods should be designed as small mini-neighborhoods, with no through streets and a limited number of entryways. In this way, the neighbors know who belongs there and who is an intruder, and criminals will fear being trapped in a neighborhood that has only one exit.

These and other urban design features are important to consider in the fight against crime because, as social scientists have demonstrated, social behaviors such as crime are significantly influenced by the nature of the physical surroundings. Yet, the use of urban design to attack crime has its limits because such programs may only deflect crime to another location rather than reduce it: The criminal merely victimizes someone else. So the crime-fighting efforts that focus on social reform are still critical because these have a better chance of reducing the absolute amount of crime committed.

Future Prospects

Population Problems

Throughout human history, many societies have been at or near **zero population growth (ZPG),** according to which *birth and death rates are nearly equal, producing a zero rate of natural increase.* Although fully developed nations such as the United States are approaching ZPG, other societies are far from it, and this is where much of the world's population problem exists. As new cures for diseases are discovered and implemented and living conditions improve in developing nations, death rates will continue to fall, and improvements in life expectancy for them will probably continue. Consequently, efforts to control world population growth will have to focus on fertility. Furthermore, current attitudes about fertility around the world suggest that nations with high birthrates are ready to do what needs to be done to bring them down. Most developing nations—the nations with high birthrates—feel that their national level of fertility is too high, and most of the nations that view their fertility rate to be too high are in favor of policies designed to reduce it (Salas, 1984).

Given these attitudes, fertility has declined and will probably continue to decline in all regions where it is high. For this to occur quickly enough to avoid the worst of the problems discussed earlier, however, a number of programs and policies that work to lower fertility will have to be pursued aggressively. We will review the major things that can be done. If they are, there is some optimism that the worst consequences of rapid population growth can be avoided.

FAMILY PLANNING In the United States, the relatively high fertility in the years following World War II declined precipitously after 1957. The reason? Certainly the widespread use of effective contraceptives played an important part. Given the effectiveness of contraception in reducing fertility, the solution to the world's population problem might appear to be providing contraceptives to everyone who desires them. However feasible this approach might appear at first, technology is of secondary importance in this realm when compared to cultural values. The prevention of conception and the termination of pregnancies through abortion are not merely technological feats. Conception and abortion are social events that represent decisions that people have made based in part on what their culture has taught them is desirable. After all, the birthrate in the United States was relatively low during the 1930s—almost as low as today—well before the pill, intrauterine devices (IUDs), and other modern contraceptive techniques were available. This low fertility rate occurred because people decided on the basis of the severe economic conditions that they wanted to postpone having children or to have smaller families.

Some modern population control efforts, then, have focused on encouraging people to consciously decide how many children they want, with the hope that people will choose to have smaller families. Such family planning programs encourage couples to have children when and if they are desired. Experience with such programs has shown that, when women realize they have a choice of whether to have children, they most often choose to have fewer children than they would have had otherwise. Research on the effectiveness of family planning services generally shows that they increase contraceptive use, reduce fertility, and result in smaller families (Jacobson, 1988; Mauldin, 1975; Robey, Rutstein, and Morris, 1993). However, the provision of such services is not a total answer to the world's population problem. In many countries with active family planning efforts, such as China, South Korea, and Costa Rica, social and economic changes—to be discussed in a moment—probably account for much of the lowering of fertility. In other countries, such as Kenya, India, and the Dominican Republic, family planning programs have had little observable effect. Why? One reason is that many of these countries failed to allocate the resources necessary to make the programs effective. In addition, as noted earlier, values are a critical element in reducing fertility—people must want to have fewer children before family planning efforts will work. In many countries, however, women have large numbers of children because they have been taught to want them, and cultural values are supportive of large families. In such settings, family planning will probably have only a marginal effect.

ECONOMIC DEVELOPMENT The social and economic changes referred to in the preceding paragraph are generally called *economic development*. Developing nations that are actively involved in programs to control population growth today have placed a major emphasis on economic development. Although these countries recognize the need for family planning, they argue that no program of population control can be completely effective unless it is a part of a more general program of economic development. A number of changes that accompany economic development—especially urbanization, increasing levels of education, and a rising standard of living—lead people to view large families as less desirable. In urban settings and since the passage of child-labor laws, there is no longer a distinct economic advantage to having many children. In fact, in urban, industrial societies, large families lead to crowded housing and a drain on family finances. Furthermore, when women receive more education, they usually want to pursue a career or develop talents other than domestic ones, and large families make this more difficult. Finally, economic development affords people a more affluent lifestyle, and large families are expensive. This affects their standard of living, leading many couples to decide to spend their resources on consumer goods or leisure activities rather than raising large families. Even with economic development, most people want to become parents, but they are more likely to opt for a smaller number of children. And as small families become common, they are viewed increasingly as "normal," and people feel social pressures not to have large families.

Recent research suggests, however, that economic development may not be as critical to reducing fertility as once thought (Robey, Rutstein, and Morris, 1993). Many of today's developing nations have reduced their fertility significantly even though they have not experienced significant economic development. In fact, some nations have experienced declining fertility even though their economic circumstances have become worse. It appears that some of the elements originally linked with economic development, such as urbanization, also influence fertility in the absence of economic development: Even in less developed nations, people in cities have fewer children because there are fewer advantages to having children in such settings. In addition, the mass media have contributed to the spread of information about contraception and to the propagation of values regarding small families in less developed nations, and this has helped bring down fertility levels. What is uncertain at this point is whether fertility levels can be brought down to the level in industrial nations without significant economic development. The International Perspectives insert explores the role of both family planning and economic development in lowering fertility in China.

INCENTIVES Some programs have been proposed and a few established that would provide people with some incentives, usually economic, for preventing births. This might involve giving people cash payments or gifts for being sterilized, or it might take the form of annual payments to women for each year they do not have children. This might be done by giving tax breaks to people with smaller families or no children at all, rather than increasing their tax exemptions as we currently do for each child that is born. A program introduced into several private tea plantations in India involved placing money in a retirement trust fund for each year that passed in which a woman did not have any children (Ridker, 1980). This program did result in lower fertility, although the effect was not dramatic. Once again, unless the social and cultural forces that lead people to want fewer children are present, declines in fertility tend to be small. The incentives approach has also been criticized on the grounds that large families, which also tend to be poorer, would suffer the most and their poverty would be further exacerbated.

THE STATUS OF WOMEN Another important element in controlling population growth is the status of women. As noted in Chapter 7, the United Nations has for decades vigorously promoted programs to improve women's lives by providing them with opportunities in education, employment, and political participation, as well as support in their domestic and maternal roles. Research has shown consistently that educational attainment and labor force participation of women are particularly important elements in a population policy: Educated women who work outside the home have fewer children than do less educated women who are not part of the labor force (Sen, 1999). Research conducted in the United States also shows that better educated women who have careers, or at least are a part of the labor force, desire smaller families and are more sensitive to the overall issue of population growth (Houseknecht, 1987). So programs intended to advance sexual equality around the world will likely have a positive impact on controlling population growth.

Urban Problems

FEDERAL GRANTS AND PROGRAMS Until the 1980s, urban policy in the United States was based on the assumption that the federal government is in the best position to fund programs to attack urban problems. Cities and states have fewer funds for such efforts and more incentives to underfund such programs. Cities and states, for example, try to keep taxes low in the competition with other states to attract businesses and industry. Cities and states might be tempted to cut urban programs to keep taxes low. Generally, interventionists have supported an active role on the part of the federal government in the attack on urban problems.

In the past 20 years, urban policy has changed dramatically, with a decided shift toward a more laissez-faire approach (Caraley, 1992). The Reagan and Bush administrations argued that a strong and healthy economy is a far more promising approach to solving urban problems than direct federal intervention. For laissez-faire advocates, the key role of the federal government in solving urban problems is to keep the economy healthy, not to intervene directly with federal programs and funding. States and cities should be allowed to choose which services they need and want. The result of this shift has been a catastrophic decline in federal support for cities. Federal programs have been turned over to the states and cities, and the states and cities—in poor financial shape themselves—have drastically cut or eliminated the programs. Federal aid has dropped from 22 percent of large cities' general expenditures in 1980 to 6 percent, but aid given by state governments has not increased to take up the slack.

Despite this shift toward a decidedly laissez-faire policy, some significant federal urban programs persist. The many federal programs that provide direct funds or services to the poor are a significant form of assistance to urban areas. These programs include Medicaid, Social Security, Temporary Assistance to Needy Families, housing assistance, food stamps, and many others (see Chapter 5). All these programs are key resources used by cities to alleviate the problems their citizens face. The Housing Act of 1949 initiated a program of *urban renewal,* which has been a prominent approach to urban problems over the years (Hawley, 1971). The major purpose of urban renewal has been to rebuild blighted areas of cities, to provide low-cost housing for urban poor, and to stimulate private investment in the inner city through the physical redevelopment of deteriorated

Population Policy and Family Planning in China

China has a tremendous problem on its hands. Geographically, it is about the same size as the United States, but with more than four times as many people! Whereas the United States has about 300 million people, China has 1.3 billion: 22 percent of the world's population with only 7 percent of the earth's arable land. To make matters worse, China's population is much younger than the U.S. population, which means a larger proportion of the Chinese are still planning to have children. So, even if China were to bring its birthrate down to U.S. levels, China's population would still grow much faster than the U.S. population. Population experts expect China's population to peak at 1.9 billion by the middle of the next century.

Such population growth puts an enormous strain on China's environment in terms of whether it can produce sufficient food for its population and absorb the pollutants generated. Rapid population growth also hinders economic development because whatever economic growth occurs is absorbed supporting the growing population rather than being available for investment in new industries or machinery. For these reasons, the Chinese authorities have been deeply concerned for decades about controlling population growth. By the end of the 1970s, they were sufficiently concerned to institute a "one-child family" program for all couples who did not already have more than one child. Incentives were created for families that achieved this goal, such as a government stipend for one-child families payable until the youngster is fourteen years old; there were also penalties for families with more than two children, including salary deductions and tax surcharges. Even more controversial was the use of government-employed family planning workers to consult with, and in some cases cajole, couples about their sexual behavior and use of contraceptives.

Through the 1980s, the birthrate in China came down but not nearly as quickly as the authorities had hoped. By the late 1980s, it began to look like the Chinese would not reach the targets they had set for themselves. Alarmed authorities, pushing for a renewed effort to achieve the goals, introduced a "responsibility system" in which district and township officials would be held personally responsible if the people under their jurisdiction did not achieve the goals (Kristof, 1993). These officials could lose bonuses or be fined or dismissed. Another part of the program was compulsory, organized sterilizations, in which family-planning cadres would descend on a village and take all women who already had a child to a clinic to be fitted with an IUD or sterilized. A

areas. Government funds were used to acquire and clear land, and this renewal was supposed to attract private investors.

After many years of operation, urban policymakers recognized that urban renewal had probably not produced its intended benefits. Many older buildings were torn down and often replaced with luxury apartments or office buildings that are more profitable to private-sector developers. The poor, who had originally occupied a neighborhood, were driven into other neighborhoods, which then often began to deteriorate. Because of these problems, urban renewal funds declined over the years, and in the 1980s the programs were combined into the Community Development Block Grant (CDBG) program (Wong and Peterson, 1986). The CDBG program has goals similar to those of urban renewal, but it gives local officials a larger role in developing urban renewal projects and greater flexibility in how federal funds are used. Compared to urban renewal, the CDBG program shifted emphasis from providing direct assistance to low-income residents to a focus on economic development.

These and other federal programs continue and have channeled significant resources to cities with serious problems. However, the laissez-faire posture in the United States' urban policy in recent years has meant fewer funds than in the past. Interventionists argue, however, that federal assistance with urban problems is still appropriate because the cities, for the most part, did not create the problems that now ravage them: poverty, drug addiction, homelessness, AIDS, and so on. It is the cities that suffer from these problems most seriously, and interventionists argue

third part of the program focused on women who became pregnant without authorization, with strong social pressure exerted on them to have an abortion. Out of fear that they would not achieve their goals, some overly zealous local officials got carried away, forcing some women to have abortions and smashing the huts of a few women who had unauthorized births.

This draconian program had an effect. By the end of the 1990s, the birthrate in China was about the same as in the United States. In addition, the number of sterilizations went way up, and very few births involved third or subsequent children. However, these successes have not been without costs, a major one of which may have been to increase female infanticides. The Chinese, especially in rural areas, want sons so they can extend the male line into the future; some even believe they have dishonored their ancestors if they fail to do so.

Female infanticide is a way to try again for a male child when the government strongly encourages one-child families. Information on the sex ratio in China supports the idea that some female infanticide is occurring. Biologically, in human populations, about 94 females are born for every 100 males. However, in recent years in China, as few as 85 to 89 females were reported born for each 100 males. Now, some of this involves families just not reporting a female birth to authorities so they can try again to have a male. But some of it is undoubtedly due to infanticide (Secondi, 2002).

By the end of the twentieth century, the one-child policy had begun to lose some of its force (Yardley, 2005). One reason for this is that the birthrate has declined substantially. In addition, economic development is enhancing the trend toward smaller families, as it did in the currently developed

countries. In fact, economic development may have contributed as much to China's declining birth rate as did the government-promulgated one-child policy. However, the experience of China highlights the importance of cultural values in influencing people's behavior. Even when the government provides benefits for those who lower their fertility and penalties for those who do not cooperate, people will continue to have more children if they value them. When government intervention is contrary to people's deeply held values, it is not likely to be very effective unless strongly repressive and authoritarian measures are used. Even these measures may not remain effective for long. So, programs of family planning and population control are likely to be less effective when they fail to gain the backing of the citizenry.

that society as a whole has a responsibility to assist cities with them.

PRIVATE INVESTMENT Despite the prominent role of the federal government in attacking urban problems over the years, there has been a trend over the past two decades to turn to private investment as a means of improving the conditions of cities. A major thrust of these efforts is the use of private funds to develop shopping centers and malls in cities that can compete with suburban shopping malls and to construct housing that can draw people away from suburban tract homes. In this way, it is hoped, people—and financial resources—can be attracted back into the city. Many cities now boast such developments: the Water Tower mall in Chicago, the Union Station in Cincinnati, the Quincy Market in Boston, the Renaissance Center in

Detroit, and Pier 39 in San Francisco. Although some of these developments used federal funds, private financing has been central to their completion. The idea behind them is that, if cities can be made into enjoyable places to live and work, decentralization might be slowed or halted and the financial problems that are at the core of so many urban difficulties alleviated.

Another approach to encouraging private development in cities through minimal government action is variously called "enterprise zones," "urban free-enterprise zones," or "empowerment zones" (Beck, 2001). The basic idea is to designate a neighborhood as an "enterprise zone" based on high levels of unemployment or poverty and little economic development. Businesses locating in such zones would be taxed at a lower rate than other areas of the city and

Early efforts at urban renewal in U.S. cities often did not produce its intended effects. The destruction of this housing complex symbolizes the realization that effective urban renewal must involve more than building large dwellings for people.

would be subject to less stringent regulation than businesses outside the zone. This approach is based on the laissez-faire assumption that the tax and regulatory systems stifle initiative and self-improvement. Remove these inhibitors, proponents argue, and new businesses will arise to take advantage of the opportunities for economic development that exist even in blighted neighborhoods. These new ventures will then help rebuild the neighborhood economy, providing jobs that will help improve the general economic conditions in the city.

At this point, the impact of such zones is difficult to assess because the research results have been contradictory (Beck, 2001; Greenbaum and Engberg, 2000; Greenbaum and Engberg, 2004). Some research shows that they have little impact on job growth and business development while other research shows they have a modest positive impact. Other research suggests that, at least in some cases, what appears to be job growth is actually due to businesses that existed elsewhere or were planning to expand finding the zones an attractive place to set up shop. So, in some cases, the zones may not result in a net increase in jobs and economic activity, but a shuffling of them from one locale to another. This

is not necessarily bad if the goal of policy is to shift jobs from low-unemployment areas to high-unemployment areas. If the community losing the jobs, however, begins to suffer, then the urban problems have merely been shifted from one community to another. The Policy Issues insert explores some further possibilities in terms of government regulation of urban development.

COMMUNITY DEVELOPMENT EFFORTS Another approach to urban problems that has proven to be very effective is to combine private and public resources and to direct them toward grassroots community efforts to revitalize blighted neighborhoods (Grogan and Proscio, 2000). One important stimulus to this effort was the Community Reinvestment Act of 1977, which requires banks to meet the credit needs of the entire community that they serve. In practice, this has meant that banks and other financial institutions have provided loans and investment funds for housing and small businesses in low-income and moderate-income neighborhoods, as well as to community groups in those neighborhoods.

As these sources of credit have become available over the past few decades, they contributed to the

Should the Government Regulate Growth and Development in Urban Areas?

In the past few decades, cities in the South, Rocky Mountain region, and West have been among the fastest growing cities in the nation. Since 1970, for example, Phoenix and the metropolitan areas of Denver and Seattle have doubled in size. This phenomenal growth has presented these urban areas with tremendous challenges. Some of these cities have staggering air pollution problems, traffic congestion, crowded schools, and dwindling open space. In most of these areas, voices have been raised in support of some government intervention to control population growth or at least to regulate it so that some of its worst consequences are minimized (Egan, 1996; Orfield, 1997). Should the government regulate such growth?

Opponents of regulation argue that the economic marketplace is the best regulator of the uses to which land should be put. People need to live somewhere, and limiting growth will make it difficult for some people to find a place to live. It will also discourage the free movement of people and jobs from one location to another. Employers would be disinclined to move to an urban area that limits growth because their employees may find it difficult to find affordable dwellings. So, limiting population growth means stunting economic growth and development, which results in fewer jobs for people. In addition, limits on growth will increase the cost of housing as people compete for a scarce commodity. Furthermore, programs to limit growth inevitably mean that the government must tell people what they can do with their property. Many opponents of limits to growth believe that, barring some substantial public interest, people should not be prohibited from using their land in ways they see as appropriate. So, there are strong economic interests, in the form of landowners and commercial developers, that support unfettered urban growth.

Some opponents of government regulation have suggested a way in which market forces could be relied on to limit urban sprawl: Require developers to pay the full cost of development, including the costs of new streets, highways, sewers, water mains, schools, and the other infrastructure that must accompany development. In most cases, this infrastructure is provided by the government as a way of encouraging growth and development. If developers had to pay this, it would make many developments prohibitively expensive, and developers would choose to build in areas where such infrastructure already exists—in other words, within the existing urban area.

Supporters of government controls on urban growth argue either that the problems raised by opponents won't occur or that the problems produced by uncontrolled growth are worse. Supporters of regulation argue that unlimited growth will worsen air pollution and congestion and lower the overall quality of life for residents of urban areas. They point to the experience of cities like Phoenix and Las Vegas to support their arguments. They also show how many cities have rapaciously consumed the open land surrounding them and transformed what were once pristine wildernesses into housing developments, shopping malls, and parking lots.

Communities that have attempted to control growth have tried a number of different strategies. Some have purchased open land surrounding the city in order to keep it from the hands of developers; some have set a limit on how many new residential dwellings can be built in a year; some have tried lower taxes and development fees for those who build in the city rather than in outlying areas. The most ambitious plan to date has been in Oregon, which in the 1970s passed a law requiring cities to prepare land-use plans that limit urban sprawl and protect surrounding areas and farms from development. Cities such as Portland simply drew boundary lines around the city and decreed that development could occur only inside the boundary. This forced the developed parts of urban areas to become more densely populated and heavily utilized. With less sprawl and denser populations, public transportation becomes a more feasible, efficient, and less polluting transportation system. Portland has also limited the amount of parking that can be developed in order to save space for other development and encourage people to abandon their cars and use public transportation.

It is hard to say at this point what the impact of programs such as the one in Portland will be. It may produce higher housing costs, and it might result in people choosing smaller homes and lots than they might have chosen otherwise. In the long run, such policies might result in more apartment dwelling and condominium development because these involve a more efficient use of space. At the same time, it would leave more open land surrounding cities and would reduce the despoliation of the environment. This is an issue about which the interventionist and laissez-faire positions are clearly in opposition.

Interventionist		**Laissez-Faire**
Government regulates growth	Government supports growth by providing infrastructure	Market-driven development with no government regulation or support

emergence of Community Development Corporations (CDCs). These are grassroots, citizen-formed, neighborhood organizations that work to revitalize their own neighborhoods and communities. CDCs seek development money wherever they can find it: bank loans, religious donations, corporate capital, or government grants. They work closely with local governments, businesses, religious groups, and other stakeholders in a community in creating a development plan and seeking resources to implement the plan. The key difference of CDCs in comparison to some other efforts at urban redevelopment is that they are much more locally controlled; they emerge out of, and remain under significant control of, people in the community being redeveloped. Thousands of independent CDCs across the United States have contributed significantly to the revitalization of their communities by promoting the development of businesses, jobs, and clean and affordable housing.

RESETTLEMENT OF THE CITIES A number of programs have focused on encouraging homeowners and affluent residents to move back to the city and purchase homes or apartments. **Urban homesteading** refers to *programs to increase home ownership by private citizens in certain neighborhoods by selling them houses at little or no cost*. The homes are usually those that have been abandoned or foreclosed for failure to pay a mortgage or taxes and thus are the property of the city or the federal government. Usually, the buyer agrees to live in the house for a specified period of time and sometimes make certain improvements to the property. The government makes some money through the sale, an abandoned piece of property is placed back on the tax rolls, and best of all a homeowner has a vested interest in keeping up both his or her property and the neighborhood. A vacant house could be a target for vandals and a haven for drug dealers. Homeowners have an incentive to keep their property up and to discourage drug dealers from coming into the area. Overall, although it is no panacea, homesteading has helped some neighborhoods in some cities (Weinstein, 1990).

Urban homesteading and other policies have produced a trend called **gentrification:** *the return of relatively affluent households to marginal neighborhoods*

Some urban planners argue that gentrification—bringing affluent households back into urban neighborhoods—will help to revive cities and can be done by providing attractive housing for them, like these remodeled brownstones.

where run-down housing is being rehabilitated or new housing constructed (Freeman and Braconi, 2004; Vigdor, 2001). In some cases, gentrification is encouraged by the policies of local, state, or federal governments; in other cases, it is driven by the actions of private developers looking for a profitable business deal; in some places, private–public partnerships have been the catalyst. Gentrification is also fueled by the decisions of affluent families who may find suburban life too expensive or who do not feel the need for large houses because they have smaller families than their parents had. For others, especially professional couples with fairly substantial incomes, the city affords easy access to restaurants, cultural events, and the like.

This gentrification has been hailed as the beginning of the rebirth of urban areas in the United States. Although it will probably help to stem the flow of economic resources out of the city, the numbers involved are difficult to calculate but are probably somewhat small. Nevertheless, it should contribute to increasing the tax base of the city, restoring neighborhoods through the rehabilitation of housing, and enhancing neighborhood businesses. Some urban planners argue that these renovated neighborhoods will serve as a magnet that will attract more affluent people into the city. However, not all the effects of gentrification are beneficial. As affluent people move into and renovate neighborhoods, the value of property increases and both rent and property taxes escalate. As a result, the people who lived in the neighborhood prior to gentrification—often the poor, the elderly, and minorities—can no longer afford it and are forced to move, sometimes from homes they have occupied for decades. The only housing these people can afford may be more dilapidated than their previous residence.

REGIONAL PLANNING AND COOPERATION Many cities have recognized that some urban problems can best be solved with regional planning and cooperation (Orfield, 1997). After all, the geographic boundaries of cities were established many years ago, and today they are rather arbitrary designations. Some have proposed a metropolitan government that would have political jurisdiction over a city and its suburbs and would consolidate all government services. Such an overarching political structure is probably not feasible in most cases. One problem is deciding where one city and its suburbs ends and another begins. In addition, few cities or suburbs would be willing to accede to such a centralized authority. They prefer to retain political power and patronage in their own hands.

On a smaller scale, however, cooperation between political entities in metropolitan areas has been established over specific issues. Issues such as transportation, water pollution, and the like affect the whole metropolitan region and can benefit from regional decision making. In some cases, the courts have even ruled that school segregation is a regional problem and called for transfers of students between city and suburban schools.

LINKAGES

The spread of slums and urban deterioration is made worse by poverty (Chapter 5), crime (Chapter 9), and drug addiction (Chapter 10). It is also enhanced when large and unresponsive corporations (Chapter 2) move jobs away from the cities where people live.

STUDY AND REVIEW

Summary

1. Fertility, mortality, and migration are the three basic elements that affect the size, composition and distribution of human populations. Fertility and mortality are key elements in evaluating world population growth.

2. The demographic transition refers to the changing patterns of birthrates and death rates brought about by industrialization. The demographic transition has four stages: preindustrial, transitional or early industrial, industrial, and postindustrial. The largest increases in population occur in the less industrialized nations that have not yet experienced the transition.

3. Cities arose after human beings had developed agriculture and domesticated animals. With industrialization, cities grow very large because industrial economic organization benefits from the concentration of people and resources. Suburbanization and urban decentralization have occurred because technological change has made it possible for people to live far from where they work and because federal policies have encouraged the building of new homes outside the cities.

4. From the functionalist perspective, population growth and urban conditions become social problems when they become dysfunctional and lead to social disorganization. According to the conflict perspective, population and urban problems become social problems due to the inequitable distribution of resources. The interactionist perspective sensitizes us to the fact that population and urban problems are in part matters of social definition.

5. There are many consequences of population growth: crowding, food shortages, depletion of resources, and intergroup conflict. A key issue is whether population growth exceeds the carrying capacity of the environment.

6. Among the major problems confronting cities in the United States are economic decline, insufficient low-income housing, racial segregation, crime, and educational problems.

7. The future of population problems will depend on the ability to control fertility. Major issues in reducing fertility are family planning, economic development, incentives, and the status of women.

8. Although the federal government has played a significant role in finding solutions to urban problems over the years, recently there has been a push to find solutions in which government involvement is small or nonexistent. The government has attacked urban problems with such programs as urban renewal and community development block grants. Private investment has focused on developing cities as better places to live, sometimes through the establishment of "urban free-enterprise zones." Urban homesteading and regional planning have also been used to improve conditions in cities.

RESEARCHING SOCIAL PROBLEMS ON THE INTERNET

The United Nations is an excellent source of information about population and immigration problems around the world. Two good Web sites are the UN's Development Programme (www.undp.org/) and its Population Fund (www.unfpa.org). Report to the class about the information that is available at each site. What other UN sites can you find, and what information about population issues do they contain?

Other organizations that play a part in developing policy about population problems are the Population Council (www.popcouncil.org/), the Population Reference Bureau (www.prb.org/), and the Population Institute (www.populationinstitute.org/). Report to the class on what information is contained at their Web sites. Locate the Web sites of other organizations that focus on population policy.

The Allyn and Bacon Social Problems Web site (wps.ablongman.com/ab_socialprob_sprsite_1) contains material on population and urbanization and their impacts on the environment.

Key Terms

carrying capacity

city

communities

demographic gap

demographic transition

demography

fecundity

fertility

gentrification

ghetto

migration

mortality

population

suburbs

urban homesteading

zero population growth

Multiple-Choice Questions

1. In analyzing world population growth, which element of demographic change is least critical in evaluating overall population growth?
   a. fertility
   b. mortality
   c. migration
   d. population
   e. zero population growth

2. The United States is currently entering which stage of the demographic transition?
   a. the preindustrial stage
   b. the transitional stage
   c. the early industrial stage
   d. the industrial stage
   e. the postindustrial stage
3. Which region of the world will see its proportion of the world population grow most significantly in the next fifty years?
   a. Africa
   b. Asia
   c. North America
   d. Europe
   e. the Caribbean
4. According to the text, agricultural villages and then cities emerged in human history because of
   a. industrialization.
   b. capitalism.
   c. domestication of plants and animals.
   d. technological developments in transportation.
5. For the functionalist perspective, population growth and urban change become social problems when
   a. they lead to social disorganization.
   b. they produce a demographic gap.
   c. powerful groups no longer believe their interests are being served.
   d. people define their environment as too crowded.
6. The Green Revolution has to do with
   a. expanding food harvests from the sea.
   b. increasing crop yields.
   c. expanding the amount of farmland available.
   d. reducing the demographic gap.
7. One major cause of the financial problems in cities in the United States is
   a. the growing demographic gap in cities.
   b. the flight of people and jobs from cities.
   c. the overpopulation of cities.
   d. the gentrification of cities.
8. The combination of social and economic changes that probably accounts for a significant decline in fertility in nations is called
   a. family planning.
   b. fecundity.
   c. demography.
   d. economic development.
   e. urban homesteading.
9. Programs to promote gender equality around the world will probably have which effect?
   a. a positive impact on controlling world population growth
   b. a negative impact on controlling world population growth
   c. little impact on world population growth
   d. a reduction in fecundity

10. Urban policy since 1980 in the United States has been characterized by
   a. an increasingly interventionist stance.
   b. a growing dependence on the federal government to solve problems.
   c. the dominance of the conflict perspective.
   d. a shift toward a more laissez-faire approach.

True/False Questions

1. The fertility of a society is usually at about the same level as its fecundity.
2. The life expectancy of women in the United States is about six years longer than that of men.
3. Cities are communities, but communities are not necessarily cities.
4. In the 1930s and 1940s, the United States government, to promote racially integrated communities, attempted to discourage people from moving to the suburbs.
5. The interactionist perspective stresses the idea that urban problems are defined as much by subjective definitions of reality as by objective conditions.
6. The carrying capacity is something that should be exceeded if population growth is to be controlled.
7. According to most observers, the sea will not be a very important source of expanding food supplies in the years to come.
8. The extent of residential segregation in cities in the United States has been declining since the 1960s.
9. Family planning is probably more effective than economic development in helping to bring down fertility levels in third-world nations.
10. Research has shown that the main impact of urban free-enterprise zones in cities in the United States will probably be the creation of new jobs rather than the movement of jobs from one locale to another.

Fill-In Questions

1. The difference between the crude birthrate and the crude death rate is referred to as the _____.
2. The United States is the third largest nation in the world today, behind _____ and _____.
3. The _____ stage of the demographic transition is characterized by high birthrates and high death rates.
4. From the _____ perspective, cities have deteriorated because those most directly affected have few political and economic resources with which to change things.
5. A _____ is a neighborhood in a city inhabited largely by members of a single ethnic or racial group.

6. _____ is a situation in which birthrates and death rates in a society are nearly equal, producing a zero rate of natural increase.
7. China's "one-child family" program for reducing population growth appears to have resulted in an increase in _____.
8. In the last twenty years, urban policy in the United States has changed dramatically, with a decided shift toward a more _____ approach.
9. Zones of a city where new businesses are given tax breaks or are subject to less stringent regulation are called _____.
10. _____ refers to programs to increase home ownership by private citizens in certain neighborhoods by selling them houses at little or no cost.

Matching Questions

_____ 1. demography
_____ 2. mortality
_____ 3. emigration
_____ 4. China
_____ 5. Thomas Malthus
_____ 6. Karl Marx
_____ 7. carrying capacity
_____ 8. Club of Rome
_____ 9. family planning
_____ 10. urban renewal

A. world's largest nation
B. study of human populations
C. conflict approach to population dynamics
D. population control program
E. report on depletion of resources
F. moving out of a particular country
G. government urban program
H. number of deaths in a population
I. functionalist approach to population dynamics
J. upper limit on population

Essay Questions

1. Define the field of demography. What are the elements of demographic change? How have they been changing in the United States during the twentieth century?
2. What is the demographic transition? Describe the stages that are a part of it and what happens at each one.
3. Describe the policies of the federal government that contributed to the growth of the suburbs in the United States.
4. How is the postindustrial city different from cities in an industrial era?

5. What is the interactionist perspective on population and urban problems?
6. Choose two of the consequences of world population growth discussed in the text and summarize what those consequences are.
7. What factors have produced the economic decline of cities in the United States?
8. What are the negative consequences of the residential segregation by race that persists in cities in the United States?
9. What is family planning? How does the program work? How effective is it at achieving its goals?
10. What federal government programs are currently in operation to help alleviate urban problems?

For Further Reading

Edward Banfield. *The Unheavenly City Revisited.* Prospect Heights, IL: Waveland Press, 1990. This sociologist offers a very positive assessment of America's cities, saying that they are healthy, enjoyable, and fulfilling places to live.

Herbert J. Gans. *People, Plans, and Policies: Essays on Poverty, Racism, and Other National Urban Problems.* New York: Columbia University Press, 1991. This is an excellent set of essays by a well-respected specialist in urban affairs. The issues discussed range from problems of architecture to poverty and the underclass.

Joel Garreau. *Edge City: Life on the New Frontier.* New York: Doubleday, 1991. "Edge city" is the author's name for those suburbs that have grown large enough to be considered self-sufficient. He provides an interesting perspective on this part of urban life, suggesting that edge cities reflect such American values as individualism and homesteading.

John D. Kasarda and Allan M. Parnell (eds.). *Third World Cities: Problems, Policies, and Prospects.* Newbury Park, CA: Sage Publications, 1993. These two sociologists have brought together some of the most recent research being done on the problems confronting cities in third-world nations. This volume views the problems of cities from a global perspective.

William H. McNeil. *Plagues and People.* Garden City, NY: Doubleday/Anchor, 1976. This is a detailed and well-documented history of epidemics through history. It demonstrates in a very interesting fashion how social practices can influence disease and how disease can work to control population growth.

Donella H. Meadows, Dennis L. Meadows, and Jorgen Randers. *Beyond the Limits: Confronting Global Collapse, Envisioning a Sustainable Future.* Post Mills, VT: Chelsea Green Pub. Co., 1992. This is a recent assessment by the same scientists who conducted the study for the Club of Rome thirty years ago. Their conclusions are a little more optimistic now, but with the caveat that there be changes in both lifestyle and technology.

Alejandro Portes and Alex Stepick. *City on the Edge: The Transformation of Miami.* Berkeley: University of California Press, 1993. This is an excellent analysis of the development of Miami as its Cuban population has grown. It is a complex story that ties in urban development, ethnicity, and socioeconomic status.

Terry Williams and William Kornblum. *The Uptown Kids: Struggle and Hope in the Projects.* New York: Putnam, 1994. This is an intimate portrait of what life is like for youth who grow up in crowded and dangerous urban public housing projects. The authors make suggestions for how the projects could be improved.

ENVIRONMENTAL PROBLEMS

One major consequence of rapid population growth, discussed in Chapter 12, is its impact on the earth's environment. In the past century, many disturbing problems have emerged that call our attention again and again to the fragility of the world's environment: air and water pollution, acid rain, the accumulation of toxic wastes, and many others. Lurking behind all of this is the frightening realization that we may be damaging the environment in irreversible ways, that human beings may soon reach (or have already reached) a point at which the destruction already done cannot be completely corrected. This chapter reviews the evidence for how extensive and irreversible the damage actually is and what can be and is being done about it.

The Ecosystem

To understand modern environmental problems, it is useful to begin with a brief look at some of the concepts that modern biology uses to understand the world and how it operates. **Ecology** is *the branch of biology that studies the relationships between living organisms and their environment*. The term **environment** refers to *the conditions and circumstances surrounding and affecting a particular group of living creatures*. Human beings, of course, are one of the living organisms that ecologists study, but from an ecological perspective all of the other organisms—plants, fish, bacteria, and so on—are equally important. Now, many cultures place human beings in a special and superior position as the most important creature in the environment. In fact, some cultures set human beings completely apart from the environment, as if they lived independently of the other living organisms and could destroy them at will, without regard to the consequences. Certainly, such cultural attitudes can be found in the Judeo-Christian heritage that is the underpinning of values for much of the United States and other Western cultures. This heritage stresses the superiority of humans over other creatures and the mastery of humans over the earth and its living creatures. Passages in the Bible, for example, have been interpreted as justifying human exploitation of the environment:

> And God said, Let us make man in our image, after our likeness: . . . Be fertile and increase, fill the earth and master it; and rule the fish of the sea, the birds of the sky, and all the living things that creep on the earth. (Genesis 1:26–28)

Modern ecologists recognize that such attitudes ignore the extent to which human beings are only one part of a complex environment and are inextricably dependent on the other creatures in that environment. A few simple examples can illustrate this. **Photosynthesis** is *the process by which plants capture light and heat energy from the sun and turn it into food*. Other animals survive by consuming these plants. Still other animals, including human beings, get sustenance by consuming both plants and animals. The same process of photosynthesis produces oxygen, which plants, animals, and humans need to breathe. In breathing, plants and animals discharge carbon dioxide into the atmosphere, and it is carbon dioxide that plants use to produce oxygen in photosynthesis. Bees pollinate plants that other animals live off. Human beings even have microorganisms in their intestines that help them digest food. Even though human beings may not be aware of this interdependent network of life, it is the indispensable core

Myths & Facts

About the Environment

Myth: Environmental pollution did not become a problem until the 1960s and 1970s.

Fact: This depends on what is meant by pollution becoming a problem. Environmental pollution existed long before modern times, and it caused people health and other problems. For most of this time, however, people did not recognize pollution as a social problem that deserved attention. They ignored it or accepted it. It was not until the 1960s that serious and widespread attention was focused on the issue. Today, many more people are inclined to see environmental degradation as an unacceptable condition and thus define it as a social problem.

Myth: Native peoples in premodern societies were more sensitive to environmental issues than are modern people in industrial societies, and native peoples worked to avoid exploiting their environments.

Fact: People in most human societies behave in much the same way as their industrial counterparts: They protect resources in short supply but take a wasteful stance toward those resources that appear to be plentiful. In addition, most premodern peoples engaged in at least some practices that would have been highly destructive to the environment if their population size had been larger or their technology more intrusive.

Myth: Environmental conditions deteriorated in the last half of the twentieth century.

Fact: Any assessment of environmental conditions is complicated and depends on which conditions are observed. Whereas many conditions have deteriorated, there have also been many significant improvements. Lead emissions into the atmosphere in the United States, for example, have dropped dramatically in the last 30 years, and the worldwide production of ozone-depleting chemicals has dropped significantly.

of life on earth. Ecologists recognize this by pointing out that all living creatures, including human beings, live in an **ecosystem:** *a complex, interrelated network of life forms and nonlife forms that interact with one another to produce an exchange of materials between the living and the nonliving parts.*

The concept of an ecosystem helps us to understand that all parts of the environment interact with one another and are, to a degree, dependent on one another. The cycle of photosynthesis illustrates this: Plants produce oxygen, which animals need, while animals expire carbon dioxide, which plants need to produce oxygen in photosynthesis. Each ecosystem achieves a natural balance among all the living creatures in it, and maintaining that equilibrium requires that all the parts be in some necessary, functional balance. An ecosystem might be relatively small, such as a section of swamp or part of a rain forest, or extensive, as when the whole earth is considered one ecosystem. A self-sufficient ecosystem also interacts with other ecosystems at the overlap of their borders. Ecologists also recognize that changes in one part of the ecosystem will likely produce changes in the other parts. This likelihood is at the core of the environmental problems discussed in this chapter; that is, the extent to which changes introduced into ecosystems because of human activities have produced further changes with severely detrimental consequences. Such human-induced changes in the ecosystem could be minor, but ecologists recognize that, if the human activities are sufficiently intrusive, they could dramatically alter the ecosystem, possibly to the point that its ability to support human life would be threatened.

Social Sources of Environmental Problems

The actions of human beings, of course, are at center stage in this assessment of environmental problems. Although environmental problems can be caused by nonhuman intervention, as when severe weather devastates an ecosystem, the most severe environmental damage in the past century has been the product of human activities. The social and cultural conditions that tend to lead human beings to behave in ways that have detrimental consequences for the environment have actually been discussed in a number of other chapters in this book. They will be reviewed here in terms of their consequences for the environment.

Biologists Paul Ehrlich and Anne Ehrlich (1990) have developed a formula that summarizes some of the social conditions that affect the impact that human beings have on their environment:

$$I = P \times A \times T$$

Or, Impact = Population $\times$ Affluence $\times$ Technology. These key factors are reviewed, along with some others.

Population Growth

Without question, the sheer number of people on the earth today is a key factor in environmental damage. If the human population were one-tenth or one-fiftieth of what it is, the same social and economic activities that people engage in today would likely produce relatively little damage. The concept of **carrying capacity** is introduced in Chapter 12: *an upper-size limit that is imposed on a population by its environmental resources and that cannot be permanently exceeded.* Exceeding the carrying capacity of an ecosystem means that people are depleting or destroying resources at a more rapid rate than they can be replaced. Forests are being cut down faster than nature can replace them, or air is being polluted at higher levels than the actions of photosynthesis can cleanse it. The carrying capacity can be exceeded for brief periods so long as population drops below that level in time for the environment to regenerate itself. However, exceeding the carrying capacity on a long-term or permanent basis may do sufficient damage to threaten the capacity of the ecosystem to support human life.

Determining the carrying capacity of an ecosystem is complicated because it depends in part on levels of affluence and technology, to be discussed in the following sections. It also depends on what people consider to be socially acceptable environmental conditions. The level of environmental damage in some very crowded nations, such as India, would horrify many people in the United States. Yet people become used to some level of air and water pollution, especially if it is seen as the cost of getting a desired job or maintaining a way of life. Even in the United States, many people are willing to accept some level of air pollution if it means they are free to use their automobiles as they wish. However, even if people can live with pollution, it may still be detrimental to society through, for example, increased health consequences.

So, it is no simple task to define what the carrying capacity of an ecosystem is. At an extreme, exceeding the carrying capacity for a long period could result in an ecological catastrophe in which the ability of an ecosystem to support human life is in danger. Such a catastrophe has probably not yet occurred on the earth due to population size alone, although some ecosystems have been made unlivable for other reasons, such as nuclear accidents. However, as human populations continue to grow, ecologists look at this possibility: When are there too many people for the earth to support? Have we already done some irreparable damage simply because the earth must support so many people?

Affluence

To achieve high levels of affluence and material comfort, people have to consume the earth's resources and pollute its environment. The industrial nations of the world today have achieved levels of affluence that have been unheard of for most people at most times in history. The list of things that contribute to this lifestyle is almost endless: automobiles, airplanes, large and well-heated homes, air-conditioning, clothing, refrigerators, and on and on. Each of these products consumes natural resources and energy when built, consumes more energy resources when operated, pollutes the air or water as a by-product of its operation, and then pollutes streams or fills landfills when it is discarded.

If few people had these material goods, of course, the environmental problems would be minimal. Today, however, as was just noted, there are so many people to purchase these goods that the problem has become dire. In addition, less-developed nations around the globe are desirous of achieving the same levels of affluence that have become routine in North America, Western Europe, and Japan. It is disturbing to consider the environmental consequences were the two most populous nations in the world, China and India, with a combined population of over 2 billion people, to achieve the same level of affluence as the United States. Looking at automobiles alone, this would mean another 1 billion automobiles on the earth, consuming fossil fuels and polluting the air, not to mention the tires and highways that would have to be built. Some ecologists think we may exceed the carrying capacity of the earth if we combine current and future world population sizes with Western levels of affluence.

Of course, if people were willing to forego the affluence that is possible in the world today, environmental damage would be reduced. But most people do not consider this to be an option; they want the best life possible for themselves and their families. In fact, if anything, people hope for progress, with life for future generations being even more affluent than it is now. This is the "phenomenon of rising expectations": Especially when things are improving, people come to expect continued improvement in the future. So affluence is a very tempting thing, much too tempting for most people to avoid.

Technology

Technology is a double-edged sword: Advances in technology result in new products that produce additional environmental damage, but at the same time technological developments can result in less polluting ways of doing things. Any technological development that brings a new product into the world that many people will buy and use is almost inherently polluting. It consumes resources in its production and use, and it pollutes the environment with its byproducts along the way. And if it supports the affluent lifestyle that many people seek, many millions of these new products will be produced and consumed. So, although modern technology does some wonderful things, it can also be very damaging. The wonders of electricity exist all around us, as it lights homes, heats buildings, and runs the computer on which these words are being written. Yet the cost is the gouging of coal out of the earth in strip mines that pollute nearby streams and ultimately results in air pollution as the coal is burned to generate electricity. The greater the number of technological wonders that are invented, the more threats to the environment will exist.

Yet, technology clearly has its positive side: It makes our lives more comfortable and enables us to produce foods and medicines to keep us healthy. It can also help to reduce environmental damage: The gasoline consumed today is far less polluting than in the past, and scrubbers have been invented to prevent many of the pollutants of burning coal from escaping into the air. The problem is not technology by itself, but rather uncontrolled technology that is harnessed to gain the greatest short-term reward without consideration of its impact on the environment.

Economic Growth

Most nations in the world today pursue a policy of economic growth, which means that the total goods and services produced is growing from year to year. Economic growth is important if a nation's population is growing because the economy must produce more to provide the same standard of living for more people. Economic growth also provides for increasing levels of affluence: Even if population size does not change, the economy needs to produce more if it is to provide higher levels of material affluence in the future. Beyond these reasons, capitalism as an economic system also stresses the ideology of growth, as it drives to expand and find new markets for its goods. Economic growth provides for higher profits for corporations.

With the emergence of the global capitalist economy, discussed in Chapter 2, worldwide pressures toward economic growth and competition have become intense. Organizations such as the World Bank and the International Monetary Fund (IMF) have expended money and resources around the globe—especially in the less developed nations of Asia, Africa, and Latin

America—to encourage economic growth and development and the exploitation of natural resources. Economic growth itself can have a disastrous impact on the environment, but critics accuse the World Bank, IMF, and other international financial organizations of promoting economic growth that is ruinous to the environment (Danaher, 2001; Stiglitz, 2006). They have been accused of mounting campaigns to build giant, unsustainable energy projects, to destroy millions of acres of rain forests, and to forcibly relocate millions of people.

So, there are many pressures toward economic growth, and such growth is not inherently bad. However, it can result in more products produced and more environmental damage. In addition to the additional products produced, corporations also tend to ignore some of the costs of doing business, and these costs often involve environmental damage. So, for example, the cheapest way for a factory to dispose of toxic wastes may be to discharge them into a nearby river, but someone will pay for the easy disposal of those wastes. It might be people living downstream who get sick from swimming in the wastes or it might be future generations who have to cleanse the river to make it usable again (Hawken, 1993). Unless regulated in some fashion, capitalists have a strong profit incentive to push these costs off onto others.

Especially in less developed nations, the pressure is intense to pursue economic growth as a means of raising low living standards. Whereas many nations have come to recognize that unregulated growth can be very destructive, all too often national leaders place short-term gains in living standards ahead of long-term protection of the environment. So, there is controversy today regarding policies of economic growth. Some environmentalists take the position that continued economic growth, especially when accompanied by continued population growth, will eventually produce an ecological catastrophe when the carrying capacity of the earth is exceeded (Hardin, 1993). Supporters of economic growth, on the other hand, while agreeing that environmental problems warrant concern and that some regulation of economic activity may be essential, argue that growth will provide the foundation for new technological discoveries that will help us reduce environmental damage. New products will be less polluting, or new technologies will arise to correct the damage from pollution. In addition, if some natural resources are depleted, they argue, technological developments will provide us with new resources or products to replace them (Easterbrook, 1995).

Cultural Values

In many nations, a constellation of cultural values exists that supports practices that are damaging to the environment, or at least the values do not discourage such practices. Earlier in this chapter, it was mentioned that some religious beliefs and cultural values stress the notion that human beings are superior to and have mastery over the earth and its creatures. This stance opens the door for radical alterations in the environment, which can be highly destructive if not closely regulated. A second cultural value that has risen to prominence is that of progress—that people's standard of living should rise over time. This notion of progress is a recent one in human societies, with most people in preindustrial societies being content to maintain a traditional way of life that is handed down from one generation to the next with little change. By the twenty-first century, the value of progress has become entrenched in many societies around the world and fuels the pursuit of economic growth.

A third cultural value that plays a part in environmental issues is individualism, the belief that individual desires and achievements are more important than collective accomplishments and goals. Individualism is a very powerful ethic in the United States, leading people to believe that they should be able to do as they wish, without regard to what other people or government agencies believe is appropriate. This notion was very prominent in the antigovernment rhetoric of the 1990s. As for environmental issues, if a person wants to drive a car that pollutes the air or depletes resources, individualists believe this should be his or her choice. If a property owner wishes to fill in a wetland on his or her property, the government should not stand in the way. In other words, environmental concerns often focus on collective goals—what is good for the whole ecosystem—whereas individualism can lead people to behave in ways contrary to those broader goals.

These values of mastery, progress, and individualism do not automatically translate into environmental damage, but they do open the door for human goals, such as economic growth, to be pursued in such a way as to disregard the importance of protecting the ecosystem.

Perspectives on Environmental Problems

The Functionalist Perspective

The functionalist perspective views society as a system made up of interrelated and interdependent parts, each working toward the maintenance of the system. In the case of environmental issues, the system consists of the land, air, water, people, and other resources in a particular ecosystem. Another part of the system comprises people's cultural beliefs and values and the resulting social behaviors. All of the parts exist in a delicate balance, and an injudicious treatment of some parts of the system may have negative consequences for other parts. For functionalists, a highly technological social organization has many benefits but also many dysfunctions. It can overuse resources, for example, and deplete them, making them unavailable for future generations. The excessive use of some resources may pollute a part of the environment to the point at which it is unhealthy to humans or not usable for some purposes. High technology and environmental preservation are at odds with one another—the parts of the system are not well integrated.

As mentioned, an important part of the system is made up of the human cultural beliefs and values that fuel behavior. If cultural values encourage people in a careless use of the environment, then this may lead to serious environmental problems. From the functionalist perspective, then, environmental problems become social problems when they produce social disorganization, making it difficult for societies to survive or to achieve desired goals. Although improvements in technology may alleviate some of the destructiveness, because technology tends to be inherently intrusive, solutions may require that technology and industrialism adapt to fit the needs of society.

The Conflict Perspective

From the conflict perspective, environmental problems have less to do with the limited amount of resources available than with their distribution. The problem is not how much is available but who gets a share of what is available. Decisions that affect the environment are not made on the basis of maintaining a balance in an ecosystem but on the basis of how successfully interest groups compete for a share of the resources available. The manner in which the environment is used emerges out of this competition of groups for varying amounts of power and other resources.

So, a central idea of the conflict perspective on environmental problems is that groups have competing interests when it comes to how to treat environmental resources: If one side gets what it wants, the other side loses. If community residents successfully oppose the location of a toxic waste incinerator in their neighborhood, the owners of the incinerator lose. On the other hand, if the incinerator is built, the residents lose. The interests of the two groups compete directly, and the outcome is determined by which group can successfully wield the most power. In addition, there are always groups who will benefit, at least in the short term, by exploiting the environment by polluting and using up resources. Oil corporations benefit when the world's oil reserves are tapped heavily, and timber interests benefit by the extensive cutting of timber. In a highly competitive environment, these corporations may feel it an essential business practice to pollute and deplete, at least to an extent, to corner markets and make a profit. In the competitive global economy, enormous pressures exist to consider concerns about environmental degradation to be secondary to the needs of business.

Environmental conditions become social problems when groups with some power feel that their interests are not being served by current environmental policies and practices. The discharge of pollutants from a factory into a stream may not be considered a problem by the corporation that owns the factory—in fact, it may be an economically efficient means of handling industrial wastes. Such discharges become a problem if there are groups with sufficient resources to mount a campaign against the pollution and direct societal attention toward the problem.

The Interactionist Perspective

The interactionist perspective stresses the importance of social definitions and subjective assessments of reality. Environmental problems are not solely objective conditions in the physical world; to become social problems, they must be identified and defined by people as problems about which something ought to be done. After all, human beings have polluted their environments even before the current era. In the early industrial period in Great Britain and Europe, for example, factories spewed pollutants into the air with abandon, and many cities had far worse air quality than cities in the United States today. Yet air pollution was not defined as a social problem but as one of the possibly unfortunate but necessary costs of economic progress. People may not have liked it, but they accepted it. However, social definitions can change over time. The media, for example, may publish articles that cast pollution as an evil about which people can do something, or biologists and ecologists might publish books showing the serious damage pollution does to the environment and how it could be alleviated. Sometimes a very powerful image can help evoke a new definition of reality. This occurred when photographs taken from space showed the earth floating alone in the immense void of space and looking very fragile indeed. The expression "spaceship earth" emerged, suggesting that the earth was alone in space with its finite supply of resources that could not be replaced and that needed to be guarded carefully.

As these and other influences gradually change people's perceptions of environmental problems, the social construction of environmental problems emerges. This does not mean that everyone agrees or that all people view environmental problems in the same way. The next section explores how these social definitions of the environment developed and changed in the United States.

The Social Construction of Environmental Problems

The interactionist perspective suggests that social problems do not really exist until people identify and define them as social problems. The conflict perspective points to the important role of the clash of competing interest groups in shaping what is considered a social problem. A brief review of changing concerns about the environment in the United States will illustrate how social problems are socially constructed by people.

A popular belief holds that premodern people had a keen understanding of nature and a harmonious relationship with their environment. American Indians, for example, have been described as the "first environmentalists." Historical evidence belies this notion, however (Krech, 1999). Most American Indians treated their environment the way that most humans have done through the centuries—they worked hard to protect those resources in short supply and took a wasteful approach toward those that they believed to be plentiful. For example, some popular images depict ruthless whites shooting buffalo for "sport" from railroad trains, but after the Indians acquired horses and firearms, they also sometimes slaughtered the buffalo, eating the best meat and taking the hides but leaving the rest to decompose. In short, American Indians at times exploited their environment before the Europeans got into the act. One of the major differences between then and now is that, with the much larger population and more elaborate technology in the United States today, people's actions are far more able to do serious damage to the environment.

People's consciousness of environmental problems has fluctuated over time. For example, at the beginning of the twentieth century, the air in cities in the United States was being polluted by the smoke and waste from the growing number of factories. But people of that era did not perceive this environmental pollution as a threat. One of the key factors that began to heighten people's awareness of these problems since

then has been the establishment of a wide variety of environmental interest groups. The oldest of these groups is the Sierra Club, which was founded in 1892 by a group of affluent San Franciscans who had an interest in hiking and camping in the Sierra Nevada Mountains of California. Today, the Sierra Club is one of the best-known environmental groups in the political and legal arena. Another older environmental association is the Audubon Society, which was founded in 1905 by affluent women and men on the East Coast, with the initial purpose of halting the commercial hunting of wild birds for plumage for the women's fashion industry. These early groups focused more on issues of conservation, or protecting wilderness areas for use by human beings, rather than environmental degradation. Despite these organizations, the general public in the United States was not aware of or responsive to environmental concerns prior to the 1950s.

The modern environmental movement really took off in the 1960s. It was then that biological ecologists such as Rachel Carson and Paul Ehrlich began writing for popular audiences about how the growth in human societies was producing an ecological disaster in nature. In 1962, Carson published *Silent Spring*, which dealt with the hidden dangers that pesticides and herbicides hold for the environment. In 1968, Ehrlich's best-selling *The Population Bomb* hit the market. Using a distinctly Malthusian approach (see Chapter 12), Ehrlich proposed that world population growth is responsible for pollution and other modern environmental problems. A bit later, Barry Commoner joined the ranks of environmental critics and, in contrast to Ehrlich's approach, blamed technology and growing corporate power structures for the expanding ecological woes of the world.

The 1960s and 1970s also saw the emergence of major nationwide environmental groups such as Friends of the Earth, the League of Conservation Voters, the Environmental Defense Fund, the Natural Resources Defense Council, and Greenpeace. These groups engaged in lobbying, demonstrations, and sometimes disruptive actions that brought environmental problems to the public eye and created a great deal of political pressure to address environmental issues with legislation.

The fervor generated by these organizations set the stage for some very important legislation in the 1970s. In 1969, for example, the National Environmental Policy Act (NEPA) was passed, which required that public hearings be held on matters that might adversely affect the environment and that environmental impact studies be conducted to assess these possible effects. Also in the early 1970s, the Clean Air Act and the Water Pollution Control Act were passed,

Greenpeace is one of the modern environmental groups that have contributed to the social construction of social problems. Through its lobbying, demonstrations, and disruptive actions, Greenpeace has helped promote the belief that environmental issues are social problems to which we should direct our attention.

and these laws led to the establishment of the Environmental Protection Agency (EPA). Originally, the Clean Air Act empowered the EPA to monitor and regulate standards of air quality, but as time went on, the EPA acquired authority over almost all matters dealing with environmental quality. Had it not been for the establishment and operation of these various environmental organizations, legislation such as this would probably not have been passed.

This brief history, then, suggests how the social problem of environmental degradation was socially constructed. It came to be identified as a problem by more people because they learned about the nature and extent of assaults on the ecosystem from biologists like Ehrlich and Commoner. In addition, the various environmental organizations were able to pressure newspapers, magazines, and television into publicizing the problems, and the prominence of this issue in the media is important in convincing people that environmental degradation should be addressed. Finally, the organizations were able to pressure the government into action, and the resulting laws and government bureaus serve as sounding boards that keep the issue before the public's attention.

Extent of Environmental Problems

Water Supply and Pollution

Water is present in the atmosphere as a vapor; it then condenses and falls to the earth as rain, dew, or snow; it collects underground and drains into streams, rivers, and the oceans; finally, it evaporates into the atmosphere once more as vapor. This *process, by which nature purifies water,* is called the **hydrologic cycle.** There are various mechanisms by which water is purified during this cycle. In a single pass through the hydrologic cycle, these mechanisms make water suitable for reuse. But this natural process is interfered with by various kinds of human pollution, including raw sewage, pesticides and other chemicals, nitrate and phosphate fertilizers, and waste products from factories and nuclear power generators. As population and technology have grown, the resulting pollution has become so massive that the hydrologic cycle cannot fully cleanse the water, although techniques exist to assist nature in this process (Abramovitz et al.,

2001). The EPA issues thousands of warnings each year not to drink, swim in, or eat fish from chemically contaminated rivers and lakes.

A dramatic example of such water pollution is found in the phenomenon of acid precipitation, or acid rain, which refers to a type of air pollution made up of sulfurous and nitrous oxide emissions from the burning of fossil fuels (Environmental Protection Agency, 2007a). These pollutants come mostly from coal-burning power plants, motor vehicles, and other industrial facilities. They combine with oxygen in the atmosphere to produce sulfuric and nitric acids that fall to the earth as acidic rain, snow, fog, or particulates. Acidity can destroy plant and animal life in an ecosystem. The environmental damage and economic costs associated with acid rain are enormous. For example, millions of acres of European and eastern U.S. forests now show severe damage linked to acid rain, as do some forests in remote parts of China. This type of air pollution may result in the extermination of valuable forests all over the world. Approximately 85 percent of the sulfur dioxide in the atmospheres of the United States and Canada is of U.S. origin, although all nations that burn fossil fuels contribute to the problem. In addition to its harmful effects on forests, acid rain also releases lead from the interior of steel pipes into drinking and irrigation water, has killed fish and other wildlife in once-thriving lakes, and has elevated the incidence of respiratory ailments in the population.

The acid rain problem can be alleviated by a reduction in the burning of fossil fuels. This would happen if people drove their automobiles less and relied less on electricity produced by burning high-sulfur coal. Many countries have begun to do this. In the United States,

the amount of nitrogen oxide released into the air grew substantially until 1980 and has since leveled off; the amount of sulfur dioxide grew until about 1970 and has since dropped to below 1940s levels (see Figure 13.1). In the past decade, Russia and the other nations that made up the former Soviet Union have significantly reduced their use of highly polluting coal as their economies have been restructured (Flavin, 1992). Another approach is to put scrubbers on the smokestacks of coal-burning plants to clean the emissions, but this is a very expensive proposition and tends to be resisted. At the same time that efforts to deal with the problem have emerged, new concerns have been felt along another front: increased use of fossil fuels by developing countries such as China and the former Soviet Union as they try to emulate the more affluent lifestyles of the industrial nations. If they follow the high-energy-consumption, no-energy-conservation route the United States has taken, worldwide sulfurous and nitrous oxide emissions will increase substantially in the future, and the acid rain problem will become more severe.

Another example of the effects of pollution on our water supply involves a process called *eutrophication*, the depletion of oxygen in a body of water because of an overabundance of plant and animal life (Environmental Protection Agency, 2006). It can happen like this: Many modern farms use nitrate and phosphate fertilizers. When these fertilizers run off into rivers and lakes, they stimulate the growth of algae and other plants that eventually decay at the bottoms of these bodies of water. In the same fashion as decomposing sewage, these algae formations consume increasing amounts of oxygen, and they compete with fish and other animals for the oxygen in the water. If the

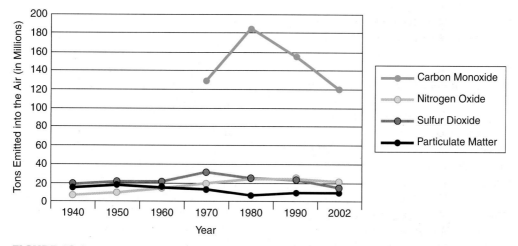

FIGURE 13.1 **Levels of Various Air Pollutants in the United States, 1940–2002.**

Sources: U.S. Environmental Protection Agency, *National Emissions Inventory, Air Pollution Emission Trends,* www.epa.gov/ttn/chief/trends.index.html, July 8, 2007; U.S. Bureau of the Census, *Statistical Abstract of the United States, 2007,* (Washington, DC: U.S. Government Printing Office, 2006), p. 222.

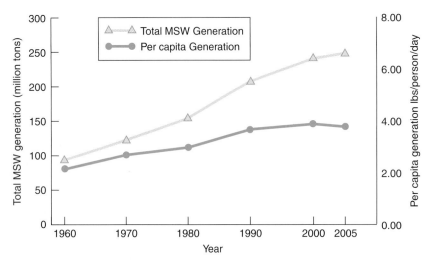

FIGURE 13.2 **Total and Per Capita Municipal Solid Waste (MSW) Generated in the United States, 1960–2005.**

Source: U.S. Environmental Protection Agency, *Municipal Solid Waste Generation, Recycling, and Disposal in the United States: Facts and Figures for 2005.* (Washington, DC: U.S. Government Printing Office, 2006), www.epa.gov/epaoswer/non-hw/muncpl/msw99.htm.

competition is too fierce, oxygen in the water is depleted rather than replaced, and nothing may be able to survive in the water. This happened to Lake Erie in the 1950s and 1960s with disastrous results. The lake had an algae bottom that was over one hundred feet thick, which was also laden with nitrous and phosphorous compounds. Fishing in the lake was ended. By halting the various forms of pollution flowing into the lake, total destruction was avoided, and Lake Erie has recovered substantially today. In the 1990s, a "dead zone" the size of New Jersey emerged in the Gulf of Mexico off the coast of Louisiana and caused a dramatic reduction in fishing and shrimping (Gardner, 1998). It was caused by the nutrient fertilizers used in agriculture throughout the Midwest that drain through the Mississippi River. Experiences such as these document that care and effort must be devoted to protecting water supplies from the harmful effects of population growth and technological development.

Solid and Toxic Wastes

The average person in the United States throws away between four and five pounds of waste every day, amounting to an incredible three tons per year for the typical family of four people, which translates to almost 250 million tons yearly for the country as a whole. This amount has tripled in the last four decades (see Figure 13.2). One hundred sixty million additional tons are added every year in industrial waste, along with between 2 and 3 billion tons yearly from mining operations. This enormous waste-disposal figure led one observer to call people in the United States

"the world's trashiest people." Disposing of this waste in a way that does not degrade the environment poses a very serious problem.

Rather than disposing of waste, it may be possible to reuse some of it (Environmental Protection Agency, 2007c). For example, some states have passed "bottle bills," which require that a deposit be paid for soda and beer bottles and other containers when a beverage is bought. This encourages people to return the bottles and cans for the deposit and contributes to the recycling of glass, plastic, and aluminum containers. In addition to not filling up landfills, recycled materials are substantially less expensive to produce, thus saving energy in the process.

Toxic waste disposal presents an even more ominous problem in terms of the pollution of our environment. Toxic wastes are the residues of the production of things such as plastics, pesticides, and nuclear energy. The tragedy at Love Canal near Niagara Falls, first coming to public attention in the late 1970s, is one of the more dramatic instances of the consequences of dumping chemical waste products. The wastes had been buried many years before, and homes were later built at Love Canal where the wastes had accumulated. Contaminants seeped into the water supply and the homes of the residents and caused severe and lingering health problems. Eventually many residents were forced to move, with the government buying their houses from them. However, many residents believed that their or their children's health had been permanently damaged and that they had not been adequately compensated for their suffering and dislocation. Even though regulation of toxic wastes began more than 20 years ago, not all

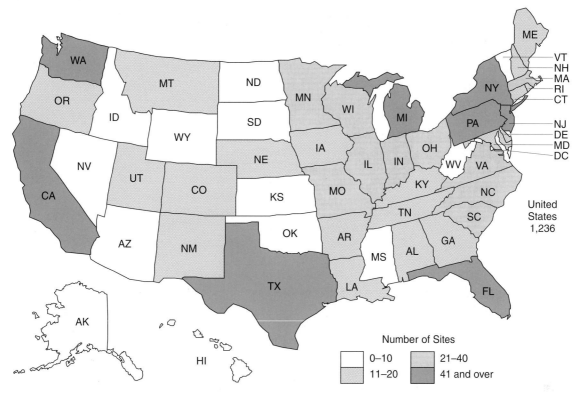

FIGURE 13.3 Sites of the Worst Hazardous Waste Dumps in 2004.

Source: U.S. Environmental Protection Agency, *Final National Priorities List (NPL) Sites, 2004,* www.epa.gov/superfund/sites/index.htm.

hazardous wastes are covered by the regulations, and there are still no answers to basic questions regarding the numbers and amounts of such wastes polluting the environment (Gerrard, 1994). Consequently, the data on this subject are extremely limited, which is disturbing considering the extent and severity of the problem.

Thousands of toxic waste dumps exist in the United States, with heavy concentrations in the industrial states of the Great Lakes region and the East and West Coasts. Figure 13.3 shows the regional concentrations of over one thousand dumps that are currently on the government's National Priorities List, which are sites that pose severe hazards and about which something must be done. However, there may be as many as thirty thousand sites that will eventually need to be cleaned up, with total cleanup costs difficult to estimate but probably in the hundreds of billions of dollars. Congress has appropriated only a fraction of that to clean up the worst sites. In addition, the Applied Research insert points to some factors that influence where these sites are located, with disturbing consequences for racial and ethnic minorities.

Radioactive Wastes

Radioactive wastes are a particularly serious form of toxic waste because they can stay so deadly for so long.

There are three sources of radioactive wastes: the lethal by-products of manufacturing nuclear weapons, the radioactive wastes from nuclear power plants, and the low-grade radioactive wastes that are by-products of our health and other industries (Nuclear Regulatory Commission, 2007; Gerrard, 1994). As of this writing, no plan for the permanent disposal of these wastes has been agreed to, even though the wastes are accumulating at an alarming rate. One problem with nuclear wastes is that they remain deadly for thousands of years, and for some wastes even tens of thousands of years. Plutonium, for example, remains radioactive for 240,000 years! That is a time span that is at least as long as *Homo sapiens* has existed on the earth. It is absurd to imagine that we could ensure the integrity of a vault or the safety of the materials over such a vast expanse of time. A successful repository for the wastes must seal them completely for all this time, and no one has yet figured out how to do that. Another problem with nuclear wastes is the NIMBY syndrome: Not in My Backyard. Few people want the waste repository near where they live, so communities have tended to resist when efforts are made to put a repository near them. A third problem with nuclear wastes is transporting them. Even if we have permanent storage facilities, wastes will be shipped there from all over the country, and that presents an image of an accident waiting to

Assessing the Extent of Environmental Justice: Race, Class, and Pollution

In 1984, methyl isocyanate, a lethal gas, escaped from a storage tank in Bhopal, India, owned by Union Carbide, a corporation based in the United States. More than two thousand people who lived in the neighborhood where the tank was located, mostly poor Indians, were killed as the gas spread through the neighborhood, and an additional one hundred thousand people were injured. In the United States, many sources of pollution tend to be more prominent in communities where low-income people and racial and ethnic minorities live. In Los Angeles, for example, freeway off-ramps, where idling cars pour out pollution, are more common in poor inner-city neighborhoods, as are the highly polluting metal plating and furniture factories (Mann, 1990).

These examples point to a problem that has been referred to as **environmental justice,** *the idea that environmental hazards should be shared equally by various groups in society or at least that no group or community should bear the burden of environmental hazards at a level disproportionate to their numbers in the population or their contributions to creating the hazard.* Environmental injustice occurs when some racial, ethnic, or social class group is disproportionately exposed to these hazards. Beyond identifying examples of such injustice, like the ones in India and Los Angeles just described, applied researchers have gathered systematic data to assess the extent to which environmental injustice occurs. The area that has

been most extensively studied in this regard is the locating of hazardous waste facilities, such as the Superfund sites on the National Priorities List described in the text (Allen, 2001; Zahran, Hastings, and Zilney, 2004). Although many factors influence the locating of hazardous waste facilities, the research clearly suggests that, at least in many cases, such sites are more likely to be located in neighborhoods with heavily African American and Hispanic American populations. In addition, race and ethnicity of the neighborhood appear to be more important than the income level in influencing where hazardous waste sites are located. And it seems that this disparity was more prominent in the 1990s than in the 1970s.

happen. A final problem with nuclear wastes is the temporary storage we use for lack of permanent storage. The nuclear industry has had a history of spreading radioactive and chemical wastes over the open ground, pouring it in rivers and lakes, and dumping it wherever it is most convenient and least expensive.

Land Degradation

As was observed at the beginning of this chapter, the future of the environment depends on a delicate balance in nature, and upsetting this equilibrium can lead to serious consequences. One of the more ominous of these is *desertification*, referring to what happens when intensification of food production, such as by continuous cropping and overgrazing, leads to the spread of desert areas, thus reducing the quantity of arable land (United Nations Convention to Combat Desertification, 2004). It has been estimated that over the past 50 years, 100 million acres of usable farmland have been degraded to the point where they are no longer arable, with another 100 million acres having lost their topsoil covers. Data on this subject show that this

problem is growing much more serious over time. In 1882, for example, about 10 percent of the earth's land was classified as desert or wasteland; by the 1990s, this figure had expanded to almost 35 percent.

Deforestation is another example of land degradation that comes from human tampering with the environment (Mattoon, 2001). Environmentalists Paul and Anne Ehrlich describe the consequences of forests being cleared:

> Numerous animals that depend on the trees for food and shelter disappear. Many of the smaller forest plants depend on the trees for shade; they and the animals they support also disappear. With the removal of trees and plants, the soil is directly exposed to the elements, and it tends to erode faster. Loss of topsoil reduces the water-retaining capacity of an area, diminishes the supply of fresh water, causes silting of dams, and . . . flooding. (Ehrlich and Ehrlich, 1970:202)

In a number of African countries, the demand on forests (to use the wood as fuel or to clear land for agriculture) is from two to five times greater than the

How do these racial and ethnic disparities in exposure to environmental hazards occur? In some cases, it is a product of direct discrimination, where a location is selected because of the racial, ethnic, or social class characteristics of its population. More specifically, when corporations or government agencies are identifying potential sites, they are often advised to choose locations where the population would be least resistant to such a facility. So, a location with existing industrial plants might be chosen because residents are not likely to resist an additional intrusion, and such locations are also likely to have residents who are low income or people of color. Or, a low-income neighborhood might be selected because its residents are less likely than people in an affluent neighborhood to have the educational and organizational resources to resist effectively such an intrusion into their community.

Beyond direct discrimination, the location of hazardous waste sites is influenced by indirect discrimination, where economic and social forces produce discrimination against a group even though that outcome was not the intent or purpose of the forces. This is a form of institutionalized discrimination discussed in Chapter 6. For example, low-income people and people of color have less freedom in choosing where to live and go to school than do more affluent people; they possess fewer job skills that would enable them to move to new communities where jobs are, and they have fewer financial resources to support moves to communities free of environmental hazards. In other cases, housing discrimination based on race may limit the opportunities of people of color. Although the intent of these factors is not to expose minorities to higher proportions of environmental hazards, that is the consequence: Low-income people and people of color are less able to move away from polluted environments and into nonpolluted communities.

Whether it is produced by direct or indirect discrimination, many people refer to the environmental injustices produced as "environmental racism" because people are being exploited and treated inequitably because of their race or ethnicity. In some of these communities, grassroots environmental organizations have formed to fight against such injustices (Bullard and Johnson, 2000).

growth rate of new trees. This imbalance between demand and supply is due largely to growing populations and will obviously lead to a shortage of wood if it continues for long. Deforestation is rapidly converting Brazil's Amazon forest to low-value, nonproductive cattle pasture, and policies for slowing this process are currently being debated. Each year, deforestation claims 17 million hectares of land, about the equivalent of the state of Washington in one year! Half of all forests on the planet have been destroyed.

Declining Biodiversity

Some of the trends previously discussed—particularly overpopulation, deforestation, overgrazing of cleared lands, and global warming—have a consequence that is difficult to notice now but may be overwhelming in the near future: the annihilation of many species of animals around the globe (McKee, 2003). Researchers estimate that 27,000 species per year are obliterated from the earth, which translates into 74 species every day of the year. Although the elimination of some species is expected as a part of normal evolutionary develop-

ment, the current rate is staggeringly high. For most of the earth's history, the number of species was increasing, resulting in greater biological diversity. Today, according to one estimate, three-quarters of the world's bird species are declining in population, all species of wild cats and most bears are declining seriously in numbers, and over two-thirds of the world's 150 primate species are threatened with extinction (Mattoon, 2001). At the current rate of destruction, biologists estimate, biodiversity on the earth is actually declining. Twenty percent of the earth's species will be extinct 30 years from now, giving the current period the distinction of having one of the largest die-offs of species in the history of the earth.

Declining biodiversity creates two major problems. One is that we are losing species that might be of some use to humans, such as in producing pharmaceuticals. Some materials can be produced only from living species, and once a species is gone it is irreplaceable. The second problem is more subtle: At some point, declines in biodiversity may threaten the ability of the ecosystem to support human life. Ecosystems thrive, in part, because of the complexity and diversity of life that

A key environmental problem is the accumulation of radioactive wastes that are a byproduct of weapons development, nuclear power generation, or other economic activity. This is a radioactive waste storage facility in Germany where wastes are held temporarily until a plan for their ultimate disposal can be agreed on.

they harbor. One species thrives by eating another while a third species survives by the wastes of the other two. Elaborate those simple interchanges many thousands of times and one can begin to see the complex interactions involved in ecosystems. As species are removed from a system, it becomes more difficult to sustain such complex life forms as human beings. The problem is that we do not know how much decline in biodiversity the earth can sustain without precipitating a biological disaster. Some experts are convinced that we are in imminent danger, that a complete dismantling of the global life-support system is under way.

Air Pollution, Global Warming, and Climate Change

There can be no question that modern technology taxes the earth's atmosphere. According to the Census Bureau, for example, as much as 85 percent of the air pollution in urban areas is attributable to the internal combustion engine, despite efforts to control these emissions by using such devices as the catalytic converter (U.S. Bureau of the Census, 2006:222). On the other hand, pollution from automobiles has already been reduced considerably. Today's new vehicles emit 96 percent less hydrocarbons, 75 percent less nitrogen dioxides, and 96 percent less carbon monoxide than their 1960 counterparts (see Figure 13.1). As Figure 13.4 shows, the amounts of lead released into the air has dropped precipitously. The contribution of all vehicles to ozone pollution is now down to 29 percent of the total, and will soon reach 20 percent under the rules now in effect, as new cars replace older ones (French and Mastny, 2001).

At the same time, there are hydrocarbons, nitrous and sulfurous oxides, lead, and various forms of particulate matter, such as soot and ash, emitted from industrial production operations and the burning of coal and wood. According to the EPA, the healthiness of air quality in the United States has generally improved over the past few decades, and manufacturers have reduced their releases of toxic chemicals into the air by 43 percent. Nevertheless, over 40 percent of residents in the United

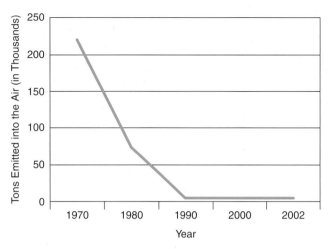

FIGURE 13.4 **Levels of Lead Emitted into the Air in the United States, 1970–2002.**

Source: U.S. Environmental Protection Agency, *National Emissions Inventory, Air Pollution Emission Trends,* www.epa.gov/ttn/chief/trends/index.html, Sept. 4, 2003.

States live in areas exceeding acceptable levels of one or more of the pollutants just mentioned (Stevens, 1995).

In the past decade, research has begun to make more clear one dimension of the air pollution problem: The earth is experiencing an alarming accumulation of ozone depleting gases and greenhouse gases in the atmosphere that are producing some degree of global warming and possibly climate change (Intergovernmental Panel on Climate Change, 2007). Chlorine- and bromine-containing chemicals, such as chlorofluorocarbons (CFCs), are often used in aerosol cans and refrigeration units. When these chemicals escape into the atmosphere, they destroy the ozone that surrounds the earth. Ozone is important because it screens out harmful ultraviolet rays from the sun. If this ultraviolet radiation gets through, it can cause skin cancer, damage marine life, lower crop yields, and contribute to global warming. Recent measurements by the National Aeronautics and Space Administration indicate that the earth may have lost a stunning 5 percent of its ozone layer in 13 years. However, some developments are promising: The United States is phasing out its production of some of these chemicals, and worldwide production declined dramatically in the 1990s (French and Mastny, 2001).

Another dimension of this problem is the "greenhouse effect" (Philander, 1998). Modern technology depends on the production and consumption of fossil fuels as a source of energy, and this releases great quantities of carbon dioxide and methane, among other gases, into the atmosphere. Various greenhouse gases act like the glass roof of a greenhouse, allowing sunlight to reach the earth's surface but preventing the escape of solar infrared radiation back into space. If these gases, along with the ozone depleting gases, continue to accumulate in the atmosphere, as scientists project that they will, the temperature of the earth's atmosphere could rise as much as 5 degrees over the next 100 years—a process called "global warming." This could substantially alter weather patterns and climate. It could also melt much of the earth's water that is now stored as ice at the poles and in glaciers. This could cause the world's oceans to rise seven feet or more from their current levels, with devastating flooding of low-lying coastal regions. There would be more, and more severe, heat waves, storms, floods, and droughts. It could cause some of the great food-producing regions of the world to dry up into dust bowls, and result in disastrous extinctions of many species of plants and animals (Thomas et al., 2004). Some scientists are concerned that this global warming has, or soon will have, progressed to the point where it produces a long-term, possibly permanent, change in the earth's climate. If so, human beings would have to live with the negative consequences of this climate change for the foreseeable future.

Many factors contribute to this accumulation of greenhouse gases, some of them natural processes such as the decay of materials in forests. But there is a growing consensus among scientists that human activities of the past few centuries have made a significant and growing contribution to the accumulation of these gases. Among these human activities is the consumption of energy, especially in the form of fossil fuels, deforestation, the burning of forests, and the burning and decay of biomass.

There has been lively debate over global warming and climate change. Some economists and scientists even argue that it is not a serious problem, that the fluctuations in temperature and various gases that we see are part of a normal cycle, or that it will produce only mild disruptions to which human societies can adapt. They also argue that some of the consequences will be positive (such as longer growing seasons in some agricultural regions) and that significant efforts to reduce greenhouse gases could stunt economic growth. However, at this point in time, the preponderance of scientific opinion is that global warming has the potential to create serious problems and that it will have many more negative consequences than positive ones (Intergovernmental Panel on Climate Change, 2007). In response to this, most nations of the world approved a treaty in 2001, called the Kyoto Protocol, that requires the industrialized nations to reduce their emissions of greenhouse gases, principally carbon dioxide, to levels below what they were in 1990. If implemented, this treaty will produce a substantial drop in greenhouse gases emitted into the atmosphere in comparison to what would occur without the treaty. The treaty was not approved by the United States and has yet to be ratified and implemented.

Pesticides and Other Chemicals

As in most instances of human beings' attempts to control their environment, efforts to cope with insects interfering with crop production began on a small scale and became increasingly complex. For example, one early strategy was the use of lead arsenate. This compound was effective in exterminating a narrow range of insects, but it was biodegradable and had no long-lasting negative effects on the environment. About 50 years ago, chemists put together a series of chlorinated hydrocarbons to produce the well-known insecticide DDT. Such chemical substances are much more effective in killing bugs, but they are also much longer lasting and less biodegradable. DDT and compounds like it remain stable for many years after application. They also accumulate in the fatty tissues of insects and fish, and then move up the food chain to affect higher animals. When consumed by human beings, these substances can cause serious health problems, such as cancer and birth defects. Furthermore, insects eventually build up immunity to pesticides, and these compounds become useless for the control of insects after a while.

The volume of synthetic organic chemicals produced in the world has skyrocketed in the past

50 years (Abramovitz et al., 2001; Environmental Protection Agency, 2007b). In the United States alone, such production has grown from less than 7 million tons in 1945 to over 100 million tons today. There are currently 70,000 such chemicals in daily use, with as many as 1,000 new ones added each year. Although not all of these chemicals are harmful, many are, and with devastating consequences: The World Health Organization estimates that 3 million severe cases of pesticide poisoning occur each year, resulting in 20,000 deaths, mostly among farmers in developing nations.

There are often alternatives to using chemicals as pesticides. One approach, known as *integrated pest management,* views a field of crops as an ecosystem in which natural forces can be used to control pests and weeds and thus enhance crop growth (Environmental Protection Agency, 2007b). This can be done by introducing natural predators of the pests or using genetic manipulations that result in pest-resistant crop varieties. This approach may not eliminate the use of chemicals, but it does focus on keeping their levels below the point at which significant crop damage and economic loss occur. A major barrier to the development of these programs is that it is generally cheaper for the private sector to use chemicals.

Energy Resources

The affluent industrialized nations of the world consume an inordinate share of the world's energy, and the United States is among the largest consumers, per person, even among the industrial nations (see Figure 13.5). Most existing energy resources are finite. There is no question that they will eventually be exhausted; the only debate is over when this depletion will occur (Goodstein, 2004). Most nations of the world are dependent on a few particular energy resources, primarily the fossil fuels: coal, petroleum, and natural gas. These fill 95 percent of the United States' energy needs, and the United States and other nations continue to place higher and higher demands on them.

Geologists have calculated that coal will be our longest lasting nonrenewable resource, with the earliest date of depletion occurring well into the twenty-first century. Although coal is an excellent ongoing energy resource, we must avoid becoming overly optimistic because the costs, both economic and social, of continuing to use it could be prohibitive. Economically, coal will become more costly to mine; and socially, the vast wastelands created by strip mining operations, increased air pollution, and deaths and injuries from the mining process itself provide further reasons for hesitancy. Although alternative sources of energy have been identified, some of these also have detrimental consequences

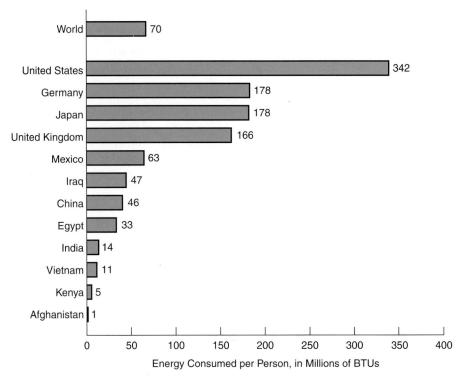

FIGURE 13.5 **Energy Consumption Among Various Nations, 2004.**

Source: U.S. Department of Energy, Energy Information Administration, *International Energy Annual, 2004,* www.eia.doe.gov/emeu/iea/wecbtu.html.

for the environment. For example, the use of wood fuel instead of oil or gas seems like an excellent alternative because this resource is renewable. But widespread burning of wood leads to increased air pollution. We may actually be overlooking some alternative sources of energy, however. Various forms of garbage, for example, have been wasted for many years. It has been conservatively estimated that the United States could save up to 2 million barrels of oil every day by using garbage as a combustible fuel source (Dunn, 2001).

Regarding nuclear energy, there are some very serious risks in using it: illness and death from radiation leakage, possible disaster from nuclear accidents, and the problem of disposing of nuclear wastes. Perhaps the most reasonable course of action involves the exploration of new energy sources, utilizing techniques that do not involve the risks and hazards that many previous strategies have entailed.

Future Prospects

In the preceding discussion, mention was made of some victories in the fight against environmental degradation, cases in which pollution has been reduced. Yet, most authorities agree that serious problems still confront the world. The victories so far may have been the easy ones

against clear-cut and readily conquered threats. More difficult and complex battles may lie ahead. In fact, as we embark on the twenty-first century, many people in the United States are stunned by the accumulating evidence of ecological damage. When asked recently whether protection of the environment should be given priority even if that meant curbing economic growth, half the people in the United States said the environment should be protected (Gallup News Service, 2004). In addition, two-thirds of the public in some surveys identified themselves as active participants in, or at least sympathetic to, the environmental movement; almost nobody was unsympathetic to that movement. Finally, two-thirds of the public believe that the government, corporations, and the public itself are currently doing too little to protect the environment. This base of substantial support for environmental causes has contributed to many significant developments to attack ecological decline.

Collective Action by Interest Groups

Collective action by the environmental groups discussed earlier in the chapter along with new groups that have emerged continues to be a significant source of pressure in the environmental realm. In Washington, DC, and across the country, groups such as the World Wildlife Fund, the Environmental Defense Fund, the Natural Resources Defense Council, and others lobby for environmental legislation and take polluters to court. Some environmentalists argue that these groups are too timid in that they disdain public demonstrations and civil disobedience as tactics to fight environmental issues. These established environmental groups also may be timid because they get significant support from the corporations that are major polluters. These environmentalists argue that the real passion in the movement today is at the grassroots level where people organize, protest, and demonstrate to stop a toxic waste landfill or a waste incinerator from being placed in their community.

At a global level, environmental interest groups such as Greenpeace have pressured corporations, nations, and the United Nations to reduce pollution and preserve the environment. They have been joined by the many nongovernmental organizations (NGOs) described in Chapter 2. Pressures from NGOs and activists around the world have resulted in some environmentally destructive projects being canceled or changed to make them more environmentally sensitive.

These environmental groups have met opposition from numerous groups that believe that the environmental problems are not that great or that the proposed solutions go too far (Ehrlich and Ehrlich, 1996). The Wise Use Movement, for example, is a coalition of business interests and citizens whose goals are, as the movement's name implies, to promote the judicious use of resources in ways that do not unnecessarily hinder economic activity and growth but that also protect the environment from excessive damage. The movement has vigorously opposed environmental regulation in areas such as oil and gas exploration, the use of rangeland by cattle farmers, and the harvesting of timber in national forests. Needless to say, environmental interest groups loudly disagree with what the Wise Use proponents call "judicious" use of resources and "excessive" damage to the environment. Nonetheless, the environmental policies of the twenty-first century will be forged out of the clash between these various interest groups.

Moderating Economic Growth

Some environmental problems are created or made worse by the unrestrained pursuit of economic growth and short-term economic goals. Some would argue that capitalism itself, especially if unrestrained, is inherently detrimental to the environment (Hawken, 1993). The reason for this is that capitalists thrive on continuous economic growth and the fact that profits can be enhanced by pursuing short-term goals. One solution is

to regulate the activities of capitalists, and this is a major element of our environmental policy and will be discussed in the next section. A more radical question, which is addressed by only a few today, is whether individualism, profit seeking, and permanent growth can be reconciled with the limited resilience of our ecosystem to respond to the assaults on it. Will the products of our social and economic organization inevitably overwhelm the ability of the earth to recoup itself? All our policies assume that some form of restrained capitalism is compatible with protection of the environment.

Government Regulation

One of the major battlegrounds of environmental issues is the extent of government regulation that should be adopted. Over the decades, laws and court rulings have placed limits on most of the pollution and degradation of the environment discussed in this chapter. The Endangered Species Act, for example, protects 700 plant and animal species from actions that might threaten their survival, and 4,000 more are being considered for such protection (Mann and Plummer, 1995). The Clean Air Acts of 1970 and 1990 limited the amount of pollutants that automobiles, industries, and electric utilities can release into the environment.

This regulation is one of the cornerstones of U.S. environmental policies, but it has also been controversial. There are continuing battles over how far to extend such regulation and over whether the costs of regulation in some cases are worth the benefit it affords the environment. This controversy is explored in the Policy Issues insert. The International Perspectives insert looks at some of the government regulations imposed in other societies.

Environmental Partnerships

Another approach to attacking environmental problems that emerged in the 1980s and 1990s is called "environmental partnerships," which involve voluntary collaborative efforts among a number of organizations that have a stake in environmental issues (Long and Arnold, 1995). The partners in such an effort might include corporations, government agencies, environmental interest groups, and landowners or other groups of people most directly affected by an environmental problem. The goal of the partnership is to identify an environmental problem and develop a solution acceptable to all the stakeholders. This is a less coercive approach to finding ways of alleviating environmental problems than government regulation, and in some situations it offers more flexibility. Such partnerships have been used to develop plans to conserve energy by utility companies, eliminate chlorofluoro-carbons, and protect salmon in the Pacific Northwest. Although such partnerships will probably not replace government regulation in the fight for a better environment, they have been useful in cases where regulation has been weak or ineffective, or, in some cases, in implementing regulations.

Radical environmentalists mistrust this approach because of the deep-seated belief that corporations tend to pursue their short-term interests in maximizing profits and to downplay the significance of environmental problems. And many advances could not have been achieved through environmental partnerships. Yet, as one prong of a many-pronged attack on environmental problems, they have proven their value.

Reduce, Reuse, Recycle

The most environmentally sensitive thing that a person can do is to consume fewer products. An automobile that is not purchased or a bottle of beer that is not bought produces no pollution. When people do consume, the focus should be on reusing and recycling what is consumed. Only recently have people in the United States become attentive to issues of reusing and recycling products. In some locales, there are effective recycling programs, such as the one thousand or more aluminum reclamation centers in operation. Many cities also have paper collection programs, which lead to the successful reuse of such products. Almost one-third of the garbage generated in 2005 (see Figure 13.6) was

reused in some fashion, up from less than 10 percent in 1980 and before. Almost half of all paper and paperboard produced in the United States is now recovered and recycled, up from only 21 percent in 1980 (U.S. Bureau of the Census, 2006:224). Half of all people in the United States are now served by a curbside recycling program. Industry in the United States has also made significant strides in recycling water. In the past thirty years, the number of times that each cubic meter of water is used by industry before it is discarded has risen from 1.8 to 8.6 (Postel and Vickers, 2004).

However, many environmentalists argue that much more could be done. For example, the recycling of materials and products could be considered in the design and production stages, and few things would be manufactured that could not be reused (Gardner, 2001). Denmark has banned throwaway beverage containers, and in the Canadian province of Ontario almost all beer is sold in standardized refillable bottles. In both places, the containers produced are standardized and sturdy, which makes their reuse easy and inexpensive. Of course, national legislation and enforcement would be necessary to make such a plan work.

New Approaches To Energy

Since energy consumption is a major cause of global warming and climate change, significant reductions in the levels of energy usage would help alleviate these problems. However, people in the United States have been reluctant thus far to support energy policies that

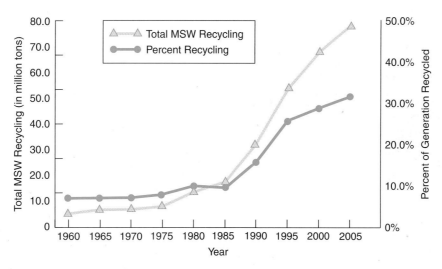

FIGURE 13.6 Recycled Municipal Solid Waste (MSW), as Total and as Percentage of MSW Generated in the United States, 1960–2005.

Source: U.S. Environmental Protection Agency, *Municipal Solid Waste Generation, Recycling, and Disposal in the United States: Facts and Figures for 2005.* (Washington, DC: U.S. Government Printing Office, 2006), www.epa.gov/epaoswer/non-hw/muncpl/msw99.htm.

Do We Need Government Regulation to Control Environmental Problems?

The use of the automobile may in some ways be symbolic of the difficulties and intricacies of finding solutions to environmental problems. For many people, the private automobile represents freedom and independence—the ability to go where you want, when you want, with whom you want. Yet, automobiles also produce pollutants that contribute significantly to global warming, acid rain, and many other environmental problems discussed in this chapter. But how do you convince people to use their cars less, or for that matter to change other behaviors that degrade the environment? One approach has been government regulation through laws, court rulings, or administrative procedures. However, it has become highly controversial whether, or to what extent, we should rely on such regulation.

Opponents of government regulation argue that it unnecessarily and unfairly impinges on people's freedoms and that it can be a very expensive fix for a problem. Extreme laissez-faire advocates argue that the mechanisms of the marketplace can alleviate many environmental problems (Anderson and Leal, 2001). When environmental problems become costly, corporations will find ways to reduce pollution in order to lower costs, and entrepreneurs will innovate by developing inexpensive technologies and services that will reduce pollution without threatening profits. However, except in a few cases, this extreme hands-off approach won't work, at least not as our current economy is organized, because many of the costs of pollution are borne by society as a whole rather than by the corporations that produce the polluting products. For example, the public pays for pollution produced by automobiles through health costs produced by smog; the auto companies or the individual automobile purchaser doesn't pay directly for the resulting pollution. So in most cases, it is more profitable for the corporation to ignore the pollution problem.

Yet, opponents of government regulation still argue that market-based solutions can be effective if polluters are required to foot the costs of their pollution. One proposal based on this "polluter pays" principle is to use the tax code to encourage businesses to operate in an environmentally sound manner (Hawken, 1993). If a business emits pollutants, dumps wastes in a stream, or uses nonrenewable resources, it will be taxed for doing so. Proponents of such plans argue that this would force businesses to pay for all the costs of doing business rather than passing some costs on to the taxpayer or future generations. Some of the increase in costs of doing business would likely be passed on to the consumer, but this makes the corporation and the consumer economically responsible for pollution. Consumers could choose to buy from companies that follow environmentally sound practices, and corporations could reduce costs and increase profits by reducing environmental damage.

Interventionists do not dispute that market-based solutions can work in some situations, but this does require government intervention in the form of tax and regulatory policies to make sure that the polluter does in fact pay for the pollution created. In addition, interventionists argue that would produce such significant reductions. People tend to support the use of technology to make our refrigerators and buildings more energy efficient, but there is less support for policies such as a large tax on fuel or a carbon tax that would probably force people to change their lifestyles substantially. Some of these policies are discussed in the Policy Issues insert and the International Perspectives insert.

Other, newer approaches to reducing people's "carbon footprint" are being tried. For example, carbon ranching or carbon offsets allows industries or individuals that spew carbon into the atmosphere to make up for it by paying a country with forests to preserve those forests. Another approach is carbon trading, in which an overall cap is placed on the amount of carbon that can be produced in a nation; then industries that produce too much carbon must pay for it by purchasing credits from low polluting industries. Yet another approach is carbon sequestration, in which carbon dioxide is captured when fossil fuels are burned and then pumped into the ground to keep it out of the atmosphere. While these are all important efforts in trying to reduce the amount greenhouse gases in the atmosphere, it is controversial at this point how substantial their impact will be.

Another approach to global warming would be to switch from finite, but exhaustible and polluting, resources, such as coal and oil, to renewable energy resources that have no inherent limit on how long humans can exploit them and generally do not increase global warming (Sawin, 2004). Solar energy is perhaps the best example of a virtually inexhaustible resource. It can be used to produce two very important types of energy: heat and electrical power. Other sources of renewable energy are waterpower, wind power, and geothermal energy (terrestrial heat). Other renewables, such as wood and vegetable fuels, can contribute to global warming. Unlike coal, wood can be replaced

some problems are so severe or the costs and consequences so far in the future, that market-based solutions will probably not work. The automobile again provides a good illustration of this. The burning of fossil fuels has already produced severe problems in the form of acid rain and global warming, but many of the consequences are not yet noticeable to most people. Despite the problems they create, it has been difficult to wean people in the United States from their cars. Part of the reason for this difficulty is that, over the decades, an infrastructure has emerged in the United States that encourages the widespread use of cars. In particular, urban sprawl with a lack of effective mass transit has left people with few choices but to use their cars. In most cases, people cannot voluntarily give up their cars because they have few alternate ways to get to work, school, or shopping centers. This problem becomes even more disturbing when we recognize that the automobile industry is looking at countries such as China and India as locations to reproduce this "car culture" and create new markets for its products. If these nations go down this car-centered path, given their population sizes, it would produce an enormous increase in the consumption of fossil fuels and the attendant environmental

problems. However, once the automobile infrastructure is in place in these countries, it will be difficult to choose another path.

It is in circumstances like this, interventionists argue, that market-based solutions are unlikely to be effective in the long run and more direct government regulation is called for. The Los Angeles basin, of course, has very severe air pollution problems, partly because of its geography and climate but also because its infrastructure is so "car oriented." This has led some policy analysts to consider government regulations that are much more severe than the current requirements for various kinds of pollution control and gas mileage devices. For example, it has been proposed that people be required to use cars that run on less polluting fuels than gasoline, such as methane or electricity, that commuters be required to carpool, and that a limit be placed on the number of cars that a family would be allowed to own. Another approach might be to allow each school or business only a limited number of parking stalls. If policies such as these were established, it would force people to find other modes of transportation, such as mass transit, and reduce the amount of pollution from automobiles.

Interventionist			Laissez-Faire
Government regulation of numbers and types of cars	Limit parking spaces	"Polluter pays" laws	Open market controls pollution

through reforestation. Organic wastes, such as corn fiber, manure, and some garbage, is sometimes called *biomass* and can be burned, converted into methane or ethanol, or processed into fuel cells that produce electrical energy. In the 1970s, the government encouraged the development of some renewable energy resources by requiring utilities to use some renewables in electricity generation in order to get large contracts. By the 1990s, however, declining oil and gas prices along with a less favorable political climate in Washington had deflated much of the enthusiasm for such efforts, and the required use of renewables has been dropped.

International Cooperation

Environmental problems are clearly global in nature. Because of this, much attention has been directed in the past two decades to international cooperation as a way to control environmental problems (French and

Mastny, 2001). From 1972, when the United Nations Conference on the Human Environment was held in Stockholm, to 2001, when the Kyoto Protocol to control greenhouse gases was approved, a steady record of international agreements and policies to protect the environment has been established. For example, in 1990, an international accord to phase out the production of ozone-depleting CFCs by the end of the twentieth century was signed. That same year, 23 nations agreed to freeze or reduce levels of carbon emissions in an effort to attack the problem of global warming. In 1994, most nations of the world signed the Convention on Biological Diversity, which commits each nation to finding strategies for protecting the plants, animals, and microorganisms, and their habitats, within its borders.

Despite progress, many of the goals of these international agreements remain unmet. The wealthy nations of the world have not come forward with the funds they had committed to fight environmental

These wind turbines in the San Gorgonio Pass in California represent the use of renewable energy resources to reduce the environmental degradation and loss of nonrenewable resources that results when energy is produced by burning coal, oil, or natural gas.

problems. Many nations are still inclined to pursue their own short-term interests. (The United States has opted out of the Kyoto Protocol.) The international accords are important, however, because they create an international climate that pressures nations to do more about these problems than they would be inclined to do on their own. In addition, the accords recognize that solving environmental problems must be a united, worldwide effort if it is to succeed.

New Cultural Values and Social Institutions

Throughout this chapter, the importance of values in environmental issues has been emphasized. In fact, some new cultural values have appeared that may have important implications in these realms. Some values related to environmental problems derive from the Western Judeo-Christian heritage, discussed earlier in the chapter, that emphasizes the desirability of procreation and the mastery of human beings over the earth. The conventional environmental ideology that has emerged in the past fifty years is in sharp contrast with this view. This environmental ideology emphasizes that human beings should live in harmony with their environment rather than "mastering" or "ruling over" it; that people should serve as stewards who protect and conserve the environment so that it will be available for future generations to use. A key notion that many environmentalists use today is "sustainability": A sustainable society is one that satisfies its needs without jeopardizing the prospects of future generations (Renner, 2004). Attaining sustainability may call for some groups to moderate their needs. Modifications in one or more elements of the $I = P \times A \times T$ formula mentioned earlier may be called for: reducing Populations, accepting a less Affluent standard of living, and using a simpler and less polluting Technology.

Some environmentalists take a more radical stance than this. For example, the following quotation is

Environmental Practices and Policies in Other Societies

Societies differ in the extent to which they utilize government regulations to encourage behavior that is less environmentally destructive. With regard to the automobile, for example, we could ask why the United States has become so oriented toward the automobile whereas people in Finland, Japan, Brazil, and most other nations have not. Part of the answer, of course, is our affluence, but other factors are equally important. First, we have designed our cities such that transportation without cars is difficult. Most cities in the United States are spread out, with places of work and school far away from where most people live. European cities, on the other hand, tend to be much more concentrated, which makes public transit less expensive and more feasible.

Second, we keep taxes on gasoline low, which encourages people to drive. In 2007, when gasoline cost around $3 per gallon in the United States, it cost between $6 and $8 in most European countries and Japan (Energy Information Administration, 2007). Seventy-five percent of the cost of gas in many European countries is taxes, whereas only one-quarter of the cost in the United States goes to taxes. So, people in the United States drive rather than ride public transit in part because it is so inexpensive to do so. The U.S. approach to controlling gasoline consumption is to place limits on the fuel economy of cars. Most experts see this approach as considerably less effective in bringing down gas usage than the European approach: high taxes on gasoline.

The combination of affluence along with a lack of effective policies to discourage the use of fossil fuels means that the United States is one of the heaviest users of energy resources. The United States burns ten times the energy resources that China consumes for each person and twice what even Japan, another industrialized and affluent nation, consumes (see Figure 13.5). With less than 5 percent of the world's population, the United States produces almost one-quarter of the world's carbon dioxide emissions, the most important component of gases causing global warming (Dunn, 2001).

One policy that could help reduce the use of fossil fuels and the amount of air pollution would be a tax on the use of energy. There are two justifications for this. One is that societies can change people's behaviors by making it more costly for them to do things that use up scarce resources or pollute the environment. Protection of resources and the environment is in everyone's interest. The second justification is that those producing the pollution—namely, users of a polluting energy source—should pay taxes to help pay for the damage to the environment and to people's health caused by the pollution. One approach to such a policy is to place a substantial tax on gasoline to discourage its use, as we have seen many other nations do. This would encourage people to use mass transit and to build communities that are not dependent on automobiles for transportation. Another approach would be to tax energy sources that produce more carbon dioxide emissions, the major culprit in the greenhouse problem. Coal would be taxed the heaviest, followed by oil and then natural gas; nuclear power and renewable energy sources could go untaxed under such a policy because they release no carbon dioxide. Finland, Denmark, and Sweden already have such taxes and many other European nations are considering them (Dunn, 2001). Such a carbon tax was considered by the Clinton administration but never implemented.

Many European nations have other so-called "green taxes" on such things as air and water pollution, waste, and noise. Norway has a tax on fertilizers and pesticides. However, many of these taxes are too low to change people's behavior significantly, although they do raise revenues to support important environmental programs. The policies in many societies other than the United States reflect an interventionist stance: The government uses its various powers to shape behaviors that conserve resources and protect against environmental degradation. Policy in the United States, on the other hand, has placed a greater emphasis on the laissez-faire position: The government should step back and let the marketplace determine the amounts and types of energy that are used.

taken from a public information bulletin published by Greenpeace:

> Ecology teaches us that humankind is not the center of life on the planet. Ecology has taught us that the whole earth is part of our "body" and that we must learn to respect it as we respect life—the whales, the seals, the forests, the seas. (Simon, 1981:335)

This philosophy, called "deep ecology" or "biocentrism," is based on the following principles (Sessions, 1995):

- All life on earth, both human and nonhuman, has equal value, and humans have a right to destroy life forms only to meet *vital* needs.

- Given the size of human populations and the technology currently available to them in industrial societies, humans have become destructively intrusive in the earth's ecosystem and substantial population reduction is necessary.

- To come into harmony with the environment, human economic, political, and social structures need to be changed so that they shift emphasis from stressing growth, bigness, and material wealth to valuing smallness, spirituality, and the nonmaterial quality of life.

Clearly, deep ecologists are calling for a radical change in people's way of life. In fact, some of these groups, such as the Earth Liberation Front and Earth First!, have resorted to action in their efforts to protect the earth. Some members of these groups have been accused of burning down a ski resort thought to be threatening an endangered species and blowing up power lines and destroying logging equipment in hopes of stopping unwanted development. In their view, human activities have become so destructive to the earth, and protecting the earth is of sufficiently high value, that the use of violence is warranted, even if it means the destruction of human property and maybe even human lives.

Although the deep ecologists (and certainly groups such as Earth First!) take a more extreme stand than most people would feel comfortable with, they do suggest that permanent, long-term solutions to environmental problems may require a change in traditional cultural values and social institutions. If we retain the biblical ideology of human mastery and domination over the earth, we may be unwilling to take extreme measures when they are warranted. In addition, we need to consider the possibility that industrial capitalism is at least part of the problem. When profits can be made by polluting the air or destroying the forests, then the unhindered operation of capitalist mechanisms such as free enterprise, competition, and profit making may destroy the environment beyond repair. It may be necessary to take a significantly interventionist stance, with the government enforcing some higher values that emphasize the protection of the environment. In fact, as we have seen, this is already happening to a degree. The controversy today is over how much further down this road it will be necessary to go to achieve environmental goals.

LINKAGES Environmental problems can be intensified when technology becomes more complex and intrusive (Chapter 15) or when there are few restraints on the profit-seeking activities of large and unresponsive corporations (Chapter 2).

STUDY AND REVIEW

Summary

1. Modern biology views the world as an ecosystem, and at the core of environmental problems is the issue of the extent to which human activities have changed the ecosystem with severely detrimental consequences.

2. The functionalist perspective views the ecosystem in terms of the interdependence among the land, air, water, people, and other resources in it; problems arise when changes in the ecosystem produce social disorganization or dysfunctional consequences. The conflict perspective sees environmental problems in terms of groups having competing interests in terms of how the environment is to be used; pollution becomes a problem when a group with some power feels that its interests are not being served. The interactionist perspective stresses the importance of social definitions and subjective assessments of reality rather

The Environmental Protection Agency has a Web site (**www.epa.gov**) that has much useful information about environmental problems and government policies to alleviate them. Look, for example, for the EPA page on global warming. The Internet has also proved to be valuable for NGOs and other groups working to reduce environmental problems. All of the major environmental organizations, of course, have Web sites: The Sierra Club's site is at **www.sierraclub.org**. A helpful exercise is to search for the Web sites of such organizations. Compile a list of the organizations and the information that can be found at their Web sites. Evaluate whether the Web sites, as designed, provide a significant resource for mobilization that would not be available otherwise. Or does the technology mostly seem to provide a public relations vehicle for the organization?

Another good source of material is the Web site for the online environmental magazine *Grist:* **www.grist.org**. Also, the Sightline Institute

(**www.sightline.org**) is an independent, nonprofit organization that has current information and links, although focused more on issues relevant to the Northwest. It also publishes some excellent books and other materials that can be downloaded. The Global Footprint Network (**www.globalfootprint.org**) has a wide range of informative materials on how to advance toward a more sustainable society. Yet another good portal to environmental issues on the Internet is Envirolink: The Online Environmental Community (**www.envirolink.org**). Once you have gathered a list of Web sites related to environmental issues, organize them according to their sponsorship: Are they mainline? radical? supported by some corporate entity? How do their proposed policies rank in terms of the laissez-faire versus interventionist debate?

The Allyn & Bacon Social Problems Supersite (**http://wps.ablongman.com/ab_socialprob_sprsite_1**) contains material on environmental problems.

than the objective amount of pollution or degradation of the environment.

3. The key social and cultural conditions that contribute to environmental problems are population growth, affluence, technology, economic growth, and cultural values.

4. According to the interactionist perspective, environmental problems do not exist as social problems until people identify and define them as such. This social construction happens as the media, influential people, and the government publicize the problems and enact social policies.

5. The major environmental problems discussed are water supply and pollution, solid and toxic wastes, radioactive wastes, land degradation, declines in biodiversity, air pollution and global warming, pesticides and other chemicals, and energy resources.

6. Collective action by various interest groups will be a key to how environmental problems are handled in the future. Other efforts to alleviate environmental problems have focused on moderating economic growth, using government regulation, using environmental partnerships, recycling, developing new approaches to energy, and international cooperation and treaties.

7. Successfully alleviating environmental problems may call for the emergence of new cultural values that emphasize living in harmony with the environment and conserving resources rather than mastery over the earth.

Key Terms

carrying capacity	**environmental justice**
ecology	**hydrologic cycle**
ecosystem	**photosynthesis**
environment	

Multiple-Choice Questions

1. _____ refers to the conditions and circumstances surrounding and affecting a particular group of living creatures.
   a. Ecology
   b. Fecundity
   c. Biosphere
   d. Demography
   e. Environment

2. The concept of _____ helps us to understand that all parts of the environment interact with one another and are dependent on one another.
   a. an ecosystem
   b. a demographic gap
   c. economic growth
   d. demography
   e. manifest functions

3. In looking at environmental problems, the functionalist perspective would focus most directly on
   a. the competing environmental goals of various interest groups.

    b. the interdependence of the land, air, water, people, and other resources in an ecosystem.

    c. how the successful wielding of power determines the outcome of environmental conflicts.

    d. the importance of social definitions and subjective assessments of environmental problems.

4. In the formula $I = P \times A \times T$, the A stands for

    a. alterations in the environment.

    b. aspirations of people.

    c. affluence of people.

    d. age structure of a society.

5. Which of the following is one of the oldest environmental interest groups?

    a. Sierra Club

    b. Greenpeace

    c. Environmental Defense Fund

    d. World Wildlife Fund

    e. Natural Resources Defense Council

6. The hydrologic cycle has to do most directly with which of the following environmental problems?

    a. depletion of energy resources

    b. declining biodiversity

    c. land degradation

    d. water pollution

7. All of the following were problems associated with the disposal of nuclear wastes *except*

    a. the wastes remain deadly for thousands of years.

    b. the NIMBY syndrome.

    c. the wastes encourage eutrophication.

    d. transportation of the wastes is risky.

8. The main problem with chlorofluorocarbons (CFCs) is that they

    a. destroy ozone.

    b. increase the greenhouse effect.

    c. reduce eutrophication.

    d. increase deforestation.

    e. inhibit photosynthesis.

9. Some critics argue that capitalism is detrimental to the environment because

    a. capitalism pursues biocentrism.

    b. capitalism thrives on economic growth.

    c. capitalism supports the ecosystem.

    d. capitalism discourages economic growth.

    e. capitalism ignores short-term goals in favor of long-term gain.

10. Environmental policy in the United States has tended to

    a. stress the interventionist approach more than European nations have.

    b. stress the laissez-faire approach more than European nations have.

    c. stress the functionalist approach more than European nations have.

    d. stress the conflict approach more than European nations have.

True/False Questions

1. The Judeo-Christian heritage in Western cultures stresses that human beings should live in harmony with their environment.

2. For the functionalist perspective, human cultural beliefs and values are an important part of the ecosystem.

3. The carrying capacity of an ecosystem can be exceeded occasionally but not permanently.

4. Premodern peoples generally lived in harmony with the environment and avoided practices that were destructive to the environment.

5. The National Environmental Policy Act (NEPA) was passed in the late nineteenth century to preserve wilderness areas in the United States for people to use.

6. Acid rain is produced by the leaking of nuclear wastes into the atmosphere.

7. The amount of municipal garbage generated in the United States has more than doubled since 1960.

8. Desertification and deforestation are types of land degradation.

9. The influence wielded by interest groups in the United States working to protect the environment has declined since the 1970s.

10. Environmental partnerships are a less coercive approach to environmental problems than is government regulation.

Fill-In Questions

1. The process by which plants capture light and heat energy from the sun and turn it into food is called _____.

2. According to the _____ perspective, the manner in which the environment is used emerges out of a competition among groups with varying amounts of power.

3. The carrying capacity of an ecosystem depends in part on levels of affluence and levels of _____.

4. _____ refers to the spread of deserts as a consequence of intensive food production on land.

5. Declining _____ refers to the elimination of species at a rate greater than expected by normal evolutionary development.

6. _____ is the heating of the atmosphere because carbon dioxide prevents solar radiation from escaping back into space.

7. _____ uses natural predators rather than pesticides to control pests and weeds in agriculture.

8. _____ are voluntary collaborative efforts to solve environmental problems by a number of organizations that have a stake in the issue.

9. List two kinds of renewable energy resources: _____ and _____.

10. The philosophy of _____ argues that all life on earth has equal value.

Matching Questions

_____ **1.** eutrophication
_____ **2.** toxic wastes
_____ **3.** branch of biology
_____ **4.** economic growth
_____ **5.** Western cultural value
_____ **6.** Paul Ehrlich
_____ **7.** Barry Commoner
_____ **8.** EPA
_____ **9.** DDT
_____ **10.** sustainability

A. ecology
B. population growth causes pollution
C. Love Canal
D. pesticide
E. mastery over the environment
F. key notion of environmentalists
G. growing amount of goods and services
H. Lake Erie
I. government agency
J. corporations cause pollution

Essay Questions

1. Describe the concepts that are important to understanding how modern biologists explain the world and how it operates.

2. Compare and contrast the functionalist and conflict views on environmental problems.

3. What is the impact of economic growth and cultural values on environmental problems?

4. Describe the process of the social construction of environmental problems.

5. What is acid rain? How is it produced? What can be done about it?

6. What are the sources of nuclear wastes? What problems do they present?

7. What is the problem of declining biodiversity? Why is it a problem?

8. Assess the greenhouse effect. What is it? How much of a problem is it? What can be done about it?

9. Describe the kinds of government regulation that have been enacted or proposed to control environmental problems. How well do they work?

10. What kind of environmental policies or practices in other nations were described that might be considered for the United States?

For Further Reading

Donald A. Brown. *American Heat: Ethical Problems with the United States' Response to Global Warming.* Lanham, MD: Rowman & Littlefield, 2002. This author focuses on environmental problems from a global perspective and explores how the United States has lost its role as world leader on environmental issues.

Jeff Goodell. *Big Coal: The Dirty Secret Behind America's Energy Future.* New York: Houghton Mifflin, 2006. The United States and the world are still heavily dependent on coal to produce energy, and this book identifies the enormously negative consequences of using this energy source.

Paul Hawken, Amory Lovins, and L. Hunter Lovins. *Natural Capitalism: Creating the Next Industrial Revolution.* New York: Little, Brown, 1999. This book argues that new business approaches and technological processes create the possibility for an industrial capitalism that can protect the environment rather than degrade it.

Jane Holtz Kay. *Asphalt Nation: How the Automobile Took Over America, and How We Can Take It Back.* New York: Crown, 1997. This is a readable and provocative book detailing how suffused our culture is with the automobile, the environmental and other problems that it creates, and what social policies could wean us from an overreliance on cars.

Elizabeth Kolbert. *Field Notes From a Catastrophe: Man, Nature and Climate Change.* New York: Bloomsbury, 2006. This book provides a readable overview of the causes and consequences of global warming and climate change. Even if only some of Kolbert's projections come true, the consequences will be dire.

J. R. McNeill. *Something New Under the Sun: An Environmental History of the Twentieth-Century World.* New York: W. W. Norton, 2000. A comprehensive overview of the enormous impact humans have had on their environment over the past century—an impact unlike almost anything that has occurred before.

Philip Shabecoff. *Earth Rising: American Environmentalism in the 21st Century.* Washington, DC: Island Press, 2000. This book is an excellent overview of the environmental movement, discussing what it has done, what it can do, and what some of its strengths and weaknesses are.

James Gustave Speth. *Red Sky at Morning: America and the Crisis of the Global Environment.* New Haven: Yale University Press, 2004. This is a sobering overview of the extent of a number of environmental problems, but especially of man-made climate change.

VIOLENCE, WAR, AND TERRORISM

The central concern of this chapter is **violence:** *behavior that is intended to bring pain or physical injury to another person or to harm or destroy property.* Actually, the topic of violence has been addressed at numerous points in this book. Criminal violence such as homicide and assault is discussed in Chapter 9, and family violence such as spouse and child abuse is analyzed in Chapters 3 and 8. In fact, the number of times the issue of violence is taken up while discussing various social problems suggests how pervasive violence is in human life. In addition to family violence and violent crime, terrorists kidnap, maim, and murder people; mobs riot in the streets and loot stores; citizens take up arms and attack their governments; and nations go to war with one another. The focus of this chapter is on these types of violence, called **collective violence:** *organized violence by relatively large groups of people to promote or resist some social policies or practices.* This is different from the interpersonal violence of most crime and spouse abuse where small numbers of people are pursuing their own personal goals or are responding to the stresses of an immediate situation.

The Extent of Violence

Civil Disorders

The United States has been fortunate to have had a fairly stable government and society over the past 200 years. Yet there have been periodic upheavals involving violent clashes between opposing groups in the United States. The term **civil disorder** refers to *strife or conflict that is threatening to the public order and that involves the government in some fashion, either as a party to the conflict or as a guardian of the public interest.*

Some civil disorders are relatively unorganized and have vague or short-term goals, such as race riots or labor conflicts. Other episodes of civil strife are quite organized and may threaten basic changes in the foundations of the social order, such as civil war or revolution. How extensive has civil disorder been in the United States? The rate at which civil disorders occur fluctuates from year to year, but there is no long-term trend. In fact, although one might expect the decade of the 1960s to be especially violent because of civil rights activities and antiwar riots, other decades approach or surpass that era in violence—the 1880s, for example, when labor strife was widespread (Levy, 1969).

Much civil disorder in the United States has arisen out of racial conflict. As long ago as the eighteenth century, mobs of white people, motivated by a fear that black slaves might revolt against their owners, viciously attacked blacks in the streets of cities such as New York. Some slaves were hanged; others were driven out of the city. In the final 20 years of the nineteenth century, nearly two thousand blacks were killed by lynch mobs in the South. In the twentieth century, many cities in the United States, both large and small, experienced severe race riots, virtually always involving black–white clashes. In the early part of the century, the riots were sparked when blacks began to move into white neighborhoods or to use recreational areas that were previously used only by whites. These **communal riots** typically began when *whites attacked blacks in the racially contested areas* (Janowitz, 1969). The Detroit riot in 1943, for example, began on Belle Isle Park, a public beach. Detroit, like many northern cities of the period, had for decades been experiencing a large influx of blacks from the South. Frictions arose as the growing population of blacks spilled over into previously all-white areas. Thirty-four people (mostly blacks) were killed and more than one thousand were injured.

Since World War II, most race riots in the United States have been **commodity riots,** in which *the focus of hostility is the property, merchandise, or equipment rather than people of another racial group.* These riots have occurred in neighborhoods that had been inhabited mostly by African Americans for some time rather

Myths & Facts

About Collective Violence and War

Myth: The United States is a peaceful nation that has been in the forefront of efforts to stop wars around the world.

Fact: Statistics show that the United States is one of the more war-prone nations in the world: In addition to the declared wars in which we have been involved, troops from the United States have been sent abroad for military purposes by the president an average of at least once a year.

Myth: Over the past two hundred years, people in the United States have been exposed to increasing levels of violence in the form of riots, labor strife, and racial conflict.

Fact: Although the number of such events has risen over the years, the rate of such violence has not increased considering the growing population, although violence does fluctuate substantially from one period to the next. Even the decade of the 1960s, which is viewed as extremely violent because of the conjunction of civil rights activities with protest against the Vietnam War and riots among university students, is not extraordinary: Other decades, such as the 1880s and the 1900s when labor violence was prominent, approach or surpass the 1960s in violence.

Myth: Entertaining television shows and movies that contain some violence, such as *NYPD Blue, The Sopranos,* or *The Patriot,* do not harm young people who watch them as long as the shows are clearly fictional and fanciful.

Fact: Most research evidence concludes that young people, especially males, who watch violent television shows or movies are more likely to behave aggressively or violently themselves.

Myth: The major contributors to the global trade in armaments are the so-called rogue states of Iran, North Korea, and Syria, which support terrorist networks.

Fact: Over the years, the United States has been the largest contributor to the global arms trade, selling far more weapons to other countries than any other nation.

than in areas of racial transition or contest. Although police officers or whites who wander into the neighborhood might be attacked, the focus of mobs' attention is on looting merchandise and burning buildings, usually those owned by people who do not live in the community. Most deaths and injuries arise from the efforts of police or the National Guard to quell the riot. Many riots of this sort occurred in the 1960s during the struggle over civil rights, and Miami exploded into commodity riots several times during the 1980s. Then, in 1992, a severe commodity riot occurred in south central Los Angeles in response to the acquittal of four police officers in the beating of an African American motorist.

Labor strife has been another significant source of civil disorder in the United States. This was particularly true from 1880 to the 1930s, as working people struggled hard to establish the principle of collective bargaining as a basis for governing worker–employer relationships. Before collective bargaining was legalized, it was illegal for workers to conspire to stop work at a factory or business. This obviously left enormous power in the hands of the business managers and owners who could simply fire individual workers who resisted their demands or complained about wages or working conditions. In the late 1800s and early 1900s, new power and authority relations were being forged between workers and industrial managers as the United States industrialized. Violence was sometimes a key ingredient in shaping these new social relations. In 1913, for example, miners in Colorado went on strike against the Colorado Fuel and Iron Company, which would not recognize the workers' right to unionize. The strikers lived in a tent city in Ludlow. On April 20, 1914, National Guard troops attacked the tent colony and burned it to the ground. In the holocaust, which became known as the Ludlow Massacre, five men, twelve children, and two women died. Before the strike was over, 74 in all would lose their lives (Taft and Ross, 1969).

Ludlow is hardly a household word today. Yet it was a key link in the forging of a new industrial order. Such incidents illustrate the extent to which labor violence has been a common outgrowth of the industrialization process.

Political Violence

The race riots and labor violence just discussed have, for the most part, not been organized efforts to change the basic political and economic institutions of the United States. At times, however, groups have resorted to violence as a means of changing the government or economy. One form that this can take is **insurrection**: *an organized action by some group to rebel against the existing government and to replace it with new political forms and leadership.* The independence of the United States, of course, was forged in an insurrection against England in 1776.

Once the independence of the United States was established, the most serious insurrection the nation faced was, of course, the Civil War, the effort of the southern states to secede from the Union (Leckie, 1990). Although the 1860 election of President Abraham Lincoln, an avowed opponent of slavery, played an important part in precipitating the Civil War, its exact causes have been debated at length by scholars and historians. Nonetheless, it was without question the most catastrophic military clash to occur within our boundaries. There was tremendous loss of life and destruction of property in battle.

Beyond the Revolutionary War and the Civil War, insurrections in the United States have been relatively small and less threatening. Shortly after the American Revolution, for example, there were a number of insurrections involving battles over land and taxes, such as Shays' Rebellion in Massachusetts in the 1780s and the Whiskey Rebellion in Pennsylvania in the 1790s. Somewhat later, Dorr's Rebellion in the 1840s was an attempt by a group of dissidents in Rhode Island to gain the right for all men (although not women) to vote. The turmoil of the 1960s spawned a number of insurrectionary groups, such as the Black Liberation Army and the Weather Underground, but these groups gained little public support and produced little political or economic change in the United States.

War

Most people in the United States probably think of their nation as powerful but also as peaceful and not aggressive. Yet political scientists J. David Singer and Melvin Small (1972) concluded from their research that the United States is among the more war-prone nations in the world. Between 1816 and 1965, they calculate, the United States was involved in six wars, not counting the Indian wars and the Vietnam War. Between 1798 and 1945, U.S. troops were sent abroad for military purposes by the president, without the approval of Congress, 163 times—an average of more than once a year (Leckie, 1992; Pinkney, 1972). The United States invaded Nicaragua 20 times, and U.S. troops once occupied Mexico City. At home, the Indian wars were particularly brutal affairs. They involved many campaigns by whites to force Indians from lands sought by white settlers. If Indians refused to sign treaties and peacefully move to reservations, the army was called in to force the issue.

Among the major wars the United States has been involved in during the past 100 years were World War I, World War II, the Korean War, the Vietnam War, the Persian Gulf War, and the Iraq War. The cost

This field displays some of the carnage that resulted from the Battle of Antietam during the American Civil War in the 1860s. The Civil War was the most serious insurrection the United States has faced since gaining independence from England.

in casualties from these wars has been high, and the decimation of civilian populations has been much greater than in earlier wars based on a simpler technology (see Table 14.1). The discovery of air flight, for example, made possible the aerial bombing of not only enemy troop concentrations but also cities and towns. One particularly devastating instance of the latter was the saturation bombing of Dresden, Germany, during World War II, in which an estimated 135,000 civilians were killed, mainly by asphyxiation and burning. The development of the atomic bomb resulted in the deaths of almost 200,000 people at Hiroshima and Nagasaki in 1945. Overall, World War II produced 30 million deaths among military combatants and civilians worldwide. Beyond these major wars, U.S. troops landed in the Dominican Republic in 1965 to forestall what was thought to be an imminent communist takeover of that country. More recently, the

TABLE 14.1 United States' Casualties in Major Wars

War	Battle Deaths	Wounded	Veterans Receiving Disability Compensation, 2004
Civil War	140,000	282,000	
World War I	53,000	204,000	<500
World War II	292,000	671,000	385,000
Korean conflict	34,000	103,000	163,000
Vietnam conflict	47,000	153,000	883,000
Persian Gulf War	<500	<500	536,000

SOURCES: U.S. Bureau of the Census, *Statistical Abstract of the United States, 2003* (Washington, DC, U.S. Government Printing Office, 2003), pp. 348, 352; Office of Policy, Planning, and Preparedness, Veteran's Administration, *VA Disability Compensation Program: Literature Review,* December 2004.

United States briefly entered conflicts in Lebanon, the Caribbean island of Grenada, and Panama. In 2001, the United States attacked the Al Qaeda terrorist network in Afghanistan in response to the terrorist attacks in New York and Washington, DC, and in 2003, the Iraq War was initiated in response to the threat that Iraq was perceived to pose to the United States.

Many of these war activities were justified as a reaction to a threatened attack on or invasion of the United States, to repel aggression, or to protect freedom. Other war activities have been more controversial, with the threat less clear and the focus more on sending troops around the world to maintain a world order that does not threaten U.S. political and economic interests. All of this suggests that the United States does get involved in the violence associated with wars. And the United States seems to get involved more than most other nations. In recent decades, military expenditures by the United States have varied from 22 percent to 47 percent of all the money spent by all the nations of the world on military expenditures (see Figure 14.1)—and we have less than 5 percent of the world's population! We spend $1,500 on military expenditures for each man, woman, and child in the United States, whereas the worldwide figure is only $140 per capita.

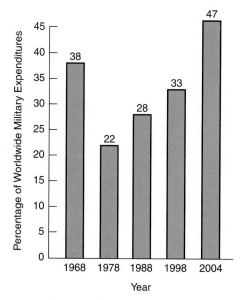

FIGURE 14.1 **United States Military Expenditures as a Percentage of Worldwide Military Expenditures, 1968–2004.**

Sources: U.S. Department of State. Bureau of Verification and Compliance, *World Military Expenditures and Arms Transfers* (Washington, DC: U.S. Government Printing Office, annual). www.state.gov/T/VL/RLS/Rpt/WMEAT; World Council of Churches, World Military Expenditures (Geneva, Switzerland, 2005).

These protesters are marching against nuclear weapons in San Francisco in 2006—symbolically on the 61st anniversary of the atomic bombing of Nagasaki, Japan, by the United States. Significant opposition to nuclear weapons persists because of their enormously destructive power.

The Global Arms Trade and the Military–Industrial Complex

Manufacturing weapons is no simple task. Certainly producing simple guns and rifles is not difficult, but making more sophisticated weaponry, such as modern jet aircraft or surface-to-air missiles is beyond the capacity of many nations around the world. Yet, when the demand for such weaponry exists—and it does—then nations that are capable of producing it step forward and export it to those nations in need. The global trade in armaments averages around $50 billion per year. The United States is the major player in this global trade. The U.S. contribution has over the years accounted for one- to two-thirds of the worldwide trade in arms (Stockholm International Peace Research Institute, 2007; U.S. Dept. of State, Bureau of Verification and Compliance, 2002). Over the years, the United States has been, by far, the largest contributor to this trade, followed distantly by the United Kingdom, Germany, France, and Russia. The United States sells twice as many arms to other nations as do all the nations of Europe.

The largest recipients of arms in this global trade are Saudi Arabia, Egypt, Turkey, South Korea, and Japan. Some of these nations have been supported so heavily over the years because they played a key role in the Cold War (Turkey and South Korea). Other nations received support because they were special allies of a particular supplier nation (Saudi Arabia as ally of the United States in the Persian Gulf War). For some of these recipient nations, arms imports constitute a large proportion of their total imports: Arms are 14 percent of Egypt's total imports and almost one-quarter of Saudi Arabia's total imports. The number of dollars spent in the global arms trade has declined appreciably since the end of the Cold War, and some corporations in the defense industry have shifted to producing for other markets. Despite this, the arms trade is still enormous, providing the capability of supporting many wars and conflicts around the globe. Especially disturbing is that many buyers in the global arms trade are poor nations who could better spend that money on education, health care, or other services to improve their people's quality of life.

One reason this global arms trade thrives is that many nations are looking to buy arms. In addition, many corporations benefit from this trade in arms, and many nations gain needed trade revenue by exporting arms. The outcome is lively global arms bazaars where companies can show their wares to potential buyers and nations can see what kind of armaments are available. Chapter 2 introduced the concept of a military–industrial complex; clearly, this military–industrial complex is global in scope, consisting of corporations that make profits from selling arms and governments that pursue military solutions to problems. The danger, of course, is that the existence and influence of this military–industrial complex will work to encourage nations to consider military solutions to internal and external conflicts and to ignore nonmilitary solutions that might be feasible. When nations possess an arsenal of guns, planes, and missiles, those nations may decide that all problems require the use of those weapons for their solution.

Many instances can be found around the world where nations were emboldened to attack other nations because they possessed the weapons to do so, and this at times has created serious problems for the United States. For example, the United States gave military support to Iraq in its war with Iran in the 1980s, and this military equipment played a part in Iraq's invasion of Kuwait, a U.S. ally, in 1990. As a result of that invasion, the United States mounted the Persian Gulf War to remove Iraq from Kuwait.

The Spread of Weapons of Mass Destruction

Whether the United States goes to war, of course, depends in part on what other nations do, and unfortunately there is a thriving worldwide trade in arms to provide nations with the means to go to war. This trade, and the U.S. role in it, is discussed in the International Perspectives insert.

One of the horrendous legacies of twentieth-century technology has been the emergence of highly frightening and destructive weapons: nuclear, chemical, biological, and toxin weapons (Langewiesche, 2007). In the last few decades, the world has seen the proliferation of these weapons to more countries, sometimes to nations with unstable or megalomaniacal leaders, and to nonstate entities such as terrorist networks. Some of the nations acquiring these weapons are involved in serious and entrenched conflicts with other nations, which could produce conditions that would lead to their use. Israel has nuclear capability, for example, and has been in conflict with many Arab countries; Iraq used chemical weapons in its war with Iran and has tried to produce nuclear weapons; India and Pakistan have nuclear weapons and have been engaged in serious territorial disputes for a number of years. At least 12 nations have or are developing biological or toxin weapons, and 20 are doing so with chemical weapons.

The international framework to prevent the spread of these weapons is weak (Falkenrath, Newman, and Thayer, 1998; Kuhr and Hauer, 2001). The Geneva Protocols of 1925 prohibit the use of chemical weapons but not their production and stockpiling. The Biological Weapons Convention of 1972 banned biological weapons, and the Chemical Weapons Convention of 1993 called on nations to destroy their stocks of chemical weapons. The 178 nations that have signed the Treaty on the Non-Proliferation of Nuclear Weapons of 1968 agree not to permit the spread of these weapons to countries currently without them. However, when the weapons have been stockpiled or used, as in the Iran–Iraq War of the 1980s, sanctions have usually not been applied against the user by the international community. In addition, some countries have not signed these various treaties, and others have ignored many of their provisions.

Terrorism

Terrorism refers to *the attempt to achieve political goals by using fear and intimidation to disrupt the normal operations of a society* (Cooper, 2001). In the past few decades, terrorist attacks in the United States have been infrequent but sometimes highly destructive. In 1993, the World Trade Center in New York City was bombed, and in 1995, a federal building in Oklahoma City was destroyed by a horrific bomb explosion that killed 167 people and wounded another 442. In 2001, terrorists piloted airplanes into the Pentagon in Washington, DC, and the

World Trade Center in New York. The horrendous result was the death of 3,000 innocent people.

Terrorist attacks have been more common outside the United States, often targeted at U.S. citizens. One of the more horrifying incidents was the 1988 terrorist bombing of a Pan Am jet as it was flying over Scotland headed for the United States, killing hundreds of passengers and a few bystanders on the ground. In 1998, bombs exploded simultaneously at the U.S. embassies in Nairobi, Kenya, and Dar es Salaam, Tanzania, killing 12 U.S. citizens and hundreds of Africans. Terrorist bombings at tourist spots in Bali, Indonesia in 2002 and 2005 and in commuter trains and buses in Madrid in 2004 and London in 2005 killed hundreds and injured thousands more. Terrorist bombings, killings, and kidnappings have become routine in Iraq and Afghanistan since the United States invaded each of those nations. As Figure 14.2 illustrates, while the number of terrorist attacks worldwide has fluctuated over time, they have increased considerably in the past few years because of episodes in Iraq and Afghanistan.

Governments sometimes engage in or support terrorism. The U.S. Department of State Office of the Coordinator for Counter Terrorism (2007) considers Syria, Iran, Cuba, North Korea, and Sudan to be among the major supporters of terrorism in the world currently. These countries provide varying levels of support to terrorist groups, from supplying arms, training, and technical expertise to providing travel documents or a hideout. This government-supported terrorism is something new and especially unsettling on the world scene.

Terrorism is a particularly unnerving form of violence because it is so difficult to control. Yet we need to recognize that terrorism often has its origins in some kind of perceived injustice, the elimination of which is the terrorists' goal. Terrorism is often resorted to by people who have little power and few resources with which to attack what they see as injustice. However, in addition to the traditional political motives and goals of terrorists, some terrorists today are motivated by ethnic loyalties, others by religious fervor, and still others are basically criminals who use the intimidation of innocent civilians to achieve criminal goals. So, some terrorists in Iraq today are motivated by fundamentalist Islamic beliefs, but other terrorist bombings and kidnappings in Iraq are done by criminal gangs whose goal is financial gain. In addition, some "narcoterrorists" have bombed buildings in South America to intimidate the police and politicians and protect their drug dealings. Another change in

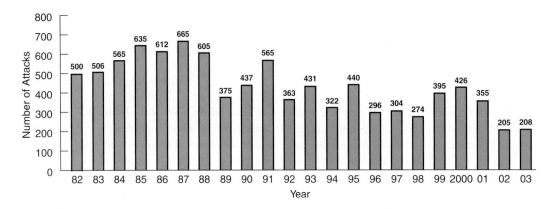

A. Total International Terrorist Attacks, 1982–2003

B. Worldwide Terrorism Incidents, 2005–2006

		2005	2006
Incidents of Terrorism	Incidents of terrorism worldwide	11,153	14,338
	Incidents resulting in the death of at least one individual	5,135	7,332
	Incidents resulting in the death of at least ten individuals	228	291
	Incidents resulting in the injury of at least one individual	3,838	5,718
	Incidents resulting in the kidnapping of at least one individual	1,152	1,334
Individuals affected	Individuals worldwide killed, injured, or kidnapped	74,217	74,543
	Individuals killed	14,614	20,498
	Individuals injured	24,761	38,191
	Individuals kidnapped	34,838	15,854

FIGURE 14.2 **Patterns of Global Terrorism, 1982–2006.**

Sources: U.S. Department of State, *Patterns of Global Terrorism, 2003* (Washington, DC: U.S. Government Printing Office, 2004), www.state.gov/s/ct/rls/crt/2003; U.S. Department of State, Office of the Coordinator for Counter Terrorism, *Country Reports on Terrorism, 2006*, April 30, 2007, www.state.gov/s/ct/rls/crt/.

terrorism is being brought about by technology. Nuclear, chemical, and biological weapons of mass destruction have become more accessible and easier to produce, making them available to more groups who might wish to use them.

Societies have made efforts to protect themselves against terrorist attacks. Such attacks can occur at any of the many points at which people are vulnerable in modern societies: flying in an airplane, eating in a restaurant, or walking along the street. Of course, nations today are doing many things to prevent terrorist attacks—including enhanced security procedures, surveillance efforts, and police interventions—and these efforts have been greatly enhanced since the September 11, 2001, attacks. And these efforts have undoubtedly stopped numerous terrorist attacks from occurring. However, short of advocating a costly and authoritarian society, it is difficult to build in the kind of controls that can provide assured protection in all these settings.

Only utter devastation remained at the site of the World Trade Center after the terrorist attacks of September 11, 2001. These attacks made people in the United States acutely aware of how vulnerable they are to terrorist attacks in the modern world.

Explanations of Collective Violence and War

If collective violence and war are to be controlled, we need to know what causes them to occur. What will be found is that the causes are complex, and there is often a chain of multiple causation, with numerous factors—social, psychological, and possibly even biological—contributing to particular outbursts of violence and war.

Biological Approaches

Other chapters review efforts to explain such social behaviors as crime (Chapter 9), drug abuse (Chapter 10), and the differences between men and women (Chapter 7) on biological grounds. People also have been intrigued by the possibility that violence and war may be part of our biological nature as human beings. Violence is so common and so nearly universal in human cultures that it seems plausible that biology plays a part. Some support for this position can be found in studies of the behavior of animals of various species. A male stickleback fish, for example, will protect against all intruders a nest containing fertilized eggs deposited by the female stickleback. Anything approaching the nest that resembles another stickleback will be viciously attacked (Tinbergen, 1955). Such protection of territory can be found in many species, and it is clearly an instinctive behavior in these species rather than a product of learning. Robert Ardrey (1967) popularized such behavior as the "territorial imperative," suggesting that such protection is necessary for some species to survive. In fact, he argued, it is so necessary that evolution imprints these behavior patterns into the genes of species. Without this instinct to defend territory, mating would be disrupted and the survival of species would be threatened. Aggressiveness in struggling for food or competing for mates also may have an evolutionary advantage for many species.

Applications of these ideas to human beings have been labeled **sociobiology,** *a field based on the idea that the genetic makeup of human beings plays a powerful role in shaping human social behavior* (Nielson, 1994). Sociobiologists maintain that there are many parallels between human and animal behavior. For example, animals of a number of species exhibit altruism, which refers to doing things that benefit others of one's species even though it may be dangerous or deadly to oneself. So, kamikaze bees will die defending their hive, soldier termites will end their lives in order to spray a deadly liquid at their enemies, and human beings will place their own lives in danger to protect their children. Other behavioral tendencies that are common in both animals and humans include aggressiveness, territoriality, selfishness, and the formation of dominance hierarchies.

Sociobiologists argue that these tendencies are common in species because they are inborn traits determined by genes. These various traits exist because they enhance the chances of survival for the species. The stronger, more powerful, and more aggressive members of a species are more likely to survive, mate, and pass on their genes to the next generation. A mother will die to save her children because this enhances the likelihood that her genes will survive in the gene pool even though she herself dies. Sociobiologists reason that aggressiveness and altruism are a part of our genetic makeup because people who behave aggressively or altruistically increase the chances for the survival of their genes. Over long periods of time, those aggressive and altruistic genes come to predominate in the gene pool.

Is violence or war programmed into human genes as sociobiologists suggest? There are a number of reasons to be cautious about their arguments (Wolfe, 1993). First, there is no direct evidence linking any specific genes to particular forms of human behavior. Although their arguments are plausible, there is no definitive proof that they are accurate. Second, there are few human traits that are found universally among human beings. The prevalence of behaviors such as altruism and aggressiveness vary widely from person to person and culture to culture. Although every kamikaze bee will die protecting its hive, for example, some human beings protect their children, whereas others neglect, abuse, and abandon them. Whereas some cultures are very warlike, other cultures rarely if ever go to war. If altruism, aggressiveness, and war were truly instinctive, this variation would not occur. Finally, even if genetically determined behavioral tendencies exist, sociobiologists recognize that they create only general tendencies to behave in certain ways. Whether people actually behave aggressively or go to war depends on numerous psychological and social forces. In fact, sociobiologists admit that these genetic tendencies, if they exist, can probably be altered or even overcome by learning and other social forces.

Social Sources of Collective Violence and War

The social sources of violence can be organized into three categories: characteristics of the structure of society that serve as preconditions to violence, the frustrations that these preconditions can create in people that push them toward violence, and mediating factors that increase the likelihood that people will react violently to frustration. We will look at each of these factors, relating them where appropriate to the three sociological perspectives.

STRUCTURAL PRECONDITIONS Most outbursts of collective violence can be traced to some social conditions that serve as preconditions for violence. One such precondition is the existence of some social strain or social deprivation. For example, strain exists when some groups in society do not have the opportunity to achieve their goals through socially acceptable means. This is discussed in Chapters 9 and 10 as Robert Merton's anomie theory of crime and drug abuse. For instance, racial or ethnic discrimination

may limit the jobs that are available to some people, or poverty may make it difficult to attain the education necessary to find a respectable job. Whatever its source, this strain or deprivation leaves people vulnerable to participating in collective violence should the opportunity arise.

Another precondition for violence is competition between people over money, jobs, territory, and other scarce but valued resources. This is discussed in Chapters 6 and 7 as a source of prejudice and discrimination against minorities. The more intensely groups compete, the more threatening each becomes to the other and the more likely one side or the other will resort to violence or terrorism. Oftentimes, the competition is economic, over jobs or money, such as the split labor market discussed in Chapter 6 and the labor disputes discussed earlier in this chapter. However, there can also be conflict over values and lifestyle. Such competition need not culminate in violence if society provides everyone with the opportunity to achieve at least some of his or her goals. Violence also can be avoided by providing people with nonviolent means to achieve an acceptable lifestyle. However, groups will resort to violence if they perceive it as a superior and effective strategy in the clash over scarce resources.

A third precondition of violence and war is ethnocentrism, or the tendency to view one's own group or culture as superior to other groups or cultures (see Chapter 6). Although some ethnocentrism can be beneficial by promoting group cohesion, excessive amounts can lead to the belief that others are not only different but also dishonest, disreputable, and possibly even not fully human. Such beliefs open the door to hostile and violent actions. Especially if the members of a group are defined as subhuman, violence, terrorism, or war against them may not be seen as bad or immoral. Thus, Adolf Hitler and the Nazis became so thoroughly convinced of the superiority of the Aryan "race" that they felt justified in brutalizing Jews and others and going to war against other nations. Likewise, many people in the United States in the eighteenth and nineteenth centuries believed that their European heritage and values were far superior to those of American Indians in the New World, and this view legitimized wars against Indians that few people are proud of today.

The structural preconditions just described—deprivation, competition, and ethnocentrism—are general statements about the factors behind collective violence and war. In specific instances of insurrections or wars, these preconditions have appeared in a number of specific forms:

1. Religious conflicts
2. Racial and ethnic conflicts
3. Conflicts over scarce land or natural resources

4. Conflicts over beliefs and ideologies

5. Protection against attack or invasion

6. Protection of national pride

People have supported revolutions, engaged in terrorist actions, or gone to war for all of these reasons.

FRUSTRATION AND AGGRESSION How are these preconditions translated into violence? Psychologists have shown that there is a clear, though complex, link among frustration, aggression, and violence. **Frustration** refers to *an inability to achieve sought-after goals.* The preconditions of violence discussed in the previous section are structured sources of frustration that can influence many people. When people are frustrated, there is a buildup of tension that may be released in aggressive and sometimes violent behavior (Baron and Richardson, 1994). This aggressive or violent reaction can release the tension created by frustration even though it fails to alleviate the real source of the frustration. For example, in the South in the United States between 1882 and 1903, nearly 2,000 blacks were killed by lynch mobs, some by hanging, others by being burned alive (Soule, 1992). Some of the impetus for such violence was the fluctuating economic conditions in the South: Unemployment and poor economic conditions frustrated southern whites, and some responded with racial violence against blacks. The violence did not alleviate the underlying economic problems, but it did provide a release for poor whites.

Chapter 9 observes that what is considered deviant is relative to the judgments of some group. What is considered frustrating is also relative. **Relative deprivation** refers to the fact that *people tend to feel deprived or frustrated in comparison to what others have or what they believe they deserve.* In other words, a sense of deprivation arises when there is a discrepancy between what people have come to expect or feel they deserve and what they actually receive. So the conditions that are frustrating or depriving for one group or at one point in history may not be so for another group or at another point. It depends on the standards that people use in assessing their circumstances. A century ago, miners in the United States went on strike because they were being maimed and killed by unsafe working conditions and for wages that barely provided the essentials of life. In the past decade, violence has accompanied labor disputes in which the workers would have been considered affluent by the standards of a century ago. The point is that the standards for what is an acceptable lifestyle and what is acceptable in the workplace have changed and so have the conditions that might precipitate violence.

The notion of relative deprivation reflects the emphasis of the interactionist perspective on the construction of social reality through human perception and interpretation. Social conditions become a problem—even one warranting a violent response—if people define them as threatening their values or disruptive of their lifestyle. These definitions are based on the meanings that groups attach to people or events. The Applied Research insert in this chapter focuses on the preconditions and frustrations that are among the social roots of terrorism.

MEDIATING FACTORS The preconditions to violence and the frustration that have been discussed do not lead inexorably to violent behavior. In fact, most people experiencing such conditions do not become violent. Rather, there are a number of mediating factors that increase the likelihood of violence. For one thing, whether violence occurs and the form that it takes depend on learning and socialization. Culture can teach people that violence is an acceptable and useful way of dealing with interpersonal problems. Some cultures, such as the Zuni Indians in the American Southwest, view aggression as an evil force that threatens group unity, and people discourage any displays of aggression (Westie, 1964). In U.S. culture, on the other hand, people are often rewarded for engaging in aggressive or violent behavior. Children, especially boys, may be cheered on when they play especially hard and aggressively at some sport. They may even be encouraged to "act like a man" and stand up to people who give them trouble—even if that means fighting.

It has been argued that some groups or subcultures in the United States tend to be very accepting of violence as a means of resolving disputes and that this atmosphere serves as an important mediating factor in producing violence or war (Wolfgang and Ferracuti, 1967). In fact, there may even be a **subculture of violence** involving *norms and values that condone and legitimize the use of violence in resolving conflicts.* Thus, aggression and violence may be viewed by some groups as the acceptable and possibly even the preferred and "manly" way of resolving disputes. Yet the subculture of violence theory should not be extended too broadly. Research suggests that such subcultures may not be as extensive as once thought and that the social class, racial, and regional variation in the propensity to use violence that was once thought to exist may not be that strong (Ball-Rokeach, 1973; Vigil, 2003). Still, for many groups, violence is considered an appropriate response in some circumstances.

There seems little doubt at this point that the mass media contribute to the levels of violence in society.

The date of September 11, 2001, has been seared into the memories of many people. The terrorist attacks on the World Trade Center in New York and the Pentagon in Washington, DC, on that day were horrific, in both their intent and their scale. Three thousand people died. It was a wrenchingly painful and tragic way for people in the United States to be made aware that terrorism could happen here. Of course, everyone knew that terrorism was relatively common in the world. The World Trade Center had been bombed almost exactly eight years earlier. In fact, in an ironic coincidence, when the planes crashed into the World Trade Center in 2001, four men were on trial in a courtroom a few blocks from the World Trade Center in Manhattan for terrorist bombings of U.S. embassies in Africa. Yet, people seemed to believe either that terrorism would not happen or that its scale would be small.

There has been, sadly, enough terrorism around the world that social scientists have had much data to analyze to help them understand it. What they have found about the social sources of terrorism reflects the social sources of violence discussed in the text (Calhoun, Price, and Timmer, 2002; White, 2002).

Terrorism is most likely to be resorted to by people who are desperate and fairly powerless. They see no other way to advance toward their goals. They may be materially bereft or have little in the way of armies or other conventional ways of influencing events. In addition, they lack the political alliances with more powerful groups that might be used to advance goals. Terrorism is a relatively inexpensive way to attack an enemy.

Terrorists typically have perceived grievances that serve as justification in their minds for their actions. Although others may disagree that the grievances are real,

or that they justify terrorism, it is important to recognize that the terrorists believe these things. The United States, as the world's predominant superpower, is often a major focal point of these grievances. As for the September 11 terrorists, as best we know, their grievances focused on some U.S. policies toward the Arab world and the Middle East. In particular, they were angered by U.S. support for Israel in the struggle with the Palestinians; the stationing of U.S. troops in Saudi Arabia, which is some of the holiest land in the Islamic religion; and U.S. bombing and blockading of Iraq.

Economic deprivation and social dislocation provide fertile ground for widespread support for terrorism. Although terrorism can occur without economic deprivation or popular support (as evidenced by Timothy McVeigh's killing of hundreds of people in the Oklahoma City bombing in 1995), it is more likely to gain recruits among

In the past 40 years, much research has been conducted on the relationship between violence on television and violence in society (Felson, 1996; Huesmann, Moise-Titus, Podolski, and Eron, 2003; Potter, 2003). Most of this research concludes that when children and youths watch violence on television, they are more likely to act aggressively or violently themselves, especially in situations that are conducive to violence. The impact is greater for males than for females, and it is more substantial for children who are more aggressive to begin with (Josephson, 1987). Children between the ages of eight and twelve seem to be especially vulnerable to the effects of watching violence on television.

Television encourages people toward violence in three ways. First, action dramas can be arousing to viewers and may stimulate them in the direction of physical activity and release. This effect is probably of short

duration, from hours to days. Second, television provides viewers with legitimizing models for violence in much the same way that parents or peers can serve as models. In fact, it is difficult to watch television without being exposed to models of violence. Thus, children learn the potential for acting violently in particular situations, and the amount of such violence on television has not declined in the past few decades and may have actually increased. Also, the violence seen on television has some unreal or surrealistic qualities. People bleed little, and the actual pain and agony resulting from a violent attack are rarely portrayed. The consequences of violence often seem antiseptic and rather unimportant. Third, television conveys attitudes and values, and it can teach children to view violence or antisocial behavior as a desirable or "manly" way to behave.

Even with all of the preconditions and mediating factors that have been discussed thus far, collective

desperate and deprived people. As we have discussed elsewhere in this book, a substantial gap persists in the world between the well-to-do and the poor. Such people can be attracted by groups or ideologies that demonize the rich as the source of their economic distress and that propose destruction of the "enemy" as relief from their problems.

Technological advances have also contributed to the expansion of terrorist activities. One impact of modern technology is that it can put highly destructive weapons into the hands of anyone willing to invest time, effort, and modest financial resources in learning how to develop and use them. Some chemical and biological weapons can be acquired by small groups of people. There is also fear that nuclear weapons might become available. The terrorists who attacked the World Trade Center and the Pentagon turned commercial aircraft into powerful and destructive weapons; they needed only to gain some rudimentary

knowledge of how to fly such aircraft and sneak simple weapons on board to take over the planes in flight. It was a very inexpensive, but well-organized, operation.

Modern communications technology, especially the Internet, also provides an assist for terrorist groups. It provides an instantaneous, worldwide mechanism of communication that enables terrorist groups to maintain contact and coordinate activities. The Internet also can be used to recruit new members, maintain contact with them, and maintain morale among individuals or groups who must remain isolated in order to carry out a mission.

Although many terrorist beliefs are purely secular in nature, religion was a powerful legitimation for the September 11 terrorists. Although many Muslims would disagree with them, the terrorists believed that their religion justified the most extreme actions against what they perceived as infidels who were intent on destroying them and their religious values. With religious justi-

fications such as this, terrorists can approach their tasks with certainty, single-mindedness, and ferocity. Their actions are supported by a transcendent justification and are seen as a road to cosmic salvation (Calhoun, Price, and Timmer, 2002; White, 2002).

Reducing the extent of terrorism or eliminating it altogether is no simple task. An important part of this involves police, intelligence, and military activities in numerous locations around the world that prevent or disrupt the mobilization of terrorist groups. Equally important, however, is to focus on the grievances, dislocations, and deprivations that make some people sympathetic to terrorists. In some cases, these grievances arise from economic disparities, whereas in other cases they emerge from disagreements with policies or actions of the United States or other powerful nations in the world. At numerous places in this book, we have discussed proposals for dealing with such problems.

violence is not likely to occur without mobilization: social mechanisms for bringing the affected people into coordinated and organized activity. Depending on the context, leaders have to emerge, money must be collected, and ways of exercising power must be discovered. Organization, administration, procedures, and strategies must also evolve. If the essential mix of resources is not mobilized, collective violence or war will not occur, even when the predisposing factors are substantial and the deprivation is severe.

Theoretical Perspectives on Collective Violence and War

The sources of violence just described relate in good measure to the functionalist perspective. They view violence as arising in part from social disorganization:

frustration, deprivation, and the like. When people are frustrated in achieving their goals, it means that the various parts of the social system are not well integrated; people learn to want things but then are not given the means to achieve them. The violence that arises may then contribute to further disorganization, and this is what makes it a social problem from the functionalist perspective. As a mechanism for redressing grievances, violence is very unstable and dangerous. It means, first of all, that more peaceful mechanisms for resolving problems have broken down. Second, violence always has the potential for getting out of hand and escalating to dangerously destructive levels. At an extreme, this can threaten the stability of the social order, as occurred during the Civil War when the United States was threatened with being split apart. Some also believe that levels of violence rose dangerously high during the 1960s with race riots and antiwar riots becoming common events. For functionalists, then, violence is a social problem because it threatens societal stability and increases social disorganization.

The conflict perspective points to a somewhat different view of violence: It is a tool that any group might use to protect or enhance its own interests. According to the conflict perspective, dominant groups use violence whenever a subordinate group begins to threaten their position. For example, business interests in the late 1800s turned to the police and National Guard troops to stop workers who were organizing to oppose the substantial power of their employers. As seen earlier in this chapter, workers were often harassed, beaten, and shot in the process. When dominant groups resort to violence, they tend to view it as socially acceptable and appropriate. Subordinate groups can also resort to violence when they have few other means of redressing grievances. Rioting, for example, has been one way that subordinate minority groups in the United States have been able to force some concessions from the powers that be. Terrorism has also been used by those with few resources in an attempt to force changes. Hamas and Islamic Jihad have done this in support of Palestinians in Israel. So, from the conflict perspective, violence itself is not a social problem; in fact, violence is an important mechanism for bringing about social change. It comes to be viewed as a problem when it threatens the interests of some group and that group is in a position to do something about it.

Constructing War: The Role of the Mass Media

A preceding discussion explored one way in which the mass media impact violence and war: Viewing violence increases the likelihood that people will model that violence in their own lives. The mass media have an additional, and more subtle, impact: shaping people's perceptions and definitions of war and military solutions to problems. The interactionist perspective stresses how people's definitions of situations serve as mechanisms of social control, shaping their thoughts, desires, and behaviors. Access to, and control over, the mass media has today become a key determinant of a group's ability to persuade or influence.

A good example of the role of the media can be found in the Persian Gulf War of 1991 (Hallin, 1991; Mowlana, Gerbner, and Schiller, 1992). As a means of controlling potential opposition to the war, U.S. political and military leaders decided to strictly control the media's access to information and to the war zone. The policy was to keep the media as far away from the war

zone as possible and to place maximum restrictions on their activities. A great deal of information about the war came from political and military press briefings; staged news events such as political speeches; and tapes, graphics, and interviews supplied to the press by the military or government. This meant that the information and images that the media had available were mostly those approved by military and political leaders and those that placed the war in the most positive light.

The outcome was remarkable: For people in the United States watching the war on television, it appeared to be an astonishingly "clean" war, devoid of the bloodshed, terror, pain, and horror that normally accompany war. Almost no one reported from or sent images back directly from the field of battle. People were not to see the suffering and death that accompanies war. The images available to the media also stressed the role of technology in the form of smart bombs and laser-guided missiles. Battles appeared to be fought by experts and technicians, and people saw fuzzy but dramatic pictures taken from planes of buildings blowing up. The television networks hired their own military commentators, usually retired military or Defense Department officials who claimed the status of "independent expert." Even the images of soldiers going into battle stressed the mastery of technology: They were the pilots of highly sophisticated jet fighters or the monitors of sophisticated radar in surveillance planes.

The media experience was quite different during the Vietnam War when reporters, photographers, and television crews were given fairly free rein to go where they wished. They could ride helicopters into battle and join soldiers on dangerous patrols. The more realistic, and certainly more sobering, media portrayal of that war undoubtedly helped to turn some public opinion against the war. In fact, the tight controls on the media in the Gulf War were clearly a reaction on the part of the government and military to what was seen as a loss in the battle to influence the public during the Vietnam War.

In the Iraq War of 2003, individual journalists were "embedded," which means they were permitted to join particular military units and lived and traveled with them for some period of time (Schechter, 2003). While providing more access than during the Persian Gulf War, it also involved less freedom and access than during the Vietnam War. First of all, the military agreed to embed journalists only if the press would agree to restrictions on what would be reported. Embedded journalists could only travel with the unit in which they were officially embedded and limits were placed on what they could report and how they could do so. Because they lived with the same soldiers for a long period of time and because they were dependent on the soldiers for protection and physical survival, there was a natural tendency for journalists to view the soldiers positively or at least to show some reluctance to portray the soldiers and the war in a negative light. In addition, military press officers worked closely with journalists to encourage positive reporting. Gruesome images of the dead or maimed were minimized. In addition, just as in the Persian Gulf War, the military worked hard to present to the media as sanitized and positive a view of the war as possible. Retired military officers once again stood out prominently as military analysts who news organizations relied heavily on for information and interpretation.

So, without question, politicians and military leaders exploit the media to persuade the U.S. public to support wars and military solutions to international conflicts. Yet, the media also constitute an independent institutional force in society with its own agenda. After all, the media could choose not to broadcast any images rather than giving the one-sided portrayal that was available to them in the Persian Gulf War. However, sociologist David Altheide points out that, in the modern mass media, "marketing logic, or what the audience approves of or 'buys,' informs message selection or production" (1993:54). A primary motivation of the media, even in the news divisions, is an economic one: to increase audience share, which enhances advertising revenue. In this view, the media were not the "exploited" but the "co-conspirators": They willingly work with political and military leaders to present a certain image of the war because the media elite believe it would be the most marketable image (MacArthur, 1992).

So the media can be powerful players in the construction of war and violence as social problems. In fact, the media can be thought of as "contested territory" that is battled over by various groups, each hoping to control the images communicated by the media. But at the same time, political and economic elites clearly have more opportunities and resources with which to control and shape media images, and their images can be a powerful force in influencing people to support war and violence as acceptable alternatives in international conflicts.

The Consequences of War and Terrorism

Death, Injury, and Social Dislocation

One of the most obvious costs of war and terrorism is the death and injury that it produces. Table 14.1 presents the number of battle deaths and injuries suffered by Americans in a variety of wars. To this, we also have to add the deaths and injuries suffered by other combatants as well as by civilians. One estimate is that more than 100 million people have been killed by wars in the twentieth century (Porter, 1994). This is probably a low estimate. Estimates are that 20 million Russians were killed during World War II, and 500,000 people died in the ethnic conflicts in Rwanda in the early 1990s. These examples give some indication of the massive killing that occurs during human wars.

To this death toll, we also have to add the injuries and the social dislocations that result from war and terrorism (Neier, 1998). Women and children are often the special victims of these problems. Some injuries are a by-product of military battles, but others occur long after battles are over—for example, when children or adults have limbs blown off by land mines left over from battles. In some cases, civilian injuries are imposed as part of a conscious effort to intimidate or humiliate a population. The Japanese forced women into prostitution during World War II, and there were widespread rapes of women in Bosnia-Herzegovina and in Rwanda in the 1990s.

Crime

Crime often accompanies war because warfare brings with it social disruption and upheaval—an environment in which crime thrives. Theft, robbery, and assault may be resorted to as a way of obtaining food, clothing, and other necessities that are difficult to obtain in the midst of a war. Crime rates also rise in the years immediately following wars. Homicide rates, for example, increase after wars, whether the wars are large or small (Archer and Gartner, 1976). The increase is not because of adverse economic conditions because it occurs when wars are followed by economic expansion. The increase is also found among both men and women. Surprisingly, the rise in crime is more likely among nations that are victorious in war, and nations with a large number of battle deaths have shown substantial crime increases.

We do not fully understand why this increase in crime occurs following wars. It may be that the violence of war tends to generate a general legitimation of violence—an expansion of the subculture of violence—and this may reduce people's inhibitions toward engaging in violence. Or it may be that a condition of anomie pervades society following a war as civilians struggle to secure food, clothing, and shelter and large numbers of soldiers return home looking for work and trying to reestablish familial and friendship ties (see Chapter 9). It may take society some time to reabsorb and help these soldiers readjust.

Political Turmoil

In addition to crime, political turmoil often increases during war. In some cases, this arises because disenchantment over the war leads to widespread discontent with the government. The government loses legitimacy in the eyes of both those who find the war morally offensive and those who feel that the government should prosecute the war more intensely. Such people may withhold support for the government, support opposition candidates, or possibly even engage in collective protest or rebellious actions. War also may have the effect of reducing people's tolerance for public dissent. When a country has gone to war with a foe, many people believe a united front is essential and are willing to allow the government to use repressive means to control dissent. As a consequence of all these things, wars generally tend to produce increases in domestic political violence (Stohl, 1976). Opponents of the war may engage in demonstrations, sit-ins, or, in extreme cases, terrorist bombings as a way of disrupting the war effort. Supporters of the government and the war may harass and attack demonstrators, and the police arrest the dissenters.

During the Civil War, for example, there was substantial dissent and conflict. In New York City, a three-day riot involving 50,000 people resulted in 1,300 deaths (Brooks, 1969). Much of the hostility was focused on the unfairness of the draft as then implemented. There was also considerable opposition to World War I. In 1917, for example, 8,000 protestors marched in Boston against the war. The pattern of violence at this march was typical: Patriotic mobs attacked the demonstrators, but it was the demonstrators who were arrested for breaching the public order. The Vietnam War was associated with substantial domestic political violence. Early in the war, the violence took the same form that it did during World War I: Nonviolent demonstrators were attacked by either citizens or the police. Later, some antiwar protestors became more violent by burning buildings and attacking police with rocks and sticks.

Economic Problems

War can have a severe impact on a nation's economy. The destruction of factories, railroads, and other economic resources can be terribly damaging, but economic problems are created even in combatant nations that suffer little or no such physical destruction. One source of economic problems is that resources devoted to the war effort must be withdrawn from some other economic realm. The labor and material resources used to build tanks and guns are not available for housing construction or leisure pursuits (Cranna, 1994). World War II drew substantial resources from the civilian realm, with nearly half of the gross national product being spent for military needs. It is estimated that the direct costs of World War II were $360 billion, at a time when the federal budget each year was less than $100 billion (U.S. Bureau of the Census, 1994:357). By comparison, Korea and Vietnam were less intrusive on the economy: They cost $50 billion and $140 billion, respectively. Depending on the state of the economy, wars can also produce high inflation, high interest rates, recessions, and other economic damages that negatively affect practically everyone.

Even when war is not fought, the preparations for war can be costly. Outfitting the United States's military machine to be prepared to intervene around the globe, for example, means diverting resources and innovation away from civilian industries and into the military–industrial complex. What has resulted is a huge industry of corporations, engineers, and workers who are dependent on government contracts and tooled to build only very specialized weapons systems. With government assistance siphoned off into the military–industrial complex, some other industries have languished, with plants closing and jobs going overseas.

Nuclear Devastation

In one major respect, many would consider the twentieth century to have been the "winter of despair": For the first time in human history, the technological capability exists for destroying life on earth, as we know it. The harnessing of nuclear power has made possible the unleashing of unimaginable destruction. In a sense, we can only speculate about the impact of nuclear war on life on earth because no other equivalent calamities have occurred to serve as examples. Of course, there were Hiroshima and Nagasaki, but these were limited attacks and the survivors could depend on support for survival and rebuilding from those not immediately affected. In a large-scale nuclear war, there would be no outside support because the explosions would spread devastation all across the United States, Europe, and Russia. Millions of people would likely die in such a war.

Another possible effect of nuclear war is what a group of scientists labeled a "nuclear winter" (Ehrlich et al., 1983). The thousands of detonations of nuclear warheads would toss tremendous amounts of dust and soot into the atmosphere and cause fierce fires that would send smoke and particulate matter into the

One atomic bomb produced this scene of utter devastation in Hiroshima, Japan, in 1945. It shows the awesome power unleashed by modern atomic and nuclear weapons.

atmosphere. This dust and soot could coalesce into a monstrous dark cloud shrouding much of the Northern Hemisphere. Little sunlight would penetrate this cloud. Even a limited nuclear exchange could reduce sunlight by 95 percent. The cold and the darkness could have disastrous effects on plants and animals, and the food supply would be seriously threatened. Based on their calculations, then, these scientists project that nuclear war could constitute a severe assault on the ecosystem and could threaten its ability to support human life.

On a smaller scale, nuclear technology creates the possibility for small groups of terrorists to produce substantial death and destruction. If they could obtain a small nuclear device and detonate it in a crowded location, the impact would be devastating. Short of a nuclear explosion, terrorist may gain access to radioactive nuclear materials that could be released in a crowded setting and cause considerable death, injury, and illness. Such radioactive nuclear materials are increasingly available in today's world, and the security of these materials is sometimes appallingly weak. So, modern technology puts the possibility of massive destruction into the hands of fairly small groups of determined people (Langewiesche, 2007).

Future Prospects
Social Reform and Social Justice

As has been seen, violence, war, and terrorism often spring out of social strain, frustration, or injustice. Collective violence may represent an effort by people to correct those injustices or to gain what they feel is an equitable share of resources. Efforts to control violence, then, need to begin by changing the social conditions that are the seedbeds of violence. In fact, the sociological investigation of social problems is an attempt to do just this. In this book, many of the conditions that can cause collective violence have been analyzed, and it is not necessary to review all of those discussions here. By way of illustration, prejudice and discrimination, discussed in Chapter 6, produce violence in the form of lynchings and race riots. Social reforms that focus on reducing discrimination, then, will affect levels of collective violence. The inequitable distribution of resources in society, discussed in Chapter 5, has resulted in violence in the form of labor strife, riots, and in a few cases, rebellion. Programs to provide people with greater opportunities and a broader distribution of resources in society will reduce the likelihood of these forms of violence.

There is no consensus regarding which social reforms are appropriate or what constitutes social justice, and this book will not presume to answer those questions. In most cases, reform programs mean that some groups benefit, whereas others lose. In fact, interventionists presume that this will be the case and that the government should serve as arbiter over the allocation of resources. The government then becomes the forum in which various groups exercise what influence they have to gain a share of resources. Laissez-faire advocates, on the other hand, would argue that the unfettered operation of impersonal economic forces can provide equity and justice for all. The government, they believe, will simply become the tool of one interest group or another. These issues are debated in other chapters in the context of specific forms of social injustice. The point here is that, although social reform is essential to controlling violence, such reforms are not easy to accomplish and are not without controversy.

Gun Control

A variety of gun control measures have been implemented in the United States, primarily in the form of prohibiting some individuals such as convicted felons from owning guns or requiring the registration of guns. To date, research on whether such measures can reduce the amount of violence in society has generally shown either a very modest impact or no impact at all (Carter, 1997; Kleck, 1991). This may be because there are so many guns available and so many jurisdictions with loose gun regulations that strict gun regulation in one city or county cannot control how many people in those locales have guns in their hands. Especially in terms of the collective violence discussed in this chapter—riots, rebellions, and wars—limiting the availability of handguns or rifles in the hands of citizens is not likely to have a major impact. These outbursts arise from long-term and entrenched social conditions, discussed earlier in this chapter, and will likely produce collective responses even when guns and rifles are less available. The availability of military arms is another matter to be discussed shortly.

Media Control

There has been considerable pressure over the years, especially from groups of parents and educators, to establish controls over the portrayal of violence in the media. This would reduce the number of models for violence that the young are exposed to. The media

have generally resisted any such controls. One reason for the resistance is that the violent movies and television shows are often the most popular and profitable ones. In 1990, Congress passed the Children's Television Education Act. It is the first legal effort to require the television industry to take steps to provide for the educational and informational needs of children and youth in their programming (Huston et al., 1992). Licensees must demonstrate at the time of their license renewal that their programs meet these needs, although there is little specific in the act about what they must do. The act does not address the issue of violence directly but instead permits television broadcasters, networks, and cable companies to collaborate to reduce the amount of violent content without being subject to antitrust laws. In 1992, the three networks did agree to some guidelines to reduce violence on television. The guidelines suggest that violence should be relevant to the development of the plot and should not be gratuitous, excessive, or depicted as glamorous. However, there is no enforcement mechanism attached to the guidelines, and the networks will probably continue to air shows that get the best ratings, which are typically those with sex and violence in them.

Resistance to controls over the media also arises among those who view such controls as an infringement on the First Amendment rights of freedom of speech and freedom of the press. As was shown when discussing the censorship of pornography in Chapter 11, it is very difficult to distinguish between what is acceptable and what should be censored. Violence is, of course, a fact of life, and to eliminate it from the media altogether would be a tremendous distortion of reality. But what level of violence is "too much"? If we can censor violence, then what about some other ideas or practices that we find offensive? The door to censorship, once ajar, may be very difficult to keep from opening further. Such censorship could easily threaten the free press and the open expression of ideas that are so essential to a democracy. So the desirability of controlling media violence needs to be weighed against the threat it may present to democratic institutions.

Preventing War

THE BALANCE OF POWER During the Cold War, which began at the end of World War II, the world was dominated by two superpowers, the Soviet Union on one side and the United States, along with its allies, on the other. U.S. foreign policy was directed toward preventing a nuclear catastrophe while at the same time maintaining U.S. political and military dominance in the world. In the early 1950s, Secretary of

State John Foster Dulles (1954) developed the policy of **massive retaliation:** *War could be avoided if the enemy realized that any aggressor against the United States would suffer overwhelming damages from the massive retaliation with the U.S. military might.* So the United States strove to prevent war by amassing weaponry to use as a threat. The threat would serve to deter unwanted actions by the Soviet Union and contain the spread of Soviet influence to new regions in the world. The Soviet bloc nations also amassed incredible military force. By the 1980s, the foreign policies of both the United States and the Soviet Union were based on the concept of **mutually assured destruction** (MAD): *War can be prevented when each side has the might to destroy the other.* Any first-strike effort would result in retaliation and the mutual destruction of both sides. What was supposed to have resulted from this policy is a **balance of power:** *A nuclear holocaust is avoided because the military capability of one side roughly balances that of the other side.*

It would seem that the balance of power approach worked. There has not been a world war nor have nuclear weapons been used in 60 years. Yet there are reasons for pessimism about such a policy. After all, 60 years is not a very long time. If another 100 years pass without a nuclear war and one occurs then, it would still have devastating consequences. In addition, more conventional wars such as the Korean conflict, the decade-long Vietnam War, the Gulf War, and our involvement in places such as Lebanon and Grenada have not been prevented. These conflicts held the potential to escalate into a nuclear exchange. Finally, there remains the possibility that nuclear war could start by accident. Although the chances of this are considered by many to be small, they cannot be ignored.

Two key events in recent history—the collapse of the Soviet Union and the terrorist attacks of September 11, 2001—have had a profound impact on policies related to war and its prevention. In fact, they have stimulated one of the great debates over foreign policy and national security of the past century. The Policy Issues insert is devoted to exploring the issues in this debate and their import.

ARMS CONTROL AND DISARMAMENT Another policy designed to protect the world from war and possible nuclear destruction would be to limit the number of weapons in existence or to eliminate them altogether. Nations are naturally reluctant to enter into agreements to limit their weaponry when they fear that the other side will take advantage of this situation. It is also often politically dangerous for elected officials to appear to compromise defensive strength.

Yet there has been some progress in arms control (Falkenrath, Newman, and Thayer, 1998). In 1963, most nations signed a treaty banning nuclear testing in the atmosphere, outer space, underwater, and in some cases underground. The focus of this treaty was on protecting the environment from radioactive contamination. In the Strategic Arms Limitation Talks (SALT I and SALT II in the 1970s), the United States and the Soviet Union agreed to place limits on their defensive weapons systems and on their most powerful land- and submarine-based offensive nuclear weapons. Although these treaties probably contributed to reducing the chances of a nuclear exchange, they left the nuclear powers with enormous stockpiles of weapons.

Then in the late 1980s, we saw the beginning of the collapse of the Soviet Union, and Presidents Mikhail Gorbachev and Ronald Reagan signed the Intermediate-Range Nuclear Forces (INF) treaty, which bans intermediate range nuclear weapons. This resulted in some of the existing nuclear stockpiles in both countries being destroyed. Both countries also agreed on certain procedures for the mutual verification of the results, something that had always been a serious hitch in negotiations between the United States and the Soviet Union. Then, in the 1990s, the United States and Russia reached agreement on two strategic arms reduction treaties, START I and START II. If fully implemented, these treaties will produce dramatic reductions in the number of nuclear warheads stockpiled by both countries. Through the 1990s, both nations have been withdrawing nuclear weapons from ships, and Russia has been bringing them back from most of the nations of the former Soviet Union. Weapons are being destroyed at a rapid rate. However, even if the reductions planned by the treaties occur, the nations known to possess nuclear weapons will still possess enough warheads to do massive destruction.

NONPROLIFERATION OF WEAPONS In the past, some nations chose not to develop nuclear or other weapons of mass destruction because they had security arrangements and guarantees that offered them protection from attack by others without the need to have weapons of their own. For example, the North Atlantic Treaty Organization (NATO) provided a nuclear defense for West Germany, and the U.S. nuclear umbrella restrained South Korea from developing its own weapons. With the end of the Cold War, many of the old security arrangements around the world are changing or disintegrating. This leaves a very unsettled international environment as far as the proliferation of weapons goes and calls for new international efforts to

American Empire: A New World Order?

The collapse of the Soviet Union left the United States as the sole superpower in the world and with overwhelming political, economic, and military predominance. September 11, 2001, produced a redirection in U.S. foreign and military policy away from a focus on wars against nations and toward a much more amorphous worldwide war on terrorism. In the modern world, terrorism and technology combine to change substantially the threats the U.S. faces. Instead of clearly identifiable nation states with armies and weapons systems, the threats we face today are amorphous terrorist networks that are difficult to identify and locate but who may be supported by weak or failed nations, such as Sudan in the 1990s and Afghanistan in 2001. Modern technology makes it possible for these relatively small and amorphous groups to do substantial damage, as the attacks of September 11, 2001, demonstrated. Add to the mix the possibility that terrorists might use nuclear or chemical weapons, and the threat becomes intensified. So, what rose to prominence after September 11 is the policy notion that, in a highly dangerous world with threats that are difficult to identify, the United States needs to use its military might to act quickly, decisively, aggressively, and massively against any targets around the world that might be, or might become, a threat. In the eyes of many policy analysts, the containment and deterrence strategies of the Cold War have become outmoded (Newhouse, 2003).

These policy directions were formulated in a new National Security Strategy published by the Bush Administration in 2002. This new policy was founded on a number of principles. One such principle is embodied in the desirability of U.S. global *preeminence,* namely that the United States should maintain its position as the sole superpower and as the nation whose military might is second to none in the world. Another principle at the foundation of this new approach is the acceptability, even necessity, of *pre-emptive* and *preventive wars.* A pre-emptive war is one that is fought against a nation that is believed about to attack but has not yet done so. A preventive war is one fought against a nation not about to attack but that it is believed might pose a threat in the future, for example, by developing a weapons system that could be threatening. President Bush portrayed the Iraq War of 2003 as a pre-emptive war (Iraq would attack the United States or its allies soon if nothing was done), whereas critics argued that the war was, at best, a preventive war (Iraq might attack the United States at some point in the future if it were permitted to develop weapons systems that it did not possess at the time of the war). A third principle of Bush's National Security Strategy is *unilateralism,* the idea that the United States should and will act alone if it feels it necessary and will not feel constrained by any ties or treaties with other nations or international organizations. While we might work with other nations and organizations when it serves U.S. interests, this will always be on U.S. terms and toward U.S. interests.

---

discourage such proliferation (Reiss, 1995). One option to reducing proliferation would be to extend the U.S. or Russian nuclear umbrella over some countries that might be tempted to develop their own. If their security needs were satisfied, then a major motivation for developing weapons would be eliminated. However, this may clash with the pressure in both countries to reduce their nuclear armaments. A second option might be to encourage the development of regional agreements that prohibit the development of effective delivery systems, such as intermediate range ballistic missiles that are hard to defend against. Without the delivery system, the weapons would be less of a threat. A third option would be to encourage open debate about the development of nuclear weapons, especially on how costly they are to develop. Experience in some countries, such as Sweden, suggests that the public tends to strongly oppose them when they learn how expensive they are. Fourth, when nations violate existing nonproliferation treaties, there should be certain and substantial international sanctions against them, such as trade embargoes. Finally, the spread of weapons can be controlled through restricting the trade in technical knowledge or materials that are necessary to produce the weapons.

WORLD GOVERNMENT One of the major obstacles to preventing war among nations is that each nation functions on the basis of protecting its own national interest and pursuing its own short-term goals.

What might be emerging, then, is a policy of the United States ruling the world with its overwhelming military force in pursuit of U.S. interests and promoting free market capitalism and democracy (Daalder and Lindsay, 2004). The United States is sufficiently rich and powerful that its forces can reach around the world and remake it as it pleases. Some argue that such a policy will have the greatest likelihood of controlling and possibly preventing war in a world where our enemies are failed states, rogue states, and the terrorist groups that those states support (or at least permit to operate). While the balance of power may have worked when more than one superpower existed in the world, a single, pre-eminent superpower can more effectively control violence and war by stretching its military tentacles around the globe and using both persuasion and naked force to shape a world in which the United States prospers and is not threatened. Some policy analysts have dubbed this approach "the new imperialism" or "the American empire." Now, words such as "imperialism" and "empire" are fraught with meaning, both positive and negative, but supporters of this policy argue that, like it or not, the United States is the sole superpower in the world and its might does dwarf the capabilities of other nations. And that military power will be used to influence and shape the world. If that produces an American empire, it will be an empire that promotes changes that will benefit many peoples around the world.

This new policy is highly controversial, with many critics arguing for a much more multilateral approach to the exercise of power (Brzezinski, 2004). Most agree that the United States will be the dominant power in the world, but they argue that it should exercise that power through cooperation with other nations, international alliances, and the rule of international law. Working together with a global community of shared interests would be the most effective way of achieving peace and security. There is also the danger that an overzealous and unrelenting focus on military solutions to security problems will contribute to the growth of a powerful military–industrial complex that takes control of political and military decisions and promotes its own interests (Johnson, 2004). These critics argue that the unilateral approach of the Bush Administration will generate resentment, encourage other nations to develop weapons systems and create alliances to protect themselves from the United States, and provide the rationale for other nations to engage in pre-emptive and preventive wars that they see as benefiting themselves. Finally, critics argue that a sole superpower, with no constraints by international organizations or alliances, will be tempted to promote policies that serve its interests even though they bring disadvantage to other peoples and nations in the world.

This foreign policy and national security debate is just beginning, and its outcome will have a profound effects on the lives of all people.

Nations do not typically pursue policies that are guided by the common long-term interests of all nations, especially when those policies have a negative impact on the achievement of their own goals. One way around this obstacle might be to establish an international organization that would do for the nations of the world something like what the U.S. federal government does for the states: serve as a forum where competing interests can be hammered into a coherent policy without resorting to violence. This was attempted with the League of Nations following World War I and with the United Nations following World War II in 1945.

For such efforts at world government to be effective, there must be a body of international law that is accepted and adhered to by all nations. There must also be some means of enforcing that law. Regarding international law, the many treaties that the members of the United Nations have signed over the years stand as a sound beginning of an agreement regarding how nations will relate to one another. Although nations disagree over the interpretation or applicability of particular parts of the laws in particular cases, there are judicial bodies, such as the International Court of Justice at The Hague (the World Court), for resolving these disputes. A major flaw in the system at this point is that nations can ignore the Court's jurisdiction in particular cases. The United States did this in 1985 when the World Court ruled that the United States had broken international law by aiding the antigovernment rebels (the contras) in Nicaragua. The World

Court ordered the United States to stop arming and training the contras, but the Reagan administration said that the Court had no jurisdiction in this area. A second major flaw in the existing system of international law is that the United Nations has no means of enforcing its laws unless individual nations consent to its enforcement. The United Nations can send its peacekeeping forces into disputes when all parties agree to let them in, and Table 14.2 shows that U.N. troops and observers are active in many places around the globe in attempting to prevent conflicts from beginning or escalating. However, the United Nations cannot move in and settle disputes without the consent of the nations involved. To this point, nations have been unwilling to surrender their sovereignty and their right to use force to any international body. So the mechanism for some form of world government is in place, but the nations have not yet agreed to use it fully.

Despite the failings of the United Nations, many supporters of world government are not discouraged because they fully expect the transition to take a long time. After all, the history of the evolution of political structures has been toward larger and more complex forms of organization. Over the past few thousand years, human societies have developed from family- and kin-based political structures to larger units such as nation-states. With the increasing complexity and interdependence of the modern world, they argue, the next natural step is to some form of supranational organization. The importance of international trade and multinational corporations to the economies of all countries illustrates the extent to which cooperation is essential and warfare increasingly destructive. However, shifting people's allegiances from a nation to a "united nations" will involve a long and possibly difficult transition, as was the transition in the United States from a federation of states to the "united states."

COLLECTIVE ACTION When it comes to issues of war and peace, citizens around the world have not left matters solely in the hands of national governments or the United Nations. As in so many other matters, nongovernmental organizations (NGOs) have been actively working to reduce armaments and promote peace (Roth, 1998). One recent example of this was the International Campaign to Ban Land Mines. Land mines planted during wars maim and kill thousands of people each year—often civilians, often children, and often long after the war is over. The International Campaign was begun by groups such as Human Rights Watch in New York, Physicians for Human Rights in Boston, and the Vietnam Veterans of America Foundation in Washington. These groups worked for years to gain support for their cause around the world and to pressure governments to back a land-mine treaty. The result was a treaty to ban the use of land mines that was signed by most nations of the world in 1997. Other NGOs worked to establish an International Criminal Court that will have the authority to try people and governments for genocide, war crimes, and crimes against humanity. This is an effort to hold people accountable for, and possibly prevent, such atrocities as the Holocaust during World War II and the campaigns of ethnic cleansing in Bosnia and Herzegovina and in Rwanda in the 1990s.

The effectiveness of these NGOs depends in part on their use of modern technologies such as the

TABLE 14.2 Examples of United Nations Peacekeeping Operations, 2007

Place	Troops/Observers	Goal
India and Pakistan	64	Monitor cease-fire between India and Pakistan
Cyprus	954	Prevent fighting between Greek and Turkish communities
Lebanon	13,435	Serve as a buffer between Israel and Lebanon and monitor the ceasefire between the two
Democratic Republic of the Congo	17,175	Monitor cease-fire agreement between government, rebel troops, and surrounding states
Georgia	284	Monitor cease-fire agreement between government of Georgia and Abkhaz authorities in Georgia
Sierra Leone	1,358	Implement a peace agreement and help disarm, demobilize, and reintegrate fighters from various factions

SOURCE: United Nations Department of Public Information, *Current Peacekeeping Operations,* 2007, www.un.org/Depts/dpko/dpko/ops.htm.

Internet and e-mail to contact people, organize, and build alliances among organizations around the world. They also need to use the media skillfully to get their message out and pressure governments to support their cause. In addition, NGOs no longer limit themselves to reacting to practices or policies initiated by governments or corporations; instead, they now initiate their own programs, such as the land-mine treaty, and often force governments and the United Nations into more of a reactive posture. Although NGOs are not always as successful as the campaign against land mines, NGOs have now become a significant force in the global political arena regarding issues of war and peace.

LINKAGES

Violence and war have an impact on race relations (Chapter 6) because dominant racial groups can use violence and war as a part of a campaign to oppress a subordinate racial group. War especially can affect people's jobs and the economy (Chapter 2); changing defense needs push some industries into decline.

STUDY AND REVIEW

Summary

1. Unlike interpersonal violence, collective violence is organized violence involving relatively large groups of people working to promote or resist some social policies and practices. There are various types of collective violence: civil disorders (race riots and labor strife), political violence, wars, and terrorism.

2. There are a number of biological explanations for violence, especially that of sociobiology, which argues that certain characteristics—such as territoriality, aggressiveness, and selfishness—are genetically determined because these traits enhance the survival of the species.

3. There are a number of social sources of violence. Among them are structural preconditions that increase the likelihood of violence: social strain or deprivation, competition, and ethnocentrism. These preconditions are translated into violence because the frustration that they produce can lead to aggressive behavior. This involves relative deprivation because people tend to feel deprived or frustrated relative to what others have or they believe they deserve.

4. The likelihood that the preconditions and the frustration will lead to violence is influenced by some mediating factors: learning in a particular culture or subculture to view violence as an acceptable way of dealing with problems, portraying violence in the mass media in a positive way.

5. War and terrorism are very disruptive to society: They cause death, disability, and social dislocation; crime and political turmoil increase during and after wars; and wars can be disruptive to the economy. The devastation accompanying a nuclear war would be a severe assault to the ecosystem and might threaten civilization as we know it.

6. One of the keys to controlling violence is to correct the strains, frustrations, and injustices that lead to collective violence. However, there is often little consensus about what social reforms would do the job or about what constitutes social justice.

7. Controlling guns and limiting the amount of violence in the media have been portrayed as partial solutions to the problem of violence. However, there is no consistent evidence that gun control would have a great effect, and many people are opposed to the censorship that would be necessary to limit violence in the media.

8. Currently, there are four major approaches to preventing war, especially nuclear war: maintain a balance of power, develop treaties for arms control and disarmament, control the proliferation of weapons, and establish a world government that would be able to stop nations from going to war. Nongovernmental organizations also work actively to promote peace.

The Web site of the U.S. State Department **(www. state.gov)** has a lot of information about terrorism, both in the United States and around the world. The data in Figure 14.2 are taken from that site; gather other relevant information from the site and bring it to class. Other important agencies for these issues are the Central Intelligence Agency **(www.cia.gov)** and the United Nations **(www.un.org)**. Search through their sites for information on international treaties, organizations (such as the World Court), and peacekeeping efforts.

A good nongovernmental Web site that is more focused on research is the home page of the Hoover Institution on War, Revolution, and Peace at Stanford University **(www.hoover.org)**. Although this institute is a bit on the conservative side, it does publish some good policy and research papers that explore important issues

in the world today in regard to war and peace. Another good site is the National Security Archive at George Washington University **(www.gwu.edu/~nsarchiv)**. Can you find any other research and policy institutes on the Internet that focus on issues of collective violence, war, and peace? Particularly in regard to terrorism, can you find any Web sites that seem to promote terrorism (or at least look upon it favorably) or that support particular terrorist groups?

Good Web sites for grassroots organization on these issues can be found. One is for Peace Action **(www.peace-action.org)**, and the other is the Student Peace Action Network **(www.webcom.com/ peaceact)**. Can you locate the Web sites of any other NGOs focused on issues of war and peace? Bring what you find to class.

Key Terms

balance of power

civil disorder

collective violence

commodity riots

communal riots

frustration

insurrection

massive retaliation

mutually assured
  destruction

relative deprivation

sociobiology

subculture of violence

terrorism

violence

Multiple-Choice Questions

1. In most cases, spouse abuse would be an instance of
   a. collective violence.
   b. interpersonal violence.
   c. commodity violence.
   d. relative deprivation.
2. Since World War II, most race riots in the United States could be characterized as
   a. whites attacking blacks in racially contested residential areas.
   b. insurrections.
   c. attacks against property, merchandise, or equipment rather than people.
   d. interpersonal rather than collective violence.

3. According to the text, one problem with international treaties to prevent the spread of weapons of mass destruction is that
   a. only a handful of nations have signed them.
   b. the United States refuses to ratify the treaties.
   c. no consistent sanctions have been used against nations that violate them.
   d. nations have failed to agree on the final wording of such a treaty.
4. Which of the following is true about the arguments of sociobiologists?
   a. Learning and other social forces can alter inborn genetic tendencies.
   b. They have identified specific genes that cause particular forms of human behavior.
   c. Sociologists have concluded that their arguments are totally implausible.
   d. Most forms of collective violence are caused by brain tumors or chemical imbalances.
5. Which of the following was identified by the text as a structural precondition to violence?
   a. violence in the media
   b. frustration
   c. the subculture of violence
   d. competition between people
6. Which of the following statements is most consistent with the conflict perspective on violence?
   a. Violence is a tool that any group might use to protect or enhance its own interests.
   b. Violence arises out of social disorganization.

c. Violence occurs because the various parts of the social system are not well integrated.

d. Violence is dysfunctional because it can escalate and get out of hand.

7. Which of the following statements is true regarding the media experience in the Persian Gulf War in 1991?

a. Substantial restrictions were placed on where the media could go in the war zone.

b. To pursue the war effort, the media were no longer considered to be "contested territory."

c. The media had more freedom of movement than did the media during the Vietnam War.

d. The media were taken over by the government in order to control what was presented about the war.

8. All of the following are among the consequences of war discussed in the text *except*

a. war is often associated with reductions in inflation.

b. war is often associated with political turmoil.

c. war is often associated with increases in crime rates.

d. war is often associated with increases in anomie.

9. Given the research that has been done, policymakers have concluded that gun control legislation would probably have which effect?

a. a substantial increase in homicides and violence

b. a substantial decrease in homicides and violence

c. a decrease in homicides but an increase in overall violence

d. little or no impact on levels of collective violence

10. President Bush's National Security Strategy emphasizes *unilateralism,* which means that

a. U.S. foreign policy will not feel constrained by ties or treaties to other nations.

b. U.S. foreign policy will work closely with the United Nations.

c. the United States will engage in pre-emptive wars but not preventive wars.

d. the United States will be reluctant to engage in foreign wars.

True/False Questions

1. The 1960s was a period in U.S. history during which levels of violence were far higher than during any other decade.

2. The Detroit race riot of 1943 was a communal riot.

3. Currently, the United States and Russia are the only nations that possess nuclear weapons.

4. Sociobiology is one of the structural preconditions that can push people toward violence.

5. Viewing violence on television is more likely to produce aggressive or violent behavior among girls than among boys.

6. The Vietnam War was the first war in U.S. history in which there was significant domestic dissent against the war.

7. Some scientists today believe that a nuclear winter of some degree of severity is a possibility after a nuclear war.

8. In controlling violence, interventionists believe that the government should be influential in determining which social reforms are pursued.

9. The problem with developing a world government today is that there is no existing body of international law for states to follow in how to relate to one another.

10. The nations in the world that currently possess nuclear weapons have established a plan for disarming themselves over a decade under the treaties known as START I and START II.

Fill-In Questions

1. _____ violence is violence that is organized and engaged in by relatively large groups of people to promote or resist some social policies or practices.

2. The two types of civil disorder discussed in the text are _____ and _____.

3. An organized action by some group to rebel against the existing government and to replace it with new political forms is a/an _____.

4. _____ refers to the fact that people tend to feel deprived or frustrated in comparison to what others have or what they believe they deserve.

5. In terms of the social sources of violence, ethnocentrism is one of the _____ in the process bringing about violence.

6. From the _____ perspective, violence is an important mechanism for bringing about social change.

7. Opponents of controls over violence in the media argue that such controls would violate the _____ Amendment to the U.S. Constitution.

8. The most recent arms control treaties that were agreed upon by the United States and Russia were the _____ treaties.

9. The _____ is an international judicial body that nations can use for resolving disputes among nations.

10. The _____ was a policy that claimed to avoid a nuclear holocaust because the military capability of one side roughly balanced that of the other side.

Matching Questions

_____ 1. Ludlow Massacre
_____ 2. Robert Ardrey
_____ 3. John Foster Dulles
_____ 4. Detroit riot of 1943
_____ 5. Dorr's Rebellion
_____ 6. mediating factor in violence
_____ 7. mass media
_____ 8. anomie
_____ 9. SALT II
_____ 10. United Nations

A. territorial imperative
B. subculture of violence
C. labor strife
D. causes crime to rise after wars
E. communal riot
F. world government
G. insurrection
H. "contested territory"
I. arms reduction
J. massive retaliation

Essay Questions

1. What are civil disorders? Describe the major civil disorders in U.S. history.
2. What is terrorism? What kinds of terrorist groups are there today? What can be done about terrorism?
3. According to sociobiologists, what are the reasons for aggression and violence in human beings? Assess their arguments.
4. How do social strain and competition between groups serve as preconditions for violence?
5. What is the subculture of violence and how does it contribute to violence in society?
6. Compare and contrast the manner in which the functionalist perspective and the conflict perspective view violence in society.
7. What kind of economic problems can war produce for society?
8. What role does social reform play in controlling the levels of violence in society?
9. Describe the new National Security Strategy proposed by the Bush Administration in 2002. What are arguments for and against this policy?
10. What is currently being done and what could be done to prevent the spread of weapons of mass destruction to nations that do not currently have them?

For Further Reading

Steven E. Barkan and Lynne L. Snowden. *Collective Violence.* Boston: Allyn & Bacon, 2001. This book provides a good exposure to the many interesting topics covered in the sociological study of collective behavior and social movements.

Carl N. Degler. *In Search of Human Nature: The Decline and Revival of Darwinism in American Social Thought.* New York: Oxford University Press, 1991. This interesting work focuses on how biological and sociobiological explanations of human behavior have gained and lost popularity in the United States over the years.

James S. Hirsch. *Riot and Remembrance: The Tulsa Race War and Its Legacy.* Boston: Houghton Mifflin, 2002. This is an excellent case study of an episode of collective violence in which white citizens of Tulsa, Oklahoma, organized to attack and destroy a good part of the African American community of the city. It documents many of the forms of collective behavior that play a role in collective violence.

Daniel Levitas. *The Terrorist Next Door: The Militia Movement and the Radical Right.* New York: Thomas Dunne Books/St. Martin's Press, 2002. This is a sobering analysis of the homegrown terrorist groups that continue to exist in the United States, including the Militia Movement, Christian Identity, and Aryan Nations. It provides a good analysis of the social sources of terrorist groups.

Clyde Prestowitz. *Rogue Nation: American Unilateralism and the Failure of Good Intentions.* New York: Basic Books, 2003. This author, who has served in government, argues that the unilateralism of the current foreign policies has caused us to lose the respect and cooperation of nations around the globe. He calls for a foreign policy that puts much more stress on multilateralism.

Louise Richardson. *What Terrorists Want: Understanding the Enemy, Containing the Threat.* New York: Random House, 2006. This author provides a detailed analysis of the ideology and the strategy of the modern terrorist threat in the world and argues that it can best be contained through effective police work, political and economic development, and counterintelligence.

George Rudé. *Ideology and Popular Protest.* New York: Pantheon, 1980. An excellent analysis of the role of ideological factors in public protest and revolution. It includes an analysis of the English, American, and French Revolutions.

Jonathan Schell. *The Unconquerable World: Power, Nonviolence and the Will of the People.* New York: Metropolitan Books, 2003. This author looks at current foreign policies based on the balance of power, prevention, and preemption and suggests approaches to conflict resolution that forsake the use of violence.

EDUCATION, SCIENCE, AND TECHNOLOGY

Education, science, and technology all provide hope for a better future. Education, for example, has traditionally been viewed in the United States as the route for personal and familial improvement. Whether one is an immigrant or comes from poor or modest background, the American dream has been that a better life can be achieved by doing well in school, learning English if one is from a non-English-speaking background, and developing the skills and knowledge that will enable one to get a good job and move up the social and economic ladder. Science and technology are also part of a promise for a better future. As science develops a greater understanding of and mastery over the physical world, the promise holds, science-based technological innovations would provide us with a more comfortable, safer, and healthier world in which people would have more leisure time to enjoy themselves. Certainly, education, science, and technology have made good on many of these promises. Yet, this chapter is about the other side to this story: the ways in which education, science, and technology have fallen short of

About Education, Science, and Technology

Myth: People need more education today than in former times because today's jobs are more complicated and the technology more sophisticated.

Fact: This belief is partly true, but reality is more complicated. Only part of the increase in educational requirements for jobs in the twentieth century can be accounted for by actual increases in the training essential to do the jobs. Educational levels for jobs have risen in part because some groups benefit from this "credentials race."

Myth: By the end of the twentieth century, because of school busing and the emergence of magnet and charter schools, significant strides had been made to achieve racial integration in the schools in the United States.

Fact: A report that came out recently argued that U.S. schools are more racially segregated than they were thirty years ago, due largely to persisting segregation in housing.

Myth: The coming of computers and a postindustrial society will usher in an era in which most people will find exciting, rewarding, and well-paying jobs.

Fact: Many experts believe that these developments will not necessarily be a boon for everyone. Many service jobs, for example, and those created by computer technology are dull, repetitive, and low paying. Also, because of technological advances involving automation and robotization, unemployment and underemployment may continue to be serious problems in the future.

Myth: It is good to develop all of the technology that scientific knowledge makes possible because then society can choose to implement those developments that are beneficial and ignore those that create problems for people.

Fact: Once a technology exists, it tends to take on a life of its own: There are powerful social pressures to use it and further develop it by those interest groups who benefit from it. In other words, once the technological cat is out of the bag, society may have little choice about whether it will be used.

---

the promise. In some cases, they fall short because they can't or don't make the promise come true for some people; in other cases, they fall short because, in the very act of carrying out the promise, education, science, or technology creates additional social problems that negatively affect some people.

Growth of Education and Technology

This book has discussed the impact of industrialization on people's lives and on society. The term **industrialization** refers to *the productive processes where fossil fuels and machines are used instead of human or animal muscle power to produce things.* When societies industrialize, they also go through a process known as **modernization:** *the economic, social, and cultural changes that occur when a preindustrial society makes the transition to an advanced industrial society.* In a sense, much of this book has been about the changes associated with modernization.

This chapter focuses on two parts of society that play a key role in the process of modernization and are

heavily impacted by the changes associated with modernization: educational institutions and science and technology. **Education** refers to *the systematic, formal process through which specialized teachers transmit skills, knowledge, and values to students.* Before the industrial revolution, schools and formal education were much less common than today, primarily because formal education was not necessary in order for a person to make a productive contribution to society. In industrial societies, the machinery and the knowledge upon which it is based become dramatically more complex. Literacy skills become essential in an economy where paperwork is pervasive, and some minimum of mathematical skills are needed in virtually all jobs.

Just as education has grown, so have science and technology become more complex and pervasive, especially in industrial societies. **Science** refers to *the process of using systematic observation to gain knowledge about the physical and social world.* **Technology** refers to *the knowledge, tools, and practices that use scientific or other organized knowledge to achieve some practical goal* (Volti, 2001). In other words, technology puts scientific and other knowledge to use. Technology can be simple—such as a shovel to dig a hole—or it can be dazzlingly complex—such as the Internet communications network that now encircles the globe. Technology can be both material and non-material. Material technology would include such things as robots, computers, and nuclear bombs, whereas nonmaterial technology includes modes of social and economic organization, such as bureaucratization, mechanization, and automation.

Science and technology, of course, were around long before industrialization, but the level of technology has become much more sophisticated and pervasive. One level of technology is **mechanization,** or *the use of tools and machinery instead of human and animal labor in the production of goods and services.* Clearly, mechanization at some level can be found in virtually all human societies, but the tools and machinery used in advanced industrial societies of the twenty-first century have become much more complex and can accomplish many more tasks than earlier levels of machinery. At another level of development, technology involves **automation,** or *the automatically controlled operation of machines by mechanical or electronic devices.* Mechanization and automation make possible enormous increases in human productivity and a highly specialized division of labor. Each worker works on only a small part of a task and becomes highly proficient at repeating that task over and over. In modern societies, another level of technological development emerges: **cybernation,** or *the use of machines, such as computers, to control other machines, to make decisions, and to monitor the production process.* These higher levels of technological organization impact people's lives profoundly. Perhaps one of the most amazing and at the same time disturbing images of technological advance is the use of robots to do the work that human beings had previously done. Robotics is based on advances in computers, automation, and cybernation and involves microelectronically controlled machines that not only can accomplish complex, multisequence tasks but also can be "taught" to do new things through reprogramming their computers. One roboticized automobile manufacturing plant was described thus:

Hardly a human works among the multitude of robots. Only forty-two hourly workers are spread over two shifts, and eventually the plant will add

Mechanization and automation have brought about some positive changes for society, but it also means that there are fewer well-paying jobs for human beings because machines do more of the work, as at this auto factory.

an overnight shift with no human presence of any kind. Overhead, perched in a glass-walled command room, a handful of engineers and technicians run the factory. (GM bets an arm and a leg on a people-free plant, 1988)

As Figure 15.1 indicates, the United States devotes an increasingly large amount of money and employs a growing number of scientists and engineers to the task of searching for more scientific and technological breakthroughs. There is little question that these developments have brought positive changes to most people's lives. The roboticized factory can produce automobiles very efficiently, but with what impact on workers and on society as a whole? This chapter will explore some of the major problems that arise in educational institutions and as a consequence of emerging technologies.

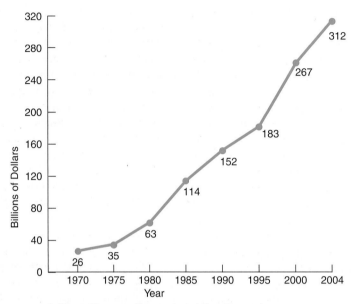

A. Expenditures on Research and Development

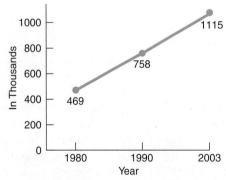

B. Scientists and Engineers Employed
in Research and Development

FIGURE 15.1 **Resources Devoted to Basic and Applied Research and Development in the United States, 1970–2004.**

Source: U.S. Bureau of the Census, *Statistical Abstract of the United States* (Washington, DC: U.S. Government Printing Office, various years).

Perspectives on Education, Science, and Technology

The three sociological perspectives can give us some insight into the role that education, science, and technology play in society and in what ways they might contribute to social problems.

The Functionalist Perspective

From the functionalist perspective, society is a system made up of interrelated and interdependent parts, each performing a function that contributes to the operation of the whole. Educational institutions perform a number of important functions in preparing people to fit into society and make productive contributions. For example, schools help to instill important cultural values in people, such as the importance of hard work or loving one's parents. Schools also train people in specific skills, such as how to be a doctor, a carpenter, or a computer programmer. Schools serve as a way to sort people into various positions in society, based on how well they perform. So people who do well in mathematics, for example, will find that they can move into positions in society that demand those skills, whereas those deficient in math skills may find their choices more limited to manual labor or other occupations where math skills are not required. Education thus functions as a mechanism for placing people in various positions in society. In industrial societies, educational institutions can become a social problem when they don't carry out their functions as effectively as desired. The schools may not transmit useful skills to some people or they may do so inequitably—educating some students but not others. The school's failure to perform its functions may be in part a consequence of social disorganization arising from an industrial social order. Poverty or racial discrimination, for example, may limit the opportunities of some people to develop valued skills and abilities. In other cases, the educational system itself may be structured such that it fails some people. This chapter will explore some of the ways in which the educational system of the United States fails to carry out its functions effectively.

Over the past few centuries, science and technology have been important sources of social change, and many of these changes have been very beneficial for society. However, industrialization and high technology have produced other changes in society that have not been as beneficial; in fact, significant social disorga-nization has been created in the process. Some of the social disorganization associated with technological change occurs because of the tendency of **cultural lag:** *a gap between the point at which one part of the social system changes and the point at which other parts adjust to compensate for that change* (Ogburn, 1957; Volti, 2001). So, technological innovations arise and create problems before other technologies or social patterns emerge to deal with the problems. William F. Ogburn, who developed the notion of cultural lag, described an example of it in the early stages of U.S. industrialization. In the 1800s, factories were built with machinery with swiftly moving wheels and belts and other highly dangerous mechanical devices. Because industrial technology was so new and because laborers of the era had little political clout, little effort was devoted to safety in the workplace. As a consequence, many industrial accidents killed or seriously maimed workers. At the time, employers were typically not held liable for on-the-job accidents, and there were no unemployment compensation or welfare benefits. So the injury or death of workers often meant financial ruin for their families. The machinery made possible advances in production, but it also placed many people at risk of losing their ability to earn a living. In short, there was a lag between the technology of production and the social policies designed to protect people from the negative consequences of the technology. Eventually, of course, workers' compensation and employer liability were established, and the cultural lag between technology and social policy was narrowed.

The Conflict Perspective

The conflict perspective is based on the idea that society consists of different groups that struggle with one another to attain the scarce societal resources that are considered valuable. Education is one of those valued resources because, in modern societies, those with better educations tend to have more access to other valued resources such as good jobs, high incomes, and important political positions. So, educational degrees become important in the struggle over scarce resources. In this view, the inequitable distribution of educational resources is not a failing of the system but rather represents the precise way in which the system operates. Educational opportunities are more available to the affluent and powerful because that is what bene-fits these groups most, and social arrangements most typically reflect what benefits the powerful. From this perspective, schools become a social problem when important groups feel that they are not getting what they deserve from the institutions of learning. Affluent families might fight to protect the use of property taxes to fund schools because this benefits more affluent schools. The poor might fight for more remedial or after-school programs because this benefits students who may be suffering from inadequate resources in schools they have attended in the past.

Scientific information and the resulting technology are also valued resources that groups compete for. This can result in a maldistribution of technological resources where some groups have access to them but others do not. In addition, particular technologies may work to the benefit of some people but to the disadvantage of others. Technological innovations, for example, may automate the work process, but they also cause unemployment for some and alienate others in boring jobs. As another example, the Internet makes possible rapid and worldwide exchange of information, but it can also reduce the control that families can exercise over their children when the children can gain access to pornographic and other materials that the parents would prefer they not have. From the conflict perspective, then, science and technology do not necessarily benefit everyone, and in analyzing their effect, it is essential to look closely at who benefits from particular technological developments and who does not, as well as what can be done to reduce the costs. Unlike the functionalist perspective, the conflict perspective assumes that there are always winners and losers when social change occurs.

The Interactionist Perspective

Chapter 1 pointed out that an important element of the interactionist perspective is human beings' ability to use symbols and thus to attach social meanings to words, objects, events, or people. This perspective focuses on the social interaction between teacher and student in the classroom and recognizes that social expectations and social meanings are a part of that interaction and play a powerful role in what students learn and accomplish in school as well as how they feel about themselves. Students in school are subjected to constant evaluation between the ages of 5 and 18, because the purpose of schooling, in addition to transmitting skills, is to judge how well students have learned and, by implication, how competent and intelligent they have become. A great deal is at stake for students because their grades and their teachers' written reports about them become an official record—a publicly stamped label—that follows them throughout their lives. According to the interactionist perspective, this labeling can have serious consequences for students (Wilkinson and Marrett, 1985). Chapter 9 noted that labeling a person as a deviant can serve as a self-fulfilling prophecy when people begin to conform to the expectations of the labels

attached to them. Likewise, a similar process can occur in the classroom when teachers label students as bright or dull. Once students are so labeled, teachers may treat them differently, possibly giving the students who are labeled bright a little more encouragement and assistance. In addition, those labeled dull may assume that there is some truth in the label and may not try very hard. The result of both the students' and the teachers' reactions may be reinforcement of the label, or a self-fulfilling prophecy as the labelers create what they thought they were merely identifying in the first place. So, schools become a social problem when these face-to-face educational encounters produce stigmatizing results, lower students' self-esteem, and make educational success more difficult to achieve.

As symbols, science and technology have taken on both very positive and very negative meanings. On the one hand, science is viewed very favorably as the source of much that is wonderful about people's lives—automobiles, modern medicine, and computers. However, there is a theme in many cultures that views science as mysterious, dangerous, and possibly even evil. This theme is probably best expressed in the science fiction or occult literature, such as Mary Shelley's *Frankenstein* or R. L. Stevenson's *The Strange Case of Dr. Jekyll and Mr. Hyde*. These portrayals have a view that science, especially if it is unleashed, might become a raging, destructive, almost maniacal uncontrolled force. The fear is that, once unharnessed, science would do things that threaten people's values or way of life. It is more stigmatized side of science that is seen as causing social problems. So, this ambivalence toward science and technology leaves people unsure about what social expectations are appropriate in this realm. In a real sense, the meaning of science and technology in our culture is uncertain, and whether they are problems is a matter of great debate.

Problems in Education

Although education can be a route of upward social mobility for some individuals, educational institutions are organized such that they also can help perpetuate patterns of social inequality. According to the conflict perspective, powerful forces in educational institutions work toward **social reproduction,** or *passing social and economic inequalities on from one generation to the next and thus perpetuating the existing stratification system.* Just as well-to-do parents can pass their money and property on to their offspring, they also pass along their social and cultural advantages in the form of access to the education that will assist their offspring (Hurn, 1993). Figure 15.2 points to one impact of this social reproduction: the effect of

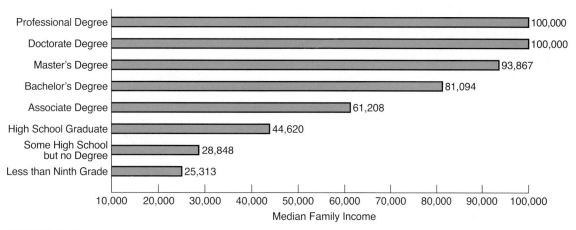

FIGURE 15.2   Median Income of Family Based on Educational Attainment of the Head of the Household, United States, 2003.

Source: U.S. Bureau of the Census, *Statistical Abstract of the United States, 2007* (Washington, DC: U.S. Government Printing Office, 2006), p. 450.

education on a person's economic position in society. The Applied Research insert describes the research that sociologists have done to document the existence and extent of inequality in the United States in access to and achievement in education. Most of the problems in education discussed in this section have to do with this issue—the tendency of the educational system to protect the advantaged while not providing opportunities for the disadvantaged—but some prob-lems, such as the effectiveness of schools and violence in schools, can also affect the advantaged.

The Credentials Race

For much of the twentieth century, there was a cre-dentials race in the United States (Collins, 1979; Dore, 1997). In 1940, less than 25 percent of adults in the United States had graduated from high school, in

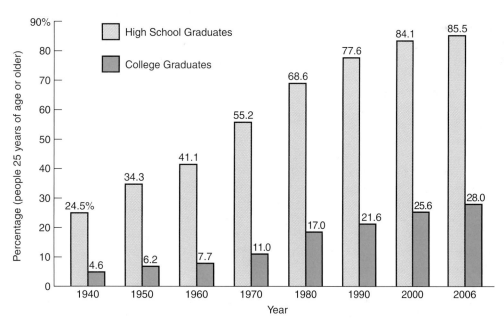

FIGURE 15.3   Percentage of Adults Who Are High School and College Graduates in the United States, 1940–2006.

Sources: U.S. Bureau of the Census, *Statistical Abstract of the United States* (Washington, DC: U.S. Government Printing Office, annual); U.S. Bureau of the Census, "Educational Attainment in the United States: 2006," *Current Population Survey, 2006 Social and Economic Supplement,* March 2007.

Evaluating the Equality of Educational Opportunities in the United States

The belief in equality in the United States rests heavily on the assumption that all people have equal access to an education. Although the doors of schools in the United States are generally open to people irrespective of social background, the chances of advancing in the educational world are powerfully affected by a person's socioeconomic status (McClendon, 1976). In 1957, sociologist William Sewell (1971) began an ambitious research project on the career plans of nine thousand high school seniors in Wisconsin. Dividing them into four socioeconomic groups, he followed their educational experiences for fourteen years. The differences among the groups were dramatic. Those whose families had the highest SES were four times more likely than those with the lowest status to attend college. They were nine times more likely to receive some graduate or professional training. In other words, the higher the educational attainment, the greater the divergence between the achievement of people at different levels in the stratification system. Furthermore, these differences were not entirely a function of ability. Among high-income students with high abilities, only 10 percent chose not to attend college, whereas 25 percent of the low-income students of similar

ability failed to go to college (Jencks et al., 1972).

These findings have been supported by all sociological research on this topic over the decades: The best predictor of the grades people get and how far they advance in their schooling is their family's socioeconomic standing. Some of these differences are undoubtedly due to economic opportunities, with low-income families less able to purchase books, computers, or special lessons and tutors and to afford college. Yet in many cases, parents and teachers fail to develop the desire for educational achievement in students of low SES; they may not expect low SES students to do well in school or go to college, and this becomes a self-fulfilling prophecy as the students themselves respond by not trying as hard as they might be capable of. In addition, low SES parents are less likely to be involved in their children's schools and education, by meeting with teachers or joining parent–teacher organizations, even though research clearly shows that parental involvement in the schools has a very positive effect on children's academic performance (Funkhouser and Gonzales, 1997). In addition, most poor children have parents with limited academic experiences who are less equipped to help their children with homework or other assignments. Finally,

children in low SES families are more likely to have health problems or nutritional inadequacies that make it more difficult for them to study and learn.

Inequalities in educational experience affect people throughout their lives, because those with better educations tend to have more desirable jobs and higher lifetime earnings (see Figure 15.2). Although this link between SES and occupational achievement still exists, recent investigations have concluded that it is weaker today than it was 40 years ago, primarily because of the wider availability of college educations to people at all levels of the socioeconomic scale (Baker and Velez, 1996). Sociological research has also documented the role that race plays in shaping educational opportunities. Going back to the Coleman Report in the 1960s, discussed in Chapter 6, research has shown that African Americans are more likely to attend schools with poor facilities, less well-trained teachers, and a motivational atmosphere that does not encourage academic achievement and aspirations to attend college. In Chapter 6, we saw that, although improvements have been made in educational accomplishments, African Americans and Hispanic Americans still lag significantly behind whites in educational achievements (see Figure 6.1 on p. 155).

comparison with 85 percent today (see Figure 15.3 on page 407). The number of college degrees conferred rose from fewer than 500,000 in 1950 to more than 1 million per year today, and the number of doctorates from 6,000 to 50,000. Functionalists argue that this "credentialing" of U.S. society reflects the higher level of skill and education needed for occupations today.

Yet, evidence exists that the minimum educational requirements for many jobs today are higher than are actually necessary to do the job. This means that only a part of the increase in educational requirements for jobs during the twentieth century can be accounted for by *actual* increases in skills and expertise needed to perform these tasks (Brown, 1995; Lowe, 2000).

Why, then, has there been such a race for higher educational credentials? Conflict theorists argue that this credentials race occurs because some groups have a vested interest in placing greater emphasis on the importance of educational degrees. For example, raising the educational threshold for particular jobs is an easy out for harried personnel managers who can use educational degrees as a simple sifting device in selecting employees. In addition, educational institutions have a vested interest in this degree inflation because it generates a greater demand for their educational services. Students may not need the degrees to *do* the job, but they need the degrees to *get* the job. Most important, however, degree inflation serves as a way of maintaining the privileges of some while controlling the aspirations of others. By elevating degree requirements for particular jobs, people who have earned the degrees, or who are in a position to obtain them, protect their own positions and those of their offspring by restricting competition. Fifty years ago, it was the affluent who were likely to have a high school diploma and thus had access to the better jobs that required a high school education. Today, college or graduate degrees represent the minimum requirement for many jobs. The less affluent and minority group members have more difficulty obtaining those degrees and thus getting the jobs that require them. Furthermore, argue conflict theorists, because the inequities result from differences in educational levels, they have legitimacy in the eyes of people who believe that educational opportunities are open to everyone. However, as the Applied Research insert documents, educational opportunities are not equally available to all in the United States.

Tracking

Another practice common in elementary and secondary schools that has important effects on students is tracking (Hallinan, 1996; Jones, Vanfossen, and Ensminger, 1995). *Tracking,* or *ability grouping,* refers to clustering people together into classes or tracks within classes that contain students of comparable abilities or students with similar educational goals (for example, academic versus nonacademic tracks). Tracking is done in some cases on the assumption that students will be better able to learn if they are in a classroom with others who have equal ability. In other cases, the tracking is based on directing students into curricular paths where it is presumed they are capable of succeeding. Decisions about tracking are based on the student's performance in class or on standardized tests, the teachers' judgments about students, and in some cases the students and their parents' choices. The danger in tracking, however, is that the track becomes a label that creates expectations on the part of both the teacher and the students regarding how well individual students are capable of performing. Teachers may tend to encourage performances that are consistent with the track a student is in, and students assume that being placed in a track indicates the performance level of which they are capable. In addition, research shows that lower-class students and minority students are considerably more likely to be placed in the lower tracks than are other students, even among students of equal abilities and performance levels (Oakes, Gamoran, and Page, 1992). This suggests that tracking decisions are made, at least in part, on the basis of stereotypes about social class and race and that racism may influence the outcome. It certainly raises troubling questions about how fair the process is. Because of these problems, some schools have discarded formalized ability grouping.

Effectiveness: Low Performance and Dropouts

Over the years, criticism of what and how well students learn in school has been almost constant. In 1986, for example, the Carnegie Forum on Education and the Economy released a report indicating that the schools were failing to prepare students adequately for work-related positions in an increasingly technological society. Performance on standardized tests, such as the Scholastic Assessment Test (SAT), has fallen substantially since the 1960s, although verbal SAT scores have been steady and math scores have risen some since 1980 (U.S. Department of Education, 2006). A study by the National Center for Improving Science Education, funded by the National Science Foundation and released in 1996, concluded that high school students in Europe and Japan take more demanding science courses than do U.S. students, and they do better in those more difficult courses than U.S. students do in the easier courses (Study finds U.S. students lag foreigners, 1996). U.S. students also do poorer on science and mathematics tests than do students in many other nations (see Figure 15.4). Most studies on this topic conclude that students in the United States display a disturbing lack of knowledge about science, geography, history, and government; many students, for example, cannot locate Greece on a map or state when Abraham Lincoln was president. Also in 1996, the National Commission on Teaching and America's Future published a report that concluded that many teachers in U.S. schools have not been adequately trained in teaching skills or in the subjects that they teach (Applebome, 1996). Some teachers have neither a college major nor a minor in the main subjects they teach.

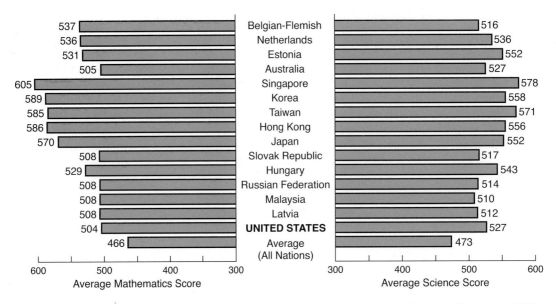

FIGURE 15.4 **Math and Science Test Scores for Eighth Graders, in Various Nations, 2003.**

Source: Patrick Gonzales et al. *Trends in International Mathematics and Science Study (TIMSS) 2003.* NCES Pub. No. 2005–005. U.S. Department of Education, National Center for Education Statistics. Washington, DC: U.S. Government Printing Office, 2004.

Yet, controversy rages over whether and in what realms U.S. schools are failing. Psychologist David Berliner and sociologist Bruce Biddle (1995) argue that much of the criticism is based on a misunderstanding of the data, or in some cases a deliberate attempt to ignore the facts in order to trash the schools. They argue, for example, that SAT scores are no longer falling, that school spending has gone up because we ask so much of the schools in terms of special education programs, and that many standardized tests, such as the SAT, are poor measures of educational quality and achievement. The schools may not be getting any better, Berliner and Biddle argue, but they probably haven't been getting any worse either.

An issue about which most researchers will agree is that, although some students attend good schools and get an excellent education, other students are definitely failed by the educational system. Students who are espe-cially likely to be failed by the schools are those from low-income families, those whose parents have low educational attainment, those from single-parent families, and those who cannot speak English well (Orfield, 2004). The result is an unacceptably large high school dropout rate in the United States, with Hispanic American students especially hurt (see Figure 15.5). The landscape of opportunities for people who drop out of school is bleak. The unemployment rate for dropouts is about twice as high as for those who graduate from high school; the unemployment rate among African Americans who have not completed high school is almost 50 percent; in addition, dropouts earn less when they do work, are more likely to commit crimes, and use more public assistance (U.S. Bureau of the Census, 2006). So, a person without a high school diploma today confronts virtually insurmountable obstacles in terms of finding social and economic opportunities.

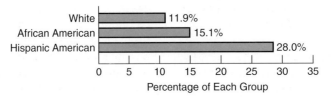

FIGURE 15.5 **High School Dropouts in the United States, Eighteen to Twenty-Four Years Old, by Race and Ethnic Origin, 2004.**

Source: U.S. Bureau of the Census, *Statistical Abstract of the United States, 2007* (Washington, DC: U.S. Government Printing Office, 2006), p. 169.

Race, Ethnicity, and Segregation

Schools in the United States tend to be highly segregated along the lines of both social class and race. Despite efforts to integrate the schools, the Civil Rights Project at Harvard's Graduate School of Education reports that schools in the United States have become substantially more segregated over the past few decades, especially for African Americans in the South and Hispanic Americans everywhere (Orfield and Lee, 2004). This situation results from a number of factors: segregated housing patterns, court decisions that have freed school districts from desegregation orders, and a public that is indifferent to the desirability of integrated schools. Another reason for this segregation is that affluent families are more likely to move in order to find a good school for their children or send them to private schools. In Chapter 6, we discussed sociological research, especially the Coleman Report, which documented the corrosive effect of racial segregation in the schools on the performance of minority students. One reaction to these findings was a program of school busing in order to achieve greater school integration. Although school busing has had some modest benefits (discussed in Chapter 6), it has been highly controversial and contributed to the flight of white families from cities with busing programs. The result has been increased residential segregation in the United States and even further separation of the races in schools.

Programs to promote school integration have been controversial not only because of the forced busing issue but also because some minority families believe the programs are inherently racist. To these families, these programs seem to be based on the assumption that African American students can do well only when whites are the majority in a school. Although this was never a conclusion drawn by Coleman and other sociologists, it seemed to be an implication of such programs. In addition, some minority families opposed school integration policies on the grounds that majority white schools are not necessarily the best environment for minority students. After all, minorities in integrated schools often have little social contact with white students and are placed in curriculum tracks heavily populated by minorities. In addition, majority white schools often don't provide support for minority culture nor teachers and school administrators of color who can serve as role models. Many minority students feel isolated and alienated in majority white schools. Given these problems, some critics argue, it might be better to take the money devoted to school integration and busing and spend it to improve schools with large minority populations.

A racially and ethnically diverse student body confronts schools in the United States with problems other than segregation: Millions of schoolchildren either speak little English, or English is their second language and is often not spoken at home. Poor English competency can compromise the ability of these students to learn in school and achieve the good grades that are essential to success later in life. To assist some of these students, programs of **bilingual education** have been established: *Students are taught in both English and their native language until their English competency is sufficient to become the sole language of instruction* (Zehr, 2004).

Bilingual education has been intensely controversial. Supporters argue that it is essential for students who come into U.S. schools with weak or nonexistent English skills; without some help, these students will fall irretrievably behind, and their future opportunities will be compromised. These supporters present data showing that students in bilingual programs perform better in school and exhibit higher self-esteem than similar students without access to the programs. Opponents of bilingual education argue that it is expensive, that it inhibits students from developing adequate English competency, and that it actually makes it more difficult for students to achieve in an educational and work environment where most people use English. In fact, some opponents say, bilingual education often turns into a cultural preservation program; transition to English never does occur and instruction in the native language becomes a vehicle for promoting identification with the native culture.

So, bilingual education remains controversial and its future uncertain. Voters in California in 1998 dumped their bilingual program in favor of a rapid immersion program where students are expected to quickly learn enough English to get by in school and then be instructed solely in English. Other states still support their bilingual programs.

Violence in the Schools

In recent years, some highly publicized acts of violence in schools have produced outrage among the public. In Oregon, a student brought multiple guns to school and opened fire in a cafeteria; in Colorado, two students entered their high school with automatic weapons and shot many of their fellow students before killing themselves. In these and other tragic events, many students were killed and wounded. As appalling and public as these events were, they represent only a small part of the problem of violence in the schools. For most students, the threat of violence may be less lethal, but it is a daily one and can cast a pall over the schools, which can destroy the educational environment. The U.S. Department of Education (2006) has documented that over half of all U.S. public schools experienced at least one episode of crime during the school year that was reported to the police and 10 percent had at least one serious violent crime incident. Twenty percent of the schools reported six or more crimes during the school year. Physical attacks were common, with 190,000 incidents without a weapon being reported and 11,000 incidents with a weapon. A quarter of U.S. high schools now have metal detectors to search for guns. Crime and violence are more serious problems in large schools, in urban schools, and in schools with a large minority population.

Certainly some of the crime and violence in schools is a product of youthful exuberance and routine conflicts as adolescents deal with the difficulties of biological and social maturation. But the schools also reflect the larger society, and, as other chapters in this book have documented, U.S. society experiences high levels of crime, drugs, and gun possession. It is inevitable that some of these social ills spill over into the schools. The illegal drug trade promotes some degree of violence, and the widespread availability of guns means that youths can too easily find them at home or steal them in the streets.

Problems of Science and Technology

The idea of technology as potentially dangerous and threatening is not new. Classical Greek mythology expressed some ambivalence toward technology: Prometheus stole fire from Olympus in defiance of the gods, and as punishment he was chained to a rock where an eagle tore at his body for eternity; Icarus tried to fly with wings made of wax and feathers, and he paid for such presumption with his life. In nineteenth-century England, rioting workers, called Luddites after the name of one of their leaders, smashed machines in factories in the futile belief that this would prevent the dislocations and unemployment that were plaguing England as it industrialized. Even in the United States today, there is, at best, equivocal support for science and technology. In a survey in the year 2004, people in the United States were asked how much confidence they had in the scientific community, and considerably less than one-half of those responding said they had a great deal of confidence in it (see Figure 15.6).

Fear of science and technology, then, can probably be found wherever technology shapes people's lives. Yet many feel that the potential dangers of technology

As violence has pervaded schools in the United States, security issues have become a routine part of the school landscape for many youngsters.

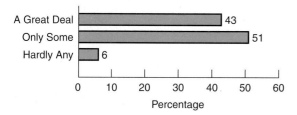

FIGURE 15.6 **People's Degree of Confidence in the Scientific Community in the United States, 2004.**

Sources: James Allen Davis and Tom W. Smith, *General Social Surveys, 1972–2004*. Chicago: National Opinion Research Center (producer), Storrs, CT; The Roper Center for Public Opinion Research, University of Connecticut (distributor); www.icpsr.umich.edu/GSS.

today are quantitatively greater than and possibly qualitatively different from what they were in the past. This section will review some of the major problems that concern people today regarding scientific and technological developments.

Unemployment

For many, the fundamental fear of technology is that machines will replace people in the workplace. Chapter 2 showed that the labor force in the United States has changed since the early twentieth century. Early in that century, as agricultural employment dwindled, the surplus labor was taken over by mining, manufacturing, transportation, and services. More recently, with advances in technology, employment in areas such as mining and manufacturing has stopped growing and in some cases has begun to decline, and workers have shifted into the service sector. Yet technology has also made the service sector more efficient and less labor intensive. So there may be fewer or no economic sectors to absorb the surplus labor of the future. As robots replace factory workers, word processors replace secretaries and typists, and computer-assisted instruction replaces teachers, where will all of these people find work? We saw in Chapter 2 that unemployment, underemployment, and temporary or contract work have become a more widespread problem today than they were in earlier decades and that this is an especially serious problem among those who are least able to acquire work skills or advance their education: the poor, minorities, the young, and women.

What some people fear, then, is that unemployment, underemployment, and temporary work are becoming more serious problems, in part, because machines are taking the place of people (Volti, 2001). Not everyone agrees with this argument. Supporters of technological development argue that technology may create dislocations for some workers, who may have to

move to a new city or state to find a job, but that it does not increase overall unemployment. Although technology ends some jobs, it also creates new ones.

The pessimists' rejoinder is that the jobs made available by the new technology are often worse than the jobs eliminated. Many jobs in the service sector, for example, are low paying, such as working in a fast-food restaurant or in an amusement park. By the beginning of the twenty-first century, more workers were stuck with low-paying jobs than had been the case decades earlier (Mishel, Bernstein, and Schmitt, 2001; Rank, 2004).

Alienation

Jobs in automated work settings are often boring, repetitive, and unfulfilling. Employees have little control over the pace of their work, what they produce, or what happens to it once it is produced. This type of work organization may be efficient and profitable for employers, but it can result in considerable discontent among employees. One consequence of working in such settings is **alienation,** *a feeling that one is powerless to control one's surroundings and that what one does has little meaning or purpose* (Vallas, 1988).

Alienation is epidemic in some occupations, especially among unskilled blue-collar workers. Yet even among white-collar workers, less than half would stay in the same occupation if they had the opportunity to change, and job dissatisfaction and alienation are common (Burke, 1999; Shin, 2001). African Americans and people with less education are likely to experience greater declines in job satisfaction, but people in professional and managerial occupations are also affected. Feeling the effects of automation, workers are likely to view themselves as mere cogs in the bureaucratic machinery.

Loss of Control

Some people fear that modern technology has become so unbelievably complex that it can take on a life of its own (Mazur, 1993). When this happens, the outcome may actually work counter to the interests and goals of those people the technology is supposed to benefit. A classic portrayal of this is the movie *2001: A Space Odyssey,* in which a highly sophisticated computer named HAL runs virtually all the functions of a spaceship on a long voyage. When the human crew attempts to take over from the computer, HAL fights against and even kills some of the crew in the process. Although this is an extreme portrayal, it illustrates the notion of an "autonomous technology" that gets away from people's control, and the way this can happen is quite complex.

There is little question that people become highly dependent on technology. This was true for the hunters and gatherers who used stone clubs to slay animals, and it is true for modern writers who use computers to make a living. But modern technology places us in a far more complex web of technological dependence in which machines do many more things for us, and our lives would be profoundly changed without them. Without computers, for example, we would be without such instruments for medical diagnoses as CAT scanners, magnetic resonance imaging, and many others. Yet computers can have very negative consequences. People have been arrested because a computer misidentified them as a suspect in a crime; others have been unable to obtain credit because a computer record indicated, based on weak or false information, that they were poor credit risks.

Yet we are not really free to remove computers from some parts of our lives and not from other parts. Once the technology is introduced and people become dependent on it, there are social forces that cause it to grow as if it had a life of its own. One of these forces is the tendency by various interest groups to use technology to their own benefit. Technological developments that are detrimental to some may be quite beneficial to others. Nuclear power, for example, could be a boon to the power companies because it offers a way to generate power very inexpensively. At the same time, it works to the detriment of those who live in communities where nuclear waste dump sites are established. So with a large array of interest groups with competing goals and values, there are likely to be many groups who favor the development of a given technology even though it has a negative impact on other groups. This explains why, once a technology exists, there is strong pressure to use it and develop it further.

Another element contributing to the complexity of technology in our lives is that responsibility for decisions about the role of technology tends to be very diffuse. This means that individuals have little control over the impact new technologies will have on them personally. Computers, for example, first came on the scene because some large corporations and some scientists believed that these machines would increase efficiency and productivity. Over time and as the technology became more accessible, computers were introduced into other realms: Someone saw the potential for putting police records on the computer, and others recognized that credit check companies could operate more efficiently with computers. Recently, an entrepreneur opened a computerized service for landlords that would enable them to learn whether prospective renters might be a "problem" because they had once sued a landlord or missed a rent payment.

Computers can also have a detrimental effect on the workplace by becoming another mechanism through which supervisors can control and regulate the activities of those under them (Parenti, 2004). More and more employees are being subjected to "computer-assisted productivity measurement." The activities of reservations clerks and customer service agents, for example, can be tracked with call-recording software that saves a complete record of everything the employee does: a voice recording of the interaction with the customer, every computer screen viewed, every mouse click made. So, the software produces a permanent record of how long the employee spent on each call, what transpired during the call, how much time was spent between calls doing paperwork, and how long they are away during breaks. At one airline, data-entry clerks are expected to make 9,000 to 16,000 strokes on their computer keyboard per hour. The three fastest workers are used to set the pace, and all others are expected to achieve at least 75 percent of that speed. All of this can be logged continuously by computers, and those who fall short can be disciplined or dismissed. Such electronic monitoring is not always disliked by employees, but it can be used to intimidate workers when supervisors manipulate the computer system to threaten people's jobs.

Who is responsible for extending computers into these many realms? Who has control over this burgeoning technology? The autonomous technology viewpoint is that the responsibility is so diffuse that there is, in fact, little control over it.

Loss of Privacy

Automatic systems are now in operation to collect bridge and highway tolls. With them, a driver need not stop at a tollbooth, because a computer reads an electronic tag mounted on the car or a radio signal sent from a unit installed in the car. The toll is then automatically deducted from a preestablished account. Plans call for a national system with standardized tags or radio signals. Some trucking and car rental companies have equipped their vehicles with signals that can be read continuously by global positioning satellites (GPS), providing a minute-by-minute record of where their vehicles are. Such computerized systems create a permanent record of your travels, showing everywhere you go, when, and for how long. Likewise, credit card purchases establish a computer trail of a person's whereabouts, travels, and purchases—a permanent record of a person's lifestyle accessible to others for whatever purpose. This information could be used by insurance companies in setting insurance rates (showing that you drive your car more than you claim or that you drove to high-crime areas that call for higher insurance rates), or they could be used in divorce settlements or workers' compensation claims.

Modern technology opens the door for intrusions into people's lives in massive ways (Rosen, 2004). With computers and telecommunications technology, it is possible to store vast amounts of information about people, access the information very quickly, and send the information anywhere on the globe almost instantaneously. Powerful information institutions, such as medical records bureaus and credit reporting companies, have emerged to gather this data wherever they can and then sell this information to those willing to pay for it. The potential for abuse is tremendous (Rothfeder, 1992). People often must spend considerable time and resources trying to identify and correct inaccurate information that is causing problems for them. Many times, the inaccuracies cannot be corrected or people are not even aware of the inaccuracies that are causing problems for them. It is impossible to know how many insurance applications are denied or jobs not gotten because of inaccurate information in a computer database. Another problem is that these companies collect and synthesize vast amounts of very intimate information about people with little federal regulation of their activities, and significant decisions are made about people's lives based on this information.

So millions of people in the United States are short-changed or otherwise abused—often without realizing it—by large bureaucracies acting on inaccurate information bought from computerized data banks. Computer records, such as the landlord service just mentioned, make it difficult for people to hide or put behind them things that have occurred in their lives. In addition, the USA PATRIOT Act of 2001, a direct response to the September 11, 2001, terror attacks, makes it possible for the government to intrude on people's privacy in ways that were more difficult or impossible before (Rosen, 2004). It empowers the government to search people's homes without notifying the homeowner and to have access to people's personal medical, business, library, and other records. As intrusive as this is, it is also clear that many Americans are willing to give up some of their privacy in the interests of feeling they have achieved more security.

An increasing number of businesses and government bureaus are requiring that people take lie-detector tests to gain employment and to remain employed. Employers require this for security or to protect against theft. But for the employee or prospective employee, it means that even our very thoughts are less private. Those little lies that we might tell to put ourselves in the best possible light can be detected by the machine. In professional sports, the military, and some industries, there are mandatory urine checks to detect the use of drugs. The goal, of course, is a laudable one—to control the use of drugs on the job—but the impact is again an assault on a person's privacy and sense of personal integrity.

The technological developments of the past 50 years may have only scratched the surface of what is possible in terms of limitations on privacy. It may not be long before it will be possible to keep permanent records of everyone's activities so that our social lives, political beliefs, leisure pursuits, and idiosyncrasies are a matter of record available to anyone having access to this information. Every mistake, minor or major, that you make during your life will be recorded and you might be accountable for it throughout your life.

Should We Play God? The Case of Genetic Engineering

Scientific developments of the past century have produced some truly amazing things, but some critics have suggested that we are treading in some areas that we should not, areas that could produce disastrous consequences if matters get out of hand. One such area is **biotechnology:** *the use of organisms or parts of organisms to make products or carry out tasks* (Rifkin, 1998).

Biotechnology is based on a very important discovery: the identification in 1953 of the nature of deoxyribonucleic acid, or DNA, as the basic genetic material that is found in each cell and contains the "blueprint" for the entire organism. DNA has been mapped and catalogued with great precision. By manipulating DNA, scientists have been able to create organisms that perform new tasks or that produce substances they would not normally produce. This is called **genetic engineering,** or *manipulating the genes of organisms to alter the organisms' characteristics in ways that would not have occurred naturally.* One way of doing this is **recombinant DNA** or **gene splicing** in which *some DNA from one organism is spliced into the genetic material of another organism to produce some new characteristics in the host or even a novel form of life.* Gene splicing has been used, for example, to produce large quantities of insulin and interferon, used in the treatment of diabetes and cancer, respectively. This is done by introducing human genes that govern the natural production of insulin or interferon into a bacterium that is then induced by this new genetic material to produce insulin or interferon. Insulin and interferon are expensive to produce by conventional means, and their genetically engineered counterparts play an important role in medicine. In addition to medicine, biotechnology is also expected to have an impact on such areas as agriculture, forestry, energy, and chemical feedstocks.

What problems do such advances create? One problem relates to potentially unpredictable consequences of genetic engineering (Fukuyama, 2002; National Research Council, 2004). Releasing genetically modified organisms into the environment could create unforeseen and very hazardous consequences.

After all, genetic modifications in nature occur very slowly over many thousands of generations of a species. With such a time span, existing flora and fauna are able to adapt gradually to new developments. Genetic engineering, however, enables us to make substantial genetic changes in a very short period. And, unlike many other forms of environmental pollution, biological pollutants reproduce themselves and are much more difficult to remove from the ecosystem. In fact, some scientists have called for a halt to gene splicing experiments because of such fears. Despite these concerns, the National Academy of Sciences has recommended that research on genetically manipulated materials should proceed, including the release of some such products into the environment, and that each biotechnology product should be closely assessed to detect any negative consequences that might occur. Lively debate over this policy continues, with some scientists claiming that such biotechnology advances are but an extension of practices, such as animal breeding, that have gone on for thousands of years whereas other scientists believe we are moving too rapidly into some unknown territory. Because the commercial application of this technology is likely to be worth billions of dollars in profits to corporations around the world, there is strong pressure to push ahead with the technology.

Other problems with biotechnology crop up when consideration is given to applying the technology to human beings (Fukuyama, 2002; McKibben, 2003). Today, parents can learn before birth whether their offspring will have certain genetic defects. This gives them the option of having an abortion rather than giving birth to children with health problems. In the future, parents may be able to alter their own genetic traits or in other ways determine the genetic characteristics of their children. Scientists have already succeeded in making clones, or multiple genetic replicas of a parent organism. It may be only a matter of time before cloning humans is possible. These technologies offer people the capability to shape their characteristics in ways never before possible. Such advances not only offer the opportunity to stamp out certain diseases, they also open the door to eliminating characteristics deemed socially undesirable by those in positions of power.

The Nazis engaged in some notorious experiments during World War II in efforts to create a "master race." Similarly, in recent years, suggestions have been made along the same lines in the United States. William Shockley, an engineer who became interested in genetic

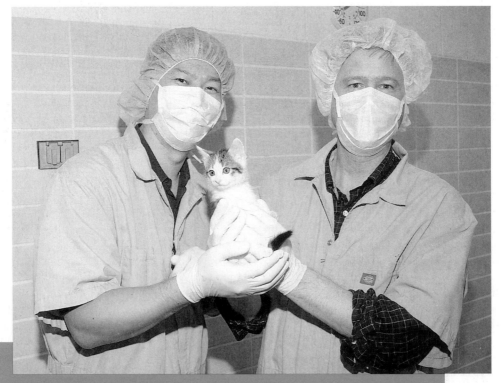

Scientists have now produced a number of animals through cloning, including this cat. The availability of this technology produces strong pressures to also clone human beings, which raises serious moral and social policy considerations.

engineering, has argued forcefully that people of low intelligence constitute a "dysgenic threat" to society because they reduce the average intelligence of society (Shockley, 1980). His solution is to encourage people with low intelligence—or anyone with genetic characteristics deemed detrimental to society—to be sterilized.

Efforts along these lines in the United States today are quite sporadic and disorganized, and most people are opposed to cloning human beings: Eighty-seven percent of those surveyed in 2005 said that cloning of human beings was morally wrong (Gallup Poll, 2007a). However, there is no reason to believe that some organization or government of the future might not institute such measures in an organized and widespread fashion. A government might pass legislation making it illegal for people with certain characteristics to have children. Or genetic engineering might be used to enhance certain human characteristics and downplay others. Or, even if left to the marketplace, well-to-do parents could afford the genetic engineering that would enhance desired qualities in their children. One scenario on these issues is that it could produce a two-class society consisting of the "GenRich" (people whose parents can afford the genetic engineering to enhance desired or valuable characteristics) and the "Naturals" (people who must depend on the old-fashioned, and much more haphazard and random, mechanism for gaining genetic material) (Silver, 1997). It might even become fashionable to use genetic engineering to enhance aggressiveness or passivity, strength or frailty, obesity or lithesomeness—whatever characteristics were fashionable at a given time. Over long periods of time, such genetic differences that originally arose from class differences may produce the emergence of distinct species, with the GenRich viewing the Naturals in much the same way that humans now view chimpanzees.

The point is that the genetic traits of the human race have been determined thus far by impersonal evolutionary forces that operate over eons and are largely unaffected by cultural values, religious beliefs, or political or economic ideology. Biotechnology may make it possible to change all of this in the near future. It might be possible to create people with certain characteristics or tailor people to certain jobs. Some people might be gene spliced for ferocity and made into soldiers, whereas others would be gene spliced to show little initiative and curiosity and made into assembly-line workers. If there were some objective and sure way of determining which characteristics are beneficial to society, then biotechnological capabilities might not be so fearsome. But there is no single set of characteristics that benefits society. And, as the conflict perspective makes us aware, not all groups benefit from the same social practices and policies. Genetic engineering that benefits one group may well work to the disadvantage of others. Biotechnology, then, could become a tool for the more powerful groups in society to exercise domination over the less powerful.

With biotechnology, human beings are beginning to tinker with the very foundations of life.

> It is now a matter of a handful of years before biologists will be able to irreversibly change the evolutionary wisdom of billions of years with the creation of new plants, new animals, and new forms of human and posthuman beings. (Howard and Rifkin, 1977:8)

Should we play "god"? We may be doing it to an extent already, as the Policy Issues insert (pp. 418–419) illustrates. When considering this, the word *hubris* comes to mind, deriving from the Greek word meaning "insolence." In current usage, *hubris* means excessive self-confidence or arrogance. The Greeks used it to mean the presumption of human beings that they could act like the gods. The fear of some is that scientists today may be showing hubris by moving into biotechnological realms that might be best left alone. The Greeks used the term *nemesis* to refer to the divine punishment visited upon humans who had presumed to invade the realms reserved for the gods. Critics of biotechnology fear that we'll confront a nemesis in some as yet unknown form if we invade the biotechnological frontier without great patience and caution.

Future Prospects

Reforms and Trends in Education

Educators and laypeople alike seem to be constantly tinkering with the U.S. educational system, and there are many ideas for reforms to make it more effective. This section explores the major innovations, with an eye on evidence regarding their effectiveness. The International Perspectives insert (pp. 420–421) makes some comparisons between schools in the United States and those in some other industrial societies.

PARENTAL CHOICE AND CHARTER SCHOOLS Some educators and politicians have suggested that education is like any other consumer market and that schools should compete for students in the same way that other businesses compete for customers—in free and open competition. If schools had to attract students by convincing them and their parents that they had the best education to offer, then the schools would be motivated to provide the best product: superior teachers, excellent resources, and solid programs. If schools have a mediocre curriculum or lackluster faculty, their enrollments would decline, and they would either close their doors or

Biotechnology Raises the Issue: Whose Life Is It, Anyway?

With recombinant DNA techniques, it is now possible for human beings to *create* life forms—new species or variants on old species—that do not occur in nature. DuPont did this in 1988 when it produced a mouse, called "oncomouse," that was genetically engineered to be unusually susceptible to cancer. The year before, the Patent and Trademark Office (PTO) of the United States government said that it would henceforth consider patenting all forms of life on the earth, including nonnaturally occurring, nonhuman multicellular living organisms. DuPont received the patent to oncomouse in 1988 (Rifkin, 1998).

To explore the implications of these developments, consider the legal ramifications of patents. When the government grants a patent over some thing, product, or process, those holding the patent have the exclusive right to make, use, license, or sell it. In other words, the patent holder legally "owns" the commodity, at least for a period of time, and others cannot use it without permission. When oncomouse was patented, DuPont became the owner of that species, that particular life form.

The PTO ruling has generated a firestorm of controversy that raises some practical and very fundamental philosophical issues. One observer of technological trends, Jeremy Rifkin, president of the Foundation on Economic Trends, sees the ruling as symbolic of a profound transition in social and economic organization:

> In economic terms, the Patent Office decision signals the beginning of a long-term transition out of the age of fossil fuels and petrochemicals and into the age of biological resources. . . . The Patent Office decision provides the necessary government guarantee that the raw materials of the biotechnology age—that is, all living things on the planet—can now be exploited for commercial gain by chemical, pharmaceutical, and biotechnology companies. (Rifkin, 1987:2)

Rifkin believes that corporations will now rush to patent as many life forms as they can. The struggle among corporate giants will be to control the planet's gene pool, so to speak, patenting everything that lives and breathes. Requests have already been made for patents for genes found in the human brain and for women who are genetically engineered to produce useful human proteins in their mammary glands (Kimbrell, 1993). Because large and powerful corporations have the resources to patent life forms, this affords them yet another mechanism to concentrate power in their own hands. Corporations have gained patent control over newly developed agricultural seeds and plants, and they have requested patent protection for hundreds of

improve. This reform is sometimes called *parental choice;* private schools in the United States already operate in such an environment. One way of implementing choice in the public schools would be to permit students to attend any school they wish, whether in their district or elsewhere in the state, and many states now allow this to occur. In some cases, schools offer special programs in particular areas, such as computer applications or performing arts, in order to attract students.

A recent variation on the choice issue is the charter schools that have been established in a number of states (U.S. Department of Education, 2004a). Charter schools are basically schools that operate autonomously with a charter directly from the state instead of being under local school district control. They receive state funding but are free from many school district rules and have more freedom than mainstream schools in budgeting, hiring, and curriculum decisions. Charter schools have been set up with diverse goals: experiential learning, team teaching, and online distance learning using the Internet, to name a few. There are over 1600 charter schools in 32 states.

Some critics have proposed extending the idea of choice to all of education by having the government give parents a voucher worth enough to pay for a child's education at any public school. Parents would then send their child to the school of their choice, paying for it with the voucher money. Some supporters of voucher plans even propose that parents be able to use the vouchers at private religious schools as partial payment of their tuition. Milwaukee schools have experimented with a voucher plan that allows some inner-city youth to spend state money to attend private or religious schools chosen by their parents. However, it is not clear yet whether this violates the constitutional separation of church and state.

There is both strong support for and opposition to choice, charter schools, and vouchers (Astin, 1992; Smith and Meier, 1995). Proponents argue that these educational innovations offer students more choices, and the competition among schools will enhance the quality. In addition, charter schools encourage parents to become active in their children's school and are more responsive to the needs of the community. Critics

genetically engineered animals. Of course, humans have owned animals since animals were first domesticated many thousands of years ago. The difference today with DuPont's ownership of oncomouse is that the corporation has exclusive ownership rights over not just this particular mouse but any mouse produced anywhere with the same genetic characteristics. In the past, anyone could purchase cows, pigs, or chickens if they had the financial resources to do so. In the future, such ownership may be limited to the patent holder when the cow, pig, or chicken has been genetically engineered with unique characteristics.

There are also some more fundamental, philosophical issues regarding the nature and meaning of life on the earth. In its ruling, the PTO argued that life could be considered a "manufacture or composition of matter." When biotechnology creates a new life form by implanting a foreign gene into an animal's genetic code, the resulting animal is merely a human invention—no different than a toaster, a golf ball, or a tie tack, according to the Patent Office ruling. The danger, some argue, is that it promotes a *materialist* conception of life: the notion that life consists only of a particular arrangement of physical matter, with no spiritual or transcendent significance (Rifkin, 1998). Of course, many people—both religious and nonreligious—believe that life is more than an arrangement of atoms and molecules; that life involves a

measure of dignity, respect, and maybe even awe. Yet the Patent Office has ruled that life is simply a "composition of matter." As a result, the line between animate life and inanimate matter has become considerably weaker. This suggests that the fundamental building blocks of life—possibly life itself—could eventually come to be seen as belonging not to impersonal nature, not to humankind in general or to supernatural spirits, but to corporate patent holders.

If animal life is merely materialist, then what about human life? Is life merely an economic commodity that can be bought and sold in the marketplace? According to the PTO, human genetic traits, if implanted in the genes of another life form, are patentable (a "composition of matter"). However, constitutional safeguards protect humans from being patented. But, in a time when some patented animals are carrying human genetic materials, is the line between humans and other animals as clear as it once was? The PTO has ruled that human embryos and fetuses are patentable, as are genetically engineered human cells and genes. If a scientist were to change the genetic structure of a human being, might some future Patent Office ruling make it possible to put a patent on that "composition of matter"? We cannot currently answer many of these questions, but what is clear is that the technology is speeding us toward a point at which we may have to come up with an answer.

of these innovations, however, argue that they may promote more segregation and divisiveness because some parents, both white and nonwhite, would likely choose their children's school on the basis of its racial or ethnic composition. A second criticism is that parents may not always be in the best position to assess the quality of schools. As in other arenas of open competition, desperate schools might sometimes resort to exaggeration, trickery, or downright fraud in their efforts to attract students, and the educations of some children would likely suffer. A third criticism is that some families would be forced to use schools near their homes, especially the poor without access to transportation. These schools would have meager resources and be poorly run because they could not attract students from other communities, but they would survive by getting enough students from poor families in the neighborhood to keep their doors open.

Research with which to assess the performance of charter schools is now beginning to accumulate, and it does not support the hopes of the proponents of charter schools (Frankenberg and Lee, 2003; Renzulli and

Evans, 2005; Rimer, 2003). Charter schools tend to rely on a much younger, less-experienced faculty that is considerably less likely to have a teaching credential and is less well paid than faculty in public schools. And, this is especially true in schools with low-income and minority students. In addition, charter schools tend to be highly segregated—much more so than public schools. As for student achievement, studies are now accumulating that show consistently that charter school students do not perform better academically than do public school students, and by many measures they do worse. In addition, these findings have been supported even when comparing students of similar races and socioeconomic backgrounds (Braun, Jenkins, and Grigg, 2006; Nelson, Rosenberg, and Van Meter, 2004; U.S. Department of Education, 2004a). As for vouchers, research doesn't find much difference in academic performance between students who use vouchers to attend private schools and equivalent students who remain in public schools (Dillon, 2007; Metcalf et al., 2002). So, charter schools and vouchers, to this point, do not appear to be a panacea for the problems found in public

Education in Other Societies

All advanced industrial societies have systems of formal education that look similar in many ways to schools in the United States, but the differences can also be instructive (Brint, 1998; Feinberg, 1993). One way in which school systems vary is in terms of the centrality of the planning and decision making. In France, Sweden, and Japan, for example, the central government, through ministries of education, controls educational policy, curriculum design, and even textbook selection. Such education ministries also determine personnel policies, ensuring that teachers with equivalent training are available to all students. Centralized systems generally spend the same amount of money on students, no matter where their school is. The United States, on the other hand, has a very decentralized educational system where state and local school boards make most decisions. Decentralization provides parents with more control over the schools their children attend, and decentralized schools are more responsive to the needs of the community in which they are located. However, decentralized school systems also tend to have greater disparities in the resources available to students and in levels of achievement from one school to another. In some cases, central-city schools may spend less than half the money spent in affluent suburbs on each student.

Another way in which schools vary is in terms of how open the school system is, especially at the high school level, to allowing large numbers of students to follow an academic curriculum and try for college. The United States has one of the most open systems in this regard, offering academic training to most students and sending a larger number of students to college than in most industrial nations. In Germany, on the other hand, students are divided into academic and vocational tracks at an early age, and by high school as many as half of students may be in vocational apprenticeship programs. In Germany, only half as many people graduate from college as in the United States. The German educational system also devotes many more resources to apprenticeships for students, including a system where many students spend part of their time working in an apprenticeship learning a trade and part of their time in school. This has provided for a much stronger link between vocational training and the labor market and has produced students with higher levels of vocational skills that are needed by employers. By contrast, many

---

schools. This lack of impact probably reflects the fact that many of the factors that influence school performance (socioeconomic status, family environment, and so on) are not changed just because a student attends a charter school or a private school through vouchers.

BACK TO BASICS Social science research shows that students in Roman Catholic schools perform better than children in public schools, even when racial and social class differences between the schools are taken into account (Bryk, Lee, and Holland, 1993; Coleman, Hoffer, and Kilgore, 1982). One reason for this is that Catholic schools place more emphasis on a strong core curriculum and require students to take more academically demanding course work. Thus, students in Catholic schools take more academic basics, such as science, math, and history, and fewer nonacademic courses, such as auto mechanics or physical education. Another reason for the better performance in Catholic schools is that they have more effective discipline, with more emphasis on obedience and respect for authority. This emphasis creates a climate that enables teachers to do their job with less disruption or fear of danger and encourages students to learn.

Many educational reformers and parents have pushed for such a back-to-basics approach, with an emphasis on the traditional core curriculum and a return to strong discipline. Many schools have adopted some of these changes, reducing elective courses, having more required courses, and in some cases establishing strict dress codes with punishments for violation. Some states have established standardized examinations that students must pass before receiving a high school diploma.

EARLY CHILDHOOD INTERVENTIONS Virtually all criticism of education in the United States recommends devoting more resources to the early educational experiences of young children, especially low-income children, to create a developmental foundation that will support later learning and achievement. Since the Coleman Report in the 1960s, research has documented that some children come to school educationally handicapped because their

U.S. high school students take academic courses in high school even though they will not go to college upon graduation, but rather into a line of work where vocational skills could be useful. Although some U.S. high schools have academic and vocational tracks, they are much less rigid and more fluid than in the German school system. One consequence of this is that students in the German system are forced to consider career decisions while in high school because they have to choose between the academic track and a number of career tracks. In the United States, high school students can put that decision off until after high school graduation and then choose between college, a vocational track at a community college, or work.

A third way in which school systems differ is in the use of exams to filter who makes the transition into high school or into college. In Japan, for example, students take a high school entrance examination during their last year in junior high school. Performance on this exam is the key determinant of entrance into high school. Students can take the exam for any public, academic high school in their district, but if they flunk the exam, they will probably have to attend a lower-prestige private school or public, vocational high school. The high school entrance exam is so important to Japanese teenagers that a whole industry of private tutors, "cram schools," and magazines and materials has emerged to help them choose the right school and pass the exam. Entrance into the government-run national universities and higher-prestige private universities is also determined almost entirely by an entrance examination. Students are allowed to take the exam for only two universities during a given year. Because of the stakes involved in the examinations at the end of junior high and high school, Japanese students tend to be very serious and to study much harder than do students in the United States. Junior high and high school curricula in Japan are also more advanced in science, mathematics, and foreign languages. In some areas, Japanese high school graduates probably have the same knowledge level as college graduates in the United States.

A final difference among school systems is how hard they push their students. Japanese students attend school on Saturday, and in nations as varied as Japan, Germany, England, Scotland, France, and Israel, students are required to attend school on more days of the year than are students in the United States—40 days more per year in Japan!

home environment does not provide them with the support and assistance that would make learning more effective. Early childhood educational interventions can overcome many of these handicaps (Karoly et al., 1998). One such program, discussed in Chapter 5, is Head Start, a preschool program to help poor children prepare for school. Head Start children are taught reading and language skills that most preschool children learn at home from their parents. Research over the years has provided strong evidence that Head Start gives poor children some significant advantages. Head Start children, when compared to other poor children, are less likely to be assigned to special education classes or to be kept back a grade in school, and they do better on mathematics achievement tests and show more improvement in IQ scores. Head Start children are also less likely to repeat a grade, get in trouble with the law, or become teenage mothers. In addition, they have a better family life and a more positive self-concept. Finally, as young adults, Head Start children are more likely to go to college and hold a steady skilled job.

With benefits like these, Head Start children should be better equipped to support themselves and their family as adults. Many educational reformers argue that the benefits of extending such compensatory educational programs to all low-income children would be enormous and well worth the expense.

PRIVATIZATION AND HOME SCHOOLING Dissatisfaction with education in the United States, especially public education, has led to two important trends that have grown in prominence in the last two decades. Each, in its own way, represents a rejection of public education. One trend is an effort to privatize education—hire private corporations to run public schools. The primary motivation behind this trend has been the poor performance of some schools. Private education companies have argued that private, competitive companies, confronting the rigors of the marketplace, will be motivated to provide better education for the students in their schools and do it less expensively than the state can. If the private companies don't

This Mississippi family is home schooling their children. Home schooling has grown in the United States in part because of a dissatisfaction with traditional public education, which is seen by some as ineffective and by others as promoting values that conflict with the values that parents wish to expose their children to.

succeed at this, states will stop contracting with the companies to provide educational services.

Now, private education has been around for some time, in the form of private or religious schools where parents pay the tuition of their children. However, this new trend retains the public school system and the government's responsibility to provide education for all, but it achieves this by contracting out to private companies to provide the educational services. Does it work? Research done to this point does not provide any evidence that these private companies do better at educating children than do traditional public schools (U.S. General Accounting Office, 2002). They also don't seem to do worse. Opponents of such privatization argue that education of the young is a moral obligation of society, working through government, and that it should not be put into the hands of a private company. In addition, opponents argue that the rigors of the marketplace will inevitably tempt some of the private companies to cut corners in order to enhance profits—to the detriment of the children. For example, there are some cases where privately run schools have discouraged the enrollment of disadvantaged and disabled students, presumably because they were too expensive to educate.

The second educational trend is home schooling, which has also grown, in part, as a rejection of traditional public education (Lines, 2000; Wichers, 2001). As many as 2 million children are home schooled each year, possibly 4 percent of all school-age children. Some children are taught at home for only a few years, whereas others may go through high school being taught at home. Some school systems provide supports for home-schooled children, such as letting them participate in athletics or other school programs that would not be available to the children at home. Parents' motivations for home schooling their children are varied: to provide what they believe is a more rigorous education; to provide moral, ethical, or religious training that they see as lacking in the public schools; to provide a safe place free of drugs or violence; or to provide a racial, ethnic, or cultural identity for their children that is lacking in the schools.

Modern technology has assisted the growth of the home-schooling movement. Through computer software and the Internet, parents can now gain access to educational materials and programs that greatly expand the educational activities that parents can provide in the home. And research evidence to this point suggests that home schooling does a pretty good job of educating children. Most research shows that home-schooled students do at least as well, academically and in college, as students who go to traditional public schools. Both of these trends—privatization and home schooling—are likely to be around for some time and need to be assessed with further research to see how they contribute to alleviating some of the problems of education in the United States.

SCHOOL INTEGRATION In part because of the Coleman Report's conclusions about the negative effect of school segregation on student performance, efforts at school integration, sometimes by busing students from one school to another, have been made since the 1960s. Has school integration worked? As reviewed in Chapter 6, overall, integration has probably made modest improvements in school achievement by African American students, especially when students are integrated in the early grades. The reason that the impact has not been more uniformly positive is because so many other factors—socioeconomic status, family background, racial tensions in the schools, and the manner in which integration is accomplished—also influence achievement.

BETTER COMMUNITIES AND FAMILIES The educational aspirations and accomplishments of low-income and minority students would be vastly improved if the communities and families in which those students live provided the support that is found in the strongest families and communities in the United States (Comer, 1997; Funkhouser and Gonzales, 1997). If those communities and families had economic opportunities, better health care, substance-abuse counseling, and a crime-free environment, then they would be better equipped to offer students the support and attention they need. It is important to recognize that the failings of the schools reflect in part the torn fabric of society that has been the focus throughout this book. As we make progress in alleviating some of these other problems—lack of job opportunities, crime, shattered families, alcohol and drug abuse, and the other problems—the resulting strengths in communities and families will make educational achievement vastly more attainable.

Science and Technology

What does the future hold regarding science and technology and the problems they create? A few would opt for fleeing from complex technology altogether and seeking a simpler way of life that does not depend on elaborate technological innovations. In the 1960s and 1970s, a loose collection of groups advocating something like this was referred to as the "back-to-the-earth" movement. These groups favored the rejection of most technology and promoted a simple and self-sufficient lifestyle. They grew their own food and avoided the use of large farm equipment and chemical fertilizers and pesticides; they harvested by hand, built their own tools, and educated their children at home. Their goal was subsistence and simplicity, not profit making, economic growth, or material comfort.

Many people still today lead such a lifestyle in the United States and in places around the world, although how many is difficult to know (Sale, 1995). The Old Order Amish communities in Pennsylvania and some traditional Indian communities that can be found on some reservations represent, to one degree or another, a rejection of, or at least an unwillingness to fully embrace, much of modern technology. Other less visible groups live in small communities and stress simplicity and limited technology. Neo-Luddites or techno-resisters, as such opponents of technology have been called, can also be found in the ranks of radical environmentalists and those fighting nuclear power and destruction of the rain forests. One of their messages is that, whatever the benefits of technology, it comes at a high price—the crime, pollution, stress, and drug abuse that seem to plague industrial societies.

Supporters of technology argue that, if such a low-technology lifestyle were adopted on a widespread scale, it would probably represent a step backward that few would want to take. Without agricultural technology, we would not be able to produce nearly the amount of food that we do, and many people would be condemned to a life of illness, starvation, and poverty. We also need modern technology to help us cope with the waste products of a large population, and without that technology disease would undoubtedly spread. So a mass rejection of modern technology, these supporters of technology argue, is neither feasible nor likely. At the same time, technology is not about to mutate into some clearly benign creature. The problem, then, is how to live with and control the negative consequences of technology. Much of the debate on this issue revolves around whether controlling technology should be accomplished without significant government intervention—the laissez-faire position—or whether the government should be a major decision maker in that arena—the interventionist approach.

LEGAL PROTECTIONS Some of the problems of modern technology are created or made worse because the legal and political systems have not been able to keep up with the changing nature of the problems that emerging technologies create. New technologies often develop in a legal void where there is little legislative direction as to what is acceptable. This is true of the massive invasions of privacy made possible by modern computer and other technologies. Some legislation in the United States does offer protection in these areas (Eder, 1994; Rothfeder, 1992). The Freedom of Information Act of 1966 provides people with the right to access almost any records that federal agencies have on them. The Privacy Act of 1974 prohibits the government from maintaining secret databanks and requires the government to keep the information it gathers about people confidential. The law also gives people the right to see information about them held by most government agencies and the right to correct information that they can show is inaccurate. The Computer Matching and Privacy Protection Acts of 1988 and 1990 update some of these earlier laws by restricting the manner in which government agencies can use computer data files to identify people for purposes of denying or terminating benefits that they receive.

However, the United States could go much further than this, as do many other industrial nations. One thing that could be done is to extend the same privacy protection rules that are imposed on the federal government to all organizations, private or government, that profit from the sale of information about people. If this were done, privacy safeguards would extend to all medical, bank, telephone, computer, or other records. A second step that could be taken is to establish a data protection board, the job of which would be to search out and challenge the validity and legality of questionable corporate or government databases, such as those that include speculative, inaccurate, or unverified data. Canada, Great Britain, France, and other industrial nations have permanent data-protection agencies that ensure that people's privacy is protected. Another measure that would go a long way to protect people's privacy is to require companies that sell credit reports, marketing services, or medical records to others to pay a royalty to a person each time that person's name is sold. This would discourage the widespread sale of information and limit it to sales that are important or essential. At the same time, it would let people know who is selling information about them and to whom it is being sold.

However, despite what could be done to further extend privacy protections, as we have seen, the USA PATRIOT Act of 2001 produced a significant erosion of these protections in order to extend security against terrorism.

The above policies and proposals deal with protecting information after it has been collected. What about collecting less information in the first place? Just because computerization makes it easy to collect data does not mean that collecting data is either essential or wise. So, technology could be designed to achieve its goal, such as levy a charge, without adding to the mountain of data that is accumulating. Credit cards, for example, could be redesigned as "cash" cards instead of charge cards, loaded with prepaid electronic cash, which is then deducted from the card as each purchase is made. There would be no need for an electronic record to be kept because the appropriate amount of cash would be instantly transferred from the card to the seller's account at the time of the transaction.

So, some combination of legal protection of data collected and technological innovations to avoid collecting data would help significantly in alleviating the problems of a loss of privacy and loss of control. Interventionists would also see a significant role for the government in protecting people who might be hurt by particular technological developments. Those, for example, who find themselves intimidated or oppressed by workplace computers should be able to turn to the government for protection against the unfair uses of these technologies. Issues relating to workplace justice were discussed in Chapter 2.

APPROPRIATE TECHNOLOGY One proposed solution to deal with many of the problems associated with modern technology is to develop what has been called **appropriate technology,** or *a technology appropriate to the human scale, to what people can comprehend and relate to; it would be a technology that is limited in size, decentralized, and responsive to human values and needs.* In most cases, an appropriate technology would be considerably smaller than what exists today. In fact, one of the early proponents of such a technology, E. F. Schumacher, wrote a book titled *Small Is Beautiful.* An appropriate technology would avoid the tendency of technology to alienate people, and it would return control to the hands of individuals (Sale, 1980). An example of an appropriate technology is solar energy, which is discussed in Chapter 13. Solar energy does not require the building of large centralized power plants as do nuclear and coal-fired facilities. The technology is decentralized, with each household or community producing some of its own energy rather than having energy production controlled by large corporations. Appropriate technology is also less injurious or damaging, and the damage it does cause is smaller in scale. Solar energy, for example, does not cause the air pollution of coal-fired energy plants or the contamination hazard of nuclear power production.

Few would argue that large-scale technology can or should be completely eliminated. Centralized power plants, for example, are helpful where solar, wind, or geothermal energy cannot fully meet a community's needs. In addition, large-scale technology is often the discovery ground for developing new alternative technologies. What advocates of appropriate technology argue for is not a rejection of technology but rather a rejection of some of the forms of social organization that are created to make use of the technology: the bigness, the bureaucracy, the centralization, and the impersonality. To achieve this may require a change in people's lifestyle. People might, for example, have to rethink their energy needs and develop a lifestyle that can be largely satisfied with alternative energy sources. As an illustration, people might design communities so that bicycles are more feasible than cars as means of transportation. The bicycle would be an appropriate technology in that it is small in scale, comprehensible by most people, and relatively nondamaging. Some communities have tried to encourage bicycle use by closing off some streets to vehicular traffic or establishing bicycle lanes. The point is that proponents of appropriate technology have an ideology that, like the "back-to-the-earth" people, values a simpler and to some extent more self-sufficient way of life. They do not, however, accept the back-to-the-earth rejection of technology; in fact, they embrace technology in its simpler and more human forms.

This debate over appropriate technology revolves to an extent around the laissez-faire versus interventionist controversy. Many advocates of appropriate technology argue that the government can play a role in its development. Through tax write-offs and other policies, the government can make it more attractive to develop appropriate technology. In fact, this has been done by some states and the federal government by allowing people to deduct from their taxes some of the costs of installing solar or wind energy. The government has also discouraged the development of nuclear power (although that was not its original intention) by requiring costly safety procedures at nuclear power plants.

TECHNOLOGY ASSESSMENT **Technology assessment** refers to *research that studies the impact of technology on our physical, social, and ethical environments and seeks solutions to social problems that arise from technological development.* Technology assessment uses extensive studies to forecast the effects of technological developments before they are implemented (Coates, 2001). This makes it possible either to alleviate the negative impact or to decide that the negatives outweigh the benefits of the technology and leave the technology unimplemented. The National Environmental Policy Act of 1969, discussed in Chapter 13, included provisions for the assessment of any environmental impact due to new technology implemented by agencies or legislation of the federal government. Today, any public or private project that requires funds from or the permission of any branch of government must prepare an Environmental Impact Statement. In 1973, the Office of Technology Assessment was established to provide Congress with information about the impact of technology that it could use in its deliberations.

When an Environmental Impact Statement must be prepared in order to initiate a project, the research is typically funded by the government or the organization wishing to initiate the project. This sort of technology assessment, however, typically has a very short time perspective: What is the likelihood that this nuclear power plant will develop a radiation leak? How many patients will survive a trial of 50 artificial heart implants? These questions address the consequences of a particular application of a technology. However, there are broader issues regarding the wisdom of developing a particular technology at all: Should society stress centralized power production, such as nuclear power, or decentralized power production, such as solar and wind energy? Should societal resources be spent on further technological improvements in crisis medicine (such as coronary bypass surgery) or on preventive medicine (such as programs to reduce cigarette smoking)? These broader assessment issues are often much more difficult to research, more speculative and value oriented in nature, and less likely to receive financial support. Especially in recent years, research on these general issues of technology assessment has had to compete for funding with other sorts of research, and the amount of money available for all such government research has been dwindling. In fact, the Office of Technology Assessment was shut down in 1995 as a budget-cutting strategy. With less of such research conducted in the future, we may be less prepared to cope with the consequences of technology.

FUTUROLOGY At the opposite extreme from the back-to-the-earth advocates are people who enthusiastically embrace technological development and advocate the active pursuit of technological innovation. These people argue that we should devote resources to studying ways in which we can achieve the maximum incorporation of technology into society with the minimum costs. In fact, a field of study has emerged called "futurology," which has attracted scholars and researchers from the natural sciences, social sciences, engineering, and business (Bell, 2001). Most of these people tend to be very optimistic about the future and about the role of science and technology in shaping the future. Many futurists envision the United States developing into a postindustrial society whose foundation will be information, communication, and knowledge. Science will play an ever more important role as it serves as a foundation for technological development and change. The findings of the social sciences will be increasingly used to establish the most effective ways of organizing and managing people and solving social problems such as crime and violence. The people with expertise in managing information and knowledge—scientists, technicians, information specialists, and educators—will develop into a distinct class with special privileges and rewards. With rapid technological change occurring, culture and social life will also have to adapt, or at least the negative impacts on people's lives will have to be alleviated. For example, the skills necessary in the occupational realm will likely change a few times during a person's life. This means that people will require periodic reeducation to keep current and competitive in their jobs. Educational institutions will have to change by viewing education as a lifelong process rather than as a product that is accomplished by young adulthood.

Not all futurists agree on these issues. Some, for example, believe that nuclear power will usher in an era of unheard-of wealth and comfort, whereas others argue that problems inherent in generating nuclear power necessarily make it a limited source of power in the future. Some futurists are very enthusiastic about the role of the government in planning the direction of technological and social change of the future; others believe that the government should stand aside and let the economic marketplace—competition and profit making—determine the best way to maximize the utility of technology and minimize its negative impact. Despite their disagreements, however, futurists tend to be very positive about our technological future and to advocate a very activist approach toward technological change.

LINKAGES Science and technology can help alleviate some problems, such as finding new ways to clean up the environment (Chapter 13) or providing new remedies for disease (Chapter 4). However, they can also intensify the same problems by, for example, elaborating the range of polluting technologies or making it possible to prolong life even when people might prefer to die.

STUDY AND REVIEW

Summary

1. Industrialization and modernization are closely related to the growth in formal education and in science and technology. Growth in technology has included mechanization, automation, and cybernation.

2. From the functionalist perspective, educational institutions become a social problem when they don't perform their proper functions, such as transmitting useful skills to people in an equitable fashion. Likewise, problems surrounding science and technology have to do with the social disorganization that results when some parts of society do not adapt sufficiently fast to changes that are occurring.

3. For the conflict perspective, schools become a social problem when influential groups believe that they are not getting what they deserve from education. Likewise, science and technology are problems when some groups use scientific and technological developments to their advantage whereas other groups are hurt by them.

4. The interactionist perspective suggests that education becomes a social problem when it produces stigmatizing results, lowering students' self-esteem and making educational success more difficult to achieve. Likewise, science and technology become problems when they acquire more negative meanings than positive ones.

5. The problems in educational institutions today include social reproduction, a lack of educational opportunities for low-income people and minorities, the credentials race, tracking, effectiveness, low performance, dropouts, segregation, and violence.

6. Some of the major problems that concern people today regarding scientific and technological developments are unemployment, alienation, loss of control due to extreme dependency on technology, loss of privacy, and problems created by genetic engineering.

7. A number of reforms have been proposed that would improve schools: parental choice through charter schools and vouchers, back-to-basics curricula, early childhood educational interventions, privatization, home schooling, school integration, and improving communities and families.

8. Regarding the future of technology, some would opt for fleeing from technology and attempting to find a simpler way of life. Others search for ways to live with and control the negative consequences of technology through legal protections, appropriate technology, technology assessment, and futurology.

Key Terms

alienation

appropriate technology

automation

bilingual education

biotechnology

cultural lag

cybernation

education

The U.S. Department of Education makes available numerous publications on the Internet and can be a good source of information about educational data, trends, and policies. Log on to the home page of the National Center for Education Statistics **(nces.ed.gov).** At this point, you are free to explore. As a start, click "Search NCES" and type in "Student Outcomes." You will get a list of publications (some available online) reporting research on the factors that influence how well students do in school. Summarize the results of some of this research. Also, search for terms like "social promotion" and "drug-free schools." How does what you find relate to some of the educational issues discussed in this chapter? What other material can you uncover that relates to issues of this chapter?

Among the most influential groups in education policy in the United States are the National Education Association **(www.nea.org),** the American Federation of Teachers **(www.aft.org),** and the National Parent Teachers Association **(www.pta.org).** Explore their Web sites for information on the topics discussed in this chapter. The Allyn & Bacon Social Problems Supersite **(wps.ablongman. com/ab_socialprob_sprsite_1)** contains material on educational institutions and their problems.

On technology issues, explore the Web site of the Privacy Foundation **(www.privacyfoundation.org),** a nonprofit educational organization that addresses issues of workplace surveillance and the threat to privacy posed by modern communication technologies.

Two other very useful Web sites that provide information and discuss policy issues relating to technology and privacy are the Electronic Privacy Information Center **(www.epic.org)** and Privacy.Org **(www.privacy.org).**

---

gene splicing

genetic engineering

industrialization

mechanization

modernization

recombinant DNA

science

social reproduction

technology

technology assessment

Multiple-Choice Questions

1. Which of the following best characterizes the current status of science and technology in the United States?
   a. More money is spent on research and development than twenty years ago.
   b. Less money is spent on research and development than twenty years ago.
   c. Fewer scientists and engineers are employed in research and development than twenty years ago.
   d. The number of scientists is increasing but the number of engineers is decreasing, suggesting a drift away from applied technology.

2. Which of the following statements would be most consistent with the conflict perspective on science and technology?
   a. Public attitudes toward science and technology are relative and vary from time to time.
   b. Science and technology create problems because parts of society do not adapt to changes quick enough.
   c. Science and technology creates problems because they produce social disorganization.
   d. Powerful groups' use of science and technology for their own benefit often works to the disadvantage of others.

3. The best predictor of how far people will advance in their schooling in the United States is
   a. their age.
   b. their family's socioeconomic standing.
   c. their religion.
   d. the region in which they were born.

4. Which of the following is true in regard to the "credentials race" in the United States?
   a. The educational requirements for most jobs today are lower than they need to be to do the job.
   b. The educational credentials required for jobs have been going down in the past few decades.
   c. The educational requirements for many jobs today are higher than they need to be to do the job.
   d. The race actually ended a couple of decades ago.

5. Alienation from one's job is especially high among
   a. skilled white-collar workers.
   b. managers and professionals.
   c. unskilled blue-collar workers.
   d. government employees.

6. As far as genetic engineering is concerned, the National Academy of Sciences has recommended that
   a. the release of some genetically manipulated materials into the environment be allowed.
   b. the release of all genetically manipulated materials into the environment be prohibited.
   c. the amount of recombinant DNA research be reduced.
   d. corporations not be allowed to patent genetically engineered animals.

7. Charter schools are
   a. schools that centralize all the educational functions in a school district.
   b. schools that attract the largest number of students in a school district.
   c. schools that receive their authority directly from the state.
   d. schools that have reduced the extent of bureaucracy in their organization.
8. Research on education has shown that
   a. students in Catholic schools perform better than students in public schools.
   b. students in public schools perform better than students in Catholic schools.
   c. students in U.S. schools do better in math and science than students in most other industrial nations.
   d. more highly bureaucratic schools encourage more creativity among their students than less bureaucratic schools.
9. Interventionists would support the position that
   a. private industry should set the standards for protecting the privacy of people.
   b. the government should play a significant role in protecting people from the negatives of technological development.
   c. cultural lag is generally not a serious problem with advances in technology.
   d. the back-to-the-earth movement has taken an appropriate stance on the issue of technological developments.
10. Which of the following would generally be true of futurists?
   a. They all support nuclear power.
   b. They are very positive about the technological future.
   c. They all agree that nuclear power will be a limited source of power in the future.
   d. They are all enthusiastic about the role of government in planning the direction of technological change.
   e. They all oppose government intervention in planning the direction of technological change.

True/False Questions

1. Mechanization and automation work at cross-purposes so that, as the automation of society has increased, the extent of mechanization has declined.
2. According to the functionalist perspective, science and technology become a social problem when the extent of cultural lag in society declines.
3. The danger of tracking in schools is that the track can become a label that creates expectations for how teachers and students should behave.

4. Among those students who are especially at risk for failure in schools in the United States are those whose parents have low educational attainment.
5. Most people agree that advances in technology and computerization in the next few decades will provide enjoyable and well-paying jobs for most people who want them.
6. An effective strategy to deal with the loss of control to computers would be to remove computers from those parts of society where this is a problem.
7. Although significant advances have been made in recombinant DNA techniques, genetic engineering has not yet produced any products that are usable by people.
8. In Japan, educational policy and curriculum design are controlled by the central government.
9. Overall, integration of schools in the United States has probably resulted in modest improvements in school achievement by African American students.
10. The appropriate technology movement stresses that technology, where possible, should be limited in size and decentralized.

Fill-In Questions

1. The term _____ refers to knowledge, tools, and practices that are employed as means of achieving clearly identifiable goals.
2. _____ involves the use of machinery to replace human and animal labor in the production of goods and services.
3. According to the _____ perspective, advances in science and technology have produced significant social disorganization.
4. Powerful forces in educational institutions work toward _____, or passing social and economic inequalities on from one generation to the next.
5. _____ refers to feeling that you are powerless to control your surroundings and that what you do has little meaning.
6. One form of genetic engineering is _____.
7. _____ is the making of multiple genetic replicas of a parent organism.
8. The school reform that is based on the notion that schools should compete for students in an open marketplace is called _____.
9. Solar energy or the use of bicycles as a means of transportation would be examples of _____.
10. People who enthusiastically embrace technological development and advocate the active pursuit of technological innovation are called _____.

Matching Questions

_____ 1. social reproduction
_____ 2. modernization
_____ 3. tracking
_____ 4. early childhood educational intervention
_____ 5. cultural lag
_____ 6. opposition to industrialization
_____ 7. back-to-the-earth movement
_____ 8. Freedom of Information Act
_____ 9. E. F. Schumacher
_____ 10. oncomouse

A. Luddites
B. conflict perspective
C. appropriate technology
D. ability grouping
E. genetic engineering
F. protection of privacy
G. antitechnology
H. transition to advanced industrial society
I. Head Start
J. functionalist perspective

Essay Questions

1. According to the conflict perspective, in what ways does education work as a mechanism to limit the opportunities of the less powerful in society?
2. Compare and contrast the functionalist and conflict perspectives on science and technology. In what ways does each perspective see science and technology becoming a social problem?
3. Assess both sides of the argument about whether advances in technology will produce more unemployment in the future.
4. In what ways does technological advance lead to a loss of privacy in people's lives?
5. What is genetic engineering? What issues does it raise and what problems does it create for society?
6. How are schooling and education in Japan and other industrial nations similar to or different from schooling and education in the United States?
7. What reforms are being implemented, or might be implemented, in schools in the United States to overcome some of the problems discussed in the text?
8. What legal protections have been implemented and could be implemented in order to protect people from the negative effects of technological advances?
9. What is appropriate technology? What are the arguments for and against it?
10. Describe the process of technology assessment in terms of what it is, how it operates, and what is currently being done in that realm in the United States.

For Further Reading

Stanley Aronowitz and Jonathan Cutler, eds. *Post-Work: The Wages of Cybernation.* New York: Routledge, 1997. The readings in this book give one vision of what the workplace in a highly technological future will look like. For most workers, it is a rather negative and dreary vision.

Jeanne Ballantine. *The Sociology of Education: A Systematic Analysis.* 5th ed. Upper Saddle River, NJ: Prentice Hall, 2001. This comprehensive textbook on the sociology of education provides a complete overview of the topics, theories, research, and problems that sociologists focus on in the institution of education.

Peter W. Cookson and Caroline Hodges Persell. *Preparing for Power: America's Elite Boarding Schools.* New York: Basic Books, 1985. These sociologists document how elite schools prepare the offspring of the powerful to take over positions of power in American society and thus contribute to the process of social reproduction.

Simon Head. *The New Ruthless Economy: Work & Power in the Digital Age.* New York: Oxford University Press, 2003. This eye-opening book argues that the new information technology is producing huge social and economic disparities as well as other serious problems in the work place.

Robert O'Harrow, Jr. *No Place To Hide.* New York: The Free Press, 2005. This journalist reviews the disturbing extent to which personal privacy in the modern world has been virtually destroyed by the modern technologies of information collection and retrieval.

Richard Rothstein. *Class and Schools: Using Social, Economic and Educational Reform to Close the Black–White Achievement Gap.* New York: Economic Policy Institute, Teachers College, Columbia University, 2004. This author focuses on the reasons for the persistent gap in educational achievement between whites and African Americans in the United States and how it can be narrowed. In doing so, the book tells a lot about how social class influences educational achievement.

Michael J. Sandel. *The Case Against Perfection: Ethics in the Age of Genetic Engineering.* Cambridge. MA: Harvard University Press, 2007. This philosopher explores the many ethical issues that arise in a world where the possibilities for genetic manipulation seem almost endless and makes the case for caution in implementing many of these possibilities.

Lee M. Silver. *Remaking Eden: Cloning and Beyond in a Brave New World.* New York: Avon Books, 1997. This book offers a good overview of what we are likely to see as a consequence of emerging biotechnologies. One of the author's points is that the technology to make dramatic changes in our lives is already available.

Absolute definition of poverty A definition of poverty based on a fixed economic level below which people are considered poor; this level does not necessarily change as society on the whole becomes more or less affluent.

Acute diseases Diseases with a fairly quick, and sometimes dramatic and incapacitating, onset and from which a person either dies or recovers.

Ageism An ideology or set of beliefs holding that people in a particular age group are inferior, have negative attributes, and can be dominated and exploited because of their age.

Age structure The distribution of people into various age categories in society.

Alcoholism The consumption of alcohol at a level that produces serious personal, social, or health consequences, such as marital problems, occupational difficulties, accidents, or arrests.

Alienation A feeling of powerlessness in regard to controlling one's surroundings and the feeling that what one does has little meaning or purpose.

Androgyny The view that there should be a blending of the traits and roles of both sexes; people should express themselves as human beings rather than in traditionally masculine or feminine ways.

Anomie Inconsistencies that arise when people are taught to strive for certain goals but are not provided with the culturally approved means necessary to attain those goals.

Anomie theory The theory stating that inconsistencies and contradictions in the social system contribute to many forms of crime.

Appropriate technology A technology appropriate to the human scale, to what people can comprehend and relate to; a technology that is limited in size, decentralized, and responsive to human values and needs.

Assimilation The process by which a racial or ethnic minority loses its distinctive identity and way of life and becomes absorbed into the dominant group.

Authoritarian personality A constellation of personality characteristics including a rigid adherence to conventional lifestyles and values, admiration of power and toughness in interpersonal relationships, submission to authority, cynicism, an emphasis on obedience, and a fear of things that are different.

Authority Legitimate power that is obeyed because people believe it is right and proper that they obey.

Automation The automatically controlled operation of machines by mechanical or electronic devices.

Balance of power A foreign policy based on the idea that a nuclear holocaust can be avoided if the military capability of one side roughly balances that of the other side.

Bilingual education Students are taught in both English and their native language until their English competency is sufficient to become the sole language of instruction.

Bioethics The study of ethical questions that relate to the life and biological well-being of people.

Biotechnology The use of organisms or parts of organisms to make products or carry out tasks.

Blended family A family based on kinship ties that accumulate as a consequence of divorce and remarriage.

Capitalism An economic system in which the means of economic production and distribution are privately held; the profit motive is the primary force guiding people's economic behavior; and there is free competition among both producers and consumers of goods.

Career deviance See *Secondary deviance.*

Carrying capacity An upper-size limit that is imposed on a population by its environmental resources and that cannot be permanently exceeded.

Causality One factor has an effect on or produces a change in some other factor.

Chronic diseases Diseases that progress over a long period of time and often exist long before they are detected.

City A relatively large, permanent community of people who rely on surrounding agricultural communities for their food supply.

Civil disorder Strife or conflict that is threatening to the public order and that involves the government in some fashion, either as a party to the conflict or as a guardian of the public interest.

Cohabitation Relationships in which two people live in the same household and share sexual, emotional, and often economic ties but are not legally married.

Collective violence Organized violence by relatively large groups of people to promote or resist some social policies or practices.

Commodity riots Race riots in which the focus of hostility is property, merchandise, or equipment rather than people of another racial group.

Communal riots Race riots in which whites attack blacks in racially contested areas.

Communism The term used by Marx to describe the end stage of the struggle over capitalism; a system in which all goods would be communally owned; people would not work for wages but would give according to their abilities; and there would be no scarcity of goods and services, allowing people to receive whatever they needed; in addition, the state would become less important and its role would dwindle.

Communities Groups of people who share a common territory and a sense of identity or belonging and who interact with one another.

Conflict perspective The sociological perspective centered on the idea that society consists of different groups who struggle with one another to attain the scarce societal resources that are considered valuable, be they money, power, prestige, or the authority to impose one's values on society.

Corporation A business enterprise that is owned by stockholders, many of whom are not involved in running the daily affairs of the business.

Crime An act that violates a criminal code enacted by an officially constituted political authority.

Crisis medicine Medical treatment that focuses on treating people's illnesses after they become ill.

Cross-dependence A situation in which the withdrawal symptoms of one drug are alleviated by another drug in the same pharmacological class.

Cross-tolerance A situation in which a tolerance built up to one drug leads to a reduced response to another drug in the same pharmacological class.

Cultural analysis of poverty A focus on the values, attitudes, and psychological orientations that may emerge among groups of people who live under conditions of poverty.

Cultural definition of poverty A definition of poverty that views it not only in terms of how many resources people have, but also in terms of why they have failed to achieve a higher economic level.

Cultural lag A gap between the point at which one part of the social system changes and the point at which other parts adjust to compensate for that change.

Cultural transmission theories The theories that posit that crime and delinquency are learned and culturally transmitted through socialization.

Curative medicine See *Crisis medicine*.

Cybernation The use of machines, such as computers, to control other machines, to make decisions, and to monitor the production process.

Definition of the situation A person's perception and interpretation of what is important in a situation and what actions are appropriate.

Demographic gap The gap between the high birthrates and low death rates that results in explosive population growth during the early industrial period of the demographic transition.

Demographic transition The changing patterns of birth and death rates brought about by industrialization.

Demography The study of the size, composition, and distribution of human populations and how these factors change over time.

Dependence A mental or physical craving for a drug and withdrawal symptoms when use of the drug is stopped.

Dependency ratio A statistic that shows the relative size of the group in society that is economically dependent for support on others who are working.

Depressants Psychoactive drugs that depress the central nervous system and have some analgesic, or painkilling, properties.

Deviance Behaviors or characteristics that violate important group norms and as a consequence are reacted to with social disapproval.

Differential association theory The theory that posits that crime and delinquency are learned in interaction with other people, for the most part within intimate primary groups such as families and peer groups.

Discrimination The unequal treatment of people because they are members of a particular group.

Drug Any substance that, when consumed, alters one or more of the functions of the human body.

Drug abuse The continued use of a psychoactive substance at a level that violates approved social practices.

Drug addiction Physical dependence on a drug.

Ecology The branch of biology that studies the relationships between living organisms and their environment.

Economics The social processes through which goods and services are produced and distributed.

Ecosystem A complex, interrelated network of living and nonliving things that interact with one another to produce an exchange of materials between the living and the nonliving parts.

Education The systematic, formal process through which specialized teachers transmit skills, knowledge, and values to students.

Egalitarian family A family in which power and authority are shared somewhat equally by husband and wife.

Environment The conditions and circumstances surrounding and affecting a particular group of living creatures.

Environmental justice The idea that environmental hazards should be shared equally by various groups in society or at least that no group or community should bear the burden of environmental hazards at a level disproportionate to their numbers in the population or their contributions to creating the hazard.

Ethnic group A people who share a common historical and cultural heritage and sense of group identity and belonging.

Ethnocentrism The tendency to view one's own culture or subculture as the best and to judge other cultures or subcultures in comparison to it.

Expressive tasks Activities focused on the relationships between people and on maintaining happiness, harmony, and emotional stability in a group.

Extended family A family involving three or more generations of people who live together or in close proximity and whose lives and livelihoods are closely intertwined.

Family A social institution based on kinship that functions to replace members of society and to nurture them.

Fecundity The biological maximum number of children that could be born in a society.

Feminist movement The collective activities of individuals, groups, and organizations whose goal is the fair and equal treatment of women and men around the world.

Fertility The actual number of children born in a society.

Frustration An inability to achieve sought-after goals.

Full employment A situation in which everyone or nearly everyone who wants to work can find a job.

Functionalist perspective The sociological perspective based on the idea that society is a system made up of a number of interrelated elements, each performing a function that contributes to the operation of the whole.

Gender Learned behavior involving how we are expected to act as males and females in society.

Gene splicing See *Recombinant DNA.*

Genetic engineering Manipulating the genes of organisms to alter the organisms' characteristics in ways that would not have occurred naturally.

Gentrification The return of relatively affluent households to marginal neighborhoods in cities where run-down housing is being rehabilitated or new housing constructed.

Gerontology The scientific study of aging.

Ghetto A neighborhood inhabited largely by members of a single ethnic or racial group.

Hallucinogens Psychoactive drugs that produce hallucinations, often of a visual nature.

Health maintenance organization (HMO) An organization that agrees to provide for all of a person's health-care needs for a fixed, periodic premium.

Homophobia An intense dislike of or prejudice against homosexuals.

Homosexuality Sexual feelings, attractions, and actions directed toward members of the same sex.

Hydrologic cycle The processes by which nature purifies water.

Hypotheses Tentative statements that can be tested regarding relationships between two or more factors.

Industrialization The productive processes where fossil fuels and machines are used instead of human or animal muscle power to produce things.

In-group A group that we feel positively toward, that we identify with, and that produces a "we feeling."

Institutionalized discrimination The inequitable treatment of a group resulting from practices or policies that are incorporated into social, political, or economic institutions and that operate independently from the prejudices of individuals.

Instrumental tasks The goal-oriented activities of a group, such as hunting, building something, or managing a work team.

Insurrection An organized action by some group to rebel against the existing government and to replace it with new political forms and leadership.

Interactionist perspective The sociological perspective that focuses on everyday social interaction among individuals rather than on large societal structures such as politics, education, and the like.

Interest group A group whose members share distinct and common concerns and who benefit from similar social policies and practices.

Internal colonialism A type of exploitation in which a subordinate group provides cheap labor that benefits the dominant group and is then further exploited by having to purchase expensive goods and services from the dominant group.

Labeling theory The theory based on the idea that whether other people define or label a person as deviant is a critical determinant in the development of a pattern of deviant behavior.

Lesbians Female homosexuals.

Life course A succession of statuses and roles that people in a particular society experience in a fairly predictable pattern as they grow older.

Life stages See *Life course.*

Managed care A health-care system that focuses on controlling costs by monitoring and controlling the health-care decisions of doctors and patients.

Massive retaliation A foreign policy based on the idea that war could be avoided if the enemy realized that any aggressor against the United States would suffer overwhelming damages from massive retaliation with U.S. military might.

Mechanization The use of tools and machinery instead of human and animal labor in the production of goods and services.

Medicaid A joint federal–state program to provide medical care for low-income people of any age.

Medical–industrial complex A coincidence of interests between physicians and other health-care providers and the industries producing health-care goods and services, with both parties profiting from the increased use of these commodities and the health-care consumer paying enormous costs for inadequate care.

Medicare Government health insurance for those over sixty-five years of age.

Migration A permanent change of residence.

Military–industrial complex The relationship between the military that wants to purchase weapons and the corporations that produce the weapons. Both the military and the corporations benefit from a large military budget and policies favoring military solutions to international problems.

Minority group A group whose members share distinct physical or cultural characteristics; are denied access to power and resources available to other groups; and are accorded fewer rights, privileges, and opportunities.

Mixed economy Economic system in which there are strong elements of both capitalism and socialism.

Modernization The economic, social, and cultural changes that occur when a preindustrial society makes the transition to an advanced industrial society.

Modified extended family Families in which elaborate networks of visitation and support are found even though each nuclear unit lives separately.

Monogamy Family systems in which people have only one spouse at a time.

Mortality The number of deaths that occur in a particular population.

Mutually assured destruction A foreign policy based on the idea that war can be prevented when each side has the might to destroy the other.

Narcotics Psychoactive drugs whose main use is as analgesics, or painkillers.

National health insurance A program of government health insurance covering all citizens.

Norms Rules of conduct that guide people's behavior.

Nuclear family A family consisting of parents and their children.

Opiates See *Narcotics.*

Patriarchy A family in which males dominate in the regulation of political and economic decision making, whereas women and children are subordinate.

Photosynthesis The process by which plants capture light and heat energy from the sun and turn it into food.

Pluralism A situation in which a number of racial and ethnic groups live side by side, each retaining a distinct identity and lifestyle while still participating in some aspects of the larger culture.

Pluralistic family A family system in which a number of different family types exist side by side, each having an attraction for some segment of the populace.

Pluralist model The view of power in America as being spread over a large number of groups with divergent values, interests, and goals.

Politics The agreements in society over who has the right to exercise control over others, who can establish laws to regulate social life, and how conflicting interests in society will be resolved.

Polygamy Having more than one spouse at the same time.

Population The total number of people inhabiting a particular geographic area at a specified time.

Pornography Sexually "explicit" writings, still or motion pictures, and similar products designed to be sexually arousing.

Poverty The uneven distribution of the resources available.

Power The ability of one group to realize its will, even in the face of resistance from other groups.

Power elite model The view of power in America that says that there exists a small group of very powerful people who make just about all of the important decisions in the United States.

Prejudice An irrational attitude toward certain people based solely on their membership in a particular group.

Preventive medicine Changes in lifestyle or other steps that help avoid the occurrence of disease.

Primary deviance The violation of social norms in which the violator is not caught or is excused rather than labeled as a deviant.

Primary prevention Preventing drug problems before they begin.

Prison–industrial complex The correctional corporations and authorities, along with correctional officers and the communities in which prisons are built, who see it to

their advantage when more people are sent to prison and given longer sentences.

Prostitution Sexual activity in exchange for money or goods, in which the primary motivation for the prostitute is neither sexual nor affectional.

Psychedelics See *Hallucinogens.*

Psychoactive drugs Drugs that can produce major alterations in the mood, emotions, perceptions, or brain functioning of the person who takes them.

Public assistance Social programs for which a person must pass a "means" test to be eligible.

Race A group of people who are believed to be a biological group sharing genetically transmitted traits that are defined as important.

Racism The view that certain racial or ethnic groups are biologically inferior and that practices involving their domination and exploitation are therefore justified.

Recidivism The repeat of an offense after having been convicted of a crime.

Recombinant DNA The practice in which some DNA from one organism is spliced into the genetic material of another organism to produce some new characteristics in the host or even a novel form of life.

Refined divorce rate The divorce rate that is determined by dividing the number of divorces each year by the total number of existing marriages in that year.

Relative definition of poverty The definition of poverty based on the idea that people are poor relative to some standard, and that standard is partially shaped by the lifestyles of other citizens.

Relative deprivation The idea that people tend to feel deprived or frustrated in comparison to what others have or what they believe they deserve.

Research The systematic examination of empirical data.

Sample Elements that are taken from a group or population and that serve as a source of data.

Science A method of obtaining objective and systematic knowledge through empirical observation.

Secondary deviance Behavior that a person adopts in reaction to being labeled as a deviant.

Secularization The process through which the influence of religion is removed from many institutions in society and dispersed into private and personal realms.

Serial monogamy A family system in which people are allowed to have more than one spouse, but not at the same time.

Sex The biological role that each of us plays in reproduction.

Sexism An ideology based on the belief that one sex is superior to and should dominate the other sex.

Sick role A set of expectations intended to guide the behavior of people who are ill.

Social institutions Relatively stable clusters of social relationships that involve people working together to meet some basic needs of society.

Social insurance Social programs offering benefits to broad categories of people, such as the elderly or injured workers, who presumably were working and paying for the insurance before becoming eligible for it.

Socialism Economic systems in which the means of production and distribution are collectively held so that the goods and services that people need are provided and equitably distributed.

Social mobility The movement of people from one social position to another in the stratification hierarchy.

Social movement A collective, organized effort to promote or resist social change through some noninstitutionalized or unconventional means.

Social policy Laws, administrative procedures, and other formal and informal social practices that are intended to promote social changes focused on alleviating particular social problems.

Social problem A social condition is a social problem when an influential group defines it as threatening its values; when the condition affects a large number of people; and when it can be remedied by collective action.

Social reproduction The process of passing social and economic inequalities on from one generation to the next and thus perpetuating the existing stratification system.

Social stratification The ranking of people into a hierarchy in which the resources considered valuable by society are unequally distributed.

Sociobiology A field of study based on the idea that the genetic makeup of human beings plays a powerful role in shaping their social behavior.

Sociological imagination The ability to understand the relationship between what is happening in people's personal lives and the social forces that surround them.

Sociology The scientific study of societies and human social behavior.

Split labor market A situation in which there are two groups of workers willing to do the same work, but for different wages.

Stimulants Psychoactive drugs whose major effect is to stimulate the central nervous system.

Structural unemployment A predictable condition of unemployment resulting from changes in the occupational structure of society.

Subculture A group within a culture that shares some of the beliefs, values, and norms of the larger culture but also has some that are distinctly its own.

Subculture of violence Norms and values that condone and legitimize the use of violence in resolving conflicts.

Suburbs Less densely populated areas, primarily residential in nature, on the outskirts of a city.

Technology Knowledge, tools, and practices that use scientific or other organized knowledge to achieve some practical goal.

Technology assessment Research that studies the impact of technology on our physical, social, and ethical environments and seeks solutions to social problems that arise from technological development.

Terrorism The attempt to achieve political goals by using fear and intimidation to disrupt the normal operations of a society.

Theoretical perspectives General views of society that provide some fundamental assumptions about the nature and operation of society and commonly serve as sources of the more specific theories.

Theory A set of statements that explains the relationship between phenomena.

Third-party medicine A health-care payment scheme in which the patient pays a premium into a fund and the doctor or hospital is paid from this fund for each treatment provided to the patient.

Tolerance Physical changes that result in the need for higher and higher doses of a drug to achieve the same effect.

Urban homesteading Programs to increase home ownership by private citizens in certain neighborhoods by selling them houses at little or no cost.

Values People's ideas about what is good or bad, right or wrong.

Violence Behavior that is intended to bring pain or physical injury to another person or to harm or destroy property.

Women's movement See *Feminist movement.*

World-system theory A theory that posits that the world's nations have become increasingly interdependent, both economically and politically, and are now linked in a worldwide system, with some nations having more power and resources than others.

Zero population growth A situation in which birth and death rates are nearly equal, producing a zero rate of natural increase.

Abadinsky, H. (2007). *Organized crime* (8th ed.). Belmont, CA: Wadsworth.

Abel, E. K. (1991). *Who cares for the elderly? Public policy and the experiences of adult daughters.* Philadelphia: Temple University Press.

Abrahamson, M. (2004). *Global cities.* New York: Oxford University Press.

Abramovitz, J. N., et al. (2001). *Vital signs 2001: The trends that are shaping our future.* New York: W. W. Norton.

Acuna, R. (1987). *Occupied America: A history of Chicanos* (3rd ed.). New York: Harper and Row.

Adams, R. E., & Serpe, R. T. (2000). Social integration, fear of crime, and life satisfaction. *Sociological Perspectives, 43,* 605–629.

Aday, L. A. (1993). *At risk in America: The health and health care needs of vulnerable populations in the United States.* San Francisco: Jossey-Bass.

Adelman, C. (1991). *Women at thirtysomething: Paradoxes of attainment.* Washington, DC: U.S. Department of Education.

Adler, F., Mueller, G. O. W., & Laufer, W. S. (2007). *Criminology,* (6th ed.). New York: McGraw-Hill.

Adorno, T. W., Frenkel-Brunswik, E., Levinson, D. J., & Sanford, R. N. (1950). *The authoritarian personality.* New York: Harper and Row.

Agnew, R. (1991). A longitudinal test of social control theory and delinquency. *Journal of Research in Crime and Delinquency, 28,* 126–156.

Albert, A. (2001). *Brothel: Mustang Ranch and its women.* New York: Random House.

Alesina, A., & Glaeser, E. L. (2004). *Fighting poverty in the U.S. and Europe: A world of difference.* Oxford: Oxford University Press.

Alex-Assensoh, Y. (1995). Myths about race and the underclass: Concentrated poverty and "underclass" behaviors. *Urban Affairs Review, 31* (September), 3–19.

Allan, E. A., & Steffensmeier, D. J. (1989). Youth underemployment, and property crime: Differential effects of job availability and job quality, on juvenile and young adult arrest rates. *American Sociological Review, 54,* 107–123.

Allen, D. W. (2001). Social class, race, and toxic releases in American counties, 1995. *The Social Science Journal, 38,* 13–25.

Alperovitz, G. (2004). *America beyond capitalism: Reclaiming our wealth, our liberty, and our democracy.* New York: Wiley.

Alsop, R. (2001, July 25). Business schools struggle to add more female students to bottom line. *Wall Street Journal,* B1–B4.

Altheide, D. L. (1993). Electronic media and state control: The case of Azscam. *Sociological Quarterly, 34,* 53–69.

Amato, P. R. (1987). Family processes in one-parent, step-parent, and intact families: The child's point of view. *Journal of Marriage and the Family, 49,* 327–337.

Amato, P. R. (1993). Children's adjustment to divorce: Theories, hypotheses, and empirical support. *Journal of Marriage and the Family, 55,* 23–38.

Amato, P. R., & Booth, A. (1997). *A generation at risk: Growing up in an era of family upheaval.* Cambridge, MA: Harvard University Press.

Amato, P. R., & Rezac, S. J. (1994). Contact with nonresident parents, interparental conflict, and children's behavior. *Journal of Family Issues, 15,* 191–207.

American Psychiatric Association. (1994). *Diagnostic and statistical manual of mental disorders* (4th ed., rev.). Washington, DC: American Psychiatric Association.

Anderson, D. C. (1998). *Sensible justice: Alternatives to prison.* New York: New Press.

Anderson, T. L., & Leal, D. R. (2001). *Free market environmentalism* (Rev. ed.). New York: Palgrave.

Anstett, P. (1992, June 23). U.S. consumers pay for health care ills. *Detroit Free Press,* p. 1.

Antonovsky, A. (1972). Social class, life expectancy, and overall mortality. In E. G. Jaco (Ed.), *Patients, physicians, and illness* (2nd ed.). New York: Free Press.

Applebome, P. (1996, September 13). Report on training of teachers gives the nation a dismal grade. *New York Times,* p. Al.

Archer, D., & Gartner, R. (1976). Violent acts and violent times: A comparative approach to postwar homicide rates. *American Sociological Review, 41,* 937–963.

Ardrey, R. (1967). *The territorial imperative.* New York: Atheneum.

Arias, E. (2004, February 18). United States life tables, 2001. *National Vital Statistics Reports,* Vol. 52, PHS Pub. No. 2004–1120. Hyattsville, MD: National Center for Health Statistics.

Aries, E. (1996). *Men and women in interaction.* New York: Oxford University Press.

Aries, P. (1962). *Centuries of childhood* (R. Baldick, trans.). New York: Random House.

Association of American Colleges. (1982). *The classroom climate: A chilly one for women?* Washington, DC: Program on the Status and Education of Women.

Astin, A. W. (1992). Educational "choice": Its appeal may be illusory. *Sociology of Education, 65,* 255–260.

Atchley, R. C., & Barusch, A. S. (2004). *Social forces and aging: An introduction to social gerontology* (10th ed.). Belmont, CA: Wadsworth.

Austin, J., & Irwin, J. (2001). *It's about time: America's imprisonment binge* (3rd ed.). Belmont, CA: Wadsworth/Thomson Learning.

Axinn, W. G., & Thornton, A. (2000). The transformation in the meaning of marriage. In L. J. Waite et al. (Eds.), *The ties that bind: Perspectives on marriage and cohabitation.* New York: Aldine de Gruyter.

Bagdikian, B. H. (2000). *The media monopoly* (6th ed.). Boston: Beacon Press.

Bagdikian, B. H. (2004). *The new media monopoly.* Boston: Beacon Press.

Bailey, W. C. (1974). Murder and the death penalty. *Journal of Criminal Law and Criminology, 65,* 416–423.

Bailey, W. C. (1990). Murder, capital punishment, and television: Execution publicity and homicide rates. *American Sociological Review, 55,* 628–633.

Baker, D., & Weisbrot, M. (2001). *Social Security: The phony crisis.* Chicago: University of Chicago Press.

Baker, T. L., & Velez, W. (1996). Access to and opportunity in postsecondary education in the United States: A review. *Sociology of Education* (Special issue), 82–101.

Baldwin, R. E. (2003). *The decline of U.S. labor unions and the role of trade.* Washington, DC: Institute for International Economics.

Bales, K. (2003). Because she looks like a child. In B. Ehrenreich & A. R. Hochschild (Eds.), *Global woman: Nannies, maids, and sex workers in the new economy.* New York: Metropolitan Books.

Bales, W., et al. (2003). *Recidivism: An analysis of public and private state prison releases in Florida.* Rockville, MD: National Criminal Justice Reference Service (www.ncjrs.gov).

Ball-Rokeach, S. J. (1973). Values and violence: A test of the subculture of violence hypothesis. *American Sociological Review, 38,* 736–749.

Banfield, E. C. (1990). *The unheavenly city revisited.* Prospect Heights, IL: Waveland Press.

Barakat, H. (1993). *The Arab world: Society, culture, and state.* Berkeley, CA: University of California Press.

Barnet, R. J., & Cavanagh, J. (1994). *Global dreams: Imperial corporations and the new world order.* New York: Simon & Schuster.

Barnett, R. C., & Rivers, C. (1996). *She works/he works: How two-income families are happier, healthier, and better off.* San Francisco: HarperSanFrancisco.

Baron, J. M., & Newman, A. E. (1990). For what it's worth: Organizations, occupations, and the value of work done by women and nonwhites. *American Sociological Review, 55,* 155–175.

Baron, L. (1990). Pornography and gender equality: An empirical analysis. *Journal of Sex Research, 27,* 363–380.

Baron, R. A., & Richardson, D. R. (1994). *Human Aggression* (2nd ed.). New York: Plenum.

Barongan, C., & Hall, G. C. N. (1995). The influence of misogynous rap music on sexual aggression against women. *Psychology of Women Quarterly, 19,* 195–207.

Barringer, H. R., Takeuchi, D. T., & Xenos, P. (1990). Education, occupational prestige, and income of Asian Americans. *Sociology of Education, 63,* 27–43.

Bartsch, U., & Müller, B. (2000). *Fossil fuels in a changing climate: Impacts of the Kyoto Protocol and developing country participation.* Oxford, UK: Oxford University Press.

Bates, E. (1999, March 29). The shame of our nursing homes: Millions for investors, misery for the elderly. *The Nation,* pp. 11–19.

Baum, A., & Davis, G. (1976). Spatial and social aspects of crowding perception. *Environment and Behavior, 8,* 527–544.

Beck, F. D. (2001). Do state-designated enterprise zones promote economic growth? *Sociological Inquiry, 71,* 508–532.

Bell, A. P., & Weinberg, M. S. (1978). *Homosexualities: A study of diversity among men and women.* New York: Simon & Schuster.

Bell, R. L., Cleveland, S. E., Hanson, P. G., & O'Connell, W. E. (1969). Small group dialogue and discussion: An approach to police–community relationships. *Journal of Criminal Law, Criminology, and Police Science, 60,* 242–246.

Bell, W. (2001). Futures studies comes of age: Twenty-five years after *The Limits to Growth. Futures, 33,* 63–76.

Belluck, P. (2003, Feb. 9). Methadone, once the way out, suddenly grows as a killer drug. *New York Times,* p. A1.

Belsky, J. (2006). Early child care and early child development: Major findings of the NICHD study of early child care. *European Journal of Developmental Psychology, 3.*

Bennett, A., & Adams, O. (1993). *Looking north for health: What we can learn from Canada's health care system.* San Francisco: Jossey-Bass.

Bennett, S. F. (1995). Community organizations and crime. *Annals of the American Academy of Political and Social Science, 539* (May), 72–84.

Benokraitis, N. V., & Feagin, J. R. (1995). *Modern sexism: Blatant, subtle and covert discrimination* (2nd ed.). Upper Saddle River, NJ: Prentice Hall.

Bergen, R. K. (1999). *Marital rape.* Harrisburg, PA: National Online Resource Center on Violence Against Women, www.vawnet.org.

Berger, P. L. (1963). *Invitation to sociology: A humanistic perspective.* Garden City, NY: Anchor Books.

Bergmann, B. R. (1996). *Saving our children from poverty: What the United States can learn from France.* New York: Russell Sage Foundation.

Berliner, D. (1988). Math teaching may favor boys over girls. *Education Digest, 53* (January), 29.

Berliner, D. C., & Biddle, B. J. (1995). *The manufactured crisis: Myths, fraud, and the attack on America's public schools.* Reading, MA: Addison-Wesley.

Bernstein, D. S. (1998). Strategies of equalization, a neglected aspect of the split labour market theory: Jews and Arabs in the split labour market of mandatory Palestine. *Ethnic and Racial Studies, 21,* 449–475.

Bernstein, J. (2003, Sept. 26). Who's poor? Don't ask the Census Bureau. *New York Times*, p. A25.

Berrill, K. T. (1992). Anti-gay violence and victimization in the United States: An overview. In G. M. Herek & K. T. Berrill (Eds.), *Hate crimes: Confronting violence against lesbians and gay men*. Newbury Park, CA: Sage Publications.

Bertram, E., Blachman, M., Sharpe, K., & Andreas, P. (1996). *Drug war politics: The price of denial*. Berkeley: University of California Press.

Best, R. (1983). *We've all got scars: What boys and girls learn in elementary school*. Bloomington: Indiana University Press.

Betz, M., Davis, K., & Miller, P. (1978). Scarcity, income advantage, and mobility: More evidence on the functional theory of stratification. *The Sociological Quarterly, 19*, 399–413.

Biagi, S., & Kern-Foxworth, M. (Eds.). (1997). *Facing difference: Race, gender and mass media*. Thousand Oaks, CA: Pine Forge Press.

Billy, J. O. G., Tanfer, K., Grady, W. R., & Keplinger, D. H. (1993). The sexual behavior of men in the United States. *Family Planning Perspectives, 25*, 52–60.

Bird, C. E., & Rieker, P. P. (1999). Gender matters: An integrated model for understanding men's and women's health. *Social Science and Medicine, 48*, 745–755.

Bishop, D. M., & Frazier, C. E. (1984). The effects of gender on charge reduction. *Sociological Quarterly, 25*, 385–396.

Black, F. L. (1978). Infectious diseases in primitive societies. In M. H. Logan & E. E. Hunt, Jr. (Eds.), *Health and the human condition*. North Scituate, MA: Duxbury Press.

Blau, F. D., Ferber, M. A., & Winkler, A. E. (1998). *The economics of women, men, and work* (3rd ed.). Upper Saddle River, NJ: Prentice Hall.

Blinder, A. S. (Ed.). (1990). *Paying for productivity: A look at the evidence*. Washington, DC: Brookings Institution.

Bloom, J. (1987). *Class, race, and the civil rights movement*. Bloomington: Indiana University Press.

Blum, K., & Payne, J. E. (1991). *Alcohol and the addictive brain*. New York: Free Press.

Blume, J., Eisenberg, T., & Wells, M. T. (2004). Explaining death row's population and racial composition. *Journal of Empirical Legal Studies, 1*, 165–207.

Blumer, H. (1962). Society as symbolic interaction. In A. M. Rose (Ed.), *Human behavior and social processes*. Boston: Houghton Mifflin.

Boccuti, C., & Moon, M. (2003). Comparing Medicare and private insurers: Growth rates in spending over three decades. *Health Affairs, 22*, 230–237.

Boeringer, S. B. (1994). Pornography and sexual aggression: Associations of violent and nonviolent depictions with rape and rape proclivity. *Deviant Behavior, 15* (July–September), 289–304.

Bogard, C. J. (2003). *Seasons such as these: How homelessness took shape in America*. New York: Aldine de Gruyter.

Bohmer, C., Brandt, J., & Bronson, D. (2002). Domestic violence law reforms: Reactions from the trenches. *Journal of Sociology and Social Welfare, 29*, 71–87.

Boli, J., and Thomas, G. M. (1997). World culture in the world polity: A century of international non-governmental organization. *American Sociological Review, 62*, 171–190.

Bonacich, E. (1972). A theory of ethnic antagonism: The split-labor market. *American Sociological Review, 37*, 547–559.

Bonner, R., & Fessenden, F. (2000, September 22). States with no death penalty share lower homicide rates. *New York Times*, p. 1.

Bornschier, V., & Trezzini, B. (1997). Social stratification and mobility in the world system. *International Sociology, 12*, 429–455.

Botvin, G. J. (1998). Preventing adolescent drug abuse through life skills training: Theory, methods, and effectiveness. In J. Crane (Ed.), *Social programs that work*. New York: Russell Sage Foundation.

Boulding, K. E. (1989). *Three faces of power*. Newbury Park, CA: Sage Publications.

Bourgois, P., Lettiere, M., & Quesada, J. (1997). Social misery and the sanction of substance abuse: Confronting HIV risk among homeless heroin addicts in San Francisco. *Social Problems, 44* (May), 155–173.

Bowen, W. G., & Bok, D. (1998). *The shape of the river: Long-term consequences of considering race in college and university admissions*. Princeton, NJ: Princeton University Press.

Braddock, J. H. (1985). School desegregation and black assimilation. *Journal of Social Issues, 41*, 9–22.

Braddock, J. H., Crain, R. L., & McPartland, J. M. (1984). A long-term view of desegregation: Some recent studies of graduates as adults. *Phi Delta Kappan, 66*, 259–264.

Braun, H., Jenkins, F., & Grigg, W. (2006). *A closer look at charter schools using hierarchical linear modeling*. U.S. Department of Education, National Center for Education Statistics, Institute of Education Sciences, Pub. No. NCES 2006–460. Washington, DC: U.S. Government Printing Office.

Brehm, S. S. (1985). *Intimate relationships*. New York: Random House.

Brennan, D. (2003). Selling sex for visas: Sex tourism as a stepping-stone to international migration. In B. Ehrenreich & A. R. Hochschild (Eds.), *Global woman: Nannies, maids, and sex workers in the new economy*. New York: Metropolitan Books.

The Brethren's first sister. (1981, July 20). *Time*, pp. 8–19.

Brewer, M. B., & Miller, N. (1996). *Intergroup relations*. Pacific Grove, CA: Brooks/Cole.

Brint, S. (1998). *Schools and society*. Thousand Oaks, CA: Pine Forge Press.

Britton, D. M. (1990). Homophobia and homosociality: An analysis of boundary maintenance. *The Sociological Quarterly, 31* (3), 423–439.

Broder, M. S., Kanouse, D. E., Mittman, B. S., & Bernstein, S. J. (2000). The appropriateness of recommendations for hysterectomy. *Obstetrics and Gynecology, 95*, 199–205.

Brooks, R. (1969). Domestic violence and America's wars: A historical interpretation. In H. D. Graham & T. R. Gurr (Eds.), *Violence in America*. New York: Bantam Books.

Brown, D. (1998a). Senior power. *Social Policy, 28*, 43–45.

Brown, J. (1970). A note on the division of labor by sex. *American Anthropologist, 72*, 1073–1078.

Brown, L. R. (1987). Analyzing the demographic gap. In L. R. Brown et al. (Eds.), *State of the world, 1987: A Worldwatch Institute report on progress toward a sustainable society*. New York: W. W. Norton.

Brown, L. R. (1998b). Struggling to raise cropland productivity. In L. R. Brown et al. (Eds.), *State of the world, 1998: A Worldwatch Institute report on progress toward a sustainable society*. New York: W. W. Norton.

Brown, M. K., Carnoy, M., Currie, E., Duster, T., Oppenheimer, D. B., Shultz, M. M., & Wellman, D. (2003). *Whitewashing race: The myth of a color-blind society*. Berkeley: University of California Press.

Brown, P. (1995). Cultural capital and social exclusion: Some observations on recent trends in education, employment and the labour market. *Work, Employment and Society, 9*, 29–51.

Brown, R. S., Clement, D. G., Hill, J. W., Retchin, S. M., & Bergeron, J. W. (1993). Do health maintenance organizations work for Medicare? *Health Care Financing Review, 15*, 7–23.

Brownell, P., & Wolden, A. (2002). Elder abuse intervention strategies: Social service or criminal justice? *Journal of Gerontological Social Work, 40*, 83–100.

Brownmiller, S. (1975). *Against our will: Men, women and rape*. New York: Simon & Schuster.

Brownstein, H. H. (2000). Drug distribution and sales as a work system. In C. Faupel and P. M. Roman (Eds.), *Encyclopedia of criminology and deviant behavior: Vol. 4. Self-destructive behavior and disvalued identity*. Philadelphia and London: Taylor and Francis.

Bruce, J., Lloyd, C. B., & Leonard, A. (1995). *Families in focus*. New York: The Population Council.

Brus, W., & Laski, K. (1989). *From Marx to the market: Socialism in search of an economic system*. Oxford: Clarendon Press.

Bryk, A. S., Lee, V. E., & Holland, P. B. (1993). *Catholic schools and the common good*. Cambridge, MA: Harvard University Press.

Brzezinski, Z. (2004). *The choice: Global domination or global leadership*. New York: Basic Books.

Bullard, R. D., & Johnson, G. S. (2000). Environmental justice: Grassroots activism and its impact on public policy decision making. *Journal of Social Issues, 56*, 555–578.

Bullock, C. S. III, Anderson, J. E., & Brady, D. W. (1983). *Public policy in the eighties*. Monterey, CA: Brooks-Cole.

Bullough, V. L. (1976). *Sexual variance in society and history*. New York: John Wiley & Sons.

Burby, R. J., & Rohe, W. M. (1990). Providing for the housing needs of the elderly. *Journal of the American Planning Association, 56*, 324–340.

Burchinal, M. R. (1999). Child care experiences and developmental outcomes. *The Annals of the American Academy of Political and Social Science, 563*, 73–97.

Burchinal, M. R., & Caskie, G. I. L. (2001). Maternal employment, child care, and cognitive outcomes. In E. L. Grigorenko & R. J. Sternberg (Eds.), *Family environment and intellectual functioning: A life-span perspective*. Mahwah, NJ: Lawrence Erlbaum Associates.

Burke, R. J. (1999). Career success and personal failure feelings among managers. *Psychological Reports, 84*, 651–653.

Burkett, E. (1996). *The gravest show on earth: America in the age of AIDS*. New York: Houghton Mifflin.

Burn, S. M., O'Neil, A. K., & Nederend, S. (1996). Childhood tomboyism and adult androgyny. *Sex Roles, 34* (March), 419–428.

Burtless, G., & Smeeding, T. M. (2001). The level, trend, and composition of poverty. In S. H. Danziger & R. H. Haveman (Eds.), *Understanding poverty*. New York: Russell Sage Foundation and Cambridge, MA: Harvard University Press.

Butterfield, F. (1992, July 19). Are American jails becoming shelters from the storm? *New York Times*, sec. 4, p. 4.

Button, J. W., Rienzo, B. A., & Wald, K. D. (1997). *Private lives, public conflicts: Battles over gay rights in American communities*. Washington, DC: Congressional Quarterly Press.

Cabaj, R. P., & Stein, T. S. (Eds.). (1996). *Textbook of homosexuality and mental health*. Washington, DC: American Psychiatric Press.

Calhoun, C., Price, P., & Timmer, A. (Eds.). (2002). *Understanding September 11*. New York: New Press.

Califano, J. A., Jr. (1994). *Radical surgery: What's next for America's health care*. New York: Times Books.

Camp, S. D., et al. (2002). Using inmate survey data in assessing prison performance: A case study comparing private and public prisons. *Criminal Justice Review, 27*, 26–51.

Campbell, C. A. (1991). Prostitution, AIDS, and preventive health behavior. *Social Science and Medicine, 32*, 1367–1378.

Campbell, F. A., Pungello, E. P., Miller-Johnson, S., Burchinal, M. R., & Ramey, C. T. (2001). The development of cognitive and academic abilities: Growth curves from an early childhood educational experiment. *Developmental Psychology, 37*, 231–242.

Canada, K., & Pringle, R. (1995). The role of gender in college classroom interactions: A social context approach. *Sociology of Education, 68*, 161–186.

Cancian, M., & Reed, D. (2001). Changes in family structure: Implications for poverty and related policy. In S. H. Danziger & R. H. Haveman (Eds.), *Understanding poverty*. New York: Russell Sage Foundation and Cambridge, MA: Harvard University Press.

Caraley, D. (1992). Washington abandons the cities. *Political Science Quarterly, 107*, 1–30.

Carling, P. J. (1995). *Return to community: Building support systems for people with psychiatric disabilities*. New York: Guilford Press.

Carlson, D. K. (2005, June 14). Do Americans give women a fighting chance? *The Gallup Poll*. Princeton, NJ: The Gallup Organization, **www.gallup.com**.

Carpenter, B. J. (2000). *Re-thinking prostitution: Feminism, sex, and the self.* New York: Peter Lang Publishing.

Carr, L. G., & Zeigler, D. J. (1990). White flight and white return in Norfolk: A test of predictions. *Sociology of Education, 63,* 272–282.

Carter, G. L. (1997). *The gun control movement.* New York: Twayne.

Cavender, G. (1991). Alternative theory: Labeling and critical perspectives. In J. F. Sheley (Ed.), *Criminology: A contemporary handbook.* Belmont, CA: Wadsworth.

Center for American Women and Politics. (2007). *Women in Elected Office, 2007: Facts and Findings.* Rutgers, The State University of New Jersey, **www.cawp.rutgers.edu**.

Centers for Disease Control and Prevention. (2006, June 2). Twenty-five years of HIV/AIDS—United States, 1981–2006. *Morbidity and Mortality Weekly Report, 55,* 585–592.

Chagnon, N. A. (1996). *The Yanomamo.* Belmont, CA: Wadsworth.

Chambliss, W. J. (1975). Toward a political economy of crime. *Theory and Society, 2,* 149–170.

Chambliss, W. J. (1991). Biology and crime. In J. F. Sheley (Ed.), *Criminology: A contemporary handbook.* Belmont, CA: Wadsworth.

Chase-Dunn, C., & Grimes, P. (1995). World-systems analysis. *Annual Review of Sociology, 21,* 387–417.

Cheng, L., & Bonacich, E. (1984). *Labor immigration under capitalism: Asian workers in the United States before World War II.* Berkeley: University of California Press.

Cherlin, A. J., Chase-Lansdale, P. L., & McRae, C. (1998). Effects of parental divorce on mental health throughout the life course. *American Sociological Review, 63,* 239–249.

Cherlin, A. J., & Furstenberg, F. F., Jr. (1994). Stepfamilies in the United States: A reconsideration. In J. Hagan and K. S. Cook (Eds.), *Annual Review of Sociology,* Vol. 20. Palo Alto, CA: Annual Reviews Inc.

Children Now. (2004). *Fall colors 2003–04: Prime time diversity report.* Oakland, CA: Children Now, **www.childrennow.org**.

Cisneros, H. G. (1995). *Defensible space: Deterring crime and building community.* Washington, DC: U.S. Department of Housing and Urban Development.

Clark, C., & Walter, B. O. (1991). Urban political cultures, financial stress, and city fiscal austerity strategies. *Western Political Quarterly, 44,* 676–697.

Clark, J., Austin, J., & Henry, D. A. (1997). "Three strikes and you're out": A review of state legislation. *National Institute of Justice: Research in brief* (September). Washington, DC: U.S. Department of Justice, Office of Justice Programs.

Clark, R., Lennon, R., & Morris, L. (1993). Of Caldecotts and kings: Gendered images in recent children's books by black and non-black illustrators. *Gender and Society, 7,* 227–245.

Clinard, M. B., & Meier, R. F. (2004). *Sociology of deviant behavior* (12th ed.). Belmont, CA: Wadsworth/Thompson.

Clines, F. X. (2001, February 28). Fighting Appalachia's top cash crop, marijuana. *New York Times,* p. A10.

Clore, G. L., Bray, R. M., Itkin, S. M., & Murphy, P. (1978). Interracial attitudes and behavior at a summer camp. *Journal of Personality and Social Psychology, 36,* 107–116.

Cloward, R. A., & Ohlin, L. E. (1960). *Delinquency and opportunity.* New York: Free Press.

Cnaan, R. A., Olsson, S. E., & Wetle, T. (1990). Cross-national comparisons of planning for the needs of the very old: Israel, Sweden, and the United States. *Journal of Aging and Social Policy, 2* (1), 83–108.

Coates, V. T. (2001). The need for a new Office of Technology Assessment. *The Futurist, 35,* 42–43.

Cochran, J. K., Chamlin, M. B., & Seth, M. (1994). Deterrence or brutalization? An impact assessment of Oklahoma's return to capital punishment. *Criminology, 32,* 107–134.

Cockerham, W. C. (2006). *Sociology of mental disorder* (7th ed.). Upper Saddle River, NJ: Prentice Hall.

Cockerham, W. C. (2007). *Medical sociology* (10th ed.). Upper Saddle River, NJ: Prentice Hall.

Cohen, J. E. (1995). *How many people can the Earth support?* New York: W. W. Norton.

Cohen, L. E., Broschak, J. P., & Haveman, H. A. (1998). And then there were more? The effect of organizational sex composition on the hiring and promotion of managers. *American Sociological Review, 63,* 711–727.

Cohen, L. E., & Felson, M. (1979). Social change and crime rate trends. *American Sociological Review, 44,* 588–609.

Coleman, J. S., Campbell, J. E., Hobson, L., McPartland, J., Mood, A., Weinfield, F., & York, R. (1966). *Equality of educational opportunity.* Washington, DC: U.S. Government Printing Office.

Coleman, J. S., Hoffer, T., & Kilgore, S. (1982). *Public and private high schools: An analysis of high schools and beyond.* Washington, DC: National Council for Education Statistics.

Coleman, J. W. (2005). *The criminal elite: Understanding white-collar crime* (6th ed.). New York: Worth.

Collins, R. (1971). A conflict theory of sexual stratification. *Social Problems, 19,* 3–21.

Collins, R. (1979). *The credential society.* New York: Academic Press.

Collins, R. (1990). Conflict theory and the advance of macro-historical sociology. In G. Ritzer (Ed.), *Frontiers of social theory: The new synthesis.* New York: Columbia University Press.

Coltrane, S., & Collins, R. (2001). *Sociology of marriage and the family: Gender, love, and property* (5th ed.). Belmont, CA: Wadsworth/Thompson.

Colvin, M. (1991). Crime and social reproduction: A response to the call for "outrageous" proposals. *Crime and Delinquency, 73,* 436–448.

Comer, J. P. (1997). *Waiting for a miracle: Why schools can't solve our problems—and how we can.* New York: Dutton.

Comstock, G. D. (1991). *Violence against lesbians and gay men.* New York: Columbia University Press.

Conlin, M. (2002, November 25). Mommy is really home from work. *Business Week,* 101–102.

Cooper, H. H. A. (2001). Terrorism: The problem of definition revisited. *American Behavioral Scientist, 44,* 881–893.

Costanzo, M. (1997). *Just revenge: Costs and consequences of the death penalty.* New York: St. Martin's Press.

Costells, M. (1977). *The urban question: A Marxist approach.* (Ann Sheridan, trans.). Cambridge, MA: MIT Press.

Crabb, P. B., & Bielawski, D. (1994). The social representation of material culture and gender in children's books. *Sex Roles 30,* 69–79.

Cranna, M. (Ed.). (1994). *The true cost of conflict: Seven recent wars and their effects on society.* New York: New Press.

Crawford, M., & MacLeod, M. (1990). Gender in the college classroom: An assessment of the "chilly climate" for women. *Sex Roles, 23,* 101–122.

Craypo, C., & Nissen, B. (Eds.). (1993). *Grand designs: The impact of corporate strategies on workers, unions, and communities.* Ithaca, NY: ILR Press.

Crossman, R. K., Stith, S. M., & Bender, M. M. (1990). Sex role egalitarianism and marital violence. *Sex Roles, 22* (5–6), 293–304.

Crowe, T. D. (1991). *Crime prevention through environmental design.* Boston: Butterworth-Heinemann.

Crystal, S. (1986). Measuring income and inequality among the elderly. *The Gerontologist, 26,* 56–59.

Cuklanz, L. M. (1996). *Rape on trial: How the mass media construct legal reform and social change.* Philadelphia: University of Pennsylvania Press.

Cullen, F. T., Link, B. G., & Polanzi, C. W. (1982). The seriousness of crime revisited: Have attitudes toward white-collar crime changed? *Criminology, 20,* 83–102.

Cullen, J. B., & Novick, S. M. (1979). The Davis-Moore theory of stratification: A further examination and extension. *American Journal of Sociology, 84,* 1414–1437.

Currie, E. (1985). *Confronting crime: An American challenge.* New York: Pantheon Books.

Currie, E. (1993). *Reckoning: Drugs, the cities, and the American future.* New York: Hill and Wang.

Currie, E. (1998). *Crime and punishment in America.* New York: Metropolitan Books.

Daalder, I. H., & Lindsay, J. M. (2004). *America unbound: The Bush revolution in foreign policy.* Washington, DC: Brookings Institution Press.

Dahrendorf, R. (1959). *Class and class conflict in industrial society.* Stanford, CA: Stanford University Press.

Danaher, K. (2001). *Democratizing the global economy: The battle against the World Bank and the IMF.* Monroe, ME: Common Courage Press.

Daniels, R. (1988). *Asian America: Chinese and Japanese in the United States since 1850.* Seattle: University of Washington Press.

Danigelis, N. L., & Fengler, A. P. (1990). Homesharing: How social exchange helps elders live at home. *The Gerontologist, 30,* 162–170.

Danziger, S., & Waldfogel, J. (Eds.). (2000). *Securing the future: Investing in children from birth to college.* New York: Russell Sage Foundation.

Darrow, W. W., et al. (1987). *Multicenter study of human immunodeficiency virus antibody in U.S. prostitutes.* Paper presented at the Third International Conference on AIDS. Washington, DC.

Davenport, W. H. (1977). Sex in cross-cultural perspective. In F. A. Beach (Ed.), *Human sexuality in four perspectives.* Baltimore: Johns Hopkins University Press.

Davenport-Hines, R. (2002). *The pursuit of oblivion: A global history of narcotics.* New York: W. W. Norton.

Davis, J. A., & Smith, T. W. (2004). *General social surveys, 1972–2004.* Chicago: National Opinion Research Center, producer; Storrs: University of Connecticut, Roper Center for Public Opinion Research, distributor.

Davis, K. (1971). Sexual behavior. In R. K. Merton & R. Nisbet (Eds.), *Contemporary social problems* (4th ed.). New York: Harcourt Brace Jovanovich.

Davis, K., & Moore, W. (1945). Some principles of stratification. *American Sociological Review, 10,* 242–249.

Dekker, P., & Ester, P. (1991). Authoritarianism, sociodemographic variables and racism: A Dutch replication of Billig and Cramer. *New Community, 17,* 287–293.

DeLaat, J. (1999). *Gender in the workplace.* Thousand Oaks, CA: Sage.

De Leon, G. (1995). Therapeutic communities for addictions: A theoretical framework. *International Journal of Addictions, 30,* 1603–1645.

Demers, D. (2002). *Global media: Menace or Messiah?,* (Rev. ed.). Cresskill, NJ: Hampton Press.

Devine, J. A., Sheley, J. F., & Smith, M. D. (1988). Macroeconomic and social-control policy influences on crime rate changes, 1948–1985. *American Sociological Review, 53,* 407–420.

Devine, J. A., & Wright, J. D. (1993). *The greatest of evils: Urban poverty and the American underclass.* Hawthorne, NY: Aldine de Gruyter.

DeVries, R., & Subedi, J. (Eds.). (1998). *Bioethics and society: Constructing the ethical enterprise.* Upper Saddle River, NJ: Prentice Hall.

Diamond, P. A., & Orszag, P. R. (2004). *Saving Social Security: A balanced approach.* Washington, DC: Brookings Institution Press.

Diana, L. (1985). *The prostitute and her clients: Your pleasure is her business.* Springfield, IL: Charles C. Thomas.

Dickens, C. (1924). *A tale of two cities.* New York: Charles Scribner's Sons.

Dillon, S. (2007, June 22). Voucher use in Washington wins praise of parents. *New York Times,* p. A13.

Dobrzynski, J. H. (1996, November 6). Somber news for women on corporate ladder. *New York Times,* p. C1.

Domhoff, G. W. (1998). *Who rules America: Power and politics in the year 2000* (3rd ed.). Mountain View, CA: Mayfield.

Donnelly, P. G., & Kimble, C. E. (1997). Community organizing, environmental change, and neighborhood crime. *Crime and Delinquency, 43,* 493–511.

Donnerstein, E., Linz, D., & Penrod, S. (1987). *The question of pornography: Research findings and policy implications.* New York: Free Press.

Doob, C. B. (1999). *Racism: An American cauldron,* (3rd ed.). Boston: Allyn & Bacon.

Dore, R. (1997). *The diploma disease: Education, qualification and development* (2nd ed.). London: Institute of Education.

Dorr, A., Kovaric, P., & Doubleday, C. (1990). Age and content influences on children's perceptions of the realism of television families. *Journal of Broadcasting and Electronic Media, 34*, 377–397.

Dowd, N. E. (1997). *In defense of single-parent families.* New York: New York University Press.

Draper, D. A., Hurley, R. E., Lesser, C. S., & Strunk, B. C. (2002). The changing face of managed care. *Health Affairs, 21*, 11–23.

Duke, J. T. (1976). *Conflict and power in social life.* Provo, UT: Brigham Young University Press.

Dukes, R. L., Stein, J. A., & Ullman, J. B. (1997). Long-term impact of Drug Abuse Resistance Education (D.A.R.E.): Results of a 6-year follow-up. *Evaluation Review, 21* (August), 483–500.

Dulles, J. F. (1954). Police for security and peace. *Foreign Affairs, 32*, 353–364.

Dunbar, L. W. (1988). *The common interest: How our social-welfare policies don't work, and what we can do about them.* New York: Pantheon.

Duncan, G., & Brooks-Gunn, J. (1997). *Consequences of growing up poor.* New York: Russell Sage Publications.

Dunford, F. W., Huizinga, D., & Elliott, D. S. (1990). The role of arrest in domestic assault: The Omaha police experiment. *Criminology, 28*, 183–206.

Dunifon, R., Kalil, A., & Danziger, S. K. (2003). Maternal work behavior under welfare reform: How does the transition from welfare to work affect child development? *Children and Youth Services Review, 25*, 55–82.

Dunlap, D. W. (1994, December 21). Survey on slayings of homosexuals finds high violence and low arrest rate. *New York Times*, p. A10.

Dunn, S. (2001). Decarbonizing the energy economy. In L. R. Brown et al. (Eds.), *State of the world, 2001: A Worldwatch Institute report on progress toward a sustainable society.* New York: W. W. Norton.

Durand, A. M. (1992). The safety of home birth: The farm study. *American Journal of Public Health, 82*, 450–453.

Durfee, A., & Rosenberg, K. (2004). Domestic violence in the United States: Current research, new directions. In R. Perrucci, K. Ferraro, J. Miller, & P. C. Rodriguez Rust (Eds.), *Agenda for Social Justice, 2004.* Knoxville, TN: Society for the Study of Social Problems.

Duster, T. (1987). Crime, youth unemployment, and the black urban underclass. *Crime and Delinquency, 33* (2), 300–316.

Dye, T. R. (2002). *Who's running America: The Bush restoration* (7th ed.). Upper Saddle River, NJ: Prentice Hall.

Easterbrook, G. (1995). *A moment on the Earth: The coming age of environmental optimism.* New York: Viking.

Eder, P. F. (1994). Privacy on parade: Your secrets for sale! *The Futurist, 28*, 38–42.

Egan, T. (1996, December 30). Drawing a line against urban sprawl. *New York Times*, p. A1.

Egan, T. (2000, October 23). Technology sent Wall Street into market for pornography. *New York Times*, p. A1.

Eggert, L. L., & Herting, J. R. (1991). Preventing teenage drug abuse: Exploratory effects of network social support. *Youth and Society, 22*, 482–524.

Egley, L. C. (1991). What changes the societal prevalence of domestic violence? *Journal of Marriage and the Family, 53*, 885–897.

Ehrlich, P. R., & Ehrlich, A. H. (1970). *Population, resources, environment.* San Francisco: W. H. Freeman.

Ehrlich, P. R., & Ehrlich, A. H. (1990). *The population explosion.* New York: Simon & Schuster.

Ehrlich, P. R., & Ehrlich, A. H. (1996). *Betrayal of science and reason: How anti-environmental rhetoric threatens our future.* Washington, DC: Island Press/Shearwater Books.

Ehrlich, P. R., et al. (1983). Long-term biological consequences of nuclear war. *Science, 222*, 1293–1300.

Ellickson, P. L. (1998). Preventing adolescent substance abuse: Lessons from the Project ALERT program. In J. Crane (Ed.), *Social programs that work.* New York: Russell Sage Foundation.

Elliott, D. S., & Huizinga, D. (1983). Social class and delinquent behavior in a national youth panel: 1976–1980. *Criminology, 21*, 149–177.

Energy Information Administration. (2007). *International Energy Price Information.* Washington, DC: Department of Energy, **eia.doe.gov.**

England, P. (1992). *Comparable worth: Theories and evidence.* New York: Aldine de Gruyter.

Entman, R. M. (1997). Modern racism and images of blacks on local television news. In S. Iyengar & R. Reeves (Eds.), *Do the media govern? Politicians, voters, and reporters in America.* Thousand Oaks, CA: Sage.

Entwisle, D. R., & Alexander, K. L. (1994). Winter setback: The racial composition of schools and learning to read. *American Sociological Review, 59*, 446–460.

Environmental Protection Agency. (2006). *Eutrophication.* Washington, DC: U.S. Government Printing Office, **www.epa.gov/maia/html/eutroph.html.**

Environmental Protection Agency. (2007a). *Acid rain.* Washington, DC: U.S. Government Printing Office, **www.epa.gov/acidrain/index.html.**

Environmental Protection Agency. (2007b). *Pesticides.* Washington, DC: U.S. Government Printing Office, **www.epa.gov/pesticides.**

Environmental Protection Agency. (2007c). *Wastes.* Washington, DC: U.S. Government Printing Office, **www.epa.gov/osw.**

Eshleman, J. R. (2006). *The family: An introduction* (11th ed.). Boston: Allyn & Bacon.

The ESOP Association. (2007). *ESOP statistics.* Washington, DC: The ESOP Association, **www.esopassociation.org.**

Estes, R. J., & Weiner, N. A. (2001). *The commercial sexual exploitation of children in the U.S., Canada, and Mexico.* Philadelphia: Center for the Study of Youth Policy, University of Pennsylvania.

Eysenck, H. J., & Gudjonsson, G. H. (1989). *The causes and cures of criminality.* New York: Plenum.

Fagan, J., Piper, E. S., & Cheng, Y-T. (1987). Contributions of victimization to delinquency in inner cities. *Journal of Criminal Law and Criminology, 78* (3), 586–609.

Falkenrath, R. A., Newman, R. D., & Thayer, B. A. (1998). *America's Achilles' heel: Nuclear, biological, and chemical terrorism and covert attack.* Cambridge, MA: The MIT Press.

Faludi, S. (1991). *Backlash: The undeclared war against American women.* New York: Crown Publishers.

Fausto-Sterling, A. (1992). *Myths of gender: Biological theories about women and men.* New York: Basic Books.

Fay, B. (1987). *Critical social science: Liberation and its limits.* Ithaca, NY: Cornell University Press.

Feagin, J. R. (1998). *The new urban paradigm: Critical perspectives on the city.* Lanham, MD: Rowman and Littlefield.

Feagin, J. R., & Sykes, M. P. (1994). *Living with racism: The black middle-class experience.* Boston: Beacon Press.

Feagin, J. R., Vera, H., & Batur-VanderLippe, P. (2000). *White racism.* New York: Routledge.

Featherman, D. L., & Hauser, R. M. (1978). *Opportunity and change.* New York: Academic Press.

Federal Bureau of Investigation. (2006). *Uniform crime reports: Crime in the United States, 2005.* Washington, DC: U.S. Government Printing Office.

Federal Interagency Forum on Child and Family Statistics. (2006). *America's children in brief: Key national indicators of well-being, 2006.* www.childstats.gov.

Feinberg, W. (1993). *Japan and the pursuit of a new American identity: Work and education in a multicultural age.* New York: Routledge.

Feldman, R., Wholey, D., & Christianson, J. (1996). Effect of mergers on health maintenance organization premiums. *Health Care Financing Review, 17* (Spring), 171–190.

Felson, R. B. (1996). Mass media effects on violent behavior. In J. Hagan & K. S. Cook (Eds.), *Annual Review of Sociology, 22.* Palo Alto, CA: Annual Reviews, Inc.

Ferree, M. M. (1991). The gender division of labor in two-earner marriages: Dimensions of variability and change. *Journal of Family Issues, 12,* 158–180.

Ferree, M. M., & Hall, E. J. (1990). Visual images of American society: Gender and race in introductory sociology textbooks. *Gender and Society, 4,* 500–533.

Ficarrotto, T. J. (1990). Racism, sexism, and erotophobia: Attitudes of heterosexuals toward homosexuals. *Journal of Homosexuality, 19* (1), 111–116.

Finnegan, W. (2003). The economics of empire. *Harper's Magazine,* May, 41–54.

Fiorentine, R. (1988). Increasing similarity in the values and life plans of male and female college students? Evidence and implications. *Sex Roles, 18,* 143–158.

Fishman, M. (1978). Crime waves as ideology. *Social Problems, 25* (June), 531–543.

Fitzpatrick, J. P. (1987). *Puerto Rican Americans: The meaning of migration to the mainland* (2nd ed.). Upper Saddle River, NJ: Prentice Hall.

Flavin, C. (1992). Building a bridge to sustainable energy. In L. R. Brown et al. (Eds.), *State of the world, 1992: A Worldwatch Institute report on progress toward a sustainable society.* New York: W. W. Norton.

Flewelling, R. L., Rachal, J. V., & Marsden, M. E. (1992). *Socioeconomic and demographic correlates of drug and alcohol use.* National Institute on Drug Abuse (DHHS Pub. No. [ADM] 92-1906). Washington, DC: U.S. Government Printing Office.

Flowers, R. B. (2000). *Domestic crimes, family violence and child abuse.* Jefferson, NC: McFarland & Company, Inc.

Flowers, R. B. (2001a). *Runaway kids and teenage prostitution: America's lost, abandoned, and sexually exploited children.* Westport, CN: Greenwood Press.

Flowers, R. B. (2001b). The sex trade industry's worldwide exploitation of children. *Annals of the American Academy of Political and Social Science, 575* (May), 147–157.

Ford, C. S. (1970). Some primitive societies. In G. H. Seward & R. C. Williamson (Eds.), *Sex roles in society.* New York: Random House.

Forero, J. (2006, August 19). Columbia's coca survives U.S. plan to uproot it. *New York Times,* p. A1.

Frankenberg, E., & Lee, C. (2003). *Charter schools and race: A lost opportunity for integrated education.* Cambridge, MA: The Civil Rights Project, Harvard University.

Franks, V., & Rothblum, E. D. (Eds.). (1983). *The stereotyping of women: Its effects on mental health.* New York: Springer.

Freedman, J. L. (1975). *Crowding and behavior.* San Francisco: W. H. Freeman.

Freeman, L., & Braconi, F. (2004). Gentrification and displacement. *Journal of the American Planning Association, 70,* 39–52.

Freeman, R. B. (1993). How much has de-unionization contributed to the rise in male earnings inequality? In S. Danziger & P. Gottschalk (Eds.), *Uneven tides: Rising inequality in America.* New York: Russell Sage Foundation.

Freeman, R. B., & Holzer, H. J. (Eds.). (1986). *The black youth employment crisis.* Chicago: University of Chicago Press.

French, H., & Mastny, L. (2001). Controlling international environmental crime. In L. R. Brown et al. (Eds.), *State of the world, 2001: A Worldwatch Institute report on progress toward a sustainable society.* New York: W. W. Norton.

Freund, P. E. S., & McGuire, M. B. (1995). *Health, illness, and the social body: A critical sociology* (2nd ed.). Upper Saddle River, NJ: Prentice Hall.

Friedlander, D., & Burtless, G. (1995). *Five years after: The long-term effects of welfare-to-work programs.* New York: Russell Sage Foundation.

Fritschner, L. M. (2000). Inside the undergraduate college classroom: Faculty and students differ on the meaning of student participation. *Journal of Higher Education, 71,* 342–362.

Fuchs, V. R., & Reklis, D. M. (1992). America's children: Economic perspectives and policy options. *Science, 255,* 41–46.

Fukuyama, F. (2002). *Our postmodern future: Consequences of the biotechnology revolution*. New York: Farrar, Straus, & Giroux.

Funkhouser, J. E., & Gonzales, M. R. (1997). *Family involvement in children's education: Successful local approaches*. Washington, DC: Office of Educational Research and Improvement, U.S. Department of Education.

Furstenberg, F. F., Jr., & Cherlin, A. J. (1991). *Divided families: What happens to children when parents part*. Cambridge, MA: Harvard University Press.

Furstenberg, F. F., Jr., & Teitler, J. O. (1994). Reconsidering the effects of marital disruption: What happens to children in early adulthood? *Journal of Family Issues, 15*, 173–190.

Galliher, J. F. (2004). A report card to the nation on capital punishment. In R. Perrucci, K. Ferraro, J. Miller, & P. C. Rodriguez Rust (Eds.), *Agenda for Social Justice, 2004*. Knoxville, TN: Society for the Study of Social Problems.

Gallup, G. H. Jr. (2003, June 24). Current views on premarital, extramarital sex. *The Gallup Poll Tuesday Briefing*. Princeton, NJ: The Gallup Organization, **www.gallup.com**.

Gallup News Service. (2001). *Attitudes about what should be done to help the have-nots*. Princeton, NJ: The Gallup Organization, **www.gallup.com/poll/socialaudits/should_be_done.asp**.

Gallup News Service. (2004). *Poll analyses*. Princeton, NJ: The Gallup Organization, **www.gallup.com**.

Gallup Poll. (2007a, July 17). *Poll topics A to Z: Cloning*. Princeton, NJ: The Gallup News Service, **www.gallup.com**.

Gallup Poll. (2007b, April 10). *Poll topics A to Z: Homosexual relations*. Princeton, NJ: The Gallup News Service, **www.galluppoll.com**.

Gans, H. J. (1988). *Middle American individualism: The future of liberal democracy*. New York: Free Press.

Gans, H. J. (1994). Positive functions of the undeserving poor: Uses of the underclass in America. *Politics and Society, 22* (September), 269–283.

Gardner, G. (1998). Recycling organic wastes. In L. R. Brown et al. (Eds.), *State of the world, 1998: A Worldwatch Institute report on progress toward a sustainable society*. New York: W. W. Norton.

Gardner, G. (2001). Accelerating the shift to sustainability. In L. R. Brown et al. (Eds.), *State of the world, 2001: A Worldwatch Institute report on progress toward a sustainable society*. New York: W. W. Norton.

Gastil, J. (1990). Generic pronouns and sexist language: The oxymoronic character of masculine generics. *Sex Roles, 23* (11–12), 629–643.

Gelles, R. J. (1987). What to learn from cross-cultural and historical research on child abuse and neglect: An overview. In R. J. Gelles & J. B. Lancaster (Eds.), *Child abuse and neglect: Biosocial dimensions*. New York: Aldine de Gruyter.

Gelles, R. J. (1992). Poverty and violence toward children. *American Behavioral Scientist, 35*, 258–274.

Gelles, R. J. (1997). *Intimate violence in families* (3rd ed.). Newbury Park, CA: Sage Publications.

Gelles, R. J., & Conte, J. R. (1990). Domestic violence and sexual abuse of children: A review of research in the eighties. *Journal of Marriage and the Family, 52*, 1045–1058.

Gendreau, P., & Ross, R. R. (1987). Revivification of rehabilitation: Evidence from the 1980s. *Justice Quarterly, 4*, 349–407.

Gennetian, L. A., & Morris, P. A. (2003). The effect of time limits and make-work-pay strategies on the well-being of children: Experimental evidence from two welfare reform programs. *Children and Youth Services Review, 25*, 17–54.

Gentry, C. S. (1991). Pornography and rape: An empirical analysis. *Deviant Behavior, 12*, 277–288.

Gerrard, M. B. (1994). *Whose backyard, whose risk: Fear and fairness in toxic and nuclear waste siting*. Cambridge, MA: MIT Press.

Gerstel, N., Riessman, C. K., & Rosenfield, S. (1985). Explaining the symptomatology of separated and divorced men and women: The role of material conditions and social networks. *Social Forces, 64*, 84–101.

Giele, J. Z. (1978). *Women and the future*. New York: Free Press.

Gilliam, F. D., Jr., Iyengar, S., Simon, A., & Wright, O. (1997). Crime in black and white: The violent scary world of local news. In S. Iyengar and R. Reeves (Eds.), *Do the media govern? Politicians, voters, and reporters in America*. Thousand Oaks, CA: Sage.

Gilmore, S., & Crissman, A. (1997). Video games: Analyzing gender identity and violence in this new virtual reality. *Studies in Symbolic Interaction, 21*, 181–199.

Ginn Daugherty, H., & Kammeyer, K. C. W. (1995). *An introduction to population*, (2nd ed.).New York: Guilford Press.

The Glass Ceiling Commission. (1995). *Good for business: Making full use of the nation's human capital: A fact-finding report of the federal glass ceiling commission*. Washington, DC: U.S. Government Printing Office.

Glazer, N. (1995). Making work work: Welfare reform in the 1990s. In D. S. Nightingale & R. H. Haveman (Eds.), *The work alternative: Welfare reform and the realities of the job market*. Washington, DC: The Urban Institute Press.

"Global 500: World's Largest Corporations." (2004, July 26) *Fortune*, 163–180

GM bets an arm and a leg on a people-free plant. (1988, September 12). *Business Week*, pp. 72–73.

Godwin, M. (1998). *Cyber rights: Defending free speech in the digital age*. New York: Times Books.

Goff, C., & Nason-Clark, N. (1989). The seriousness of crime in Fredericton, New Brunswick: Perceptions toward white-collar crime. *Canadian Journal of Criminology, 31* (1), 19–34.

Gold, M. (2003). Can managed care and competition control Medicare costs? *Health Affairs, 22*, 176–188.

Goldstein, A., & Kalant, H. (1990). Drug policy: Striking the right balance. *Science, 249*, 1513–1521.

Goldstein, M. C. (1971). Stratification, polyandry, and family structure in central Tibet. *Southwest Journal of Anthropology, 27,* 65–74.

Golombok, S., & Tasker, F. (1996). Do parents influence the sexual orientation of their children? Findings from a longitudinal study of lesbian families. *Developmental Psychology, 32,* 3–11.

Gonzalez, J. (2000). *Harvest of empire: A history of Latinos in America.* New York: Viking.

Goode, E. (2001). *Deviant behavior.* (6th ed.). Upper Saddle River, NJ: Prentice Hall.

Goodstein, D. (2004). *Out of gas: The end of the age of oil.* New York: W. W. Norton & Company.

Gordon, M. (1978). *The American family: Past, present, and future.* New York: Random House.

Gordon, M. M. (1964). *Assimilation in American life.* New York: Oxford University Press.

Gordon, M. M. (1988). *The scope of sociology.* New York: Oxford University Press.

Gornick, J. C., & Meyers, M. K. (2003). *Families that work: Policies for reconciling parenthood and employment.* New York: Russell Sage Foundation.

Gornick, M. E., Eggers, P. W., Reilly, T. W., Mentnech, R. M., Fitterman, L. K., Kucken, L. E., & Vladeck, B. C. (1996). Effects of race and income on mortality and use of services among Medicare beneficiaries. *New England Journal of Medicine, 335* (September 12), 791–799.

Gottlieb, M. (1988). *Comparative economic systems: Preindustrial and modern case studies.* Ames, IA: Iowa State University Press.

Gouldner, A. W. (1976). The dark side of the dialectic: Toward a new objectivity. *Sociological Inquiry, 46,* 3–16.

Greenbaum, R., & Engberg, J. (2000). An evaluation of state enterprise zone policies: California, Florida, New Jersey, New York, Pennsylvania, and Virginia. *Policy Studies Review,* 17, 29–46.

Greenbaum, R., & Engberg, J. (2004). The impact of state enterprise zones on urban manufacturing establishments. *Journal of Policy Analysis and Management,* 23, 315–339.

Greenberg, D., Linksz, D., & Mandell, M. (2003). *Social experimentation and public policymaking.* Washington, DC: The Urban Institute Press.

Greenberg, D. F. (1988). *The construction of homosexuality.* Chicago: University of Chicago Press.

Greenberg, J. R., McKibben, M., & Raymond, J. A. (1990). Dependent adult children and elder abuse. *Journal of Elder Abuse and Neglect, 2* (1–2), 73–86.

Greenfield, S., Rogers, W., Mangotich, M., Carney, M. F., & Tarlov, A. R. (1995). Outcomes of patients with hypertension and non-insulin dependent diabetes mellitus treated by different systems and specialties: Results from the medical outcomes study. *Journal of the American Medical Association, 274* (November 8), 1436–1444.

Greenman, M. (1990). Survivors of prostitution find PRIDE. *Families in Society, 71,* 110–113.

Gregory, R. F. (2003). *Women and workplace discrimination: Overcoming barriers to gender equality.* New Brunswick, NJ: Rutgers University Press.

Greider, W. (1992). *Who will tell the people: The betrayal of American democracy.* New York: Simon & Schuster.

Greider, W. (2003). *The soul of capitalism: Opening paths to a moral economy.* New York: Simon & Schuster.

Grogan, P. S., & Proscio, T. (2000). *Comeback cities: A blueprint for urban neighborhood revival.* Boulder, CO: Westview Press.

Haglund, R. M. J., & Schuckit, M. A. (1981). The epidemiology of alcoholism. In N. Estes & E. Heineman (Eds.), *Alcoholism: Development, consequences and interventions.* St. Louis: Mosby.

Hallin, D. (1991). TV's clean little war. *The Bulletin of the Atomic Scientists, 47* (May), 17–19.

Hallinan, M. T. (1996). Track mobility in secondary school. *Social Forces 74,* 983–1002.

Hamer, D., & Copeland, P. (1994). *The science of desire: The search for the gay gene and the biology of behavior.* New York: Simon & Schuster.

Hanson, D. J. (1975). The influence of authoritarianism upon prejudice: A review. *Resources in Education, 14,* 31.

Hardin, G. (1993). *Living within limits: Ecology, economics, and population taboos.* New York: Oxford University Press.

Harding, R. W. (1997). *Private prisons and public accountability.* New Brunswick, NJ: Transaction Publishers.

Harrington, C., Woolhandler, S., Mullan, J., Carrillo, H., & Himmelstein, D. U. (2001). Does investor ownership of nursing homes compromise the quality of care? *American Journal of Public Health, 91,* 1452–1455.

Harrington, M. (1989). *Socialism: Past and future.* New York: Arcade Publishing.

Harrison, B. (1994). *Lean and mean: The changing landscape of corporate power in the age of flexibility.* New York: Basic Books.

Harrison, P. M., & Beck, A. J. (2006, November). Prisoners in 2005. *Bureau of Justice Statistics Bulletin,* U.S. Department of Justice.

Hawken, P. (1993). *The ecology of commerce: A declaration of sustainability.* New York: HarperCollins.

Hawkins, G., & Zimring, F. E. (1988). *Pornography in a free society.* Cambridge: Cambridge University Press.

Hawley, A. H. (1971). *Urban society: An ecological approach.* New York: Ronald Press.

Hawley, W. D., et al. (1983). *Strategies for effective desegregation.* Lexington, MA: Lexington Books.

Headley, B. D. (1991). Race, class and powerlessness in world economy. *The Black Scholar, 21,* 14–21.

Heckman, J. J., & Lochner, L. (2000). Rethinking education and training policy: Understanding the sources of skill formation in a modern economy. In S. Danziger & J. Waldfogel (Eds.), *Securing the future: Investing in children from birth to college.* New York: Russell Sage Foundation.

Heimer, K., & Matsueda, R. L. (1994). Role-taking, role commitment, and delinquency: A theory of differential social control. *American Sociological Review, 59,* 365–390.

Henderson, N. J., Ortiz, C. W., Sugie, N. F., & Miller, J. (2006). *Law enforcement and Arab American community relations after September 11, 2001: Engagement in a time of uncertainty.* New York: Vera Institute of Justice, **www.vera.org/policerelations**.

Hendry, J. (1995). *Understanding Japanese society* (2nd ed). London: Routledge.

Hertz, R. (1986). *More equal than others: Women and men in dual-career marriages.* Berkeley: University of California Press.

Hewitt, J. P. (2007). *Self and society: A symbolic interactionist social psychology* (10th ed.). Boston: Allyn & Bacon.

Hewlett, S. A. (1991). *When the bough breaks: The cost of neglecting our children.* New York: Basic Books.

Hick, S., & Halpin, E. (2001). Children's rights and the Internet. *Annals of the American Academy of Political and Social Science, 575* (May), 56–70.

Hijab, N. (1988). *Womanpower: The Arab debate on women at work.* New York: Cambridge University Press.

Himmelstein, D., Woolhandler, S., & Hellander, I. (2001). *Bleeding the patient: The consequences of corporate health care.* Monroe, ME: Common Courage Press.

Hindelang, M. J. (1981). Variations in sex-race-age-specific incidence rates of offending. *American Sociological Review, 46,* 461–474.

Hirschel, J. D., Hutchison, I. W. III, & Dean, C. W. (1992). The failure of arrest to deter spouse abuse. *Journal of Research in Crime and Delinquency, 29,* 7–33.

Hirschi, T. (1969). *Causes of delinquency.* Berkeley: University of California Press.

Hirschman, C., & Wong, M. G. (1986). The extraordinary educational achievement of Asian Americans: A search for historical evidence and explanations. *Social Forces, 65,* 1–27.

Hoffmann, J. P., Larison, C., & Sanderson, A. (1997). *An analysis of worker drug use and workplace policies and programs.* Rockville, MD: Office of Applied Studies, Substance Abuse and Mental Health Services Administration, Department of Health and Human Services.

Holden, K. C., & Smock, P. J. (1991). The economic costs of marital dissolution: Why do women bear a disproportionate cost? In W. Richard Scott & J. Blake (Eds.), *Annual Review of Sociology, 17,* 51–78.

Holley, D. (2001, August 21). Portugal takes away prison as a penalty for using drugs. *Los Angeles Times,* p. A1.

Holstein, J. A., & Miller. G., Eds. (2003). *Challenges and choices: Constructionist perspectives on social problems.* Hawthorne, NY: Aldine de Gruyter.

Hooker, E. (1969). Parental relations and male homosexuality in patient and nonpatient samples. *Journal of Consulting and Clinical Psychology, 33,* 141.

Hooks, G., Mosher, C., Rotolo, T., & Lobao, L. (2004). The prison industry: Carceral expansion and employment in U.S. counties, 1969–1994. *Social Science Quarterly, 85,* 37–57.

Horrocks, S., Anderson, E., & Salisbury, C. (2002, April 6). Systematic review of whether nurse practitioners working in primary care can provide equivalent care to doctors. *British Medical Journal, 324,* 819–823.

Horwitz, A. V. (2002). *Creating mental illness.* Chicago: University of Chicago Press.

Hourani, A. (1991). *A history of the Arab peoples.* Cambridge, MA: Harvard University Press.

Houseknecht, S. (1987). Voluntary childlessness. In M. B. Sussman & S. K. Steinmetz (Eds.), *Handbook of marriage and the family.* New York: Plenum.

Houseknecht, S. K., Vaughan, S., & Macke, A. S. (1984). Marital disruption among professional women: The timing of career and family events. *Social Problems, 31,* 273–284.

Hout, M. (1988). More universalism, less structural mobility: The American occupational structure in the 1980s. *American Journal of Sociology, 93,* 1358–1400.

Howard, I. (2002). Power sources: On party, gender, race, and class, TV news looks to the most powerful groups. *Extra!,* (May/June).

Howard, J. R., & Henney, A. L. (1998). Student participation and instructor gender in the mixed-age college classroom. *Journal of Higher Education, 69,* 384–405.

Howard, T., & Rifkin, J. (1977). *Who should play God? The artificial creation of life and what it means for the future of the human race.* New York: Delacorte Press.

Huesmann, L. R., Moise-Titus, J., Podolski, C., & Eron, L. D. (2003). Longitudinal relations between children's exposure to TV violence and their aggressive and violent behavior in young adulthood: 1977–1992. *Developmental Psychology, 39,* 201–221.

Huff-Corzine, L., Corzine, J., & Moore, D.C. (1991). Deadly connections: Culture, poverty, and the direction of lethal violence. *Social Forces, 69,* 715–732.

Hurn, C. J. (1993). *The limits and possibilities of schooling* (3rd ed.). Boston: Allyn & Bacon.

Huston, A. C., et al. (1992). *Big world, small screen: The role of television in American society.* Lincoln: University of Nebraska Press.

Illich, I. (1976). *Medical nemesis.* New York: Bantam Books.

Ima, K. (1982). Japanese Americans: The making of "good" people. In A. G. Dworkin & R. J. Dworkin (Eds.), *The Minority Report* (2nd ed.). New York: Holt, Rinehart and Winston.

Inciardi, J. A., Horowitz, R., & Pottieger, A. E. (1993). *Street kids, street drugs, street crime: An examination of drug use and serious delinquency in Miami.* Belmont, CA: Wadsworth.

Intergovernmental Panel on Climate Change. (2007). *Climate change 2007: Mitigation of climate change.* Cambridge, UK: Cambridge University Press.

Intriligator, M. D. (1993). A way to achieve national health insurance in the United States: The Medicare expansion proposal. *American Behavioral Scientist, 36,* 709–723.

Investment Company Institute. (2001). *2001 Profile of Mutual Fund Shareholders.* Washington, DC: Investment Company Institute, **www.ici.org**.

Irelan, L. M., Moles, O. C., & O'Shea, R. M. (1969). Ethnicity, poverty, and selected attitudes: A test of the "culture of poverty" hypothesis. *Social Forces, 47,* 405–413.

Jacobsen, C., & Hanneman, R. A. (1992). Illegal drugs: Past, present and possible futures. *The Journal of Drug Issues, 22,* 105–120.

Jacobsen, J. P., & Levin, L. M. (1992). The effects of intermittent labor force attachment on female earnings. Paper presented at a meeting of the American Economic Association, New Orleans.

Jacobson, J. (1988). Planning the global family. In L. R. Brown et al. (Eds.), *State of the world 1988: A Worldwatch Institute report on progress toward a sustainable society.* New York: W. W. Norton.

Jaffe, H. W., et al. (1983). National case-control study of Kaposi's sarcoma and *pneumocystis carinii* pneumonia in homosexual men: 1. Epidemiological results. *Annals of Internal Medicine, 99,* 145–151.

Janowitz, M. (1969). Patterns of collective racial violence. In H. D. Graham & T. R. Gurr (Eds.), *The history of violence in America.* New York: Bantam Books.

Jargowsky, P. A. (1997). *Poverty and place: Ghettos, barrios, and the American city.* New York: Russell Sage Foundation.

Jekielek, S. M. (1998). Parental conflict, marital disruption and children's emotional well-being. *Social Forces, 76,* 905–935.

Jencks, C. (1992). *Rethinking social policy: Race, poverty, and the underclass.* Cambridge, MA: Harvard University Press.

Jencks, C., et al. (1972). *Inequality: A reassessment of the effect of family and schooling in America.* New York: Basic Books.

Jenness, V., & Broad, K. (1997). *Hate crimes: New social movements and the politics of violence.* New York: Aldine de Gruyter.

Jesilow, P., Pontell, H. N., & Geis, G. (1993). *Prescription for profit: How doctors defraud Medicaid.* Berkeley: University of California Press.

Johnson, C. (2004). *The sorrows of empire: Militarism, secrecy, and the end of the Republic.* New York: Metropolitan Books/Henry Holt.

Johnson, J. D., Adams, M. S., Ashburn, L., & Reed, W. (1995). Differential gender effects of exposure to rap music on African American adolescents' acceptance of teen dating violence. *Sex Roles, 33,* 597–605.

Johnson, S. M., & O'Connor, E. (2002). *The gay baby boom: The psychology of gay parenthood.* New York: New York University Press.

Jones, J. D., Vanfossen, B. E., & Ensminger, M. E. (1995). Individual and organizational predictors of high school track placement. *Sociology of Education, 68,* 287–300.

Joseph, J. (1997). Fear of crime among black elderly. *Journal of Black Studies, 27,* 698–717.

Josephson, W. L. (1987). Television violence and children's aggression: Testing the priming, social script, and disinhibition predictions. *Journal of Personality and Social Psychology, 53* (5), 882–890.

Jost, K. (2003, March 15). Medical malpractice: The crisis question. *Congressional Quarterly Weekly, 61,* 648–653.

Judd, D. R. (1991, December 9). Segregation forever? *The Nation,* pp. 740–743.

Kagan, S. L. (1991). Examining profit and nonprofit child care: An odyssey of quality and auspices. *Journal of Social Issues, 47* (2), 87–104.

Kalmuss, D. S., & Straus, M. A. (1982). Wife's marital dependency and wife abuse. *Journal of Marriage and the Family, 44,* 277–286.

Kamerman, S. B., & Kahn, A. J. (1991). *Innovations in European parenting policies.* Westport, CT: Greenwood.

Karoly, L. A., et al. (1998). *Investing in our children: What we know and don't know about the costs and benefits of early childhood interventions.* Santa Monica, CA: RAND.

Kate, N. T. (1992). Filling the corporate day-care gap. *American Demographics, 14,* 19–20.

Kay, F. M., & Hagan, J. (1998). Raising the bar: The gender stratification of law-firm capital. *American Sociological Review, 63,* 728–743.

Kennedy, L. W. (1990). *On the borders of crime: Conflict management and criminology.* New York: Longman.

Kerschner, P. A., & Hirschfield, I. S. (1983). Public policy and aging. In D. S. Woodruff & J. E. Birren (Eds.), *Aging: Scientific perspective and social issues* (2nd ed.). Monterey, CA: Brooks-Cole.

Kessler, R. C., House, J. S., & Turner, J. B. (1987). Unemployment and health in a community sample. *Journal of Health and Social Behavior, 28,* 51–59.

Kett, J. F. (1977). *Rites of passage: Adolescents in America, 1970 to the present.* New York: Basic Books.

Kiecolt-Glaser, J. K., et al. (1987). Marital quality, marital disruption, and immune function. *Psychosomatic Medicine, 49,* 13–34.

Killias, M., & Clerici, C. (2000). Different measures of vulnerability in their relation to different dimensions of fear of crime. *British Journal of Criminology, 40,* 437–450.

Kimbrell, A. (1993). *The human body shop: The engineering and marketing of life.* New York: HarperSanFrancisco.

Kimmel, M. (1996). *Manhood in America: A cultural history.* New York: Free Press.

King, R. S., & Mauer, M. (2001). *Aging behind bars: "Three strikes" seven years later.* Washington, DC: The Sentencing Project.

Kirby, D. (2001). *Emerging answers: Research findings on programs to reduce teen pregnancy (summary).* Washington, DC: National Campaign to Prevent Teen Pregnancy.

Kirk, S. A., & Kutchins, H. (1992). *The selling of DSM: The rhetoric of science in psychiatry.* New York: Aldine de Gruyter.

Kitano, H. H. L. (1976). *Japanese Americans* (2nd ed.). Upper Saddle River, NJ: Prentice Hall.

Kleck, G. (1991). *Point blank: Guns and violence in America.* New York: Aldine de Gruyter.

Kleinknecht, W. (1996). *The new ethnic mobs: The changing face of organized crime in America.* New York: Simon & Schuster.

Kletzer, L. G. (2001). *Job loss from imports: Measuring the costs.* Washington, DC: Institute for International Economics.

Kluegel, J. R., & Bobo, L. (1991). Modern American prejudice: Stereotypes of blacks, Hispanics, and Asians.

Paper presented at the annual meeting of the American Sociological Association, Cincinnati, Ohio.

Kooistra, P. G., Mahoney, J. S., & Westervelt, S. D. (1998). The world of crime according to "Cops." In M. Fishman & G. Cavender (Eds.), *Entertaining crime: Television reality programs*. New York: Aldine de Gruyter.

Koppel, R. (2002). American public policy: Formation and implementation. In R. A. Straus (Ed.), *Using sociology: An introduction from the applied and clinical perspectives*, (3rd ed.). Lanham, MD: Rowman & Littlefield.

Kornhauser, W. (1966). "Power elite" or "veto groups." In R. Bendix & S. M. Lipset (Eds.), *Class, status and power* (2nd ed.). New York: Free Press.

Kosberg, J. I. (Ed.). (1992). *Family care of the elderly: Social and cultural changes*. Newbury Park, CA: Sage Publications.

Kozol, J. (2005). *The shame of the nation: The restoration of Apartheid schooling*. New York: Crown.

Krech, S., III. (1999). *The ecological Indian: Myth and history*. New York: W. W. Norton.

Kristof, N. D. (1993, April 25). China's crackdown on births: A stunning and harsh success. *New York Times*, p. 1.

Kuhn, C., Swartzwelder, S., & Wilson, W. (1998). *Buzzed: The straight facts about the most used and abused drugs from alcohol to ecstasy*. New York: W. W. Norton.

Kuhr, S., & Hauer, J. M. (2001). The threat of biological terrorism in the new millennium. *American Behavioral Scientist, 44*, 1032–1041.

Kull, S. (1994). *Fighting poverty in America: A study of American public attitudes*. Washington, DC: Center for the Study of Policy Attitudes.

Kutchinsky, B. (1991). Pornography and rape: Theory and practice? *International Journal of Law and Psychiatry, 14*, 47–64.

Kutner, N., & Kutner, M. (1987). Ethnic and residence differences among poor families. *Journal of Comparative Family Studies, 18* (3), 463–470.

Land, K. C., et al. (2007). *The child and youth well-being index (CWI)*. Durham, NC: Duke University, **www.soc. duke.edu/~cwi**.

Langewiesche, W. (2007). *The atomic bazaar: The rise of the nuclear poor*. New York: Farrar, Straus, & Giroux.

Lanier, J. R. (2003). The harmful impact of the criminal justice system and war on drugs on the African American family. In National Urban League, *The State of Black America, 2003*. Washington, DC: National Urban League, **www.nul.org**.

Lasswell, H. D. (1936). *Politics: Who gets what, when, and how*. New York: McGraw-Hill.

Lattimore, P. K., Trudeau, J., Riley, K. J., Leiter, J., & Edwards, S. (1997). *Homicide in eight U.S. cities: Trends, context, and policy implications*. Washington, DC: National Institute of Justice, Office of Justice Programs.

Laumann, E. O., Gagnon, J. H., Michael, R. T., & Michaels, S. (1994). *The social organization of sexuality: Sexual practices in the United States*. Chicago and London: University of Chicago Press.

Laws, G. (1995). Understanding ageism: Lessons from feminism and postmodernism. *The Gerontologist, 35*, 112–118.

Lawson, R., & George, V. (1980). An assessment. In V. George & R. Lawson (Eds.), *Poverty and inequality in common market countries*. London: Routledge and Kegan Paul.

Leavitt, G. C. (1992). General evolution and Durkheim's hypothesis of crime frequency: A cross-cultural test. *Sociological Quarterly, 33*, 241–263.

Leckie, R. (1990). *None died in vain: The saga of the American Civil War*. New York: HarperCollins.

Leckie, R. (1992). *The wars of America*. New York: Harper-Collins.

Lee, J. (2002). From civil relations to racial conflict: Merchant–customer interactions in urban America. *American Sociological Review, 67*, 77–98.

Lee, S. M. (1994). Poverty and the U.S. Asian population. *Social Science Quarterly, 75*, 541–559.

Le Grand, J., & Estrin, S. (Eds.). (1989). *Market socialism*. Oxford: Clarendon Press.

Lemert, E. (1951). *Social pathology*. New York: McGraw-Hill.

Lempert, R. (1983). The effect of executions on homicides: A new look in an old light. *Crime and Delinquency, 29*, 88–115.

Levin, J., & Levin, W. C. (1994). *The functions of discrimination and prejudice* (2nd ed.).New York: Harper & Row.

Levine, L. (2001). *The gender wage gap and pay equity: Is comparable worth the next step?* Washington, DC: Congressional Research Service Report for Congress, The Library of Congress.

Levy, S. G. (1969). A 150-year study of political violence in the United States. In H. D. Graham & T. R. Gurr (Eds.), *Violence in America: Historical and comparative perspectives*. New York: Bantam Books.

Lewes, K. (1988). *The psychoanalytic theory of male homosexuality*. New York: Simon & Schuster.

Lewin, T. (1998a, April 15). Men assuming bigger share at home, new survey shows. *New York Times*, p. A16.

Lewin, T. (1998b, April 29). From welfare role to child care worker. *New York Times*, p. A14.

Lewis, D. A., Stevens, A. B., & Slack, K. S. (2002). *Welfare reform in Illinois: Is the moderate approach working?* Evanston, IL: Institute for Policy Research, Northwestern University, **www.northwestern.edu/ ipr/research**.

Lewis, O. (1966). The culture of poverty. *Scientific American, 2* (5), 19–25.

Lichter, D. T., & Jayakody, R. (2002). Welfare reform: How do we measure success? *Annual Review of Sociology, 28*, 117–141.

Light, W. J. H. (1986). *Psychodynamics of alcoholism: A current synthesis*. Springfield, IL: Charles C. Thomas.

Lindorff, D. (1992). *Marketplace medicine: The rise of the for-profit hospital chains*. New York: Bantam Books.

Lindsey, L. L. (1997). *Gender roles: A sociological perspective* (3rd ed.). Upper Saddle River, NJ: Prentice Hall.

Lines, P. M. (2000). Homeschooling comes of age. *Public Interest*, 140, 74–85.

Linz, D., & Donnerstein, E. (1992). Research can help us explain violence and pornography. *The Chronicle of Higher Education*, 39 (September 30), B3–B4.

Loeb, S., et al. (2004). Child care in poor communities: Early learning effects of type, quality, and stability. *Child Development*, 75, 47–65.

Loeb, S., et al. (2007). How much is too much? The influence of preschool centers on children's social and cognitive development. *Economics of Education Review*, 26, 52–66.

Loftus, J. (2001). America's liberalization in attitudes toward homosexuality, 1973 to 1998. *American Sociological Review*, 66, 762–782.

Lohr, S. (2003, Dec. 22). Offshore jobs in technology: Opportunity or a threat? *New York Times*, p. C1.

Long, F. J., & Arnold, M. B. (1995). *The power of environmental partnerships*. Fort Worth, TX: Dryden Press.

Longman, P. (1987). *Born to pay: The new politics of aging in America*. Boston: Houghton Mifflin.

Longshore, D., & Prager, J. (1985). The impact of school desegregation: A situational analysis. *Annual Review of Sociology*, 11, 75–91.

Loomis, L. S., & Landale, N. S. (1994). Nonmarital cohabitation and childbearing among black and white American women. *Journal of Marriage and the Family*, 56, 949–962.

Loseke, D. R. (2003). *Thinking about social problems: An introduction to constructionist perspectives*. Edison, NJ: Aldine Transaction.

Love, J. M., et al. (2002). *Making a difference in the lives of infants and toddlers and their families: The impacts of Early Head Start*. Washington, DC: Administration of Children and Families, Department of Health and Human Services, and Mathematica Policy Research, Inc., **www.acf.hhs.gov/programs/core/ongoing-research/ehs/ehsreports.html**.

Lowe, J. (2000). International examinations: The new credentialism and reproduction of advantage in a globalising world. *Assessment in Education*, 7, 363–377.

Lowman, J. (1992). Street prostitution control: Some Canadian reflections on the Finsbury Park experience. *The British Journal of Criminology*, 32, 1–16.

Luckenbill, D. F. (1989). Deviant career mobility: The case of male prostitutes. In D. H. Kelly (Ed.), *Deviant behavior* (3rd ed.). (pp. 485–503). New York: St. Martin's Press.

Luker, K. (1996). *Dubious conceptions: The politics of teenage pregnancy*. Cambridge, MA: Harvard University Press.

Lynch, J. W., Kaplan, G. A., & Shema, S. J. (1997). Cumulative impact of sustained economic hardship on physical, cognitive, psychological, and social functioning. *New England Journal of Medicine*, 337 (December 25), 1889–1895.

Lyon, L. (1999). *The community in urban society*. Prospect Heights, IL: Waveland Press.

MacArthur, J. R. (1992). *Second front: Censorship and propaganda in the Gulf War*. New York: Hill and Wang.

MacDonald, K., & Parke, R. (1986). Parent–child physical play: The effects of sex and age of children and parents. *Sex Roles*, 15, 367–378.

MacKenzie, D. L. (1997). Criminal justice and crime prevention. In L. W. Sherman, D. Gottfredson, D. MacKenzie, J. Eck, P. Reuter, & S. Bushway (Eds.), *Preventing crime: What works, what doesn't, what's promising*. Washington, DC: Office of Justice Programs, U.S. Department of Justice.

MacKinnon, C. A. (1993). *Only words*. Cambridge, MA: Harvard University Press.

Macklin, E. (1987). Non-traditional family forms. In M. Sussman & S. Steinmetz (Eds.), *Handbook of marriage and the family*. New York: Plenum.

Maguire, K., & Pastore, A. L. (Eds.). (2004). *Sourcebook of criminal justice statistics, 2002*. Washington, DC: U.S. Department of Justice, Bureau of Justice Statistics, **www.albany.edu/sourcebook**.

Malamuth, N. M., Addison, T., & Koss, M. (2000). Pornography and sexual aggression: Are there reliable effects and can we understand them? *Annual Review of Sex Research*, 11, 26–91.

Malthus, T. R. (1960, originally published 1798). In G. Himmelfarb (Ed.), *On population*. New York: Modern Library.

Mann, C. C., & Plummer, M. L. (1995). *Noah's choice: The future of endangered species*. New York: Alfred A. Knopf.

Mann, E. (1990, September 17). L. A.'s smogbusters. *The Nation*, 257, pp. 257–274.

Mansfield, P. K., Koch, P. B., Henderson, J., Vicary, J. R., Cohn, M., & Young, E. W. (1991). The job climate for women in traditionally male blue-collar occupations. *Sex Roles*, 25 (1–2), 63–79.

Marden, C. F., Meyer, G., & Engel, M. H. (1992). *Minorities in American society* (6th ed.). New York: HarperCollins.

Marks, C. (1981). Split-labor markets and black–white relations, 1865–1920. *Phylon*, 42, 293–308.

Marks, C. (1991). The urban underclass. *Annual Review of Sociology*, 17, 445–466.

Marks, P. M. (1998). *In a barren land: American Indian dispossession and survival*. New York: William Morrow.

Marshall, D. S. (1974). Too much sex in Mangaia. In E. Goode & R. Troiden (Eds.), *Sexual deviance and sexual deviants*. New York: William Morrow.

Martin, C. L. (1990). Attitudes and expectations about children with nontraditional and traditional gender roles. *Sex Roles*, 22 (3–4), 151–165.

Martin, S. E. (Ed.). (1993). *Alcohol and interpersonal violence: Fostering multidisciplinary perspectives*. National Institute on Alcohol Abuse and Alcoholism (NIH Pub. No. 93-3496). Rockville, MD: U.S. Department of Health and Human Services.

Martin, S. E., Maxwell, C. D., and White, H. R. (2004). Trends in alcohol use, cocaine use, and crime: 1989–1998. *Journal of Drug Issues*, 34, 333–359.

Martinez, R., & Dukes, R. L. (1991). Ethnic and gender differences in self-esteem. *Youth and Society*, 22, 318–338.

Martinez, T. A. (1997). Popular culture as oppositional culture: Rap as resistance. *Sociological Perspectives, 40,* 265–286.

Marx, K. (1964, originally published 1848). In T. B. Bottomore & M. Rubel (Eds.), *Selected writings in sociology and philosophy.* Baltimore: Penguin.

Marx, K. (1967, originally published 1867–1895). *Das kapital.* New York: International Publishers.

Massey, D. S. (2001). Residential segregation and neighborhood conditions in U.S. metropolitan areas. In N. J. Smelser, W. J. Wilson, & F. Mitchell (Eds.), *America becoming: Racial trends and their consequences, Vol. I.* Washington, DC: National Research Council, National Academy Press.

Mattoon, A. (2001). Deciphering amphibian declines. In L. R. Brown et al. (Eds.), *State of the world, 2001: A Worldwatch Institute report on progress toward a sustainable society.* New York: W. W. Norton.

Mauer, M., & Chesney-Lind, M., Eds. (2002). *Invisible punishment: The collateral consequences of mass imprisonment.* New York: The New Press.

Mauldin, W. P. (1975). Assessment of national family planning programs in developing countries. *Studies in Family Planning, 6,* 30–36.

Maume, D. J., Jr. (1991). Child-care expenditures and women's employment turnover. *Social Forces, 70,* 495–508.

Maume, D. J., Jr. (1998). Occupational constraints on women's entry into management. In D. Vannoy & P. J. Dubeck (Eds.), *Challenges for work and family in the twenty-first century.* New York: Aldine de Gruyter.

Maxwell, C. D., Garner, J. H., and Fagan, J. A. (2001, July). The effects of arrest on intimate partner violence: New evidence from the spousal assault replication program. *Research in Brief.* Washington. D.C.: National Institute of Justice, U.S. Department of Justice.

Mazur, A. (1993). Controlling technology. In A. H. Teich (Ed.), *Technology and the future* (6th ed.). New York: St. Martin's Press.

McChesney, R. W. (2004). *The problem of the media: U.S. communication politics in the 21st century.* New York: Monthly Review Press.

McClendon, M. J. (1976). The occupational status attainment process in males and females. *American Sociological Review, 41,* 52–64.

McConnell, S. R. (1983). Retirement and employment. In D. S. Woodruff & J. E. Birren (Eds.), *Aging: Scientific perspectives and social issues* (2nd ed.). Monterey, CA: Brooks-Cole.

McCoy, N. L. (1985). Innate factors in sex differences. In A. G. Sargent (Ed.), *Beyond sex roles* (2nd ed.). St. Paul, MN: West Publishing Company.

McGinn, A. P. (1998). Promoting sustainable fisheries. In L. R. Brown et al. (Eds.), *State of the world, 1998: A Worldwatch Institute report on progress toward a sustainable society.* New York: W. W. Norton.

McKee, J. K. (2003). *Sparing nature: The conflict between human population growth and earth's biodiversity.* New Brunswick, NJ: Rutgers University Press.

McKeown, T., Brown, R. G., & Record, R. G. (1972). An interpretation of the modern rise of population in Europe. *Population Studies, 26,* 345–382.

McKeown, T., Brown, R. G., & Turner, R. D. (1975). An interpretation of the decline of mortality in England and Wales during the twentieth century. *Population Studies, 29,* 391–422.

McKibben, B. (2003). *Enough: Staying human in an engineered age.* New York: Times Books/Henry Holt.

McKinlay, J. B. (1997). A case for refocusing upstream: The political economy of illness. In P. Conrad (Ed.), *The sociology of health and illness: Critical perspectives* (5th ed.). New York: St. Martin's Press.

McKinlay, J. B., & McKinlay, S. M. (1977). The questionable contribution of medical measures to the decline of mortality in the United States in the twentieth century. *Milbank Memorial Fund Quarterly/ Health and Society, 55,* 405–428.

McLanahan, S., & Sandefur, G. (1994). *Growing up with a single parent: What hurts, what helps.* Cambridge, MA: Harvard University Press.

McManus, P. A., & DiPrete, T. A. (2001). Losers and winners: The financial consequences of separation and divorce for men. *American Sociological Review, 66,* 246–268.

McNeil, J. (2001). Americans with disabilities: 1997. *Current Population Reports,* Pub. No. P70–73. Washington, DC: U.S. Bureau of the Census.

Mead, L. M. (1994). Poverty: How little we know. *Social Service Review, 68,* 322–350.

Melman, S. (2001). *After capitalism: From managerialism to workplace democracy.* New York: Knopf.

Merrill, J. C., & Cohen, A. B. (1989). Explicit rationing of medical care: Is it really needed? In J. D. McCue (Ed.), *The medical cost-containment crisis: Fears, opinions, and facts.* Ann Arbor, MI: Health Administration Press.

Merton, R. K. (1949). Discrimination and the American creed. In R. M. MacIver (Ed.), *Discrimination and national welfare.* New York: Harper & Row.

Merton, R. K. (1968). *Social theory and social structure* (2nd ed.). New York: Free Press.

Mesarovic, M., & Pestel, E. (1974). *Mankind at the turning point.* New York: Dutton.

Metcalf, K. K., West, S. D., Legan, N., Paul, K., & Boone, W. J. (2002). *Evaluation of the Cleveland Scholarship and Tutoring Program, 1998–2001.* Bloomington: Indiana Center for Evaluation, Indiana University.

Middleton, R. (1976). Regional differences in prejudice. *American Sociological Review, 41,* 94–117.

Milhausen, R. R., & Herold, E. S. (1999). Does the sexual double standard still exist? Perceptions of university women. *Journal of Sex Research, 36,* 361–368.

Milhorn, H. T. (1994). *Drug and alcohol abuse.* New York and London: Plenum.

Miller, A. D., & Ohlin, L. E. (1985). *Delinquency in the community: Creating opportunities and controls.* Beverly Hills, CA: Sage Publications.

Miller, R. L. (1991). *The case for legalizing drugs.* New York: Praeger.

Miller, S. C. (1969). *The unwelcome immigrant.* Berkeley: University of California Press.

Mills, C. W. (1956). *The power elite*. New York: Oxford University Press.

Mills, C. W. (1959). *The sociological imagination*. New York: Oxford University Press.

Min, P. G. (Ed.). (1994). *Asian Americans: Contemporary trends and issues*. Thousand Oaks, CA: Sage Publications.

Mincer, J. (1985, August 9). Those hurt by drunken drivers press suits against drivers' hosts. *New York Times*, p. 1.

Miringoff, M., & Miringoff, M. L. (1999). *The social health of the nation: How America is really doing*. New York: Oxford University Press.

Mirkinson, J. (1997). The global trade in women. *Earth Island Journal, 13* (Winter), 30–31.

Miron, J. A. (2004). *Drug war crimes: The consequences of prohibition*. Oakland, CA: The Independent Institute.

Mirowsky, J., & Ross, C. E. (2003). *Social causes of psychological distress*. Hawthorne, NY: Aldine de Gruyter.

Mishel, L., Bernstein, J., & Schmitt, J. (2001). *The state of working America: 2000/2001*. Ithaca, NY, and London: ILR Press and Cornell University Press.

Monbiot, G. (2004). *Manifesto for a new world order*. New York: New Press.

Montagu, A. (1998). *Man's most dangerous myth: The fallacy of race* (6th ed.). Thousand Oaks, CA: Altamira Press.

Moody, K. (1997). *Workers in a lean world: Unions in the international economy*. London, New York: Verso.

Moore, T. S. (1996). *The disposable work force: Worker displacement and employment instability in America*. New York: Aldine de Gruyter.

Morris, A. D. (1984). *The origins of the civil rights movement: Black communities organizing for change*. New York: Free Press.

Morris, J. R. (1999). Market constraints on child care quality. *The Annals of the American Academy of Political and Social Science, 563*, 130–145.

Mowlana, H., Gerbner, G., & Schiller, H. I. (Eds.). (1992). *Triumph of the image: The media's war in the Persian Gulf—A global perspective*. Boulder, CO: Westview Press.

Murdock, G. P. (1967). *World ethnographic atlas*. Pittsburgh: University of Pittsburgh Press

Myers, S. L. (1994, September 11). Tough laws urged on X-rated shops in New York City. *New York Times*, p. A1.

Nace, T. (2003). *Gangs of America: The rise of corporate power and the disabling of democracy*. San Francisco: Berrett-Koehler Publishers.

Nadelmann, E. A. (1998). Commonsense drug policy. *Foreign Affairs, 77* (January–February), 111–126.

Najjar, O. A. (1992). Between nationalism and feminism: The Palestinian answer. In J. M. Bystydzienski (Ed.), *Women transforming politics: Worldwide strategies for empowerment*. Bloomington and Indianapolis: Indiana University Press.

National Center for Health Statistics. (2006). *Health, United States, 2006*. Hyattsville, MD: National Center for Health Statistics.

National Council of La Raza. (1997). Don't blink: Hispanics in television entertainment. In S. Biagi & M. Kern-Foxworth (Eds.), *Facing difference: Race, gender and mass media*. Thousand Oaks, CA: Pine Forge Press.

National Institute of Child Health and Human Development Early Child Care Research Network. (2003). Does amount of time spent in child care predict socio-emotional adjustment during the transition to kindergarten? *Child Development, 74*, 976–1005.

National Low Income Housing Coalition. (2006). *Out of reach 2006*. Washington, DC: National Low Income Housing Coalition, www.nlihc.org/.

National Research Council. (2004). *Biological confinement of genetically engineered organisms*. Washington, DC: The National Academies Press.

Neckerman, K. M., & Kirschenman, J. (1991). Hiring strategies, racial bias, and inner-city workers. *Social Problems, 38*, 443–447.

Neier, A. (1998). *War crimes: Brutality, genocide, terror, and the struggle for justice*. New York: Times Books.

Nelson, F. H., Rosenberg, B., & Van Meter, N. (2004). *Charter school achievement in the 2003 National Assessment of Educational Progress*. Washington, DC: American Federation of Teachers, www.aft.org.

Neugarten, B. L. (1982). Age or need? *National Forum: The Phi Kappa Phi Journal, 62*, 25–27.

Newhouse, J. (2003). *Imperial America: The Bush assault on the world order*. New York: Alfred A. Knopf.

Newman, K. S. (1999). *No shame in my game: The working poor in the inner city*. New York: Knopf & the Russell Sage Foundation.

Newman, O. (1972). *Defensible space*. New York: Macmillan.

Nielson, F. (1994). Sociobiology and sociology. *Annual Review of Sociology, 20*, 267–303.

Nuclear Regulatory Commission. (2007). *Radioactive Waste*. Washington, DC: U.S. Government Printing Office, www.nrc.gov/waste.html.

Nusberg, C., Gibson, M. J., & Peace, S. (1984). *Innovative aging program abroad: Implications for the United States*. Westport, CT: Greenwood Press.

Oakes, J., Gamoran, A., & Page, R. N. (1992). Curriculum and differentiation: Opportunities, outcomes and meanings. In P. W. Jackson (Ed.), *Handbook of research on curriculum*. Washington, DC: American Educational Research Association.

O'Brien, D. J., & Fugita, S. S. (1991). *The Japanese American experience*. Bloomington: Indiana University Press.

Office of National Drug Control Policy. (1997). *Pulse check: National trends in drug abuse*. Washington, DC: U.S. Government Printing Office.

Office of National Drug Control Policy. (2007). *National drug control strategy: 2007*. Washington, DC: U.S. Government Printing Office.

Ogburn, W. F. (1938). The changing family. *The Family, 19*, 139–143.

Ogburn, W. F. (1957). Cultural lag as theory. *Sociology and Social Research, 41*, 167–174.

O'Kelly, C. G., & Carney, L. S. (1986). *Women and men in society: Cross cultural perspectives in gender inequality* (2nd ed.). Belmont, CA: Wadsworth.

Olasky, M. N. (1992). *The tragedy of American compassion*. Washington, DC: Regnery Gateway.

Oliver, M. B., & Armstrong, G. B. (1998). The color of crime: Perceptions of Caucasians and African-Americans' involvement in crime. In M. Fishman and G. Cavender (Eds.), *Entertaining crime: Television reality programs*. New York: Aldine de Gruyter.

Olzak, S. (1992). *The dynamics of ethnic competition and conflict*. Stanford, CA: Stanford University Press.

Orcutt, J. D., & Turner, J. B. (1993). Shocking numbers and graphic accounts: Quantified images of drug problems in the print media. *Social Problems, 40* (May), 190–206.

Orfield, G. (2004). *Dropouts in America: Confronting the graduation rate crisis*. Cambridge, MA: Harvard Education Press.

Orfield, G., & Lee, C. (2004, January 17). Brown *at 50: King's dream or Plessy's nightmare*. Cambridge, MA: The Civil Rights Project, Harvard University.

Orfield, M. (1997). *Metropolitics: A regional agenda for community and stability*. Washington, DC: Brookings Institute Press; Cambridge, MA: Lincoln Institute of Land Policy.

Osborne, D., & Gaebler, T. (1992). *Reinventing government: How the entrepreneurial spirit is transforming the public sector*. Reading, MA: Addison-Wesley.

Padilla, F. M. (1985). *Latino ethnic consciousness: The case of Mexican Americans and Puerto Ricans in Chicago*. Notre Dame, IN: University of Notre Dame Press.

Page, B. I., & Simmons, J. R. (2000). *What government can do: Dealing with poverty and inequality*. Chicago: University of Chicago Press.

Pallas, A. M., Entwisle, D. R., Alexander, K. L., & Weinstein, P. (1990). Social structure and the development of self-esteem in young children. *Social Psychology Quarterly, 53*, 302–315.

Parenti, C. (2004). *The soft cage: Surveillance in America from slavery to the war on terror*. New York: Basic Books.

Parsons, T. (1951). *The social system*. New York: Free Press.

Patterson, O. (1997). *The ordeal of integration: Progress and resentment in America's "racial" crisis*. Washington, DC: Counterpoint Press.

Pelton, L. (1978). The myth of classlessness in child abuse cases. *American Journal of Orthopsychiatry, 48*, 569–579.

Perrone, D., and Pratt, T. C. (2003). Comparing the quality of confinement and cost-effectiveness of public versus private prisons: What we know, why we do not know more, and where to go from here. *Prison Journal, 83*, 301–322.

Perrucci, R., & Wysong, E. (2002). *The new class society: Goodbye, American dream*. Lanham, MD: Rowman & Littlefield.

Petersen, W. (1975). *Population* (3rd ed.). New York: Macmillan.

Petersilia, J. (1985). Racial disparities in the criminal justice system: A summary. *Crime and Delinquency, 31*, 15–34.

Peterson, I. (1991, November 3). Why older people are richer than other Americans. *New York Times*, sec. 4, p. 3.

Peterson, J. (1990). The challenge of comparable worth: An institutionalist view. *Journal of Economic Issues, 24*, 605–612.

Peterson, R. D., & Bailey, W. C. (1991). Felony murder and capital punishment: An examination of the deterrence questions. *Criminology, 29*, 367–395.

Peterson, S. B., & Kroner, T. (1992). Gender biases in textbooks for introductory psychology and human development. *Psychology of Women Quarterly, 16*, 17–36.

Peterson, S. B., & Lach, M. A. (1990). Gender stereotypes in children's books: Their prevalence and influence on cognitive and affective development. *Gender and Education, 2* (2), 185–197.

Petrocelli, W., & Repa, B. K. (1992). *Sexual harassment on the job*. Berkeley, CA: Nolo Press.

Pettigrew, T. F. (1988). Integration and pluralism. In P. A. Katz & D. A. Taylor (Eds.), *Eliminating racism: Profiles in controversy*. New York: Plenum.

Pettigrew, T. F. (1998). Intergroup contact theory. *Annual Review of Psychology, 49*, 65–85.

Phelan, T. J., & Schneider, M. (1996). Race, ethnicity, and class in American suburbs. *Urban Affairs Review, 31* (May), 659–680.

Philander, S. G. (1998). *Is the temperature rising? The uncertain science of global warming*. Princeton, NJ: Princeton University Press.

Phillips, U. B. (1963). *Life and labor in the old South*. Boston: Little, Brown.

Pillemer, K., & Finkelhor, D. (1988). The prevalence of elder abuse: A random sample survey. *The Gerontologist, 28* (1), 51–57.

Pillemer, K., & Finkelhor, D. (1989). Causes of elder abuse: Caregiver stress versus problem relatives. *American Journal of Orthopsychiatry, 59*, 179–187.

Pinkney, A. (1972). *The American way of violence*. New York: Random House.

Piven, F. F., & Cloward, R. A. (1997). *The breaking of the American social compact*. New York: New Press.

Plakans, A. (1994). The democratization of unstructured time in western societies: A historical overview. In M. W. Riley, R. L. Kahn, & A. Foner (Eds.), *Age and structural lag*. New York: Wiley Interscience.

Plotnick, R. D. (1993). The effect of social policies on teenage pregnancy and childbearing. *Families in Society, 6*, 324–328.

Popenoe, D., & Whitehead, B. D. (2003). *The state of our unions, 2003: The social health of marriage in America*. Piscataway, NJ: The National Marriage Project, Rutgers, The State University of New Jersey.

Porter, B. D. (1994). *War and the rise of the states: The military foundations of modern politics*. New York: Free Press.

Postel, S., & Vickers, A. (2004). Boosting water productivity. In L. Starke et al. (Eds.), *State of the world, 2004: A Worldwatch Institute report on progress toward a sustainable society*. New York: W. W. Norton.

Potter, W. J. (2003). *The 11 myths of media violence*. Thousand Oaks, CA: Sage.

Pouncy, H. (2000). New directions in job training strategies for the disadvantaged. In S. Danziger & J. Waldfogel (Eds.), *Securing the future: Investing in children from birth to college*. New York: Russell Sage Foundation.

Project on Government Oversight. (2004). *The politics of contracting.* Washington, DC: Project on Government Oversight, **www.pogo.org.**

Project on Government Oversight. (2005). *Homeland and national security whistleblower protections: An unfinished agenda.* Washington, DC: Project on Government Oversight, **www.pogo.org.**

Purcell, P., & Stewart, L. (1990). Dick and Jane in 1989. *Sex Roles, 22* (3–4), 177–185.

Quadagno, J. (2005). *One nation, uninsured: Why the U.S. has no national health insurance.* New York: Oxford University Press.

Quinney, R., & Shelden, R. G. (2001). *Critique of the legal order: Crime control in capitalist society.* Princeton, NJ: Transaction Books.

Rahman, Q., & Wilson, G. D. (2003). Born gay? The psychobiology of human sexual orientation. *Personality and Individual Differences, 34,* 1337–1382.

Ramey, S. L., & Ramey, C. T. (2000). Early childhood experiences and developmental competence. In S. Danziger & J. Waldfogel (Eds.), *Securing the future: Investing in children from birth to college.* New York: Russell Sage Foundation.

Ramstad, J. (2000, March 15). Congress needs to face facts about America's War on Drugs. *Congressional Record, 146,* 1062–1063.

Rank, M. R. (1994). *Living on the edge: The realities of welfare in America.* New York: Columbia University Press.

Rank, M. R. (2004). *One nation, underprivileged: Why American poverty affects us all.* New York: Oxford University Press.

Rankin, D. (1985, March 24). Protecting your pension—and spouse. *New York Times,* p. 11.

Rankin, J. H. (1983). The family context of delinquency. *Social Problems, 30,* 466–479.

Ray, B. A. (Ed.). (1988). *Learning Factors in Substance Abuse.* NIDA Research Monograph 84, DHHS Pub. No. [ADM] 88–1576. Rockville, MD: National Institute on Drug Abuse.

Ray, O., & Ksir, L. (2004). *Drugs, society, and human behavior.* (10th ed.). New York: McGraw Hill.

Read, J. G. (2004). *Culture, class, and work among Arab-American women.* New York: LFB Scholarly Publishing LLC.

Reiman, J. (2007). *The rich get richer and the poor get prison: Ideology, class, and criminal justice,* (8th ed.). Boston: Allyn & Bacon.

Reiss, M. (1995). *Bridled ambition: Why countries constrain their nuclear capabilities.* Baltimore: Johns Hopkins University Press.

Relman, A. S. (1980). The new medical–industrial complex. *New England Journal of Medicine, 303,* 963–970.

Renner, M. (2004). Moving toward a less consumptive economy. In L. Starke et al. (Eds.), *State of the world, 2004: A Worldwatch Institute report on progress toward a sustainable society.* New York: W. W. Norton.

Rennison, C. M. (2003). Intimate partner violence, 1993–2001. *Crime Data Brief,* NCJ 197838. Washington, DC: U.S. Department of Justice, Bureau of Justice Statistics.

Renzulli, L. A., & Evans, L. (2005). School choice, charter schools, and white flight. *Social Problems, 52,* 398–418.

Repetto, R. (1994). *The "second India" revisited.* Washington, DC: World Resources Institute.

Reynolds, A. J., Temple, J. A., Robertson, D. L., & Mann, E. A. (2001, May 9). Long-term effects of an early childhood intervention on educational achievement and juvenile arrest. *Journal of the American Medical Association, 285,* 2339–2346.

Reynolds, H. (1986). *The economics of prostitution.* Springfield, IL: Charles C. Thomas.

Rhode, D. L. (2001). *The unfinished agenda: Women and the legal profession.* Chicago: American Bar Association.

Richmond-Abbott, M. (1992). *Masculine and feminine: Gender roles over the life cycle* (2nd ed.). New York: McGraw-Hill.

Ridker, R. (1980). The no-birth bonus scheme: The use of savings accounts for family planning in south India. *Population and Development Review, 6,* 31–46.

Riesman, D. (1961). *The lonely crowd.* New Haven, CT: Yale University Press.

Rifkin, J. (1987, April 26). Is nature just a form of private property? *New York Times,* sec. 3, p. 2.

Rifkin, J. (1998). *The biotech century: Harnessing the gene and remaking the world.* New York: Jeremy P. Tarcher/Putnam.

Riley, M. W., Kahn, R. L., & Foner, A. (Eds.). (1994). *Age and structural lag.* New York: Wiley Interscience.

Rimer, S. (2003). Study finds charter schools lack experienced teachers. *New York Times,* April 8, p. A12.

Rimmerman, C. A. (2005). *The new citizenship: Unconventional politics, activism, and service* (3rd ed.). Boulder, CO: Westview Press.

Rist, R. C. (1979). *Desegregated schools: Appraisals of an American experiment.* New York: Academic Press.

Roane, K. R. (1998, February 23). Prostitutes on wane in New York streets but take to Internet. *New York Times,* p. 1.

Robey, B., Rutstein, S. O., & Morris, L. (1993). The fertility decline in developing countries. *Scientific American, 269* (December), 60–67.

Robinson, B. E., Skeen, P., Hobson, C. F., & Herrman, M. (1982). Gay men's and women's perceptions of early family life and their relationships with parents. *Family Relations, 31,* 79–83.

Robinson, J. D., & Skill, T. (2001). Five decades of families on television: From the 1950s through the 1990s. In J. Bryant & J. A. Bryant (Eds.), *Television and the American family* (2nd ed.). Mahwah, NJ: Lawrence Erlbaum Associates.

Roblin, D. W. et al. (2004). Use of midlevel practitioners to achieve labor cost savings in the primary care practice of an MCO. *Health Services Research, 39,* 607–626.

Rodgers, H. L., Jr. (1990). *Poor women, poor families: The economic plight of America's female-headed households.* Armonk, NY: M. E. Sharpe.

Rodriguez Rust, P. C. (2004). Civil unions, domestic partnerships, and the extension of marital rights to same-sex partners. In R. Perrucci, K. Ferraro, J. Miller, & P. C. Rodriguez Rust (Eds.), *Agenda for Social Justice, 2004.* Knoxville, TN: Society for the Study of Social Problems.

Rose, A. M. (1967). *The power structure: Political process in American society.* New York: Oxford University Press.

Rosen, C., & Youngs, K. M. (Eds.). (1991). *Understanding employee ownership.* Ithaca, NY: ILR Press.

Rosen, J. (2004). *The naked crowd: Reclaiming security and freedom in an anxious age.* New York: Random House.

Ross, J. W. (1991). Elder abuse. *Health and Social Work, 16,* 227–229.

Ross, M. W., Paulsen, J. A., & Stalstrom, O. W. (1988). Homosexuality and mental health: A cross-cultural review. *Journal of Homosexuality, 15,* 131–152.

Rossi, A. (1984). Gender and parenthood. *American Sociological Review, 49,* 1–19.

Roth, K. (1998, April 13). New minefields for N.G.O.s. *The Nation,* pp. 22–24.

Rothfeder, J. (1992). *Privacy for sale: How computerization has made everyone's private life an open secret.* New York: Simon & Schuster.

Rounsaville, B. J., et al. (1984). Psychiatric disorders in treated opiate addicts. In G. Serban (Ed.), *Social and medical aspects of drug abuse.* New York: SP Medical and Scientific Books.

Rowe, A. R., & Tittle, C. R. (1977). Life cycle changes and criminal propensity. *Sociological Quarterly, 18,* 223–236.

Rowe, J. W., & Kahn, R. L. (1998). *Successful aging.* New York: Pantheon Books.

Russell, K. K. (1998). *The color of crime: Racial hoaxes, white fear, black protectionism, police harassment, and other macroaggressions.* New York: New York University Press.

Saad, L. (1997). Majority of Americans unfazed by Ellen's "coming out" episode. *The Gallup Poll Monthly* (April), 24–26.

Sacco, V. F. (1995). Media constructions of crime. *Annals of the American Academy of Political and Social Science, 539* (May), 141–154.

Sadik, N. (1989). Discrimination against girls. In *State of the world population report.* New York: United Nations.

Sadker, M., & Sadker, D. (1994). *Failing at fairness: How America's schools cheat girls.* New York: Charles Scribner's.

Salas, R. M. (1984). *Reflections on population.* New York: Pergamon Press.

Sale, K. (1980). *Human scale.* New York: Coward, McCann, and Geoghegan.

Sale, K. (1995). *Rebels against the future: The Luddites and their war on the industrial revolution: Lessons for the machine age.* Reading, MA: Addison-Wesley.

Sawin, J. L. (2004). *Mainstreaming renewable energy in the 21st century.* Washington, DC: Worldwatch Institute, Paper 169.

Saxton, L. (1980). *The individual, marriage, and the family* (4th ed.). Belmont, CA: Wadsworth.

Schaefer, R. T. (2004). *Racial and ethnic groups.* (9th ed.). Upper Saddle River, NJ: Prentice Hall.

Schaeffer, R. K. (1997). *Understanding globalization: The social consequences of political, economic, and environmental change.* Lanham, MD: Rowman & Littlefield.

Schechter, D. (2003). *Embedded: Weapons of mass deception: How the media failed to cover the war on Iraq.* Amherst, NY: Prometheus Books.

Scheff, T. J. (1999). *Being mentally ill: A sociological theory* (3rd ed.). New York: Aldine de Gruyter.

Schlesinger, A. M., Jr. (1986). *The cycles of American history.* Boston: Houghton Mifflin.

Schmid, C. L. (1981). *Conflict and consensus in Switzerland.* Berkeley: University of California Press.

Schnall, P. L., & Kern, R. (1986). Hypertension in American society: An introduction to historical materialist epidemiology. In P. Conrad & R. Kern (Eds.), *The sociology of health and illness: Critical perspectives* (2nd ed.). New York: St. Martin's Press.

Schochet, P. Z., Burghardt, J., & Glazerman, S. (2000). *National Job Corps study: The short-term impacts of Job Corps on participants' employment and related outcomes.* Princeton, NJ: Mathematica Policy Research, Inc.

Schuckit, M. A. (2006). *Drug and alcohol abuse* (6th ed.). New York: Springer.

Scott, J., & Leonhardt, D. (2005, May 15). Class in America: Shadowy lines that still divide. *New York Times,* pp. 1, 16–17.

Scott, W. J. (1985). The equal rights amendment as status politics. *Social Forces, 64* (2), 499–506.

Scott, W. J., & Stanley, S. C. (1994). *Gays and lesbians in the military: Issues, concerns, and contrasts.* New York: Aldine de Gruyter.

Scully, D. (1994). *Men who control women's health: The miseducation of obstetrician-gynecologists.* New York: Teachers College Press.

Secondi, G. S. (2002). Biased childhood sex ratios and the economic status of the family in rural China. *Journal of Comparative Family Studies, 33,* 215–234.

Segal, L. (1990). Pornography and violence: What the "experts" really say. *Feminist Review, 36,* 29–41.

Sen, A. (1999). *Development as freedom.* New York: Knopf.

Servicemembers Legal Defense Network. (2007). *Total "Don't ask, don't tell" discharges: 1994–2006.* Washington, DC: Servicemembers Legal Defense Network, **www. sldn.org**.

Sessions, G. (Ed.). (1995). *Deep ecology for the twenty-first century.* New York: Random House.

Sewell, W. H. (1971). Inequality of opportunity for higher education. *American Sociological Review, 36,* 793–808.

Shanas, E. (1972). Adjustment to retirement: Substitution or accommodation. In F. Carp (Ed.), *Retirement.* New York: Behavioral Publications.

Shane, S. (2007, February 4). In Washington, contractors take on biggest role ever. *New York Times,* p. A1.

Sheley, J. F. (1985). *America's "crime problem": An introduction to criminology.* Belmont, CA: Wadsworth.

Sherman, L. W. (1997). Policing for crime prevention. In L. W. Sherman, D. Gottfredson, D. MacKenzie, J. Eck, P. Reuter, & S. Bushway (Eds.), *Preventing crime: What works, what doesn't, what's promising.*

Washington, DC: Office of Justice Programs, U.S. Department of Justice.

Sherman, L. W., & Berk, R. A. (1984). The specific deterrent effects of arrest for domestic violence. *American Sociological Review, 49,* 261–271.

Sherrill, R. (1995, January 9–16). Dangerous to your health: The madness of the market. *The Nation,* pp. 45–72.

Shilts, R. (1987). *And the band played on: Politics, people, and the AIDS epidemic.* New York: St. Martin's Press.

Shin, J. H. (2001). Is there work alienation in post-industrial America: An analysis of technical and social relations in today's changing labor force. *Dissertation Abstracts International,* 61, February, 3375-A.

Shipler, D. K. (2004). *The working poor: Invisible in America.* New York: Alfred A. Knopf.

Shockley, W. B. (1980). Playboy interview: William Shockley. *Playboy* (August), 73.

Shostak, A. (2001). Applied sociology and organized labor: On going better together. In W. Du Bois & R. D. Wright (Eds.), *Applying sociology: Making a better world.* Boston: Allyn & Bacon.

Sigerist, H. E. (1977). The special position of the sick. In D. Landy (Ed.), *Culture, disease, and healing: Studies in medical anthropology.* New York: Macmillan.

Silver, L. M. (1997). *Remaking Eden: Cloning and beyond in a brave new world.* New York: Avon Books.

Simmons, J. L. (1969). *Deviants.* Berkeley, CA: Glendessary Press.

Simon, J. L. (1981). *The ultimate resource.* Princeton, NJ: Princeton University Press.

Simons, R. L., & Gray, P. A. (1989). Perceived blocked opportunity as an explanation of delinquency among lower-class black males: A research note. *Journal of Research in Crime and Delinquency, 26* (1), 90–101.

Simpson, G. E., & Yinger, J. M. (1985). *Racial and cultural minorities* (5th ed.). New York: Plenum.

Sims, C. (1995, July 11). Defying U.S. threat, Bolivians plant more coca. *New York Times,* p. A3.

Singer, J. D., & Small, M. (1972). *The wages of war, 1816–1965: A statistical handbook.* New York: John Wiley and Sons.

Skocpol, T. (1995). *Social policy in the United States: Future possibilities in historical perspective.* Princeton, NJ: Princeton University Press.

Small, M. L., & Newman, K. (2001). Urban poverty after *The Truly Disadvantaged:* The rediscovery of the family, the neighborhood, and culture. *Annual Review of Sociology,* 27, 23–45.

Smedley, B. D., Stith, A. Y., & Nelson, A. R. (2002). *Unequal treatment: Confronting racial and ethnic disparities in health care.* Washington, DC: National Academy Press, Institute of Medicine.

Smeeding, T. M. (1997). American income inequality in a cross-national perspective: Why are we so different? Luxembourg Income Study Working Paper No. 157, Center for Policy Research, The Maxwell School. Syracuse, NY: Syracuse University.

Smith, D. (1997, May 1). Study looks at portrayal of women in media. *New York Times,* p. A17.

Smith, D. A., & Klein, J. R. (1984). Police control of interpersonal disputes. *Social Problems, 31,* 468–481.

Smith, K. B., & Meier, K. J. (1995). *The case against school choice: Politics, markets, and fools.* Armonk, NY: M. E. Sharpe.

Smitherman, G. (1997). "The chain remain the same": Communicative practices in the Hip Hop nation. *Journal of Black Studies, 28,* 3–25.

Smock, P. J., & Wilson, F. D. (1991). Desegregation and the stability of white enrollments: A school-level analysis, 1968–84. *Sociology of Education, 64,* 278–292.

Snipp, C. M. (1989). *American Indians: The first of this land.* New York: Russell Sage Foundation.

Sobel, L. A. (Ed.). (1979). *Pornography, obscenity and the law.* New York: Facts on File.

Solorzano, D. G. (1991). Mobility aspirations among racial minorities, controlling for SES. *Sociology and Social Research, 75,* 182–188.

Sommers-Flanagan, R., Sommers-Flanagan, J., & Davis, B. (1993). What's happening in music television? A gender role content analysis. *Sex Roles, 28,* 745–753.

Soule, S. A. (1992). Populism and black lynching in Georgia, 1890–1900. *Social Forces, 71,* 431–449.

Sowell, T. (1981). *Ethnic America: A history.* New York: Basic Books.

Spector, M., & Kitsuse, J. I. (2000). *Constructing social problems* (3rd ed.). Piscataway, NJ: Transaction Books.

Spencer, J. W., & Drass, K. A. (1989). The transformation of gender into conversational advantage: A symbolic interactionist approach. *Sociological Quarterly, 30,* 363–383.

Springstead, G. R., & Wilson, T. M. (2000). Participation in voluntary individual savings accounts: An analysis of IRAs, 401(k)s, and the TSP. *Social Security Bulletin, 63,* 34–39.

Stacey, J. (1998). Gay and lesbian families: Queer like us. In M. A. Mason, A. Skolnick, & S. D. Sugarman (Eds.), *All our families: New policies for a new century.* New York: Oxford University Press.

Stacey, J., & Biblarz, T. J. (2001). (How) does the sexual orientation of the parents matter? *American Sociological Review, 66,* 159–183.

Stack, S. (1990). Execution publicity and homicide in South Carolina: A research note. *Sociological Quarterly, 31,* 599–611.

Stanko, E. A. (1995). Women, crime, and fear. *Annals of the American Academy of Political and Social Science, 539* (May), 46–58.

Stark, L. P. (1991). Traditional gender role beliefs and individual outcomes: An exploratory analysis. *Sex Roles, 24,* 639–650.

Steffensmeier, D. J., & Allan, E. A. (1988). Sex disparities in arrests by residence, race, and age: An assessment of the gender convergence/crime hypothesis. *Justice Quarterly, 5* (1), 53–80.

Steinem, G. (1980). Erotica and pornography: A clear and present difference. In L. Lederer (Ed.), *Take back the night: Women on pornography.* New York: William Morrow.

Steiner, J. (1990). Power-sharing: Another Swiss "export product"? In J. V. Montville (Ed.), *Conflict and peacemaking in multiethnic societies.* Lexington, MA: Lexington Books.

Steinmetz, S. K. (1987). Family violence. In M. B. Sussman & S. K. Steinmetz (Eds.), *Handbook of marriage and the family.* New York: Plenum.

Stets, J. E. (1991). Cohabiting and marital aggression: The role of social isolation. *Journal of Marriage and the Family, 53,* 669–680.

Steurer, S. J., & Smith, L. G. (2003). *Education reduces crime: Three-state recidivism study.* Lanham, MD: Correctional Education Association.

Stevens, W. K. (1995, April 18). The 25th anniversary of Earth Day: How has the environment fared? *New York Times,* p. B5.

Stiglitz, J. E. (2004, Jan. 6). The broken promise of NAFTA. *New York Times,* p. A27.

Stiglitz, J. E. (2006). *Making globalization work.* New York: W. W. Norton.

Stitt, B. G. (1988). Victimless crime: A definitional issue. *Journal of Crime and Justice, 11* (2), 87–102.

Stockholm International Peace Research Institute. (2007). *The SIPRI arms transfers database.* **armstrade. sipri.org.**

Stohl, M. (1976). *War and domestic political violence: The American capacity for repression and reaction.* Beverly Hills, CA: Sage Publications.

Stolberg, S. G. (2001, April 19). Researchers find a link between behavioral problems and time in child care. *New York Times,* p. A18.

Stolberg, S. G. (2002, August 8). Patient deaths tied to lack of nurses. *New York Times,* p. A14.

Straus, M. A., Gelles, R. J., & Steinmetz, S. K. (1980). *Behind closed doors: A study of family violence in America.* Garden City, NY: Anchor Press/Doubleday.

Straus, R. A. (2002). Using what? The history and nature of sociology. In R. A. Straus (Ed.), *Using sociology: An introduction from the applied and clinical perspectives,* (3rd ed.). Lanham, MD: Rowman & Littlefield.

Strong, B., DeVault, C., & Cohen, T. F. (2008). *The marriage and family experience,* (10th ed.). Belmont, CA: Wadsworth/Thomson Learning.

Strossen, N. (1995). *Defending pornography.* New York: Charles Scribner's Sons.

Strug, D., Wish, E., Johnson, B., Anderson, K., Miller, T., & Sears, A. (1984). The role of alcohol in the crimes of active heroin users. *Crime and Delinquency, 30* (4), 551–567.

Struyk, R. J., Page, D. B., Newman, S., Carroll, M., Ueno, M., Cohen, B., & Wright, P. (1989). *Providing supportive services to the frail elderly in federally assisted housing.* Washington, DC: Urban Institute Press.

Study finds U.S. students lag foreigners. (1996, March 24). *New York Times,* p. 18.

Sugarman, S. D. (1998). Single-parent families. In M. A. Mason, A. Skolnick, & S. D. Sugarman (Eds.), *All our families: New policies for a new century.* New York: Oxford University Press.

Sullivan, T. J. (1992). *Applied sociology: Research and critical thinking.* New York: Macmillan.

Sullivan, T. J. (2001). *Methods of social research.* Fort Worth, TX: Harcourt.

Suro, R. (1998). *Strangers among us: How Latino immigration is transforming America.* New York: Alfred A. Knopf.

Sutherland, E. H., & Cressey, D. R. (1978). *Criminology* (10th ed.). Philadelphia: Lippincott.

Swain, C. M. (2001). Affirmative action: Legislative history, judicial interpretations, public consensus. In N. J. Smelser, W. J. Wilson, & F. Mitchell (Eds.), *America becoming: Racial trends and their consequences,* Volume I. Washington, DC: National Academy Press.

Switzer, J. Y. (1990). The impact of generic word choices: An empirical investigation of age- and sex-related differences. *Sex Roles, 22,* 69–82.

Sykes, G. M., & Cullen, F. T. (1992). *Criminology.* (2nd ed.). Fort Worth, TX: Harcourt Brace Jovanovich.

Szasz, T. S. (1987). *Insanity: The idea and its consequences.* New York: John Wiley & Sons.

Taft, P., & Ross, P. (1969). American labor violence: Its causes, character, and outcome. In H. D. Graham & T. R. Gurr (Eds.), *Violence in America.* New York: Bantam Books.

Tannen, D. (1994). *Gender and discourse.* New York: Oxford University Press.

Tavris, C. (1992). *The mismeasure of woman.* New York: Simon & Schuster.

Thio, A. (2004). *Deviant behavior* (7th ed.). Boston: Allyn & Bacon.

Thistlethwaite, A., Wooldredge, J., & Gibbs, D. (1998). Severity of dispositions and domestic violence recidivism. *Crime & Delinquency, 44,* 388–398.

Thoits, P. A. (1995). Stress, coping, and social support processes: Where are we? What next. *Journal of Health and Social Behavior* (Special issue), 53–79.

Thomas, C. D., et al. (2004). Extinction risk from climate change. *Nature, 427,* 145–148.

Thomas, W. I., & Thomas, D. S. (1928). *The child in America.* New York: Alfred A. Knopf.

Thorne, B. (1993). *Gender play: Girls and boys in school.* New Brunswick, NJ: Rutgers University Press.

Thornton, A. (1985). Changing attitudes toward separation and divorce: Causes and consequences. *American Journal of Sociology, 90,* 856–872.

Thornton, R. Y., & Endo, K. (1992). *Preventing crime in America and Japan: A comparative study.* Armonk, NY: M. E. Sharpe.

Tienda, M. (1989). Puerto Ricans and the underclass debate. *Annals of the American Academy of Political and Social Science, 501,* 105–119.

Tietze, W., & Cryer, D. (1999). Current trends in European early child care and education. *Annals of the American Academy of Political and Social Sciences, 563,* 175–193.

Tinbergen, N. (1955). The curious behavior of the stickleback. In *Twentieth century bestiary.* New York: Simon & Schuster.

Tittle, C., & Meier, R. (1990). Specifying the SES/delinquency relationship. *Criminology, 28,* 271–301.

Tjaden, P., & Thoennes, N. (2000). *Full report of the prevalence, incidence, and consequences of violence against women: Findings from the National Violence Against Women Survey.* Washington, DC: National Institute of Justice, U.S. Department of Justice.

Tonelson, A. (2000). *The race to the bottom: Why a worldwide worker surplus and uncontrolled free trade are sinking American living standards.* Boulder, CO: Westview Press.

Tonry, M. (1995). *Malign neglect: Race, crime, and punishment in America.* New York: Oxford University Press.

Torbet, P., Gable, R., Hurst, H., IV, Montgomery, I., Szymanski, L., & Thomas, D. (1996). *State responses to serious and violent juvenile crime.* Washington, DC: Office of Juvenile Justice and Delinquency Prevention, U.S. Department of Justice.

Trebach, A. S. (1982). *The heroin solution.* New Haven, CT: Yale University Press.

Trenholm, C., et al. (2007). *Impacts of four Title V, section 510 abstinence education programs: Final report.* Princeton, NJ: Mathematica Policy Research, Inc.

Troiden, R. R. (1989). The formation of homosexual identities. *Journal of Homosexuality, 17,* 43–73.

Turner, J., & Maryanski, A. (1979). *Functionalism.* Menlo Park, CA: Benjamin/Cummings.

Turner, M. A., et al. (2002–2003). *Discrimination in metropolitan housing markets.* Washington, DC: The U.S. Department of Housing and Urban Development and The Urban Institute.

Uchitelle, L. (2006). *The disposable American: Layoffs and their consequences.* New York: Knopf.

United Nations. (2000). *The world's women, 2000: Trends and statistics* (Pub. No. E00.XVII.3). New York: United Nations, Department of Economic and Social Affairs.

United Nations. (2006). *Human development report, 2006: Beyond scarcity: Power, poverty and the global water crisis.* Gordonsville, VA: Palgrave Macmillan.

United Nations Convention to Combat Desertification. (2004). *Desertification in the world.* New York: United Nations, **www.unccd.int/main.php**.

United Nations Development Fund for Women. (2002). *Progress of the world's women: Gender equality and the millennium development goals.* New York: United Nations, **www.unifem.undp.org**.

U.S. Advisory Board on Child Abuse and Neglect, U.S. Department of Health and Human Services. (1995). *A nation's shame: Fatal child abuse and neglect in the United States.* Washington, DC: U.S. Government Printing Office.

U.S. Bureau of Indian Affairs. (2005). *Orientation to the U.S. Department of Interior: Bureau of Indian Affairs.* Washington, DC: U.S. Department of the Interior, www.doiu.nbc.gov/orientation/bia2.cfm.

U.S. Bureau of the Census. (1978). *Statistical abstract of the United States, 1978.* Washington, DC: U.S. Government Printing Office.

U.S. Bureau of the Census. (1984). *Statistical abstract of the United States, 1985.* Washington, DC: U.S. Government Printing Office.

U.S. Bureau of the Census. (1994). *Statistical abstract of the United States, 1994.* Washington, DC: U.S. Government Printing Office.

U.S. Bureau of the Census. (2000). *Statistical abstract of the United States, 2000.* Washington, DC: U.S. Government Printing Office.

U.S. Bureau of the Census. (2003a). Poverty in the United States: 2002. *Current Population Reports,* Series P60-222. Washington, DC: U.S. Government Printing Office.

U.S. Bureau of the Census. (2003). *Statistical abstract of the United States, 2003.* Washington, DC: U.S. Government Printing Office.

U.S. Bureau of the Census. (2005). *We the people of Arab ancestry in the United States: Census 2000 special reports.* Washington, DC: U.S. Government Printing Office.

U.S. Bureau of the Census. (2006). *Statistical abstract of the United States, 2007.* Washington, DC: U.S. Government Printing Office.

U.S. Bureau of the Census. (2006a). *Current population survey, 2006 annual social and economic supplement.* Washington, DC: U.S. Government Printing Office.

U.S. Department of Commerce. (2001). *Survey of women-owned business enterprises, 1997.* Washington, DC: U.S. Government Printing Office.

U.S. Department of Education. (2004a). *The nation's report card: America's charter school report,* NCES 2005–456. Washington, DC: National Center for Education Statistics.

U.S. Department of Education, National Center for Education Statistics. (2004b). *The condition of education, 2004.* NCES 2004077. Washington, DC: U.S. Government Printing Office.

U.S. Department of Education, National Center for Education Statistics. (2006). *Digest of education statistics, 2005.* Pub No. NCES 2006030. Washington, DC: U.S. Government Printing Office, **nces.ed.gov/programs/digest/**.

U.S. Department of Health and Human Services. (2006). *National survey on drug use and health, 2005.* Rockville, MD: Substance Abuse and Mental Health Services Administration, Office of Applied Studies, **www.oas.samhsa.gov/nhsda.htm**.

U.S. Department of Health and Human Services, Office of the Assistant Secretary for Planning and Evaluation. (2002). *Trends in the well-being of America's children and youth: 2002.* Washington, DC: U.S. Government Printing Office.

U.S. Department of Justice. (1992a). *Combating violent crime: 24 recommendations to strengthen criminal justice.* Washington, DC: U.S. Government Printing Office.

U.S. Department of Justice. (1992b). *Drugs, crime, and the justice system: A national report from the Bureau of Justice Statistics* (Pub. No. NCJ-133652). Washington, DC: U.S. Government Printing Office.

U.S. Department of Justice. (2006). *Criminal victimization in the United States, 2005: Statistical tables.* Washington, DC: Bureau of Justice Statistics, **www.ojp.usdoj.gov/bjs/**.

U.S. Department of Labor. (2000). *By the sweat and toil of children, Vol. VI: An economic consideration of child labor.* Washington, DC: U.S. Government Printing Office, Bureau of International Labor Affairs.

U.S. Department of Labor. (2001). *Report on the youth labor force.* Washington, DC: U.S. Government Printing Office, Bureau of Labor Statistics.

U.S. Department of State. (2007). *International narcotics control strategy report: 2007.* Washington, DC: Bureau for International Narcotics and Law Enforcement Affairs, **www.state.gov/**.

U.S. Department of State, Bureau of Verification and Compliance. (2002). *World military expenditures and arms transfers, 1999–2000.* Washington, DC: U.S. Government Printing Office.

U.S. Department of State, Office of the Coordinator for Counter Terrorism. (2007a, April 30). *Country reports on terrorism, 2006.* Washington, DC: U.S. Government Printing Office, **www.state.gov/s/ct/rls/crt/**.

U.S. Equal Employment Opportunity Commission. (2004). *Age Discrimination in Employment Act (ADEA) charges: FY 1992–FY 2002.* Washington, DC: U.S. Government Printing Office, **www.eeoc.gov/stats/charges.html**.

U.S. General Accounting Office. (2001). *Women in management: Analysis of selected data from the Current Population Survey,* report no. GAO-02-156. Washington, DC: U.S. Government Printing Office.

U.S. General Accounting Office. (2002). *Public schools: Insufficient research to determine effectiveness of selected private education companies,* report no. GAO-03-11. Washington, DC: U.S. Government Printing Office.

Urbina, I. (2007, March 23). Court rejects law limiting pornography on the Internet. *New York Times,* p. A11.

Vallas, S. P. (1988). New technology, job control, and worker alienation: A test of two rival perspectives. *Work and Occupations, 15,* 148–178.

Vannoy-Hiller, D., & Philliber, W. W. (1989). *Equal partners: Successful women in marriage.* Newbury Park, CA: Sage Publications.

Verbrugge, L. (1979). Marital status and health. *Journal of Marriage and the Family, 41,* 267–285.

Verbrugge, L. M. (1983). Multiple roles and physical health of women and men. *Journal of Health and Social Behavior, 24,* 16–30.

Vigdor, J. L. (2001). *Does gentrification harm the poor?* Duke University, NC: Terry Sanford Institute of Public Policy.

Vigil, J. D. (2003). Urban violence and street gangs. *Annual Review of Anthropology, 32,* 225–242.

Vinovskis, M. A. (1978). Angels' heads and weeping willows: Death in early America. In M. Gordon (Ed.), *The American family in social-historical perspective.* New York: Random House.

Volti, R. (2001). *Society and technological change* (4th ed.). New York: Worth.

Waldron, I. (1997). What do we know about the causes of sex differences in mortality? A review of the literature. In P. Conrad (Ed.), *The sociology of health and illness: Critical perspectives* (5th ed.). New York: St. Martin's Press.

Walker, S., Spohn, C., & DeLone, M. (2003). *The color of justice: Race, ethnicity, and crime in America* (3rd ed.). Belmont, CA: Wadsworth/Thomson Learning.

Wallerstein, I. (1979). *The capitalist world-economy.* New York: Cambridge University Press.

Wallerstein, J. S., Lewis, J. M., & Blakeslee, S. (2000). *The unexpected legacy of divorce: A 25-year landmark study.* New York: Hyperion.

Wanner, R. A., & Lewis, L. S. (1978). The functional theory of stratification: A test of some structural hypotheses. *The Sociological Quarterly, 19,* 414–428.

Ware, J. E., Jr., Bayliss, M. S., Rogers, W. H., Kosinski, M., & Tarlov, A. R. (1996, October 2). Differences in 4-year health outcomes for elderly and poor, chronically ill patients treated in HMO and fee-for-service systems. *Journal of the American Medical Association, 276,* 1039–1047.

Weber, M. (1958, originally published 1919). *From Max Weber: Essays in sociology.* H. H. Gerth & C. W. Mills (trans. & ed.). New York: Oxford University Press.

Weil, A., & Finegold, K. (2002). *Welfare reform: The next act.* Washington, DC: The Urban Institute Press.

Weinstein, J. I. (1990). Homesteading: A solution for the homeless? *Journal of Housing* (May–June), 125–164.

Weisberg, D. K. (1985). *Children of the night: A study of adolescent prostitution.* Lexington, MA: Lexington Books/D.C. Heath.

Weisner, T. S., Garnier, H., & Loucky, J. (1994). Domestic tasks, gender egalitarian values, and children's gender typing in conventional and nonconventional families. *Sex Roles, 30,* 23–54.

Wells, L. E., & Rankin, J. H. (1991). Families and delinquency: A meta-analysis of the impact of broken homes. *Social Problems, 38,* 71–93.

Westermann, W. L. (1955). *The slave systems of Greek and Roman antiquity.* Philadelphia: American Philosophical Society.

Westie, F. R. (1964). Race and ethnic relations. In R. E. L. Faris (Ed.), *Handbook of modern sociology.* Chicago: Rand McNally.

White, J. R. (2002). *Terrorism: An introduction,* (3rd ed.). Belmont, CA: Wadsworth.

Whitebook, M. (1999). Child care workers: High demand, low wages. *The Annals of the American Academy of Political and Social Science, 563,* 146–161.

Wichers, M. (2001). Homeschooling: Adventitious or detrimental for proficiency in higher education. *Education, 122,* 145–151.

Widom, C. S., & Kuhns, J. B. (1996). Childhood victimization and subsequent risk for promiscuity, prostitution, and teenage pregnancy: A prospective study. *American Journal of Public Health, 86,* 1607–1612.

Wilkinson, L. C., & Marrett, C. B. (Eds.). (1985). *Gender influences in classroom interaction.* Orlando, FL: Academic Press.

Williams, D. R., & Collins, C. (1995). U.S. socioeconomic and racial differences in health: Patterns and explanations. *Annual Review of Sociology, 21,* 349–386.

Wilson, C. C., II., Gutiérrez, F., & Chao, L. (2004). *Racism, sexism, and the media: The rise of class communication in multicultural America.* Thousand Oaks, CA: Pine Forge Press.

Wilson, W. J. (1987). *The truly disadvantaged: The inner city, the underclass, and public policy.* Chicago: University of Chicago Press.

Wilson, W. J. (1991). Studying inner-city social dislocations: The challenge of public agenda research. *American Sociological Review, 56,* 1–14.

Wilson, W. J. (1996). *When work disappears: The world of the new urban poor.* New York: Alfred A. Knopf.

Wilson, W. J. (1999). *The bridge over the racial divide: Rising inequality and coalition politics.* Berkeley and New York: University of California Press/Russell Sage Foundation.

Wolfe, A. (1993). *The human difference: Animals, computers, and the necessity of social science.* Berkeley: University of California Press.

Wolfe, A. (1998). *One nation, after all: What middle-class Americans really think about: God, country, family, racism, welfare, immigration, homosexuality, work, the right, the left, and each other.* New York: Viking.

Wolff, E. N. (1995). *Top heavy: A study of the increasing inequality of wealth in America.* New York: The Twentieth Century Fund.

Wolfgang, M. E., & Ferracuti, F. (1967). *The subculture of violence: Toward an integrated theory in criminology.* London: Tavistock.

Wong, K. K., & Peterson, P. E. (1986). Urban response to federal program flexibility: Politics of community development block grant. *Urban Affairs Quarterly, 21,* 293–310.

World Bank. (2003). *World development report, 2004: Making services work for poor people.* New York: Oxford University Press.

World Bank. (2004). *World development report, 2005: A better investment climate for everyone.* New York: Oxford University Press.

World Commission on the Social Dimensions of Globalization. (2004). *A fair globalization: Creating opportunities for all.* New York: United Nations, International Labour Organization, www.ilo.org.

Wren, C. S. (1998, January 9). Alcohol or drug link found in 80% of U.S. prisoners. *New York Times,* p. A15.

Wright, J. D., Rubin, B. A., & Devine, J. A. (1998). *Beside the golden door: Policy, politics, and the homeless.* New York: Aldine de Gruyter.

Wysong, E., & Wright, D. W. (1995). A decade of DARE: Efficacy, politics and drug education. *Sociological Focus, 28* (August), 283–311.

Yancovitz, S. R., et al. (1991). A randomized trial of an interim methadone maintenance clinic. *American Journal of Public Health, 81,* 1185–1191.

Yardley, J. (2005, January 31). Fearing future, China starts to give girls their due. *New York Times,* p. A3.

Yergin, D., & Stanislaw, J. (1998). *The commanding heights: The battle between government and the marketplace that is remaking the modern world.* New York: Simon & Schuster.

Yinger, J. (1995). *Closed doors, opportunities lost: The continuing costs of housing discrimination.* New York: Russell Sage Foundation.

Young, R. K., Gallaher, P., Belasco, J., Barr, A., & Webber, A. W. (1991). Changes in fear of AIDS and homophobia in a university population. *Journal of Applied Social Psychology, 21,* 1848–1858.

Young, T. K. (1994). *The health of Native Americans: Toward a biocultural epidemiology.* New York: Oxford University Press.

Zahran, S., Hastings, D. W., & Zilney, L. A. (2004). In R. Perrucci, K. Ferraro, J. Miller, & P. C. Rodriguez Rust (Eds.), *Agenda for Social Justice, 2004.* Knoxville, TN: Society for the Study of Social Problems.

Zebrowitz, L. A., Tenenbaum, D. R., & Goldstein, L. H. (1991). The impact of job applicants' facial maturity, gender, and academic achievement on hiring recommendations. *Journal of Applied Social Psychology, 21,* 525–548.

Zehr, M. A. (2004, Feb. 4). Study gives advantage to bilingual education over focus on English. *Education Week, 21,* 10.

Zhang, Z., Huang, L. X., & Brittingham, A. M. (1999). *Worker drug use and workplace policies and programs: Results from the 1994 and 1997 National Household Survey on Drug Abuse.* Rockville, MD: Office of Applied Studies, Substance Abuse and Mental Health Services Administration, Department of Health and Human Services.

Zill, N., & Nord, C. W. (1994). *Running in place: How American families are faring in a changing economy and an individualistic society.* Washington, DC: Child Trends, Inc.

Zimbardo, P. G. (1973). A field experiment in auto shaping. In C. Ward (Ed.), *Vandalism.* New York: Van Nostrand Reinhold.

Zimmer, L., & Morgan, J. P. (1997). *Marijuana myths marijuana facts: A review of the scientific evidence.* New York: The Lindesmith Center.

Zussman, R. (1997). Sociological perspectives on medical ethics and decision-making. *Annual Review of Sociology, 23,* 171–189.

ANSWERS TO CUMULATIVE PRACTICE TESTS

Chapter 1

Multiple-Choice

1. A;   **2.** E;   **3.** C;   **4.** A;   **5.** B;
6. B;   **7.** B;   **8.** D;   **9.** D;   **10.** C

True/False

1. F;   **2.** T;   **3.** T;   **4.** F;   **5.** F;
6. T;   **7.** T;   **8.** F;   **9.** T;   **10.** F

Fill-In

1. an influential group
2. subcultures
3. sociological imagination
4. dysfunctional
5. interest, power, dominance, conflict, coercion
6. the definition of the situation
7. hypotheses
8. the time sequence be correct
9. validity
10. applied sociology, applied social research, evaluation research

Matching

1. A;   **2.** E;   **3.** B;   **4.** C;   **5.** D;
6. J;   **7.** G;   **8.** F;   **9.** I;   **10.** H

Chapter 2

Multiple-Choice

1. A;   **2.** C;   **3.** B;   **4.** C;   **5.** B;
6. D;   **7.** B;   **8.** A;   **9.** A;   **10.** D

True/False

1. F;   **2.** F;   **3.** F;   **4.** T;   **5.** F;
6. F;   **7.** T;   **8.** T;   **9.** F;   **10.** F

Fill-In

1. profit
2. mixed economies
3. a monopoly
4. conglomerate
5. the highly industrialized capitalist nations of North America, Europe, and Asia
6. C. Wright Mills
7. the military–industrial complex
8. displaced workers
9. laissez-faire
10. stakeholders

Matching

1. B;   **2.** D;   **3.** A;   **4.** E;   **5.** C;
6. J;   **7.** I;   **8.** F;   **9.** G;   **10.** H

Chapter 3

Multiple-Choice

1. A;   **2.** E;   **3.** D;   **4.** B;   **5.** C;
6. B;   **7.** B;   **8.** D;   **9.** A;   **10.** C

True/False

1. F;   **2.** F;   **3.** T;   **4.** F;   **5.** F;
6. T;   **7.** F;   **8.** F;   **9.** T;   **10.** F

Fill-In

1. modified extended
2. declined
3. participant-run
4. serial monogamy
5. very young
6. blended
7. both parents
8. alone
9. pluralistic
10. privatization

Matching

1. D;   **2.** A;   **3.** G;   **4.** B;   **5.** J;
6. C;   **7.** I;   **8.** E;   **9.** F;   **10.** H

Chapter 4

Multiple-Choice

1. A;   **2.** C;   **3.** D;   **4.** B;   **5.** A;
6. D;   **7.** C;   **8.** B;   **9.** E;   **10.** D

True/False

1. F;   **2.** F;   **3.** T;   **4.** F;   **5.** T;
6. T;   **7.** F;   **8.** T;   **9.** F;   **10.** F

Fill-In

1. functionalist
2. acute; or parasitic and infectious
3. secondary
4. community treatment; or community mental health
5. third-party
6. medical–industrial complex
7. dental hygienists
8. prolongation of life and whom to treat
9. government health insurance
10. iatrogenic illness

Matching

1. H;   **2.** E;   **3.** B;   **4.** G;   **5.** C;
6. J;   **7.** D;   **8.** A;   **9.** F;   **10.** I

Chapter 5

Multiple-Choice

1. B;   **2.** D;   **3.** E;   **4.** A;   **5.** D;
6. A;   **7.** A;   **8.** C;   **9.** B;   **10.** C

True/False

1. F;   **2.** F;   **3.** T;   **4.** F;   **5.** T;
6. F;   **7.** T;   **8.** T;   **9.** T;   **10.** F

Fill-In

1. relative
2. social stratification

3. white
4. functionalist
5. structural unemployment
6. culture of poverty
7. Head Start
8. an entitlement, workfare
9. social insurance
10. Supplemental Security Income; Temporary Assistance to
    Needy Families; General Assistance; Medicaid

Matching
1. E;   2. A;   3. J;   4. B;   5. C;
6. I;   7. D;   8. G;   9. F;   10. H

Chapter 6

Multiple-Choice
1. B;   2. A;   3. C;   4. D;   5. A;
6. D;   7. A;   8. C;   9. C;   10. B

True/False
1. T;   2. F;   3. F;   4. T;   5. T;
6. F;   7. F;   8. T;   9. F;   10. F

Fill-In
1. belief
2. racism
3. ethnocentrism
4. lower-priced workers
5. *Brown v. Board of Education of Topeka, Kansas*
6. 1920s
7. Asia
8. pluralism
9. reverse
10. white flight

Matching
1. E;   2. A;   3. J;   4. D;   5. B;
6. G;   7. C;   8. I;   9. H;   10. F

Chapter 7

Multiple-Choice
1. B;   2. B;   3. A;   4. D;   5. C;
6. C;   7. A;   8. B;   9. C;   10. D

True/False
1. F;   2. F;   3. T;   4. F;   5. T;
6. F;   7. T;   8. T;   9. T;   10. F

Fill-In
1. achieved
2. sexism
3. instrumental
4. interactionist
5. gender
6. occupation, income
7. secretaries or dental hygienists (Ch. 4)
8. 77
9. comparable worth
10. 16

Matching
1. H;   2. A;   3. E;   4. B;   5. I;
6. C;   7. D;   8. J;   9. F;   10. G

Chapter 8

Multiple-Choice
1. A;   2. D;   3. B;   4. C;   5. D;
6. B;   7. C;   8. A;   9. C;   10. C

True/False
1. F;   2. F;   3. T;   4. T;   5. F;
6. T;   7. F;   8. T;   9. F;   10. T

Fill-In
1. life course *or* life stages
2. adolescence
3. lower
4. roleless
5. vested pension
6. homophobia
7. IRAs *or* SEPs *or* 401(k)s
8. Medicare
9. AARP *or* NRTA
10. collective action

Matching
1. J;   2. A;   3. C;   4. B;   5. I;
6. D;   7. G;   8. E;   9. F;   10. H

Chapter 9

Multiple-Choice
1. C;   2. A;   3. B;   4. E;   5. A;
6. E;   7. D;   8. C;   9. B;   10. A

True/False
1. F;   2. T;   3. F;   4. T;   5. F;
6. T;   7. T;   8. T;   9. T;   10. F

Fill-In
1. psychological
2. Anomie
3. innovation
4. cultural transmission
5. secondary *or* career
6. white-collar
7. status
8. gender
9. adversary
10. swift, certain, equitable, *or* fair

Matching
1. A;   2. E;   3. B;   4. F;   5. I;
6. C;   7. D;   8. G;   9. H;   10. J

Chapter 10

Multiple-Choice
1. C;   2. A;   3. B;   4. B;   5. D;
6. A;   7. D;   8. C;   9. C;   10. D

True/False
1. F;   2. F;   3. F;   4. T;   5. T;
6. F;   7. T;   8. F;   9. T;   10. T

Fill-In
1. tolerance
2. cross-dependence
3. stimulants
4. stimulant
5. depressant
6. the occasional use of heroin
7. Social learning *or* Reinforcement
8. interactionist
9. Methadone
10. educational programs

Matching
1. C;   2. F;   3. A;   4. J;   5. B;
6. G;   7. D;   8. I;   9. E;   10. H

Chapter 11

Multiple-Choice
1. B;   2. C;   3. D;   4. B;   5. E;
6. A;   7. A;   8. A;   9. B;   10. C

True/False
1. F;   2. T;   3. T;   4. F;   5. F;
6. F;   7. F;   8. T;   9. T;   10. T

Fill-In
1. revolution
2. double standard
3. secularization
4. pimp
5. 100,000; 500,000
6. Nevada
7. peer-delinquent; gay
8. poverty
9. Obscene material
10. 37

Matching
1. B;   2. I;   3. D;   4. E;   5. A;
6. H;   7. C;   8. J;   9. G;   10. F

Chapter 12

Multiple-Choice
1. C;   2. E;   3. A;   4. C;   5. A;
6. B;   7. B;   8. D;   9. A;   10. D

True/False
1. F;   2. T;   3. T;   4. F;   5. T;
6. F;   7. T;   8. F;   9. F;   10. F

Fill-In
1. rate of natural increase
2. China, India
3. preindustrial
4. conflict
5. ghetto
6. Zero population growth
7. female infanticide *or* abortion
8. laissez-faire
9. urban free-enterprise zones
10. Urban homesteading

Matching
1. B;   2. H;   3. F;   4. A;   5. I;
6. C;   7. J;   8. E;   9. D;   10. G

Chapter 13

Multiple-Choice
1. E;   2. A;   3. B;   4. C;   5. A;
6. D;   7. C;   8. A;   9. B;   10. B

True/False
1. F;   2. T;   3. T;   4. F;   5. F;
6. F;   7. T;   8. T;   9. F;   10. T

Fill-In
1. photosynthesis
2. conflict
3. technology
4. Desertification
5. biodiversity
6. Global warming
7. Integrated pest management
8. Environmental partnerships
9. solar, wood, wind, water power, geothermal
10. deep ecology *or* biocentrism

Matching
1. H;   2. C;   3. A;   4. G;   5. E;
6. B;   7. J;   8. I;   9. D;   10. F

Chapter 14

Multiple-Choice
1. B;   2. C;   3. C;   4. A;   5. D;
6. A;   7. A;   8. A;   9. D;   10. A

True/False
1. F;   2. T;   3. F;   4. F;   5. F;
6. F;   7. T;   8. T;   9. F;   10. F

Fill-In
1. Collective
2. race riots, labor strife
3. insurrection
4. Relative deprivation
5. structural preconditions
6. conflict
7. First
8. START
9. World Court
10. balance of power

Matching
1. C;   2. A;   3. J;   4. E;   5. G;
6. B;   7. H;   8. D;   9. I;   10. F

Chapter 15

Multiple-Choice
1. A;   2. D;   3. B;   4. C;   5. C;
6. A;   7. C;   8. A;   9. B;   10. B

True/False
1. F;   2. F;   3. T;   4. T;   5. F;
6. F;   7. F;   8. T;   9. T;   10. T

Fill-In
1. technology
2. mechanization
3. functionalist
4. social reproduction
5. alienation
6. recombinant DNA or gene splicing
7. cloning
8. parental choice
9. appropriate technology
10. futurists or futurologists

Matching
1. B;   2. H;   3. D;   4. I;   5. J;
6. A;   7. G;   8. F;   9. C;   10. E

P. vii, © Paul Colangelo/Corbis; **p. viii**, AP Wide World Photos; **p. ix**, Rafael Macia/Photo Researchers, Inc.; **p. x**, Mike Derer/AP Wide World Photos; **p. xi**, AP Wide World Photos; **p. xii**, Bob Daemmrich/The Image Works; **p. xiii**, AP Wide World Photos; **p. xiv**, © Mary Lyons/Corbis Digital Stock; **p. xv**, © Bill Fritsch/Brand X Pictures/Punchstock; **p. xvi**, Chris Anderson/Aurora & Quanta Productions, Inc.; **p. xvii**, Stephen Ferry/Getty Images; **p. xviii**, Peter Menzel Photography; **p. xix**, © Danny Lehman/Corbis; **p. xx**, AP Wide World Photos; **p. xxi**, PNC/Digital Vision/Getty Images; **p. 3**, © Paul Colangelo/Corbis; **p. 6**, Sylvain Grandadam/Photo Researchers, Inc.; **p. 10**, AP Wide World Photos; **p. 19**, Simon Maina/Stringer AFP/Getty Images; **p. 29**, AP Wide World Photos; **p. 39**, AP Wide World Photos; **p. 43**, Courtesy Richard Pini/elfquest.com; **p. 48**, Joe Raedle/Getty Images, Inc.–Liaison; **p. 59**, Rafael Macia/Photo Researchers, Inc.; **p. 67**, Raghu Rai/Magnum Photos; **p. 75**, ©Viviane Moos/ Corbis/ Bettmann; **p. 77**, © Jupiter Images/ Creatas / Alamy; **p. 82**, © Picture Partners /Alamy; **p. 89**, AP Wide World Photos; **p. 93**, Robert Harbison; **p. 100**, AP Wide World Photos; **p. 106**, Nancy Louie; **p. 108**, Brian Bohannon/AP Photo; **p. 121**, AP Wide World Photos; **p. 130**, AP Wide World Photos; **p. 132**, George Cohen; **p. 133**, Christine Gonsalves/Jupiter Images; **p. 137**, © Greg Wahl-Stephens/Associated Press; **p. 149**, Bob Daemmrich/The Image Works; **p. 151**, Billy E. Barnes/PhotoEdit; **p. 154**, © Reuters/Danilo Krstanovic; **p. 164**, John Nordell/Index Stock Imagery; **p. 165**, A. Ramey/Woodfin Camp & Associates; **p. 177**, © Itsuo Inouye/Associated Press; **p. 180**, Library of Congress; **p. 184**, © American Broadcasting Companies, Inc.; **p. 194**, AP Wide World Photos; **p. 203**, © Mary Lyons/Corbis Digital Stock; **p. 208**, © JP Laffont/Sygma/Corbis; **p. 215**, Deborah Davis/PhotoEdit; **p. 219**, Cleve Bryant/PhotoEdit; **p. 233**, © Bill Fritsch/Brand X Pictures/Punchstock; **p. 243**, AP Wide World Photos; **p. 247**, A. Ramey/Woodfin Camp & Associates; **p. 249**, AP Wide World Photos; **p. 263**, Chris Anderson/Aurora & Quanta Productions Inc.; **p. 267**, Andrew Lichtenstein/The Image Works; **p. 281**, Knut Mueller/Das Fotoarchiv /Peter Arnold, Inc.; **p. 285**, Tony Savino/The Image Works; **p. 286**, John Boykin/PhotoEdit; **p. 293**, Stephen Ferry/Getty Images; **p. 301**, © Andrew Medichini/Associated Press; **p. 305**, Ezio Peterson/Corbis/Bettmann; **p. 311**, © Michael Newman/PhotoEdit; **p. 317**, Peter Menzel Photography; **p. 324**, © Chad Ehlers/Alamy; **p. 328**, © Ajit Solanki/Associated Press; **p. 338**, AP Wide World Photos; **p. 340**, David Forbert/Superstock; **p. 347**, © Danny Lehman/Corbis; **p. 354**, AP Wide World Photos; **p. 360**, © Soeren Stache/dpa/Corbis; **p. 368**, Getty Images—Digital Vision; **p. 375**, AP Wide World Photos; **p. 378**, Courtesy of the Library of Congress; **p. 379**, © Benjamin Sklar/Associated Press; **p. 383**, AP Wide World Photos; **p. 391**, Hulton Archive/Stringer/Getty Images; **p. 403**, PNC/Digital Vision; **p. 405**, Ken Osburn/Index Stock Imagery; **p. 414**, Bob Daemmrich/The Image Works; **p. 418**, AP Wide World Photos; **p. 424**, AP Wide World Photos.

Marden, C. F., 148
Marks, C., 134, 154
Marks, P. M., 158, 173
Marrett, C. B., 406
Marsden, M. E., 264
Marshall, D. S., 292
Marshall, J., 288
Martin, C. L., 180
Martin, S. E., 263, 273
Martinez, R., 153, 180
Martinez, T. A., 77
Marx, K., 7, 14, 132, 234
Maryanski, A., 6
Massey, D. S., 328
Mastny, L., 358, 359, 365
Matsueda, R. L., 236
Mattoon, A., 356, 357
Mauer, M., 245, 246
Mauldin, W. P., 332
Maume, D. J., Jr., 185, 193
Maxwell, C. D., 18, 273
Mazur, A., 413
McChesney, R. W., 31, 40
McClendon, M. J., 408
McConnell, S. R., 209
McCoy, N. L., 176
McGinn, A. P., 325
McGuire, M. B., 109
McKee, J. K., 357
McKeown, T., 93
McKibben, B., 416
McKibben, M., 76
McKinlay, J. B., 93, 94
McKinlay, S. M., 93
McKinney, K. D., 173
McLanahan, S., 72, 207
McManus, P. A., 68
McNeil, J., 128
McNeil, W. H., 342
McNeill, J. R., 371
McPartland, J., 166
McRae, C., 68
McVeigh, T., 384
Mead, L. M., 134
Meadows, D. H., 342
Meadows, D. L., 342
Meier, K. J., 418
Meier, R., 242
Meier, R. F., 295, 297
Melman, S., 49
Merrill, J. C., 108
Merton, R. K., 7, 150, 233, 276, 382
Mesarovic, M., 326
Messner, M. A., 199
Metcalf, K. K., 419
Meyer, G., 148
Meyers, M. K., 79, 80, 81
Michael, R. T., 313
Middleton, R., 151
Milhausen, R. R., 294
Milhorn, H. T., 271, 272, 275
Miller, A. D., 233
Miller. G., 10
Miller, N., 160
Miller, P., 129
Miller, R. L., 281

Miller, S. C., 159
Mills, C. W., 2, 5, 38, 39, 47
Mills, R. J., 103
Min, P. G., 159
Mincer, J., 284
Miringoff, M. L., 208
Miringoff, M.-L., 208
Mirkinson, J., 298
Miron, J. A., 277, 278, 282
Mirowsky, J., 100, 117
Mishel, L., 45, 122, 413
Moen, P., 85
Moise-Titus, J., 384
Mokhiber, R., 55, 258
Moles, O. C., 134
Monbiot, G., 51
Montagu, A., 149
Moody, K., 49
Moon, M., 107
Moore, D. C., 243
Moore, L. J., 117
Moore, T. S., 45
Moore, W., 129
Morgan, J. P., 267, 280
Morris, A. D., 165
Morris, J. R., 63
Morris, L., 180, 332
Morris, P. A., 139
Mowlana, H., 386
Mueller, G. O. W., 232
Müller, B., 326
Murdock, G. P., 293
Myers, S. L., 307

Nace, T., 30, 36, 50
Nadelmann, E. A., 279, 280, 281
Nader, R., 48
Najjar, O. A., 189
Nason-Clark, N., 238
Neckerman, K. M., 133, 156
Nederend, S., 180
Neier, A., 387
Nelson, A. R., 98
Nelson, F. H., 419
Neugarten, B. L., 220
Newhouse, J., 392
Newman, A. E., 193
Newman, K., 133, 134, 145
Newman, O., 330
Newman, R. D., 379, 391
Nielson, F., 381
Nightingale, C. H., 228
Nissen, B., 32
Nord, C. W., 72, 79
Novick, S. M., 129
Nusberg, C., 222

Oakes, J., 409
O'Brien, D. J., 159, 173
O'Connor, E., 74
Ogburn, W. F., 59, 405
O'Harrow, R., Jr., 429
Ohlin, L. E., 233, 277
O'Kelly, C. G., 177, 189, 191
Olasky, M. N., 138
Oliver, M. B., 250

Olsson, S. E., 222
Olzak, S., 150
O'Malley, P. M., 266, 267, 268, 270, 275
O'Neil, A. K., 180
Orcutt, J. D., 250
Orenstein, P., 199
Orfield, G., 168, 410, 411
Orfield, M., 337, 339
Orshansky, M., 121, 122
Orszag, P. R., 221
Osborne, D., 48
O'Shea, R. M., 134

Padavic, I., 199
Padilla, F. M., 157
Page, B. I., 136
Page, R. N., 409
Pallas, A. M., 153
Parenti, C., 414
Parke, R., 179
Parnell, A. M., 342
Parsons, T., 6, 88, 177
Pastore, A. L., 240, 243, 249, 296
Patterson, O., 154
Pattillo, M., 258
Paulsen, J. A., 15, 214
Payne, J. E., 275
Peace, S., 222
Pelton, L., 76
Penrod, S., 304
Perrone, D., 250, 251
Perrucci, R., 132
Persell, C. H., 429
Pestel, E., 326
Petersen, W., 319
Petersilia, J., 247
Peterson, I., 209
Peterson, J., 185
Peterson, P. E., 334
Peterson, R. D., 246
Peterson, S. B., 180
Petrocelli, W., 195
Pettigrew, T. F., 160, 164
Phelan, T. J., 329
Philander, S. G., 359
Philliber, W. W., 70
Phillips, K., 145
Phillips, U. B., 154
Phoenix, R., 261
Pillemer, K., 76
Pinkney, A., 375
Piper, E. S., 243
Piven, F. F., 141
Plakans, A., 203
Plotnick, R. D., 79
Plummer, M. L., 362
Podolski, C., 384
Polakow, V., 229
Polanzi, C. W., 238
Pontell, H. N., 109
Popenoe, D., 63
Porter, B. D., 387
Portes, A., 343
Postel, S., 363
Potter, W. J., 384
Pottieger, A. E., 263, 295

Ghettos, 154–155, 328
Global corporations, 19, 30–32,
    188–189
Global economy, 30–35, 41, 49–51,
    133–134, 188–189, 206
Global warming, 358–360, 363–368
Government,
    abuse of authority in, 27–28, 33–35,
        45–47
    deficit spending and, 47
    growth of, 33–35
    regulation, 29–30, 33–35, 155–157,
        192–195, 337, 364–365
    reorganization of, 47–48
    world, 392–394
Gray Panthers, 221, 224
Great Britain, 280–281
Great Society, 137
Greenhouse effect, 358–360
Greenpeace, 14, 48, 351, 362, 368
Green Revolution, 325–326
Gun control, 390

Hallucinogens, 266, 274
Hashish. *See* Marijuana
Head Start, 80, 81, 136, 252, 421
Health,
    children and, 76
    divorce and, 67
    drugs and, 264, 271–274, 280–281,
        295–296
    elderly and, 212, 221
    gender and, 95–98, 103–105
    lifestyle and, 98, 113–114
    minorities and, 89, 97–98, 156–159
    social factors affecting, 91–98
    societal development and, 92–94
Health care,
    access to, 102–103
    corporatization of, 105–107, 110–111
    cost of, 88–91, 101–102, 108–111
    ethics and, 107–108
    financing of, 101–102, 108–111
    fraud, 109
    gender inequality in, 103–105
    perspectives on, 88–91
    practitioners in, 112–113
    quality of, 103, 106–107
    right vs. privilege, 113
    socialized, 110–111
    technology and, 107–108
    unnecessary or harmful, 102, 104–105,
        111–112
Health insurance, 102, 108–112,
Health–Maintenance Organizations
    (HMOs), 110–112
Heroin, 263, 272–274, 276–277,
    280–281
    See also Narcotics
Hispanic Americans,
    criminal justice system and, 247, 276
    discrimination against, 156–160,
        356–357
    education and, 156–158, 183–184, 408,
        410–411
    income and, 154–157, 185–187

media and, 161–163
poverty and, 72, 125–127, 154–157,
    207, 209–210, 328–329
segregation of, 328–329
unemployment and, 45
See also Minority groups
Homeless, 93, 122, 129, 328, 333
Home schooling, 421–423
Homophobia, 217–218
Homosexuality, 213
    attitudes toward, 215–217, 224–225
    causes of, 15, 213–214
    as deviance, 215–216
    discrimination against, 74–75, 215–218,
        224–225
    labeling theory and, 214
Homosexuals, 12–13, 90–93
Hospitals, 100–101, 105–107
Housing, 211, 221–223, 328, 333, 411
Hydrologic cycle, 352–353
Hypothesis, 11
Hysterectomies, 105

Iatrogenic illness, 114
Illiteracy, 189
Immigrants, 159–161, 163–164, 317–318
Income,
    distribution, 122–124
    education and, 406–409, 411
    elderly and, 209–211, 219–221
    gender inequality and, 185–187
    minorities and, 12–13, 45, 154–159,
        210
Indian Citizenship Act, 158
Indians. *See* Minority groups
Individualism, 19, 58, 349, 364–365
Individual Retirement Accounts, 221
Industrialization, 1–2, 51, 401–403
    age and, 202–204
    birth and death rates and, 318–320
    cities and, 321–323
    crime and, 233
    education and, 401–403
    the family and, 4, 59–60, 64–65, 72–73,
        233
    health and, 92–94, 98
    religion and, 4, 233
    sex roles and, 177–180, 190–191
Inequality. *See* Social inequality
Infanticide, 335
Infant mortality, 92–95, 317
In-group, 150
Innovation, 233, 276
Institutional racism, 356–357
Instrumental tasks, 177
Insurrection, 375
Interactionist perspective, 6, 9–11
    cities and, 324
    crime and, 234–236, 249
    drugs and, 276–277
    education and, 406
    environment and, 350–351
    family and, 61–62
    gender inequality and, 179
    health care and, 89–91
    mental illness and, 99–100

minorities and, 150, 161–163
population and, 324
poverty and, 134
science and technology and, 406
sexual deviance and, 303–306
social constructionism and, 10–11
violence and war and, 383, 386–387
Interest groups, 8, 14, 89, 351–352
Internal colonialism, 151
International Bank for Reconstruction and
    Development. *See* World Bank
International Court of Justice, 393–394
International Monetary Fund, 36–37, 43,
    48–49, 348–349
Internet, 299, 308–309, 385
Interpersonal violence. *See* Violence
Interventionist approach, 19, 30, 49–51,
    81, 135–136, 138–139, 167,
    250–251, 281, 306–309, 333–337,
    364–365, 390, 424
Intimate partner violence. *See* Domestic
    violence; Spouse abuse
Iran–Contra scandal, 46
Iraq War, 187, 375–377, 386–387

Japan, 252–253, 420–421
Japanese Americans. *See* Minority groups
Job Corps, 136, 139
Juvenile delinquency. *See* Delinquency

Kinship, 202–203
Korean Americans, 159–160
Korean War, 375–376, 388
Kubu people of Sumatra, 90
Kyoto Protocol, 360, 365–366

Labeling, 9, 99–100, 214, 235–236, 406,
    409
Labor, 32–33, 44–46, 49
Laissez–faire approach, 19, 29–30, 47,
    50–51, 81, 135–136, 138–139, 167,
    250–251, 281, 306–309, 333–337,
    364–365, 390, 424
Language, gender inequality and, 179
Latent functions, 7, 322
Latinismo, 157
Latinos. *See* Hispanic Americans
Law, gender and the, 188, 192–193
Law enforcement. *See* Criminal justice
    system; Police
League of Conservation Voters, 351
League of Nations, 393
League of United Latin American Citizens,
    157
Lesbianism. *See* Homosexuality
Life course, 202–204
Life expectancy, 92–97, 317–318
Life stages. *See* Life course
Lifestyles, health and, 90–97
Living wills, 108
Lynchings, 153

Macrosociological approach, 6
Mafia, 237
Managed health care. *See* Health
    Maintenance Organizations

Manifest function, 7, 322
Maquiladoras, 45
Marijuana, 262–263, 265–269, 276–281
Market economies, 28–29
Marriage, 63–65, 69–70, 74–75, 78–79, 98
   See also Family
Masculine mystique, 188
Master status, 176
Maternity leaves, 79–81
MDMA, 274
Measurement, scientific, 15–16
Mechanization, 403
Media,
   concentration of power and, 31, 40–41
   constructing social problems and, 10–11, 40–41
   crime and, 249–251
   family and, 77–78, 182–183
   gender inequality and, 182–183
   minorities and, 161–163, 249–252
   population growth and, 332–333
   the power elite and, 40–41
   technology and, 249–251
   violence and war and, 383–384, 386–387, 390
Medicaid, 97, 102–103, 106, 108–109, 113, 137, 221
Medical care. *See* Health care
Medical-industrial complex, 107
Medicare, 97, 102–103, 106, 108–109, 113, 137, 219–221
Melting pot, 164
Men, discrimination against, 188
Mental illness, 97–101, 129, 214, 232–233
Methadone maintenance programs, 280–281
Methaqualone, 272
Mexican American Political Alliance, 156–157
Mexican Americans. *See* Hispanic Americans
Microsociological approach, 6
Midwives, 112
Migration, 317–318
Military, 187–188, 216–217, 298, 375–378
Military-industrial complex, 39, 107, 378, 388
Minority Groups, 148–149
   American Indians, 157–158, 351, 375, 382
   Arab Americans, 160–161
   Asian Americans, 125, 154–155, 157, 158–161, 210
   Chinese Americans, 158–159
   crime and, 212, 241–243, 250–251, 276
   education and, 154–159, 183–184, 405–411
   environmental problems and, 356–357
   health of, 89, 96–98, 155–157
   income and, 154–159, 185–187
   Japanese Americans, 159
   media and, 161–163, 250–251

poverty and, 125–127, 154–159
unemployment of, 44–45
women as, 183
   See also African Americans; Hispanic Americans
Mixed economies, 30
Modernization, 402–404
   See also Industrialization
Modified extended family, 58
"Mommy track", 193
Monogamy, 58, 62, 66, 74
Monopoly, 31–32
Morphine. *See* Narcotics
Mortality, 76, 92–98, 317
Mothers Against Drunk Driving (MADD), 284
Multinational corporations, 31–33
Music, 77, 183
Mutually Assured Destruction (MAD), 391

Nader's Raiders, 48
Narcotics, 272–274, 275–275, 278–281
   See also Heroin
National Council of La Raza, 157, 162
National Environmental Policy Act, 351–352, 425
National Organization for Women (NOW), 190–191
National Retired Teachers Association, 224
National Rifle Association, 8
National Welfare Rights Organization, 141
Native Americans. *See* Minority groups
Natural resources, depletion of, 326–327
Natural Resources Defense Council, 351, 362
Nazis, 149–150, 382, 416–417
Netherlands, drug policy, 280–281
New Deal, 35, 137
Nongovernmental organizations (NGOs), 48–49, 191–192, 362, 394–395
Norms, 3, 9, 99–100, 293–294
North American Free Trade Agreement (NAFTA), 36, 49, 51
Nuclear energy, 355–356, 361
Nuclear family, 58–61, 77
Nuclear weapons, 88, 355–356, 376–380, 388–389, 390–393
Nuclear winter, 388–389
Nurse practitioners, 112
Nurses, 89, 99, 102–104, 112
Nursing homes, 21–213, 222–223

Obesity, 208
Objectivity. *See* Scientific objectivity
Obscenity, 300
   See also Pornography
Occupational structure, 33
Office of Technology Assessment, 425
Old–Age, Survivors, Disability, and Health Insurance. *See* Social Security
Oligopoly, 31–32, 112
One–parent families. *See* Single–parent families
Opiates. *See* Narcotics

Opium. *See* Narcotics
Organized crime, 237, 277–280
Ozone depletion, 358–359, 365

Palimony, 71
Patriarchy, 61, 189–191, 303–304
PCP, 274
Pensions. *See* Retirement
People for the Ethical Treatment of Animals, 3
Persian Gulf War, 187, 375–377, 386–387
Pesticides, as pollutants, 360
Phencyclidine. *See* PCP
Phenomenon of rising expectations, 348
Physicians, 88–89, 103–106, 110–113
Physicians' assistants, 112
Plessy v. Ferguson, 154
Pluralism, 163–164, 168–169
Pluralist model, 38–41, 50
Police, 18, 234, 243–244, 249–251, 252–253
Political discontent, 375, 388
Political economy of drug use, 378–379
Politics, 28, 35–41, 189, 194–195, 224
Pollution. *See* Environmental problems
Polygamy, 66–67
Poor, 124–129
Population, 317
   doubling time, 321
   economic development and, 332–335
   environmental problems and, 347–348, 351
   growth, 316–321
   perspectives on, 323–324
   problems of, 325–327
   solution to problems of, 331–333
Pornography, 300
   aggression and, 12–13, 302, 304–305
   children and, 207, 298–299, 301
   censorship and, 300–301, 308–309
   Internet and, 299, 308–309
   perspectives on, 302–306
   social policy and, 308–309
   violence and, 12–13, 302, 304–305
Postindustrial society, 33
Poverty, 120–122
   causes of, 122–124, 153
   children and, 72, 123, 126–127, 129
   crime and, 233, 251–252
   disabled and, 128
   domestic violence and, 72–76
   drugs and, 270–271, 278–279
   the economy and, 130–133, 135
   elderly and, 125–127, 209–210
   extent of, , 122–124
   functions of, 130–131
   health and, 89, 95–97, 106–107, 108–111
   homelessness and, 129
   international perspectives on, 124, 140
   minorities and, 125, 154–159, 209–210, 329–329
   perspectives on, 129–134
   programs to combat, 135–140
   prostitution and, 297–299, 306–307
   women and, 125–128, 209–210

Power, 5, 7–8, 10, 28, 71–74
  concentration of, 30–36, 44–49
  perspectives on, 35–41
Power elite, 37–39, 50
Preindustrial society, 58–60, 64–65, 92–95
Prejudice, 149–153, 160–161
Premarital sex, 293–294
Preventive medicine, 94, 102
Primary deviance, 99, 235
Primary prevention of drug abuse, 281–282
Prison-industrial complex, 250–251
Prisons, 231, 248–251, 254
Privacy, 414, 423–424
Privatization of services, 19, 47, 50–51,
  80–81, 105–107, 113, 250–251,
  335–337, 421–423
Profit making, 29
  cities and, 329, 335–337
  day care and, 63, 80–81
  environment and, 362
  health care and, 89, 105–107, 113
  media and, 249–250
  nursing homes and, 212–213, 222–223
  population and, 324
  prisons and, 250–251
Progress, 349
Property crimes, 237–241, 329
Prostitution, 294
  controlling, 306–307
  extent of, 238, 295–296
  health and, 93, 295–296
  legalization of, 295–296, 306–307
  male, 297
  perspectives on, 302–306
  poverty and, 297–299, 303–307
  recruiting and, 299
  teenage, 207, 298–299
  types of, 294
Psychedelics. See Hallucinogens
Psychoactives drugs. See Drugs
Psychological approaches,
  to alcohol and drug abuse, 275–276
  to crime, 232–233
  to sexual orientation, 214, 217–218
  to prejudice and discrimination,
  151–153
Public assistance, 137–140
Puerto Rican Organization for Political
  Action, 157
Puerto Ricans. See Hispanic Americans

Quebec, 164
Quaaludes. See Methaqualone

Race, 148–149
  crime and, 241, 243, 247
  education and, 411
  environment and, 356–357
  health and, 98
  income and, 186–187
  poverty and, 125–127, 132–133
  riots, 159–160, 374–375
  See also Minority groups
Racial discrimination. See Discrimination
Racism, 132–133, 149, 160–161,
  164–165, 356–357, 409

Radioactive waste, 355–356
Rape, 188, 237, 240, 303–305, 330,
  387
Reagan Administration, 90, 130, 301,
  333, 393–394
Recidivism, 248–250, 252–255
Recycling, 354–355, 363
Rehabilitation, 243, 248–249, 254,
  282–283
Relative deprivation, 121, 383
Religion, 190–191, 217, 233, 252,
  264–265, 293–294, 346, 349, 366,
  368, 382, 384–385, 418–420
Research, 11–16
  See also Science
Retirement, , 188, 202–203, 208–211,
  219–221
Retirement Equity Act, 219
Retreatism, 276
Riots. See Race riots
Robbery. See Crime
Robotization, 33, 402–404

Sampling, 14–15
Saudi Arabia, 190–191
Scapegoating, 152
School integration. See Desegregation
Schools,
  busing, 166–169, 411
  charter, 417–420
  choice, 417–420
  crime and, 252, 411–412
  drop outs, 409–410
  functions of, 405
  gender inequality and, 183–185
  home, 421–423
  integration of, 166–169, 423
  privatized, 421–423
  violence in, 411–412
  vouchers, 418–419
Science, 2, 11–16, 401–406
  attitudes toward, 412–413
  future of, 423–425
  perspectives on, 405–406
  problems with, 13–15, 412–417
  values and, 13–15
Scientific objectivity, 13–15
Secondary deviance, 99, 235
Secularization, 294
Segregation, 163, 166–169, 221–222,
  328–329, 411
Self-concept, 153, 214, 235–236
Self esteem, 153, 180–181
Self-fulfilling prophecy, 99, 214, 235–236,
  330, 406, 409
Sentencing policies, 245–248, 253–254
Serial monogamy, 66
Sex, defined, 176, 179
Sex industry, 189, 292, 298–299
Sexism, 103–104, 176–179
Sexual behavior, 59, 292–294
Sexual deviance, 292–294, 302–306
Sexual exploitation, 189, 207
Sexual harassment, 194–195
Sexual inequality. See Gender inequality
Sexual orientation, 213–215

Sexual revolution, 293–294
Shay's Rebellion, 375
Sick role, 89
Sierra Club, 8, 48, 351
Singlehood, 63–65, 70
Single-parent families, 62–63, 69, 71–72,
  77, 79–81, 125–127, 207
Slavery, 151, 154
Social change, 6–10, 35–36
Social class, 7, 12, 123–134, 164–165,
  356–357
  See also Socioeconomic status
Social constructionism. See Constructing
  social problems
Social control theory, 233
Social disorganization, 7, 10, 35–36,
  59–61, 89, 130, 150, 203, 233, 323,
  350, 385–386, 405
Social inequality, 405–409
Social institutions, 4, 7
Social insurance, 137
Socialism, 29–30, 111
Social isolation, 77, 211
Socialization,
  as cause of racial discrimination, 151
  crime and, 235
  drugs and, 275–276
  in the family, 59–61
  gender and, 97
  sex and, 292–294
  violence and, 384–385
Social learning theory, 275–276, 283
Social mobility, 133–134
Social movement, 17–19, 224–225
Social policy, 16–19, 283–284
Social problems, 2–5
  international perspectives on, 20
  research on, 11–16
  solving, 16–20
  theoretical perspectives on, 6–11
  See also Constructing social problems
Social reform, 16, 251–252, 283–284,
  389–390
Social reproduction, 406
Social Security, 137, 209–211, 219–221,
  224
Social stratification, 39, 42, 120, 129–130,
  148, 153, 176, 178, 183
Sociobiology, 381–382
Socioeconomic status,
  alcoholism and, 264
  crime and, 242–243
  divorce and, 67
  education and, 406–407
  elderly and, 209–211
  gender and, 183
  health and, 95–97
Sociological imagination, 5
Sociology, 2–6
Speed. See Amphetamines
Split labor market, 151, 178, 382
Spouse abuse, 18, 73–77, 78–79
  See also Domestic violence
Spurious relationship, 15
Status offenders, 238
Status politics, 191